Imaam Ali bn Abi-Taalib's

Sermons, Letters & Sayings as
Compiled by
Sayyid Shareef ar-Razi

in

NAHJ Al-BALAAGHA

Peak of Eloquence

Translated by **Sayyid Ali Reza**
Includes Introductory Notes by
Sayyid Mohammad Askari Jafery

بسم الله الرحمن الرحيم

IN THE NAME OF ALLAH,

THE MOST BENEFICENT, THE MERCIFUL

Contents

Introduction

THE BOOK

This book is a translation of the sermons, letters, orders and some of the sayings of Hazrat Ali (A.S.) as compiled by Sayyid Razi and named "Nahjol-Balaagha". These sermons and preachings of Hazrat Ali (A.S.) were so highly valued and venerated in the Islamic world that within a century of his death they were taught and read as the last word on the Philosophy of monotheism, as the best lectures for character building, as exalted sources of inspiration, as very persuasive sermons towards piety, as guiding beacons towards truth and justice, as marvellous eulogies of the Holy prophet (A.S.) and the Holy Quraan, as convincing discourses on the spiritual values of Islam, as awe inspiring discussions about the attributes of God. as master-piece of literature, and as models of the art of rhetorics.

1st Century

According to the famous book of biographies ar-Rejalol-al-Kabeer, the first person to collect these sermons in a book form was Zayd bn Wahab Jenny, who died in 90 A.H. and who was regarded as a narrator of Ahaadeeth (Traditions). Thus within thirty years of Hazrat Ali's death and during the first century of hijra his sermons, letters, sayings, Ahaadeeth etc. were collected quoted and preserved.

2nd Century

With the dawn of 2nd Century bn Wahab's example was followed by 1 The famous calligraphist of the early Abbasites regime, Abdl-Hameed bn Yahya (132 A.H.).

2 bn-Moqaffa (142 A.H.) took up this work of compilation. Jaahiz Othmaani says: bn-Moqaffa had very carefully studied these sermons and used to say that he had saturated himself from the fountains head of knowledge and wisdom and was daily getting fresh inspirations from these sermons 3 bn-Nadeem in his biographies "The Fahrist" says that Hishaam bn Saaib Kalbi (146 A.H.) had also collected these sermons (Fahrist bn-Nadeem, section VII p.251).

Thence onward century after century Moslim scholars, theologians, historians and michaditheen were ciiing these sermons, quoting them, discussing the meanings of the words and phrases used by Hazrat Ali (A.S.), and referring them when they needed an authority on theology, ethics, the teaching of the Holy prophet (A.S.) and the Holy Quraan or on literature and rhetorics.

3rd Century

During the third century five famous men took up this work.

1. Abo-Othmaan Omaro bn Bahrol-Jahiz, who died in 255 A.H. (868 A.D.), quoted many sermons in his book al-Bayan wat-Tabyeen.
2. bn-Qotayba Daynoori, who died in 276 A.H., in his books Oyoonol-Akhbaar and Ghareebol-Hadeeth quoted many sermons and discussed meanings of many words and phrases used by Hazrat Ali (A.S.).
3. bn-Wazeh Yaqoobi, who died in 278 A.H., cited many sermons and sayings of Hazrat Ali (A.S.) in his history.
4. Abo-Haneefa Daynoori (280 A.H.) in his history al-Akhbaar at-Tiwaal quoted many sermons and sayings.
5. Abol-Abbas al-Mobarrad (286 A.H.) in his book Kitaab al-Mobbed collected many sermons and letters.

4th Century

1. The famous historian bn-Jareer Tabari who died in 310 A.H. quoted some of these sermons in his Taareekh kabeer.
2. Abo-Mohammad Hasan bn Ali bn Shoba Halabi (320 AH.) had collected some sermons in his book "Tohafol-oqool. This book was later printed in Persia. The following writers have also extensively quoted the sermons and sayings of Hazrat Ali in their respective books.
3. bn-Wareed (321 A.H.) in his book al-Mojtabni.
4. bn-Abd Rabbih (328 A.H.) in al-Iqdol-Fareed.
5. Thiqatol-Islam Kolayni (329 A.H.) in Kaafi.
6. Ali bn Mohammad bn Abdillah Madani (335 A.H.) collected sermons, letters and sayings of Hazrat in his book. Yaqoot Hamwi mentions of this book in Mojam al-Odabaa p.313 Volume V.
7. The Historian Masoodi (346 A.H.), in Morooj az-Zahab, has quoted some of the letters and sermons of Hazrat.
8. Abol-Faraj al-Isbahaani (356 A.H.) in Aghaani,
9. Abo-Ali (356 A.H.) in Nawaadir, and

10 Shaykh Sadooq (381 A.H.) in Kitaab at-Tawheed, have extensively quoted these sermons, letters and sayings.

5th Century

1. Shaykh Mofeed (413 A.H.) in Irshaad has quoted many sermons, Ahaadeeth (traditions) sayings and letters of Hazrat.
2. Sayyid Razi (420 A.H.) compiled the book "Nahjol-Balaagha.
3. Shaykh at-Taayefa Abo-Jafar Mohammad bn-Hassan Toosi (460 A.H.) was a contemporary of Sayyid Razi and had collected some of these sermons etc., long before Sayyid took up his work.

What Sayyid Razi could compile in Nahjol-Balaagna does not contain all the sermons letters and sayings of Hazrat Ali (A.S.). Masoodi (346 A.H.) in his famous history Morooj az-Zahab (vol.i p.33 printed at Cairo) says: Only sermons of Hazrat Ali, which have been preserved by various people, number more than four hundred and eighty. These were extempore orations, people have copied them one from another and have compiled thera in book forms; they have cited them and have quoted passages from them in their books.

Apparently out of these four hundred and eighty sermons some were lost and Sayyid Razi could lay hand on only about 245 sermons, besides them he collected about 75 letters and more than 200 sayings. Almost everyone of the sermons, letters and sayings collected in Nahjol-Balaagha is to be found in bools of authors who died long before Sayyid Razi was born, while some are found in works of such authors who, though his contemporaries, yet were older to him and had written their books before Nahjol-Balaagha was compiled.

If I quote all of what has been said by the Moslim and the Christian Arab scholars, Theologians, Philosophers and Historians in praises of these sermons, sayings and Letters it will cover a volume as big as this book, therefore I shall briefly quote only a few of them.

1. Abo-Saadat Mobaarak Majdoddeer bn Atheer Jazaairi (606 A.H.) is recognised even today only as a narrator of Ahaadeeth (tradition) but also as a lexicologist of great eminence. His book "Nehaaya, is a study of the history and meanings of the difficult words of Holy Quraan and the traditions. In this book he has at great length discussed many words, phrases and the sentences of Hazrat Ali's sermons from the book Nahjol-

Balaagha. He says: So far as comprehensiveness is concerned Ali's words come next only to the Quraan.

2. Allama Shaykh Kamaloddeen bn Mohammad bn Talha Shaaf: (died in 652 A.H.) in his famous book "Mataalibos-Soaal" writes:The fourth attribute of Hazrat Ali (A.S.) was his eloquence and rhetorics. He was such an Imaam in these arts that none can aspire to rise up to the level cs the dust of his shoes. One who has studied Nahjol-Balaagha can form some idea of his supreme eminence in this sphere.

3. Allama Abo-Hamid Abdl-Hameed bn Hibatollah, known as bn-abil-Hadeed al-Miotaz.li, who died in 655 A.H., and who has written a really great commentary on these sermons says:

(i) His speeches, letters and sayings are so supremely eminent that they are above the sayings of man and below only to the words of God. None can surpass it but the Holy Quraan.

At another place he says that His (Hazrat Ali) sayings are miracle of the Holy prophet (A.S.). His prophecies show that his knowledge was superhuman.

4. Allama Saaddodeen Taftazaani (791 A.H.) in "Sharh al-Maqaasid" says: Ali had supreme command over language, over ethics and over tenets of religion, at the same time he was a great orator, his sermons compiled in Nahjol-Balaagha bear witness to these facts.

5. Allama Alaoddeen (875 A.H.) in Sharh Tajreed says: The book Nahjol-Balaagha that is the sermons and sayings contained therein prove that none can surpass it on these lines but the Holy Quraan.

6. Mofti of Egypt, Shaykh Mohammad Abda (1323 A.H.) has written a commentary on the book Nahjol-Balaagha. He was among those modern thinkers, who made the modern world realise the beauties of the teaching of Islam. His introduction on his own commentary of Nahjol-Balaagha deserves careful study.

In this introduction he says: Everyone who fully understands Arabic language must agree that the sermons and sayings of Hazrat (A.S.) are next only to the words of God and the Holy prophet (A.S.). Ali's words are so full of meanings and they convey such great ideas that this book Nahjel-Balaagha should be very carefully studied, referred and quoted by students as well as teachers. This professor of Arabic literature and philosophy persuaded the Universities of Cairo and Beirut to include the book Nahjol-Balaagha in their courses for advance studies of literature and philosophy.

7. The famous author and orator Shaykh Mostafa Ghaali" Ayni of Beirut, who is considered as an authority on commentaries (Tafseer) of the Quraan and also on Arabic literature in his book "Areejoz-Zahr" in chapter "The styles of language writes:

Who can write better than Ali except the Holy prophet (A.S.) and God. Those who want to study eminent standards of literature should study the book Nahjol-Balaagha. It contains such depth of knowledge and such wonderful advises on the subjects of ethics and religion that itsconstant siudy will make a man wise, pious and noble minded and will train him to be an orator of great siandіng.

8. Ostaad Mohammad Moheeddeen, professor of the Arabic language, al-Azhar University of Cairc says: Nahjol-Balaagha is a collection of the works of Hazrat Ali. It is compiled by Sayyid Razi. It contains such examples of chaste language, noble eloquence and superior wisdom that none but Ali can produce such a work because next to the Holy prophet (A.S.), he was the greatest orator, the greatest authority on language and literature and the greatest source of wisdom of the religion (Islam). He was such a philosopher that from his words flow streams of knowledge and wisdom.

9. Ostaad Abdl-Wahab-Hamada, an authority on Arabic literature and the "traditions, and a professor of the Fooaad i University of Cairo, in 1951 writes: The Book Nahjol-Balaagha contains all that great scholars, professor of ethics, philosophers, scientists, authorities on religions and politicians can say or write. The wonderful force of advises and the superfine way of presenting arguments and the depth of vision prove that it is the work of a super mind like that of Ali. 10. Abdl-Maseeh-al-Antaaki, in his famous book "Sharh Qasaaid al-Awliyya" writes: It cannot be denied that Ali was the Imaam of speakers and crators, and he was the teacher and the leader of writers and philosophers. There is truth in this assertion that his sayings are superior to that of any man and are inferior only to the sayings of God the Almighty. He undoubtedly was the man from whom writers, speakers, philosophers, theologians and poets have drawn inspirations, have improved their styles and have mastered their arts. The compilation of his work is named Nahjol-Balaagha, which should be read often. 11. Fooaad ai-Bostaani, professor of Arabic literature in the Qideese Osqof College of Beirut, is a Roman Catholic Christian. He has compiled a

book containing selections from the works of philosophers, scientists, theologians and essayists. He starts this book with the following words: I want to start this work of mine with the selections from the book Nahjol-Balaagha. It is a work of the greatest thinker of the world Imaam Ali bn Abi Talib.

12. The famous Christian moralist, author and poet, Polos Salama in his famous book "Awal-lay-Molhama al-Arabia" (printed at al-Naseer Press of Beirut) says:

The famous book Nahjol-Balaagha is the work which makes one realise the great mind of Ali bn Abi-Talib. No book can surpass it but the Quraan. In it you will find pearls of knowledge strung in beautiful chains, flowers of language making ones mind fragrant with sweet and pleasing smell of heroism and nobility, and streams of chaste language sweeter and cooler than the famous stream of the Kawther flowing constantly and refreshing minds of readers.

Hazrat Ali bn Abi-Talib (A.S)

His Genealogy

Hazrat Ali (A.S.) the lord of the faithful was the first cousin of the Holy prophet (A.S.). His father. Abo-Talib, and the father of the Holy prophet (A.S.), Abdillah, were sons of Abdi-Mottalib, and children of the same mother, Fatima, the daughter of Asad son of the famous Hashim. Thus his (Hazrat Ali) parents were cousins. His genealogical table is as follows.

His Birth

Hazrat Ali (A.S.,) was born on the 13th Rajab 30 (Aamol-Feel) about 610 A.D. i.e. 23 years before Hijra of the Holy prophet (A.S.). Historians say that he was born in the precincts of Kaba. See:

1 Imaam Hakim in Mostadrak

2 Masoodi, in Morooj az-Zahab p. 125,

3 Izalutul-Khifa-2nd subject p.251, and

4 Allama Aaloosi in Sharh Ayniyya.

His Name

At the time of his birth his father and his cousin, Mohammad, the Holy prophet (A.S.), were out of Mecca, his mother gave him the names of Asad and Hayder, when his father returned he called him Zayd. But when the Holy prophet (A.S.) came back to the city he took his young cousin in his change and gave him the name of Ali, saying that it was the name decreed for him by God.

1 Imaam Noodi, the commentator of Bokhaari.

2 bn-Arabi in his book Yoowakheeth.

3 Sabt bn Jawzi in his book Tazkirat-Khawaas al-Aimma. Hazrat Ali has called himself Ali and Hayder.

His Konya

Among various Konyas, the most famous were Abol-Hasan, Abos-Sibtayn, and Abo-Torab.

Names derived on account of some relation or some connection. It is an Arab systein that respectable people are addressed with their Konya and not with their names.

His Algaab

His Alqaab were, Mortaza (the chosen one), Ameer al-Momineen (the Commander of the faithful), imaamol-Mottaqeen (the leader of the pious and God fearing persons).

His features

Famous historian and biographist Allama Ali bn Mohammad in his book Ostol-Ghaaba Fee Tamyeez Sahaba (book iv p.398) says: He was a man of middle height with very black and very big and piercing eyes, very handsome cast of face, very clear and fair complexion, broad shoulders, powerful arms, vast chest, strong and roughened hands, a long ruscular neck, a broad forehead and he had few hairs on the iop of his head.

Imaam Hakim in his Mcsiadrak (book III), Kaamil bn Atheer in his Taareekh al-Khamees, bn Abdi-Bar in his al-Isteeaab (book ! p.486) and Allama Tabarani in his ar-Riyaaz an-Nazira (book !! p. 202 and 218) agree with the above description. Tabarani further says: He used to walk with very light tread and was very agile in his movements, had a very smiling face, very pleasing manner, a jovia! temperameni, very kind disposition and very courteous behaviour. He would never lose his temper.

His Upbringing

He was born three years before the marriage of the Holy prophet (A.S.) with Hazrat Khadeeja (A.S.). Scon after his birth the Holy prophet (A.S.) took him under his holy care and Ali was like a son unto him. He used to live with the prophet, used to sleep with him, was fed by him, washed and dressed by him, and even carried by him on a sling whenever he would go out. The historian Masoodi in Ithbaat al-Waseeyya (page119) says: When the Holy prophet (A.S.) married Khadeeja, she adopted this child as her son. Hazrat Ali, himself, has described his childhood in Khotba Qaaseeaa; saying: I was still a new born baby when the prophet took me from my parents. I used to cling to him, he would made me sleep in his bed, pressing my body against his and making me smell his fragrance and felt its warmth; he used to feed me, and (when I grew a little older) he never found me uttering a lie or feigning a deceit. To me he was like a guiding star and I used to carefully follow his actions and deeds. I was attached to him like a young camel attached to its mother. He used to place before me high values of morality, and used to advise me to follow them, every year he would spend some days at the grotto of the Hera mountain. And I used to be with him, I was his only companion then and none else could meet him at Hera, there I used to see the light of revelation, and used to smell the fragrance of apostlehood. Once the Holy prophet (A.S.) told me that "Ali, you have attained a very eminent place. You see what I see and you hear what I hear

. Hafiz Abo-Naeem in his book Hilyatol-Awliyaa, (book 1 p.67) and Imaam Seyooti in his Tafseer Ad-Dorrol-Manthoor say that once Holy prophet (A.S.) told Hazrat Ali: O Ali! God hath ordered me to keep you near me. You are to me like an ear that retain everything, because your are the retaining ears that the Holy book (Quraan) has praised.

The Holy Prophet and Hazrat Ali loved each other

bn-abil-Hadeed al-Motazili, the commentator of Nahjol-Balaagha, cites Abdillah bn Abbas asking his father:

Father!, my cousin Mohammad had many sons, all of whom died in babyhood, which of them he loved the most?

- Ali bn Abi Talib. Sir I was enquiring about his sons

- The Holy prophet (A.S.) loved Ali more than all of his sons. When Ali was a child I never saw himn separated from Mohammad for half an hour, unless Mohammad went out of the house for some work. I never saw a father love his son so much as the Holy Prophet (A.S.) loved Ali, and I never saw a son so obedient, so attached and so loving to his father as Ali was to Mohammad.

The same author cites the companion of the Holy prophet (A.S.), Jobayr bn Moo's bn Adi bn Nawfal, saying that once his father addressed him and some young men of his family:

Have you noticed the child Ali loving, venerating and obeying that young man, Mohammad, instead of his own father, what an intensity of love and veneration. I swear by our gods, the Lath and the Ozza, that instead of having so many offsprings of Nawfal around me I had a son like Ali.

Allama Tirmizi (Jaami". Tirmizi, vol.i p.33, ivishkaat vol.ii p.8 and Mosnad Imaam Ahmed vol.i p. 146), quotes the Holy prophet (A.S.) saying:

O Ali, I wish to achieve every such thing for you that I desire to acquire myself and I want to keep you away from all those things whose contact I abhor.

Allama Tabarani (in his Aasit) and Imaam Hakim (in his Saheeh) say:

Whenever the Holy prophet (A.S.) was in anger nobody dare addressed him but Ali.

bn-abil-Hadeed (commentary of Nahjol-Balaagha vol.iii p.251) once again quotes the uncle of Holy prophet (A.S.), Abbas saying:

The prophet was so fond of Ali that once when Ali was a young boy he sent him out on some errand and the child took long time to return, he started getting worried and anxious and in the end he prayed to God "Please Lord do not let me die unless I behold Ali once again

Ali staited acting as the bodyguard of the Holy prophet (A.S.) even when he was just a boy of 13 or 14 years. The young men of Quraysh under instigation of their parents used to stone the Holy prophet (A.S.). Ali took up the work of acting as his defender, he fell upon those young men, broke the nose of one, teeth of the other, pulled the ears of the third and threw down the fourth. He often fought against those who were older than him, was often himself hurt, but he never forsook the self imposed duty. After some days he got the nick name of Gaazim (the breaker of thrower) and nobody dared throw anything at Holy prophet (A.S.) when Ali was with him and he would not allow the Holy prophet (A.S.) to go out of the house alone. Ayan vol.i p.280:

Offering himself as a sacrifice at the night of Hijra (migration) and his subsequent behaviour in all the battles are enough proofs of the intensity of Ali's love to the Holy prophet (A.S.)

His Character

Joriy Zaydan (George Gordan) who died recently was a famous Christian historian, linguist, philosopher and poet of the modern Egypt. Arabic was his mother tongue, but he was so well versed in English, French, Germany,

Persian and Latin that he used to contribute to historical and philosophical Magazines of France, Germany and England. About Hazrat Ali he says:

None can praise to the extent that he (Ali) deserves. So many instances of his piety and fear of God are cited that one starts loving and venerating him. He was a true, strict and scrupulous follower of Islam. His words and deeds bore stamps of nobility, sagacity and courage of conviction. He was a great man having his own independent views about life and its problems. He never deceived, misled, or betrayed anybody. In various phases and periods of his life he exhibited marvellous strength cí body arid nind which were due to his true faith in religion and in his sincere belief in truth and justice. He never had servant and never allowed his slaves to work hard. Ofter he would carry his household goods himself and if anybody offered to relieve liim of the weight he would refuse.

The famous Egyptian philosopher and Professor of Islamic of al-Azhar University, Allama Mohammad Mostafa Beck Najeeb in his equally famous book "(Himaato! Islam, part I, p.98)" says:

What can be said about this Imaam? It is very difficult to fully explain his attributes and qualities. It is enough to realise that the Holy prophet (A.S.) had named him the gateway of knowledge and wisdom. He was the most learned person, the most brave man and the most eloquent speaker and orator. His piety, his love of God, his sincerity and fortitude in following religion were of such high order that none could aspire to reach him. He was the greatest politician because he hated diplomacy and loved truth and justice, his was the policy as taught by God. On account of his sagacity and through knowledge of human mind he always arrived at correct conclusion and never changed his opinions. His was the best judgement, and had he no fear of God he would have been the greatest diplomat amongst the Arabs. He is loved by ail, and everyone has a place for him in his heart. He was a man of such surpassing and pre-eminent attributes and such transcending and peerless qualities that many learned men got perplexed about him and imagined him to be an incarnation of God. Several men amongst Jews and Christians love him and such philosophers who came to know of his teachings bow down before his incomparable vast knowledge. Roman kings would have his pictures in their palaces and great warriors would engrave his name on their swords.

Another philosopher and historian of Egypt Ostaad (professor) Mohammad Kaamil, (in a review on the character of Ali p.40) pays his tributes in the following words:

His life is a agglomeration of pleasing incidents, bloody encounters and sad episodes. His personality is very prominent on account of his transcending and high qualities. Each aspect of his life is so lofty and glorious that a study of one phase would make you feel that it was the best phase of his character and the most beautiful picture of his personality, while contemplation of any other phase will enchant you more and you will come to the conclusion that no human being car attain that height, and a third aspect will fascinate you equally and you will realise that before you is a personality of such great eminence that you cannot fully appreciate its greatness and you will feel that Ali was an Imaam (Leader) in battlefield, was an Imaam (Leader) in politics, was an Imaam (leader) in religion, and also an Imaam in ethics, in philosophy, in literature, in learning and wisdom. It is not difficult for God to create such a person

The historian John J. Pool (author of the life of H.M. Queen Victoria) in his book Studies in Mohammadanism says:

This prince was a man of mild and forbearing character, wise in counsel and bold in war. Mohammad had given him the surname of "Lion of God... Ali and his sons Hasan and Hosayn were truly noblemen-men of righteousness man of a brave, a humble, and a forgiving spirit. Their lives deserve to be commemorated; for there was a peculiar pathos about them (their lives) which were not spent selfishly or in vain.

As Mathew Arnold (Essays in Criticism) says:

The sufferers of Karbala had aloft to the eyes of millions the lesson so loved by the sufferer of Calvary (Representation of Crucification):Learn of Me for I am meek and lowly in heart, and Ye shall find rest unto your souls.

He further says:

Ali was the first Caliph to protect and encourage national literature. This prince was a scholar himself and many of his wise saying and proverbs are published in a book. It is a remarkable work and deserves to be more widely read in the West.

bn-abil-Hadeed, the Motazili commentator of Nahjol-Balagha, says:

Hazrat Ali had a personality in which opposite characteristics had so gathered that it was difficult to believe a human mind could manifest such a combination. He was the bravest man that history could cite and such brave persons are always hard hearted, cruel, and eager for blood-shed. On the contrary Ali was kind, sympathetic, responsive and warm hearted person, qualities quite contradictory to the other phase of his character and more suited to pious and God fearing persons.

He was very pious and God fearing person and often pious and religious persons avoid society and do not care to mix with men of sins and men of wrath, similarly warriors, kings and dictators are usually arrogant and haughty, they consider it below themselves to mix with poor, lowly and humble persons. But Ali was different. He was friend to all. As a matter of fact he had a tender spot in his heart for poor and humble, and for orphans and cripples. To them he always was a kind friend, a sympathetic guide and a fellow sufferer; he was meek unto thern but haughty and arrogant against famous warriors and generals, so many of whom he had killed in hand to hand combats. He was always kind but strict with wayward persons, sympathetically teaching then the ways to God. He always smiled and passed happy and witty rejoinders, it was difficult to overcome him in debates or repartees, his rejoinders and retorts always bore high mark of culture, education and knowledge.

He was a scion of a very illustrious, rich and noble clan, as well as son-in-law and great favourite of the Holy prophet (A.S.), at the same time he was the greatest warrior and marshal of his time, yet in spite of his riches he ate, dressed and lived like a poor person to him wealth was for the use of other needy persons, not for himself and his family. Change of times and change of circumstances did not bring any change in his bearing, mien, or character. Even when he ascended the throne of Arabia and was acclaimed as the Caliph, he was the same Ali as they had found him to be during the previous regimes. Once in the society of Abdillah, son of Imaam Maalik bn Hambal a discussion took place about Ali and his caliphate, Abdillah brought the discussion to an end saying that the caliphate did not bring any honour or glory to Ali, but it was itself honoured and glorified by Ali and it received the status actually due to it.

I want to add one more point to the points discussed by bn-abil-Hadeed. World cannot quote an example other than that of Ali a first class warrior and a marshal who is also a philosopher, a moralist and a great teacher of religious principles and theology. A study of his life shows that his sword was the only help that Islam received during its early days of struggle and its wars of self-defence. For Islam he was the first line of defence, the second line of defence and the last line of defence. Who was with him in the battles of Badr, Ohod, Khandaq, Khaybar and Honayn? This is one aspect of his life. While the other phase of his character is portrayed by his sermons, orders, letters and sayings. What high values of morality they teach, what ethics they preach, what intricate problems of Unitarianism they elucidate, how rich they are in philosophy; how they try to train us to be kind, good, benevolent and God fearing rulers, and faithful, sincere and law abiding subjects, how they persuade us to be warriors who can fight only for God, truth and justice, and not mercenaries murdering and plundering for wealth and riches, and how they instruct us to be teachers who can teach nothing injurious and harmful to mankind. Was there any such combination before and will there ever be?

Oelsner, the famous French Orientalist and author of "Les Effects de La Religion de Mohammad" says:

Pure, gentle and learned without fear and without reproach, he set the world the noblest example of chivalrous grandeur of character. His spirit was a pure reflection of that of Mohammad, it overshadowed the Islamic world and formed the animating genius of succeeding ages.

Osborne, in "Islam under the Arabs" says:

Ali had been advised by several of his counsellors to defer the dismissal of the corrupt governors previously appointed until he himself was sure against all eneinies. The Bayard of Islam, the hero without fear and without reproach, refused to be guilty of any duplicity or cornpromise with in justice. This uncompromisingly noble attitude cost him his state and his life; but such was Ali, he never valued anything above justice and truth.

Gibbon, in "The History of the Decline and Fall of the Roman Empire (vol.v)" says:

The zeal and virtues of Ali were never out stripped by any recent proselyte. He united the qualification of a poet, a soldier and a saint. His wisdom still breaths in a collection of moral and religious saying; and every antagonist in the combats of tongue or of sword was subdued by his eloquence and valour. From the first hour of mission to the last rites of his funeral, the apostle was never forsaken by this generous friend, whom he delighted to name his brother, his vicegerent and the faithful Aaron of second Moses.

Masoodi, the famous historian of Islam says:

If the glorious name of being the first Moslims, a comrade of the prophet in exile, his faithful companion in the struggle for the faith, his intimate associate in life, and his kinsman, if a true knowledge of the spirit of his teachings and of the Book, if self-abnegation and practice of justice, if honesty, purity, and love of truth and if knowledge of law and science constitute a claim to pre-eminence, then all must regard Ali as the foremost Moslim. We shall search in vain to find, either among his predecessor (save the Holy prophet, A.S.), or among his successor, those virtues with which God had endowed him.

His Religion

As has been declared by all the historians of Islam, Ali from his babyhood was adopted and looked after by the Holy Prophet (A.S.). Therefore naturally his religious tendencies from his childhood were those of the Holy prophet (A.S:).

The question as to when he embraced Islam is out of consideration. He was Moslim from the very beginning. His religion was the religion of the Holy prophet (A.S.).

Al-Imaamol-Kabeer Nooroddeen Ali bn Ibraheem Shaafii in his book Seera Halabiyya says:

Ali was like a son unio the Holy prophet (A.S.) therefore his religion from the very beginning was the religion followed by the Holy prophet (A.S.)".

The famous historian Masoodi says:

The general census of opinion amongst the Moslims historians and theologians is that Ali was never a non-Moslim and never prayed before idols, therefore the question of his embracing Islam does not and cannot arise.

His Wife, Children and Home Life

In the words of the spirit of Islam:

Hazrat Ali was married to Hazrat Fatima, the only daughter of the Holy prophet (A.S.) from Hazrat Khadeeja. He had been betrothed to her several days before the expedition to Badr. But the inarriage was celebrated three months later, Hazrat Ali being in his 21st year and Hazrat Fatima in 15th year of her life.

It was very happy marriage. The transcendental distinctiveness of their respective characters biended so weil with each other that they never quarrelled and complained of one another and led a happy and contended life. Each one of them was rich in his own rights; Fatima was the only heir of one of the richest women of Arabia, Khadeeja, and had inherited many orchards and gardens in Mecca and Madeena, besides that she was the daughter of the head of a rich clan and a king of a fast growing kingdom. Ali was a marshal who had very handsome shares from the spoils of wars. Yet all that they owned went to the poor, cripples and orphans, and they themselves often starved. Their only luxury in life was prayers, and the company of each other and their children, and they willingly shared the sorrows and suffering of poor. They were given a slave girl, Fizza, but the Holy prophet (A.S.) had made arrangement that every alternate day was the off day of Fizza and her mistress would do all the household work. Even when Hazrat Fatima was ill on Fizza's off day, Fizza would not be allowed to attend to the duties, but Hazrat Ali would work, and the hero of Badr, Ohod, Khandaq, Khaybar and Honayn was shen grinding oats lighting the oven, preparing the pread and looking after the children, Salmaan says:

What a household, the only daughter of the Holy prophet (A.S.) and wife of his vicegerent leading the life of a poor labourer. If they had spent one-tenth of what they were distributing daily they would have led a life of ease and comfort.

From Hazrat Ali the Lady of Light (Fatima) had four children and the fifth (Mohsin) was a stil! birth. The causes of this mishap and also that of her death are very sad and pathetic incidents of their lives. The names of these four children were Hassan, Hosayn, Zaynab (wife of Abdillah bn-Jafar) and Ommi- Kolthoom (wife of Obaydillah bn-Jafar). During the life time of Hazrat Fatima (A.S.) Hazrat Ali did not marry another woman. After her death he married Yamama and at her death another lady, having the name of Hanafiyya, from whom he had a son, Mohammad Haneefa and after her death he married again, thus he had many children some of whom had unparalleled place in the history of mankind, e.g. Hasan, Hosayn (the hero of Karbala), Zaynab (the defender of true Islam in Koofa and Damascus). Abbas (the commander of Hosayn's army in Karbala) and Mohammad Haneefa, the hero of Nahrawan.

Ali and his Foes

I have cited below a few cases which go to show what type of man was "Ali bn Abi Talib. As Pool says: He was truly a noble man, a man of righteousness, and a man of brave, humble and forgiving spirit, And as Oelsner says: - Pure, gentle and learned without fear and without reproach, setting the noblest example of character to the world. Out of hundreds and hundreds of cases to select I find it rather difficult which to choose and which not to choose. I have selected a few according to the standard of my knowledge and visualisation. Talha bn Abi Talha was not only a bitter enemy of Islam, but was personal enemy of the Holy prophet (A.S.) and Ali. His exertions to harm these two and their mission is a legion. In the battle of Ohod he was the flag-bearer of the army of Quraysh. Ali faced him and in a hand to hand encounter dealt him such a severe blow that he reeled and fell down. Ali left him like that and walked away from him. Many Moslim warriors ran up to Ali and advised him to finish Talha, saying that he was Ali's worst enemy, Ali replied: Enemy or no enemy he cannot defend himself now, and I cannot strike a man who is not in a position to defend himself. If he survives he is welcome to live as long as his life lasts. in the battle of "Jamal" in the thick of the encounter his slave Qamber brought some sweet syrup saying: My lord the sun is very hot and you have been constantly fighting, have a glass of this cold drink to refresh yourself.

Ali looked around himself and replied:

Shall I refresh myself when hundreds of people around me are lying wounded and dying of thirst and wounds? Instead of bringing sweet syrup for me take a few men with you and give each of these wounded persons a cool drink.

- My lord, they are all our enemies.

- They may be but they are human beings and attend to them.

In the battle of "Siffeen" Moaawiya reached the river Euphrates before the army of Hazrat, and took position of the river. When Hazrat's army reached there he was informed that they would not be allowed a drop of water from the river. Hazrat sent a messenger to Moaawiya saying that this action was against the canons of humanity and orders of Islam. Moaawiya's reply was:

A war is a war and therein one cannot accept principles of humanity and doctrines of Islam. My sole aim is to kill Ali and to demoralise his army and this stoppage of water will bring about these results easily and quickly.

Hazrat ordered Imaam Hosayn to attack and get back the river. The attack took place and river side position was captured. It was then Moaawiya's turn to beseech permission to get water from the river. His messengers arrived and Ali told them to take as much water as they like and as often as they require. When his officers told him that those were the very people who had refused water to them, should they be allowed a free run of the river? He replied:

They are human beings and though have acted inhumanely yet I cannot follow their example and cannot refuse a man food and drink because he happens to be my worst enemy.

It was the battle of Nahrawan and he himself was fighting like any other ordinary soldier. During this battle a man came to face him and in the encounter lost his sword. He realised his hopeless plight of standing before Ali without any weapon in hand. Ali's hand was raised for a blow when he saw the antagonist trembling with fear he lowered his hand slowly and said:

Run away friend you are not in a position to defend yourself.

This attitude made the man bold and he said:

Ali! why do not you kill me? it would have made one enemy less for you.

- I cannot strike a man, who cannot defend himself. You were begging for your life and it was spared.

The opponent got bolder and said:

I am told that you have never rerused a beggar. Now I beg you of your sword will you grant it to me?

Ali handed him over the sword. Taking possession of the sword he said:

- Now Ali! who is going to defend you against me and save you from my killing blow?

- Of course God, He will defend me if He so wills. He has appointed my death to be my guarding angei none can harm before it is due and none can save me when it arrives.

Nobility of thought and action effected the foe and he kissed the bridle of Ali's horse and said:

O lord, you are a great man indeed. You cannot only forsake the life of your enemy in a battle-field but also you can grant him your sword. May I have the honour to act as your body-guard and to fight for you?

- Friend! fight for truth and justice and do not fight for persons.

During 39 and 40 A.H. Moaawiya organised bands of murderers and brigands to enter border towns and to carry on loot, plunder, arson and rape. Komay! was at that time the governor of Heet. He asked Hazrat's permission to organise similar bands and carry plunder in the province of Circiea which was under the control of Moaawiya. Hazrat Ali replied:

I never expected such a suggestion from a man like you. It is more noble and more moral to guard your people and province than to plundei' others. They might be our enemies but they are human beings. They consist of civil population comprising of women and children how can one kill, loot and plunder them. No, never even dream of such a venture.

It was the month of Ramazaan, the month of fasting. It was the time of the morning prayers; the mosque was full of Moslims. Ali was kneeling before God and when he raised his head a terrible blow fell upon it giving a very deep cut. There was a great disturbance and commotion in the mosque. The murderer started running. The Moslims followed, caught and bound him in ropes and brought him before Ali who was on the prayer carpet drenched in blood and was reclining upon his sons. He knew the blow was fatal and he could not survive it but when the murderer was brought before him, he saw that the rope which had bound him was so tightly bound that it was cutting into his flesh. He turned towards those Moslims and said:

You should not be so cruel with your fellow being slacken his ropes, do not you see that they are cutting into his flesh and he is in agony.

So was Ali. History of Islam is full of the incidents of his chivalrous and merciful behaviour against his enemies.

Ali and his friends and relatives

Abdillan, son of his brother jafar. was his favourite nephew, whom he had brought up since the death of Jafar and to whom he had given his most favourite daughter, Zaynab, into marriage. This Abdillah once came to hirr requesting for an advance instalment of his share from Baytol-Mal. Ali refused and when the young man persisted he said:

No my son, not a day before all the others and not a pie more.

Aqeel, his elder brother was financially in a very unhappy condition, he asked for something more than his share and before the time was due. Hazrat refused, saying that he could not resort to dishonesty. Aqeel must wait till the time of distribution, and must bear the sufferings patiently. He had cited this incident in one of his sermons.

Bn-Haneefa was his trusted disciple and a faithful follower. He was governor o? a province and was once invited to a function which was followed by sumptuous dinner. When Hazrat hear of this he wrote him a very severe letter, criticising his action and saying:

You went to a dinner where only rich people were invited and poor were scornfully excluded.

Ali and his 2 servants: Qamber and Saocd

After his death Qamber related that he very seldom had the occasion to serve his master. Hazrat used to do his work for himself, used to wash his own clothings, used even to patch them whenever needed. He would draw water from the well for his daily use. He would give them good food and decent dresses, and would himself eat and dress like a very poor man. Let alone whipping or beating he never even got angry with us. He never used a cane even on his horse, camel or mule. These animals apparently understood his mood and desire and would trot and walk as he wished them to do. His oiten used phrase with them was "go easy child. Continuing Qamber said:

Once and only once he got annoyed with me. It was the occasion when I showed him the money that I had hoarded. It was from my share of income given to me like others from the Moslim treasury and the girls I had received from the members of his family. I had no immediate uss of it and had collected the amount. It was not much, being barely 100 Dirhams. When I showed him the amount he looked annoyed and what pained me more he looked very sad. I enquired as to why he was so sad, he said: "Qamber, if you had no use of this money, were there not people around you who were in need of it, some of them might have been starving and some ill and infirm, could you not have helped them. I never thought that you could be so heartless and cruel, and could love wealth for the sake of wealih. Qamber I am afraid you are not trying to acquire much from Isları, try more seriously and sincerely.Take these coins out of my house. I took them out and distributed them amongst the beggars in the Koofa mosque.

Saeed says:

it was a very hot day, Hazrat was writing some letters, he wanted to send me to call some of his officers, he called me, once, twice and thrice and each time I purposely kept silent and did not reply. He got up to go himself and saw me sitting not very far away from him. He asked me as to why I did not respond to his call, I replied: "Sir, I want to find out when and how you get angry. A smile played on his lips and he replied: "You cannot rouse my anger with such childlike tricks, Then he set me free and kept on supporting me till his death.

Ali amongst his subjects

Once Obaydillah bn Abbas, as governor, ill-treated the Bani-Tameem clan. They complained to Hazrat. He wrote to bn-Abbas:

You should not behave like a beast with your subjects. They are respectable people ard should be treated respectfully. You are representing me and your treatment is considered as that of mine. Your first consideration should be the welfare of those over whom you rule and then to treat them with due respect and consideration.

Once a group of non-Moslim subjects waited on Hazrat complaining, that Abdillah bn Abbas always treated them with contempt and scorn. They were agriculturists and agricultural labour. It had then become a practice that non-Moslims were usually treated scornfully. Hazrat wrote to Abdillah: Agricultural population of you province complain about your harsh, contemptuous and cruel treatment. Their complaints require careful consideration. I feel that they deserve better treatment than what was met out to them, give them a change to approach you and meet them kindly and politely. They may be heathens, and polytheists but being our subjects and human beings they do not deserve to be driven from us and to be treated harshly and contemptuously.

Hazrat Ali was passing through Ambar, with his army. The rich men of the province, as was the custom of those times, came out to greet him. They offered the best Persian horses as presents, and requested his permission to act as hosts to his army. He met them very courteously, but very politely refused to accept the gifts and the invitation, saying:

You have paid your taxes, to receive anything more from you, even when you offer it voluntarily and willingly, is a crime against the state. But when they persisted and pressed their request, he ordered that the horses could be accepted against their taxes, and so far as the feast was concerned it must be paid out of the war expenses.

In the Magazine "al-Hakam" vol.ii No.47 of 1906, there appeared an article (Apparently translated from the Magazine al-Hablol al-Mateen) saying:

The Russians in 1905 found an order of Hazrat Ali, in his own hand-writing which was in Koofi script. This was found in a monastery of Ardabeel, chief town of Azarbaijaan. This letter was an amnesty deed to the monastery and the Christians of Ardabeel. Translation of this deed appeared in the Russian newspapers and thence it was translated in the Turkish papers and in the Arabic Magazines of Cairo and Beirut, and lots of commentating articles on the spirit of toleration and the treatment of conquered by Islam were written by the Russians and Arab Christians.

In this deed Hazrat says that as a caliph and a ruler, he promises safety and security of life, property, honour, social status and religious freedom of Armenian Christians. This order should be obeyed by his officers and by his successors. The Christians should not be maltreated or looked down because they are non-Moslims. So long as they do not try to betray and injure the cause of the state or Islam they should not be molested and should be allowed to practice their religion and trades freely and openly.

Islam teaches us to carry a message of peace with us and improve the status of society wherever we go and the best way to achieve this is to create amity, friendliness and concord between human beings; therefore, Moslims should try to develop friendship of these people and should never resort to wrong use of power, force and arrogance. They should not be over-taxed, should not be humiliated and should not be forced out of their homes, lands and trades. Their priests should be treated with due respects, their monasteries should be protected, they should be allowed to carry on their lectures, teachings and preachings as usual and their religious ceremonies should not be prohibited. If they want-to build their places of Worship then fallow and ownerless lands should be allotted to them. One, who disobeys this order is going against the orders of God and the Holy prophet (A.S.) and will deserve His Wrath.

Haarith bn Sohayl, one of the governor of the provinces, was in Koofa, once he was riding through the city and saw Hazrat Ali also riding. He got down from his horse to accompany Hazrat on foot. Hazrat stopped his horse and said:

It ill-becomes a man to lower himself before anybody but his God, please get upon your horse, even had you not been an officer of the state I would not have allowed you to lower yourself like this, the sight of such humiliation of man before man never pleases me. It is the worst form of tyranny which can be practised.

There is a letter of Hazrat, which is actually a system of rules and regulations for the administration of a benign government and a code for higher values of morality, it is included in Nahjo-Salaagna and is referred so oftea hy historians of Europe and Philosorhers of Argola, and even by Justice Kayari in his presidential address in Karachi Bar on April 16, 1930 that it now needs no Introduction. In this lettei there are orders which show that he wanted his officers to remember thai the people over whom they rule are the trust entrusted to them by God and should be treated as such.

Ali and the poor

He had a very sofi corner in his heart for old, weak, infirin, disabled and poor, and children were always his favourites.

It was the hottest day of the season, he had finished his noon-prayers in the mosque and was passing through the bazaar, he saw a young slave-girl piteously weeping on the road. He asked her the reason. She said that her master had given her some money to get dates from the bazaar; the dates which she brought were not liked by her master, he wanted them to be returned and get back the money. The fruit-seller refused to take them back, her master was beating her for the money and fruit-selier had also caned her for going to him cver and over again. She did not know what to do and whom to approach for helo. Hazrat accompanied her to the fruit-seller to advise him to take back the dates. He vas a new comer to Koofa and did not recognise Hazrat and was ude to tim, some passer-by intervened and told him who Hazrat was. He umped froin his shop and begged of Hazrat to excuse him and said that he vould give back the money immediately to her. Hazrat replied that it was really mean of him to eat honest st'ggestion disdainfully and haughtily and to cow down before power and might so atjectly and humiliatingly. The owner of the slave-girl had also heard the news of this incident and ran to meet Hazrat to apologise for the trouble caused by the slave-gir. Hazrat told him:

You have no mercy for a person who is under your power and carnot forgive her inistake, have you a right to expect Mercy and Forgiveness from the Lord? You people have Kquired nothing from Islam but its name.

One day he saw an old woman carrying a heavy load of firewood which she coulú ill-alford to lift, she was tottering under the weight. Hazrat relieved her of her weight carried it to her hamlet and on her request lighted her oven for her and gave her some money also. She did not know who Hazrat was and was thanking him for his kindness when a neighbour entered the hamlet, recognised Hazrat and told her, who he was, only then she realised that who had served ter like an obedient servart was the caliph and the king.

Orily after his death the world came to know that he had provided a shelter for o leper in an advanced stage of the disease. The shelter was outside the town, he used to go there daily, dress his wounds, feed him with his own hands (because the leper had lost his hands), wash him, put his bed in order and carry him out of the sheiter for itúe time, so that he may get fresh air. Accidentaily relatives and friends of Hazrat came across this shelter and found a leper in it, learned his history and told him Hazrat was murderer and they had just then by The 90 aserted the poor oriple that he died on the spot.

Ali's Food

Hazrat Ali (A.S.) always ate such kind of food and dressed in such a way thai even the poorest can afford better than that. It was not because he was poor but it was because he wanted to lead the life of the poorest person and spend all that could thus be spared on poor. I have noted below certain cases quoted by the historians, these incidents are of the time when he was the ruler and king of the entire Moslim Empire except Syria.

Imaam Ahmad bn Hambal in his "Masnad" cited Soweda bn Ghafla" saying:

One day I went to see Ali (A.S.) in the Government House (Darol-Imarah). It was the time of breakfast and before him there was a cup of milk and some barley bread. The bread was dry, stale, hard and did not contain any butter, or oil. It could not be easily broken into pieces. Hazrat was exerting himself to break it and to sosteni. I turned towards his slave, Fizza and said: Fizza! have you no pity upon you! old master and why cannot you give him softer bread and add some butter or oil to it? She replied: "Why should I pity limn when he never pities himself. He has given strict orders that nothing is to be added to his bread and even chail and husks are not to be separated from the flour. We, ourselves, eat much better food than this, though we are his slaves. Hearing this I told him O Lord, have pity on yourself, look at your age, your responsibilities, your hard work and your food. Hie replied "O Soweda, you have no idea what the Holy prophet

(A.S.) used to eat. He never ate full stomach for three consecutive days. Allama Kamaloddeen Mohammad bn Talha Shaafii in his book Mataəlibos-Soaal quotes Abdillah bn Zorara saying:

I went to see Hazrat Ali (A.S.) on an Eed day. He asked me to join in his breakfast. I agreed. A very poor kind of food was served before us. I told him, O Lord, you are such a rich man, a caliph and a king. I was expecting that game would be served before us but what do I see? Hazrat replied "bn-Zorara, you have heard of mighty kings who have lead life of luxury. Let me be a ruler leading the life of a poor and humble personi-a humble labourer.

Meelaani in his book "Seera" and Iraaam Ahmad in his Mosnad quote the famous "Tabayi bn Abi-Rafay, who says:

I went to Hazrat ori an Eed day and while I was sitting there a bag was brought before Hazrat, I thought that it might contain jewels. Hazrat opened the bag, it contained dried pieces of bread, which he softened with water. I asked him as to the reason of sealing such a kind of food which even a beggar would not care to stea! Hazrat smiler aid said: "I keep it sealed because my children try to substitute softer bread, containing oil or butter in it. I said "Has God prohibited you to eat better kind of food? He replied: "No, but I want to eat the kind of food which the poorest of this realm can afford at least once a day. I shall improve it after I have improved their standards of life. I want to live, {vel and suffer like them.

His Dress

Imaam Ahmad in his book "al-Manaaqib" and bn-Atheer in his history quote Haroon bn Anza saying that he accompanied his father (Anza) to the "Khorniq" castle to meet Hazrat Ali, those were winter days, and the winter was very severe, he found Hazrat in a very thin cotton garment, and the cold wind was making him shiver. Anza asked him:

O Commander of faithful! God has reserved a share for you and your family from Baytol-Mal (Moslim Treasury) why do you not make use of it?.

He replied:

O Anza! I do not want anything from your treasury, this is the dress I have brought with me from Madeena.

Imaam Ahmad quotes Zayd bn Wahab saying that once Hazrat came out of his house and there were patches sewn to his dress. bn-Noaja, who was a Kharijite and an enemy and yet was allowed to lead a peaceful and comfortable life by Hazrat at Koota taunted Hazrat on the very poor and coarse kind of dress put on by him. He replied:

Let go, what have you to find objection in my dress, it is the kind which our masses can afford, why can you not think of their lives and dresses, I shall improve my standard after I have succeeded in improving theirs. I shall continue to live like them. Such kind of dress makes one feel humble and meek and give up vanity, haughtiness and arrogance

Aliol-Mottaqi in his books Kanz al-Ommaal and Tabari in ar-Riyaaz an-Nazira quote Omar bn Qays saying that once he asked Hazrat as to the reason of his having patches in his dress, he replied:

o Omar, such type of dress makes you soft hearted, vanishes vanity from your mind and it is the kind which poor Moslims can conveniently afford.

Shaykhol-Islam Imaam Abo-Omar Yoosof bn Abdl-Birr in his book al-Isteeaab quotes Hasan bn Jermooz saying that his father once saw Hazrat coming out of Koofa mosque in a shirt made of jute cloth and around him were people so well dressed that compared to him they looked like princes, he was advising them as to how understand religion.

Imaam Ahmad quotes Abo-Naziya, the ready-made cloth merchant of Koofa saying that Hazrat purchased two shirts from his shop, one was of superior quality, which he handed over to his slave Qamber to put on and the other which was of a rough cloth, very coarse and cheap, he reserved it for himself.

His services to Islam

The first occasion on which Ali offered his services to the cause of Islam was when the Holy Prophet (A.S.) was first ordered by God to preach Islam openly.

For three years the Holy prophet (A.S.) was preaching Islam under absolute secrecy, at the end of the third year (i.e. the fourth year after "Bayat, in 45 Aamol Feel) he received orders to preach his near relations and to admonish them. John Devonport in his book "An apology for Mohammad and Quraan) writes:

The Holy Prophet (A.S.) directed Ali to prepare an entertainment and to invite the sons and grandsons of Abdi-Mottalib. This was done and about forty of them came, but Abo-Lahab, made the company break up before Mohammad (A.S.) had an opportunity to speak. Next day a second invitation was issued and when they came and the frugal meal was served the Holy prophet (A.S.) rose and declared his sacred character, offered the treasures of time and of eternity to whomsoever should become his disciples, and concluded by demanding, who among you will aid me to bear this burden, who will be my Lieutenant, and Vazeer, as Aaron was unto Moses? The assembly remained mute with astonishment, not one venturing to accept the offered perilous office, until Ali, Mohammad's cousin, stood up and exclaimed:

O prophet! I will, though I am indeed the youngest of these present, the most rheum of them as to the eyes and the slenderest of them as to the legs; 1, O prophet, will be thy Vazeer over them.

On which throwing his arms around the generous and courageous youth, and pressing him to his bosom, Mohammad (A.S.) declared;

Behold my brother and my Vazeer and obey him.

Many historians are of opinion that it was a momentous declaration at a momentous occasion. The first and the greatest service done to the cause of Islam. If the appeal of the Holy prophet (A.S.) was then left unanswered, the propagation of Islam would have been nibbled in the bud. Carlyle is of the opinion:

Though all the people gathered there, were not enemies of the Holy prophet (A.S.) yet most of them were dead against this religion and some were quite uninterested. To them the whole thing (and adult person preaching a few religion dild a yourg courageous youth offering his servicce vebememly) looked like a big farce. They laughed at both of them and dispersed advising Ali's father to obey his youngest son fror inat day onward. But these two pecple (Holy prophet and Hazrat Ali) proved to the world that there was nothing laughable in their deciaration and they had wisdom and courage enough to make their mission a success.

He further says:

Youns Ali had realiy such a personality as could be liked, loved and venerated by everybody. He was the man of excellent character loving and loveable, so intensely brave that if anything stood against his bravery it was consumed as if by tire, yet he was so gentle and kind that he represented the model of a Christian Knight.

As was said this was really the first and the greatest service of Islam. From this day to the last day of his life, Hazrat Ali sincerely, bravely and nobly acted as the defender of the faith. The second great cccasion was when the Holy prophet (A.S.) was forced to leava Mecca, making somebody stay in his place in such a way that his enemies would believe that he was still in his house and thus he might safely go away in the darkness of the night. This departure to Madeena is called Hijra and the Mosiim era is named after this event. It took place during the month of September, 662 AD. Thursday the 26th Safar (thirteen years after the Holy propher started preaching Islam). People of Madeena were favourably inclined towards Islam and some had embraced this religion and had promised every kind of support to the Holy Prophet (A.S.). Many Moslims had left for Madeena and were handsomely treated by Ansaars of Madeena. Quraysh realising that !ciam was gaining a good support and a firm hold at Madeena and those who had led from Mecca were being happily settled there, decided to strike at the root cause. Their hatred of the Holy prophet (A.S.) was so intense that nothing would satisfy them but his death. They gathered at Nadwa and decided that a few people froin each clan of Quraysh would jointly attack the Holy prophet (A.S) and strike him with their swords at one and the same time. Thus no individual of any single clan would be responsible of his death, and Bani-Hashim would not be able to kill any one person in return or to fight against any single cian and as they were not strong enough to fight against all the clans of Quraysh at the same time they would be forced to be satisfied with blood-money (Diyat). They further decided to surround the house of the Holy prophet (A.S.) during ne night so that he may not go away and then to kill him next morning. Thus Porty men got ready and surrounded his house. God revealed to His apostle of the intrigue planned against him and ordered him to leave Mecca the very same night. It was a serious and dangerous occasion. He was ordered by God to go and to go in such a way that none of his enemies might suspect his departure and, if possible, none of his friends might know of it. The walls of his house were barely seven leo high and shyone placing a stone and standing upon it could easily peep into the house. He knew the house was surrounded. Whom could he ask to sleep in his bed covering himself with his (Holy prophet's) coverlet, such a person should not expose his identify till the dawn (till the prophet was safe and out of danger) and should be unarmed, so that he might not rouse the suspicion of peeping enemies, he should thus be willing to bear the brunt of the enemies" anger in the morning and be ready to be killed. To whom but to Ali, could the Holy prophet (A.S.) turn at this most dangerous moment. In details he informed Ali of the whole plan and of the positive danger of taking his place saying that the least could be expected of those enemies would be death without torture. Ali asked:

If I take your place and leave you alone to go through the gathered enemies will your life be safe?

The Holy prophet (A.S.) replied:

Yes. God has promised me a safe passage through them.

Ali bowed his head before God as a sign of thanks-giving. He lied down on the bed of the Holy prophet (A.S.) and covered himself with the prophet's coverlet. During the night many stones and arrows were aimed at him. Stones hit him in the back and on the head and arrows embedded in his legs but he did not even turn in his bed. In the morning he was found out by the enemies only when one of them pulled the coverlet. When they wanted to attack him knowing that he was Ali not Mohammad (A.S.), only then he unsheathed his sword.

In Madeena the Holy prophet (A.S.) was forced to defend himself and his followers, and was thus forced to fight many battles. At each and every battle Ali was the hero. And it was he who fought single-handed with famous worriers of Arabia, defeated the enemies and brought a victory to Islam.

Records of these battles carry with them chronicles of his bravery, courage and chivalry.

Even the enemies sang songs of his valour and gallantry. Every one of these battles was an outcome of very grave circumstances and conditions, and combination of very serious events and very harmful forces against the safety of the Moslims and Islam. There were many such encounters but I have briefly mentioned only five of those instances where the events had far reaching effects. In each of them Ali alone broke through evil combinations and carried the Moslims and Islam to position of safety, eminence and power.

The first of these battles was Badr. It took place in the month of Ramazaan of the 2nd year of Hijra. Moslims were not prepared for a battle and could ill-afford to fight against superior forces. But Madeena was being invaded and necessarily the Holy prophet (A.S.) was forced to defend himself and his followers. He decided to leave Madeena and fight out the battle in an open field. He had only 313 Moslims who were not adequately armed for a battle, many of them were nervous of an encounter, and were suffering from inferiority complex. The Quraysh had come with an army of about 1000 warriors which fact had frightened the Moslims even more. The battle took place and about 36 Quraysh were killed by Ali; some of them were very important persons and famous warriors of Quraysh.

Ali killed every one of those 36 antagonis's in hand to hand combat, and most of them were the persons who had surrounded the house of Holy prophet (A.S.) on the night of Hijra. During this elicounter he was wounded, but by his bravery and courage he brought home to Moslims that he would act as the first line of defence for Islam, that they had no cause to suffer from inferiority compex and that God would defend them against heavy odds. Amongst Quraysh there were two worst enemies of Islam, Abo-Jahal and Abo-Sofyaan; and in this battle Abo-Jahal was killed. Ali was hero of this battle and brought the first victory to Seiam in armed encounters with its enemies.

The second most important battle was that of Ohod. Quraysh and their leader Abo-Sofyaan were smarting under the defeat of Badr and had sworn to retaliate, The idolaters were burning for revenge. They made formidable preparations for another encounter and succeeded in obtaining assistance of Tihama and Kinana tribes. Abo-Sofyaan's wife Kinda, mother of Moaawiya, took keen interest in all arrangements and preparations. She had written poerns to excite Quraysh against Islam and had organised a band of women minstrels who accompanied the army of Quraysh to the battle field. Thus they had mobilised an army of 3000 infantry and 2000 cavalry: The Holy prophet (A.S.) could muster only 700 Moslims to face this horde. They faced each other in the battle-field of Ohod. The battle took place on the 11th Shawwal 3 A.H. (a year after the battle of Badr). The command of Moslim army was divided between Ali and Hamza and Abo-Sofyaan had appointed Khaalid bn Waleed, Akrama bn Abi-Jahal and Oinar bn Ass as the three commanders to command the right and left wing and the centre respectively.

The first encounter took place between Ali and Talha bn Talha. This encounter carries with it an incident of marvellous chivalry by Ali, which I have narrated elsewhere. Talha suffered defeat at the hands of Ali and died. He was flag bearer of Quraysh's army.

His death brought his four sons and one grandson to face Ali, and each one of them was killed by him and other flag bearers followed them and were in turn killed by Ali; then a general encounter took place in which Ali and Hamza carried the day and Moslims came out victorious. "But eagerness for spoils threw the ranks of Moslim army into disorder, Ali however tried to keep them in order, but it was not to be. Knaalid bn Waleed immediately attacked them from the rear and the flank, he wounded the Holy prophet (A.S.) with a Javelin; and had also stoned him, face of the prophet was also wounded and he had fallen down from the horse. Khaalid bn Waleed started shouting with a loud voice "the lying prophet is slain" upon which without stopping to ascertain the followers of Islam fled panic stricken" (Devonport).

The wounded prophet was left in the battle-field with only Ali, Hamza, Abo-Dajana and Zakwaan to defend him. These brave warriors fought fiercely and during this encounter Hamza was killed, Zakwaan and Abo-Dajana lay seriously wounded and Ali was left alone in the battle-field. He had received 16 wounds but he searched and found the Holy prophet (A.S.) lying wounded and surrounded by enemies under command of Khaalid who were trying to kill him; he fought against these six men, killed two of them and scattered the rest; he bodily lifted the Holy prophet (A.S.) and carried him to a mount; he kept on attacking the rallying armies of the enemy; and kept on shouting that "the Holy prophet (A.S.) is alive and calling Moslims to come back." Those Moslims who had not fled very far came back, saw the wounded prophet, saw his daughter, Fatima (who had come out of Madeena hearing the rumour of her father's death) attending him, they took heart and gathered again under the command of Ali and started fighting again, and victory was gained. The most peculiar aspect of this battle was that the greed of the Moslim Warriors had converted a hard earned victory into a ignominious defeat and Ali had reconverted this defeat into a glorious victory. He thus once again saved the day, saved the face of the fleeing Moslims and the most important of all he saved was the life of the Holy prophet (A.S.), but without Ali the Holy prophet would have been killed.

Twenty eight famous warriors of Arabia were killed by Ali in this battle of whom seventeen were flag bearers of Quraysh. The Holy Prophet (A.S.) declared that the Angel Gabriel was loud in the praise of Ali and had said: There is no braver youth than Ali and no better sword than his Zol-Fiqaar.

A detailed account of this battle may be read in:

1 Wagaadi's history of Prophets

2 Shah Ismaaeel Hamwi's history "Abol-Fida

3 Tabari's history

The third momentous armed encounter of Moslims with Quraysh is called the battle of clans (Ahzaab) or battle of the moat or ditch (Khandacy. It is so called because many clans of Arabs were persuaded by Abo-Sofyaan to help him to annihilate Islam and the Moslims and because when these forces invaded Madeena, the Holy prophet (A.S.) was obliged to dig a moat or ditch around his army. This battle also proves that the Holy prophet (A.S.) was forced to take up arms in defence of his followers and his mission. It took place on the 23rd Zil-Quda in the year 5 A.H.

The defeat at Ohod was great blow to Quraysh and their leader Abo-Sofyaan. While retreating from Ohod he had promised that he will come back again to avenge the defeat. He instigated the clans of Bani-Nazeer, Bani-Ghatafaan, Bani-Saleem and Bani-Kinana and also succeeded in persuading Bani-Quryza, who till then had not sided with any party, to join their forces against Isiam. Abo-Sofyaan was very sure of his success. He specially relied upon the fame of Omar bn Abd-Wod, who was as famous in Arabia as Rostam was in Persia. He had gathered an army of about 9 to 10 thousand soldiers under command of this famous warrior. They marched upon Madeena.

The Holy prophet (A.S.) could barely muster 2000 Moslims to face this army. For nearly a month the armies stood facing each other and one day Omar jumped the moat and faced the Moslim army, challenging them for an encounter. He was accompanied by Akrama bn Abi-Jahal, Abdillah bn Mogheera, Zarar bn Khattaab, Nawfal bn Abdillah and others. His bravery, his valour and courage were so well known in Arabia that none of the Moslims except Ali dared face him. The assemblage of famous warrior tribes and the presence of Omar bn Abd-Wod as their commanderhad made the Moslims so nervous that even the Quraan says:

Their eyes were petrified and their hearts were beating violently and they were thinking of running away.

Thrice Omar bn Abd-Wod challenged them to out and every time none but Ali stood up and asked the permission of the Holy prophet (A.S.) to face him. Twice the Holy prophet (A.S.) refused him the permission, but in the end he allowed him, saying:

Today faith in embodiment is facing embodied infidelity.

Then he raised his hands in prayers and beseeched God, saying:

Lord! I am sending Ali alone in the battle-field, do not allow me to be left alone, you are the best Companion and the best Guardian.

Moslims were so certain of Ali being killed by Omar that some of them came forward to have a last look at his face. The encounter ended in Ali's success and Omar's death, after Omar he faced Abdillah bn Mogheera and Nawfal bn Abdillah and killed them both. Thus a victory was won without any Moslims, except Ali, coming out of the ranks. In the encounter with Omar and the defeat and death of this great warrior Ali again exhibited such a chivalrous attitude that the sister of Omar composed a poem in praise of the man who faced her brother, fought bravely against him and paid such a noble and chivalrous tribute to his vanquished enemy. In it she said:

if anyone else than Ali had killed her brother, she would have wept over the infamy her life long, but not now.

The death of Omar had completely demoralised the various clans gathered and they started leaving the army and going back to their countries. Quraysh went back to Mecca sad and dejected.

Thus Ali brought an end to the hostilities of Quraysh in three encounters of Badr, Ohod and Khandaq. Their best warriors were killed, their unity against Islam was crushed, their pride was humiliated and their prestige before Arab Clans lowered by him and by him alone.

He further raised the status of Moslims among the haughty, merciless and warring tribes of Arabia. In all these three battles not more than sixty Moslims were killed, and he alone had killed more than seventy enemies of Islam, every one of whom was the head of some clan or a sub-clan, a warrior famous for his bravery or a deadly enemy of the Holy prophet (A.S.) and Islam.

For a detailed account of this battle, the following books may be consulted.

1 Shah Waliollah Dahlaawi's Izabatol-Khifa.

2 Kaamil bn Atheer's History vol.ii

3 Seyooti's ad-Dorrol-Manthoor.

4 Tabari's History

In their struggle for existence Moslims had to face a very serious opposition from Jews. In the beginning they tried to help Quraysh against Islam surreptitiously and then openly. But when Ali broke through the enmity of Quraysh and when Holy prophet (A.S.) was forced to banish the Jews from Madeena, they decided to try their fate against Islam with the help of Bani-Asad, Bani-Kinana and Bani-Ghatafaan. Khaybar was the province, which they had occupied since the times of their banishment from Palestine. It contained a few fortresses, the biggest of them was called Qumoose, which was on a steep hill. In these fortresses they started gathering in large-numbers and in the end they raised an army of about 10 to 12 thousand warriors and were scheming to march on Madeena. Hearing these serious news the Holy prophet (A.S.) decided to face them at Khaybar only. He marched at the head of an army of 3000 soldiers. This battle took place in Moharram of the year 7 A.H.

Ali then was suffering from sour eyes and was left at Madeena. The Moslim army succeeded in defeating the Jews in minor skirmishes but when they tried to capture the main fort of Qumoose they had to face a set back; they could not succeed though they tried for days at a stretch. The defeats sustained there, were sadly demoralising the Moslim army. Holy prophet (A.S.) had allowed every important person to command the Moslim forces day by day, but each day the result was fresh defeat, fresh demoralisation, fresh boldness of Jews and daily increasing danger of some more clans, emboldened by the weakness and defeats of Moslims, joining hands with the Jews. There were still many such tribes who were deadly against Islam and wanted to harm it, but Moslims victories at Badr, Ohod and Khandaq had made them nervous. The news of the defeats at Khaybar were making them bold. In the words of The Spirit of Islam:

The Jews of Khaybar united by an ancient alliance with Bedouin horde of the Bani-Ghatafaan were incessantly working for the formation of a powerful coalition against the Moslims, and the Holy prophet (A.S.) knew fully well the power possessed by the desert races to injure Moslims.

There was further danger of Monafiqeen (hypocrites and double dealers) staging a revolt in Madeena. Promp measures were needed to avert these evils. Only a victory could have saved the situation which was getting more and more critical day by day. The prophet was himself ill and sadly felt the need of Ali at his side. He knew that though ill yet Ali had not left him alone and had followed him, therefore ill or not ill Ali had to come to the succour of Moslims, Islam and the Holy prophet (A.S.). When the news of the last disastrous repulse of the Moslims were brought to him, the Holy prophet (A.S.) said:

Tomorrow I shall give the command (the flag, an ensignia of the command) of this army to a man who is brave, who will keep on attacking, who will not run away from the battle-field, who loves God and His prophet and is beloved by God and His prophet and who will not come back to me without success.

Next day Ali was called from his bed and was handed over the command. He took the fort by storm; killed Marhab, Anther Morra, Harris and four other chieftains of the Jew tribes in hand to hand combats, broke the door of the fort single handed, carried his army inside the fort and within four hours he flew the flag of the Holy crophet (A.S.) on the biggest fortress of Arabia and thus once more saved Islam from a disastrous end.

The news of success so pleased the Holy prophet (A.S.) that he, though ill, came out to greet the victor embraced him and said:

Ali had I not been afraid that Moslims will start regarding you as Christians regard the Christ, I would have said things about you which would have made the Mcslims venerate you and to consider the dust of your feet as something worth venerating; but it will suffice to say that you are from me and I am from you; you will inherit me and I will inherit you; you are unto me what Aaron was unto Moses; you will fight for my cause, you will be nearest to me on the day of Judgement; you will be next to me on the fountain of Kawther, enmity against you is enmity against me: a war against you is a war against me; your friendship is my friendship; to be at peace with you is to be at peace with me; your flesh is my flesh; your blood is my blood; who will obey you will obey me. Truth is on your tongue, in your heart and in your mind. You have as much faith in God as I have. You are door to me. As per orders of God I give you these tidings that your friends will be rewarded in the Heaven and your enemies will be punished in the Hell.

For further details of the above Hadeeth and the battle of Khaybar, the following books may be consulted:

1 Meraaj an-Nobowwa vol.i p.216

2 al-Manaaqib of Khawaarizmi

3 Molla Ali Hamdani's Yanaabee al-Mawadda

4 bn-Hishaain's Seera p.187

5 Tabari's History

The victory which Ali brought to Islam in Khaybar proved of great consequence to its mission and its followers. It gave such an importance and prestige over the infidels of the Quraysh that they, who till then had complete control and sway over Mecca and did not even allow the Holy prophet (A.S.) and his followers to come for Haj and Omra and had forced them for the treaty of Hodaybiyya, were now obliged to surrender the city to him and Mecca fell before the superior forces of Islam.

The causes of the invasion and fall of Mecca are not to be discussed here; suffice it to say that Abo-Sofyaan who had brought it all upon the heads of Quraysh, later leaving the country and countrymen to the devil started running after every important person to secure his own and his family's freedom of life and property from the Holy prophet (A.S.) and through the mediation of Abbas (uncle of Holy prophet) he received the pardon sought for. The behaviour of the Holy prophet (A.S.) against these murderers of Moslims and the enemies of Islam was sc merciful benign and humane that he pardoned every one of them, a clemency and kindriess which was and shall ever remain unparalleled in the history of mankind. But Mecca was taken over by the Moslims, the precincts of Kaba were cleared of all idols by the person of the Holy prophet (A.S.) and Ali, and it ceased to exist as the centre of infidelity and polytheism in Arabia.

The fall of Mecca which took place in the Ramazaan of 8 A.H. (January 630 A.D.) was accompanied witi, serious repercussions. The success of Islam since the Hijra had brought many followers to its fold. Those were of three types, some had seen the truth in its preaching and had accepted it sincerely and faithfully, some were such that they wanted to bask in the glory of a religion which was fast becoming a mighty temporal power and they wished to make their worldly positions good through its influence and had accepted it with those ulterior motives, while there were some whose conversion was under false impression that unless they had accepted Islam their lives and properties were not safe. The fall of Mecca had very sad effect upon those two latter groups. They were not expecting that Abo-Sofyaan and Quraysh would succumb so easily to the pressure of Moslim invasion. Clearing of idols from the precir.cts of Kaba and closing its doors to the infidels was a sadder blow, it became more poignant when they found that their age long enemy, the mail whose valour and whose sword brought all these victories to Islam and disastrous defeats to their side, that is, Ali was the flag bearer a (commander) of the Holy prophet's (A.S.) forces on the occasion of the fall of Mecca, and along with the Holy prophet (A.S.) he was the man who cleared Kaba of its idols. There still were many polytheist clans in Arabia, to them Mecca was the centre of worship, amongst them there were two powerful Bedouin tribes, Bani-Hawazan and Bani-Thaqeef. They now were joined by Bani-Nasser, Bani-Saad, Bani-Hishaam and Bani-Hilaal. Those tribes decided to stage a come back and were quietly promised help by the hypocrites.

The whole thing was arranged so quickly and so stealthily that by the time the Moslims could come out of the sweet pleasure of success at Mecca there was an army of 20,000 warriors at Taaif ready to face them. The Holy prophet (A.S.) marched to Taaif at the head of an army of 15,000 Moslims. Some of them were freed slaves of Moslims conquest of Mecca and many more were the hypocrites of the types mentioned above, and there were few thousand of those Moslims who had accompanied him from Madeena.

The hostile tribes decided to attack the Moslim army at a point of vantage at Honayn and selected two prominences where they concealed their archers. Moslims were very proud of their strength and were very sure of their success, but their behaviour during the encounter was shamelessly timorous and cowardly. The Almighty Lord discussing their attitude in this battle says (section 9, Sorat-Tawba):

God came to your help on so many occasions, on the day of Honayn, your vanity in the number of your soldiers and your arrogance did not prove of any avail to you, you were badly defeated and could not find any place of shelter, you started running away without shame.

This encounter took place in the month of Shawwal 8, AH. (January/February 030 A.D.). When the Moslim army marched towards the place where archers were concealed. The enemy opened the campaign with such a severe onslaught of their archery that Moslim army could not stand it. The assault was fierce and the confusion in the Moslim ranks made the archers bolder and they came nearer and attacked from both the back and from the front. Moslims could not stand the attack any longer. They started running without putting up any resistance and did not care to leave even the Holy prophet (A.S.) alone (Saheeh Bokhaari).

The first battalion to run in pell-mell was the one in command of Khaalid bn Waleed (Rawzatos-Safa, vol.ii, p. 137, Taareekh al-Ambiaa, vol.i p.388). He was accompanied by Bani-Saleem and freshly converted Quraysh of Mecca. This was followed by such a disorderly and tumultuous flight of Moslims that only ten persons out of an army of 15000 were left with the Holy prophet (A.S.). Eight of them were Bani-Hashim (Abbas and his two sons, Ali, Aqeel and three other Cousins of the Holy prophet, A.S.).

Abbas was shouting the Moslims to come back, reminding them of oaths of allegiance taken and promises made, but it was of no avail. Those who had accepted Islam for wealth and power or under false fears were not willing to risk their lives. They ran as fast as they could. Many of them who had carefully hidden their enmity of the rising power were happy at the defeat, they gathered round Abo-Sofyaan, started congratulating him and saying that "the magical circle of the lying prophet is broken. They were praying for the come back of polytheism (Abol-Fida, p.349-Rawzatos-Safa, p. 136 vol.i-Taareekh al-Ambiaa, p.389 vol.ii).

Once again it fell to the lot of Ali to save the Holy prophet (A.S.) and the Islam. Armies of Bani-Hawazan and Bani-Thaqeef under cover of their archers were rushing down the hillock, and were getting ready for a fierce onslaught. Ali divided the small band of faithful Moslims in three divisions; to Abdillah bn Masood, Abbas bn Abdi-Mottalib and his nephew Abo-Sofyaan bn Harris, he assigned the duty of guarding the Holy prophet (A.S.), to three others he ordered to guard the rear and he faced the onslaught with only three Warriors along with him. He fought and fought, he was wounded, but he faced the commander of hostile army, Abo-Jerdal in a hand to hand combat and killed him with one stroke of sword; he attacked the enemy's rank once again, bringing the number of those whom he had slain on that day to forty. His aides had a glorious example before them, they also fought bravely and killed thirty more men.

The day was saved, the commander of the enemy's army was killed, their ranks were broken, they had no courage to face Ali and started retreating. They sight of a powerful enemy under retreat, made the fleeing Moslims bold and they came back after as victory was won for them.

A detailed account of this encounter is to be found in:

1 Rawzatos-Safa vol.ii, p. 136.

2 Taareekh Al-Ambiaa vol.ii, p.388

3 Seera bn Hishaam vol.i p.621

4 Kanz al-Ommaal vol.v, p.307

During the life time of Holy prophet (A.S.) Hazrat Ali was sent on many occasions for propagation of Islam and on many missions of mercy and peace. He carried out these duties to the satisfaction of the Holy prophet (A.S.) and God. For instance in the words of "The Spirit of Islam:

The men of Khaalid bn Waleed, under the order of this newly converted warrior killed Bani-Jazima Bedouin. The news of this wanton blood-shed deeply grieved the prophet and he prayed “O Lord! I am innocent of what Khaalid has done. He immediately despatched Hazrat Ali to make every possible preparation for the outrage committed. Such mission was congenial to Ali's nature and he executed it faithfully. He made careful enquiries as to the number of persons killed, their status, and the losses incurred by their families, and paid the “Diyat” strictly. When every loss was made good he distributed the remainder of the money he had brought among the kinsman of the victims and other members of the tribe, gladdening every heart by his gentleness and benevolence, carrying with him the blessings of the whole people he returned to the prophet who overwhelmed him with thanks and praises.

Similarly in 8 A.H. when other missions failed to bring the powerful Yamani tribe of Bani-Hamdan to the folds of Islam, Ali was sent there. bn Khaldoon says:

On the first occasion he gathered the tribesmen some of whom were very learned and spoke before them of the truths which Islam preached. This sermon was so effective that some of those learned persons immediately embraced Islam. This was followed by long discussions with others, he made them realised the rationality of the doctrines of Islam. The discussions ended in the whole-hearted conversion of Bani-Hamdan, who followed their learned leaders. These news so pleased the Holy prophet (A.S.) that he bowed down before God in thanks and thrice said "Peace be to Bani-Hamdan and to Ali. Again in 10 A.H. his sermons and preachings proved so effective that the whole province embraced Islam as one man.

Designation of Ali as Vicegerent

The Spirit of Islam p.292 says:

It is generally supposed that the Holy prophet (A.S.) had not expressly designated anyone as his successor in the spiritual and temporal government, but this notion is framed on an incorrect apprehension of fact, for there is abundant evidence that many a time the Prophet (A.S.) had openly indicated Ali for Vicegerency.

The first occasion was when he was ordered by God to openly and unreservedly invite his kith and kin to Islam. This occasion is called Dawat Asheera (propagation of the religion amongst the relatives). In the words of Rev-Sale the Holy prophet (A.S.) said:

God hath commanded me to call you unto Him; who therefore, among you will be assisting to me herein and become my brother and my vicegerent?

All of them hesitating and declining the matter, Ali at length rose up, and declared that he would be his assistant and threatened those who should oppose him. Mohammad upon this embraced Ali, with great demonstration of affection, and desired all those present to hearken to and to obey him as his Deputy.

Thus at this occasion of the introduction of Islam as a religion Hazrat Ali was declared by the Holy prophet (A.S.) as his Deputy. The value of Ali's support to the Holy prophet (A.S.) and his designation as a vicegerent at this stage is fairly well assessed by theologians, historians and thinkers of the West and the East. See

1 Tafseer Tabari vol.19 p.68
2 Tafseer Maalim at-Tanzeel p.663
3 Masnad Imaam Ahmad bn Hambal vol.i p. 163
4 Mostadrak Imaam Hakim vol.iii p.133
5 History of Tabari vol.i p.216
6 History of Kaamil vol.i p.25
7 History of Abol-Fida vol.i p. 116

The second occasion was at the time of Ali's conquest of Khaybar. The words of the Holy prophet (A.S.) quite clearly, positively and expressively give out his opinion about Hazrat Ali and his desire to leave Hazrat Ali as the guardian and the propagator of his mission. He said:

You are from me and I am from you, you will inherit me.. you are urto me what Aaron was unto Moses... you will be nearest to me on the day of Judgement and next to me on the fountain of Kawther, enmity against you is enmity against me, a war against you is a war against me... you have as much faith in God as I have. You are door to me.

What more can one say? Can there be anything more forceful, more eloquent, more pregnant with clear indications and more categorical than the words which the Holy prophet (A.S.) has used? Do they leave any shadow of doubt? Has the Holy prophet (A.S.) ever used such words for anybody else?

The third instance was the accasion of the invasion of Tabook. To understand the occasion and the cause of remarks of the Holy prophet (A.S.) it is necessary to know the historical back-ground of the incident. It was the summer of 9 A.H. and the Holy prophet (A.S.) had received the information that the Roman King was mobilising his forces to invade the Islamic State and many Arab tribes were gathering round him. He decided to face them in their own land and not to allow them the run of the Moslim state so that they might not lay waste to the lands through which they pass. The situation had become very serious because there was famine in Hijaaz, Taaif and Yaman.

The Hypocrites (the Monafiqeen) were carrying on intensive propaganda campaign and trying to make the people believe that the famine was the sign that God was angry with Moslims and wants to exterminate them with the worst form of death (cannibalism). And in case of a defeat against the Roman armies there was eminent danger of revolt. It was imperative that the state should be left in the hands of a faithful and powerful guardian otherwise there was every possibility of being sandwiched between the two enemies. The Holy prophet (A.S.) therefore decided that Hazrat Ali should act as a regent in his place and the world might also realise that in the opinion of the Holy prophet (A.S.) none could look after the temporal as well as spiritual welfare of the Moslims during his absence but Ali. He called Ali and told him that he would have to act as the last line of defence for him and Islam, saying:

O Ali; nobody could look after this centre of Moslim state but I or you

See: Imaam Haakim in al-Mostadrak, Allama bn Abdl-Birr in Istecaab, Shah Waliollah in Izalatol Khifa, Sibt bn Jawzi in Tazkirat Khawaas al-Aimma and Allama Ali Mottaqi in Kanz al-Ommaal).

Hazrat Ali's stay at Madeena disappointed the Monafiqeen (hypocrites and double-dealers) and as they constituted the majority of those left behind by the Holy prophet (A.S.) they started a whispering campaign. It was to the effect that the Holy prophet (A.S.) had lost faith in Hazrat Ali and had therefore left him behind and that it was positively certain that the Holy prophet (A.S.) was going to suffer a defeat. Hazrat Ali naturally felt anxious for the Holy prophet (A.S.) and annoyed at aspersions against him. He left Madeena immediately, met the Prophet at the place of Jerf and told him all that was said at his back. Thereupon the Holy prophet (A.S.) said:

Ali! they are lying against you as they have lied against me, they have called me an epileptic, a magician, a sorcerer and a necromant and have always styled me as a liar. I have appointed you as my vicegerent and my caliph over all which I have left behind. Are you not satisfied to realise that you are unto me what Aaron was unto Moses.

See Saheeh Bokhaari pp. 145 p.387 and pp.18 p.89

The fourth time was in the words of the Spirit of Islam p.292):

Notably the occasion of the return journey from the performance of "The Farewell Pilgrimage, during a halt at a place called Khom, he had convoked an assembly of the people accompanying him, and used the words which could leave little doubt as to his intention regarding a successor. "Ali, said he, is to me what Aaron was to Moses. The Almighty God be a friend to his friends and a foe to his foes; help those who help him and frustrate those who betray him).

I would be doing a great disservice to the cause of truth and to the history of Islam if I do not sketch at least a bare outline of this incident. Because more than fifty thousand people had gathered on that occasion and many of them narrated all that took place there; among those narrators we find such luminaries as Hazrat Abo-baker Siddeeq, Hazrat Omar Farooq, Hazrat Othmaan Ghani, Zobayr bn Awwam, Abdillah bn Omar, Abdillah bn Abbas, Ommol-Momineen Bibi Aysha, Ommol-Momineen Bibi Om-Salama, Abdillah bn Masood and Hasan bn Thabit (The book Arjah al-Mataalib cites 100 names of the companions of the Holy prophet (A.S.). From these narrators about 153 historians, biographist collectors of the Holy prophet's traditions and authors of Sehahas, Moojams and Massaaneed from the 1st Century A.H. right upto 1300 A.H., have narrated the whole incident in details and have drawn practically the same inference as the author of the Spirit of Islam. The book Arjah al-Mataalib again gives a list of them in chronological order of 13 Centuries, from which I have quoted a few names at the end of this section.

The Holy prophet (A.S.) was returning from the "Farewell Pilgrimage" and had reached the place Khom, (which in the words of the famous historian and geographist bn-Khallikan is a valley lying between Mecca and Madeena). It contains a pond, Ghadeer, near which the prophet pronounced his invocation. This took place on the 18th of Zil-Hijja and the 18th of this month is the anniversary of the Feast of Ghadeer (Eedol-Ghadeer) ".

There the Holy prophet (A.S.) suddenly made his camel stop and said that just then a message of God was revealed unto him which must be immediately conveyed to the Moslims. He despatched messengers towards those who had gone ahead and those who were following him leisurely to come back or to hurry up and join him at once. When all of them were gathered he performed the Noon-prayers in that blazing hot summer sun. A pulpit was erected for him and from this eminence he preached a sermon which is rightly considered as a masterpiece of Arabic literature and a brief survey of what the Holy prophet (A.S.) had taught and achieved for the Moslims. Then he said that he had just then received the revelation which said:

O Apostle! proclaim the whole of what which hath been sent down to thee from Thy Lord, for if thou dost it not, it will be as if thou hast not at all performed the duty of His prophet-hood. And God will protect thee (thy mission) from evil men, verily God guideth not the unbelievers,

He was standing there to convey that message to the Moslims and to perform the duty he was ordered to perform. Continuing the sermon he said:

O people! shortly I shall be called (to the Heaven), and if I go back I shall have to give an account as to how I have conveyed His Message to you and you in your turn) will also be asked as to how you have accepted and carried out my teachings. Now tell me what you will say.

Thereupon all the gathering as one man declared:

O Apostle of God! we testify and declare that you have conveyed the message of Cod in full details, you have striven your utmost to guide us to the right path, and taught us, to follow it, you were most kind to us and you never wished for us but our good, may God repay you for all that

Thereupon he asked the gathering:

Do you not testify that there is no god but God, that Mohammad is His creature, His servant and His apostle, that there is the Heaven and the Hell, that death will overtake every one of you, that you will be brought back from your graves, that the day of resurrection will surely dawn and human beings will be resurrected from their graves to account for their deeds.

The gathering declared:

We believe and testify all of this.

Hearing this declaration he said:

I am leaving amongst you two most important things worthy of obedience, the Quraan and my progeny (descendants). Take care how you treat them, they will not separate from each other till they reach me on the Fountain of Kawther. Then said he "The Almighty God is my Lord (Mawla) and I am the Lord of all Moslims and have more right and power on their lives than they themselves; do you believe in this assertion of mine?

They all in one voice replied:

Yes O Apostle of God

Thrice he asked the same question and thrice he received the same reply.

On this solemn affirmation he said:

Hear and remember that to whomover I am Lord or Mawla Ali is the Lord and Mawla to him. He is to me what Aaron was unto Moses. The Almighty God be a friend to his friends and a foe to his foes, help those who help him and frustrate those who betray him

While saying this he raised Hazrat Ali so that the gathering may have a look at the man, who will be Lord and Mawla of those who believe the Holy prophet (A.S.) to be their Lord and Mawla. Thereupon the Holy prophet (A.S.) received the revelation:

This day I have perfected your religion for you and have filled up the measure of my bounties upon you and I am pleased with Islam to be your religion.

After performing this ceremony and receiving the above revelation the Holy prophet (A.S.) came down the pulpit prostrated before God in prayers and ordered a tent to be fixed. In this tent Hazrat Ali was made to take his seat and pecple were ordered to pay homage to him and to address him as Ameer al-Momineen (Lord of the faithful). The first person to congratulate and address him as such was Hazrat Omar-al-Khattaab, saying:

I congratulate you, O Ali. Today you have become my Mawla (Lord) and Lord of every Moslim man and woman.

See: 1 Mosnad Imaam Ahmad bn Hambal (vol.v p.28)

2 Imaam Ghazaali in Seerol-Aalameen.

3 The rerriarks of Imaam Ghazaali about this event and the inferences he has drawn are instructive readings.

List of some out of the famous 153 authors and books which contain the above:

1 bn-Shihaab-az-Zohri(125 A.H.)

2 Mohammad bn Ishaag(IS2 A.H.)

3 br-Rahooya(238 A.H.)

4 Imaam Ahmad br Hambal Mosnad vol.v, p.281 (243 A.H.)

5 Jareer-Tabari(310 A.H.)

6 Hakeem Tirmizi (320 A.H.)

7 Imaam Hakim (al-Mostadrak) (400 A.H.)

8 Imaarn Ghazaali (Seerol-Aalameen) (505 A.H.)

9 Sibt bn Jawzi (654 A.H.)

10 bn-Sabbagh Maaliki (855 A.H.)

11 Seyooti (1011 A.H.)

12 Shaykh Abdl-Haq Mohaddith Dahlaawi (IOS2 A.H.)
13 Shah Waliollah Mohaddith Dahlaawi (1176 A.H.)
14 Allama Mohammad Moeen (1280 A.H.)

A brief survey of Hazrat Ali's life from Hijra to the death of the Holy Prophet (A.S) 40A.H.

When the Holy prophet (A.S.) left his house at Mecca in the night and Ali was found in his bed, the Quraysh at first thought of killing him, but when they found him ready to defend himself they gave up idea and dispersed in search of the Holy prophet (A.S.)

Ali as per orders of the Holy prophet (A.S.) stayed three days at Mecca and handed back all the articles which were entrusted to the Holy prophet (A.S.) for sale custody, mostly by his enemies, secured their receipts and left the city in broad daylight.

He was entrusted by the Holy prophet (A.S.) for safe transport of Holy prophet's daughter Hazrat Fatima, daughter of Hamza, another Fatima, his own mother, a third Fatima, and his aunt, that was the daughter of Abdi-Mottalib, a fourth Fatima. The Quraysh wanted to prevent the departure of these four ladies. Eight prominent people came out to fight. Ali fought single handed with them. He killed Jonah with a stroke of his sword and scattered the rest and continued the journey. On account of scarcity of mounts he had to travel on foot and thus he reached Madeena with bleeding feet. Awaiting the arrival of Hazrat Ali the Holy prophet (A.S.) was staying at Qubba, two miles away from Madeena, when he reached Qubba, on the 12th of Rabiol-Awwal (probably the end of June) the Holy prophet (A.S.) embraced him, dressed his bleeding feet and entered Madeena along with him.

Before his migration to Madeena the Holy prophet (A.S.) had created a bond of brotherhood between the Moslims. He had fraternised Hazrat Abi-Baki to Hazrat Omar, Hazrat Othmaan to Abdr-Rahmaan bn Awf, Hazrat Hamza to Zayd bn Haretha and Talha to az-Zobayr. On that occasion he had fraternised Hazrat Ali to himself, saying,

O Ali, you are my brother in this world as well as in the next See: Taareekh Khamees vol.i p.398)

Ist A.H.

Five months after his arrival at Madeena he fraternised the Mohajirs (the Migrators) with the Ansaars (the citizens of Madeena). On that occasion again he called Ali and said:

O Ali you are my brother in this world and hereafter.

The historian bn Hishaam says:

The Holy prophet (A.S.) caught the hand of Hazrat Ali and said "he alone is my brother" thus the apostle of God, who was actually the leader of all the prophets as well as of all the pious men of the world and who had no parallel among human beings by fraternising with Hazrat Ali, showed that Ali also had no parallel among mankind except the Holy prophet (A.S.)

See: Seera bn Hishaam vol.ii, Abol-Fida vol.i p. 127, al-Mostadrak of Imaam Hakim vol.iii and Fat-hol-Baari, commentary of Saheeh Bokhaari vol.vii p.211.

2nd A.H.

The battle of Badr took place. See p.:

During the 2nd year of Hijra Hazrat Ali's marriage took place with the Holy prophet's daughter Fatima. Holy prophet (A.S.) was receiving many offers for his daughter from very rich people of Madeena, from some of the Mohajirs and from chiefs of mighty clans of Arabia. He had refused even to consider these offers and sometimne felt annoyed at them and at the end he closed the door by saying that he was awaiting the orders of God. The book Osdol-Ghaaba Fi Tamyeez Sahaba, gives a detailed account of these offers and the way of refusai by the Holy prophet (A.S.). Some of the Ansaars suggested to Hazrat Ali to place a proposal for himself before the Holy prophet (A.S.). Hazrat Ali went before him feeling shy and modest. This was the first time in his life that he talked reservedly to a man who was like a father unto him and to whom he was like a dear son. When the Holy prophet (A.S.) heard the proposal he was so pleased that he siniled and said it is a welcome and happy proposal)

See: Taareekh-al-Khamees vol.i p.407, bn-Saad Vol.v p.11 and 12, and Osdol-Ghaaba).

The Holy prophet (A.S.) took the consent of Hazrat Fatima for this proposal. The marriage ceremony was very simple and without pomp and ostentation. There was a Khotba from the Holy prophet (A.S.) in which he praised God mentioning some of His attributes and citing verses of the Quraan and concluding with the remarks that he was ordered by God to give Hazrat Fatima into marriage with Hazrat Ali. This was followed by a Khotba from Hazrat Ali, praising God and the Holy prophet (A.S.) and desiring the gathering to witness his marriage with Hazrat Fatima, the daughter of Holy prophet (A.S.). After this happy ceremony somebody reminded the Holy prophet (A.S.) of his late companion in life, the mother of Hazrat Fatima, Hazrat Khadeeja, and he said:

Khadeeja! where is Khadeeja, who can be like Khadeeja, she testified me when the world was falsely accusing me as a liar, she relieved me of much of my weight, she was my partner in my work and she helped me when others were creating obstruction in my mission.

After reaching Madeena the Holy prophet (A.S.) stayed in the house of Kolthoom bn Haddam for seven months and Hazrat Ali was staying with him. When the Holy prophet (A S.) finished the coristruction of mosque he built houses for his wives around it and in the centre of them he built a house for Hazrat Ali. (Salveg; Bokhaari, pp.14 p.387).

Following his example many of his companions except Hazrat Abo-Baker built their houses around the mosque. Hazrat Abo-Baker was staying in the locality of Bani. Abde-Awf where the marriages of both of his daughters took place and later on he shifted to Sokh (Bokhaari vol.1). The doors of all the houses built around the mosque opened in the mosque. One day the Holy prophet (A.S.) ordered that except the doors of his houses and that of Ali all the other doors should be closed. Some of the companions requested him to allow them to keep a small window open. He replied "No, not a pin hole, God so willed it"

See: Mosnad Imaam Ahmad and Mostadrak Imaam Hakim fee Khasaais Nisaa)

3rd A.H.

The battle of Ohod took place which was followed by despatch of expeditionary force to Homrol-Asad under Hazrat Ali.

In the same year the first child to Hazrat Ali and Hazrat Fatima was born and he was named Hassan (Imaam Hassan) by the Holy prophet (A.S.).

4th A.H.

Hazrat Ali and Hazrat Fatima had the second child Hosayn (Imaam Hosayn) who was also named by the Holy prophet (A.S.).

In the same year a battle took place with Bani-Nazeer and Hazrat Ali brought it to a successful and and Bani-Nazeer were forced to vacate their fortress.

5th A.H.

Three battles took place, battle with Bani-Mostalaq, battle of Khandaq (the moat) and battle with Bani-Kanza. In all three of them Ali was the commander of the army. Most important of them was the battle of Khandaq.

6 th A.H.

An expedition to Fadak was sent under the command of Hazrat Ali and without a battle or skirmish he brought the whole province under control of the Holy prophet (A.S.). In Zil-Quda of this year the Holy prophet (A.S.) along with fourteen hundred Moslims left for Mecca with the intention of pilgrimage. He had to desire to fight anybody and had left all the armaments at Madeena. When Quraysh came to know about this intending pilgrimage they refused to allow the Holy prophet (A.S.) to enter Mecca. Khaalid bn Waleed came out with a force of well equipped two hundred cavalry men to obstruct the Holy prophet (A.S.) and if necessary to fight over the issue. At an oasis called Hodaybiyya, the opponents faced each other. A chieftain named Orwa from Quraysh came out to discuss the situation with the Holy prophet (A.S.) and instead of a battle a treaty was arranged, and it was written by Hazrat Ali. The last clause of the treaty was that the present intention of the pilgrimage should be given up but next year the Holy prophet (A.S.) and Moslims can come for "Omra.

7th A.H.

Two battles took place, the Khaybar and the Wadil-Qura. The more important of them was Khaybar.

In the same year the Holy prophet (A.S.) along with Moslims went to perform Omra, it was very peaceful mission. The Holy prophet (A.S.) and many of the Moslims had their wives and children with them. The Omra was performed without any unpleasant incident taking place.

8th A.H.

This year had some important events in its fold.

The first of them as the fall of Mecca. The terms of the treaty of Hodaybiyya were dishonoured by the Quraysh. Within two years of the Treaty they killed twenty persons of Bani-Khozaa's clan without rhyme or reason. Representatives of the clans came to the Holy prophet (A.S.) asking for his promised support, he was annoyed at this flagrant dishonouring the treaty and said:

I am not be helped if I do not help them.

The arrangement for the invasion of Mecca was being carried on by the Moslims, in the meanwhile, Hatab, a companion of the Holy prophet (A.S.) who was with him in the battle of Badr, wrote a letter to his family, informing them of the intention of Moslims. This espionage, under orders of the Holy prophet (A.S.), was detected by Hazrat Ali and he brought this letter to the Holy prophet (A.S.). It was being sent through an Abysinian slave girl. Hatab confessed his crime and was mercifully pardoned by the Holy prophet (A.S.) (Bokhaari).

When all the arrangements were ready, the army of invasion, numbering

about ten thousand, marched towards Mecca. The command of the army this time was given to Saad bn Abbada Ansaari, with orders to enter Mecca as an advance party. Saad entering Mecca, said:

Today is going to be a big day, a day of retaliation, a day when Mecca will be looted.

Abbas, uncle of the Holy prophet (A.S.), hearing this came to the Holy prophet (A.S.) and said:

O Apostle of God! Saad has very serious intention against Quraysh. He may carry on a massacre.

The Holy prophet (A.S.) called Hazrat Ali and said:

O Ali! you go and take the command from Saad and do the needful. He would not be unhappy in handing over the command to you and to you alone.

Hazrat Ali took over the command of the expedition and entered the city, declared perfect amity and peace and waited for the Holy prophet (A.S.). When Holy Prophet (A.S.) entered Mecca he went straight to Kaba and started removing the idols placed there. Some of them were placed on a very high platform where his hands would not reach, he asked Ali to mount on his back and remove the idols. Ali obeyed the order, mounted on his back and was removing the idols when the Holy prophet (A.S.) asked:

O Ali! how do you find yourself?

- O Apostle of God! I find myself on such an eminent place that I feel as if my head is resting on the Empyrean of God the Almighty.

- O Ali, how fortunate you are, doing the work of God and how fortunate I am that I am bearing your burden

See Mosnad Imaam Ahmad, vol.i p.151.

At the occasion, a poet presented an eulogium in praise of Hazrat Ali. In which he said:

I am asked to praise Ali in verses,

Because recital of his praises will
Release a man from the Hell.
I replied to them, how can I praise
A man whose attributes are so sublime
That men got confused over these attributes
And started apotheosising him.
He has placed his foot at such an eminent
Place, that according to the Holy prophet (A.S.),
It is the place on which, on the night of Meraj,
God Hath placed His hand of
Grace and Mercy.

Hearing this eulogium the Holy prophet (A.S.) rewarded the poet handsomely.

The second important event was the massacre of Bani-Jazima by Khaalid bn Waleed and reparation carried by Hazrat Ali under orders of the Holy prophet (A.S.)

The Shawwal of this year saw the Moslims facing certain powerful tribes of Arabs on the battle-field of Honayn. Ali again secured a victory for them. Honayn was followed by an expedition to Taaif under command of Hazrat Ali. Those who had run away from Honayn had gathered there and wanted to measure their strength once again. The commander of their army who was the chief of Bani-Zaigham clan was killed by Hazrat Ali, which broke the back of resistance and various parties of hostile clans started dispersing. Seeing this the Holy prophet (A.S.) raised the siege and brought the expedition to an end.

In the same year Hazrat Ali was sent to Yaman on a missionary service, he carried on this work so successfuily and his speeches there proved so effective that the tribe of Bani-Hamdan embraced Islam as one man.

9th A.H.

This has to relate tour important incidents of Hazrat Ali's life:

The first was the expedition to Zaat as-Salaasil. Ali brought it to a successful end, defeated the clans gathered there to invade Madeena and brought the happy news to the Holy Prophet (A.S.). The Apostle of God came out of Madeena to welcome the warrior. Ali was riding a horse at the head of his army, saw the Holy prophet (A.S.) walking towards him and jumped from his horse. The prophet told him "keep on riding, do not dismount, God and His prophet are really pleased with your services" and made him remount his horse and he walked along with the horse.

See Meraaj an-Nobowwa.

The second event was the Holy prophet's expedition in person to Tabook. See p.

The third important event in the life of Ali and in the history of Islam was the reading of the Chapter (Sora) Baraat before the infidels of Mecca. This Sora declares that God and his apostle in future will have nothing to do with the infidels and polytheists. All the treaties which existed till then are now annulled and cancelled. No polytheist or infidel will in future be allowed to enter the city cf Mecca or the precincts of Kaba.

Imaam Hakim in his al-Mostadrak vol.iii p.32, ar-Riyaaz an-Nazira vol.ii, p.203, Mosnad Imaam Ahmad bn Hambal vol.i p.331, al-Isaaba-fee-Maryfatis-Sahaba vol.iv, p.270 and Izalatol-Khifa, Section 2, p.261 say that the Holy prophet (A.S.) first ordered Hazrat Abo-Baker to carry this Sora to Mecca and to read it at the Kaba, but immediately after him he sent Hazrat Ali to replace Hazrat Abo-Baker on the mission. When Hazrat Abo-Baker complained about this change, the Apostle of God replied:

i have done it under orders of God which came explicitly that either I should perform this duty or somebody who is like me.

The fourth event: Najraan was a city in the province of Yaman. It was centre of the Christian Missionary activities in Southern Arabia. The Holy prophet (A.S.) had written to the Chief Priest of the city to realise the blessings of Islam. In reply he wrote that he would like to personally discuss the teachings of this new religion. His name was Haarith. He was invited and came with a retinue of fourteen Priests. These Priests stayed at Madeena as guests of the Holy prophet (A.S.). Long discussion about monotheism versus trinity took place and it was realised that these Priests were not open minded on the contrary were prejudiced against Islam. The Almighty Lord ordered the Holy prophet (A.S.) to explain to them that:

Verily Jesus is as Adam in the sight of God. He created him out of dust. He then said unto him “Be" and he was. This is the truth from
Thy Lord; be not therefore one of those who doubt; and whoever shall dispute with thee after the knowledge which hath been given thee, say unto them, come let us call together our sons and your sons, our women and your women and ourselves and yourselves, then let us make imprecations and lay the curse of God upon those who lie.

Quraan Chap.ii: Family of Imran

According to Omar bn Saad and Ommol-Momineen Bibi Aysha when the above verses were revealed to the Apostle of God he called Ali, Fatima, Hasan and Hosayn and said:

Lord this is my family and progeny (Ahlil-Bayt)

See Saheeh Bokhaari, Part.vii p.77, Saheeh Moslim, vol. 11 p.278, Jaami" Tirmizi p.421, Mishkaat vol.viii p. 129).

Imaam Fakhroddeen Raazi (in At-Tafseer al-Kabeer vol. 11 p.701, printed in Egypt) says:

When the above verses were revealed the prophet of God covered himself with a black coverlet, took in it Ali, Fatima, Hasan and Hosayn and said "Lord this is my progeny, my household and my family (Ahlil-Bayt). Thereupon the Apostle of the Lord received the revelation "Verily God desireth to remove from you every abomination of sin and evil, and you are the household of the prophet, and to purify you by a perfect purification.

See also: Tafseer al-Khshshaaf vol. 1, p.308 agrees with Imaam Fakhroddeen Raazi.

Hearing the glad news of the Divine Purification, Sanctification and Consecration the Holy prophet (A.S.) decided to take only these four persons along with him for the ceremony of trial by imprecations as ordered by God; that is, Ali representing the 'selves" as mentioned in the above verses, Fatima representing "women" Hasan and Hosayn representing 'sons.

The Christian Priests were then informed of these orders of God and "They agreed next morning to abide by the trial as a quick way of deciding which of them were in the wrong. Mohammad (A.S.) met them accordingly accompanied by his daughter Fatima, his son-in-law Ali and his two grandsons Hasan and Hosayn and desired them (the Christian Priests) to wait till he had said his prayers. But when they saw him kneel down their resolution failed them and they dared not venture to curse him and his party, but agreed to sign a treaty and pay tribute to him" (Rev-Sale)

Ahlil-Bayt" people of the household (of Mohammad, A.S.), is the designation usually given to Fatima, Ali and their children and descendants. This is the name by which bn Khaldoon invariably designates them, and followers and disciples, Shiaas or adherents of the "People of the House. Sanai (the famous Soofi poet whom Mawlaana Room praises) represents the general feeling with which the descendants of Mohammad (A.S.) were regarded in the following Verses:

Excepting the book of God and his family (Descendants) nothing has been left by Ahmad the prophet, Memorial such as these can never be obtained till the day of Judgement

Kanz al-Ommaal vol.vi p. 159, Tafseer-al-Kashshaaf vol.i p.308, Ali Hamdani in Mawaddatol-Qurba, and Allama bn Hajr Makki in as-Sawaaiq al-Mohriqa, while discussing this event and the verses referred above, have given their opinion that the Holy prophet (A.S.), by translating the word "Selves" as himself and Ali, the word "Women" as Fatima and the word "Sons" as Hasan and Hosayn have shown to the Moslim the estimation in which these four persons are held by God and by himself, and that they and they alone are his Ahlil-Bayt who deserve the Divine Purification, Sanctification and Consecration.

10th A.H.

During this year Ali was sent once again on a propagation mission to Yaman and thence on an expedition against Amer bn Madi. He performed both the duties successfully. Imaam Ahmad bn-Hambal in his Masnad vol.v p.356, Imaam Nisaai in Khasaais and Allama bn Hajr Makki in as-Sawaaiq al-Mohriqa, Chap.ii, say that from the later expedition Khaalid bn Waleed sent a letter containing complaints of Hazrat Ali to the Holy prophet (A.S.). This letter was carried by Borayda, a companion of the Holy prophet (A.S.). On receipt of this letter the apostle of God was annoyed and got angry and said:

You are fabricating lies and fictitious complaints against Ali, he is from me and I am from him, he is your lord (Vali) after me. Whoever annoys him actually annoys me and whoever forsakes him forsakes me. He is made of the same material that I am made of and I am made of the same material that Abraham is made of and my status before God is superior to that of Abraham.

The end of the 10th A.H. saw the Holy prophet (A.S.) performing the "Farewell Pilgrimage" and while returning from there he for the last time designated Hazrat Ali as his Vicegerent.

11th A.H.

The year 11th A.H. was the saddest year of Hazrat Ali's life. He lost two of his best friends. One of whom he loved and venerated like a father, like a master and like the dearest friend, the Holy prophet (A.S.) who died during the early months of the year. His death was followed by the death of Hazrat Ali's dearest companion, his wife, Fatima, the lady of the Light

The last year of Holy Prophet's life was spent at Madeena. An envoy of his was killed by the Syrians and he had ordered an expedition against the Byzantines under Osaama bn Zayd and he had ordered all his companions except Hazrat Ali join this expedition, and had ordered the troops to be encamped outside the city (Taareekh Tabari, Taareekh kaamil bn Atheer. Tabaqaat bn-Sad and as-Seera al-Halabiyya, Madaarej an-Nobowwa vol.ii p. 766). Though he was ill yet in spite of his weakness he came out, arranged the flag (the Insignia of the command) with his own hands and handed it over to Osaama. He felt that people were not willing to join this expedition, because of the young age of Osaama, he got annoyed and said:

Curse of God be on those who forsake the army of Osaama.

See al-Milal-wan-Nehal of Allama Sharistaani.

Cause of this illness was the poison which had been given to him and which had slowly penetrated into his system and has now begun to show its effect, and it became evident that he had not long to live. The news of his approaching end led to the stoppage of the expedition (The Spirit of Islam). At the last stage of illness the Holy prophet (A.S.) was staying at the house of Ommol-Momineen Bibi Aysha. From there he came out for the last time to lead the prayers. He was so weak that he was actually carried there by the sons of Abbas bn Abdi-Mottalib. He, himself, led the prayers. (Fat-hol-Bari. Sharh Saheeh Bokhaari, pp.3 p.372).

This exertion proved too much for the Apostle of the Lord and when he returned home from the mosque he was fainted. His condition was very serious at that time and fainting fit was of long duration. His children and members of family, and his companions started weeping and lamenting. He came out of the swoon and looked at those tear sprinkled faces around him and said:

Bring pen, ink and paper so that I may write a will for you that will keep you on the straight path.

Some of his companions wanted to offer the pen and paper while Hazrat Omar was of opinion that he was talking insanely on account of the intensity of illness, they have the Holy Quraan with them which would suffice them. This discussion took a serious turn and people started arguing in loud voices. The Apostle of God got annoyed at this and asked them to go away and to leave him alone. (Saheeh Bokhaari pp.12 p.126, pp.8 p.100, pp.23 p.384, Minhaajol-Sonna of Allama bn Taymiyya, Sharh Saheeh Moslim of Allama Noodi, give a detailed account of this event).

This was Sunday the 27th Safar, after the above incident the Apostle of God called Ali and said:

Ali you will be first to meet me on the fountain of Kawther. After me when hardship and reverses face you then do not lose patience and when you find people running after worldly gains then you busy yourself in the way of truth and God.

See Madaarej an-Nobowwa vol. 11 p.8 551

Next day, Monday the 28th of Safar, the Apostle of God passed away to the realm of His Grace, Blessings and Majesty.

Last montent and the last rights of Holy Prophet (A.S)

Allama Mchammad bn Sad in his famous book Tabaqaat (vol. 11, Section 2, p.51 and 61) relates that during the caliphate of Hazrat Omar once the famous Jew Kabol-Ahbar (who later embraced Islami) asked of the caliph Sire please tell me what were the last words of the Holy prophet.

The caliph told him to ask Hazrat Ali about it. Kab came to him and asked him the same question. Hazrat Ali replied:

During the last moments of the Holy prophet (A.S.) his head was resting on my shoulder and his words were prayers, prayers.

Kab declared "verily last moments of prophets have always been thus, they are ordained for it and they carry the message even with their last breath. Then Kab went to Hazrat Omar and asked him:

Sire who performed the ablutions of the body of the prophet after his death.

The caliph told him to ask Hazrat Ali about that also. He again came to Hazrat Ali and repeated the question. Hazrat Ali replied:

The Apostle of God had willed that none but I should perform those ablutions; because if any other person looked at his naked body he would get blind. A curtain was hanged and from the other side of the curtair. Fazl bn Abbas and Osaama, blind-folded, were handling over water to me and I was performing the ablutions.

These facts, that Hazrat Ali was the only person to be with the Holy prophet (A.S.) at his last moments and to have performed the last rights, are also borne out by the books Tazkeratol- Khawaas al-Aimma Chap.ii p.

16, Kanz al-Ommaal vol.i p.55, al-Mostadrak of Imaam Hakim vol.iii p. 139, ar-Riyaaz an-Naazira, printed in Egypt, p.80 and al-Mojam al-Kabeer of Tabraani.

Alter the last ablutions and after shrouding the august of the Apostle of God as per his will, first Hazrat Ali performed the "Death prayers" alone and then parties of Moslims came and offered death prayers without any leader (Imaam). Allama on Abdi-Bar in !steeaab says:

Hazrat Ali offered his "Death prayers" alone then Bani-Hashim offered the prayers, then Mohajirs and then Ansaars.

Burial of the Holy Prophet (A.S.)

After the death prayers were said. Hazrat Ali, Abbas, Fazl bn Abbas and Osaaina bn Zayd got busy with the arrangements of burial of the Apostle of God, and at the request of Ansaars, Aws-al-Ansaari who was also a Badri, was allowed to join them. Osaama dug the grave in the house of Ommol-Momineen Bibi Aysha. Aws got into the grave and Hazrat Ali lifted the august body in hands and lowered it into the grave. He stayed in the grave for sometime, he was weeping bitterly, Osaama says:

I have never seen Ali weeping like that before or after this occasion, and then he came out of the grave and lifting his hands said "Lord! he was Thy first creation, his apparent death is not a sign of his mortality, he lifted the gloom prevailing before the creation started, he was a proof of Thy Glory and Benevolence, he had come to us from the Realm of Thy Love and Glory, and was our guide towards that Realm. His soul was the Emblem of Thy Supreme Might, his body was the master-piece of Thy Creation and his mind was Thy Treasure house. Then he closed the grave.

See also: Irshaad Shaykh Mofeed

When Ali with Bani-Hashim were busy with the last rites of the burial of the Apostle of God, some Mohajirs and some Ansaars gathered at "Saqeefa" and decided that Hazrat Abo-Baker be the first caliph. Hazrat Ali was asked to accede to this decision. He refused. Abo-Sofyaan came to Madeena and went to Abbas (uncle of the Holy prophet (A.S.) and told him:

These people have taken away the caliphate from Bani-Hashim. You are uncle of the Apostle of God and oldest among the Quraysh, you have been kind to them also, they will accept your lead. Let you and I swear allegiance to Ali. If anybody opposes us we shall kill him.

They both came to Ali and Abo-Sofyaan told him:

Ali, if you like I shall overflow Madeena with infantry and cavalry, accept our proposal, put out your hand and let us swear the oath of allegiance.

Hearing this Afi replied:

Abo-Sofyaan, I swear by God the Almighty that you, through this proposal, want to create serious dissension amongst the Moslims. You have always tried to harm Islam, I do not need your sympathies and your help.

A detail account of this event may be found in:

1 Tabari volji p.202 and 303

2 Taareekh al-Kholafaa p.45

3 Kanz al-Ommaal vol.iii p. 140.

Hazrat Ali realised that any serious dissension at this stage would harm the cause of Islam considerably. He had before him the example of the Holy prophet (A.S.) and treaty of Hodaybiyya and had been foretold by the Holy prophet (A.S.} of all that would happen. Allama Ali bn Mohammad (630 A.H.) in Osdol-Ghaaba Fi Tamyeez Sahaba (vol.i p.31) says that the Holy prophet (A.S.) had told Hazrat Ali:

Your status is like that of Kaba. People (Moslims) go to Kaba but that august house never approaches anybody. Therefore after my death if people come to you and swear the oath of allegiance you accept it and if they not come to you then you do not go to them.

Allama Shaykh Abdl-Haq Mohaddith Dahlaawi in Madaarej an-Nobowwa (vol.ii p.511) says that the Holy prophet had advised Hazrat Ali:

After me you will have to face extremes of suffering, do not get disheartened and do not lose patience; and when you find people craving for and trying their utmost to secure worldly power and wealth you mould your life for the hereafter.

Hazrat Ali loved Islam as intensely as the Holy prophet (A.S.) had loved it, he could not, therefore, for the sake of worldly kingdom endanger Islam. He fully well knew that a civil war at that stage would give chances to the Jew clans of Bani-Nazeer and Bani-Qurayza on one side and the Christian tribes of Najraan and Syria by the Byzantine armies on the other, and the Monafiqeen (hypocrites) and fresh converts on the third to simply take advantage of the situation. When they would find the Moslims busy killing each other they would literally cut them to pieces and Islam would totally disappear as a messenger of peace. He wanted the Arabs to remain in the fold of Islam even with the desires of making their worldly position good, and wanted the enemies of Islam to realise that Islam was powerful enough to defend itself even after the sad demise of the Apostle of the Lord. Therefore, he was willing to accept every wrong for the Islam and to retire to seclusion of his house. The advice he gave to his uncle Abbas is to be found in Nahjol-Balaagha wherein he told him not to join the turmoil.

According to the famous Arab philosopher, mathematician and physician Boo Ali Seena, Hazrat Ali and Holy Quraan were the two miracles of Mohammad (A.S.), the Apostle of God. Life of Hazrat Ali at every stage was a mirror like reflection of the life of the Holy prophet (A.S.). The days of Badr, Ohod, Khaybar, and Honayn were not long passed and their hero still had the same courage, valour, bravery and strength with him, he could have jumped at the proposal of Abo-Sofyaan. But had he done so he would not have been Ali bn Abi Talib, the man "who loved God and His apostle and was loved by God and His apostle. (Meraaj an-Nobowwa).

But, unfortunately, his feelings were not reciprocated. Following books give an account of very serious events which happened at Hazrat Ali's refusal to accede to the decision of Saqeefa.

1 Tabari vol. 111 p.198

2 Al-Idol-Fareed of bn-Abd Rabba, vol.ii p. 179, printed in Egypt.

3 History of Abol-Fida vol.i p. 156 printed in Egypt.

4 Kitaab al-Imaama-was-Siyaasa of Allama bn Qutayba Ad-Daynoori vol.i p.20, printed in Egypt (this book gives a very detailed account)

5 Morooj az-Zahab Masoodi p. 159

6 al-Milal-wan-Nehal of Shahristani vol.i p.25 printed in Bombay, India.

7 al-Farooq of Shibli Nomani, printed in India

8 bn-Abil Hadeed in commentary of Nahjol-Balaagha.

Death of Fatima (A.S.)

What one could gather, from various accounts which these books have given, is a sad and pathetic episode. It appears that though Hazrat Ali decided to retire to the seclusion of his house and not to take any part in power politics yet his house was burnt down on the head of his family, and either the burning door or a hard hit from the hilt of a sword or a heavy push or all together broke the ribs and hand of Hazrat Fatima, daughter of the Holy prophet (A.S.) and caused her such a serious injury that the baby she was carrying was a still birth. Allama Shahristani in Milal-wan-Nehal (vol.i p.25) says:

There was nobody in the house but Ali, Fatima and their children (who were between the ages of 4 to 8). Apparently the assault was sudden and unexpected, nobody was ready for it. The resulting confusion could be better imagined than narrated. The lady of the house was seriously hurt, and had fainted, the house was full of smoke, the children were frightened. Ali was attending to his wounded wife and suffocating children he was overpowered and dragged from the house. Later Hazrat Fatima was refused her heritage. The physical injury and the mental shock laid her low and after a short illness she passed away on the 14th of Jamaadil-Awwal, 11 A.H. She was buried in the dead of the night. Besides Bani-Hashim only following companions of the Holy prophet (A.S.) attended her funeral:- Salmaan, Abo-Zar, Ammaar and Miqdad. Before her death she had expressed her sufferings in a poem, a verse of which has come down in the Arabic language as a proverb. She says so many sufferings have descended upon me that if they had descended upon bright days they would have been turned into dark nights.

The account of the last day of her life clearly show what kind of a lady was this daughter of the Holy prophet (A.S.). She told the household that she was feeling better, the pain in her ribs and in her hand was not so severe and that her fever had come down. Then she started bathing the children, immediately Ali and Fizza came to her assistance. She got those children bathed, dressed and fed, then sent them away to her cousin. Then she called Hazrat Ali to her side and said:

Ali, my dear husband, you know very well why I did all that. Please excuse my fussiness, they have suffered so much with me and during my illness that I want to see them happy on the last day of my life. Yes, Ali, you know also that this is the last day of my life, I am happy and also I am sad. Happy I am that my troubles will shortly be over and I shall meet my father and sorry and I am to part with you. Please, Ali, make a note of what I say and do as I wish you to do. After me you may marry anybody you like but you must marry my cousin Yamama, she loves my children and Hosayn is very much attached to her. Let Fizza remain with you even after her marriage, if she so desires, she was more than a mere servant to me. I loved her like my daughter. Ali, bury me in the night and do not let those who have been so cruel to me attend my burial, let my death do not dishearten you, you have to serve Islam and humanity for a long time to come. Let not my sufferings embitter your life, promise me Ali.

-Yes Fatima I promise

- I know how you love my children but be very careful of Hosayn. He loves me dearly and will miss me sadly, be a mother unto him. Till my recent illness he used to sleep on my chest, he is already missing it. Ali was caressing the broken hand, his hot and big tears dropped on her hand. She looked up and said "Do not weep Ali, I know with a rough outward appearance what a tender heart you possess. You have already borne too much and will have to bear more. Farewell my lord, Farewell my dear husband, Farewell Ali.

- Farewell Fatima.

- May the Merciful Lord help you to bear these sorrows and sufferings patiently. Now let me be alone with my God

Saying this she turned towards her prayers carpet and prostrated before God. When after a little time Hazrat Ali entered the room he found her still in prostration but the soul had departed to join her Holy father in the Realm of His Grace, Mercy and Might. She died very young as Hazrat Ali says:

A flower nibbled in the bud, it was from Jannah (Heaven) and it went to Jannah, but has left its fragrance in my mind.

12th A.H-33 A.H

Thence onward till 35 A.H. Hazrat Ali led a very retired life. In the beginning he spent his days in compiling the Holy Quraan in the chronological order of chapters and verses as they were revealed to the Holy prophet (A.S.), he presented this to Moslims, but when its acceptance was refused, he advised his companions to accept this Holy Book as compiled officially, saying that his compilation would not be seen by anybody, so that there might not come into existence more than one version of the Quraan and might not create doubts about the authenticity of this august book.

When Abo-Sofyaan found that Hazrat Ali was not paying attention to him he tried to get in the good books of the government and his eldest son Yazeed was appointed as the governor of Syria and on his death his brother Moaawiya was appointed on the same post.

During the caliphate of Hazrat Abo-Baker and more often during the time of Hazrat Omar whenever Ali's advice was asked for, he, like a true Moslim, offered his. sincere advice.

Though Bani-Hashim were never given any or place of honour with the government yet Ali did not mind this in difference and whenever a serious problem arose and his counsel was sought he co-operated whole-heartedly.

The Spirit of Islam says:

From the commencement of the Islamic preaching, Hazrat Ali had extended the utmost consideration and friendship to the conquered. After the battle of Qaadisiyya, Ali used to devote his share of prize money to redemption of captives, and repeatedly with his counsels and persuasive interference he induced Hazrat Omar to lighten the burden of subjects and captives.

Imaam Hakim in al-Mostadrak and Kaamil bn Atheer in his history say that till the year 17 A.H. no era was fixed by the Moslims to designate their years. Sometimes Aamol-Feel (year of Abysinian invasion of Mecca) was considered as the beginning of era at other times, the battle of Fojjar (a pre-Islamic encounter between Arab clans), while with some year of repairs carried on to Kaba was considered the year to mark the era. When this confusion was brought to the notice of Hazrat Omar, he asked the advice of Hazrat Ali, who told him to begin the Moslim era from the year of the Hijra (emigration of the Holy prophet, A.S.) to Madeena.

People went to Hazrat Omar, saying that a lot of jewels and valuable articles and attachments are in Kaba if this could be converted into currency and be used for arming the armies it would prove a very useful asset. When Hazrat Ali's advice was sought he said:

These articles were there during the times of the Holy prophet (A.S.) but he did not touch them. Though Moslims were poorer then than now, and though they were more in need of arms and mounts then you are in need of, yet the Holy prophet (A.S.) did not make use of these ornaments for such purposes. It shows that the Apostle of God did not appreciate such appreciation. You also do not do it.

Hearing this Hazrat Omar said:

O Ali! had you not been here we would have suffered a disgrace

(Rabiol-Abraar of Allama Zamakhshari)

On the occasion of the invasion of Rome when Hazrat Omar sought his counsel as to the advisability of heading the army as the Commander-in-Chief, he advised him to be at the helm and to send some experienced general as a commander. This advice is narrated in a sermon in Nahjol-

Balaagha. Similarly at the time of invasion of Persia he counselled the caliph Omar not to leave the capital and to send somebody else.

The following books cite several such cases where his counsel was asked for and he sincerely gave his advice:

1 Izalatol Khifa (subject II p.268 and 269,
2 Riyaaz Naazira vol.ii p.194 to 197,
3 Masnad Imaam Ahmad vol. 11 p.231 (Margin),
4 Mostadrak Imaam Hakim vol.i p.438 to 460,
5 Isteeaab Allama Abdl-Bar vol.ji 474 and
6 Ihyaa Oloom of Imaam Ghazaali,

Only one case I want to relate which shows in what high esteem Ali held the value of the knowledge acquired, collected and preserved by man in the fields of philosophy, science, history, geography and ethics. Following authors give a detailed account of the famous library of Alexandria in Egypt:

1 Qazi Abdl-Qaasim Sad bn Ahmad Andalosi (462 A.H.) in Tabaqaat al-Omam.
2 Haji Khaleefa Chalapee in Kaashif az-Zonoon vol.i, preface, p.24, printed in Egypt
3 The famous biographist bn Nadeem in Al-fahrist p.334, printed in Egypt.
4 The historian Jamaloddeen, know as, bn-Qufti in Akhbaar al-Olamaa wa Akhbaar al-Hokamaa, p.s232 and 233 printed in Egypt and at Liepzig (Germany).
5 Imaam Hafizoddeen Mohammad bn Mohammad, known as bn Bazzazol-Koormi (827 A.H.) in Kitaab al-Imaamol-Azam vol.I, p.37, printed at Hayderabad, India.
6 Allama Ahmad bn Mostafa, know as Tashol-Kobra Zada (962 A.H.) in Miftaah al-Saada and Misbahol-Seyaada vol.1, p.241, printed in Hayderabad, India.

They are unanimous in saying that there was a fairly large library at Alexandria in Egypt. It contained between five to seven thousand books on papyri, pal, leaves and parchments, a very large library indeed when compared with the standard of literacy and education of those days.

It contained books on chemistry, astronomy, irrigation, engineering, physics, philosophy and on various religions etc.

When Omar bn Aas conquered Egypt, he enquired as to what was to be done with those book. Orders were issued from the Centre that "if these

books are according to the Holy Quraan (i.e. they say the same things which this Holy book has said) then we do not need them and if they say anything contrary to
the Holy Quraan then we do not want them. Therefore, in any case they ought to be burnt" (Akhbarol-Olamaa-wa-Akhbarol-Hokama of bn-Qufti p.232 and 233) printed at Cairo and Leipzig).

The history of Mohammad bn Abdoo edited by Allama Rasheed, Editor, al-Manaar, Cairo, (Egypt) vol.i p.535, Tabaqaat al-Omam of Qazi Saed Andalosi say that when Hazrat Ali heard the news of this, he tried to pursue them to refrain from issuing such order. He told them:

Those books are treasures of knowledge and they cannot say anything against the Holy Quraan on the contrary the knowledge contained therein would act as commentaries of this Holy Book and would assist and help in further explanations of the knowledge as presented by the Holy prophet (A.S.). Knowledge is an asset for human-beings and a birth right of man. It should not be destroyed. Akhbaar al-Olamaa further states that his suggestion was not accepted and those books were distributed among one thousand hot water-baths of Alexandria to be burnt as fire-wood.

At his death Hazrat Abo-Baker nominated Hazrat Omar as his successor to the caliphate and Hazrat Omar on his death had appointed a board of six members to select his successor; the board consisted:

1 Abdr-Rahmaan bn Awf,
2 Saad bn Abi Waqqaas
3 Hazrat Othmaan bn Affaan
4 Talha bn-Abdillah
5 az-Zobayr bn-Awwam and
6 Hazrat Ali bn Abi Talib. The terms of reference for this council were:

1. If they unanimously select a person he will be designated as the caliph.
2. If there is no unanimity, then that person will be caliph for whom Abdr-Rahmaan bn Awf and his party vote. 3. If any five of them agree on one man and the sixth disagrees then the dissenter should be immediately killed. 4. If any four of them agree on one man and then two disagree then two should be killed.
5. If there is equal division then the casting vote would be that of Abdillah bn Omar (his son). Abdr-Rahmaan bn Awf was cousin of Hazrat Othmaan and husband of the aunt of Saad bn Abi-Waqqaas and az-Zobayr was son-

in-law of Hazrat Abo-Baker as-Siddeeq. Abdr-Rahmaan bn Awf declared that he is not standing as a candidate to the caliphate.

See al-Imaama was-Syiasa of Mohammad bn-Qutayba Daynoori (270 A.H.) p.26 and History of bn Khaldoon, second part p. 134 to 136, printed in Egypt.

In the council opinions were equally divided in favour of Hazrat Ali and Hazrat Othmaan. Abdr-Rahmaan bn Awf asked Hazrat Ali "If you are selected as a caliph do you promise that you will act according to the Holy Quraan and the traditions and orders of the Holy prophet (A.S.) and according to the rulings and decisions of the previous two caliphs?" Hazrat Ali replied "So far as the Holy Quraan and the orders and traditions of the Holy prophet (A.S.) are concerned I agree to abide by them and follow then faithfully and sincerely, but so far as the rulings and decisions of the previous two caliphs are concerned if these are according to the Holy Book and the traditions of the Holy prophet (A.S.) who could dare refuse them and if they are against the orders of God or the Holy prophet (A.S.) who would dare accept and follow them. I refuse to bind myself with those rulings and decisions. I shall act according to my knowledge and my discretion.

Then Abdr-Rahmaan asked the same question of Hazrat Othmaan. He agreed not only to act according to the Holy Quraan and the traditions of the Holy prophet (A.S.) but also implicitly follow the rulings and the decisions of the previous two caliphs. Then Abdr-Rahmaan declared that Hazrat Othmaan is selected as a caliph.

See:

1 Tabari vol.5 p.35 to 38 vol.16 p.59

2 bn-Khaldoon p. 134 to 136,

3 Abol-Fida p.34,

4 Rawzatos-Safa vol.2 p.9.

1st Moharram 24 A.H. Justice Sayyid Ameer Ali in his book "A short history of the Saracen, p. 46, says:

The choice of electorate fell upon Othmaan, a member of the Omayyads family (First Moharram 24 A.H. the 7th November 644 A.D.) His election proved in the end the ruin of Islam. He fell at once under the influence of his clan. He was guided entirely by his secretary and son-in-law Marwaan, who had once been expelled by the prophet for the breach of trust. With his usual patriotism and devotion to the faith, Ali gave his adhesion to

Othmaan as soon as he was elected. Othmaan displaced most of the lieutenants employed by Omar and appointed in their stead incompetent and worthless members of his own family. The weakness of the centre and the wickedness of the favourites was creating a great ferment among the people. Loud complaints of exaction and oppression by the governors began pouring into the capital. Ali pleaded and expostulated several times with the caliph the manner in which he allowed the government to fall into the hands of the unworthy favourites but Othmaan under the influence of his evil genus Marwaan paid no heed to these counsels. Twice Hazrat Ali was asked to leave Madeena and to go to a village near it and twice he was called back to intervene between the ruler and the ruled, in few sermons in Nahjol-Balaagha he has related these facts.

To continue the version of the short History of the Saracen (pages 47 and 48):

At last a deputation from the provinces arrived in Madeena to demandi redress. They were sent back with promises. On their way home they intercepted a letter of Marwaan, purporting to bear the seal of the caliph, containing directions to the local governors to behead the leaders of the deputation on their arrival at their destinations. Furious at this treachery, they returned to Madeena and demanded the surrender of Marwaan. And this demand was enforced even by members of the house of Omayya (Masoodi in Morooj az-Zahab). The ill-fated Othmaan met this demand with stern refusal. Enraged at what they believed to be the complicity of the caliph, they besieged him at his home

Narrating the details of the siege and the murder, Taareekh Khamees (vol. 11 p.261 and 262) Taareekh Kholafaa Seyooti (page 108), Morooj az-Zahab of Masoodi and Riyaaz an-Nazira (vol. 11 p.125), say that at this hour of peril, the Omayyads deserted the old chief and some fled towards Syria and that Moaawiya though ordered by the caliph did not come to his help, on the contrary the contingent which he sent to Madeena came under instructions to stop and stay at a place thirty miles away from Madeena and wait for further orders which never arrived until the caliph was killed, and the contingent was called back. But Hazrat Ali sent water and food to the caliph during the siege and later as per his orders Hazrat Othmaan was bravely defended by his sons and dependants, and the insurgents had great difficulty in making any impression on the defenders; therefore on the 18th Zil-Hijja 34 A.H. some of these besiegers scaled a wall of a neighbour's house, entered the house of the caliph and killed him inside his house.

The people who were furious against the caliph were:

1. Talha: He played an important role in the siege and the stoppage of water He was commanding the group of the people who were bent upon killing Hazrat Othmaan and on that account Marwaan killed him in the battle of Jarnal. (Tabari vol.vi p.154, Kaamil bn Atheer vol.iv p.70, bn Khaldoon vol: 11 p.397). And this very Talha later came out as the avenger of murder of the caliph and carried on the propaganda that Hazrat Ali was responsible for his murder. He was one of the chief instigators of the battle of Jamal. He had insinuated people to kill Hazrat Othmaan with the hope of succeeding to the caliphate, and when he was frustrated in it he instigated a revolt against Hazrat Al (See Note to sermon 179 of Nahjol-Balaagha).

2. Zobayr bn Awwam: He was enemy number one of the caliph (Mostadrak of Imaam Hakim vol. 111 p.118, Kitaab al-Imaama wa Siyaasa vol.vi p.58, Morooj az-Zahab of Masoodi vol. 11 p. 11). Later az-Zobayr with motives like those of Talha staged a revolt against Ali and was the prime mover for the battle of Jamal in the battle-field of Jamal when Hazrat Ali reminde him of the orders given to him by the Holy prophet (A.S.) about Hazrat Ali, he left the battle-field and was riding away to Madeena when he was killed by Omar bn Jermooz, who was neither in Hazrat Ali's army nor his companion. Hazrat Ali felt sad at az-Zobayr's death, and said: i'hough he later turned into a bitter enemy of mine yet in early days of Islam he was a good defender of the cause of religion.

3. Omar bn Aas was the third bitter enemy of Hazrat Othmaan. Tabari gives a detailed account of the way he insulted the caliph in the mosque, and says:

Nobody was mere pleased at the murder of Hazrat Othmaan than Omar bn Aas. The reason was that he had been deposed from the governorship of Egypt by the third caliph. Later this Omar joined Moaawiya as a claimant for retribution of the murder of Hazrat Othinaan.

When the events from the year 11 A.H. to 34 A.H. were moulding their course Hazrat Ali took no part in the affairs of the state. In the words of the history of Saracen "He was endeavouring in Madeena to give an intellectual turn to the newly developed energy cs the Saracenic race. In the public mosque at Madeena he delivered weekly lectures on philosophy, logic, history, explanation of the traditions of the Holy prophet (A.S.) and the verses of the Holy Quraan as well as cn Moslim law and rhetorics. Thus he formed the nucleus of the intellectual movement which displayed itself in such great force in the later days. Those lectures and sermons were compiled within forty years of his death by Zayd bn Wahab Jenny (Rejaloi-Kabeer). Many of them were lost, but some of them are preserved in Nahjol-Balaagha (Mascodi).

34 A.H. --- 40 A.H.

Five days after the death of caliph Othmaan, by a unanimous election in which representatives from Basra, Koofa, Egypt and Hijaaz took part, Hazrat Ali was elected as a caliph. This took place on the 24th Zil-Hijja 34 A.H.

Eric Schroeder in "Mohammad's people, printed in England 1955, says:

Five days after the murder of caliph Othmaan, the people fathered together and decided: "We know no fitter man to be Imaam than Ali but he will take the burden of Imaama. Answered some "press him home till he consents. They all gathered at Ali's house with such eagerness that they were pushing and crushing each other, they called Ali out, and said: "If we go our homes again without an Imaam and a caliph such a strife will stir as will never again be stilled, you will have io consent to be our Imaam and caliph of God. Ali replied 'small longings have i for this authority, yet the believers roust have a chief; and right gladly will I accept temporal authority of another of Talha" "Nay thou hast more right than I" said Talha. One who stocd by forced open Ali's palm and Talha swore oath of allegiance to Ali. az-Zebayr did the like house with n ig and crushiny a anal said: "If we

and from his house they brought Ali to the mosque and everybody once again thronged round him to swear the oath of allegiance to him as their Imaam and caliph.

The Spirit of Islam says:

It might have been thought that all would submit themselves before his glory, so fine and so grand. But it was not to be, az-Zobayr and Talha, who had hoped that the choice of people rnight fall on either of them for caliphate balked in their ambitious design and smarting under the refusal of the new caliph to bestow on then the governorship of Basra and Koosa, were the first to raise the standard of revolt. They were assisted by Ommol-Momineen Bibi Aysha, who had taken a decisive part in the former elections. She was the life and soul of the insurrection and herself accompanied the insurgent troops to the field riding a carnel. Ali with his characteristic aversion to bloodshed sent his cousin Abdillah bn Abbas to adjure the insurgents by every obligation of the faith to abandon the arbitrament of war, but to no avail. az-Zobayr and Talha gave battle at a place called Khorayba and were defeated and killed. The battle is called the battle of Jamal (camel) - from Bibi Aysha's presence in a litter on a camel, Bibi Aysha was taken prisoner, was treated with courtesy and consideration and escorted with every marks of respect to Madeena. She was sent under escort of her brother Mohammad bn Abi-baker.

See also: Aasim Koofi, p. 147. Tabari vol.iv p.548 to 565, Rawzatos-Safa vol. 11, Taareekh Zahabi p.1-21. Abol-Fida p.518 to 520.

After the battle when Ommol-Momineen Bibi Aysha felt that though she had brought about this insurgence yet Hazrat Ali was treating her with utmost courtesy and kindness she requested that her nephew Abdillah bn az-Zobayr, who had been commander-in-chief of the rebel forces and was taken prisoner, to be forgiven and freed. Hazrat Ali granted the request. Marwaan got nervous and thought that two worst enemies of Hazrat Ali (Talha and az-Zobayr) were killed. One (Abdillah bn az-Zobayr) was excused and pardoned, the burden of vengeance might fall upon him. He requested Imaam Hasan and Imaam Hosayn to plead for his cause, they requested for his pardon and he was also pardoned (years afterwards the very same Marwaan made his archers shoot arrows on the dead body and bier of Imaam Hassan and later he persuaded the governor of Madeena, though unsuccessfully, to immediately kill Imaam Hosayn on his refusal to accept Yazeed as the caliph). Then an order for general amity, peace and forgiveness was issued, every opponent was forgiven and every prisoner was released (Masood, Zahabi p.28).

Besides his sons Imaam Hassan, Imaam Hosayn and Mohammad Hanafiyya, the following companions of the Holy prophet (A.S.) were Hazrat Ali's officers and commanders in this battle:

1 Abdillah bn Abbas,

2 Ammaar Yasir,

3 Abo-Ayyoob Ansaari,

4 Hazim bn Thabit (for whom the Holy prophet (A.S.) had said that his sole testimony would be equal to the testimony of two witnesses).

5 Qays bn Saad bn Abbada,

6 Obaydillah bn Abbas,
7 Mohammad bn Abi-Baker Siddeeq,
8 Hijr bn Adi al-Kindi,
9 Adi bn Hatim Taaee.

The victory gave Ali time to consolidate his kingdom in Hijaaz, Iraq and Egypt. And according to Masoodi with the honesty of purpose which always distinguished him, he disregarded all advises for temporising. Several of his advisers counselled him to defer the dismissal of the corrupt officers previously appointed until he was himself sure against all enemies, but this hero without fear and without reproach refused to be guilty of any duplicity or compromise with injustice and inequity. Therefore, immediately after his accession he had giver orders for the dismissal of corrupt and tyrannous governors, for the resumption of fiefs and states which had been previously bestowed at public revenues loss among the principle favourites of the rulers, and for the equal distribution of the public revenues amongst the Arabs and non-Arabs, black and whites, masters and siaves, heads of clan and paupers.

These orders gave great offence to those who had enriched themselves under former administrations, and his endeavours to remedy the evils, which had crept into administration, raised against him host of enemies. No sooner the rebellion of Talha and az-Zobayr was suppressed Moaawiya, an Omayyad by descent, who had held the governorship of Syria from the time of Hazrat Omar, raised the standard of revolt.

Abo-Sofyaan, his son Moaawiya and his clan Bani-Omayya had little sympathy and no faith in Islam. Masoodi, in Morooj az-Zahab vol.vi, says: When Abo-Sofyaan had grown old and blind, he was sitting in the mosque and there were Hazrat Ali, Abdillah bn Abbas and many other Moslims besides them. The Moazzin (the man who calls for prayers) started Azan (the invitation for prayers) and he reached the part "I testify thai Mohammad (A.S.) is the prophet of God" Abo-Sofyaan said look at my cousin, meaning the Holy prophet (A.S.), where he has placed his name. Hazrat Ali got annoyed and said that it was done by the order of God.

Taareekh (history) Khamees vol.ii p.97, printed in Egypt says:

Abo-Sofyaan advised Bani-Omayya to treat the caliphate like a ball and to pass it on from one to another of their clan and never let the ball out of their possession because "I swear that there is neither punishment nor judgement, neither the Heaven nor the Hell, and neither the Resurrection nor the day of Reckoning. His son and his clan accepted his teachings, followed his faith, adopted his advice and obeyed his orders.

In the very beginning Moaawiya had made fools of Talha and az-Zobayr. According to bn abil Hadeed when Moaawiya learnt that people had sworn the oath of allegiance to Hazrat Ali, he wrote to az-Zobayr that he had taken oath of allegiance for him and for Talha as his successor. The whole of Syria was ready to back them, and they should try to overthrow Hazrat Ali's regime and accept the caliphate which was awaiting them in Damascus (See Note to Sermon 12 of Nahjol-Balaagha). Thus exciting these two old men he got Hazrat Ali busy with their rebellion and secured time to make his government more powerful in Syria.

Talha and az-Zobayr by their rebellion had done a great service to his cause but they were no more in the world to serve his purpose any longer, he therefore, gathered around him Mogheera bn Shoba (who had originally tried to approach Hazrat Ali but was repulsed by him), Marwaan bn Hakam, Waleed bn Oqba, Abdillah bn Omar, Abo-Horayra and Omar bn Aas. His best find was Omar bn Aas. Though Moaawiya had to pay a heavy price (governorship of Egypt and more than 10 Laes of Dinars) to purchase the fidelity and faith of this Omar, yet the later events proved that it was the best investment that Moaawiya had made in his life. He also collected proofs that Ziad bn Abeen was actually the son of Abo-Sofyaan (born in sin) and not the son of a slave Obayd. This change of fatherhood was officially (though shamelessly) proclaimed and Zayd proudly became the natural brother of Moaawiya. He proved himself to be a man without conscience, without remorse, without faith in Islam and without any consideration of human rights, but a very useful ally to Moaawiya. He was Moaawiya's second best find.

Histories of Tabari, Rawzatos-Safa, Aasim Koofi, Morooj az-Zahab, Abol-Fida, Kaamil bn Atheer may be referred for details of the above mentioned facts. With these henchmen at his back Moaawiya staged a revolt against Hazrat Ali.

After settling Chaldea and Mesopatenisce Hazrat Ali was forced to march towards Syria to face Moaawiya's forces at a place called Siffeen. The books noted above and Simon D.Aucklay in the History of the Saracens give a detailed account of this battle which was long drawn one.

Tabari vol.vi p.577, Rawzatos-Safa vol.ii p.425, Abol-Fida p.425 narrate in details the orders issued by Hazrat Ali to his officers and soldiers before the battle. As these orders give a clear indication of the principles and methods laid down by Hazrat Ali as to how Jihaad (Holy Wars) should be carried on, I have briefly copied them here:

1 Never begin a war yourself, God does not like blood-shed, fight only in defence.

2 Never be first to attack your enemy, repulse his attacks, but do it boldly, bravely and courageously.

3 While declaring yourself and your deeds (a custom amongst hand to hand combatants), never waste your time, and instead of speaking about yourself speak about God and the Holy prophet (A.S.)

4 Never follow and kill those who run away from the battle or an encounter, life is dear to them, let them live as long as death permits them to live.

5 Never kill wounded persons who cannot defend themselves.

6 Never strip naked a dead mar for his coat of arms or dress. 7 Never cut nose or ears of dead men to humiliate them.

8 Never take to loot and arson.

9 Never molest or outrage the modesty of a woman.

10 Never hurt a woman even if she swears at you or hurts you.

11 Never hurt a child.

12 Never hurt an old or an enfeebled person.

This battle started on the 1st Safar 38 A.H. and lasted for more than two months. During this period about 18 Encounters took place.

In the beginning with his usual humanity Hazrat Ali endeavoured to bring about a peaceful settlement. But Moaawiya was inflated with pride and wanted impossible conditions. To avoid unnecessary shedding of blood, Hazrat Ali offered to end the quarrel by personal combat, but Moaawiya realising who and what Hazrat Ali was, declined the challenge. In spite of every exasperation Hazrat Ali commanded the troops to await the enemy's attack, to spare the fugitives and to respect the captives. During the encounters once Omar br Aas and at other time Bisr bn Haarith faced Hazrat Ali in the battlefield. They did not, until the encounter started realise that the warrior facing them was Hezral Ali. One blow was sufficient to send them down from their horses. When they found no way of escaping his sword immediately each one of them in his turn stripped himself naked and fell down turning their faces towards the earth and backs towards the sky. Both the armies laughed at those life-saving antics and somebody suggested Hazrat Ali to kill these arch enemies of heir. In the case of Omar bn Aas he replied "I cannot kill timid dogs, he has begged for his life though in a shameless and humiliating manner, he said:

I cannot dirty ray arms with the blood of such a cowardly and shameless person.

These rebels were defeated in three successive battles and Moaawiya was ready to fly from the field, when a trick of his accomplice Omar bn Aas saved them from destruction. He made his mercenaries tear the Holy Quraan into so many pages and to tie those pages to their lances and flags and shout for quarters. When even such pages were not available mere rags were tied to the lances. There were scme persons in the army of Hazrat Ali who were bribed by Moaawiya, for instance Ashath bn Qays etc. and as per orders of Omar bn Aas they and their soldiers desisted from the battle and forced other soldiers to desist from it. They gathered around Hazrat Ali and called upon him to refer the Uispute to arbitration. Hazrat Ali saw through the ruse practised by the rebels,and tried to make his soldiers realise it, but the clamour of the army led him to consent to the course granted. He then wanted Abdillah bn Abbas to represent his side in the arbitration, but again a part of the army, under instigation of Ashath demanded that a weak and old man, named Abo-Moosa Ashari, who was also secretly hostile to Hazrat Ali" (The History of the Saracen) be nominated as an arbitrator from this side. There was immediate danger of serious factions arising in his own army, which might have developed in blood-shed, therefore Hazrat Ali acceded to the demand and Abo-Moosa was appointed as an arbitrator. Moaawiya was represented by the astute and cunning Omar bn Aas. They both decided against Hazrat Ali, who deprived of the fruits of victories by a section of his soldiers and faithless officers, retired in disgust with a part of his army and faithful followers to Koofa.

In the battle of Siffeen, one of the famous companions of the Holy prophet (A.S.) Ammaar Yasir and another great favourite of the Holy prophet Oyas Quraani, fought for Hazrat Ali and were killed in the battle. The men who had been, with ulterior motives, most clamorous at Siffeen for the reference to arbitration, when felt that their hopes could not be realised, repudiated the arbitration and denounced it as sinful. They openly mutinied against Hazrat Ali (therefore they were called Kharijites). From Koofa they withdrew to a place called Nahrawan, which was on the border of the desert. There they assumed threatening attitude, killed some officers of the government and many respectable men as well as many women and children. They refused to hear reasonable advice, to join duty or to return home. Their conduct at last became so serious that Hazrat Ali was forced to attack them at Nahrawan, that encounter is called the battle of Nahrawan. The majority fell fighting, a few escaped to Bahrain and Ahsaa, where they formed the nucleus of a fanatical horde which later assumed various names and adopted various guises.

Abo-Moosa had also retired to Madeena where he subsequently received a handsome yearly pension from the court of Moaawiya. (Tabari, Abol-Fida, Aasim Koofi, Rawzatos-Safa, Morooj az-Zahab, Kaamil bn Atheer and the Short History of the Saracen).

From the day of ascension to the rulership to the last day of his life Hazrat Ali did not get a day's rest and peace. It is a wonder, that facing the heavy odds that he had to encounter, how and when he could get time to introduce reforms in the government; to lay out fundamentals of grammar for Arabic language, to deliver sermons on theology, on rethorics, on philosophy of religion, on wonders of creation and nature, and on duties of man to God and man; to advise people in the most persuasive style, to suppress the tendencies for innovation and schism, which had crept in the minds of Moslims, or to introduce and to bring into effect principles of a benign government.

After dealing with the revolt of Kharijites Hazrat Ali had to face the problem of consolidating his control over Egypt. He had sent Qays on Saad as a governor there, but had to call him back and to send Mohammad bn Abi-Baker Siddeeq in his stead. Unfortunately Mohammad though brave and sincere was no match to Moaawiya and Omar bn Aas. He was forced by Moaawiya for a batie. He wrote to Hazrat Ali who sent Maalik bn Ashtar for his help. But Maalik could not reach Egypt, he was on the way poisoned by a henchman of Moaawiya and he died. (Tabari voliv p.521), Mohairmad was informed címis ract. That young man faced Omar bn Aas alone, was defeated in the encounter, was killed, and by the crders of Moaawiya his dead body was burnt and his ashes were strev/n (Tabari vol.iv p.592). Hazrat Ali's words at the news of death of Mohammad show he loved the young man and how the youth loved him. After him Hazrat Ali had to send some experienced officer to Egypt. He therefore was busy with tnat problem when Moaawiya organised bands of gorillas with orders for loot, murder, arson and rape. These bards were to attack, in the form of waves the provinces of Hijaaz, Basra, Ray, Mosil and Harat. Hazrat Ali organised defences of these provinces defeated these bands and freed the country from their harassment.

It was very easy for Hazrat Ali to divert the minds of masses towards foreign invasion and thus make them busy in murder and plunder. It had always been done by rulers and is even today considered as the best form of employing energies of a rising nation as well as the easiest way to form Empire and to propagate religion. But Hazrat Ali hated bloodshed, did not believe in Imperialism, and had no faith in propagation of religion with sword in one hand and the Quraan in the other. He believed Islam to be a message of Peace and Love and wanted mankind to be ruled on the basis of equity and justice. Therefore after strengthening one province after another and fortifying their defences he got busy in introducing reforms to create a benign temporal state and never seriously thought of expanding his domain.

By the time he got complete control over those problems and could organise an army to liberate Syria and Egypt from the reign of terror which had held them in its sway the fateful month of Ramazaan 40 A.H. arrived.

40th A.H.

it was the 15th of the Ramazaan, the month of fasting of that eventful year. The Ume was that of morning prayers. The place was the mosque of Koofa. Hezrat Ali had arrived in the mosque long before the time of the prayers, had roused those who were sleeping in the mosque. Amongst them was Abdr-Rahmaan bn Moljam Moraadi. He was lying on his face and had hidden under his garment a sword, the blade of which had been poisoned. Hazrat Ali roused him, told him that it was an unhealthy way of sleeping, it hinders free breathing, and also told him that he had hidden a sword in his garment and an evil intention in his mind. Hazrat Ali then called the Moslims to morning prayers and led the service. it was the first part of the prayers and he was rising from the kneeling posture when the sword of Abdr-Rahmaan bn Moljam descended on his head. It was the same sword that Hazrat Ali had pointed out only half an hour ago, it gave him a very deep cut. The prayers were disturbed. Abdr-Rahmaan started running. People went after him. Nobody was attending the prayers. There was confusion everywhere. But Hazrat Ali finished his two prostrations and then reeled into the hands of his sons Hasan and Hosayn. The wound which was bleeding profusely was attended to. His blood drenched lips parted into thanks giving prayers and he said:

Lord! I thank Thee for rewarding me with martyrdom; how kind are Thee and how Gracious. May Thy Mercy further lead me to the Realm of Thy Grace and Benevolence.

Abdr-Rahmaan was caught by Sasaa bn Soohan and was brought before Hazrat Ali. Hands of the murderer where tied behind his back. Hazrat saw that the ropes were cutting into the flesh of the murderer. He forgot the wound of his dead, the blow which was to end his life and to cut his career in its prime, he forgot that Abdr-Rahmaan was murderer, all that he saw was a human being subjected to inhuman torture. He ordered the Moslims to loosen the hands of Abdr-Rahmaan and to treat the man more humanly. The kindness touched the murderer and he started weeping. A smile played on those lips and in faint voice he said:

It is too late to repent now, you have done your deed. Was I a bad Imaam or a unkind ruler?

They carried him to his house and when he saw the bright day he addressed it:-

O day! you can bear testimony to the fact that during the life time of Ali you have never, not even once, dawned and found him sleeping.

He lived two days after this event and in that interval whenever he found time he delivered a few sermons (sermon No.152 is one of them). In those sermons and with his dying breath he expressly ordered that no harshness should be used towards his murderer, who should be executed, if the heirs of Hazrat Ali so desire, with one blow, he should not be tortured before death, his dead body should not be mutilated, members of his family should not suffer on account of his crime and his property should not be confiscated. He designated his son Imaam Hasan (A.S.) as his Vicegerent.

Thus closed the last chapter of the history of a life which from beginning to its end was full with noble deeds, pious thoughts and sublime words, and every hour of which was a crowded hour of a glorious life.

Oelsner says:

Had Ali been allowed to reign in peace, his virtues, his firmness, and his ascendancy of character would have perpetuated the basic principles of a good government and its simple manners.

Osborn says:

The dagger of an assassin destroyed the hope of Islam. With him, perished the truest hearted and the best Moslim of whom the Mohammadi history has preserved the remembrance.

Justice Amir Ali says in "The Spirit of Islam:

Seven Centuries before, this wonderful man would have been apotheosised, and thirteen centuries later his genius and talents, his virtues ard his valour, would have exerted the admiration of the civilized world. Chivalrous, humane and forbearing to the verge of weakness, as a ruler he came before his time. He was almost no match by his uncompron.ising love of truth, his gentleness and his merciful nature to cope with Omayyads treachery and falsehood

Justice Amir Ali further says:

To quote the language of the modern French historian "But for his assassination the Moslim world might have witnessed the realisation of the prophet's teaching, in actual amalgamation of the first principles of true philosophy into positive action. The sarne passionate devotion to knowledge and learning which distinguished Mohammad (A.S.) breathed in every word of Ali. With a liberality of mind - far beyond the age in which he lived -- was joined a sincere devotion of spirit and earnestness of faith. His sermons, his psalms, his litanies portray a devout l!plooking towards the source of Ali Good, and an unbounded faith in humanity.

According to his will he was buried at Najaf a place about two miles from Koosa.

About Ali, his character, his wisdom, his teaching, his services to Islam, his love of mankind, his respect to duty, and adherence to piety, to truth and to justice, more than eight thousands books have already been written. They are in Arabic, Persian, Turkish, Ordo, English, Spanish, Italian, German, Frerich, Gujrati, Hindi, Telegu and Tamil, a sincere homage to the sincerity of his faith in the greatness and nobility of character inherent in man and in the possibility of human beings developing these traits by good thoughts and good deeds.

Hazrat Ali (A.S.) as a ruler and statesman.

Before Hazrat Asi took charge of the state the condition of the country was in a hopeless turmoil. All the most important people and the companions of the Holy prophet (A.S.) had lost sympathy with the government and were openly hostile to it. Rank favouritisin and short-sighted greed of Marwaan and his cian were responsible for this chaos.

People were embolden to rise in arms against the mismanaged and malevolent rule. Their uprising had succeeded. They had lost every respect of the authority, and had no desire to see the ruling junta back into power again. On the other hand the members of the overthrown regime had sinister designs to gain back the control which had benefited thens for so long, while some influential persons were hoping to gain caliphate for themselves.

For three days after the murder of the caliph there was anarchy in the capita! and on the fifth day Hazrat Ali was unanimously elected. He neither claimed nor contested for the temporal kingdom. It was forced upon him. But when he accepted it he openly declared his policy in his very first specon. And that was to the effect that they had elected him as their temporal ruler and so he would remain as long as they kept on obeying him. But he had grave doubts about the sincerity of their desire, therefore, he had originally twice refused to accept their request to act as their ruler, but their hopeless plight and their repeated solicitations moved him to assent to their entreaties; yet he was under no obligation to them for their election, on the contrary he had done them a service by agreeing to rule over them. He knew fully well the reasons of their persistent supplications for his rulership, they had been very badly treated by the malevolent, cruel and oppressive regime, the ruling class had insulted them and had always refused to listen to their grievances and to come to their relief. The masses had been kept under complete ignorance of the true teaching of Islam and were made to feel that such ignorance was the best thing for them, they had been made to concentrate on worldly benefits at the cost of religion and piety, the result was a rule of brutal force of which they were tired and wanted the kind of benign government which had been introduced by the Holy prophet (A.S.). That desire had made them look for somebody who could reintroduce that type of government, and they realised that he was the man in whom the Holy prophet (A.S.) had confided and entrusted more than in anybody else, and that he had been the Trustee to everyone of Holy prophet (A.S.) secrets, therefore they unanimously elected him as their ruler.

But they had not realised the responsibilities and obligations under which they had brought themselves by making him their Amir (ruler). He knew their weaknesses and also knew that they would lose their confidence in him when they would find that he attached more importance to general welfare than to personal good, when he would make them follow the path laid down by the Holy prophet (A.S.), when with the introduction of equality and equity he would make them accept the principles of brotherhood of man and general amity towards their fellow-beings, and when he would try to lead them toward sehiless discharge of duties as laid down by God and the Holy prophet(A.S.), and thus would make them a model subject of the kingdom of God, a model to be adopted by those who desire peace and prosperity under a benign rule. He was afraid that with introduction of such system of the government and the society they would revolt against him, they would clamour for personal benefits, and would crave for vicious pleasure, but which would be made impossible in his government. They did not realise that by allowing them cheap and simple pleasure, by granting them limited power and by keeping them in darkness of ignorance the rulers had actually turned them into automata to work for them, kind of slaves without vision, fore-sight and prospect of future life. He would try to make them follow the true path of religion of their own free will, to develop the habit of simple living and high thinking and to give up the desire of seeking undue favours and unjustifiable pleasures. That was the kind of men that God wanted them to be and the Holy prophet (A.S.) had tried to made them to. The task had not been easy then, the lapse of a quarter century had made it even more difficult, but he would try to achieve it. (al-Karrar of Mawlaana Reyaaz Ali).

Whatever shadow of hope was lurking in the minds of persons expecting wealth, prosperity and governorship disappeared by this very first speech of Hazrat Ali. They knew that they cannot expect unholy and ungodly concession from Ali bn Abi Talib. Their unreasonable claims on public wealth, their fiefs and their unjustifiable holdings of public property will not remain with them. The resuit was three rebellions against Ali bin Abi-Talib and a restless period of rulership for about four year.

His Reforms

But Ali with the sincerity of purpose tried to do what he had promised, that is to raise the mental uplift of the masses: the first thing was the consolidation of the state. This he successfully carried out against very heavy odds. The second thing was to create a Central Bureau where he distributed the work of training the crude Arabs into educated and civilised being. To Abol-Aswad-Dcali, he dictated basic principles and rules of grammar for the Arabic language with special instruction to concentrate on the syntax of that language. Abdr-Rahmaan Solaami was made to look after the art of reading the Quraan correctly. Komayl bn Ziyad was made responsible for the Mathematics, Engineering and Astronomy. Ornar bn-Salaama for Arabic language and literature (prose). Abada bn Sameet for poetry and logic. Abdillah bn Abbas for principles of Administration and Rhetorics, and he himself for philosophy of religion, ethics, commentary of the Holy Quraan and the traditions of the Holy prophet (A.S.). But actually he was hub of the whole activity. Though every hour of his glorious life was crowded yet he found time to teach his assistants, what to say, when and how to say it, what to teach, and when and how to teach it. Long after his death every one of nis above pupiis proved a shining star in the sky of Moslim civilisation, they have been considered as Imams.

Introduction of New System of Government

The next subject which engaged his immediate attention was the improvement of administration. To make due arrangements for security of the state from external attacks, to preserve law and order, to control corruption and bribery, to provide equaiity of opportunities and equal distribution of public wealth among his subjects, to appoint honest and pious officers, to chastise and remove from service dishonest ones, to maintain a powerful army, to avoid enrolment of mere mercenaries in it, to take care of trades and traders and treat non-Moslims with deserving leniency and respect, were apparently the items of his programme which he successfully carried out.

He divided the state Services into:

1 Finance Department

2 Army

3 Central Secretariat,

4 Judiciary, 5 Provincial offices

Finance Department

The department of the Public Finance was divided into two section: Collection section and Distribution sections.

1 Collection Section was subdivided into three heads and only three kinds of taxes were allowed to be collected by Hazrat Ali:-

1 Land Revenue: It was usually collected in coins of silver and gold or in bullion. Officers to collect this revenue were sometimes appointed by the

centre, but Hazrat had also authorised the governors to appoint such officers themselves.

2 Zakat (poor rate) and Sadaqaat (poor fund); it was usually collected in kind or in live-stock. Officers to collect this revenue were always appointed directly by Hazrat and he took great care to appoint honest and pious persons on these posts and to keep a sharp look out on their activities and behaviour.

3 Jizya: a tax from non-Moslims in lieu of Zakat etc. and in return for the security and amenities provided to them. Collection of no other kind of tax, from non Moslims, was allowed by him.

Land survey was carried on by him wherever necessary. Every tax-payer had the right to appeal and an appellate jurisdiction was brought into force. Officers for this court of appeal were directly appointed by Hazrat.

He was the first man to introduce the Budgetary system for collection of Revenues and for its Expenditure. Every province had to present its budget direct to him for approval. The incomes were divided into two heads; provincial and central. Zakat and Sadaqaat were items of the Central Revenues, Land Revenue and Jizya were Provincial Incomes.

The schedule of rate for Land Revenue was fixed by him as under in Dirhams per Jareeb=2268 3/4 sq.yd.):

1 Most fertile land One and half

2 Fertile land One

3 Grade land Half

4 Vine yards, Orchards and date-palm groves 10

Sadaqaat and Zakat were the taxes wirich only Moslims had to pay. It was a tax levied on personal income, landed property, hoarded bullion and currency and on live-stock, its rate was that which was fixed by tenets of the Moslim Law.

Jizya was a personal tax, collected per head of a person irrespective of his income or property. But such persons were divided into classes. It was an annual tax. The division of classes was as under in Dirhams per head):

1 Very rich and land-lords 48

2 Middle class people 42

3 Businessmen 40

4 General public 12

There were positive orders that no Jizya was to be collected from beggars, and persons falling in following categories:

1 Those who were above 50 years
2 Those who were below 20 years
3 All women-folks
4 All paralysed persons
5 All disabled persons
6 All blind persors
7 All mad persons

Income from the source of Zakat and Sadaqaat was reserved for the following heads:

1 Administration of the Departments of Collection and Distribution.
2 Grants, Donations and aids to poor, have-nots, orphans, aged widows and disabled persons.
3 Honorarium to volunteers who fought for the state
4 Pensions to widows and orpharis of soldiers and officers of the army
5 To acquire and to set free slaves from the bondage of slavery.
6 Reparation of government loans
7 To hielp Hais whenever and wherever they were found stranded.

items 3 to 6 were for the first time introduced by Hazrat Ali and so far as 6 was concerned previously no king ever thought his kingdom to be morally obliged to pay back a loan taken from somebody.

Hazrat Ali was the first man who declared that a ruler's share of income from the state was equal to that of any commoner.

Income from Jizya was car-marked for the following items of expenditure:

1 Maintenance of army.
2 Construction and maintenance of Forts
3 Construction and maintenance of Roads and Bridges
4 Well sinking
5 Construction of Rest houses

Land Revenue was the provincial income to be spent on maintenance of courts, offices, and other necessary items as per orders of the Centre.

Before I bring to an end the narration of his system of revenue collection I must mention a remark passed by him in this respect to one of his governors. He said:

So far as collection of land revenue is concerned you must always keep in view the welfare of the tax-payer, which is of primary importance than the taxes themselves, and as actual taxable capacity of people rests on fertility of land therefore more attention should be paid to fertility of land and prosperity of the subjects than to the collection of revenues.

Distribution of Public wealth was a subject on which Hazrat Ali spent much time and thought and which in return caused him to lose many adherents and followers.

The first reform that Hazrat Ali (A.S.) introduced was to reorganise the Treasury and the Accounts department. Dishonest officers were removed from the service. A system of accounting was introduced. Othmaan bn Haneefa was appointed as the Chief Treasury Officer. The principle of equal distribution of public money was introduced. The system of weekly distribution was for the first time adopted. Every Thursday was the distribution day or pay day so that Moslims could spend their National Holiday of Friday happily. Every Thursday accounts were closed and every Saturday started with fresh books of accounts.

Impartiality and equity were the key-notes of his policy of distribution of wealth. At the Centre (Koofa) he often supervised the distribution himself and after the work was over and accounts cleared he would say prayers in the Treasury and thank his Lord that he had performed his duty faithfully.

Imaam Shoobi says in Kitaab al-Ghaaraat:

As a young boy, once he passed the Treasury at the time when Hazrat Ali was supervising the distribution, he saw Negro-slaves standing in line with the Arab Shaykhs and getting equal shares, and within a short time the heaps of silver and gold coins disappeared, the Treasury was cleared, Hazrat Ali said the prayers and left the office empty handed. That day he had given his share to an old woman who complained that her share was not sufficing her.

Once one of his favourite and trusty companion, Othmaan bn Haneefa, told him that by introduction of the principle of Equal Distribution of wealth and bringing important persons down to the level of commoners, by raising the status of Negroes, and Persian to that of Arabs, by allotting shares to slaves equal to their masters, by depriving the rich persons of their jagirs and by stopping special grants apportioned to them according to their status, he had done more harm to himself and his cause than good. Continuing he said:

Look my Lord, these are the reasons why influential and rich Arabs are deserting you and are gathering around Moaawiya. Of what use these

poor persons, disabled people, aged widows and Negro slaves are to you. How can they help and serve you?
He replied:
I cannot allow rich and influential persons to exploit the society of this Moslim state and to run an inequitable and unjust system of distribution of wealth and opportunities. I cannot for a moment tolerate this. This is public wealth, it comes from the masses it must go back to them. The rich and powerful persons have not created any wealth, they have merely sucked it from the masses and after paying the taxes, etc., what is left to them is many times more than what they pay to the state and they are welcome to retain it. Had all this been private property I would have gladly distributed it in the same manner. So far as their desertion is concerned I am glad they have deserted me. So far as the usefulness or services of these disabled persons and have-nots is concerned, remember that I am not helping them to secure their services, I fully well know they are unable to serve me. I help them because they cannot help themselves and they are as much human-beings as you and I. May God help me to do my duty as He wishes me to do. (Kitaab al-Gharaa).

Army

Hazrat Ali was a born soldier and had started his Military career at the age of fourteen, when he acted as a bodyguard to the Holy prophet (A.S.). Thence onward he was the only Military talent on whom the Holy prophet (A.S.) would rely and all arrangements for organisation of defences and maintenance of an arity of volunteers or soldiers were totally entrusted to him by the Holy prophet (A.S.). It was his ability and valour which brought such success to Islam in its early stage against such enormous odds. Even Hazrat Omar was taking his advice on Military problems (as-Siraaj al-Mobeen, al-Mortaza and Kitaab al-Ghaaraat).

Time had not dimmed his valour or his ability to organise such an important section of the state. At the age of sixty in the battle-fields of Jamal, Siffeen and Nahrawan, he was as brave soldier, as good leader and as keen Marshal as he was in the prime of his life, in the battlefields of Badr, Ohod, Khandaq, Khaybar and Honayn.

During his short period of rulership of about four years he organised this department very carefully.

The first liability on the state exchequer was the army department. Every governor of the province besides being chief finance officer of the province was the commander of the army placed under him. When officers could not be found to look after the military as well as civil administration then the functions were divided.

Hazrat Ali did not tolerate mere mercenaries but did not let services of volunteers go unpaid. He hated murder and blood-shed and desired his soldiers to be soldiers in the service of God and religion. His strict orders to the army were:

1 Always keep fear of God in your mind,
remember that you cannot afford to do without His Grace.
2 Remember that Islam is a mission of peace and love.
3 Keep the Holy prophet (A.S.) before you as a model of bravery, valour and piety.
4 Do not kill anybody unless in self-defence.
5 Take care of your mounts and your arms, they are your best guards.
6 Work hard while you are at it and then devote sometime to rest and relaxation.
7 Rest and relaxation are as much necessary for you as hard work.
8 Do not let one overstep the time limit of the other.
9 Do not pursue those who run away from an encounter and do not kill fleeing persons.
10 Do not kill those who beg for life and mercy.
11 Do not kill civilians.
12 Do not outrage modesty of women. Do not harm old people and children. Do not accept any gifts from the civil population of any place.
13 Do not billet your soldiers or officers in the houses of civilians.
14 Do not forget to say your daily prayer. Fear God.
15 Remember that death will inevitably come to every one of you sometime or other, even if you are thousand of miles away from a battle-field; therefore be always ready to face death.

He did not appreciate heavily armed and clad soldiers. He liked lighter swords, lighter bows and arrow, lighter coat of arms and lighter chain of armours. He preferred to have an agile and a mobile army. I wish I had space at my disposal to translate parts from the books: al-Gaaraat, as-Siraaj al-Mobeen, al-Mortaza and Kitaab Siffeen (as quoted by bn abil Hadeed). They have discussed and narrated at some length his system of reorganising the army, his principles of strategy and his tactics of war: how he divided the army into six units, beginning from van guard (Moqadamat al-Jaysh) and ending it at the rear guards (Radah and Saqqah); how he arranged to cover every possibility of a retreat with the help of these units; how he subdivided the cavalry into horse and camel units; and infantry into archers, swordsmen and "Mataeen" (soldiers armed with short lances which they threw with precision, skill and force); how he made the vanguard responsible for scouting, pioneering and performing duties of sapper and Miners; how he used to arrange the army in a battle-field; how he never suffered a defeat in his life; how bold he was; how he used to fight without protecting his body with armour or shield; how he never delivered more than one blow (mostly his one blow was sufficient to kill his opponent, if not he would give the opponent chance to get up and run away) and how nobody ever dared stand before him for his second blow. To him war was a pious duty to be performed only for the purpose of defence. He often declared "A Moslim's life is a battle-field, where he is seldom required to defend his self or his cause and country at the point of sword, which is Jihaad Asghar (Holy war on a minor scale), however formidable be the forces he is to face, while in every day of his life he is to fight against evil desires, vicious cravings and inordinate wishes, which is Jihaad al-Akbar (A holy war on a major scale), take care and do not suffer a defeat in this battle; remember it is life long struggle; a success here will be honoured with martyrdom, even if one dies in his bed surrounded by his relatives.

Judicature

The principle of keeping independent of, and over and above the executive, administrative and military sections of the state was the main factor of the reforms introduced by him. He was very particular about this. So much so that historians narrate that he appeared before his Chief Justice (Qazi Sharaia) as a complainant and the Chief Justice wanted to give him a place of honour in the court and to treat him like a king or caliph. He reproached the judge for such a behaviour, saying that he was there as a plaintiff and not as a king or a caliph, and then he cheerfully accepted the decision of the court against him. The effect of upholding the prestige of the court of justice, and his adherence to the principles of equality and equity were so impressive that the person, against whom he had filed the case and had lost it, ran after him kissed the hem of his garment and said:

My Lord, teach me Islam, I am a Christian and I want to be converted.

-Why? Did any body forced you to do that?

- No My Lord, But your behaviour of treating even a non-Moslim subject as your equal, the prestige you have granted to justice and fair play and your abstention from use of power and authority made me feel that Islam is a great religion. You are a ruler and a caliph, you could have easily ordered me to be killed and my property looted, and nobody dared ask reasons of your actions, but you took the case against me to the court and cheerfully accepted the decision against you; I have never heard of such a ruler before you. What is more the thing that you claimed as yours is actually yours and not mine, but I know the persons who could provide proof of this are out of Koosa, therefore, I boldly said that it was mine and not yours. That was a lie, and now I am ashamed to feel that I lied against such an honourable person. You have heard me. Will you not allow me to enter the fold of Islam?

- Are you o your free-will entering our fold?

- Yes. Under your regime I have nothing to lose by remaining in my religion and no worldly benefit to gain by embracing Islam and by confessing my guilt and sin.

The code which he laid down for selection and enrolment of judges shows he took care of even minute requirements of the post and position, it says:

1 Only such persons should be selected who are well versed in Moslim Law and know enough of the Holy Book and traditions of the Holy prophet (A.S.) to decide according to the principles laid down therein, besides they must have knowledge of personal Laws of other religions followed in their provinces.

2 They must be men of some standing and status.

3 They must not lose temper or patience and treat litigants harshly and insultingly. The litigants must feel that their interests are well guarded and well looked after, and the doors of justice are always open for them.

4 If they feel that they have made a mistake they should not obsunately stick to it, but try to undo the injustice done by them.

5 They should be able to probe deeply before them and to reach the truth.

6 They must be able to reach decisions quickly and must not unnecessarily prolong a case.

7 They must not accept recommendadons and must not be influenced.

8 Their salaries should be so fixed that they are not tempted by bribes and gifts.

9 In audiences and levees of the governors they should be given seats of honour.

10 Greedy and avarious persons, and those who are open to flattery and cajolery should also be avoided.

11 The door of appeal to the public should not be closed. The caliph should always hear appeals against the decisions of the courts and should decide as per orders of God and the Holy prophet (A.S.).

Central and Provincial Secretariat and Subordinate Offices

Hazrat has laid down a code for the officers of the State which covers every aspect of their duties and obligations. It is embodied in the form of a letter (Letter No.53, Nahjol-Balaagha) written to one of his governors. Abdi-Maseeh Antaaki, the famous Christian Jurist, poet and Philosopher of Beirut, who died in the beginning of the 20th Century says:

It is by far a superior and better code than the ones handed down by Mosses and Hamoraabi. It explains what a humane administration should be like and how it is to be carried on and it justifies the claims of Moslims that Islam wants to introduce a Godly administration of the people, by the people and for the people and it decrees that a ruler should not rule to please himself but to bring happiness to the ruled, no religion before Islam tried to achieve this end. Ali must be congratulated for having introduced these principles in his government and for having written them down for posterity.

I quote here just a few points to illustrate what Abdi-Maseeh meant by saying that it was a better code than the codes handed down by Mosses or Hamoraabi.

1 You must create in your mind kindness and love for your subjects. Do not behave with them as if you are voracious and ravenous beast and your success lies in tearing them up and devouring them.

2 Moslims and Non-Moslims should be treated alike. Moslims are your brothers and Non-Moslims are human beings just like you.

3 Do not feel ashamed to forgive. Do not hurry over punishments. Do not quickly lose your temper over mistakes and failures of those over whom you rule. Anger and desire of vengeance are not going to be of much use to you in your administration.

4 Do not allow favouritism and nepotism force you to violate your duties to God and to man, and drive you towards tyranny and oppression.

5 While selecting officers take care that you do not select such people who have served tyrannous and oppressive rulers and have been responsible for atrocities and savage cruelties committed by the state.

6 Select honest and kind persons and from amongst them prefer those who speak out bitter truth to you unreservedly without fear or favour.

7 Appointments in the first place must be on probation.

8 Keep your officers well paid so that they may not be tempted to corruption or misappropriation.

9 Appoint confidential officers to secretly watch the activities of your officers and staff and report to you about their behaviours.

10 Your secretaries should be cream of your civil, judicial or military service. Choose the best amongst them irrespective of age or period of service.

11 All letters or applications should be dealt with by the officers and replies or orders about them should be drafted by them only, no subordinate must be allowed to work as the eyes and minds of these officers.

12 Take your subjects into your confidence and make them feel that you are their well-wisher and friend.

13 Never break a promise or go against the terms of a treaty. It is a sin. against God.

14 You must take care of your traders but should never allow them to resort to hoarding, black-marketing and profiteering.

15 Help handicraft, it reduces poverty and raises the standard of life.

16 Agriculturists are assets to the state and should be protected as an asset.

17 Remember that your sacred duty is to look after the poor, disabled and orphans. Let not your officers humiliate them, ill-treat them or oppress them. Help them, protect them and let them approach you whenever they are in need of your help.

18 Avoid blood-shed, do not kill anybody unless he deserves to be killed according to the canons of Islam.

Hazrat Ali (A.S.) and the Philosophy of Religions

A man enters a garden iaid out into beautiful flower-beds, artistically and aesthetically arranged. Flowers in each bed have been grown by persons who know the art and science of it. The beauty of their colours and the delicacy of their forms and shade are pleasing to the eyes, and their fragrance enchants the minds. He knows that he has not the knowledge and capability to cultivate and grow flowers like that and the public have no time to go through the garden and enjoy the sights and fragrance of these beds at leisure. He picks up a few flowers from each of these beds and arranges them in a bouquet as a humble homage to the grandness and beauty of the garden.

With this view in my mind's eyes I took up to write these chapters. I have drawn freely from the following books: al-Mortaza, al-Karrar, as-Siraaj al-Mobeen. Tazeedol-Mateen, Nofs Rasool, The Spirit of the Islam, The Islam under Arabs, The preaching of Islam, Khasaais Nisaaee, Ihtejaaj Tabrasi, Behaar al-Anwaar, al-Manaaqib, Sharh bn Maytham, Sharh Mirza Fat-hollah, Sharh bn abil-Hadeed and Irshaad.

I am sure the selection is not the best, but it is the best that I can do and I am sure it will provoke minds superior to mine for better efforts.

In this last chapter I try to discuss the teachings of Hazrat in the field of philosophy of religion.

With Hazrat Ali and the Imams of his descent religion was a vital and positive force of life. Their philosophy never sinks to that war of words without life and without earnestness which is main feature of the schools under Ptolemies or the vicious circles created by philosophers of the West and the East. Their ardent love of knowledge, their devotion in evolution of human mind, their sincere faith in God, and in His Mercy, Love and kindness, and their looking upwards for above the literalness of common interpretation of the law, show the spirituality and expansiveness of their philosophy of religion, Hazrat Imaam Jafar as-Saadiq (A.S.) defines knowledge "Enlightenment of heart is its essence, Truth is its principal object, Inspiration is its guide, Reason is its acceptor, God is its Inspirer, and the words of man are its utterers. To them evolution of mind was the essence of life and religion was the essence of the evolution of mind.

How correctly Hazrat Ali taught us that a man without mind is not a man, and a mind without religion is worst than the instinct of a beast, more harmful, more dangerous and more carnivorous. Devotion without understanding will not bring Blessing of God, it is useless.

He attaches so much value to mind and its correct ways of grasping truth that he says:

Your first leader and guide is your mind.

At another place he says:

Nothing is more useful to man than his intelligence, or there is nothing wealthier than wisdom, or there is no greater bounty of the Lord than the intellect granted to you, or you can dispense with everything but your mind and intelligence, or there is no better guide towards truth than wisdom, or one hour of deep and sober meditation is better than a life of prayers without understanding, or a wise man thinks first and speaks or acts afterwards.

Next to intelligence and wisdom he taught us to attach importance to sincerity of purpose in life. Once explaining a certain verse to Abdillah bn Abbas, he said:

bn- Abbas! if you sincerely and intelligently go in search of truth or religion and if you wander out of the right path even then there is a reward for you.

There is sermon in Nahjol-Balaagha in which he says:

Do not kill Kharijites after me because to go in search of truth and to iose the true path is better than to spend the entire span of ones life in pursuit of vicious pleasure and wickedness.

The natural and logical sequence of the above two attributes is to take count of yourself, your knowledge, your thoughts, your intentions, your desires and your deeds. He therefore advises us "To weight your own souls before the time of weighing of your actions arrives. Take count with yourself before you are called upon to account for your conduct in this existence.

To obtain favourable results of such weighing and taking count of oneself ore must have done good deeds. And so far as actions and reactions are concerned he wants us to understand that human conduct is not fortious, one act is the esult of another, life, destiny and character mean connected series of incidents, events and actions which are related to each other, as cause and effect by an Ordained Law. Therefore, apply yourself to good and pure actions, adhere to truth, follow the true path to salvation, before death makes you leave this abode. if you do not warn yourself and do not guide yourself none other can direct you. The Lord has pointed out to you the path of salvation and has warned you of the temptation of this world. Abstain from fouiness though it may be fair-seeming to your sight. Avoid evil however pleasant, for you know not how far it takes you away from Him.

His discourses in Nahjol-Balaagha about noble deeds are supreme reading. His warnings against sinful life are very persuasive teachings. He says:

o Ye servants of the Lord! fulfil the duties that are imposed on you for in their neglect there is abasement, your good work alone will render easy the road to death and to the Heaven. Remember each sin increases the debt and makes the chain heavier. The message of mercy has come,the path of truth (Haq) is clear, obey the command that has been laid on you; live in purity and work with nobility of purpose and ask God to help you in your endeavours and to forgive your past transgressions. Cultivate humility and forbearance, comfort yourself with sincere truth.

Next to sincere faith in the unity of God and the apostlehood of the Holy prophet (A.S.), he lays great stress on piety. He wants us to realise that piety is not a juicy morsel to be swallowed easily nor it is a dip in river to clean all dirt and filth from the body. Piety means actions and those actions in beginning may be sour, harsh, and painful to perform. Piety means to free oneself from vicious desires and wicked deeds. This freedom cannot be obtained but by constant efforts and endeavours. Such efforts are a continuous struggle and long drawn war against vicious cravings of mind. No body can be free from vices and sins unless he develops the capacity to abhor and hate them. When once this capacity develops then to adopt a pious and sober life because a habit, a second nature. Few things are forbidden to you and so many things are allowed that no one is barred from normal relaxations, ease and comfort and from sober and harmless pleasures and pursuits.

With him asceticism was a sin against self. History cites many instances where he admonished the persons who bad given up their homes and families, had severed every connection with society, had taken to a mosque, and had been praying, fasting and reciting the Holy Book morning, noon and night. He sent them back to their homes and told them that their duties lie among their fellow beings, and what they had taken to is not piety but fanatic asceticism which is not allowed in Islam. He strongly reprobated observance of asceticism and condemned the abandonment of the affairs of this life in fanatic pursuits of rituals. He says:

He who acts with piety gives rest to his soul; he who takes warning understands the truth and he who understands it attains the perfect knowledge.

His teachings do not convey any impression of predestination; on the contrary they portray a soul animated with living faith in God and yet full of trust in human development founded on individual exertion springing from human volition. Somebody one day, asked him the meaning Qaza and Qader. He replied:

Qaza means obedience to commandments of God and avoidance of sin and Qader means the ability to live a pious and Holy life, and to do that which brings one nearer to God and to shun that which throws him away from His Perfection. Say not that man is compelled, for that attribution is tyranny to God, nor say that man has absolute discretion to decide what is right and what is wrong, we are furthered by His Help and Grace in our endeavours, to act righteously and we transgress because of our neglect of His Commands.

Explaining the verse "There is no power nor help but from God" he said:

it means that I am not afraid of God's Anger, but I am afraid of His Purity: ner hove i power to coservo His Coromandments, but my strength is in His assistance. God has placed us on earth to try each according to his endowments.

Explaining the verse "We will try you to see who are strivers (after truth and purity) and who are forbearing and patient, and we will test your actions and we will help you by degrees to attain what you know not!" he says:

These verses prove the liberty of human volition.

Explaining the verse "God directs him whom He Chooses, and leads him astray whom He Chooses" he says:

This does not mean that He compels men to evil or good deeds, or thai He either gives direction or refuses it according to His caprice, for this would do away all responsibility for human action; on the contrary it means that God points out the road to truth, and lets men choose as they will.

in a sermon in Nahjol-Balaagha he says:

The theory of compulsion, predestination or predetermination of fate is a satanic insinuation and a doctrine of faith amongst enemies of God. On the contrary God hath ordained man to obey His Commands and hath given him freedom of will and action, he is at full liberty to obey His Commands or to disobey. There is no compulsion in accepting the religions preached by His apostles and no compulsion to obey His Commands. Even His Commands (like daily prayers, fasting, Zakat etc.) are not hard, harsh and unbearable and every leniency and case on account of age and health is granted to man.

The freedom of human will, based on the doctrine that man would be judged by to use he had made of his reason, was inculcated in the teachings of the Holy prophet (A.S.), along with an earnest belief in the Supreme Power ruling the universe. Hazrat Ali gave this idea a more definite form and it grew into a philosophy. In reply to a question he says:

Perhaps you consider predestination to be necessary and the particular decree to be irreversible; if it were so then would reward and punishment be vain, and the promise and the threat would be of no account; and surely blame would not have come from God for the sinner nor praise for the righteous, nor would the righteous be more worthy of the reward of his good deeds, nor the wicked be more deserving of the punishment of his sin than the righteous. God hath ordained the giving of choice to man and the putting of them in fear and He hath not laid duties upon resby force mor rent va prophets as farce;

When asked What is predestination and particular decree which drove us. He answered:

The command of God, and therein His purpose. Then he repeated the verse “The Lord hath ordained (predestined) that you worship none but Him and kindness to your parents.

Mortality of life is another point which Hazrat Ali wanted men to realise fully, sincerely and rationally. He wants us to understand that death is a biological incident of all forms of life and it is unavoidable, inevitable and sudden. No body knows when and how he is going to cross his barrier. Therefore it is foolish to imagine that it can be avoided, sinful self deception to forget it, and idiotically timid to be afraid of it. He says:

I am as fond of death as a baby is fond of his mother's breast.

The natural sequence of the mortality of life is that everything connected with it and with this world is mundane, has no lasting value. Therefore, why concentrata on pleasure and take to vicious ways to acquire them, why not try to improve your lot in the hereafter.

Hazrat Ali's teachings are gospel of work. He wants man to work, and to work honestly, sincerely and diligently. To work for the reward reserved in the Heaven. He says:

Work, work, and do good work while you still have life, health and opportunities. God ordains you to work while there is still time of work. Be thankful for the time and opportunities allotted to you and work for the good of mankind and for your own good. A life without work is a life without worth. A mind without sober thoughts and a life without programme of honest work is the most fertile soil for seeds of wickedness and vice. Work with nobility of purpose is one of the forms of prayers. His advice to his son was "exert yourself to earn an honest living. Worst form of folly is waste of opportunities. Opportunities do not repeat themselves make use of each one of them when it presents itself, but let piety guide you in all of your actions.

Thus guiding us to the problems of man in respect of self he leads us towards the solution of problem pertaining to man versus man. In a letter to Imaam Hasan (A.S.). he says:

My dear son, so far as your behaviour with other human-beings is concerned let yourself act as scales to help you judge its goodness or wickedness.

Do unto others as you wish others to do unto you. Whatever you dislike to happen to you spare others from such happenings.

At another place he advises:

Do not make yourself slave of anybody. God has created you a free man.

Do not sell away this freedom in return for anything. There is no real value or benefit that you derive by selling your honour, conscience and self respect.

Do not run after him who tries to avoid you. Remember that to oppress a weak or helpless person is the worst form of tyranny.

Do good to your brother when he is bent upon doing harm to you. Befriend him when he ignores you. Be generous to him if he is miserly to you. Be kind to him if he is harsh and cruel to you. But be very careful that you do not behave thus with undeserving, mean and wicked persons.

Hazrat Ali had a very soit corner in his noble heart for poor, disabled, aged and orphans. To Maalik he says:

I want to caution you about the poor. Fear God about your attitude towards them. Let it be remembered that their welfare is the first charge on a state and on well-to-do people.

So far as the question of man and God is concerned Hazrat Ali teaches us to believe in a God Who has created us, Who loves us, nourishes us, help us and is our well-wisher. He should be loved, adored and venerated.

Through many of his prayers Hazrat Ali has implanted in the minds of those who have faith in God the highest devotional spirit. He teaches us to love and adore him and to think of Him as "The Lord, the Adorable, the Eternal, the Ever Existing, the Cherisher, the True Sovereign, Whose Mercy and Grace overshadows the universe. Who is the Master, the Loving and Forgiving, Who bestows power and might on whom He pleases. None can lower him whom He exalted. Whose beneficence is all persuading. Whose Forgiveness and Mercy is all embracing. Who is the Helper of the afflicted, the Reliever of all distressed, the Consoler of the broken hearts. Who is present everywhere to help His Creatures. Who fulfils all needs, bestows all blessings. Who is friend of poor and bereaved. At another place he beseeches the Lord thus "Thou art my Fortress; a Castle for all who seek Thy Protection and Help. The Helper of pure and true the Refuge of the weak. The Helper of those who seek Thy help. Thank be to Thee O Lord, Whose Mercy extends to every sinner and who provides for even those who deny Him.

This is how he wants us to have faith in God, a Creator, a Nourisher, a Helper, a Refuge, a Protection. One who loves you and One to be loved, adored, venerated and worshipped.

The other aspect of his teaching is that he has clearly and emphatically condemned all anthropomorphic (to attribute human forms, qualities or personally to God) and anthropopathic (ascription of human passion and affections to God) conceptions of deity. He says:

God is not like any object that the human mind can conceive. No attribute can be ascribed to Him which bore the least resemblance to any quality of which human being have perception from their knowledge of material objects. The perfection of piety consists in knowing God; the perfection of knowledge is the affirmation of His Verity; and the perfection of verity is the acknowledgement of His Unity in all sincerity; and the persection of sincerity is to deny all attributes to the Deity. He, who resers an attribute to God believes the attributes to be God, and he who so believes an attribute to be God, regards God as two or part of one. He who asks where God is assimilates him with some object. God is the Creator, not because He Himself is created. God is Existent not because he was non-existent. He is with every object, not from resemblance or nearness. He is outside everything not from separation or indifference towards His creatures. He works and creates not in the meaning of motions or actions. He sees and hears but not with help of bodily organs or outside agencies. He was seeing when there was nothing created to see. He has no relation to matter, time and space, God is Omniscient because knowledge is His Essence, Loving because love is His Essence, Mighty because Power is His Essence, Forgiveness because Forgiveness is His Essence, and not because these are attributes apart from His Essence.

At another place he says:

O my Lord! Thou art the Creator, I am the created; Thou art the Sovereign, I am only Thy servant; I am the beseecher, Thou, my Lord art the Refuge. Thou art the Forgiver, I am the sinner, Thou my Lord, art the Merciful, All knowing, All loving; I am groping in the dark; I seek Thy knowledge and Love. Bestow my Lord all Thy Knowledge, Love and Mercy and let me approach Thee, my Lord. Thou Livest in every heart and every soul. Thy Knowledge is ingrained in every mind.

The Compiler and Some Cornentators

The last compiler of the Sermons, Letters, Orders and Sayings of Hazrat Ali was Sayyid Razi. His was the compilation which came down to us in its entire form through ten centuries. He named this compilation as Nahjol-Balaagha.

His name was Abol-Hasan Sayyid Mohammad Razi. Razi was his nickname (Laqab). He was born in Baghdad (during the year 359 A.H.) in a family famous all over the country for their connections whit the state, for their patronago of art and literature, and for their interest in history, philosophy and religion, it was a time when Baghdad was vying with Cairo and Cordoba for superiority over arts, science, philosophy and languages.

His father Abo-Ahmad Sayyid Hosayn was appointed five times as Naqeeb or chief of the members of the Family of Hazrat Ali (A.S.). His family was held in great regards by Abbasites caliphs.

His father was descendant of Hazrat Imaam Moosa al-Kaazim (A.S.) being the great grandson of the Imaam. His mother was the great grand daughter of Hazrat Imaam Zayn al-Aabideen (A.S.). She was a woman famous for her piety and her literary talents.

His elder brother Sayyid Mortaza was great theologian and poet. Sayyid Mortaza's work (poems) are still being published in Cairo and Beirut and form part of the course of Arabic literature in the universities of those two cities. Sayyid Mortaza has a great place among the Shiaa Theologians and is nick-named Alamol-Hodaa (standard or way mark of the true path of religion).

His mother took keen interest in educating her two sons, Sayyid Mortaza and Sayyid Razi. She personally took them both to the Shiaa Theologian and Mojtahid, Abo-Abdillah Shaykh Mofeed and requested him to educate these children under his personal supervision and care.

Sayyid Razi under instructions of Shaykh Mofeed, received early education in Arabic grammar, literature and lexicology from Hasan bn Abdillah Sayrafi. There at the early siage of ten he was considered as a finished product of that institutions and a good poet. Thence he joined educational institutions of Abi-shaaq-Ahmad on Mohammad-Tabari, Ali bn Esaa Robaii, Othmaan bn Jinni and Abo-Baker dohammad bn Moosa Khawaarizmi, and with them he studied the Holy Book, the Tradrtions, Theology, History of Religions, Philosophy and Literature. From asrly childhood his keen desire of acquiring knowledge and concentrating on studies was rioted and appreciated by every one of those great scholars under whom he received his training. As a matter of fact he was considered as a prodigy by many of them. At the age of iwenty his merit was recognised and respected by all of them and even Shaykh Mofeed regarded this young man as his equal. He died young at the age of forty-five or forty-seven years, but during this short period he had written many books, his commentary of the Holy Quraan is considered by the historian ba-Khaikan as peerless, and his explanation of the traditions of the Holy propile. (A.S.) is still rsspected as a great source of canino ci the words used by the My Arosis of God.

At the age of 21 he was elected in place of his father as Naqeeb of the Family of Abo-Talib and was appointed by the state as Ameer of Pilgrimage to Mecca.

He was a man of strong character, free will and independent views. During his time the Abbasites caliphate of Baghdad was on war with the Fatemite caliphate of Egypt, and had persuaded Sunni and Shiaa men of importance to sign a Mahzar (public attestation) depicting Non-Moslims tendencies and activities of the Fatemite caliphs. Even the elder brother of Sayyid Razi and his father were forced to sign it, but Sayyid Razi point blank refused to sign such a decree. This brought him under the bad-books of the government. but he cheerfully accepted the loos of political privilege and status. Four times during his life he refused to accept financial aid from the government.

In his early age he had come across sayings, sermons and letters of Hazrat All. He had found them scattered in various books of philosophy, religion, history, biography, literature and commentaries of the Holy Quraan and the Traditions of the Holy prophet (A.S.). He had also found that the collections of Hazrat Ali's work as carried on by great scholars of the first four centuries, on account of the unsettled political condition of the centres of learning in the peninsula, were lost. He therefore decided to re-collect them once again. The desire became a passion with him. He toured all over the peninsula to collect these sermons, sayings and letters, gathered all the various books containing them and classified them into sermons, letters and sayings. The letters also included orders of Hazrat Ali to his officers and two of his wills.In fact, the classification was on the basis of what Hazrat Ali preached, what he wrote and what he said. Some biographists say that for years he devoted eighteen hours a day for this work. It was a labour of love for him. His health was failing yet he continued the work without abatement of intensity.

To him this compilation was a sacred duty and he carried it out with the devotion and diligence that it deserved. He was particularly and sincerely careful not to add and not to subtract a word from the tests which he found. So much so that if he found a sermon divided into many parts he did not join these pieces into a continuos whole but let them remain as two or three or four disjointed parts. Such system of compilation annoyed the later commentators of Nahjol-Balaagha, like bn abil Hadeed and bn-Maytham, and they have in a way complained about it. Sometimes he found the middle part of a sermon missing, he left the two remaining parts as two separate sermons.

As he was collecting from a pile of books and manuscripts on various subjects and he had come across those books at various periods of his work, naturally there could not be any chronological order in his collection. The sermons which are supposed to be delivered in Madeena or in the early period of Hazrat Ali's temporal rulership are found in the later part of the book and sermons on the events of Siffeen and Nahrawan in early part. Similarly the sermon which is considered as the last sermon of Hazrat Ali proceeds many discourses which by their test may rightly be considered to be delivered in Madeena during the periods of the first and second caliphate. At places we find that the Sayyid had copied the same sermon in different places as quoted by different authors. All these discrepancies jar upon the minds of the readers. But they stand as iron clad irrefutable proof of the honest and sincere desire of Sayyid Paz to present the thing as he found it and not to interfere with it in any way however essential it might be.

Some historians and biographists are of the opinion that Sayyid Razi was helped in this work by his elder brother Sayyid Mortaza. But had this been a fact the noble minded Sayyid would have willingly mentioned it in his preface, because he has tried to mention all the sources from which he found these sermons etc.

Sayyid Razi died in the month of Moharram 404 A.H. at the age of 45 years. Some biographists are of the opinion that the year of his death was 406 A.H., his age at the time of death was 47 years. His elder brother Sayyid Mortaza and his teacher Shaykh Mofeed were so grievously stricken that they could not lead the funeral service of that great man and the service was led by the Prime Minister Abo-Ghaalib Fakhrol-Molk.

Sayyid Razi has left about 40 books as his memorial, some of them are great works, they consist of commentaries of the Holy Quraan on religion and philosophy, yet his masterpiece was the collection of the sermons, letters and sayings of Hazrat Ali.

As soon as the noble Sayyid compiled this book (Nahjol-Balaagha) his contemporaries started writing commentaries on it, and this work of commenting on the text and explanation of meanings of the words used by Hazrat Ali, and the historical events mentioned therein is continued till today. ! am citing herein the names of some of the famous commentators of Nahjol-Balaagha.

Sunni Commentators

1.Imaam Ahmad bn Mohammad-al-Wayri (about 470 A.H.)

2.Abol-Hassan Ali bn abil-Qaasim al-Bayhaqi (S65 A.H.) His commentary is quoted by Mojam al-Odabaa of Yaqoot Hamwi vol. 13, p.225, printed in Egypt.

3.Imaam Fakhroddeen Razi (606 A.H.) His commentary is quoted by:
1.Akhbarol-Hokama of bn-Quftee p.192 printed in Egypt.
2.Oyoonol-Ambiaa of bn-Abi-Sabeea p.25, printed in Egypt.
4.Abcl-Hameed Hibatollah Mohammad bn-Mohammad bn-abil Hadeed-Motazili, (know as bn-abil Hadeed 655 A.4.). His commentary is a world famous classic covering 17 volumes, printed half-a-dozen times in Cairo, Beirut, Tehran and Isfahaan.
5.Shaykh Kamaloddeen Abdr-Rahmaan Shaybani (about 705 A.H.)
6. Allama Sadroddeen Taftazaani (797 A.H.)
7.Qazi of Baghdad Shaykh Qewamoddeen.
8.Allama Shaykh Mohammad Abdoo (1323 A.H.) His commentary has been printed very often and forms a part of the university course in Cairo and Beirut.
9. Ostaad (Professor) Mohammad Hassan an-Nayyer al-Morsaai of Egypt. His commentary is printed in Darol-Kotob Press Cairo (Egypt).
10.Ostaad (Professor) Mohammad Moheeddeen Abdl-Hameed, Professor of Lexicology of al-Azhar University. His book was printed at Isteqaama Misr Press, Cairo.
11.Ostaad (Professor) Shaykh Abdillah al-Beerooni of Cairo (Egypt)

Shiaa Commentators

1.Allama Sayyid Ali bn Naasir (about 450 A.H.). He was contemporary of Sayyid Razi.
2. The famous Shiaa Mojtahid, Theologian and Philosopher Allama Qutoboddeen Raawandee. His Commentary is named Minhaajol-Braa,
3. Faazil Jaleel, Allama Sayyid bn-Taawoos
4. Allama bn-Maitham Bahraani (about 660 A.H.) He was contemporary of bn-abil-Hadeed. His commentary is famous and is considered of immense value on problems of the philosophy of Islam. He has not devoted as much time towards literary and historical aspects of Nahjol-Balaagha as bn-abil-Hadeed. His book is greatly valued by Shiaa theologians and philosophers.
5. Allama Qutoboddeen Mohammed bn Hosayn Iskandari. His commentary is named al-Islaah.
6.Shaykh Hosayn bn Shaykh Shahaboddeen Hayder Ali Aamelol-Kirki. He died in Hayderabad India in the year 1076 A.H.
7. Shaykh Nizaamoddeen Ali bn Hosayn bn Nizaamoddeen Jeelaani. He named his commentary as "Anwaar al-Fosahaa and Asraar al-Balaagha.

8. Allama Sayyid Samad Mirza Alaoddeen Mohammad bn Abo-Torab, known as Faazil Golistana (1110 A.H.). His commentary covers 20 volumes.
9. Agha Shaykh Mohammad Reza His commentary is called Badra Najafiyya. It has been printed often and very much liked in Persia.
10. Allama Sayyid Majid bn Mohammad Bahraani He was contemporary of Shaykh Bahaai and died in 1028 A.H. His commentary is greatly valued by Shiaa theologians.
11. Molla Fat-hollah Kashaani. He died in 997 A.H. He was a lexicologist, grammarian, mathematician, physicist, engineer and theologist. He had been to the court of Akbar also, and was contemporary of the famous historian of Akbar's court, Molla Abdl-Qaadir Badayooni. The Molla speaks very highly of him in his book Montakhab at-Tawareekh. He says:
Aadil Khan, governor of Deccan, Khan-al-Khan and Hakeem Abol-Fattah of the court of Akbar paid great respects to him and Akbar also had great regards for him. His commentary is printed very often, and so far as translation of words used by Hazrat Ali in Persian is concerned, it is the best book ever published.

Preface by the compiler of Nahjol-Balaagha Sayyid Razi

In the Name of Allah, the Merciful the Compassionate.

So now, praise is due to Allah who has held praise as the price of His bounties, protection against His retribution, pathway to His paradises and means for ultiplication of His good treatment, and blessings be on his Messenger, the Prophet of Mercy, the torch of the people, the chosen one from the origin of greatness and family of long-standing honours, the plantation of all-engrossing glory and the branch of sublimity full of fruits and foliage, and on the members of his family who are lanterns of darkness, protection of the peoples, brilliant iminarets of religion and high standards of greatness, Allah may shower upon them all blessings befitting their distinction as reward for their actions and suitable to the chastity of their lineage so long as the morning dawns and the stars twinkle.

In my early age at the dawn of youth I commenced writing a book on the characteristics of the Imams covering the account of their virtues and masterpieces of their utterances. The purpose of the compilation was stated by me in the beginning of the book. Therein I completed the portion relating to the account of Ameer al-liomineen Ali (peace be upon him) but I could not complete that part concerning the other Imams due to impediments of the time and obstacles of the days. I divided the book into several chapters and sections, in a manner for its last section to comprise whatever had been related to Ali's (p.b.u.h.) short utterances such as counsels, maxims and proverbs but not long lectures and detailed discourses.

A number of my friends and brothers-in-faith, while wondering at its delicate and blossoming expressions, admired the contents of this particular section, and desired me to complete a book which should cover all the forms of the utterances of Ameer al-Momineen, including diverse materials such as lectures, letters, counsels, ethics, etc., as they were convinced that the entire proceedings would comprise wonders and surprises of eloquence and rhetorics, brilliant jewels of Arabic language and shining expressions about faith; collected in any other work, nor found together in any other book, because Ameer al-Momineen was the fountain of eloquence and the source of rhetorics. Through him the hidden delicacies of eloquence and rhetorics came to light, and from him were learnt its principles and rules. Every speaker and orator had to tread on his footprints and every eloquent preacher availed of his utterances.

Even then none could equal him and so the credit for being the first and foremost Tornained with him, because his uitsances are those that carry the reflection of Divine knowledge and savour of the Prophet's utterance. Accordingly, I accedeo to their request as I knew that it meant great reward, handsoine reputaton and a treasure of recompense.

The object of this compilation is to bring forth Ameer al-Momineen's greatness and superiority in the art of thetorics, in addition to his countless qualities and innumerable distinctions, and to show that he had risen to the highest pinnacle of this attainment, was singular among all those predecessors whose utterances are quoted here and there, whereas his own utterances are such an on-rushing stream that its flow cannot be encountered and such a treasure of delicacies that cannot be matched. Since I proudly trace my descent from him I have a pleasure of quoting a couplet of al-Farazdaq:

These are my forefathers 0 Jareer.

When we get together, can you claim forth their equals? /1/

In my view Ameer al-Momineen's utterances are divisible in three categories: firstly Sermons and Decrees, secondly Letters and Communications and thirdly Maxims and Counsels, Allah willing I have decided to compile first the Sermons, then Letters, and finally the Maxims and Counsels, whilst proposing a separate Chapter for each category? leaving blank pages in between each so that it anything has been left out and becomes handy afterwards it may be inserted therein, whereas any utterance which is routine or in reply to some question or has some other aim does not fit in with any of my divisions should be included in the category for which it is most suitable or to which its subject matter is most akin. In this compilation, some sections and sentences have crept in whose arrangement savours of disarray and disorderliness. This is because am only collecting the most representative brilliant utterances but do not wish to arrange or array them.

The characteristics of Ameer al-Momineen /2/ in which he is unparalleled and is shared by no one, is that his utterances on reclusion, piety, remembrance of Allah and admonition are such that when a person peruses them without beaning in mind that they are the words of a man who enjoys great and ruling position and who controls destinies of men he can have no doubt that it is the utterance of a man who has no interest other than reclusion and no activity save worshipping, who is confined to the interior of some house or the valley of some mountain where he hears nothing save his own murmur and sees no one except himself. He would not believe that this is the utterance of one who plunges in battles with drawn sword severing heads and vai quishing the heroes and comes back with his sword dripping with blood and heart's fluid. And despits all this he is supreme among the recluse and chief among the saints This distinction is one of those astonishing characteristics of Ameer al-Momineen with which he collected in himself contradictory qualities and patched together diverse greatnesses. I often mention these to my brethren-in-faith and put them wondering over it. It is indeed a subject to ponder over and think about.

Within this compilation, some repetition of words or subject matter are to be expected, as the utterances of Ameer al-Momineen have been known to be related in numerous forms Sometimes it happeriod that a particular terance was found in a particular form in a tradition and was taken down in that very form. Thereafter, the same utterance was found in some other tradition either with acceptable addition or in a more attractive style of expression. In such a case with a view to further the object of compilation and to preserve the beautiful utterance from being lost it was decided to/repeat it elsewhere. It has also happened that a particular utterance had appeared earlier but due to remoteness it has been entered again. This is through omission, not by intent.

in spite of all this I do not claim that I have collected Ameer al-Momineen's utterances from all sources and that no single sentence of any type or construction has been left out. In fact I do not rule out the possibility that whatever has been left out might be more than what has been collected, and what has been in any knowledge and use is far less than what has remained beyond my reach. My task was to strive to the best of my capacity and it was Allah's part to make the way easy and guide me to the goal: Allah may will so.

Having completed my work, both in the collection and compliation of this manuscript Nahjol-Balaagha, the pathway of rhetorics would be the appropriate title of the book, in that it would open the doors of eloquence for the reader and shorten its approach for him; the scholar and the student would meet their needs from it while the rhetoricians as well as the recluse would find their objectives in it as well. In this book would be found a wonderful discussion on Allah's Oneness, Justness and His being free from body and form, that would quench every thirst (for learning), provide cure for every malady (of unbelief) and remove every doubt. I seek from Allah succour, protection against straying, correctness of action and His assistance. I seek His protection against mistakes of heart before mistakes of tongue and against mistakes of speech before mistakes of action. He is my Reliance and He is the best Trustee.

_1_ al-Farazdaq whose name was Homam bn-Ghaalib belonged to the tribe of Bani Darim and was a notable poet. He was generally at loggerheads with another Arab poet named Jareer bn-Atiyya and they showed their merit only in mutual abuse and boasting over each other. The quoted couplet of al-Farazdaq is a link froin that chain, wherein he addresses Jareer saying "My forefathers were such as you have just heard, now you come forward with what your forefathers were, and if there were any one like mine, name thern before all of us." Reciting this couplet about his own forefathers Sayyid Razi challenges every one to bring forth their like, if any, ai-Farazdag had addressed only Jareer but its quotation here has inade it general and universal when its addressee is no more one single individual, but every person can consider himself to be its addressee. Despite this generality and universality the challenge to "name their like" remains unresponded like the Quraanic challenge "then bring forth its Like."

Sayyid Razi has pointed at this relationship and distinction at such an appropriate moment that there can be no better occasion, because the greatness of the personality (namely Amir al-Momineen) through whom te claims pride has already been mentioned and eyes have stood dazzled at the brilliance of his status while mind has acknowledged the sublimity of his position. Now hearts can easily be made to bow before the height od greatness of this individual who bears relationship to him. Thus at the moment when heart and mind were already inclined Sayyid Razi's eloquence-conscious eyes turned the sight towards himself as he was the ray of the sun whose abundant light dazzles the eye, and a scion of the same lineal tree whose root is in the earth and whose branch extends upto the sky. Now who is there who would remain unaffected by this relationship and distinction and refuse to acknowledge his greatness and sublimity?

_2_ In the World such persons are rarely found in whom besides one or two virtuous qualities, other qualities might also attain prominence, much less the convergence of all contradictory qualities, because every temperament is not suited for the development of every quality, each quality has a peculiar tempo and each virtue needs a particular climate, and they are appropriate only for such qualities or virtues with which they accord, but where there is contradiction instead of harmony the natural tendencies act as obstacles and do not allow any other quality to grow. For example, generosity and bountifulness demand that a person should possess the feeling of pity and God-fearing so that on seeing anyone in poverty or want his heart would rend, and his feelings would be disturbed at other's tribulations while the dictates of bravery and fighting require that instead of pity and compassion there should be the passion of bloodshed and killing, prompting the person at every moment to enter into scuffles ready to kill or be killed. These two qualities differ so widely that it is not possible to fuse the delicacies of generosity into the stiff manifestations of bravery just as bravery cannot be expected from Hatim nor generosity from Rostam. But the personality of Ali-bn-Abi-Taalib (p.b.u.h) showed full accord with every greatness and complete harmony with every accomplishment, ard there was no good attribute or accomplishment which he lacked, nor any robe of greatness or beauty which did not fit his body. Thus the contradictory qualities of generosity and bravery were found in him side by side, If he rained like the cloud in generosity, he also fought bravely standing firm es a mountain. Thus his generosity and liberty of nature was of a degree that even during days of want and starvation whatever he earned as the wage of his day's toil its major part was distributed among the poor and the starving, and he would never allow a beggar to return disappointed from his door, so much so that even when in the battle field the enemy asked him his sword he threw it before him being confident of the prowess of his naked arm.

An Ordo couplet says:

The unbeliever depends on his sword but the believer fights even without it.

And his bravery and courage was such that the onslaught of armies could not shake the firmness of his foot with the result that he achieved success in every encounter and even the bravest fighter could not save his life in an encounter with him. Thus bn-Qutayba writes in al-Maarif, "Whomever he encountered was prostrated." The heartless nature of the brave is not wont to thinking or pondering nor do they have anything to do with foresight or tore-judging but `Ali (p.b.u.h.) had the quality of thinking of the highest degree. Thus, Esh-Shafii said as follows:

What can I say about a rnan in whom three qualities existed with three other qualities that were never found together in any other man - Canerosity with wani, Eravery with sagacity and Knowledge with practical achievements.

It was the result of this proper thinking and correct judgernent that when alter the death of the Prophet some people advised him to fight and promised to enlist warriors for him he rejected this advice, although on suck occasions even a slight support is enough to encourage the heartless breve, yet 'Ali (p.b.u.h.) far-sighted mind at once foresaw that if battle was saged at that moment the voice of Islam would be submerged under the ciutter of swords, and then even if success was achieved it would be said trat the position was gained by dint of sword and that there was no right for it. Thus, by withholding his sword on the one hand he provided protection to Islam and on the other saved his own right from the imputation of bloodshed.

When the veins are full of daring blood and the bosom full of fiames of siger and wrath it is extremely difficult to curb the passion of vengeance by adopting the course of forgiving and, despite authority and power, to Dardon and overlook. But 'Ali's (p.b.u.h.) metal used to shine on such occasions when his forgiving nature would accommodate even his Woodthirsty foes. Thus, at the end of the Battle of Jamal he made a general Proclamation that no one who flees away from the field or seeks ou? protection would be molested and he let go without any punishment even auch enemies as Marwaan bn-Hakam and 'Abdillah bn-az-Zobayr. And the treatment that he meted out to Aysha matchless manifestation of his nobility and high character is that in spite of her open enmity and rebellion he Sent with her women in men's garb to escort her to Madeena.

By giving his own personal inalice the garb of fundamental differences man not only deceives others but also tries to keep himself under deception, and in these conditions such a delicate situation arises that a man fails to distinguish and separate his personal malice from a fundamental difference but easily mixing them together considers that he has followed the Command of Allah, and in this way he satisfies his passion for vengeance as well. But Amir al-Momineen discerning eyes never got deceived nor did they willingly deceive theranseives. Thus, on an occasion when after prostrating the opponent he placed himself on his bosom the vanquished opponent spat on his face. As man his rage should have risen and his band should have moved quicker but instead of being enraged he got off from the man's bosom lest his action would be tarnished by personal feeling, and slayed him only after the anger had subsided.

There is nothing in common between combat and encounter and reclusion and God-fearing because one shows valour and courage while the other sapplication and submission. But Amir al-Momineen was a unique conbination of both these qualities as his hands that were bound in devodon were equally active in the battlefield, and side by side with relaxing in seclusion for devotion he was a common visitor of the field of action.The scene of the Night of Herder poi hoan wit in scoishment and wonder when closing his eyes to the bloody action around he spread his prayer cloth and engaged himself in prayer with full peace of mind and heart while arrows were darting off sometimes over his head and sometimes from his right or left. But he remained engaged in Allah's remernbrence without any fear or apprehension. After finishing he again cast his hand on the sword's handle and the fierce battle that then followed is umparalleled in history. The position was that on all sides there was such hue and cry and fleeing activity that even voices falling on the ears could not be discerned. of course, after every moment or so his own call of Allaho Akbar rose in the atmosphere and resounded in the ears, and every such call meant death of a foe. Those who counted these calls of takbeer recorded their number as five hundred and twenty three.

The taste for learning and God-knowing does not combine with material activity but Amir al-Momineen adorned the meetings of learning and scholarship along with warlike pursuits, and he watered the field of Islam with springs of learning and truth along with shedding streams of blood (in battles).

Where there is perfection of learning, then even if there is not complete absence of action, there must no doubt exist shortness of action but Amir al-Momineen treaded the field of knowledge and action equally, as has been already shown in ash-Shfai's verse.

Examples of harmony in utterance and action are quite rare but Amir al-Momineen's action preceded his utterance, as he himself says:

O people I do not exhort you to any action but that I myself first proceeds towards it before you and do not desist you from any matter but that I first desist from it myself.

As soon as we think of a recluse and a pious man we visualise a face full of frowns because for piety severity of temper and hardness of face are inseparable so much so that the thought of a smile on the lips of a pious man is regarded as a sin. But despite extreme piety and self-denial Amir al-Momineen always had such appearance that his light temper and brightness of face was apparent from his looks and his lips always bore playful smile. He never showed frowns on his forehead like the dry recluce, so much so that when people could not find any defect in him this very lightness of temper was taken to be his fault, while hard temper and bitter face was held to be a virtue.

If a man possesses cheerful heart and joyous temper he cannot command authority over others; but Amir al-Momineen's cheerful face was so full of awe and dignity that no eye could face it Once Moaawiya tauntingly said "Allah bless 'Ali. He was a man of cheerful taste," then Qays bn-Saad retorted. "By Allah despite cheerful disposition and entertaining countenance he was more awe-inspiring than a hungry lion and this awe was due to his piety not like your ave over the nondescripts of Syria.

Where there is rule and authority there is also a crowd of servants and workers, checks of grandeur and eminence with equipment of pageantry but Amir al-Momineen's period of rule was an example of the highest simplicity. In lim people saw oniy a tattered turban in place of & Royal Crown, patched apparel in place of the regai robes and the floor of earth in place of the ruler's throne. He never liked grandeur and pageantry nor allowed show of external grandiosity. Once he was passing on a horse back when Harb bn-Sharhabeel started walking with him and began talking. Then Amir al-Momineen said to him "Get back because walking on foot with me by one like you is mischievous for the ruler (me) and an insuit to the believer (you).

In short he was such a versatile personality in whom numerous contradictory qualities had joined together and all the good attributes were centred in their full brightness as though his oneself was a collection of severai selves and each self was an astounding portrait of achievement which showed forth the delineation of distinction in its untainted form, and on whose accomplishment one wonders with bewilderment.

A Persian couplet says:

The igure of my beloved is so beautiful that when I cast my glance on the body from head to foot.

Every spot thereof calls my attention claiming to be the most enchanting.

SERMONS

Selaction From the Sermons of Ameer al-Momineen Ali bn Abi-Talib (Peace be Upon him) And Utterance Delivered in the Form of Sermons at Various Meetings, Encounters and Occasions the he faced

Nahj ALBALAAGHA

Peak of Eloquence

SERMONS 1

Creation of Earth and Sky and Birth of Adam

Praise is due to Allah whose worth cannot be described by speakers, whose bounties cannot be counted by calculators and whose claim (to obedience) cannot be satisfied by those who attempt to do so, whom the height of intellectual courage cannot appreciate, and the divings of understanding cannot reach; He for whose description no limit has been laid down, no eulogy exists, no time is ordained and no duration is fixed. He brought forth creation through His Omnipotence, dispersed winds through His Compassion, and made firm the shaking earth with rocks.

The foremost in religion is the acknowledgement of Him, the perfection of acknowledging Him is to testify Him, the perfection of testifying Him is to believe in His Oneness, the perfection of believing in His Oneness is to regard Him Pure, and the perfection of His purity is to deny Him attributes, because every attribute is a proof that it is different from that to which it is attributed and everything to which something is attributed is different from the attribute. Thus whoever attaches attributes to Allah recognises His like, and who recognises His like regards Him two; and who regards Him two recognises parts for Him; and who recognises parts for Him mistook Him; and who mistook Him pointed at Him; and who pointed at Him admitted limitations for Him; and who admitted limitations for Him numbered Him.

Whoever said in what is He, held that He is contained; and whoever said on what is He held He is not on something else. He is a Being but not through phenomenon of coming into being. He exists but not from non-existence. He is with everything but not in physical nearness. He is different from everything but not in physical separation. He acts but without connotation of movements and instruments. He sees even when there is none to be looked at from among His creation. He is only One, such that there is none with whom He may keep company or whom He may miss in his absence.

Creation of Universe

He initiated creation most initially and commenced it originally, without undergoing reflection, without making use of any experiment, without innovating any movement, and without experiencing any aspiration of mind. He allotted all things their times, put together their variations gave them their properties, and determined their features knowing them before creating them, realising fully their limits and confines and appreciating their propensities and intricacies.

When Almighty created the openings of atmosphere, expanse of firmament and strata of winds, He flowed into it water whose waves were stormy and whose surges leapt one over the other. He loaded it on dashing wind and breaking typhoons, ordered them to shed it back (as rain), gave the wind control over the vigour of the rain, and acquainted it with its limitations. The wind blew under it while water flowed furiously over it.

Then Almighty created forth wind and made its movement sterile, perpetuated its position, intensified its motion and spread it far and wide. Then He ordered the wind to raise up deep waters and to intensify the waves of the oceans. So the wind churned it like the churning of curd and pushed it fiercely into the firmament throwing its front position on the rear and the stationary on the flowing till its level was raised and the surface was full of foam. Then Almighty raised the foam on to the open wind and vast firmament and made therefrom the seven skies and made the lower one as a stationary surge and the upper one as protective ceiling and a high edifice without any pole to support it or nail to hold it together. Then He decorated them with stars and the light of meteors and hung in it the shining sun and effulgent moon under the revolving sky, moving ceiling and rotating firmament.

Creation of Angels

Then He created the openings between high skies and filled them with all classes of His angels. Some of them are in prostration and do not kneel up. Others in kneeling position and do not stand up. Some of them are in array and do not leave their position. Others are extolling Allah and do not get tired. The sleep of the eye or the slip of wit, or languor of the body or the effect of forgetfulness does not effect them.

Among them are those who work as trusted bearers of His message, those who serve as speaking tongues for His prophets and those who carry to and fro His orders and injunctions. Among them are the protectors of His creatures and guards of the doors of the gardens of Paradise. Among them are those also whose steps are fixed on earth but their necks are protruding into the skies, their limbs are getting out on all sides, their shoulders are in accord with the columns of the Divine Throne, their eyes are downcast before it, they have spread down their wings under it and they have rendered between themselves and all else curtains of honour and screens of power. They do not think of their Creator through image, do not impute to Him attributes of the created, do not confine Him within abodes and do not point at Him through illustrations.

Creation of Adam

Allah collected from hard, soft, sweet and sour earth, clay which He dripped in water till it got pure, and kneaded it with moisture till it became gluey. From it He carved an image with curves, joints, limbs and segments. He solidified it till it dried up for a fixed time and a known duration. Then He blew into it out of His Spirit whereupon it took the pattern of a human being with mind that governs him, intelligence which he makes use of, limbs that serve him, organs that change his position, sagacity that differentiates between truth and untruth, tastes and smells, colours and species. He is a mixture of clays of different colours, cohesive materials, divergent contradictories and differing properties like heat, cold, softness and hardness.

Then Allah asked the angels to fulfil His promise with them and to accomplish the pledge of His injunction to them by acknowledging Him through prostration to Him and submission to His honoured position. So Allah said:

Be prostrate towards Adam and they prostrated except Eblees (Shaytan)." (Quraan, 2:34; 7:11; 17:61; 18:50; 20:116)

Self-importance withheld him and vice overcame him. So that he took pride in his own creation with fire and treated contemptuously the creation of clay. So Allah allowed him time in order to let him fully deserve His wrath, and to complete (man's) test and to fulfil the promise (He had made to Satan). Thus, He said:

Verily you have been allowed time till the known Day." (Quraan, 15:38; 38:81)

Thereafter, Allah inhabited Adam (p.b.u.h.) in a house where He made his life pleasant and his stay safe, and He cautioned him of Eblees and his enmity. Then his enemy (Eblees) envied his abiding in Paradise and his contacts with the virtuous. So he changed his conviction into wavering and determination into weakness. He thus converted his happiness into fear and his prestige into shame. Then Allah offered to Adam (p.b.u.h.) the chance to repent, taught him words of His Mercy, promised him return to His Paradise and sent him down to the place of trial and procreation of progeny.

Allah Chooses His Prophets

From his (Adam's) progeny Allah chose prophets and took their pledge for his revelation and for carrying His message as their trust. In course of time many people perverted Allah's trust with them and ignored His position and took compeers along with Him. Satan turned them away from knowing Him and kept them aloof from His worship. Then Allah sent His Messengers and series of His prophets towards them to get them to fulfil the pledges of His creation, to recall to them His bounties, to exhort them by preaching, to unveil before them the hidden virtues of wisdom and show them the signs of His Omnipotence namely the sky which is raised over them, the earth that is placed beneath them, means of living that sustain them, deaths that make them die, ailments that turn them old and incidents that successively betake them.

Allah never allowed His creation to remain without a Prophet deputised by Him, or a book sent down from Him or a binding argument or a standing plea. These Messengers were such that they did not feel little because of smallness of their number or of largeness of the number of their falsifiers. Among them was either a predecessor who would name the one to follow or the follower who had been introduced by the predecessor.

Prophethood of Mohammad

In this way ages passed by and times rolled on, fathers passed away while sons took their places till Allah deputised Mohammad (peace be upon him and his progeny) as His Prophet, in fulfillment of His promise and in completion of His Prophethood. His pledge had been taken from the Prophets, his traits of character were well reputed and his birth was honourable. The people of the earth at this time were divided in different parties, their aims were separate and ways were diverse. They either likened Allah with His creation or twisted His Names or turned to else than Him. Through Mohammad (p.b.u.h.a.h.p) Allah guided them out of wrong and with his efforts took them out of ignorance.

Then Allah chose for Mohammad, peace be upon him and on his progeny, to meet Him, selected him for His own nearness, regarded him too dignified to remain in this world and decided to remove him from this place of trial. So He drew him towards Himself with honour. Allah may shower His blessing on him, and his progeny.

Holy Quraan and Sonna

But the Prophet left among you the same which other Prophets left among their peoples, because Prophets do not leave them untended (in dark) without a clear path and a standing ensign, namely the Book of your Creator clarifying its permission and prohibitions, its obligations and discretion, its repealing injunctions and the repealed ones, its permissible matters and compulsory ones, its particulars and the general ones, its lessons and illustrations, its long and the short ones, its clear and obscure ones, detailing its abbreviations and clarifying its obscurities.

and the young grow old and the true believer acts under strain till he meets Allah (on his death). I found that endurance thereon was wiser. So I adopted patience although there was pricking in the eye and suffocation (of mortification) in the throat. I watched the plundering of my inheritance till the first one went his way but handed over the Caliphate to bn-Khattaab after himself.

Then he quoted al-Asha's verse:

My days are now passed on the camel's back (in difficulty) while there were days (of ease) when I enjoyed the company of Jaabir's brother Hayyan.[1]

It is strange that during his lifetime he wished to be released from the caliphate but he confirmed it for the other one after his death. No doubt these two shared its udders strictly among themselves. This one put the Caliphate in a tough enclosure where the utterance was haughty and the touch was rough. Mistakes were in plenty and so also the excuses therefore. One in contact with it was like the rider of an unruly camel. If he pulled up its rein the very nostril would be slit, but if he let it loose he would be thrown. Consequently, by Allah people got involved in recklessness, wickedness, unsteadiness and deviation.

Nevertheless, I remained patient despite length of period and stiffness of trial, till when he went his way (of death) he put the matter (of Caliphate)

-1- Hayyan bn Samin al-Hanafi of Yamama was the chief of the tribe Bani-Haneefa and the master of fort and army. Jabir is the name of his younger brother while al-Asha whose real name was Maymoon bn Qays bn Jandal enjoyed the position of being his bosom friend and led a decent happy life through his bounty. In this verse he has compared his current life with the previous one that is the days when he roamed about in search of livelihood and those when he led a happy life in Hayyan's company. Generally Ameer al-Momineen's quoting of this verse has been taken to compare this troubled period with the peaceful days passed under the care and protection of the Prophet when he was free from all sorts of troubles and enjoyed mental peace. But taking into account the occasion for making this comparison and the subject matter of the verse it would not be far fetched if it is taken to indicate the difference between the unimportant position of those in power during the Prophet's life time and the authority and power enjoyed by them after him, that is, at one time in the days of the Prophet no heed was paid to them because of Ali's personality but now the time had so changed that the same people were masters of the affairs of the Moslim world.

in a group[1] and regarded me to be one of them. But good Heavens! what had I to do with this "consultation? Where was any doubt about me with

-1- When Omar was wounded by Abo-Loloa and he saw that it was difficult for him to survive because of the deep wound, he formed a consultative committee and nominated for it Ali bn Abi-Talib, Othmaan bn Affaan, Abdr-Rahmaan bn Awf, az-Zobayr bn Awwam, Saad bn Abi Waqqas, and Talha bn Obaydillah and bound them that after three days of his death they should select one of themselves as the Caliph while for those three days Sohayb should act as Caliph. On receipt of these instructions some members of the committee requested him to indicate what ideas he had about each of them to enable them to proceed further in their light. Omar therefore disclosed his own view about each individual. He said that Saad was harsh-tempered and hot headed; Abdr-Rahmaan was the Pharaoh of the community; az-Zobayr was, if pleased, a true believer but if displeased an unbeliever; Talha was the embodiment of pride and haughtiness, if he was made caliph he would put the ring of the caliphate on his wife's finger while Othmaan did not see beyond his kinsmen. As regards Ali he is enamoured of the Caliphate although I know that he alone can run it on right lines. Nevertheless, despite this admission, he thought it necessary to constitute the consultative Committee and in selecting its members and laying down the working procedure he made sure that the Caliphate would take the direction in which he wished to turn it. Thus, a man of ordinary prudence can draw the conclusion that all the factors for Othmaan's success were present therein. If we look at its members we see that one of them namely Abdr-Rahmaan bn Awf is the husband of Othmaan's sister, next Saad bn Abi Waqqas besides bearing malice towards Ali is a relation and kinsman of Abdr-Rahmaan. Neither of them can be taken to go against Othmaan. The third Talha bn Obaydillah about whom Prof. Mohammad Abdo writes in his annotation on Nahjol-Balagha:

Talha was inclined towards Othmaan and the reason for it was no less than that he was against Ali, because he himself was at at-Taymi and Abi-Bakr's accession to the Caliphate had created bad blood between Bani-Taym and Bani-Hashim.

As regards az-Zobayr, even if he had voted for Ali, what could his single vote achieve. According to at-Tabari's statement Talha was not present in Madeena at that time but his absence did not stand in the way of Othmaan's success. Rather even if he were present, as he did actually reach at the meeting (of the Committee) , and he is taken to be Ali's supporter, still there could be no doubt in Othmaan's success because Omar's sagacious mind had set the working procedure that:

If two agree about one and the other two about another then Abdillah bn Omar should act as the arbitrator. The group whom he orders should choose the Caliph from among themselves. If they do not accept Abdillah bn Omar's verdict, support should be given to the group which includes Abdr-Rahmaan bn Awf, but if the others do not agree they should be beheaded for opposing this verdict. (at-Tabari, vol.1, pp.2779-2780; bn al-Athir, vol.3, p.67).

Here disagreement with the verdict of Abdillah bn Omar has no meaning since he was directed to support the group which included Abdr-Rahmaan bn Awf. He had ordered his son Abdillah and Sohayb that:

If the people differ, you should side with the majority, but if three of them are on one side and the other three on the other, you should side with the group including Abdr-Rahmaan bn Awf. (at-Tabari, vol.1, pp.2725, 2780; bn al-Athir, vol.3, pp.51, 67).

In this instruction the agreement with the majority also means support of Abdr-Rahmaan because the majority could not be on any other side since fifty blood-thirsty swords had been put on the heads of the opposition group with orders to fall on their heads on Abdr-Rahmaan's behest. Ameer al-Momineen's eye had fore-read it at that very moment that the Caliphate was going to Othmaan as appears from his following words which he spoke to al-Abbas bn Abdl-Mottalib:

The Caliphate has been turned away from us" al-Abbas asked how could he know it. Then he replied, "Othmaan has also been coupled with me and it has been laid down that the majority should be supported; but if two agree on one and two on the other, then support should be given to the group which includes Abdr-Rahmaan bn Awf. Now Saad will support his cousin Abdr-Rahmaan who is of course the husband of Othmaan's sister" (ibid)

However, after Omar's death this meeting took place in the room of Aysha and on its door stood Abo-Talha al-Ansaari with fifty men having drawn swords in their hands. Talha started the proceedings and inviting all others to be witness said that he gave his right of vote to Othmaan. This touched az-Zobayr's sense of honour as his mother Safiyya daughter of Abdl-Mottalib was the sister of Prophet's father. So he gave his right of vote to Ali. Thereafter Saad bn Abi Waqqas made his right of vote to Abdr-Rahmaan. This left three members of the consultative committee out of whom Abdr-Rahmaan said that he was willing to give up his own right of vote if Ali (p.b.u.h.) and Othmaan gave him the right to choose one of them or one of these two should acquire this right by withdrawing. This was a trap in which Ali had been entangled from all sides namely that either he should abandon his own right or else allow Abdr-Rahmaan to do as he wished. The first case was not possible for him; that is, to give up his own right and elect Othmaan or Abdr-Rahmaan. So, he clung to his right, while Abdr-Rahmaan separating himself from it assumed this power and said to Ameer al-Momineen, "I pay you allegiance on your following the Book of Allah, the Sonna of the Prophet and the conduct of the two Shaykhs, (Abi-Bakr and Omar). Ali replied, "Rather on following the Book of Allah, the Sonna of the Prophet and my own findings" When he got the same reply even after repeating the question thrice he turned to Othmaan saying, "Do you accept these conditions" He had no reason to refuse and so he agreed to the conditions and allegiance was paid to him. When Amir al Momineen saw his rights being thus trampled he said:

This is not the first day when you behaved against us. I have only to keep good patience. Allah is the Helper against whatever you say. By Allah, you have not made Othmaan Caliph but in the hope that he would give back the Caliphate to you. "

After recording the events of ash-Shoora (consultative committee) , bn-Abil-Hadeed has written that when allegiance had been paid to Othmaan, Ali addressed Othmaan and

regard to the first of them that I was now considered akin to these ones? But I remained low when they were low and flew high when they flew high. One of them turned against me because of his hatred and the other got inclined the other way due to his in-law relationship and this thing and that thing, till the third man of these people stood up with heaving breasts between his dung and fodder. With him his children of his grand-father, (Omayya) also stood up swallowing up Allah's wealth[1] like a camel

---

Abdr-Rahmaan saying, "May Allah sow the seed of dissension among you" and so it happened that each turned a bitter enemy of the other and Abdr-Rahmaan did not ever after speak to Othmaan till death. Even on death bed he turned his face on seeing him.
On seeing these events the question arises whether ash-Shoora (consultative committee) means confining the matter to six persons, thereafter to three and finally to one only. Also whether the condition of following the conduct of the two Shaykhs for Caliphate was put by Omar or it was just a hurdle put by Abdr-Rahmaan between Ali (p.b.u.h.) and the Caliphate, although the first Caliph did not put forth this condition at the time of nominating the second Caliph, namely that he should follow the former's footsteps. What then was the occasion for this condition here?
However, Ameer al-Momineen had agreed to participate in it in order to avoid mischief and to put an end to arguing so that others should be silenced and should not be able to claim that they would have voted in his favour and that he himself evaded the consultative committee and did not give them an opportunity of selecting him.
-1- About the reign of the third Caliph, Ameer al-Momineen says that soon on Othmaan's coming to power Bani-Omayya got ground and began plundering the Bayt al-Mal (public fund) , and just as cattle on seeing green grass after drought trample it away, they recklessly fell upon Allah's money and devoured it. At last this self-indulgence and nepotism brought him to the stage when people besieged his house, put him to sword and made him vomit all that he had swallowed.
The maladministration that took place in this period was such that no Moslim can remain unmoved to see that Companions of high position were lying uncared for, they were stricken with poverty and surrounded by pennilessness while control over Bayt al-Mal (public fund) was that of Bani-Omayya, government positions were occupied by their young and inexperienced persons, special Moslim properties were owned by them, meadows provided grazing but to their cattle, houses were built but by them, and orchards were but for them. If any compassionate person spoke about these excesses his ribs were broken, and if someone agitated this capitalism he was externed from the city. The uses to which zakat and charities which were meant for the poor and the wretched and the public fund which was the common property of the Moslims were put may be observed from the following few illustrations;
1) al-Hakam bn abil-Aas who had been exiled from Madeena by the Prophet was allowed back in the city not only against the Prophet's Sonna but also against the conduct of the

devouring the foliage of spring, till his rope broke down, his actions finished him and his gluttony brought him down prostrate.

At that moment, nothing took me by surprise, but the crowd of people rushing to me. It advanced towards me from every side like the mane of the hyena so much so that Hasan and Hosayn were getting crushed and both the ends of my shoulder garment were torn. They collected around me like the herd of sheep and goats. When I took up the reins of government one party broke away and another turned disobedient while the rest began acting wrongfully as if they had not heard the word of Allah saying:

---

first two Caliphs and he was paid three hundred thousand Dirhams from the public fund. (Ansab al-Ashraf, vol.5, pp.27, 28, 125)

2) al-Waleed bn Oqba who has been named hypocrite in the Quraan was paid one hundred thousand Dirhams from the Moslim's public fund. (al-Iqd al-fareed, vol.3, p.94)

3) The Caliph married his own daughter Om-Aban to Marwaan bn Hakam and paid him one hundred thousand Dirhams from the public fund. (Sharh of bn-Abil-Hadeed, vol.1, pp.198-199).

4) He married his daughter Aysha to Haarith bn Hakam and granted him one hundred thousand Dirhams from the public fund. (ibid.)

5) Abdillah bn Khaalid was paid four hundred thousand Dirhams. (al-Maarif of bn Qutayba, p.84)

6) Allowed the khums (one fifth religious duty) from Africa (amounting to five hundred thousand Dinars) to Marwaan bn Hakam. (ibid)

7) Fadak which was withheld from the angelic daughter of the Prophet on the ground of being general charity was given as a royal favour to Marwaan bn Hakam. (ibid.)

8) Mahzor a place in the commercial area of Madeena which had been declared a public trust by the Prophet was gifted to Haarith bn Hakam. (ibid.)

9) In the meadows around Madeena no camel except those of Bani-Omayya were allowed to graze. (Sharh of bn-Abil-Hadeed, vol.1, p.199)

10) After his death (Othmaan's) one hundred and fifty thousand Dinars (gold coins) and one million Dirhams (silver coins) were found in his house. There was no limit to tax free lands; and the total value of the landed estate he owned in Wadi al-Qura and Honayn was one hundred thousand Dinars. There were countless camels and horses. (Morooj az-Zahab, vol.1, p.435)

11) The Caliph's relations ruled all the principal cities. Thus, at Koofa, al-Waleed bn Oqba was the governor but when in the state of intoxication of wine he led the morning prayer in four instead of two raka and people agitated he was removed, but the Caliph put in his place a hypocrite like Saeed bn Aas. In Egypt Abdillah bn Saad bn Abi Sarh, in Syria Moaawiya bn Abi Sofyaan, and in Basra, Abdillah bn Amir were the governors appointed by him (ibid.)

That abode in the hereafter, We assign it for those who intend not to exult themselves in the earth, nor (to make) mischief (therein); and the end is (best) for the pious ones." (Quraan, 28:83)

Yes, by Allah, they had heard it and understood it but the world appeared glittering in their eyes and its embellishments seduced them. Behold, by Him who split the grain (to grow) and created living beings, if people had not come to me and supporters had not exhausted the argument and if there had been no pledge of Allah with the learned to the effect that they should not acquiesce in the gluttony of the oppressor and the hunger of the oppressed I would have cast the rope of Caliphate on its own shoulders, and would have given the last one the same treatment as to the first one. Then you would have seen that in my view this world of yours is no better than the sneezing of a goat.

It is said that when Ameer al-Momineen reached here in his sermon a man of Iraq stood up and handed him over a writing. Ameer al-Momineen began looking at it, when bn-Abbas said "O Ameer al-Momineen, I wish you resumed your Sermon from where you broke it." Thereupon he replied:

O bn-Abbas it was like the foam of a Camel which gushed out but subsided.

bn Abbas says that he never grieved over any utterance as he did over this one because Ameer al-Momineen could not finish it as he wished to

Sayyid Razi says: The words in this sermon "like the rider of a camel" mean to convey that when a camel rider is stiff in drawing up the rein then in this scuffle the nostril gets bruised, but if he lets it loose in spite of the camel's unruliness, it would throw him somewhere and would get out of control" ashnaq an-naqah" is used when the rider holds up the rein and raises the camel's head upwards. In the same sense the word 'shanaqa an-naqah" is used. bn-Sikkit has mentioned this in Islaah al-mantiq. Ameer al-Momineen has said "ashnaqa laha" instead of "ashnaqaha, this is because he has used this word in harmony with "aslasa laha" and harmony could be retained only by using both in the same form. Thus, Ameer al-

Momineen has used "ashnaqa laha" as though in place of "in rafaa laha rasaha, that is "if he stops it by holding up the reins

SERMONS 4

His Far-Sightedness and his Staunch Conviction in Belief

Through us you got guidance in the darkness and secured high position, and through us you got out of the gloomy night. The ears which do not listen to the cries may become deaf. How can one who remained deaf to the loud cries (of the Quraan and the Prophet) listen to (my) feeble voice. The heart that has ever palpitated (with fear of Allah) may get peace.

I always apprehended from you consequences of treachery and I had seen you through in the garb of the deceitful. The curtain of religion had kept me hidden from you but the truth of my intentions disclosed you to me. I stood for you on the path of truth among misleading tracks where you met each other but there was no leader and you dug but got no water.

Today I am making these dumb things speak to you (i.e. my suggestive ideas and deep musings etc.) which are full of descriptive power. The opinion of the person who abandons me may get astray. I have never doubted in the truth since it has been shown to me. Mosa[1] did not

---

-1- The reference is to that even of Moses when sorcerers were sent for to confront him and they showed their sorcery by throwing ropes and sticks on the ground and Moses felt afraid. Thus, the Quraan records:

... it seemed to him (Moses) , by their sorcery as if they were running. Then Moses felt in himself a fear. We said: Fear not! Verily thou art the uppermost. (20:66-68)

Ameer al-Momineen says that the ground for Moses fear was not that since he saw ropes and sticks moving he might have entertained fear for his life but the cause of his fear was lest people be impressed with this sorcery and get astray, and untruth might prevail on account of this craft. That is why Moses was not consoled by saying that his life was safe but by saying that he would prove superior, and his claim would be upheld. Since his fear was for the defeat of the truth and victory of the untruth, not for his own life, the consideration was given to him for the victory of truth and not for the protection of his life.

Ameer al-Momineen also means that he too had the same fear viz. that the people should not be caught in the trap of these (Talha, az-Zobayr, etc.) and fail into misguidance by getting astray from the true faith. Otherwise, he himself never feared for his own life.

entertain fear for his own self. Rather he apprehended mastery of the ignorant and away of deviation. Today we stand on the cross-roads of truth and untruth. The one who is sure of getting water feels no thirst.

SERMONS 5

Delivered when the Holy Prophet died and Abbas bn-Abd al-Mottalib and Abo-Sofyaan bn-Harb offered to pay Allegiance to him for the caliphate

O People![1] Steer clear through the waves of mischief by boats of deliverance, turn away from the path of dissension and put off the crowns

---

-1- When the Holy Prophet died Abo-Sofyaan was not in Madeena. He was coming back when on his way he got the news of this tragedy. At once he enquired who had become the leader and Chief. He was told that people had paid allegiance to Abi-Bakr. On hearing this the acknowledged mischief-monger of Arabia went into deep thought and eventually went to Abbas bn Abdl-Mottalib with a proposal. He said to him, "Look, these people have by contrivance made over the Caliphate to the Taym and deprived Bani-Hashim of it for good, and after himself this man would place over our heads a haughty man of Bani-Adi. Let us go to Ali bn Abi-Talib and ask him to get out of his house and take to arms to secure his right" So taking Abbas with him he came to Ali and said:
Let me your hand; I pay allegiance to you and if anyone rises in opposition I would fill the streets of Madeena with men of cavalry and infantry" This was the most delicate moment for Ameer al-Momineen. He regarded himself as the true head and successor of the Prophet while a man with the backing of his tribe and party like Abo-Sofyaan was ready to support him. Just a signal was enough to ignite the flames of war. But Ameer al-Momineen's foresight and right judgement saved the Moslims from civil war as his piercing eyes perceived that this man wanted to start civil war by rousing the passions of tribal partisanship and distinction of birth, so that Islam should be struck with a convulsion that would shake it to its roots. Ameer al-Momineen therefore rejected his counsel and admonished him severely and spoke forth the words, whereby he has stopped people from mischief mongering, and undue conceit, and declared his stand to be that for him there were only two courses — either to take up arms or to sit quietly at home. If he rose for war there was no supporter so that he could suppress these rising insurgencies. The only course left was quietly to wait for the opportunity till circumstances were favourable.
Ameer al-Momineen's quietness at this stage was indicative of his high policy and far-sightedness, because if in those circumstances Madeena had become the centre of war its fire would have engulfed the whole of Arabia in its flames. The discord and scuffle that had already begun among mohaajiroon (those who came from Mecca) and Ansaar (the

of pride. Prosperous is one who rises with wings (i.e. when he has power) or else he remains peaceful and others enjoy ease. It (i.e. the aspiration for Caliphate) is like turbid water or like a morsel that would suffocate the person who swallows it. One who plucks fruits before ripening is like one who cultivated in another's field.

---

locals of Madeena) would have increased to maximum, the wire-pullings of the hypocrites would have had full play, and Islam's ship would have been caught in such a whirlpool that its balancing would have been difficult; Ameer al-Momineen suffered trouble and tribulations but did not raise his hands. History is witness that during his life at Mecca the Prophet suffered all sorts of troubles but he was not prepared to clash or struggle by abandoning patience and endurance, because he realised that if war took place at that stage the way for Islam's growth and fruition would be closed. Of course, when he had collected supporters and helpers enough to suppress the flood of unbelief and curb the disturbances, he rose to face the enemy. Similarly, Ameer al-Momineen, treating the life of the Prophet as a torch for his guidance refrained from exhibiting the power of his arm because he was realising that rising against the enemy without helpers and supporters would become a source of revolt and defeat instead of success and victory. Therefore, on this occasion Ameer al-Momineen has likened the desire for Caliphate to turbid water or a morsel suffocating the throat. Thus, even where people had forcibly snatched this morsel and wanted to swallow it by forcible thrusting, it got stuck up in their throat. They could neither swallow it nor vomit it out. That is, they could neither manage it as is apparent from the blunders they committed in connection with Islamic injunctions, nor were they ready to cast off the knot from their neck.

He reiterated the same ideas in different words thus: "If had I attempted to pluck the unripe fruit of Caliphate then by this the orchard would have been desolated and I too would have achieved nothing, like these people who cultivate on other's land but can neither guard it, nor water it at proper time, nor reap any crop from it. The position of these people is that if I ask them to vacate it so that the owner should cultivate it himself and protect it, they say how greedy I am, while if I keep quiet they think I am afraid of death. They should tell me on what occasion did I ever feel afraid, or flew from battle-field for life, whereas every small or big encounter is proof of my bravery and a witness to my daring and courage. He who plays with swords and strikes against hillocks is not afraid of death. I am so familiar with death that even an infant is not so familiar with the breast of its mother. Hark! The reason for my silence is the knowledge that the Prophet has put in my bosom. If I divulge it you would get perplexed and bewildered. Let some days pass and you would know the reason of my inaction, and perceive with your own eyes what sorts of people would appear on this scene under the name of Islam, and what destruction they would bring about. My silence is because this would happen, otherwise it is not silence without reason. "

A Persian hemistch says:

Silence has meaning which cannot be couched in words. "

If I speak out they would call me greedy towards power but if I keep quiet they would say I was afraid of death. It is a pity that after all the ups and downs (I have been through). By Allah the son of Abi-Talib[1] is more familiar with death than an infant with the breast of its mother. I have hidden knowledge, if I disclose it you will start trembling like ropes in deep wells.

SERMONS 6

Delivered on being advised not to chase Talha bn-Obaydillah and az-Zobayr bn-Awwam for fighting[2]

-1- About death Ameer al-Momineen says that it is so dear to him that even an infant does not so love to leap towards the source of its nourishment while in its mother's lap. An infant's attachment with the breast of its mother is under the effect of a natural impulse but the dictates of natural impulses change with the advance of age. When the limited period of infancy ends and the infant's temperament changes, he does not like even to look at what was so familiar to him but rather turns his face from it in disgust. But the love of prophets and saints for union with Allah is mental and spiritual, and mental and spiritual feelings do not change, nor does weakness or decay occur in them. Since death is the means and first rung towards this goal their love for death increases to such an extent that its rigours become the cause of pleasure for them and its bitterness proves to be the source of delight for their taste. Their love for it is the same as that of the thirsty for the well or that of a lost passenger for his goal. Thus when Ameer al-Momineen was wounded by Abdr-Rahmaan bn Moljam's fatal attack, he said "I was but like the walker who has reached (the goal) or like the seeker who has found (his object) and whatever is with Allah is good for the pious" The Prophet also said that there is no pleasure for a believer other than union with Allah.

-2- When Ameer al-Momineen showed intention to chase Talha and az-Zobayr, he was advised to leave them on their own lest he received some harm from them. Ameer al-Momineen uttered these words in reply, the sum total whereof is: "How long can I be a mere spectator to my right being snatched and keep quiet. Now, so long as I have breath of life I shall fight them and make them suffer the consequences of their conduct. They should not think that I can be easily over-powered like the badger. "

Daboo means badger. Its nickname is Om-Amir and Om-Torrayq. It is also called "the glutton, because it swallows everything and eats up whatever it gets as if several bellies were contained in one, and they do not have their fill. It is also called Nathal. It is a very simple and silly animal. Its slyness is apparent from the way it is easily caught. It is said that the hunter surrounds its den and strikes it with his foot or a stick, and calls out softly, "Bow you head Om-Torrayq, conceal yourself Om-Amir" On repeating this sentence and patting the ground, it conceals itself in a corner of the den. Then the hunter says, "Om-

By Allah I shall not be like the badger, which feigns sleep on continuous (sound of) stone-throwing till he who is in search of it finds it or he who is on the look out for it overpowers it. Rather, I shall ever strike the deviators from truth with the help of those who advance towards it, and the sinners and doubters with the help of those who listen to me and obey, till my day (of death) comes. By Allah I have been continually deprived of my right from the day the Prophet died till today.

SERMONS 7

The hypocrites

They[1] have made Satan the master of their affairs, and he has taken them as partners. He has laid eggs and hatched them in their bosoms. He creeps and crawls in their laps. He sees through their eyes, and speaks with their tongues. In this way he has led them to sinfulness and adorned for them foul things like the action of one whom Satan has made partner in his domain and speaks untruth through his tongue.

Amir is not in its den, it is sleeping" On hearing this it stretches its limbs and feigns sleep. The hunter then puts the knot in its feet and drags it out, and if falls like a coward into his hand without resistance.

-1- Ameer al-Momineen says about the hypocrites (i. e. those who opposed him before and during his Caliphate) that they are partners in action of Satan and his helpers and supporters. He too has befriended them so much that he has made his abode with them, resides on their bosoms, lays eggs and hatches young one from them there, while these young ones jump and play in their laps without demur. He means that Satanic evil ideas take birth in their bosoms and grow and thrive there. There is no restrain on them, nor restriction of any kind. He has so permeated in their blood and mingled in their spirit that both have become completely unified. Now eyes are theirs but sight is his, the tongue is theirs but the words are his, as the Prophet had said "Verily, Satan permeates the progeny of Adam like blood" That is, just as the circulation of blood does not stop, in the same way the quick succession of Satan's evil ideas know no break and he draws man towards evil in sleep and wakefulness, and in every posture, rising or sitting. He so paints them with his dye that their word and action reflect an exact portrait of his word and action. Those whose bosoms shine with the effulgence of faith prevent such evil ideas but some are already ready to welcome those evils and these are the persons who under the garb of Islam are ever after advancement of heresy.

SERMONS 8

Said about az-Zobayr at a time for which it was appropriate

He asserts that he swore allegiance to me with his hand but did not swear with his heart.[1] So he does admit allegiance. As regards his claiming it otherwise than with his heart he should come forward with a clear argument for it. Otherwise, he should return to wherefrom he has gone out.[2]

SERMONS 9

Cowardice of the People of Jamal

They[3] thunder like clouds and shone like lightning but despite both these things they exhibited cowardice, while we do not thunder till we pounce

-1- When after swearing allegiance on the hand of Ameer al-Momineen, az-Zobayr bn Awwam broke the allegiance, then sometimes he put forth the excuse that he was forced to swear allegiance and that forced allegiance is no allegiance, and sometimes he said that allegiance was only for show. His heart did not go in accord with it. As though he himself admitted with his tongue the duplicity of his outer appearance and inner self. But this excuse is like that of the one who reverts to apostasy after adopting Islam and to avoid penalty may say that he had accepted Islam only by the tongue, not in the heart. Obviously, such an excuse cannot be heard, nor can avoid punishment by this argument. If az-Zobayr suspected that Othmaan was slain at Ameer al-Momineen's insistence, this suspicion should have existed when he was taking oath for obedience and stretching his hand for allegiance, not now that his expectations were getting frustrated and hopes had started dawning from somewhere else.

-2- Ameer al-Momineen has rejected his claim in short form thus: that when he admits that his hands had paid allegiance then until there is justification for breaking of the allegiance he should stick to it. But if, according to him his heart was not in accord with it he should produce other proof for it. Since proof about the state of heart cannot be adduced how can he bring such proof, and an assertion without proof is unacceptable to his mind.

-3- About the people of Jamal (i. e. the enemy in the battle of Jamal) Ameer al-Momineen says that they rose thundering, shouting and stampeding but when encounter took place they were seen flying like straw. At one time they made loud claims that they would do this and would do that and now they showed such cowardice as to flee from the battle-field. About himself Ameer al-Momineen says, that "We do not threaten the enemy before battle, nor utter boasts, nor terrorise the enemy by raising unnecessary cries upon the foe nor do we show flow (of words) until we have not virtually rained.

SERMONS 10

Talha and az-Zobayr

Beware! Satan[1] has collected his group and assembled his horse-men and foot-soldiers. Surely, with me is my sagacity. I have neither deceived myself nor ever been deceived. By Allah I shall fill to the brim for them a cistern from which I alone would draw water. They can neither turn away from it nor return to it.

SERMONS 11

When he gave the Standard of the Battle of Jamal to his son Mohammad bn-Hanafiyya[2]

---

because it is not the way of the brave to use the tongue instead of the hand" That is why on this occasion he said to his comrades: "Beware of excessive talk as it is cowardice. "

-1- When Talha and az-Zobayr broke away by violating the Oath of allegiance and set for Basra in the company of Aysha, Ameer al-Momineen spoke in these words which are part of the long speech.

bn-Abil-Hadeed has written that in this sermon Satan denotes the real Satan as well as Moaawiya because Moaawiya was secretly conspiring with Talha and az-Zobayr and instigating them to fight against Ameer al-Momineen but the reference to the real Satan is more appropriate, obvious and in accord with the situation and circumstances.

-2- Mohammad bn Hanafiyya was Ameer al-Momineen's son but called bn Hanafiyya after his mother. His mother's name was Khawla bnt Jafar. She was known as Hanafiyya after her tribe Bani-Haneefa. When people of Yamama were declared apostates for refusing to pay zakat (religious tax) and were killed and their women-folk were brought to Madeena as slave girls, this lady also came to Madeena with them. When her tribesmen came to know it they approached Ameer al-Momineen and requested him to save her from the blemish of slavery and protect her family honour and prestige. Consequently, Ameer al-Momineen set her free after purchasing and married here whereafter Mohammad was born.

Most historians have written his surname as Abol-Qaasim. Thus, the author of al-Isteeaab (vol.3, pp.1366, 1367-1368, 1370, 1371-1372) has narrated the opinion of Abo-Rasheed bn Hafs az-Zohri that from among the sons of the companions (of the Prophet) he came across four individuals everyone of whom was named Mohammad and surnamed Abol-Qaasim, namely (I) Mohammad bn Hanafiyya, (2) Mohammad bn Abi-Bakr (3) Mohammad bn Talha and (4) Mohammad bn Saad. After this he writes that Mohammad bn Talha's name and surname was given by the Prophet. al-Waqidi writes that the name and surname of Mohammad bn Abi-Bakr was suggested by Aysha. Apparently the Holy Prophet's giving the name of Mohammad bn Talha seems incorrect since from some traditions it appears that the Prophet had reserved it for a son of Ameer al-Momineen and he was Mohammad bn Hanafiyya.

As regards his surname it is said that the Prophet had particularised it and that he had told Ali that a son would be born to you after me and I have given him my name and surname and after that it is not permissible for anyone in my people to have this name and surname together.

With this opinion before us how can it be correct that the Prophet had given this very name and surname to anyone else since particularisation means that no one else would share it. Moreover, some people have recorded the surname of bn Talha as Abo-Solaymaan instead of Abol-Qaasim and this further confirms our view point. Similarly, if the surname of Mohammad bn Abi-Bakr was on the ground that his son's name was Qaasim, who was among the theologians of Madeena, then what is the sense in Aysha having suggested it. If she had suggested it along with the name how could Mohammad bn Abi-Bakr tolerate it later on since having been brought up under the care of Ameer al-Momineen the Prophet's saying could not remain concealed from him. Moreover, most people have recorded his surname as Abo-Abdr-Rahmaan, which weakens the view of Abo-Rasheed.

Let alone these people's surname being Abol-Qaasim, even for bn al-Hanafiyya this surname is not proved. Although bn Khallikan (in Wafayat al-Ayan, vol.4, p.170) has taken that son of Ameer al-Momineen for whom the Prophet had particularised this surname to be Mohammad bn Hanafiyya, yet Allama al-Mamaqani (in Tanqih al-Maqal, vol.3, Part 1, p.112) writes:

In applying this tradition to Mohammad bn Hanafiyya, bn Khallikan has got into confusion, because the son of Ameer al-Momineen whom the Prophet's name and surname together have been gifted by the Prophet, and which is not permissible to be given to any one else, is to the awaited last Imam (may our lives be his ransom) , and not to Mohammad bn Hanafiyya, nor is the surname Abol-Qaasim established for him, rather some of the Sonnis being ignorant of the real intention of the Prophet, have taken to mean bn al-Hanafiyya.

However, Mohammad bn Hanafiyya was prominent in righteousness and piety, sublime in renunciation and worship, lofty in knowledge and achievements and heir of his father in bravery. His performance in the battles of Jamal and Siffeen had created such impression among the Arabs that even warriors of consequence trembled at his name. Ameer al-Momineen too was proud of his courage and valour, and always placed him forward in encounters. Shaykh al-Bahaai has written in al-Kashkool that Ali bn Abi-Talib kept him abreast in the battles and did not allow Hasan and Hosayn to go ahead, and used to say, "He is my son while these two are sons of the Prophet of Allah" When a

Mountains[1] may move from their position but you should not move from yours. Grit your teeth. Lend to Allah your head (in fighting for Allah, give yourself to Allah). Plant your feet firmly on the ground. Have your eye on

---

Kharijite said to bn al-Hanafiyya that Ali thrust him into the flames of war but saved away Hasan and Hosayn he replied that he himself was like the right hand and Hasan and Hosayn like Ali's two eyes and that Ali protected his eyes with his right hand. But Allama al-Mamaqani has written in Tanqih al-Maqal that this was not the reply of bn al-Hanafiyya but of Ameer al-Momineen himself. When during the battle of Siffeen Mohammad mentioned this matter to Ameer al-Momineen in complaining tone he replied, "You are my right hand whereas they are my eyes, and the hand should protect the eyes. "
Apparently it seems that first Ameer al-Momineen must have given this reply and thereafter someone might have mentioned it to Mohammad bn Hanafiyya and he must have repeated the same reply as there could be no more eloquent reply than this one and its eloquence confirms the view that it was originally the outcome of the eloquent tongue of Ameer al-Momineen and was later appropriated by Mohammad al-Hanafiyya. Consequently, both these views can be held to be correct and there is no incongruity between them. However, he was born in the reign of the second Caliph and died in the reign of Abdl-Malik bn Marwaan at the age of sixty-five years. Some writers have recorded the year of his death as 80 A.H. and others as 81 A.H. There is a difference about the place of his death as well. Some have put it as Madeena, some Ayla and some Taif.
-1- When in the Battle of Jamal Ameer al-Momineen sent Mohammad bn Hanafiyya to the battle-field, he told him that he should fix himself before the enemy like the mountain of determination and resoluteness so that the onslaught of the army should not be able to displace him, and should charge the enemy with closed teeth because by pressing teeth over the teeth tension occurs in the nerves of the skull as a result of which the stroke of the sword goes amiss, as he said at another place also viz. "Press together the teeth. It sends amiss the edge of the sword" Then he says, "My child, lend your head to Allah in order that you may be able to achieve eternal life in place of this one, because for a lent article there is the right to get it back. Therefore, you should fight being heedless of your life, otherwise also if your mind clings to life you will hesitate to advance towards deathly encounters and that would tell upon your reputation of bravery. Look, do not let your steps falter because the enemy is emboldened at the faltering of steps, and faltering steps fastens the feet of the enemy. Keep the last lines of the enemy as your aim so that the enemy may be overawed with loftiness of your intentions and you may feel ease in tearing through their lives, and their movement should also not remain concealed from you. Look, do not pay heed to their superiority in numbers, otherwise your valour and courage would suffer" This sentence can also mean that one should not wide open the eyes to be dazzled by the shining of weapons, and the enemy may make an attack by taking advantage of the situation. Also, always bear it in mind that victory is from Allah. "If Allah helps you no one can overpower you" Therefore, instead of relying on material means seek His support and succour.
(Remember O" ye Believers!) If Allah helpeth you, none shall overcome you...(Quraan, 3:159)

the remotest foe and close your eyes (to their numerical majority). And keep sure that succour is but from Allah, the Glorified.

SERMONS 12

When[1] Allah gave Ameer al-Momineen victory over the enemy at the Battle of Jamal, one of his Comrades said on that occasion "I wish my brother had been present and he too would have seen what success and victory Allah had given you," whereupon he said:

Did your brother hold me friend? "

He said: "Yes," Then Ameer al-Momineen said:

In that case he was with us. Rather in this army of ours, even those persons were also present who are still in the loins of men and wombs of women. Shortly, time will bring them out and faith will get strength through them.

SERMONS 13

Condemning the People of Basra[2]

-1- If a person falls short in his actions despite means and equipment, this would be indicative of the weakness of his will. But if there is an impediment in the way of action or his life comes to an end as a result of which his action remains incomplete, then in that case Allah would not deprive him of the reward on the basis that actions are judged by intention. Since his intention in any case was to perform the action, therefore he should deserve reward to some extent.

In the case of action, there may be absence of reward because action can involve show or pretence but intention is hidden in the depth of heart. It can have not a jot of show or affectation. The intention would remain at the same level of frankness, truth, perfection and correctness where it is, even though there may be no action due to some impediment. Even if there is no occasion for forming intention but there is passion and zeal in the heart, a man would deserve reward on the basis of his heart's feelings. This is to what Ameer al-Momineen has alluded in this sermon, namely that "If your brother loved me he would share the reward with those who secured martyrdom for our support

-2- bn Maytham writes that when the Battle of Jamal ended then on the third day after it Ameer al-Momineen said the morning prayer in the central mosque of Basra and after finishing it stood on the right side of the prayer place reclining against the wall and delivered this sermon wherein he described the lowness of character of the people of Basra and their slyness, namely that they got enflamed at others" instigation without anything of their own and making over their command to a woman clung to a camel. They broke away after swearing allegiance and exhibited their low character and evil nature by practising double facedness. In this sermon woman implies Aysha and quadruped implies the camel (Jamal) after which this battle has been named the Battle of Jamal. "

This battle originated in this way that when although during the life time of Othmaan, Aysha used to oppose him and had left for Mecca leaving him in siege and as such she had a share in his assassination details of which would be stated at some suitable place but when on her return from Mecca towards Madeena she heard from Abdillah bn Salama that after Othmaan allegiance had been paid to Ali (as Caliph) she suddenly exclaimed, "If allegiance has been paid to Ali, I wish the sky had burst on the earth. Let me go back to Mecca" Consequently she decided to return to Mecca and began saying, "By Allah Othmaan has been killed helplessly. I shall certainly avenge his blood" On seeing this wide change in the state of affairs Abo-Salama said "What are you saying as you yourself used to say "Kill this Nathal; he had turned unbeliever" Thereupon she replied, "Not only I but everyone used to say so; but leave these things and listen to what I am now saying, that is better and deserves more attention. It is so strange that first he was called upon to repent but before giving him an opportunity to do so he has been killed"
On this Abo-Salama recited the following verses addressing her:

You started it and now you are changing and raising storms of wind and rain.

You ordered for his killing and told us that he had turned unbeliever.

We admit that he has been killed but under your orders and the real Killer is one who ordered it.

Nevertheless, neither the sky fell over us nor did the sun and moon fall into eclipse.

Certainly people have paid allegiance to one who can ward off the enemy with power and grandeur, does not allow swords to come near him and loosens the twist of the rope, that is, subdues the enemy.

He is always fully armed for combat and the faithful is never like the traitor.

However, when she reached Mecca with a passion for vengeance she began rousing the people to avenge Othmaan's blood by circulating stories of his having been victimised. The first to respond to this call was Abdillah bn Amir al-Hazrami who had been the governor of Mecca in Othmaan's reign and with him Marwaan bn Hakam, Saeed bn Aas and other Omayyads rose to support her. On the other side Talha bn Obaydillah and az-Zobayr bn Awwam also reached Mecca from Madeena. From Yemen Yala bn Monabbih who had been governor there during Othmaan's caliphate and the former governor of Basra, Abdillah bn Amir bn Korayz also reached there, and joining together began preparing their plans. Battle had been decided upon but discussion was about the venue of confrontation. Aysha's opinion was to make Madeena the venue of the battle but some people opposed and held that it was difficult to deal with Medinites, and that some other place should be chosen as the venue. At last after much discussion it was decided to march towards Basra as there was no dearth of men to support the cause. Consequently on the strength of Abdillah bn Amr's countless wealth, and the offer of six hundred thousand Dirhams and six hundred camels by Yala bn Monabbih they prepared an army of three thousand and set off to Basra. There was a small incident on the way on account of which Aysha refused to advance further. What happened was that at a place she heard the barking of dogs and enquired from the camel driver the name of the place. He said it was Hawab. On hearing this name she recalled the Prophet's admonition when he had said to his wives, "I wish I could know at which of you the dogs of Hawab would bark" So when she realised that she herself was that one she got the camel seated by patting and expressed her intention to abandon the march. But the device of her companions saved the deteriorating situation. Abdillah bn Zobayr swore to assure her that it was not Hawab, Talha seconded him and for her further assurance also sent for fifty persons to stand witness to it. When all the people were on one side what could a single woman do by opposing. Eventually they were successful and Aysha resumed her forward march with the same enthusiasm.

When this army reached Basra, people were first amazed to see the riding animal of Aysha. Jariya bn Qudama came forward and said "O mother of the faithful, the assassination of Othmaan was one tragedy but the greater tragedy is that you have come out on this cursed camel and ruined your honour and esteem. It is better that you should get back" But since neither the incident at Hawab could deter her nor could the Quraanic injunction: "Keep sitting in your houses" (33:33) stop her, what effect could these voices produce. Consequently, she disregarded all this.

When this army tried to enter the city the Governor of Basra Othmaan bn Honayf came forward to stop them and when the two parties came face to face they drew their swords out of the sheaths and pounced upon each other. When a good number had been killed from either side Aysha intervened on the basis of her influence and the two groups agreed that till the arrival of Ameer al-Momineen the existing administration should continue and Othmaan bn Honayf should continue on his post. But only two days had elapsed when they made a nightly attack on Othmaan bn Honayf, killed forty innocent persons, beat Othmaan bn Honayf, plucked every hair of his beard, took him in their custody and shut him up. Then they attacked public treasury and while ransacking it killed twenty persons on the spot, and beheaded fifty more after arresting them. Then they attacked the grain store, whereupon an elderly noble of Basra Hokaym bn Jabala could not control himself and reaching there with his men said to Abdillah bn Zobayr, 'spare some of this grain for the city's populace. After all there should be a limit to oppression. You have spread killing and destruction all round and put Othmaan bn Honayf in confinement. For Allah's sake keep off these ruining activities and release Othmaan bn Honayf. Is there no fear of Allah in your hearts? "bn az-Zobayr said "This is vengeance of Othmaan's life" Hokaym bn Jabala retorted, "Were those who have been killed assassins of Othmaan? By Allah, if I had supporters and comrades I should have certainly avenged the blood of these Moslims whom you have killed without reason" bn az-Zobayr replied, "We shall not give anything out of this grain, nor will Othmaan bn Honayf be released" At last the battle raged between these two parties but how could a few individuals deal with such a big force? The result was that Hokaym bn Jabala, his son al-Ashraf bn Hokaym bn Jabala, his brother ar-Ril bn Jabala and seventy persons of his tribe were killed. In short, killing and looting prevailed all round. Neither anyone's life was secure nor was there any way to save one's honour or property.

When Ameer al-Momineen was informed of the march to Basra he set out to stop it with a force which consisted of seventy of those who had taken part in the battle of Badr and four hundred out of those companions who had the honour of being present at the Allegiance of Rizwaan (Divine Pleasure). When he stopped at the stage of Ziqar he sent his son Hasan (p.b.u.h.) and Ammaar bn Yaasir to Koofa to invite its people to fighting. Consequently, despite interference of Abo-Mosa al-Ashari seven thousand combatants from there joined Ameer al-Momineen's army. He left that place after placing the army under various commanders. Eye witnesses state that when this force reached near Basra first of all a contingent of Ansaar appeared foremost. Its standard was held by Abo-Ayyoob al-Ansaari. After it appeared another contingent of 1000 whose commander was Khozayma bn Thabit al-Ansaari. Then another contingent came in sight. Its standard was borne by Abo-Qatada bn Rabi. Then a crowd of a thousand old and young persons was seen. They had signs of prostration on their foreheads and veil of fear of Allah on their face. It seemed as if they were standing before the Divine Glory on the Day of Judgement. Their Commander rode a dark horse, was dressed in white, had black turban on his head and was reciting the Quraan loudly. This was Ammaar bn Yaasir. Then another contingent appeared. Its standard was in the hand of Qays bn Saad bn Obada. Then an army came to sight. Its leader wore white dress and had a black turban on his head. He was so handsome that all eyes centred around him. This was Abdillah bn Abbas. Then followed a contingent of the companions of the Prophet. Their standard bearer was Qutham bn Abbas. Then after the passing of a few contingents a big crowd was seen, wherein there was such a large number of spears that they were overlapping and flags of numerous colours were flying. Among them a big and lofty standard was seen with distinctive position. Behind it was seen a rider guarded by sublimity and greatness. His sinews were well-developed and eyes were cast downwards. His awe and dignity was such that no one could look at him. This was the Ever Victorious Lion of Allah namely Ali bn Abi-Talib (p.b.u.h.). On his right and left were Hasan and Hosayn (p. b. u. t.). In front of him Mohammad bn Hanafiyya walked in slow steps carrying the banner of victory and glory, and on the back were the young men of Bani-Hashim, the people of Badr and Abdillah bn Jafar bn Abi-Talib. When this army reached the place az-Zawiya, Ameer al-Momineen alighted from the horse, and after performing four raka of prayer put his cheeks on the ground. When he lifted his head the ground was drenched with tears and the tongue was uttering these words:

O" Sustainer of earth, heaven and the high firmament, this is Basra. Fill our lap with its good and protect us from its evils.

Then proceeding forward he got down in the battle-field of Jamal where the enemy was already camping. First of all Ameer al-Momineen announced in his army that no one should attack another, nor take the initiative. Saying this he came in front of the opposite army and said to Talha and az-Zobayr, "You ask Aysha by swearing in the name of Allah and His prophet whether I am not free from the blame of Othmaan's blood, and whether I used the same words for him which you used to say, and whether I pressurised you for allegiance or you swore it of your own free will" Talha got exasperated at these words but az-Zobayr relented, and Ameer al-Momineen turned back after it, and giving the Quraan to Moslim (a young man from the tribe of Abd Qays) sent him towards them to pronounce to them the verdict of the Quraan. But people took both of them within aim and covered this godly man with their arrows. Then Ammaar bn Yaasir went to canvass and convince them and caution them with the consequences of war but his words were also replied by arrows. Till now Ameer al-Momineen had not allowed an attack as a result of which the enemy continued feeling encouraged and went on raining arrows constantly. At last with the dying of a few valiant combatants consternation was created among Ameer al-Momineen's ranks and some people came with a few bodies before him and said "O Commander of the faithful you are not allowing us to fight while they are covering us with arrows. How long can we let them make our bosoms the victim of their arrows, and remain handfolded at their excesses?" At this Ameer al-Momineen did show anger but acting with restraint and endurance, came to the enemy in that very form without wearing armour or any arm and shouted, "Where is az-Zobayr?" At first az-Zobayr hesitated to come forward but he noticed that Ameer al-Momineen had no arms he came out. Ameer al-Momineen said to him "O az-Zobayr, you must remember that one day the Prophet told you that you would fight with me and wrong and excess would be on your side" az-Zobayr replied that he had said so. Then Ameer al-Momineen enquired "Why have you come then?" He replied that his memory had missed it and if he had recollected it earlier he would not have come that way. Ameer al-Momineen said "Well, now you have recollected it" and he replied, "Yes" Saying this he went straight to Aysha and told her that he was getting back. She asked him the reason and he replied, "Ali has reminded me a forgotten matter. I had gone astray, but now I have come on the right path and would not fight Ali bn Abi-Talib at any cost" Aysha said "You have caught fear of the swords of the sons of Abdl-Mottalib" He said "No" and saying this he turned the reins of his horse. However, it is gratifying that some consideration was accorded to the Prophet's saying, for at Hawab even after recollection of the Prophet's words no more than transient effect was taken of it. On returning after this conversation Ameer al-Momineen observed that they had attacked the right and left flanks of his army. Noticing this Ameer al-Momineen said "Now the plea has been exhausted. Call my son Mohammad" When he came Ameer al-Momineen said "My son, attack them now" Mohammad bowed his head and taking the standard proceeded to the battle-field. But arrows were falling in such exuberance that he had to stop. When Ameer al-Momineen saw this he called out at him, "Mohammad, why do not you advance?" He said "Father, in this shower of arrows there is no way to proceed. Wait till the violence of arrows subsides" He said "No, thrust yourself in the arrows and spears and attack" Mohammad bn Hanafiyya advanced a little but the archers so surrounded him that he had to hold his steps. On seeing this a frown appeared on Ameer al-Momineen's fore-head and getting forward he hit the sword's handle on the Mohammad's back and said "This is the effect of your mother's veins" Saying this he took the standard from his hands and folding up his sleeves made such and attack that a tumult was created in the enemy's ranks from one end to the other. To whichever row he turned, it became clear and to whatever side he directed himself bodies were seen falling and heads rolling in the hoofs of horses. When after convulsing the rows he returned to his position he said to Mohammad bn Hanafiyya, "Look, my son, battle is fought like this" Saying this he gave the standard to him and ordered him to proceed. Mohammad advanced towards the enemy with a contingent of Ansaar. The enemy also came out moving and balancing their spears. But the brave son of the valiant father convulsed rows over rows while the other warriors also made the battle-field glory and left heaps of dead bodies.

From the other side also there was full demonstration of spirit of sacrifice. Dead bodies were falling one over the other but they continued sacrificing their lives devotedly around the camel. Particularly the condition of Bani-Dabba was that although their hands were being severed from the elbows for holding the reins of the camel, and bosoms were being pierced yet they had the following battle-song on their tongues:

a) To us death is sweeter than honey. We are Bani-Dabba, camel rearers.

b) We are sons of death when death comes. We announce the death of Othmaan with the edges of spears.

c) Give us back our chief and there is an end to it.

The low character and ignorance from faith of these Bani-Dabba, can be well understood by that one incident which al-Madaini has narrated. He writes that in Basra there was a man with mutilated ear. He asked him its reason when he said "I was watching the sight of dead bodies in the battle-field of Jamal when I saw a wounded man who sometimes raised his head and sometimes dashed it back on the ground. I approached near. Then the following two verses were on his lips:

a) Our mother pushed us into the deep waters of death and did not get back till we had thoroughly drunk.

b) By misfortune we obeyed Bani-Taym who are none but slave men and slave girls.

I told him it was not the time to recite verses; he should rather recall Allah and recite the kalimat ash-shahada (verse of testimony). On my saying this he saw me with angry looks and uttering a severe abuse and said "You are asking me to recite kalimat ash-shahada, get frightened at the last moment and show impatience" I was astonished to hear this and decided to return without saying anything further. When he saw me returning he said "Wait; for your sake I am prepared to recite, but teach me" I drew close to teach him the kalima when he asked me to get closer. When I got closer he caught my ear with his teeth and did not leave it till he tore it from the root. I did not think it proper to molest a dying man and was about to get back abusing and cursing him when he asked me to listen one more thing. I agreed to listen lest he had an unsatisfied wish. He said that when I should get to my mother and she enquired who had bitten my ear I should say that it was done by Omayr bn Ahlab ad-Dabbi who had been deceived by a woman aspiring to become the commander of the faithful (head of the state). "

However, when the dazzling lightning of swords finished the lives of thousands of persons and hundreds of Bani-Azd and Bani-Dabba were killed for holding the rein of the camel, Ameer al-Momineen ordered, "Kill the camel for it is Satan" Saying this he made such a severe attack that the cries of "Peace" and "Protection" rose from all round. When he reached near the camel he ordered Bojayr bn Dolja to kill the camel at once.

You were the army of a woman and in the command of a quadruped. When it grumbled you responded, and when it was wounded (hamstrung) you fled away. Your character is low and your pledge is broken. Your faith is hypocrisy. Your water is brackish. He who stays with you is laden with sins and he who forsakes you secures Allah's mercy. As though I see your mosque prominent, resembling the surface of a boat, while Allah has sent chastisement from above and from below it and every one who is on it is drowned.[1]

By Allah, your city would certainly be drowned so much so that as though I see its mosque like the upper part of a boat or a sitting ostrich.[2]

Your city is the most stinking of all the cities as regards its clay, the nearest to water and remotest from the sky. It contains nine tenths of evil. He who enters it is surrounded with his sins and he who is out of it enjoys Allah's forgiveness. It seems as though I look at this habitation of yours that water has so engulfed it that nothing can be seen of it except the highest part of mosque appearing like the bosom of a bird in deep sea.

Consequently, Bojayr hit him with such full might that the camel fell in agony on the side of its bosom. No sooner than the camel fell the opposite army took to heels and the carrier holding Aysha was left lonely and unguarded. The companion of Ameer al-Momineen took control of the carrier and under orders of Ameer al-Momineen, Mohammad bn Abi-Bakr escorted Aysha to the house of Safiyya bnt al-Haarith.

This encounter commenced on the 10th of Jamaad ath-Thaani, 36 A.H., in the afternoon and came to an end the same evening. In it from Ameer al-Momineen's army of twenty two thousand, one thousand and seventy or according to another version five hundred persons were killed as martyrs while from Aysha's army of thirty thousand, seventeen thousand persons were killed, and the Prophet's saying, "That people who assigned their affairs (of state) to a woman would never prosper" was fully corroborated. (al-Imaama was-Siyasa; Morooj az-Zahab; al-Iqd al-fareed; at-Taareekh, at Tabari)

-1- bn-Abil-Hadeed has written that as prophesied by Ameer al-Momineen, Basra got under floods twice — once in the days of al-Qadir-Billah and once in the reign of al-Qaim bi-Amrillah and the state of flooding was just this that while the whole city was under water but the top ends of the mosque were seen about the surface of the water and looked like a bird sitting on the side of its bosom.

2 Like the bosom of a bird in deep sea.

SERMONS 14

Also in Condemnation of the People of Basra

Your earth is close to the sea and away from the sky. Your wits have become light and your minds are full of folly. You are the aim of the archer, a morsel for the eater and an easy prey for the hunter.

SERMONS 15

After resuming the land grants made by Othmaan bn-Affaan

By Allah, even if I had found that by such money women have been married or slave-maids have been purchased I would have resumed it because there is wide scope in dispensation of justice, and he who finds it hard to act justly should find it harder to deal with injustice.

SERMONS 16

Delivered when Allegiance was sworn to him at Madeena

The responsibility for what I say is guaranteed and I am answerable for it. He to whom experiences have clearly shown the past exemplary punishments (given by Allah to peoples) is prevented by piety from falling into doubts. You should know that the same troubles have returned to you which existed when the Prophet was first sent.

By Allah who sent the Prophet with faith and truth you will be severely subverted, bitterly shaken as in sieving and fully mixed as by spooning in a cooking pot till your low persons become high and high ones become low, those who were behind would attain forward positions and those who were forward would become backward. By Allah, I have not concealed a single word or spoken any lie and I had been informed of this event and of this time.

Beware that sins are like unruly horses on whom their riders have been placed and their reins have been let loose so that they would jump with them in Hell. Beware that piety is like trained horses on whom the riders have been placed with the reins in their hands, so that they would take the riders to Heaven. There is right and wrong and there are followers for each. If wrong dominates, it has (always) in the past been so, and if truth goes down that too has often occurred. It seldom happens that a thing that lags behind comes forward.

Sayyid Razi says: In this small speech there is more beauty than can be appreciated, and the quantity of amazement aroused by it is more than the appreciation accorded to it. Despite what we have stated it has so many aspects of eloquence that cannot be expressed nor can anyone reach its depth, and no one can understand what I am saying unless one has attained this art and known its details

... No one appreciates it except those who know" (Quraan, 29:43)

He who has heaven and hell in his view has no other aim. He who attempts and acts quickly, succeeds, while the seeker who is slow may also entertain hope, and he who falls short of action faces destruction in Hell. On right and left there are misleading paths. Only the middle way is the (right) path which is the Everlasting Book and the traditions of the Prophet. From it the Sauna has spread out and towards it is the eventual return.

He who claims (otherwise) is ruined and he who concocts falsehood is disappointed. He who opposes[1] right with his face gets destruction. It is enough ignorance for a man not to know himself. He who is strong rooted[2]

-1- In some versions after the words "man abda safhatahu lilhaqqi halaka: "the words "inda jahalatin-nas" also occur. In that case the meaning of this sentence would be that he who stands in face of right dies in the estimation of the ignorant.

2 Piety is the name of heart and mind being affected and impressed by the Divine Greatness and Glory, as an effect of which the spirit of man becomes full of fear of Allah, and its inevitable result is that engrossment in worship and prayer increases. It is impossible that heart may be full of Divine fear and there be no manifestation of it in actions and deeds. And since worship and submission reform the heart and nurture the spirit, purity of heart increases with the increase of worship. That is why in the Quraan "Taqwa" (piety) has been applied sometimes to fear, sometimes to worship and devotion and sometimes to purity of heart and spirit. Thus in the verse "wa iyyaya fattaqun" (and Me you fear 16:2) Taqwa implies fear, in the verse, "ittaqol-laha haqqa tuqatihi" (worship

in piety does not get destruction, and the plantation of a people based on piety never remains without water. Hide yourselves in your houses and reform yourselves. Repentance is at your back. One should praise only Allah and condemn only his own self.

SERMONS 17

About those who sit for dispensation of justice among People but are not fit for it

Among[1] all the people the most detested before Allah are two persons. One is he who is devoted to his self. So he is deviated from the true path

---

Allah as He ought to be worshipped 3:102) , Taqwa implies worship and devotion and in the verse "wa yakhshal-laha wa yattaqhi faulaika humol-faizun" (24:52) Taqwa implies purity of spirit and cleanliness of heart.

In the traditions Taqwa has been assigned three degrees. The first degree is that a man should follow the injunctions and keep aloof from prohibitions. The second degree is that recommended matters should also be followed and disliked things should be avoided. The third degree is that for fear of falling into doubts one may abstain from the permissible as well. The first degree is for the common men, the second for the nobles and the third for high dignitaries. Allah has referred to these three degrees in the following verse:

On those who believe and do good, is no blame for what they ate, (before) when they did guard themselves and did believe, and did good, still (furthermore) they guard themselves and do good; and Allah loveth the doers of good. (Quraan, 5:93)

Ameer al-Momineen says that only action based on piety is lasting, and only that action will blossom and bear fruit which is watered by piety because worship is only that wherein the feeling of submission exists. Thus, Allah says:

Is he therefore better who hath laid his foundation on fear of Allah and (His) goodwill or he who layeth his foundation on the brink of a crumbling hollowed bank so it crumbled down with him into the fire of Hell... (Quraan, 9:109)

Consequently, every such belief as is not based on knowledge and conviction is like the edifice, erected without foundation, wherein there is no stability or firmness while every action that is without piety is like the plantation which withers for lack of watering.

-1- Ameer al-Momineen has held two categories of persons as the most detestable by Allah and the worst among people. Firstly, those who are misguided even in basic tenets and are busy in the spreading of evil. Secondly, those who abandon the Quraan and Sonna and pronounce injunctions through their imagination. They create a circle of their devotees and popularise the religious code of law concocted by themselves. The misguidance and wrongfulness of such persons does not remain confined to their own

and loves speaking about (foul) innovations and inviting towards wrong path. He is therefore a nuisance for those who are enamoured of him, is himself misled from the guidance of those preceding him, misleads those who follow him in his life or after his death, carries the weight of others" sins and is entangled in his own misdeeds.

The other man is he who has picked up ignorance. He moves among the ignorant, is senseless in the thick of mischief and is blind to the advantages of peace. Those resembling like men have named him scholar but he is not so. He goes out early morning to collect things whose deficiency is better than plenty, till when he has quenched his thirst from polluted water and acquired meaningless things.

He sits among the people as a judge responsible for solving whatever is confusing to the others. If an ambiguous problem is presented before him he manages shabby argument about it of his own accord and passes judgement on its basis. In this way he is entangled in the confusion of doubts as in the spider's web, not knowing whether he was right or wrong. If he is right he fears lest he erred, while if he is wrong he hopes he is right. He is ignorant, wandering astray in ignorance and riding on carriages aimlessly moving in darkness. He did not try to find reality of knowledge. He scatters the traditions as the wind scatters the dry leaves.

By Allah, he is not capable of solving the problems that come to him nor is fit for the position assigned to him. Whatever he does not know he does not regard it worth knowing. He does not realise that what is beyond his reach is within the reach of others. If anything is not clear to him he keeps quiet over it because he knows his own ignorance. Lost lives are crying against his unjust verdicts, and properties (that have been wrongly disposed of) are grumbling against him.

---

selves but the seed of misguidance sown by them bears fruit and growing into the form of a big tree provides asylum to the misguided and this misguidance goes on multiplying. And since these very people are the real originators the weight of other's sins is also on their shoulders as the Quraan says:

And certainly they shall bear their own burdens, and (other) burdens with their own burdens... (29:13)

I complain to Allah about persons who live ignorant and die misguided. For them nothing is more worthless than Quraan if it is recited as it should be recited, nor anything more valuable than the Quraan if its verses are removed from their places, nor anything more vicious than virtue nor more virtuous than vice.

SERMONS 18

In disparagement of the differences of view among the theologians

When[1] a problem is put before anyone of them he passes judgement on it from his imagination. When exactly the same problem is placed before

---

-1- It is a disputed problem that where there is no clear argument about a matter in the religious law, whether there does in reality exist an order about it or not. The view adopted by Abol-Hasan al-Ashari and his master Abo-Ali al-Jobbai is that in such a case Allah has not ordained any particular course of action but He assigned the task of finding it out and passing a verdict to the jurists so that whatever they hold as prohibited would be deemed prohibited and whatever they regard permissible would be deemed permissible. And if one has one view and the other another then as many verdicts will exist as there are views and each of them would represent the final order. For example, if one scholar holds that barley malt is prohibited and another jurist's view is that it is permissible then it would really be both prohibited and permissible. That is, for one who holds it prohibited, its use would be prohibited while for the other its use would be permissible. About this (theory of) correctness Mohammad bn Abdl-Kareem ash-Shahristani writes:

A group of theorists hold that in matters where ijtihad (research) is applied there is no settled view about permissibility or otherwise and lawfulness and prohibition thereof, but whatever the mojtahid (the researcher scholar) holds is the order of Allah, because the ascertainment of the view of Allah depends upon the verdict of the mojtahid. If it is not so there will be no verdict at all. And according to this view every mojtahid would be correct in his opinion. (al-Milal wan-Nehal, p.98)

In this case, the mojtahid is taken to be above mistake because a mistake can be deemed to occur where a step is taken against reality, but where there is no reality of verdict, mistake has no sense. Besides this, the mojtahid can be considered to be above mistake if it is held that Allah, being aware of all the views that were likely to be adopted has ordained as many final orders as a result of which every view corresponds to some such order, or that Allah has assured that the views adopted by the mojtahids should not go beyond what He has ordained, or that by chance the view of every one of them would, after all, correspond to some ordained order or other.

The Imaamiyya sect, however, has different theory, namely that Allah has neither assigned to anyone the right to legislate nor subjected any matter to the view of the mojtahid, nor in case of difference of views has He ordained numerous real orders. Of course, if the mojtahid cannot arrive at a real order then whatever view he takes after research and probe, it is enough for him and his followers to act by it. Such an order is the apparent order which is a substitute for the real order. In this case, he is excused for missing the real order, because he did his best for diving in the deep ocean and to explore its bottom, but it is a pity that instead of pearls he got only the sea-shell. He does not say that observers should except it as a pearl or it should sell as such. It is a different matter that Allah who watches the endeavours may price it at half so that the endeavour does not go waste, nor his passion discouraged.

If the theory of correctness is adopted then every verdict on law and every opinion shall have to be accepted as correct as Maybozi has written in Fawatih:

In this matter the view adopted by al-Ashari is right. It follows that differing opinions should all be right. Beware, do not bear a bad idea about jurists and do not open your tongue to abuse them.

When contrary theories and divergent views are accepted as correct it is strange why the action of some conspicuous individuals are explained as mistakes of decision, since mistake of decision by the mojtahid cannot be imagined at all. If the theory of correctness is right the action of Moaawiya and Aysha should be deemed right; but if their actions can be deemed to be wrong then we should agree that ijtihad can also go wrong, and that the theory of correctness is wrong. It will then remain to be decided in its own context whether feminism did not impede the decision of Aysha or whether it was a (wrong) finding of Moaawiya or something else. However, this theory of correctness was propounded in order to cover mistakes and to give them the garb of Allah's orders so that there should be no impediment in achieving objectives nor should anyone be able to speak against any misdeeds.

In this sermon Ameer al-Momineen has referred to those people who deviate from the path of Allah and, closing their eyes to light, grope in the darkness of imagination, make Faith the victim of their views and opinions, pronounce new findings, pass orders by their own imagination and produce divergent results. Then on the basis of the theory of correctness they regard all these divergent and contrary orders as from Allah, as though each of their order represents divine Revelation so that no order of theirs can be wrong nor can they stumble on any occasion. Thus, Ameer al-Momineen says in disproving this view that:

1) When Allah is One, Book (Quraan) is one, and Prophet is one then the religion (that is followed) should also be one. And when the religion is one how can there be divergent orders about any matter, because there can be divergence in an order only in case he who passed the order has forgotten it, or is oblivious, or senselessness overtakes him, or he wilfully desires entanglement in these labyrinths, while Allah and the Prophet are above these things. These divergences cannot therefore be attributed to them. These divergences are rather the outcome of the thinkings and opinions of people who are bent on twisting the delineations of religion by their own imaginative performances.

another of them he passes an opposite verdict. Then these judges go to the chief who had appointed them and he confirms all the verdicts, although their Allah is One (and the same), their Prophet is one (and the same), their Book (the Quraan) is one (and the same).

Is it that Allah ordered them to differ and they obeyed Him? Or He prohibited them from it but they disobeyed Him? Or (is it that) Allah sent an incomplete Faith and sought their help to complete it? Or they are His partners in the affairs, so that it is their share of duty to pronounce and He has to agree? Or is it that Allah the Glorified sent a perfect faith but the Prophet fell short of conveying it and handing it over (to the people)?

The fact is that Allah the Glorified says:

...We have not neglected anything in the Book (Quraan) ..." (Quraan, 6:38)

---

2) Allah must have either forbidden these divergences or ordered creating them. If He has ordered in their favour, where is that order and at what place? As for forbidding, the Quraan says:

...Say thou! "Hath Allah permitted you or ye forge a lie against Allah?" (10:59)

That is, everything that is not in accordance with the Divine orders is a concoction, and concoction is forbidden and prohibited. For concocters, in the next world, there is neither success or achievement nor prosperity and good. Thus, Allah says:

And utter ye not whatever lie describe your tongues (saying) :

This is lawful and this is forbidden, to forge a lie against Allah; verily, those who forge a lie against Allah succeed not. (Quraan, 16:116)

3) If Allah has left religion incomplete and the reason for leaving it halfway was that He desired that the people should assist Him in completing the religious code and share with Him in the task of legislating, then this belief is obviously polytheism. If He sent down the religion in complete form the Prophet must have failed in conveying it so that room was left for others to apply imagination and opinion. This, Allah forbid, would mean a weakness of the Prophet and a bad slur on the selection of Allah.

4) Allah has said in the Quraan that He has not left out anything in the Book and has clarified each and every matter. Now, if an order is carved out in conflict with the Quraan it would be outside the religious code and its basis would not be on knowledge and perception, or Quraan and Sonna, but it would be personal opinion and one's personal judgement which cannot be deemed to have accord with religion and faith.

5) Quraan is the basis and source of religion and the fountain head of the laws of sharia. If the laws of sharia were divergent there should have been divergence in it also, and if there were divergences in it, it could not be regarded as Divine word. When it is Divine word the laws of sharia cannot be divergent, so as to accept all divergent and contrary views as correct and imaginative verdicts taken as Quraanic dictates.

And says that one part of the Quraan verifies another part and that there is no divergence in it as He says:

...And if it had been from any other than Allah, they would surely have found in it much discrepancy." (Quraan, 4:82)

Certainly the outside of the Quraan is wonderful and its inside is deep (in meaning). Its wonders will never disappear, its amazements will never pass away and its intricacies cannot be cleared except through itself.

SERMONS 19

Treachery and Hypocrisy of al-Ashath al-Kindi

Ameer al-Momineen was delivering a lecture from the pulpit of (the mosque of) Koofa when al-Ashath bn-Qays[1] objected and said "O Ameer

---

-1- AL-ASHATH BN QAYS AL-KINDI:

His original name was Madi Kareeb and surname Abo-Mohammad but because of his dishevelled hair he is better known as al-Ashath (one having dishevelled hair). When after Proclamation (of Prophethood) he came to Mecca along with his tribe, the Prophet invited him and his tribe to accept Islam. But all of them turned back without anyone accepting Islam. When after hijra (immigration of the Holy Prophet) Islam became established and in full swing and deputations began to come to Madeena in large numbers he also came to the Prophet's audience with Bani-Kinda and accepted Islam. The author of al-Isteeaab writes that after the Prophet this man again turned unbeliever but when during the Caliphate of Abi-Bakr he was brought to Madeena as prisoner he again accepted Islam, though this time too his Islam was a show. Thus, Shaykh Mohammad Abdo writes in his annotations on Nahjol-Balagha:

Just as Abdillah bn Obay bn Salool was a companion of the Prophet, al-Ashath was a companion of Ali and both were high ranking hypocrites.

He lost one of his eyes in the battle of Yarmook. bn Qutayba has included him in the list of the one-eyed. Abi-Bakr's sister Om-Farwa bnt bn-Quhaafa, who was once the wife of an al-Azdi and then of Tameem ad-Darimi, was on the third occasion married to this al-Ashath. Three sons were born of her viz. Mohammad, Ismaaeel and Ishaaq. Books on biography show that she was blind. bn-Abil-Hadeed has quoted the following statement of Abol-Faraj wherefrom it appears that this man was equally involved in the assassination of Ali (p.b.u.h.) :

On the night of the assassination bn Moljam came to al-Ashath bn Qays and both retired to a corner of the mosque and sat there when Hijr bn Adi passed by that side and he heard al-Ashath saying to bn Moljam, "Be quick now or else dawn's light would disgrace you" On hearing this Hijr said to al-Ashath: "O one-eyed man, you are preparing to kill al-Momineen this thing is not in your favour but against you[1] Ameer al-Momineen looked at him with anger and said:

Ali" and hastened towards Ali bn Abi-Talib, but bn Moljam had preceded him and struck Ali with sword when Hijr turned back people were crying, "Ali has been killed

It was his daughter who killed Imam Hasan (p.b.u.h.) by poisoning him. Masoodi has written that:

His (Hasan's) wife Jada bnt al-Ashath poisoned him while Moaawiya had conspired with her that if she could contrive to poison Hasan he would pay her one hundred thousand Dirhams and marry her to Yazeed. (Morooj az-Zahab, vol.2, p.650)

His son Mohammad bn Ashath was active in playing fraud with Hazrat Moslim bn Aqeel in Koofa and in shedding Imam Hosayn's blood in Karbala. But despite all these points he is among those from whom al-Bokhaari, Moslim, Abo-Dawood, at-Tirmizi, an-Nisaaee and bn-Maaja have related traditions.

-1- After the battle of Nahrawan, Ameer al-Momineen was delivering a sermon in the mosque of Koofa about ill effects of "Arbitration" when a man stood up and said "O Ameer al-Momineen, first you desisted us from this Arbitration but thereafter you allowed it. We cannot understand which of these two was more correct and proper" On hearing this Ameer al-Momineen clapped his one hand over the other and said "This is the reward of one who gives up firm view" that is, this is the outcome of your actions as you had abandoned firmness and caution and insisted on "Arbitration" but al-Ashath mistook it to mean as though Amir al Momineen implied that "my worry was due to having accepted Arbitration" so he spoke out, "O Ameer al-Momineen this brings blame on your own self" whereupon Ameer al-Momineen said harshly:

What do you know what I am saying, and what do you understand what is for me or against me. You are a weaver and the son of a weaver brought up by unbelievers and a hypocrite. Curse of Allah and all the world be upon you.

Commentators have written several reasons for Ameer al-Momineen calling Ashath a weaver. First reason is, because he and his father like most of the people of his native place pursued the industry of weaving cloth. So, in order to refer to the lowliness of his occupation he has been called "weaver. Yamanese had other occupations also but mostly this profession was followed among them. Describing their occupations Khaalid bn Safwan has mentioned this one first of all.

What can I say about a people among whom there are only weavers, leather dyers, monkey keepers and donkey riders. The hoopoe found them out, the mouse flooded them and a woman ruled over them. (al-Bayan wat-Tabyeen, vol.1, p.130)

The second reason is that "hiyaka" means walking by bending on either side, and since out of pride and conceit this man used to walk shrugging his shoulders and making bends in his body, he has been called "hayik.

The third reason is — and it is more conspicuous and clear — that he has been called a weaver to denote his foolishness and lowliness because every low person is proverbially known as a weaver. Their wisdom and sagacity can be well gauged by the fact that their follies had become proverbial, while nothing attains proverbial status without peculiar characteristics. Now, that Ameer al-Momineen has also confirmed it no further argument or reasoning is needed.

The fourth reason is that by this is meant the person who conspires against Allah and the Holy Prophet and prepares webs of which is the peculiarity of hypocrites. Thus, in Wasail ash-Shia (vol.12, p.101) it is stated:

It was mentioned before Imam Jafar as-Saadiq (p.b.u.h.) that the weaver is accursed when he explained that the weaver implies the person who concocts against Allah and the Prophet.

After the word weaver Ameer al-Momineen has used the word hypocrite, and there is no conjunction in between them in order to emphasise the nearness of meaning thereof. Then, on the basis of this hypocrisy and concealment of truth he declared him deserving of the curse of Allah and all others, as Allah the Glorified says:

Verily, those that conceal what we have sent of (Our) manifest evidences and guidance, after what we have (so) clearly shown for mankind in the Book (they are) , those that Allah doth curse them and (also) curse them all those who curse (such ones). (Quraan, 2:159)

After this Ameer al-Momineen says that “You could not avoid the degradation of being prisoner when you were unbeliever, nor did these ignominies spare you after acceptance of Islam, and you were taken prisoner” When an unbeliever the event of his being taken prisoner occurred in this way that when the tribe of Bani-Moraad killed his father Qays, he (al-Ashath) collected the warriors of Bani-Kinda and divided them in three groups. Over one group he himself took the command, and on the others he placed Kabs bn Hani” and al-Qasham bn Yazeed al-Arqam as chiefs, and set off to deal with Bani-Moraad. But as misfortune would have it instead of Bani-Moraad he attacked Bani-Haarith bn Kab. The result was that Kabs bn Hani” and al-Qasham bn Yazeed al-Arqam were killed and this man was taken prisoner alive. Eventually he got a release by paying three thousand camels as ransom. In Ameer al-Momineen’s words, “Your wealth or birth could not save you from either” the reference is not to real “fidya” (release money) because he was actually released on payment of release money but the intention is that neither plenty of wealth nor his high position and prestige in his tribe could save him from this ignominy, and he could not protect himself from being a prisoner.

The event of his second imprisonment is that when the Holy Prophet of Islam passed away from this world a rebellion occurred in the region of Hazramawt for repelling which Caliph Abi-Bakr wrote to the governor of the place Ziyad bn Labid al-Bayadi. al-Ansaari that he should secure allegiance and collect zakat and charities from those people. When Ziyad bn Labid went to the tribe of Bani-Amr bn Moaawiya for collection of zakat he took keen fancy for a she-camel of Shaytan bn Hijr which was very handsome and of huge body. He jumped over it and took possession of it. Shaytan bn Hijr did not agree to spare it and said to him to take over some other she-camel in its place but Ziyad would not agree. Shaytan sent for his brother al-Addaa bn Hijr for his support. On coming he too had a talk but Ziyad insisted on his point and did not, by any means, consent to keep off his hand from that she-camel. At last both these brothers appealed to Masrooq bn Madi Karib for help. Consequently, Masrooq also used his influence so that Ziyad might leave

How do you know what is for me and what is against me?! Curse of Allah and others be on you. You are a weaver and son of a weaver. You are the son of an unbeliever and yourself a hypocrite. You were arrested once by the Unbelievers and once by the Moslims, but your wealth and birth could not save you from either. The man who contrives for his own people to be put to sword and invites death and destruction for them does deserve that the near ones should hate him and the remote ones should not trust him.

---

the she-camel but he refused categorically, whereupon Masrooq became enthusiastic and untying the she-camel handed it over to Shaytan. On this Ziyad was infuriated and collecting his men became ready to fight. On the other side Bani-Walia also assembled to face them, but could not defeat Ziyad and were badly beaten at his hands. Their women were taken away and property was looted. Eventually those who had survived were obliged to take refuge under the protection of al-Ashath. Al-Ashath promised assistance on the condition that he should be acknowledged ruler of the area. Those people agreed to this condition and his coronation was also formally solemnised. After having his authority acknowledged he arranged an army and set out to fight Ziyad. On the other side Abi-Bakr had written to the chief of Yemen, al-Mohaajir bn Abi Omayya to go for the help of Ziyad with a contingent. Al-Mohaajir was coming with his contingent when they came face to face. Seeing each other they drew swords and commenced fighting at az-Zorqan. In the end al-Ashath fled from the battle-field and taking his remaining men closed himself in the fort of an-Nojayr. The enemy was such as to let them alone. They laid siege around the fort. Al-Ashath thought how long could he remain shut up in the fort with this lack of equipment and men, and that he should think out some way of escape. So one night he stealthily came out of the fort and met Ziyad and al-Mohaajir and conspired with them that if they gave asylum to nine members of his family he would get the fort gate opened. They accepted this term and asked him to write for them the names of those nine persons. He wrote down the nine names and made them over to them, but acting on his traditional wisdom forgot to write his own name in that list. After settling this he told his people that he has secured protection for them and the gate of the fort should be opened. When the gate was opened Ziyad forces pounced upon them. They said they had been promised protection whereupon Ziyad's army said that this was wrong and that al-Ashath had asked protection only for nine members of his house, whose names preserved with them. In short eight hundred persons were put to sword and hands of several women were chopped off, while according to the settlement nine men were left off, but the case of al-Ashath became complicated. Eventually it was decided he should be sent to Abi-Bakr and he should decided about him. At last he was sent to Madeena in chains along with a thousand women prisoners. On the way relations and others, men and women, all hurled curses at him and the women were calling him traitor and one who got his own people put to sword. Who else can be a greater traitor? However, when he reached Madeena Abi-Bakr released him and on that occasion he was married to Om-Farwa.

Sayyid Razi says: This man was arrested once when an unbeliever and once in days of Islam. As for Ameer al-Momineen's words that the man contrived for his own people to be put to sword, the reference herein is to the incident which occurred to al-Ashath bn-Qays in confrontation with Khaalid bn-Waleed at Yamama, where he deceived his people and contrived a trick till Khaalid attacked them. After this incident his people nicknamed him "Orf an-Nar" which in the parlance stood for traitor.

SERMONS 20

Death and Taking Lessons from it

If you could see that has been seen by those of you who have died, you would be puzzled and troubled. Then you would have listened and obeyed; but what they have seen is yet curtained off from you. Shortly, the curtain would be thrown off. You have been shown, provided you see and you have been made to listen provided you listen, and you have been guided if you accept guidance. I spoke unto you with truth. You have been called aloud by (instructive) examples and warned through items full of warnings. After the heavenly messengers (angels), only man can convey message from Allah. (So what I am conveying is from Allah).

SERMONS 21

Advice to Keep Light in this World

Your aim (reward or punishment) is before you. Behind your back is the hour (of resurrection) which is driving you on. Keep (yourself) light and overtake (the forward ones). Your last ones are being awaited by the first ones (who have preceded).

Sayyid Razi says: If this utterance of Ali (p.b.u.h.) is weighed with any other utterance except the word of Allah or of the Holy Prophet, it would prove heavier and superior in every respect. For example, Ali's saying "Keep light and overtake" is the shortest expression ever heard with the greatest sense conveyed by it. How wide is its meaning and how clear its spring of wisdom! We have pointed out the greatness and meaningfulness of this phrase in our book al-Khasaais.

SERMONS 22

About those who Accused him of Othmaan's killing

Beware! Satan has certainly started instigating his forces and has collected his army in order that oppression may reach its extreme ends and wrong may come back to its position. By Allah they have not put a correct blame on me, nor have they done justice between me and themselves.

They are demanding of me a right which they have abandoned, and a blood that they have themselves shed.[1] If I were a partner with them in it

---

-1- When Ameer al-Momineen was accused of Othmaan's assassination he delivered this sermon to refute that allegation, wherein he says about those who blamed him that: "These seekers of vengeance cannot say that I alone am the assassin and that no one else took part in it. Nor can they falsify witnessed events by saying that they were unconcerned with it. Why then have they put me foremost for this avenging? With me they should include themselves also. If I am free of this blame they cannot establish their freedom from it. How can they detach themselves from this punishment? The truth of the matter is that by accusing me of this charge their aim is that I should behave with them in the same manner to which they are accustomed. But they should not expect from me that I would revive the innovations of the previous regimes. As for fighting, neither was I ever afraid of it nor am I so now. Allah knows my intention and He also knows that those standing on the excuse of taking revenge are themselves his assassins" Thus, history corroborates that the people who managed his (Othmaan's) assassination by agitation and had even prevented his burial in Moslims" graveyard by hurling stones at his coffin were the same who rose for avenging his blood. In this connection, the names of Talha bn Obaydillah, az-Zobayr bn Awwam and Aysha are at the top of the list since on both occasions their efforts come to sight with conspicuity. Thus bn-Abil-Hadeed writes that:

Those who have written the account of assassination of Othmaan state that on the day of his killing Talha's condition was that in order to obscure himself from the eyes of the people he had a veil on his face and was shooting arrows at Othmaan's house.

And in this connection, about az-Zobayr's ideas he writes:

Historians have also state that az-Zobayr used to say "Kill Othmaan. He has altered your faith" People said "Your son is standing at his door and guarding him" and he replied: "Even my son may be lost, but Othmaan must be killed. Othmaan will be lying like a carcass on Sirat tomorrow" (Sharh Nahjol-Balagha, vol.9, pp.35-36)

then they too have their share of it. But if they did it without me they alone have to face the consequences. Their biggest argument (against me) is (really) against themselves. They are suckling from a mother who is already dry, and bringing into life innovation that is already dead. How disappointing is this challenger (to battle)? Who is this challenger and for what is he being responded to? I am happy that the reasoning of Allah has been exhausted before them and He knows (all) about them. If they refuse (to obey) I will offer them the edge of the sword which is enough a curer of wrong and supporter of Right.

It is strange they send me word to proceed to them for spear-fighting and to keep ready for fighting with swords. May the mourning women mourn over them. I have ever been so that I was never frightened by fighting nor threatened by clashing. I enjoy full certainty of belief from my Allah and have no doubt in my faith.

SERMONS 23

Keeping aloof from Envy, and Good Behaviour towards Kith and Kin

Now then, verily Divine orders descend from heaven to earth like drops of rain, bringing to every one what is destined for him whether plenty or paucity. So if any one of you observes for his brother plenty of progeny or of wealth or of self, it should not be a worry for him. So long as a Moslim does not commit such an act that if it is disclosed he has to bend his eyes (in shame) and by which low people are emboldened, he is like the gambler who expects that the first draw of his arrow would secure him gain and also cover up the previous loss.

About Aysha, bn Abd Rabbih writes:

al-Mogheera bn Shoba came to Aysha when she said "O Abo-Abdillah, I wish you had been with me on the day of Jamal; how arrows were piercing through my hawdaj (camel litter) till some of them stuck my body" al-Mogheera said "I wish one of them should have killed you" She said "Allah may have pity you; why so?" He replied: 'so that it would have been some atonement for what you had done against Othmaan" (al-Iqdol-Fareed, vol.4, p.294)

Similarly, the Moslim who is free from dishonesty expects one of the two good things: either call from Allah and in that case whatever is with Allah is the best for him, or the livelihood of Allah. He has already children and property while his faith and respect are with him. Certainly, wealth and children are the plantations of this world while virtuous deed is the plantation of the next world. Sometimes Allah joins all these in some groups.

Beware of Allah against what He has cautioned you and keep afraid of Him to the extent that no excuse be needed for it. Act without show or intention of being heard, for if a man acts for some one else then Allah makes him over to that one. We ask Allah (to grant us) the positions of the martyrs, company of the virtuous and friendship of the prophets.

O people! surely no one (even though he may be rich) can do without his kinsmen, and their support by hands or tongues. They alone are his support from rear and can ward off from him his troubles, and they are the most kind to him when tribulations befall him. The good memory of a man that Allah retains among people is better than the property which others inherit from him.

Behold! If any one of you finds your near ones in want or starvation, he should not desist from helping them with that which will not increase if this help is not extended, nor decrease by thus spending it. Whoever holds up his hand from (helping) his kinsmen, he holds only one hand, but at the time of his need many hands remain held up from helping him. One who is sweet tempered can retain the love of his people for good.

Sayyid Razi says: In this sermon "al-ghafira" means plenty or abundance, and this is derived from the Arab saying "al-jamm al-ghafir" or "al-jamma" al-ghafir" meaning thick crowd. In some versions for "al-ghafira" "afwatan" appears" "afwah" means the good and selected part of anything. It is said "akaltu afwata "t-taam, to mean "I ate select meal." About "wa man yaqbid yadahu an ashiratihi" appearing towards the end he points out how beautiful the meaning of this sentence is, Ameer al-Momineen implies that he who does not help his own kinsmen withholds only his hand but when he is in need of their assistance and would be looking for their sympathy and support then he would remain deprived of the sympathies and succour of so many of their extending hands and marching feet.

SERMONS 24

Exhorting People for Jihaad

By my life there will be no regard for anyone nor slackening from me in fighting against one who opposes right or gropes in misguidance. O creatures of Allah, fear Allah and flee unto Allah from His wrath (seek protection in His Mercy). Tread on the path He has laid down for you and stand by what He has enjoined upon you. In that case Ali would stand surety for your success (salvation) eventually even though you may not get it immediately (i.e. in this world).

SERMONS 25

When his Officers were Overpowered by Moaawiya's Men

When Ameer al-Momineen received successive news that Moaawiya's men were occupying cities[1] and his own officers in Yemen namely

-1- When after arbitration Moaawiya's position was stabilised he began thinking of taking possession of Ameer al-Momineen's cities and extend his domain. He sent his armies to different areas in order that they might secure allegiance for Moaawiya by force. In this connection he sent Bishr bn Abi-Artat to Hijaaz and he shed blood of thousands of innocent persons from Hijaaz upto Yemen, burnt alive tribes after tribes in fire and killed even children, so much so that he butchered two young boys of Obaydillah bn Abbas the Governor of Yemen before their mother Jowayriyya bnt Khaalid bn Qaraz al-Kinaniyya.
When Ameer al-Momineen came to know of his slaughtering and blood shed he thought of sending a contingent to crush him but due to continuous fighting people had become weary and showed heartlessness instead of zeal. When Ameer al-Momineen observed their shirking from war he delivered this sermon wherein he roused them to enthusiasm and self respect, and prompted them to Jihaad by describing before them the enemy's wrongfulness and their own short-comings. At last Jariya bn Qudama as-Saadi responded to his call and taking an army of two thousand set off in pursuit of Bishr and chased him out of Ameer al-Momineen's domain.

Obaydillah bn-Abbas and Said bn-Nimran came to him retreating after being overpowered by Bishr bn Abi-Artat, he was much disturbed by the slackness of his own men in Jihaad and their difference with his opinion. Proceeding on to the pulpit he said:

Nothing (is left to me) but Koofa which I can hold and extend (which is in my hand to play with). (O Koofa) if this is your condition that whirlwinds continue blowing through you then Allah may destroy you.

Then he illustrated with the verse of a poet:

O Amr! By your good father's life. I have received only a small bit of fat from this pot (fat that remains sticking to it after it has been emptied).

Then he continued:

I have been informed that Bishr has overpowered Yemen. By Allah, I have begun thinking about these people that they would shortly snatch away the whole country through their unity on their wrong and your disunity (from your own right), and separation, your disobedience of your Imam in matters of right and their obedience to their leader in matters of wrong, their fulfillment of the trust in favour of their master and your betrayal, their good work in their cities and your mischief. Even if I give you charge of a wooden bowl I fear you would run away with its handle.

O my Allah they are disgusted of me and I am disgusted of them. They are weary of me and I am weary of them. Change them for me with better ones and change me for them with worse one. O my Allah melt their hearts as salt melts in water. By Allah I wish I had only a thousand horsemen of Bani-Firas bn-Ghanim (as the poet says) :

If you call them the horsemen would come to you like the summer cloud.

Thereafter Ameer al-Momineen alighted from the pulpit:

Sayyid Razi says: In this verse the word "armiyah" is plural of "ramiyy" which means cloud and "hamim" here means summer. The poet has particularised the cloud of summer because it moves swiftly. This is because it is devoid of water while a cloud moves slowly when it is laden with rain. Such clouds generally appear (in Arabia) in winter. By this verse the poet intends to convey that when they are called and referred to for help they approach with rapidity and this is borne by the first line "if you call them they will reach you

SERMONS 26

Arabia before Proclamation of Prophethood

Allah sent Mohammad (p.b.u.h.a.h.p) as a Warner (against vice) for all the worlds and a trustee of His revelation, while you people of Arabia were following the worst religion and you resided among rough stones and venomous serpents. You drank dirty water and ate filthy food. You shed blood of each other and cared not for relationship. Idols are fixed among you and sins are clinging to you.

On the attentiveness of the People after the death of the Holy Prophet

I looked and found that there is no supporter for me except family, so I refrained from thrusting them unto death. I kept my eyes closed despite motes in them. I drank despite choking of throat. I exercised patience despite trouble in breathing and despite having to take sour colocynth as food.

On the settlement between Moaawiya and Amr bn al-Aas

He did not swear allegiance till he got him to agree that he would pay him its price. The hand of this purchaser (of allegiance) may not be successful and the contract of the seller may face disgrace. Now you should take up arms for war and arrange equipment for it. Its flames have grown high and its brightness has increased. Clothe yourself with patience for it is the best to victory.[1]

-1- Ameer al-Momineen had delivered a sermon before setting off for Nahrawan. These are three parts from it. In the first part he has described the condition of Arabia before Proclamation (of Prophethood); in the second he has referred to circumstances which forced him to keep quiet and in the third he has described the conversation and settlement between Moaawiya and Amr bn Aas. The position of this mutual settlement was that when Ameer al-Momineen sent Jareer bn Abdillah al-Bajali to Moaawiya to secure his allegiance he detained Jareer under the excuse of giving a reply, and in the meantime he began exploring how far the people of Syria would support him. When he

SERMONS 27

Exhorting People for Jihaad

Now then, surely Jihaad is one of the doors of Paradise, which Allah has opened for His chief friends. It is the dress of piety and the protective armour of Allah and His trustworthy shield. Whoever abandons it Allah covers him with the dress of disgrace and the clothes of distress. He is kicked with contempt and scorn, and his heart is veiled with screens (of neglect). Truth is taken away from him because of missing Jihaad. He has to suffer ignominy and justice is denied to him.

Beware! I called you (insistently) to fight these people night and day, secretly and openly and exhorted you to attack them before they attacked you, because by Allah, no people have been attacked in the hearts of their houses but they suffered disgrace; but you put it off to others and forsook it till destruction befell you and your cities were occupied. The horsemen of Bani-Ghamid[1] have reached al-Anbaar and killed Hassan bn-Hassan al-Bakri. They have removed your horsemen from the garrison.

---

succeeded in making them his supporters by rousing them to avenge Othmaan's blood he consulted his brother Otba bn Abi Sofyaan. He suggested, "If in this matter Amr bn Aas was associated he would solve most of the difficulties through his sagacity, but he would not be easily prepared to stabilise your authority unless he got the price he desired for it. If you are ready for this he would prove the best counsellor and helper" Moaawiya liked this suggestion, sent for Amr bn Aas and discussed with him, and eventually it was settled that he would avenge Othmaan's blood by holding Ameer al-Momineen liable for it in exchange for the governorship of Egypt, and by whatever means possible would not let Moaawiya's authority in Syria suffer. Consequently, both of them fulfilled the agreement and kept their words fully.

-1- After the battle of Siffeen, Moaawiya had spread killing and bloodshed all round, and started encroachments on cities within Ameer al-Momineen's domain. In this connection he deputised Sofyaan bn Awf al-Ghamidi with a force of six thousand to attack Hit, al-Anbaar and al-Madain. First he reached al-Madain but finding it deserted proceeded to al-Anbaar. Here a contingent of five hundred soldiers was posted as guard from Ameer al-Momineen's side, but it could not resist the fierce army of Moaawiya. Only a hundred men stuck to their position and they did face them stoutly as far as they could but collecting together the enemy's force made such a severe attack that they too could no more resist and the chief of the contingent Hassan bn Hassan al-Bakri was killed along

I have come to know that every one of them entered upon Moslim women and other women under protection of Islam and took away their ornaments from legs, arms, necks and ears and no woman could resist it except by pronouncing the verse,
We are for Allah and to Him we shall return." (Quraan, 2:156)
Then they got back laden with wealth without any wound or loss of life. If any Moslim dies of grief after all this he is not to be blamed but rather there is justification for him before me.
How strange! How strange! By Allah my heart sinks to see the unity of these people on their wrong and your dispersion from your right. Woe and grief befall you. You have become the target at which arrows are shot. You are being killed and you do not kill. You are being attacked but you do not attack. Allah is being disobeyed and you remain agreeable to it. When I ask you to move against them in summer you say it is hot weather. Spare us till heat subsides from us. When I order you to march in winter you say it is severely cold; give us time till cold clears from us. These are just excuses for evading heat and cold because if you run away from heat and

---

with thirty others. When the battlefield was clear the enemy ransacked al-Anbaar with full freedom and left the city completely destroyed.
When Ameer al-Momineen got the news of this attack he ascended the pulpit, and exhorted the people for crushing the enemy and called them to Jihaad, but from no quarter was there any voice or response. He alighted from the pulpit utterly disgusted and worried and in the same condition set off for the enemy on foot. When people observed this their sense of self respect and shame was also awakened and they too followed him. Ameer al-Momineen stopped at an-Nokhayla. People then surrounded and insisted upon him to get back as they were enough with the enemy. When their insistence increased beyond reckoning, Ameer al-Momineen consented to return and Saeed bn Qays al-Hamdani proceeded forward with a force of eight thousand. But Sofyaan bn Awf al-Ghamidi had gone, so Saeed came back without any encounter. When Saeed reached Koofa then — according to the version of bn-Abil-Hadeed — Ameer al-Momineen was so deeply grieved and indisposed during those days to an extent of not wishing to enter the mosque, but instead sat in the corridor of his residence (that connects the entrance of the mosque) and wrote this sermon and gave it to his slave Saad to read it over to the people. But al-Mobarrad (al-Kaamil, vol.1, pp.104-107) has related from Obaydillah bn Hafs at-Taymi, bn Aysha, that Ameer al-Momineen delivered this sermon on a high pace in an-Nokhayla. bn Maytham has held this view preferable.

cold, you would be, by Allah, running away (in a greater degree) from sword (war).

O you semblance of men, not men, your intelligence is that of children and your wit is that of the occupants of the curtained canopies (women kept in seclusion from the outside world). I wish I had not seen you nor known you. By Allah, this acquaintance has brought about shame and resulted in repentance. May Allah fight you! You have filled my heart with pus and loaded my bosom with rage. You made me drink mouthful of grief one after the other. You shattered my counsel by disobeying and leaving me so much so that Quraysh started saying that the son of Abi-Talib is brave but does not know (tactics of) war. Allah bless them! Is any one of them more fierce in war and more older in it than I am? I rose for it although yet within twenties, and here I am, have crossed over sixty, but one who is not obeyed can have no opinion.

SERMONS 28

The Transient Nature of this World and Importance of the next World

So now, surely this world has turned its back and announced its departure while the next world has appeared forward and proclaimed its approach. Today is the day of preparation while tomorrow is the day of race. The place to proceed to is Paradise while the place of doom is Hell. Is there no one to offer repentance over his faults before his death? Or is there no one to perform virtuous acts before the day of trial?

Beware, surely you are in the days of hopes behind which stands death. Whoever acts during the days of his hope before approach of his death, his action would benefit him and his death would not harm him. But he who fails to act during the period of hope before the approach of death his action is a loss and his death is a harm to him. Beware, and act during a period of attraction just as you act during a period of dread. Beware, surely I have not seen a coveter for Paradise asleep nor a dreader from Hell to be asleep. Beware, he whom right does not benefit must suffer the harm of the wrong, and he whom guidance does not keep firm will be led away by misguidance towards destruction.

Beware, you have been ordered insistently to march and been guided how to provide for the journey. Surely the most frightening thing which I am afraid of about you is to follow desires and to widen the hopes. Provide for yourself from this world what would save you tomorrow (on the Day of Judgement).

Sayyid Razi says: If there could be an utterance which would drag by neck towards renunciation in this world and force to action for the next world, it is this sermon. It is enough to cut off from the entanglements of hopes and to ignite the flames of preaching (for virtue) and warning (against vice). His most wonderful words in this sermon are "Today is the day of preparation while tomorrow is the day of race. The place to proceed to is Paradise while the place of doom is Hell," because besides sublimity of words, greatness of meaning, true similes and factual illustrations, there are wonderful secrets and delicate implications therein.

It is his saying that he place to proceed to is Paradise while the place of doom is Hell. Here he has used two different words to convey two different meanings. For Paradise he has used the word "the place to proceed to" but for Hell this word has not been used. One proceeds to a place which he likes and desires, and this can be true for Paradise only. Hell does not have the attractiveness that it may be liked or proceeded to. We seek Allah's protection from it. Since for Hell it was not proper to say "to be proceeded to" Ameer al-Momineen employed the word "doom" implying the last place of stay where one reaches even though it may mean grief and worry or happiness and pleasure.

This word is capable of conveying both senses. However, it should be taken in the sense of "al-masir" or "al-maal, that is, last resort. Quraanic verse is 'say thou "Enjoy ye (your pleasures yet a while), for your last resort is unto the (hell) fire" (14:30). Here to say 'sabqatakum" that is "the place for you to proceed to" in place of the word "masirakum" that is, your doom or last resort would not be proper in any way. Think and ponder over it and see how wondrous is its inner implication and how far its depth goes with beauty. Ameer al-Momineen's utterance is generally on these lines. In some versions the word 'sabqa" is shown as 'subqa" which is applied to reward fixed for the winner in a race. However, both the meanings are near each other, because a reward is not for an undesirable action but for good and commendable performance.

SERMONS 29

About those who found pretexts at the time of Jihaad

O people, your bodies are together but your desires are divergent. Your talk softens the hard stones and your action attracts your enemy towards you. You claim in your sittings that you would do this and that, but when fighting approaches, you say (to war) "turn thou away" (i.e. flee away). If one calls you (for help) the call receives no heed. And he who deals hardly with you his heart has no solace. The excuses are amiss like that of a debtor unwilling to pay. The ignoble can not ward off oppression. Right cannot be achieved without effort. Which is the house besides this one to protect? And with which leader (Imam) would you go for fighting after me?

By Allah! deceived is one whom you have deceived while, by Allah! he who is successful with you receives only useless arrows. You are like broken arrows thrown over the enemy. By Allah! I am now in the position that I neither confirm your views nor hope for your support, nor challenge the enemy through you. What is the matter with you? What is your ailment? What is your cure? The other party is also men of your shape (but they are so different in character). Will there be talk without action, carelessness without piety and greed in things not right?![1]

-1- After the battle of Nahrawan, Moaawiya sent az-Zahhaak bn Qays al-Fihri with a force of four thousand towards Koofa with the purpose that he should create disorder in this area, kill whomever he finds and keep busy in bloodshed and destruction so that Ameer al-Momineen should find no rest or peace of mind. He set off for the achievement of this

SERMONS 30

In Connection with Othmaan bn-Affaan's killing[1]

---

aim, and shedding innocent blood and spreading destruction all round reached upto the place of ath-Thalabiyya. Here he attacked a caravan of pilgrims (to Mecca) and looted all their wealth and belongings. Then at al-Qutqutana he killed the nephew of Abdillah bn-Masood, the Holy Prophet's companion, namely Amr bn Oways bn-Masood together with his followers. In this manner he created havoc and bloodshed all round. When Ameer al-Momineen came to know of this rack and ruin he called his men to battle in order to put a stop to this vandalism, but people seemed to avoid war. Being disgusted with their lethargy and lack of enthusiasm he ascended the pulpit and delivered this sermon, wherein he has roused the men to feel shame and not to try to avoid war but to rise for the protection of their country like brave men without employing wrong and lame excuses. At last Hijr bn Adi al-Kindi rose with a force of four thousand for crushing the enemy and overtook him at Tadmor. Only a small encounter had taken place between the parties when night came on and he fled away with only nineteen killed on his side. In Ameer al-Momineen's army also two persons fell as martyrs.

-1- Othmaan is the first Omayyad Caliph of Islam who ascended the Caliphate on the 1st Moharram, 24 A.H. at the age of seventy and after having wielded full control and authority over the affairs of the Moslims for twelve years was killed at their hands on the 18th Zil-Hijja, 35 A.H. and buried at Hashsh Kawkab.

This fact cannot be denied that Othmaan's killing was the result of his weaknesses and the black deeds of his officers, otherwise, there is no reason that Moslims should have unanimously agreed on killing him while no one except a few persons of his house stood up to support and defend him. Moslims would have certainly given consideration to his age, seniority, prestige and distinction of companionship of the Prophet but his ways and deeds had so marred the atmosphere that no one seemed prepared to sympathise and side with him. The oppression and excesses perpetrated on high ranking companions of the Prophet had roused a wave of grief and anger among the Arab tribes. Everyone was infuriated and looked at his haughtiness and wrong doings with disdainful eyes. Thus, due to Abo-Zarr's disgrace, dishonour and exile Bani-Ghifaar and their associate tribes, due to Abdillah bn-Masood's merciless beating Bani-Hozayl and their associates, due to breaking of the ribs of Ammaar bn Yaasir, Bani-Makhzoom and their associates Bani-Zohra, and due to the plot for the killing of Mohammad bn Abi-Bakr, Bani-Taym all had a storm of rage in their hearts. The Moslims of other cities were also brimful of complaints at the hands of his officers who under intoxication of wealth and the effects of luxury did whatever they wished and crushed whomever they wanted. They had no fear of punishment from the centre nor apprehension of any enquiry. People were fluttering to get out of their talons of oppression but no one was ready to listen to their cries of pain and restlessness; feelings of hatred were rising but no care was taken to put them down. The companions of the Prophet were also sick of him as they saw that peace was destroyed, administration was topsy turvy and Islam's features were being metamorphosed. The poor and the starving were craving for dried crusts while Bani-Omayya were rolling in wealth. The Caliphate had become a handle for belly-filling and a means of amassing wealth. Consequently, they too did not lag behind in preparing the ground for killing him. Rather, it was at their letters and messages that people from Koofa, Basra and Egypt had collected in Madeena. Observing this behaviour of the people of Madeena, Othmaan wrote to Moaawiya:

So now, certainly the people of Madeena have turned heretics, have turned faith against obedience and broken the (oath of) allegiance. So you send to me the warriors of Syria on brisk and sturdy horses.

The policy of action adopted by Moaawiya on receipt of this letter also throws light on the condition of the companions. Historian at-Tabari writes after this:

When the letter reached Moaawiya he pondered over it and considered it bad to openly oppose the companions of the Prophet since he was aware of their unanimity.

In view of these circumstances to regard the killing of Othmaan as a consequence of merely enthusiasm and temporary feelings and to hurl it at some insurgents is to veil the fact, since all the factors of his opposition existed within Madeena itself, while those coming from without had collected for seeking redress of their grievances at their call. Their aim was only improvement of the position, not killing or bloodshed. If their complaints had been heard then the occasion for this bloodshed would not have arisen. What happened was that when, having been disgusted with the oppression and excesses of Abdillah bn Saad bn Abi Sarh, who was foster brother of Othmaan, the people of Egypt proceeded towards Madeena and camped in the valley of Zakhoshob near the city. They sent a man with a letter to Othmaan and demanded that oppression should be stopped, the existing ways should be changed and repentance should be offered for the future. But instead of giving a reply Othmaan got this man turned out of the house and did not regard their demands worth attention. On this these people entered the city to raise their voice against this pride and haughtiness, and complained to the people of this behaviour besides other excesses. On the other side many people from Koofa and Basra had also arrived with their complaints and they, after joining these ones, proceeded forward with the backing of the people of Madeena and confined Othmaan within his house, although there was no restriction on his going and coming to the mosque. But in his sermon on the very first Friday he severely rebuked these people and even held them accursed, whereupon people got infuriated and threw pebbles at him as a result of which he lost control and fell from the pulpit. After a few days his coming and going to the mosque was also banned.

When Othmaan saw matters deteriorating to this extent he implored Ameer al-Momineen very submissively to find some way for his rescue and to disperse the people in whatever way he could. Ameer al-Momineen said "On what terms can I ask them to leave when their demands are justified?" Othmaan said "I authorise you in this matter. Whatever terms you would settle with them I would be bound by them" So Ameer al-Momineen went and met the Egyptians and talked to them. They consented to get back on the condition that all the tyrannies should be wiped off and Mohammad bn Abi-Bakr be made governor by removing bn-Abi-Sarh. Ameer al-Momineen came back and put their demand before Othmaan who accepted it without any hesitation and said that to get over these excesses time was required. Ameer al-Momineen pointed out that for matters concerning Madeena delay had no sense. However, for other places so much time could be allowed that the Caliph's message could reach them. Othmaan insisted that for Madeena also three days were needed. After discussion with the Egyptians Ameer al-Momineen agreed to it also and took all the responsibility thereof upon himself. Then they dispersed at his suggestion. Some of them went to Egypt with Mohammad bn Abi-Bakr while some went to the valley of Zakhoshob and stayed there and this whole matter ended. On the second day of this event Marwaan bn Hakam said to Othmaan, "It is good, these people have gone, but to stop people coming from other cities you should issue a statement so that they should not come this way and sit quiet at their places and that statement should be that some people collected in Madeena on hearing some irresponsible talk but when they came to know that whatever they heard was wrong they were satisfied and have gone back" Othmaan did not want to speak such a clear lie but Marwaan convinced him and he agreed, and speaking in the Holy Prophet's mosque, he said:

These Egyptians had received some news about their Caliph and when satisfied that they were all baseless and wrong they went back to their cities.

No sooner he said this than there was great hue and cry in the mosque, and people began to shout to Othmaan, "Offer repentance, fear Allah; what is this lie you are uttering?" Othmaan was confused in this commotion and had to offer repentance. Consequently, he turned to the Kaba, moaned in the audience of Allah and returned to his house.

Probably after this very event Ameer al-Momineen advised Othmaan that, "You should openly offer repentance about your past misdeeds so that these uprisings should subside for good otherwise if tomorrow people of some other place come you will again cling to my neck to rid you of them" Consequently, he delivered a speech in the Prophet's mosque wherein admitting his mistakes he offered repentance and swore to remain careful in future. He told the people that when he alighted from the pulpit their representatives should meet him, and he would remove their grievances and meet their demands. On this people acclaimed this action of his and washed away their ill-feelings with tears to a great extent. When he reached his house after finishing from here Marwaan sought permission to say something but Othmaan's wife Naila bnt Farafisa intervened. Turning to Marwaan she said "For Allah's sake you keep quiet. You would say only such a thing as would bring but death to him" Marwaan took it ill and retorted, "You have no right to interfere in these matters. You are the daughter of that very person who did not know till his death how to perform ablution" Naila replied with fury, "You are wrong, and are laying a false blame. Before uttering anything about my father you should have cast a glance on the features of your father. But for the consideration of that old man I would have spoken things at which people would have shuddered but would have confirmed every such word" When Othmaan saw the conversation getting prolonged he stopped them and asked Marwaan to tell him what he wished. Marwaan said "What is it you have said in the mosque, and what repentance you have offered? In my view sticking

---

to the sin was a thousand times better than this repentance because however much the sins may multiply there is always scope for repentance, but repentance by force is no repentance. You have said what you have but now see the consequences of this open announcement, that crowds of people are at your door. Now go forward and fulfil their demands" Othmaan then said "Well, I have said what I have said, now you deal with these people. It is not in my power to deal with them" Consequently, finding out his implied consent Marwaan came out and addressing the people spoke out, "Why have you assembled here? Do you intend to attack or to ransack? Remember, you cannot easily snatch away power from our hands, take out the idea from your hearts that you would subdue us. We are not to be subdued by anyone. Take away your black faces from here. Allah may disgrace and dishonour you

When people noticed this changed countenance and altered picture they rose from there full of anger and rage and went straight to Ameer al-Momineen and related to him the whole story. On hearing it Ameer al-Momineen was infuriated and immediately went to Othmaan and said to him, "Good Heavens. How badly you have behaved with the Moslims. You have forsaken faith for the sake of a faithless and characterless man and have lost all wit. At least you should have regard and consideration for your own promise. What is this that at Marwaan's betokening you have set off with folded eyes. Remember he will throw you in such a dark well that you will never be able to come out of it. You have become the carrier animal of Marwaan so that he can ride on you howsoever he desires and put you on whatever wrong way he wishes. In future I shall never intervene in your affair nor tell people anything. Now you should manage your own affairs. "

Saying all this Ameer al-Momineen got back and Naila got the chance, she said to Othmaan, "Did I not tell you to get rid of Marwaan otherwise he would put such a stain on you that it would not be removed despite all effort. Well, what is the good in following the words of one who is without any respect among the people and low before their eyes. Make Ali agree otherwise remember that restoring the disturbed state of affairs is neither within your power nor in that of Marwaan" Othmaan was impressed by this and sent a man after Ameer al-Momineen but he refused to meet him. There was no siege around Othmaan but shame deterred him. With what face could he come out of the house? But there was no way without coming out. Consequently, he came out quietly in the gloom of night and reaching Ameer al-Momineen's place, he moaned his helplessness and loneliness, offered excuses, and also assured him of keeping promises but Ameer al-Momineen said "You make a promise in the Prophet's mosque standing before all the people but it is fulfilled in this way that when people go to you they are rebuked and even abuses are hurled at them. When this is the state of your undertakings which the world has seen, then how and on what ground can I trust any word of yours in future. Do not have any expectation from me now. I am not prepared to accept any responsibility on your behalf. The tracks are open before you. Adopt whichever way you like and tread whatever track you choose" After this talk Othmaan came back and began blaming Ameer al-Momineen in retort to the effect that all the disturbances were rising at his instance and that he was not doing anything despite being able to do everything.

On this side the result of repentance was as it was. Now let us see the other side. When after crossing the border of Hijaaz, Mohammad bn Abi-Bakr reached the place Ayla on the coast of the Red Sea people caught sight of a camel rider who was making his camel run so fast as though the enemy was chasing him. These people had some misgivings about him and therefore called him and enquired who he was. He said he was the slave of Othmaan. They enquired wherefore he was bound. He said Egypt. They enquired to whom he was going. He replied to the Governor of Egypt. People said that the Governor of Egypt was with them. To whom was he going then? He said he was to go to bn-Abi-Sarh. People asked him if any letter was with him. He denied. They asked for what purpose he was going. He said he did not know that. One of these people thought that his clothes should be searched. So the search was made, but nothing was found on him. Kinana bn Bishr at-Tojibi said 'see his water-skin" People said "Leave him, how can there be a letter in water! Kinana said "You do not know what cunning these people play" Consequently, the water-skin was opened and seen. There was a lead pipe in it wherein was a letter. When it was opened and read, the Caliph's order in it was that "When Mohammad bn Abi-Bakr and his party reaches you then from among them kill so and so, arrest so and so, and put so and so in jail, but you remain on your post" On reading this all were stunned and thus began to look at one another in astonishment.
A Persian hemistich says:
Mind was just burst in astonishment as to what wonder it was!
Now proceeding forward was riding into the mouth of death, consequently they returned to Madeena taking the slave with them. Reaching there they placed that letter before all the companions of the Prophet. Whoever heard this incident remained stunned with astonishment, and there was no one who was not abusing Othmaan. Afterwards a few companions went to Othmaan along with these people, and asked whose seal was there on this letter. He replied that it was his own. They enquired whose writing it was. He said it was his secretary's. They enquired whose slave was that man. He replied that it was his. They enquired whose riding beast it was. He replied that it was that of the Government. They enquired who had sent it. He said he had no knowledge of it. People then said "Good Heavens. Everything is yours but you do not know who had sent it. If you are so helpless, you leave this Caliphate and get off from it so that such a man comes who can administer the affairs of the Moslims" He replied, "It is not possible that I should put off the dress of Caliphate which Allah has put on me. Of course, I would offer repentance" The people said "Why should you speak of repentance which has already been flouted on the day when Marwaan was representing you on your door, and whatever was wanting has been made up by this letter. Now we are not going to be duped into these bluffs. Leave the Caliphate and if our brethren stand in our way we will hold them up; but if they prepare for fighting we too will fight. Neither our hands are stiff nor our swords blunt. If you regard all Moslims equally and uphold justice hand over Marwaan to us to enable us to enquire from him on whose strength and support he wanted to play with the precious lives of Moslims by writing this letter" But he rejected this demand and refused to hand over Marwaan to them, whereupon people said that the letter had been written at his behest.

However, improving conditions again deteriorated and they ought to have deteriorated because despite lapse of the required time every thing was just as it had been and not a jot of difference had occurred. Consequently, the people who had stayed behind in the valley of Zakhoshob to watch the result of repentance again advanced like a flood and spread over the streets of Madeena, and closing the borders from every side surrounded his house.

During these days of siege a companion of the Prophet, Niyar bn Eyaz desired to talk to Othmaan, went to his house and called him. When he peeped out from the above he said "O Othmaan, for Allah's sake give up this Caliphate and save Moslims from this bloodshed" While he was just conversing, one of Othmaan's men aimed at him with an arrow and killed him, whereupon people were infuriated and shouted that Niyar's killer should be handed over to them. Othmaan said it was not possible that he would hand over his own support to them. This stubbornness worked like a fan on fire and in the height of fury people set fire to his door and began advancing for entering, when Marwaan bn Hakam, Saeed bn Aas and Mogheera bn Akhnas together with their contingents pounced upon the besiegers and killing and bloodshed started at his door. People wanted to enter the house but they were being pushed back. In the meanwhile, Amr bn Hazim al-Ansaari whose house was adjacent to that of Othmaan opened his door and shouted for advancing from that side. Thus through this house the besiegers climbed on the roof of Othmaan's house and descending down from there drew their swords. Only a few scuffles had taken place when all except people of Othmaan's house, his well-wishers and Bani-Omayya ran away in the streets of Madeena and a few hid themselves in the house of Om-Habeeba bnt bn-Sofyaan (Moaawiya's sister) the rest were killed with Othmaan defending him to the last. (at-Tabaqaat, bn Saad, vol.3, Part 1, pp.50-58; at-Tabari, vol.1, pp.2998-3025; al-Kaamil, bn al-Athir, vol.3, pp.167-180; bn-Abil-Hadeed, vol.2, pp.144-161).

At his killing several poets wrote elegies. A couplet from the elegy by Abo-Horayra is presented:

Today people have only one grief but I have two griefs
the loss of my money bag and the killing of Othmaan.

After observing these events the stand of Ameer al-Momineen becomes clear, namely that he was neither supporting the group that was instigating at Othmaan's killing nor can be included in those who stood for his support and defence but when he saw that what was said was not acted upon he kept himself aloof.

When both the parties are looked at then among the people who had raised their hands off from Othmaan's support are seen Aysha, and according to the popular versions (which is not right) the then living persons out of the ten Pre-informed ones (who had been pre-informed in this world by the Prophet for their being admitted in Paradise) , out of those who took part in the consultative committee (formed for Othmaan's selection for Caliphate) , Ansaar, original mohaajiroon, people who took part in the battle of Badr and other conspicuous and dignified individuals, while on the side (of Othmaan) are seen only a few slaves of the Caliph and a few individuals from Bani-Omayya. If people like Marwaan and Saeed bn Aas cannot be given precedence over the original

If I had ordered his assassination I should have been his killer, but if I had refrained others from killing him I would have been his helper. The position was that he who helped him cannot now say that he is better than the one who deserted him while he who deserted him cannot say that he is better than the one who helped him. I am putting before you his case. He appropriated (wealth) and did it badly. You protested against it and committed excess therein. With Allah lies the real verdict between the appropriator and the protester.

SERMONS 31

Before the commencement of the Battle of Jamal, he sent Abdillah bn-Abbas to az-Zobayr bn-Awwam to advise him back to obedience

Do not meet Talha (bn Obaydillah). If you meet him you will find him like an unruly bull whose horns are turned towards its ears. He rides a ferocious riding beast and says it has been tamed. But you meet Az-Zobayr because he is soft-tempered. Tell him that your maternal cousin says that "(It looks as if) in the Hijaaz you knew me (accepted me), but (on coming here to) Iraq you do not know me (do not accept me). So, what has dissuaded (you) from what was shown (by you previously) ?! "

Sayyid Razi says: The last sentence of this sermon "fama ada mimma bada" has been heard only from Ameer al-Momineen.

SERMONS 32

Disparagement of the World and Categories of People

O people! we have been borne in such a wrongful and thankless period wherein the virtuous is deemed vicious and the oppressor goes on

---

mohaajiroon their actions too cannot be given precedence over the actions of the latter. Again, if ijma" (consensus of opinion) is not meant for particular occasions only then it would be difficult to question this overwhelming unanimity of the companions.

advancing in his excess. We do not make use of what we know and do not discover what we do not know. We do not fear calamity till it befalls.

People are of four categories. Among them is one who is prevented from mischief only by his low position, lack of means and paucity of wealth.

Then there is he who has drawn his sword, openly commits mischief, has collected his horsemen and foot-men and has devoted himself to securing wealth, leading troops, rising on the pulpit and has allowed his faith to perish. How bad is the transaction that you allow (enjoyment of) this world to be a price for yourself as an alternative for what there is with Allah for you.

And among them is he who seeks (benefits of) this world through actions meant for the next world, but does not seek (good of) the next world through actions of this world. He keeps his body calm (in dignity), raises small steps, holds up his clothes, embellishes his body for appearance of trust-worthiness and uses the position of Allah's connivance as a means of committing sins.

Then there is one whose weakness and lack of means have held him back from conquest of lands. This keeps down his position and he has named it contentment and he clothes himself with the robe of renunciation although he has never had any connection with these qualities.

Then there remain a few people in whose case the remembrance of their return (to Allah on Doomsday) keeps their eyes bent, and the fear of resurrection moves their tears. Some of them are scared away (from the world) and dispersed; some are frightened and subdued; some are quiet as if muzzled; some are praying sincerely, some are grief-stricken and pain-ridden whom fear has confined to namelessness and disgrace has shrouded them, so they are in (the sea of) bitter water, their mouths are closed and their hearts are bruised. They preached till they were tired, they were oppressed till they were disgraced and they were killed till they remained few in number.

The world in your eyes should be smaller than the bark of acacia and the clippings of wool. Seek instruction from those who preceded you before those who follow you take instruction from you, and keep aloof from it realising its evil because it cuts off even from those who were more attached to it than you.

Sayyid Razi says: Some ignorant persons attributed this sermon to Moaawiya but it is the speech of Ameer al-Momineen. There should be no doubt about it. What comparison is there between gold and clay or sweet and bitter water. This has been pointed out by the skilful guide and the expert critic Amr bn-Bahr al-Jaahiz as he has mentioned this sermon in his book, al-Bayan wat-Tabyeen (vol. 2, pp. 59-61). He has also mentioned who attributed it to Moaawiya and then states that it is most akin to be the speech of Ali and most in accord with his way of categorising people and information about their oppression, disgrace, apprehension and fear. (On the other hand) we never found Moaawiya speaking on the lives of renunciates or worshippers.

SERMONS 33

At the time of setting for the Battle of Jamal

Abdillah bn-Abbas says that when Ameer al-Momineen set out for war with the people of Basra he came to his audience at Ziqar and saw that he was stitching his shoe. Then Ameer al-Momineen said to me,

what is the price of this shoe? "

I said: "it has no value now." He then said,

By Allah, it should have been more dear to me than ruling over you but for the fact that I may establish right and ward off wrong.

Then he came out and spoke:

Verily, Allah sent Mohammad (p.b.u.h.a.h.p) when none among the Arabs read a book or claimed Prophethood. He guided the people till he took them to their (correct) position and their salvation. So their spears (i.e. officers) became straight and their conditions settled down.

By Allah, surely I was in their lead till it took shape with its walls. I did not show weakness or cowardice. My existing march is also like that. I shall certainly pierce the wrong till right comes out of its side.

What (cause of conflict) is there between me and the Quraysh? By Allah, I have fought them when they were unbelievers and I shall fight them when they have been misled. I shall be the same for them today as I was for them yesterday.

By Allah, the Quraysh only take revenge against us because Allah has given us (i.e. the Holy Prophet and his progeny) preference over them. So, we have allowed them into our domain, whereupon they have become as the former poet says:

By my life, you continued drinking fresh milk every morning, And (continued) eating fine stoned dates with butter; We have given you the nobility which you did not possess before; And surrounded (protected) you with thoroughbred horses and tawny-coloured spears (strong spears)[1]

SERMONS 34

Exhorting People to fight against the People of Syria[2]

Woe to you. I am tired of rebuking you. Do you accept this worldly life in place of the next life? Or disgrace in place of dignity? When I invite you to fight your enemy your eyes revolve as though you are in the clutches of

---

-1- In fact, the aim of the poet here is to say that the condition of the addressee's life, from the moral and material point of view, had been worse in the past, and that the poet and his tribe have given him the best means of leading their lives. But as the result of this improved condition the addressee has completely lost himself and forgotten his past condition and thinks that he had had this kind of life previously.

Now, Ameer al-Momineen wants to convey the same idea here to the Quraysh as Fatima (p.b.u.h.) the holy daughter of the Holy Prophet said in her speech on Fadak:

(O" People) ... You were on the brink of the pit of Hell Fire..." (Quraan, 3:103). You were as worthless as the mouthful of water. You were minority like the handful greedy and a spark of the hasty. You were as down-trodden as the dust under feet. You drank dirty water. You ate untanned skin. You were abased and condemned. But Allah has rescued you through my father Mohammad (p.b.u.h.a.h.p) ...

-2- The word "ash-Sham" was a name used for a vast geographical area occupied by Moslim countries in those days. This area included present-day Syria, Lebanon and Palestine. Its capital was Damascus. Wherever the word Syria is mentioned (in this book) it should be understood in its larger meaning.

death, and in the senselessness of last moments. My pleadings are not understood by you and you remain stunned. It is as though your hearts are affected with madness so that you do not understand. You have lost my confidence for good. Neither are you a support for me to lean upon, nor a means to honour and victory. Your example is that of the camels whose protector has disappeared, so that if they are collected from one side they disperse away from the other side.

By Allah, how bad are you for igniting flames of war. You are intrigued against but do not intrigue (against the enemy). Your boundaries are decreasing but you do not get enraged over it. Those against you do not sleep but you are unmindful. By Allah, those who leave matters one for the other are subdued. By Allah, I believed about you that if battle rages and death hovers around you, you will cut away from the son of Abi-Talib like the severing of head from the trunk.[1]

By Allah, he who makes it possible for his adversary to so overpower him as to remove the flesh (from his bones), crush his bones and cut his skin

---

-1- This sentence is employed for such severance after which there is no occasion or possibility of joining. The author of ad-Dorran-Najafiyya has quoted several views in its explanation:

i) bn Dorayd's view is that it means that. "Just as when the head is severed its joining again is impossible, in the same way you will not join me after once deserting me"

ii) al-Mofazzal says ar-ra's (head) was the name of a man, and a village of Syria, Bayt ar-ra's is named after him. This man left his home and went away somewhere and never again returned to his village after which the proverb sprang up "you went as ar-ra's had gone"

iii) One meaning of it is that "Just as if the joints of the bones of the head are opened they cannot be restored, in the same way you will not join me after cutting from me. iv) It has also been said that this sentence is in the sense of separating completely. After copying this meaning from the Sharh of Shaykh Qutboddeen ar-Rawandi, the commentator bn-Abil-Hadeed has written that this meaning is not correct because when the word "ar-ra's" is used in the sense of whole it is not preceded by "Alif" and "lam"

v) It is also taken to mean that "You will so run away from me as one (fleeing for life) to save his head" Besides this, one or two other meanings have also been stated but being remote they are disregarded.

First of all it was used by the philosopher of Arabia Aktham bn Sayfi while teaching unity and concord to his children. He says:

O" my children do not cut away (from each other) at the time of calamities like the cutting of head, because after that you will never get together.

into pieces, then it means that his helplessness is great and his heart surrounded within the sides of his chest is weak. You may become like this if you wish. But for me, before I allow it I shall use my sharp edged swords of al-Moshrafiyya which would cut as under the bones of the head and fly away arms and feet. Thereafter, Allah will do whatever He wills.

O people, I have a right over you and you have a right over me. As for your right over me, that is to counsel you, to pay you your dues fully, to teach you that you may not remain ignorant and instruct you in behaviourism that you may act upon. As for my right over you, it is fulfillment of (the obligation of) allegiance, well-wishing in presence or in absence, response when I call you and obedience when I order you.

SERMONS 35

Arbitration[1]

-1- When the Syrians" spirit was broken by the bloody swords of the Iraqis, and the incessant attacks of the night of al-Harir lowered their morale and ended their aspirations Amr bn Aas suggested to Moaawiya the trick that the Quraan should be raised on spears and shouts urged forth to treat it as the arbitrator. Its effect would be that some people would try to stop the war and others would like to continue it. We would thus divide them and be able to get the war postponed for another occasion. Consequently, copies of the Quraan were raised on spears. The result was that some brainless persons raised hue and cry and created division and disturbance in the army and the efforts of simple Moslims turned slow after having been near victory. Without understanding anything they began to shout that they should prefer the verdict of the Quraan over war.

When Ameer al-Momineen saw the Quraan being the instrument of their activities, he said:

O people do not fall in this trap of deceit and trickery. They are putting up this device only to escape the ignominy of defeat. I know the character of each one of them. They are neither adherents of the Quraan nor have they any connection with the faith or religion. The very purpose of our fighting has been that they should follow the Quraan and act on its injunctions. For Allah's sake do not fall in their deceitful device. Go ahead with determination and courage and stop only after vanquishing the dying foe" Nevertheless, the deceitful instrument of wrong had worked. The people took to disobedience and rebellion. Misar bn Fadaki at-Tameemi and Zayd bn Hosayn at-Tai each with twenty thousand men came forward and said to Ameer al-Momineen, "O" Ali, if you do not respond to the call of the Quraan we will deal with you in the same manner as we did with Othmaan. You end the battle at once and bow before the verdict of the Quraan. Ameer al-Momineen tried his best to make them understand but Satan was standing before them in the garb of the Quraan. He did not allow them to do so, and they compelled Ameer al-Momineen that he should send someone to call Malik bn Haarith al-Ashtar from the battlefield. Being obliged, Ameer al-Momineen sent Yazeed bn Haani to call Malik back. When Malik heard this order he was bewildered and said "Please tell him this is not the occasion to leave the position. He may wait a bit then I will come to his audience with the tidings of victory" Haani conveyed this message on return but people shouted that Ameer al-Momineen must have sent word to him secretly to continue. Ameer al-Momineen said he never got any occasion to send any secret message to him. Whatever he said was said before them. People said he should be sent again and that if Malik delayed his return Ameer al-Momineen should forsake his life. Ameer al-Momineen again sent Yazeed bn Haani and sent word that rebellion had occurred, he should return in whatever condition he was. So Haani went and told Malik "You hold victory dear or the life of Ameer al-Momineen. If his life is dear you should raise hands off the battle and go to him" Leaving the chances of victory Malik stood up and came to the audience of Ameer al-Momineen with grief and disappointment. Chaos raged there. He rebuked the people very much but matters had taken such a turn that could not be corrected.

It was then settled that either party should nominate an arbitrator so that they should settle the (matter of) Caliphate according to the Quraan. From Moaawiya's side Amr bn Aas was decided upon and from Amir al Momineen's side people proposed the name of Abo-Mosa al-Ashari. Seeing this wrong selection Ameer al-Momineen said 'since you have not accepted my order about arbitration at least now agree that do not make Abo-Mosa the arbitrator. He is not a man of trust. Here is Abdillah bn Abbas and here is Malik al-Ashtar. Select one of them" But they did not at all listen to him and stuck to his name. Ameer al-Momineen said "All right, do whatever you want. The day is not far when you will cut your own hands through your misdeeds

After the nomination of arbitrators when the deed of agreement was being written, then with Ali bn Abi-Talib (p.b.u.h.) the word Ameer al-Momineen was also written. Amr bn Aas said "This should be rubbed off. If we regarded him Ameer al-Momineen why should this battle have been fought?" At first Ameer al-Momineen refused to rub it off but when they did not in any way agree, he rubbed it off and said "This incident is just similar to the one at al-Hodaybiyya when the unbelievers stuck on the point that the words "Prophet of Allah" with the name of the Prophet should be removed and the Prophet did remove it" On this Amr bn Aas got angry and said "Do you treat us as unbelievers?" Ameer al-Momineen said "On what day have you had anything to do with believers and when have you been their supporters?" However, after this settlement, the people dispersed, and after mutual consultation these two arbitrators decided that by removing both Ali and Moaawiya from the Caliphate the people should be accorded the power to choose whomever they desired. When time came to its announcement there was a meeting at Damatol-Jandal, a place between Iraq and Syria, and then two arbitrators also reached there to announce the judgement on the fate of the Moslims. Acting cunningly

All praise is due to Allah even though time has brought (for us) crushing calamity and great occurrence. And I stand witness that there is no god but Allah the One, there is no partner for Him nor is there with Him any god other than Himself, and that Mohammad is His slave and His Prophet (May Allah's blessing and greeting be upon him and his progeny).

So now, certainly the disobedience of sympathetic counsellor who has knowledge as well as experience brings about disappointment and result in repentance. I had given you my orders about this arbitration and put before you my hidden view, if Qasir's[1] orders were fulfilled but you

---

Amr bn Aas said to Abo-Mosa, "I regard it ill manner to precede you. You are older in years and age so first you make the announcement" Abo-Mosa succumbed to his flattery and came out proudly and stood before the gathering. Addressing them he said "O Moslims we have jointly settled that Ali bn Abi-Talib and Moaawiya should be removed and the right to choose a Caliph be accorded to the Moslims. They should choose whomever they like" Saying this he sat down. Now the turn was for Amr bn Aas and he said "O Moslims you have heard that Abo-Mosa removed Ali bn Abi-Talib. I also agree with it. As for Moaawiya, there is no question of removing him. Therefore I place him in his position" No sooner that he said this there were cries all round. Abo-Mosa cried hoarse that it was a trick, a deceit and told Amr bn Aas that, "You have played a trick, and your example is that of a dog on which if you load something he would gasp, or leave him he would gasp" Amr bn Aas said "Your example is like the ass on whom books are loaded" However Amr bn Aas's trick was effective and Moaawiya's shaking feet were again stabilised.

This was the short sketch of the Arbitration whose basis was laid in the Quraan and Sonna. But was it a verdict of the Quraan or the result of those deceitful contrivances which people of this world employ to retain their authority? Could these pages of history be made a torch-guide for the future and the Quraan and Sonna be not used as a means of securing authority or as an instrument of worldly benefits.

When Ameer al-Momineen got the news of this lamentable result of arbitration, he climbed on the pulpit and delivered this sermon every word of which savours of his grief and sorrow and at the same time it throws light on soundness of his thinking, correctness of his opinion and foresighted sagacity.

-1- This is a proverb which is used on an occasion where the advice of a counsellor is rejected and afterwards it is repented. The fact of it was that the ruler of al-Heera namely Jazima al-Abrash killed the ruler of al-Jazira named Amr bn Zarib whereafter his daughter az-Zabba" was made the ruler of al-Jazira. Soon after accession to the throne she thought out this plan to avenge her father's blood, that she sent a message to Jazima that she could not alone carry on the affairs of the state and that if he could become her patron by accepting her as his wife she would be grateful. Jazima was more than puffed up at

rejected it (my orders) like rough opponents and disobedient insurgents till the counsellor himself fell in doubt about his counsel and the flint (of his wit) ceased to give flame. Consequently, mine and your position became as the poet of Hawazan says:

I gave you my orders at Monarajil-Liwa but you did not see the good of my counsel till the noon of next day (when it was too late).[1]

SERMONS 36

Warning the People of Nahrawan[2] of their fate

---

this proposal, and prepared himself to set off for al-Jazira with a thousand horsemen. His slave Qasir advised him much that this was just a deceit and trick and that he should not place himself in this danger; but his wit had been so blinded that he could not think over why az-Zabba" should select the Murderer of her father for her life companionship. Anyhow, he set off and when he reached the border of al-Jazira although az-Zabba's army was present for his reception but she neither gave any special reception nor offered any warm welcome. Seeing this state Qasir was again suspicious and he advised Jazima to get back, but nearness to the goal had further fanned his passion. He paid no heed and stepping further entered the city. Soon on arrival there he was killed. When Qasir saw this he said "Had the advice of Qasir been followed" From that time this proverb gained currency.

-1- The poet of Hawazin implies Dorayd-bn Zimma. He wrote this couplet after the death of his brother Abdillah bn Zimma. Its facts are that Abdillah along with his brother led an attack of two groups of Bani-Josham and Bani-Nasr who were both from Hawazin, and drove away many camels. On return when they intended to rest at Monarajil-Liwa, Dorayd said it was not advisable to stay there lest the enemy attacks from behind, but Abdillah did not agree and stayed there. The result was that as soon as dawn appeared the enemy attacked and killed Abdillah on the spot. Dorayd also received wounds but he slipped away alive, and after this he wrote a few couplets out of which one couplet is this wherein he has referred to the destruction resulting from his advice having been rejected.

-2- The cause of the battle of Nahrawan was that when after Arbitration Ameer al-Momineen was returning to Koofa, the people who were foremost in pleading acceptance of Arbitration began to say that appointment of anyone other than Allah as arbitrator is heresy, and that, Allah forbid, by accepting the Arbitration Ameer al-Momineen turned heretic. Consequently, by distorting the meaning of "There is no authority same with Allah" they made simple Moslims share their views and separating from Ameer al-Momineen encamped at Hanira" near Koofa. When Ameer al-Momineen learned of these plottings he sent Sasaa bn Soohan al-Abdi and Ziyad bn Nazr al-Haarithi in the company of bn Abbas towards them and afterwards himself went to the place of their stay and dispersed them after discussion.

When these people reached Koofa they began to spread the news that Ameer al-Momineen had broken the agreement of Arbitration and that he is again ready to fight against the Syrians. When Ameer al-Momineen learned this he contradicted it whereupon these people stood up in rebellion and encamped twelve miles from Baghdad in the low area of the canal called Nahrawan.

On the other side, after hearing the verdict of Arbitration Ameer al-Momineen rose for fighting the army of Syria and wrote to the Kharijites that the verdict passed by the two arbitrators in pursuance of their heart's wishes instead of the Quraan and Sonna was not acceptable to him, that he had therefore decided to fight with them and they should support him for crushing the enemy. But the Kharijites gave him this reply, "When you had agreed to Arbitration in our view you had turned heretic. Now if you admit your heresy and offer repentance we will think over this matter and decide what we should do" Ameer al-Momineen understood from their reply that their disobedience and misguidance had become very serious. To entertain any kind of hope from them now was futile. Consequently, ignoring them he encamped in the valley of an-Nokhayla with a view to marching towards Syria. When the army had been arrayed he came to know that the men desired to deal with the people of Nahrawan first, and to move towards Syria afterwards. Ameer al-Momineen, however, said that they should be left as they were, that they themselves should first move towards Syria while the people of Nahrawan could be dealt with afterwards. People said that they were prepared to obey every order of his with all their might whether he moved this way or that way. The army had not moved when news about the rebellion of Kharijites began to reach, and it was learnt that they had butchered the governor of Nahrawan namely Abdillah bn Khabbab bn Aratt and his slave maid with the child in her womb, and have killed three women of Bani-Tayyi and Om-Sinan as-Saydawiyya. Ameer al-Momineen sent al-Haarith bn Morra al-Abdi for investigation but he too was killed by them. When their rebellion reached this stage it was necessary to deal with them. Consequently, the army turned towards Nahrawan. On reaching there Ameer al-Momineen sent them word that those who had killed Abdillah bn Khabbab bn Aratt and innocent women should be handed over to him for avenging blood. Those people replied that they had killed these persons jointly and that they considered it lawful to shed the blood of all the people on his side. Even at this Ameer al-Momineen did not take the initiative for the battle, but sent Abo-Ayyoob al-Ansaari with a message of peace. So he spoke to them aloud, "Whoever comes under this banner or separates from that party and goes to Koofa or al-Madain would get amnesty and he would not be questioned. As a result of this Farwa bn Nawfal al-Ashjai said that he did not know why they were at war with Ameer al-Momineen. Saying this he separated along with five hundred men. Similarly group after group began to separate and some of them joined Ameer al-Momineen. Those who remained numbered four thousand, and according to at-Tabari's account they numbered two thousand eight hundred. These people were not in any way prepared to listen to the voice of truth, and were ready to kill or be killed. Ameer al-Momineen had stopped his men to take the

I am warning you that you will be killed on the bend of this canal and on the level of this low area while you will have no clear excuse before Allah nor any open authority with you. You have come out of your houses and then divine decree entangled you. I had advised you against this arbitration but you rejected my advice like adversaries and opponents till I turned my ideas in the direction of your wishes. You are a group whose heads are devoid of wit and intelligence. May you have no father! (Allah's woe be to you!) I have not put you in any calamity nor wished you harm.

SERMONS 37

His Steadfastness in Religion and Precedence in (acceptance of) Belief

I discharged duties when others lost courage (to do so), and I came forward when others hid themselves. I spoke when others remained mum. I stroke with Divine light when others remained standing. I was the quietest of them in voice but the highest in going forward. I cleaved to its rein and applied myself solely to its pledge, like the mountain which neither sweeping wind could move nor storm could shake. No one could find fault with me nor could any speaker speak ill of me.

The low is in my view worthy of honour till I secure (his) right for him while the strong is in my view weak till I take (other's) right from him. We are happy with the destiny ordained by Allah and have submitted to the command of Allah. Do you think I would speak lie about the Prophet of Allah? By Allah, I am surely the first to testify him, so I will not be the first

---

initiative but the Kharijites put arrows in their bows and broke and threw away the sheathes of their swords. Even at this juncture Ameer al-Momineen warned them of the dire consequences of war and this sermon is about that warning and admonition. But they were so brimming with enthusiasm that they leapt on Ameer al-Momineen's force all of a sudden. This onslaught was so severe that the foot men lost ground but they soon fixed themselves firmly that the attack of arrows and spears could not dislodge them from their position and they soon so cleared away the Kharijites that except for nine persons who fled away to save their lives not a single person was left alive. From Ameer al-Momineen's army only eight persons fell as martyrs. The battle took place on the 9th Safar, 38 A.H.

to falsify him. I looked at my affairs and found that my obedience should have precedence over my allegiance while my pledge with him is a burden on my neck.

SERMONS 38

Naming of Doubt as such and Disparagement of those in Doubt

Doubt is named doubt because it resembles truth. As for lovers of Allah, their conviction serves them as light and the direction of the right path (itself) serves as their guide; while the enemies of Allah, in time of doubt call to misguidance in the darkness of doubt and their guide is blindness (of intelligence). One who fears death cannot escape it nor can one who fears for eternal life secure it.

SERMONS 39

In Disparagement of those who Shrink from Fighting

I am faced with men who do not obey when I order and do not respond when I call them. May you have no father! (Woe to you!) What are you waiting for to rise for the cause of Allah? Does not faith join you together, or sense of shame rouse you? I stand among you shouting and I am calling you for help, but you do not listen to my word, and do not obey my orders, till circumstances show out their bad consequences. No blood can be avenged through you and no purpose can be achieved with you. I called you for help of your brethren but made noises like the camel having pain in stomach, and became loose like the camel of thin back. Then a wavering weak contingent came to me from amongst you:

as if they are being led to death and they are only watching[1] (Quraan, 8:6)

-1- Moaawiya sent a contingent of two thousand soldiers under an-Nomaan bn Basheer to assault Aynot-Tamr. This place was a defence base of Ameer al-Momineen near Koofa whose in charge was Malik bn Kab al-Arhabi. Although there were a thousand combatants under him, but at the moment only hundred men were present there. When Malik noticed the offensive force advancing he wrote to Ameer al-Momineen for help.

Sayyid Razi says: Ameer al-Momineen's word "motazaib" means "modtarib" (i.e. moved or troubled), as they say "tazaabat arrih" (i.e. the winds blow in troubled manner). Similarly the wolf is called "zib" because of its troubled movement.

SERMONS 40

In reply to the slogan of Kharijites: "No Verdict Save Allah

The sentence is right but what (they think) it means, is wrong. It is true that verdict lies but with Allah, but these people say that (the function of) governance is only for Allah. The fact is that there is no escape for men from ruler good or bad. The faithful persons perform (good) acts in his rule while the unfaithful enjoys (worldly) benefits in it. During the rule, Allah would carry everything to end. Through the ruler tax is collected, enemy is fought, roadways are protected and the right of the weak is taken from the strong till the virtuous enjoys peace and allowed protection from (the oppression of) the wicked.

When Ameer al-Momineen received the message he asked the people for his help but only three hundred men got ready as a result of which Ameer al-Momineen was much disgusted and delivered this sermon in their admonition. When Ameer al-Momineen reached his house after delivering the sermon Adi bn Hatim at-Tai came and said "O Ameer al-Momineen a thousand men of Bani-Tayyi" are under me. If you say I shall send them off" Ameer al-Momineen said "It does not look nice that people of one tribe only should meet the enemy. You prepare your force in the Valley of an-Nokhayla" Accordingly he went there and called people to Jihaad, when besides Bani-Tayyi" one thousand other combatants also assembled. They were still preparing to set off when word reached from Malik bn Kab that there was no need for help as he had repulsed the enemy.

The reason of this was that Malik had sent off Abdillah bn Hawala al-Azdi hastily to Qaraza bn Kab al-Ansaari and Mikhnaf bn Solaym al-Azdi so that if there was delay in the arrival of support from Koofa he could get help from here in time. Abdillah went to both, but got no help from Qaraza. However, Mikhnaf bn Solaym got ready fifty persons under Abdr-Rahmaan bn Mikhnaf and they reached there near evening. Upto that time the two thousand men (of the enemy) had not been able to subdue the hundred men of Malik. When an-Nomaan saw these fifty men he thought that their forces had started coming in so he fled away from the battlefield. Even in their retreat Malik attacked them from rear and killed three of their men.

When Ameer al-Momineen heard the cry of the Kharijites on the said verdict he said:

I am expecting the verdict (destiny) of Allah on you.

Then he continued:

As for good government the pious man performs good acts in it, while in a bad government the wicked person enjoys till his time is over and death overtakes him.

SERMONS 41

In Condemnation of Treason

O people! Surely fulfillment of pledge is the twin of truth. I do not know a better shield (against the assaults of sin) than it. One who realises the reality of return (to the next world) never betrays. We are in a period when most of the people regard betrayal as wisdom. In these days the ignorants call it excellence of cunning. What is the matter with them? Allah may destroy them. One who has been through thick and thin of life finds the excuses to be preventing him from orders and prohibitions of Allah but he disregards them despite capability (to succumb to them and follows the commands of Allah), while one who has no restraints of religion seizes the opportunity (and accepts the excuses for not following the commands of Allah).

SERMONS 42

Heart's Desires and Hopes

O people what I fear most about you are two things — acting according to desires and extending of hopes. As regards acting according to desires, this prevents from truth; and as regards extending of hopes, it makes one forget the next world. You should know this world is moving rapidly and nothing has remained out of it except last particles like the dregs of a vessel which has been emptied by someone. Beware, the next world is advancing, and either of them has sons i. e. followers. You should become sons of the next world and not become sons of this world because on the Day of Judgement every son would cling to his mother. Today is the Day of action and there is no reckoning while tomorrow is the Day of reckoning but there would be no (opportunity for) action.

Sayyid Razi says: "al-hazza" means rapid but some people have read it "jazza" ". According to this version the meaning would be that the cycle of worldly enjoyments would end soon.

SERMONS 43

In Reply to a Suggestion of War

After Ameer al-Momineen had sent Jareer bn-Abdillah al-Bajali to Moaawiya (for securing his allegiance) some of his companions suggested preparation to fight against him then, he said:

My preparation for war with the people of Syria (Sham) while Jareer bn-Abdillah al-Bajali is still there would be closing the door for Syria and prevention of its people from good action (i.e. allegiance) if they intend doing it. However, I have fixed a time limit for Jareer after which he would not stay without either deception or in disobedience. My opinion is in favour of patience, so wait a while. (In the meantime) I do not dislike your getting ready.

I have observed this matter thoroughly from all sides but I do not find any way except war or heresy. Certainly, there was over the people a ruler (before me) who brought about new (unIslamic) things and compelled the people to speak out. So they did speak, then rose up and thereafter changed the whole system.

SERMONS 44

When Masqala fled away to Moaawiya

Masqala[1] bn-Hobayra ash-Shaybani had purchased some prisoners of Bani-Najiyya from an executive of Ameer al-Momineen, when the price he was demanded, he avoided and fled to Syria.

-1- When after Arbitration the Kharijites rose, a man of Bani-Najiyya from them named al-Khirrit bn Rasheed an-Naji stood up for instigating people and set off towards al-Madain with a group killing and marauding. Ameer al-Momineen sent Ziyad bn Khasaafa with three hundred men to check him. When the two forces met at al-Madain they attacked each other with swords. Only one encounter or so had taken place when the gloom of evening prevailed and the battle had to be stopped. When morning appeared Ziyad's men noticed that five dead bodies of the Kharijites were lying and they themselves had cleared off the battlefield. Seeing this Ziyad set off for Basra along with his men. There he came to know that the Kharijites had gone to Ahwaaz. Ziyad did not move onwards for paucity of force and informed Ameer al-Momineen of it. Ameer al-Momineen called back Ziyad and sent Maqil bn Qays ar-Riyahi with two thousand experienced combatants towards Ahwaaz and wrote to the governor of Basra Abdillah bn Abbas to send two thousand swordsmen of Basra for the help of Maqil. Consequently, the contingent from Basra also joined them at Ahwaaz and after proper organisation they got ready for attacking the enemy. But al-Khirrit marched on along with his men to the hills of Ramhormoz. These people also followed him and overtook him near these hills. Both arrayed their forces and started attacking each other. The result of this encounter was also that three hundred and seventy Kharijites were killed in the battlefield while the rest ran away. Maqil informed Ameer al-Momineen of his performance and of the enemy's running away when Ameer al-Momineen directed him to chase them and so to shatter their power that they should not be able to raise heads again. On receipt of this order he moved on and overtook him on the coast of the Persian gulf where al-Khirrit had by persuasion secured the co-operation of the people and enlisting men from here and there, had collected a considerable force. When Maqil reached there, he raised the flag of peace and announced that those who had collected from here and there should get away. They would not be molested. The effect of this announcement was that save for his own community all others deserted him. He organised those very men and commenced the battle but valorous combatants of Basra and Koofa displayed such excellent use of swords that in a short time one hundred and seventy men of the insurgents were killed while an-Nomaan bn Sohban ar-Rasibi encountered al-Khirrit (bn Rasheed an-Naji) and eventually felled him and killed him. Soon upon his fall the enemy lost ground and they fled away from the battlefield. Thereafter Maqil collected all the men, women and children from their camps at one place. From among them those who were Moslims were released after swearing of allegiance. Those who had turned heretics

Allah may be bad to Masqala. He acted like the noble but fled away like a slave. Before his admirer could speak (about him) he silenced him and before his eulogist could testify to his good deeds he closed his mouth. If he had stayed behind we would have taken from him what he could easily pay and waited for the balance till his money increased.

SERMONS 45

Allah's Greatness and Lowliness of this World

Praise is due to Allah from Whose mercy no one loses hope, from Whose bounty no one is deprived, from Whose forgiveness no one is disappointed and for Whose worship no one is too high. His mercy never ceases and His bounty is never missed.

This world is a place for which destruction is ordained and for its inhabitants departure from here is destined. It is sweet and green. It hastens towards its seeker and attaches to the heart of the viewer. So depart from here with the best of provision available with you and do not

---

were called upon to resume Islam. Consequently except one old Christian all others secured release by accepting Islam and this old man was killed. Then he took with him those Christians of Bani-Najiyya who had taken part in this revolt together with their families. When Maqil reached Ardasheer Khorra (a city of Iran) these prisoners wailed and cried, before its governor Masqala bn Hobayra ash-Shaybani and beseeched humiliatively to do something for their release. Masqala sent word to Maqil through Zohl bn Haarith to sell these prisoners to him. Maqil agreed and sold those prisoners to him for five hundred thousand Dirhams and told him to dispatch the price immediately to Ameer al-Momineen. He said that he was sending the first instalment at once and the remaining instalments would also be sent soon. When Maqil met Ameer al-Momineen he related the whole event before him. Ameer al-Momineen ratified this action and waited for the price for some time, but Masqala observed such deep silence as if nothing was due from him. At last Ameer al-Momineen sent a messenger to him and sent him word to either send the price or to come himself. On Ameer al-Momineen's order he came to Koofa and on demand of the price paid two hundred thousand Dirhams but to evade the balance went away to Moaawiya's who made him the governor of Tabaristan. When Ameer al-Momineen came to know all this he spoke these words (as in this sermon). Its sum total is that, "If he had stayed we would have been considerate to him in demanding the price and would have waited for improvement of his financial condition, but he fled away like slaves after displaying a showy act. Talk about his high perseverance had just started when people began to discuss his baseless and lowliness."

ask herein more than what is enough and do not demand from it more than subsistence.

SERMONS 46

When he decided to march towards Syria

My Allah, I seek Thy protection from the hardships of journey, from the grief of returning and from the scene of devastation of property and men. O Allah, Thou art the companion in journey and Thou art one who is left behind for (protection of the) family. None except Thee can join these two because one who is left behind cannot be a companion in journey nor one who is in company on a journey can at the same time be left behind.
Sayyid Razi says: The earlier part of this sermon is related from the Prophet but Ameer al-Momineen has completed it very aptly by adding most eloquent sentences at the end. This addition is from "None except Thee can join" upto the end.

SERMONS 47

Calamities befalling Koofa

O Koofa, as though I see you being drawn like the tanned leather of Okaazi[1] in the market, you are being scraped by calamities and being ridden by severe troubles. I certainly[2] know that if any tyrant intends evil

-1- During pre-Islamic days a market used to be organised every year near Mecca. Its name was Okaz where mostly hides were traded as a result of which leather was attributed to it. Besides sale and purchase literary meetings were also arranged and Arabs used to attract admiration by reciting their works. After Islam, because of the better congregation in the shape of Haj this market went down.

-2- This prophecy of Ameer al-Momineen was fulfilled word by word and the world saw how the people who had committed tyranny and oppression on the strength of their masterly power had to face tragic end and what ways of their destruction were engendered by their blood-shedding and homicidal activities. Consequently, the end of Ziyad bn abih (son of unknown father) was that when he intended to deliver a speech for vilification of Ameer al-Momineen suddenly paralysis overtook him and he could not get out of his bed thereafter. The end of the bloodshed perpetrated by Obaydillah bn Ziyad

for you Allah will afflict him with worry and fling him with a killer (set someone on him to kill him).

SERMONS 48

At the time of marching towards Syria

Praise is due to Allah when night spreads and darkens, and praise be to Allah whenever the star shines and sets. And praise be to Allah whose bounty never misses and whose favours cannot be repaid.

Well, I have sent forward my vanguard[1] and have ordered them to remain in camp on this bank of the River till my order reaches them. My intention is that I should cross this water over to the small habitation of people residing on the sides of the Tigris and rouse them to march with you towards the enemy and keep them as auxiliary force for you.

Sayyid Razi says: Here by "mitat" Ameer al-Momineen has meant the direction where he had ordered the men to camp and that was the bank of the Euphrates, and "mitat" is used for the bank of a river although its literal meaning is level ground whereas by "nutfa" he means the water of the Euphrates, and these are amazing expressions.

---

was that he fell a prey to leprosy and eventually blood thirsty swords put him to death. The ferocity of al-Hajjaj bn Yoosof ath-Thaqafi drove him to the fate that snakes cropped up in his stomach as a result of which he died after severe pain. Omar bn Hobayra al-Fazari died of leucoderma. Khaalid bn Abdillah al-Qasri suffered the hardships of prison and was killed in a very bad way. Mosab bn Zobayr and Yazeed bn Mohallab bn Abi-Sofra were also killed by swords.

-1- Ameer al-Momineen delivered this sermon when he camped at the Valley of an-Nokhayla on Wednesday the 5th Shawwal 37 A.H. on his way to Siffeen. The Vanguard mentioned herein means the twelve thousand persons whom he had sent towards Siffeen under the command of Ziyad bn Nadr and Shorayh bn Haani, while the small force of al-Madain mentioned by him was a contingent of twelve hundred men who had come up in response to Ameer al-Momineen's call.

SERMONS 49

Allah's Greatness and Sublimity

Praise be to Allah Who lies inside all hidden things, and towards Whom all open things guide. He cannot be seen by the eye of an onlooker, but the eye which does not see Him cannot deny Him while the mind that proves His existence cannot perceive Him. He is so high in sublimity that nothing can be more sublime than He, while in nearness, He is so near that no one can be nearer than He. But his sublimity does not put Him at a distance from anything of His creation, nor does His nearness bring them on equal level to Him. He has not informed (human) wit about the limits of His qualities. Nevertheless, He has not prevented it from securing essential knowledge of Him. So he is such that all signs of existence stand witness for Him till the denying mind also believes in Him. Allah is sublime beyond what is described by those who liken Him to things or those who deny Him.

SERMONS 50

Admixture of Right and Wrong

The basis of the occurrence of evils are those desires which are acted upon and the orders that are innovated. They are against the Book of Allah. People co-operate with each other about them even though it is against the Religion of Allah. If wrong had been pure and unmixed it would not be hidden from those who are in search of it. And if right had been pure without admixture of wrong those who bear hatred towards it would have been silenced. What is, however, done is that something is taken from here and something from there and the two are mixed! At this stage Satan overpowers his friends and they alone escape for whom virtue has been apportioned by Allah from before.

SERMONS 51

When his men were prevented from taking water from the River Euphrates

When in Siffeen the men of Moaawiya overpowered the men of Ameer al-Momineen and occupied the bank of river Euphrates and prevented them from taking water, Ameer al-Momineen said:

They[1] are asking you morsels of battle. So either you remain in ignominy and the lowest position or drench your swords with blood and quench your thirst with water. Real death is in the life of subjugation while real life is in dying as subjugators. Beware, Moaawiya is leading a small group of insurgents and has kept them in dark about the true facts with the result that they have made their bosoms the targets of death.

-1- Ameer al-Momineen had not reached Siffeen when Moaawiya posted forty thousand men on the bank of the River to close the way to the watering place, so that none except the Syrians could take the water. When Ameer al-Momineen's force alighted there they found that there was no watering place except this one for them to take water. If there was one it was difficult to reach there by crossing high hillocks. Ameer al-Momineen sent Sasaa bn Soohan al-Abdi to Moaawiya with the request to raise the control over water. Moaawiya refused. On this side Ameer al-Momineen's army was troubled by thirst. When Ameer al-Momineen noticed this position he said "Get up and secure water by dint of sword" Consequently, these thirsty persons drew their swords out of sheaths, put arrows in their bows and dispersing Moaawiya's men went right down into the River and then hit these guards away and occupied the watering place themselves.

Now, Ameer al-Momineen's men also desired that just as Moaawiya had put restriction on water by occupation of the watering place, the same treatment should be accorded to him and his men and no Syrian should be allowed water and everyone of them should be made to die of thirst. But Ameer al-Momineen said "Do you want to take the same brutal step which these Syrians had taken? Never prevent anyone from water. Whoever wants to drink, may drink and whoever wants to take away may take away" Consequently, despite occupation of the River by Ameer al-Momineen's army no one was prevented from the water and everyone was given full liberty to take water.

SERMONS 52

Reward and Punishment in the next World

(This sermon has already appeared earlier but due to the difference between the two versions we have quoted it again here).

Beware, the world is wrapping itself up and has announced its departure. Its known things have become strangers and it is speedily moving backward. It is advancing its inhabitants towards destruction and driving its neighbours towards death. Its sweet things (enjoyments) have become sour, and its clear things have become polluted. Consequently, what has remained of it is just like the remaining water in a vessel or a mouthful of water in the measure. If a thirsty person drinks it his thirst is not quenched.

O creatures of Allah get ready to go out of this world for whose inhabitants decay is ordained, and (beware) heart's wishes should overpower you, nor should you take your stay (in life) to be long. By Allah, if you cry like the she-camel that has lost its young one, call out like the cooing of pigeons, make noise like devoted recluses and turn to Allah leaving your wealth and children as a means to secure His nearness and high position with Him or the forgiveness of sins which have been covered by His books and recorded by His angels it would be less than His reward that I expect for you or His retribution that I fear about you.

By Allah, if your hearts melt down thoroughly and your eyes shed tears of blood either in hope for Him or for fear from Him and you are also allowed to live in this world all the time that it lasts even then your actions cannot pay for His great bounties over you and His having guided you towards faith.

Qualities of the animal meant for sacrifice (on Eed al-Azha)

For an animal to be fully fit for sacrifice it is necessary that both its ears should be raised upwards and its eyes should be healthy. If the ears and the eyes are sound the animal of sacrifice is sound and perfect, even though its horn be broken or it drags its feet to the place of sacrifice.

Sayyid Razi says: Here place of sacrifice means place of slaughter.

SERMONS 53

On the Swear of Allegiance

They leapt upon me as the camels leap upon each other on their arrival for drinking water, having been let loose after unfastening of their four legs till I thought they would either kill me or kill one another in front of me. I thought over this matter in and out to the extent that it prevented me from sleeping. But I found no way except to fight them or else to reject whatever has been brought by Mohammad (p.b.u.h.a.h.p). I found that to face war was easier for me than to face the retribution, and the hardships of this world were easier than the hardships of the next world.

SERMONS 54

When his men showed impatience on his delay in giving them permission to fight in Siffeen

Well, as for your idea whether this (delay) is due to my unwillingness for death, then by Allah I do not care whether I proceed towards death or death advances towards me. As for your impression that it may be due to my misgivings about the people of Syria (Sham), well by Allah, I did not put off war even for a day except in the hope that some group may join me, find guidance through me and see my light with their weak eyes. This is dearer to me than to kill them in the state of their misguidance although they would be bearing their own sins.

SERMONS 55

Steadiness in the Battlefield

In the company of the Prophet of Allah (p.b.u.h.) we used to fight our parents, sons, brothers and uncles, and this continued us in our faith, in submission, in our following the right path, in endurance over the pangs of pain and in our fight against the enemy. A man from our side and one from the enemy would pounce upon each other like energetic men contesting as to who would kill the other; sometime our man got over his adversary and some-time the enemy's man got over ours.

When Allah had observed our truth He sent ignominy to our foe and sent His succor to us till Islam got established (like the camel) with neck on the ground and resting in its place. By my life, if we had also behaved like you, no pillar of (our) religion could have been raised, nor the tree of faith could have borne leaves. By Allah, certainly you will now milk our blood (instead of milk) and eventually you will face shame.[1]

-1- When Mohammad bn Abi-Bakr had been killed Moaawiya sent Abdillah bn Amir al-Hazrami to Basra to exhort the people of Basra for avenging Othmaan's blood because the natural inclination of most of the inhabitants of Basra and particularly of Bani-Tameem was towards Othmaan. Consequently, he stayed with Bani-Tameem. This was the time when Abdillah bn Abbas, the governor of Basra had gone to Koofa for condolence about Mohammad bn Abi-Bakr, leaving Ziyad bn Obayd (Abih) as his substitute. When the atmosphere in Basra began to deteriorate Ziyad informed Ameer al-Momineen of all the facts. Ameer al-Momineen tried to get Bani-Tameem of Koofa ready but they kept complete silence and gave no reply. When Ameer al-Momineen saw this weakness and shamelessness on their part he gave this speech namely that "During the days of the Prophet (p.b.u.h.) we did not see whether those killed at our hands were our kith and kin, but whoever collided with Right, we were prepared to collide with him. If we too had acted carelessly or been guilty of inaction like you then neither religion could have taken root nor could Islam prosper. "The result of this shaking was that Ayan bn Dabia al-Mojashii prepared himself but on reaching Basra he was killed by the swords of the enemy. Thereafter, Ameer al-Momineen sent off Jariya bn Qudama as-Saadi with fifty men of Bani-Tameem. First he tried his best to canvass his own tribe but instead of following the right path they stooped down to abusing and fighting. Then Jariya called Ziyad and the tribe of Azd for his help. Soon on their arrival (Abdillah) bn al-Hazrami also came out with his men. Swords were used from both sides for some time but eventually bn al-Hazrami fled away with seventy persons and took refuge in the house of Sabil as-Saadi. When Jariya saw no other way he got this house set on fire. When fire rose into flames they came out in search of safety but could not succeed in running away. Some of them were crushed to death under the wall while others were killed.

SERMONS 56

Moaawiya swallows whatever he gets and crave for what he does not get

Soon after me there would be put on you a man with a broad mouth and a big belly. He would swallow whatever he gets and would crave for what he does not get. You should kill him but (I know) you would not kill him. He would command you to abuse me and to renounce me. As for abusing, you do abuse me because that would mean purification for me and salvation for you. As regards renunciation, you should not renounce me because I have been born on the natural religion (Islam) and was foremost in accepting it as well as in hijra (migrating from Mecca to Madeena).[1]

-1- About the person to whom Ameer al-Momineen has alluded in this sermon some people hold that he is Ziyad bn abih; some hold that he is al-Hajjaj bn Yoosof ath-Thaqafi and some hold that he is Mogheera bn Shoba. But most of the commentators have held him to be Moaawiya and this is correct because the qualities that Ameer al-Momineen has described prove true fully on him alone. Thus bn-Abil-Hadeed has written about the gluttonous quality of Moaawiya that once the prophet sent for him and he was informed that Moaawiya was busy eating. Then a second and third time a man was sent to call him but he brought the same news. Thereupon the Prophet said “May Allah never satisfy his belly” The effect of this curse was that when he felt tired of eating he would say, “Take away, for, by Allah I am not satiated but I am tired and disgusted” Similarly, his abusing Ameer al-Momineen and ordering his officers for it are such accepted facts of history about which there is no scope of denying. In this connection such words were used on the pulpit that even Allah and the Prophet were hit by them. Thus, Om-al-Momineen Om-Salama wrote to Moaawiya, “Certainly you people abuse Allah and the Prophet, and this is like this that you hurl abuses on Ali and those who love him, while I do stand witness that Allah and the Prophet did love him” (al-Iqd al-Fareed, vol.3, p.131)

Thanks to Omar bn Abdl-Aziz who put a stop to it, and introduced the following verse in place of abuse in the sermons:

Verily Allah enjoineth justice and benevolence (to others) and giving unto the kindred, and forbidden lewdness, and evil, and rebellion; He exhorteth you that ye may take heed (Quraan 16:90)

In this sermon Ameer al-Momineen has ordered his killing on the basis of the Prophet’s order that “When you (O” Moslims) see Moaawiya on my pulpit, kill him” (Kitaab Siffeen, pp.243, 248; Sharh of bn-Abil-Hadeed, vol.1, p.348; Taareekh Baghdad, vol.12, p.181; Mizan al-Etidal, vol.2, p.128; Tahzeeb at-Tahzeeb, vol.2, p.428; vol.5, p.110; vol.7, p.324)

SERMONS 57

Addressing the Kharijites

Storm may overtake you while there may be none to prick you (for reforms). Shall I be witness to my becoming heretic after acceptance of Faith and fighting in the company of the Prophet?

In that case I shall be misguided and I shall not be on the right path." (Quran, 6:56).

So you should return to your evil places, and get back on the traces of your heels. Beware! Certainly you will meet, after me, overwhelming disgrace and sharp sword and tradition that will be adopted by the oppressors as a norm towards you.[1]

Sayyid Razi says: In the words "wala baqiya minkom abirun" used by Ameer al-Momineen the "abir" has been related with "ba" and "ra" and it has been taken from the Arab saying "rajulun abirun" which means the man who prunes the date-palm trees and improves them. In one version the word is "athir" and its meaning is "relater of good news." In my view this is more appropriate, as though Ameer al-Momineen intends to say

---

-1- History corroborates that after Ameer al-Momineen, the Kharijites had to face all sorts of ignominy and disgrace and wherever they raised their heads for creating trouble, they were met with swords and spears. Thus Ziyad bn abih, Obaydillah bn Ziyad, al-Hajjaj bn Yoosof, Mosab bn Zobayr and al-Mohallab bn Abi-Sofra left no stone unturned in annihilating them from the surface of the globe, particularly al-Mohallab chased them for nineteen years, routed them thoroughly and rested only after completing their destruction.

At-Tabari writes that when ten thousand Kharijites collected in Silla wa Sillibra (the name of a mountain in Ahwaaz) then al-Mohallab faced them so steadfastly that he killed seven thousand Kharijites, while the remaining three thousand fled towards Kirman for life. But when the Governor of Persia noticed their rebellious activities he surrounded them in Sabor and killed a good number of them then and there. Those remained again fled to Isfahaan and Kirman. From there they again formed a contingent and advanced towards Koofa via Basra. Al-Haarith bn Abi Rabeea al-Makhzoomi and Abdr-Rahmaan bn Mikhnaf al-Azdi stood up with six thousand combatants to stop their advance, and turned them out of Iraq's boundaries. In this way successive encounters completely trampled their military power and turning them out of cities compelled them to roam about in the deserts. Afterwards also, when they rose in the form of groups they were crushed. (at-Taareekh, vol.2, pp.580-591); bn al-Athir, vol.4, pp.196-206).

that there should remain none to carry news. In one version the word appears as "abiz" with "za" which means one who leaps. One who dies is also called "abiz.

SERMONS 58

When he was told that the Kharijites had crossed the bridge of Nahrawan

Their falling place is on this side of the river. By Allah, not even ten of them will survive while from your side not even ten will be killed.[1]
Sayyid Razi says: In this sermon "nutfa" implies the River Euphrates, and for water this is the nicest expression, even though water may be much.

SERMONS 59

When he was told that the Kharijites had been totally killed

By Allah, no, not yet. They still exist in the loins of men and wombs of women. Whenever a chief would appear from among them, he would be cut down till the last of them would turn thieves and robbers.[2]

-1- This prophecy cannot be attributed to wit and farsightedness, because farsighted eyes may forecast victory or defeat and preconceive the outcome of war but to tell about the correct figures of the killed on either side is beyond their capacity. This can be done only by one who can unveil the unknown future and see the coming scene with his eyes and who sees the sketches yet to appear on the page of the future with the help of the light of knowledge possessed by him as Imam.
Consequently, events occurred just according to what this inheritor of the Prophet's knowledge had said, and from among the Kharijites all except nine persons were killed. Two of them fled away to Oman, two to Sijistan, two to Kirman and two to al-Jazira while one escaped to Tall-Mawzan. Of Ameer al-Momineen's party only eight men fell as martyrs.
-2- This prophecy of Ameer al-Momineen also proved true word by word. Every chief of Kharijites who rose was put to sword. A few of their chiefs who were badly put to death are mentioned here:
1) Naafi" bn Azraq al-Hanafi: the largest group of the Kharijites namely al-Azariqa is named after him. He was killed by Salama al-Bahili during encounter with the army of Moslim bn Obays.

SERMONS 60

Do not fight the Kharijites after me!

Do not fight[1] the Kharijites after me, because one, who seeks right but does not find it, is not like one who seeks wrong and finds it.

---

2) Najda bn Amir: the an-Najadat al-Aziriyya sect of Kharijites is named after him. Abo-Fodayk al-Khaariji got him killed.
3) Abdillah bn Ibad at-Tameemi: the sect Ibadite (Ibadiyya) is named after him. He was killed during encounter with Abdillah bn Mohammad bn Atiyya.
4) Abo-Bayhas Haytham bn Jabir-ad-Zabaai: the sect of al-Bayhasiyya is named after him. Othmaan bn Hayyan al-Morri the governor of Madeena got his hands and feet severed and then killed him.
5) Orwa bn Odayya at-Tameemi: Ziyad bn abih killed him during the reign of Moaawiya.
6) Qatari bn Fojah al-Mazini at-Tameemi: when he encountered the army of Sofyaan bn Abrad al-Kalbi in Tabaristan then Sawra bn Horr ad-Darimi killed him.
7) Abo-Bilaal Mirdas bn Odayya at-Tameemi: was killed in encounter with Abbas bn Akhdar al-Mazini.
8) Shawzab al-Khariji al-Yashkori: was killed during encounter with Saeed bn Amr al-Harashi.
9) Hawthara bn Wada" al-Asadi: was killed at the hands of a man of Bani-Tayyi
10) al-Mostawrid bn Ollafah at-Taymi: was killed by Maqil bn Qays ar-Riyahi in the reign of Moaawiya.
11) Shibeeb bn Yazeed ash-Shaybani: died by being drowned in river.
12) Imraan bn Haarith ar-Rasibi: was killed in the battle of Dolab.
13, 14) Zahhaaf at-Taii and Qorayb bn Morral-Azdi: were killed in encounter with Bani-Taiyya.
15) az-Zobayr bn Ali as-Saliti at-Tameemi: was killed in encounter with Attab bn Warqa ar-Riyahi.
16) Ali bn Basheer al-Yarbooi: al-Hajjaj bn Yoosof ath-Thaqafi got him killed.
17) Obaydillah bn Basheer: was killed in encounter with al-Mohallab bn Abi-Sofra in the battle of Dolab.
18) Abol-Wazi" ar-Rasibi: a man in the graveyard of Bani-Yashkor felled a wall on him and killed him.
19) Abdo-Rabbih as-Sagheer: was killed in encounter with al-Mohallab bn Abi-Sofra.
20) Al-Waleed bn Tareef ash-Shaybani: was killed in encounter with Yazeed bn Mazyad ash-Shaybani.
21-24) Abdillah bn Yahya al-Kindi, al-Mokhtaar bn Awf al-Azdi (Abo-Hamza ash-Shari) , Abraha bn Sabbah and Balj bn Oqba al-Asadi: were killed by Abdl-Malik bn Atiyya as-Saadi in the reign of Marwaan bn Mohammad (the last of the Omayyad caliphs).
-1- The reason for stopping people from fighting the Kharijites was that Ameer al-Momineen was clearly perceiving that after him authority and power would devolve on

Sayyid Razi says: Ameer al-Momineen means Moaawiya and his men.

SERMONS 61

When he was warned of being killed by deceit

Surely, there is a strong shield of Allah over me. When my day would come it would get away from me and hand me over to death. At that time neither an arrow would go amiss nor a wound would heal up.

SERMONS 62

Transience of this World

Beware! Surely this world is a place from which protection cannot be sought except while one is in it. The action, which is performed only for this world, cannot secure salvation. People are tested in it through

---

people who would be ignorant of the proper occasion of Jihaad, and who will make use of sword only to maintain their sway. And there were those who excelled even Kharijites in holding and calling Ameer al-Momineen bad. So those who are themselves in the wrong have no right to fight others in the wrong. Again, those who are wilfully in the wrong can be allowed to fight those who are in the wrong by mistake. Thus, Ameer al-Momineen's words make this fact clear that the misguidance of Kharijites was not wilful but under Satan's influence. They mistook wrong as right and stuck to it. On the other hand, the position of misguidance of Moaawiya and his party was that they rejected right realising it as right and appropriated wrong as the code of their conduct fully knowing that it was wrong. Their audacity in the matter of religion reached the stage that it can neither be regarded as a result of misunderstanding nor can it be covered under the garb of error of judgement, because they openly transgressed the limits of religion and paid no heed to the Prophet's injunctions in comparison with their own view. Thus, bn-Abil-Hadeed has written (vol.5, p.130) that when the Prophet's companion Abo-d-Darda" saw utensils of gold and silver being used by Moaawiya he said he had heard the Prophet saying, "One who drinks in vessels of gold and silver will feel flames of the fire of Hell in his stomach" whereupon Moaawiya said "As for me, I do not find any harm in it" Similarly, creating Ziyad bn abih's blood relationship with himself by his own opinion in total disregard of the Prophet's injunction, abusing the descendants of the Prophet over the pulpit, transgressing the limits of sharia, shedding blood of innocent persons and placing over Moslims (as so called Khaleefa) a vicious individual and thus opening the way to disbelief and atheism are events that to attribute them to any misunderstanding is like wilfully closing eyes to facts.

calamities. Those who have taken worldly pleasures here will be taken out from them (by death) and will be questioned about them. And whatever (good actions) they have achieved for the other world, they will get them there and stay in them. For the intelligent this world is like the shade — one moment it is spread out and extended but soon it shrinks and contracts.

SERMONS 63

Decline and Destruction of this World

O creatures of Allah! Fear Allah and anticipate your death by good actions. Purchase everlasting joy by paying transitory things — pleasures of this world. Get ready for the journey, for you are being driven, and prepare yourselves for death, since it is hovering over you. Be a people who wake up when called, and who know that this world is not their abode, and so have it changed (with the next).

Certainly, Allah has not created you aimlessly nor left you as useless. There is nothing between anyone of you and Paradise or Hell except death that must befall him. The life that is being shortened every moment and being dismantled every hour must be regarded very short. The hidden thing namely death which is being driven (to you) by two over new phenomena, the day and the night, is certainly quick of approach. The traveler which is approaching with success or failure (namely death) deserves the best of provision. So acquire such provision from this world while you are here with which you may shield yourself tomorrow (on the Day of Judgment).

So everyone should fear Allah, should admonish himself, should send forward his repentance and should overpower his desire, because his death is hidden from him, his desires deceive him and Satan is posted on him and he beautifies for him sin so that he may commit it and prompts him to delay repentance till his desires make him the most negligent. Piety is for the negligent person whose life itself would be a proof against him and his own days (passed in sin) would lead him to punishment.

We ask Allah, the Glorified, that He may make us and you like one whom bounty does not mislead, whom nothing can stop from obedience of Allah and whom shame and grief do not befall after death.

SERMONS 64

Allah's Attributes

Praise be to Allah for Whom one condition does not proceed another so that He may be the First before being the Last or He may be Manifest before being Hidden. Everyone called one (alone) save Him is by virtue of being small (in number); and everyone enjoying honor other than Him is humble. Every powerful person other than Him is weak. Every master (owner) other than Him is slave (owned).

Every knower other than Him is seeker of knowledge. Every controller other than Him is sometimes imbued with control and sometimes with disability. Every listener other than Him is deaf to light voices while loud voices make him deaf and distant voices also get away from him. Every onlooker other than Him is blind to hidden colors and delicate bodies. Every manifest thing other than Him is hidden, but every hidden thing other than Him is incapable of becoming manifest.

He did not create what He created to fortify His authority nor for fear of the consequences of time, nor to seek help against the attack of an equal or a boastful partner or a hateful opponent. On the other hand all the creatures are reared by him and are His humbled slaves. He is not conditioned in anything so that it be said that He exists therein, nor is He separated from anything so as to be said that He is away from it. The creation of what He initiated or the administration of what He controls did not fatigue Him. No disability overtook Him against what He created. No misgiving ever occurred to Him in what He ordained and resolved. But His verdict is certain, His knowledge is definite, His governance is overwhelming. He is wished for at time of distress and He is feared even in bounty.

SERMONS 65

Ways of Fighting

Delivered during the days of Siffeen to his followers

O crowd of Moslims! Make fear of Allah the routine of your life. Cover yourselves with peace of mind and clinch your teeth because this makes the sword slip off from the skull. Complete your armour and shake your swords in their sheathes before showing them out. Have your eyes on the enemy. Use your spears on both sides and strike (the enemy) with swords. Keep in mind that you are before Allah and in the company of the Prophet's cousin. Repeat your attacks and feel ashamed of running away, because it is a shame for posterity and (cause of awarding you) fire on the Day of Judgement. Give your lives (to Allah) willingly and walk towards death with ease. Beware of this great majority, and the pitched tent and aim at its centre because Satan is hiding in its cornet. He has extended his hand for assault and has kept back his foot for running away. Keep one enduring till the light of Truth dawns upon you.

While ye have the upper hand, and Allah is with you, and never will He depreciate your deeds. (Quraan, 47:35)

SERMONS 66

On hearing the account of what took place in Saqeefa of Bani-Saaida

When after the death of the prophet news reached Ameer al-Momineen about the happening in Saqeefa of bani-Saaida,[1] he enquired what the

-1- From what happened in the Saqeefa of Bani-Saaida it appears that the greatest argument of mohaajiroon against Ansaar and the basis of the former's success was this very point that since they were the kith and kin of the Prophet no one else could deserve the Caliphate. On this very ground the big crowd of Ansaar became ready to lay down their weapons before three mohaajiroon, and the latter succeeded in winning the Caliphate by presenting their distinction of descent. Thus in connection with the events of Saqeefa at-Tabari writes that when the Ansaar assembled in Saqeefa of Bani-Saaida to swear allegiance on the hand of Saad bn Obada, somehow Abi-Bakr, Omar and Abo-Obayda bn Jarrah also got the hint and reached there. Omar had thought out something for this occasion and he rose to speak but Abi-Bakr stopped him, and he himself stood up. After praise of Allah and the immigration of the mohaajiroon and their precedence in Islam he said:

They are those who worshipped Allah first of all and accepted belief in Allah and his Prophet's friends and his Kith and Kin. These alone therefore must deserve the Caliphate. Whoever clashes with them commits excess.

When Abi-Bakr finished his speech al-Hobaab bn Monzir stood up and, turning to the Ansaar, he said:

O group of Ansaar! Do not give your reins in the hands of others. The populace is under your care. You are men of honour, wealth and tribe and gathering. If the mohaajiroon have precedence over you in some matters you too have precedence over them in other matters. You gave them refuge in your houses. You are the fighting arm of Islam. With your help Islam stood on its own feet. In your cities prayer of Allah was established with freedom. Save yourselves from division and dispersion and stick to your right unitedly. If the mohaajiroon do not concede to your right tell them there should be one chief from us and one from them

No sooner al-Hobaab sat down after saying this then Omar rose and spoke thus:

This cant be that there be two rulers at one time. By Allah, the Arabs will never agree to have you as the head of the state since the Prophet was not from amongst you. Certainly, the Arabs will not care the least objection in that the Caliphate is allowed to one in whose house Prophethood rests so that the ruler should also be from the same house. For those who dissent clear arguments can be put forth. Whoever comes in conflict with us in the matter of the authority and rulership of Mohammad (p.b.u.h.a.h.p) he is leaning towards wrong, is a sinner and is falling into destruction.

After Omar, al-Hobaab again stood up and said to the Ansaar, "Look, stick to your point and do not pay heed to the views of this man or his supporters. They want to trample your right, if they do not consent turn him and them out of your cities and appropriate the Caliphate. Who else than you can deserve it more? "

When al-Hobaab finished Omar scolded him. There was use of bad words from that side also, and the position began to worsen. On seeing this Abo-Obayda bn Jarrah spoke with the intention of cooling down Ansaar and to win them over to his side and said:

O Ansaar! You are the people who supported us and helped us in every manner. Do not now change your ways and do not give up your behaviour" But the Ansaar refused to change their mind. They were prepared to swear allegiance to Saad and people just wanted to approach him when a man of Saad's tribe Basheer bn Amr al-Khazraji stood up and said:

No doubt we came forward for Jihaad, and gave support to the religion, but our aim in doing thus was to please Allah and to obey His Prophet. It does not behove us to claim superiority and create trouble in the matter of the caliphate. Mohammad (p.b.u.h.a.h.p) was from Quraysh and they have a greater right for it, and are more appropriate for it"

As soon as Basheer uttered these words division occurred among the Ansaar, and this

Ansaar said. People said that they were asking for one chief from among them and one from the others, Ameer al-Momineen said:

Why did you not argue against them (Ansaar) that the Prophet had left his will that whoever is good among Ansaar should be treated well and whoever is bad he should be forgiven. People said: "What is there against them in it? "

Ameer al-Momineen said:

If the Government was for them there should have been no will in their favour

Then he said:

What did the Quraysh plead? "

People said: "They argued that they belong to the lineal tree of the Prophet.

Then Ameer al-Momineen said:

They argued with the tree but spoiled the fruits.

---

was his aim, because he could not see a man of his own tribe rising so high. The mohaajiroon took the best advantage of this division among the Ansaar, and Omar and Abo-Obayda decided to swear allegiance to Abi-Bakr. They had just got forward for the act when Basheer first of all put his hand on that of Abi-Bakr and after that Omar and Abo-Obayda swore the allegiance. Then the people of Basheer's tribe came and swore allegiance, and trampled Saad bn Obada under their feet.

During this time Ameer al-Momineen was occupied in the funeral bath and burial of the Prophet. When afterwards he heard about the assemblage at the Saqeefa and he came to know that the mohaajiroon had won the score over Ansaar by pleading themselves to be from the tribe of the Prophet he uttered the fine sentence that then argued on the lineal tree being one but spoiled its fruits, who are the members of his family. That is, if mohaajiroon's claim was acceded for being from the lineal tree of the Prophet, how can those who are the fruits of this tree be ignored? It is strange that Abi-Bakr who connects with the Prophet in the seventh generation above and Omar who connects with him in the ninth generation above may be held of the tribe and family of the Prophet and he who was his first cousin, he is refused the status of a brother.

SERMONS 67

When Mohammad bn-Abi-Bakr, governor of Egypt, was overpowered and killed[1]

-1- Mohammad bn Abi-Bakr's mother was Asma bnt Omays whom Ameer al-Momineen married after Abi-Bakr's death. Consequently, Mohammad lived and was brought up under the care of Ameer al-Momineen and he imbibed his ways and manners. Ameer al-Momineen too loved him much and regarded him as his son, and used to say "Mohammad is my son from Abi-Bakr" He was born in the journey for the last Haj (of the Prophet) and died as martyr in 38 A.H. at the age of twenty eight years.

On accession to the Caliphate Ameer al-Momineen had selected Qays bn Saad bn Obada as the Governor of Egypt but circumstances so developed that he had to be removed and Mohammad bn Abi-Bakr had to be sent there as Governor. The policy of Qays there was that he did not want to take any serious step against the Othmaani group but Mohammad's view was different. After the lapse of a month he sent them word that in case they did not obey him their existence there would be impossible. Upon this these people organised a front against him, and engaged themselves in secret wire-pullings, but became conspicuous soon. After arbitration they started creating trouble with the slogan of vengeance. This polluted the atmosphere of Egypt. When Ameer al-Momineen came to know these deteriorated conditions he gave the governorship of Egypt to Malik bn Haarith al-Ashtar and sent him off there in order that he might suppress insurgent elements and save the administration from getting worse, but he could not escape the evil designs of the Omayyads and was killed by poison while on his way. Thus, the governorship of Egypt remained with Mohammad bn Abi-Bakr.

On this side, the performance of Amr bn Aas in connection with the Arbitration made Moaawiya recall his own promise. Consequently, he gave him six thousand combatants and set him off to attack Egypt. When Mohammad bn Abi-Bakr knew of the advancing force of the enemy he wrote to Ameer al-Momineen for help. Ameer al-Momineen replied that he would be soon collecting help for him but in the meantime he should mobilise his own forces. Mohammad mobilised four thousand men under his banner and divided them into two parts. He kept one part with himself and on the other he placed Kinana bn Bishr at-Tojibi in command and ordered him to go forward to check the enemy's advance. When they settled down in camp before the enemy various parties of the enemy began attacking them but they faced them with courage and valour. At last Moaawiya al-Kindi made an assault with full force. These people did not turn away from the enemy's swords but faced them steadfastly and fell as martyrs in action. The effect of this defeat was that Mohammad bn Abi-Bakr's men got frightened and deserted him. Finding himself alone Mohammad fled away and sought refuge in a deserted place. The enemy however got news about him through someone and traced him out when he was dying with thirst. Mohammad asked for water but these cruel men refused and butchered him thirsty. Then they put his body in the belly of a dead ass and burnt it.

I had intended to send Hashim bn-Otba to Egypt and had I done so he would have made way for the opponents nor given them time (to get hold of him). This is without reproach to Mohammad bn-Abi-Bakr as I loved him and had brought him up.

SERMONS 68

Admonishing his Companions about Careless Behaviour

How long shall I accord you consideration that is accorded to camels with hollow hump, or to worn clothes which when stitched on one side give way on the other. Whenever a vanguard force of Syria (Sham) hovers over you, everyone of you shuts his door and hides himself like the lizard in its hole or a badger it its den. By Allah, he whom people like you support must suffer disgrace and he who throws arrows with your support is as if he throws arrows that are broken both at head and tail. By Allah, within the courtyard you are quite numerous but under the banner you are only a few. Certainly, I know what can improve you and how your crookedness can be straightened. But I shall not improve your condition by marring myself. Allah may disgrace your faces and destroy you. You do not understand the right as you understand the wrong and do not crush the wrong as you crush the right.

SERMONS 69

Spoken on the morning of the day he was fatally struck with sword

I was sitting when sleep overtook me. I saw the Prophet of Allah appear before me, and I said: "O Prophet of Allah! what crookedness and enmity I had to face from the people." The prophet of Allah said: "Invoke (Allah) evil upon them," but I said "Allah may change them for me with better ones and change me for them with a worse one.

Malik bn Kab al-Arhabi had already left Koofa with two thousand men but before he could reach Egypt it had been occupied by the enemy.

Sayyid Razi says: "al-awad" means crookedness and "al-ladad" means enmity, and this is the most eloquent expression.

SERMONS 70

In Condemnation of the People of Iraq

Now then, O people[1] of Iraq! You are like the pregnant woman who, on completion of the period of pregnancy delivers a dead child and her husband is also dead and her period of widowhood is long while only remote relation inherits her. By Allah, I did not come to you of my own accord. I came to you by force of circumstances. I have come to know that you say Ali speaks lie. May Allah fight you! Against whom do I speak lie? Whether against Allah? But I am the first to have believed in him. Whether against His Prophet? But I am the first who testified to him. Certainly not. By Allah it was a way of expression which you failed to appreciate, and you were not capable of it. Woe to you. I am giving out these measures of nice expression free of any cost. I wish there were vessels good enough to hold them.

Certainly, you will understand it after some time." (Quraan, 38:88)

-1- When after Arbitration the Iraqis displayed lethargy and heartlessness in retaliating the continuous attacks of Moaawiya, Ameer al-Momineen delivered this sermon abusing and admonishing them. Herein he has referred to their being deceived at Siffeen and has likened them to a woman who has five qualities:

i) Firstly, she is pregnant. This implies that these people had full capability to fight, and were not like a barren woman from whom nothing is expected

ii) Secondly, she has completed the period of pregnancy. That is they had passed over all difficult stages and had approached near the final goal of victory.

iii) Thirdly, she wilfully miscarries her child. That is after coming close to victory they came down to settlement and instead of achieving the coveted goal faced disappointment.

iv) Fourthly, her period of widowhood is long. That is they fell in such a state as though they had no protector or patron and they were roaming about without any ruler.

v) Fifthly, her successors would be distant persons. That is the people of Syria who had no relationship with them would occupy their properties.

SERMONS 71

How to seek Divine Blessings on the Prophet (p.b.u.h.a.h.p)

My Allah, the Spreader of the surfaces (of earth) and Keeper (intact) of all skies, Creator of hearts on good and evil nature, send Thy choicest blessings and growing favours on Mohammad Thy servant and Thy Prophet who is the last of those who preceded (him) and an opener for what is closed, proclaimer of truth with truth, repulser of the forces of wrong and crusher of the onslaughts of misguidance. As he was burdened (with responsibility of Prophethood) so he bore it standing by Thy commands, advancing towards Thy will, without shrinking of steps of weakness of determination, listening to Thy revelation, preserving Thy testament, proceeding forward in the spreading of Thy commands till he lit fire for its seeker and lighted the path for the groper in the dark.

Hearts achieved guidance through him after being ridden with troubles. He introduced clearly guiding signs and shining injunctions. He is Thy trusted trustee, the treasurer of Thy treasured knowledge, Thy witness on the Day of Judgement, Thy envoy of truth and Thy Messenger towards the people. My Allah prepare large place for him under Thy shade and award him multiplying good by Thy bounty.

My Allah, give height to his construction above all other constructions, heighten his position with Thee, grant perfection to his effulgence and perfect for him his light. In reward for his discharging Thy prophetship, grant him that his testimony be admitted and his speech be liked for his speech is just, and his judgements are clear-cut. My Allah put us and him together in the pleasures of life, continuance of bounty, satisfaction of desires, enjoyment of pleasures. ease of living, peace of mind and gifts of honour.

SERMONS 72

When Hasan and Hosayn interceded on behalf of Marwaan bn al-Hakam

When Marwaan was taken on the day of Jamal, he asked Hasan and Hosayn (p.b.u.t.) To intercede on his behalf before Ameer al-Momineen. So they spoke to Ameer al-Momineen about him and he released him. Then they said "O Ameer al-Momineen he desires to swear you allegiance" whereupon Ameer al-Momineen said:

Did he not swear me allegiance after the killing of Othmaan? Now I do not need his allegiance, because his is the hand of a Jew. If he swears me allegiance with his hand he would violate it after a short while. Well, he is to get power for so long as a dog licks his nose. He is the father of four rams (who will also rule). The people will face days through him and his sons.[1]

-1- Marwaan bn Hakam was the nephew (brother's son) and son-in-law of Othmaan. Due to thin body and tall stature he was known with the nickname "Khayt Baatil" (the thread of wrong). When Abdl-Malik bn Marwaan killed Amr bn Saeed al-Ashdaq, his brother Yahya bn Saeed said:

O" sons of Khayt Baatil (the thread of the wrong) you have played deceit on Amr and people like you build their houses (of authority) on deceit and treachery.

Although his father al-Hakam bn Abi al-Aas had accepted Islam at the time of the fall of Mecca but his behaviour and activities were very painful to the Prophet. Consequently, the Prophet cursed him and his descendants and said "Woe will befall my people from the progeny of this man" At last in view of his increasing intrigues the Prophet externed him from Madeena towards the valley of Waj (in Taif) and Marwaan also went with him. Prophet did not thereafter allow them entry in Madeena all his life. Abi-Bakr and Omar did likewise, but Othmaan sent for both of them during his reign, and raised Marwaan to such height as though the reins of caliphate rested in his hands. Thereafter his circumstances became so favourable that on the death of Moaawiya bn Yazeed he became the Caliph of the Moslims. But he had just ruled only for nine months and eighteen days that death overtook him in such a way that his wife sat with the pillow on his face and did not get away till he breathed his last.

The four sons to whom Ameer al-Momineen has referred were the four sons of Abdl-Malik bn Marwaan namely al-Waleed, Solaymaan, Yazeed and Hishaam, who ascended the Caliphate one after the other and coloured the pages of history with their stories. Some commentators have regarded this reference to Marwaan's own sons whose names

SERMONS 73

When the Consultative Committee (or Shora) decided to Swear Allegiance to Othmaan

You have certainly known that I am the most rightful of all others for the Caliphate. By Allah, so long as the affairs of Moslims remain intact and there is no oppression in it save on myself I shall keep quiet seeking reward for it (from Allah) and keeping aloof from its attractions and allurements for which you aspire.

SERMONS 74

When he learnt that the Omayyads blamed him for killing Othmaan

Omayyads" knowledge about me did not desist them from accusing me, nor did my precedence (in accepting Islam) keep off these ignorant people from blaming me. Allah's admonitions are more eloquent than my tongue. I am the contester against those who break away from Faith and the opposer of those who entertain doubts. Uncertainties should be placed before Quraan, the Book of Allah (for clarification). Certainly, people will be recompensed according to what they have in their hearts.

SERMONS 75

Preaching and Counselling

Allah may bless him who listens to a point of wisdom and retains it, when he is invited to the right path he approaches it, he follows a leader (by catching his waist band) and finds salvation, keeps Allah before his eyes and fears his sins, performs actions sincerely and acts virtuously, earns treasure of heavenly rewards, avoids vice, aims at (good) objectives and

---

are Abdl-Malik, Abdl-Aziz, Bishr and Mohammad. Out of these Abdl-Malik did become Caliph of Islam but Abdl-Aziz became governor of Egypt, Bishr of Iraq and Mohammad of al-Jazira.

reaps recompense, faces his desires and rejects (fake) hopes, makes endurance the means to his salvation and piety the provision for his death, rides on the path of honour and sticks to the highway of truth, makes good use of his time and hastens towards the end and takes with him the provision of (good) actions.

SERMONS 76

Bani-Omayya

The Bani-Omayya (Omayyads) are allowing me the inheritance of Mohammad (p.b.u.h.a.h.p) bit by bit. By Allah, if I live I would throw them away as the butcher removes the dust from the dust-covered piece of flesh.

Sayyid Razi says: In one version for "al-wizamott-tariba" (dust covered piece of flesh) the words "at-turabul-wazima" (the soil sticking on a piece of flesh) have been shown. That is, for the adjective the qualified noun and for the qualified noun the adjective has been placed. Any by the word "layufawwiqunani" Ameer al-Momineen implies that they allow him bit by bit just as a she-camel may be milked a little and then its young one may be made to suck milk so that it may be ready to be milked. And "al-wizam" is the plural of "wazama" which means the piece of stomach or of liver which falls on the ground and then the dust is removed from it.

SERMONS 77

One of his Supplications

O my Allah! Forgive me what Thou knowest about me more than I do. If I return (to the sins) Thou return to forgiveness. My Allah forgive me what I had promised to myself but Thou didst not find its fulfillment with me. My Allah forgive me that with what I sought nearness to Thee with my tongue but my heart opposed and did not perform it. My Allah forgive me winkings of the eye, vile utterances, desires of the heart and errors of speech.

SERMONS 78

Prophecy of Astrologers

When[1] he decided to set out for the Battle with thė Kharijites someone said "if you set out at this moment then according to astrology I fear you will not be successful in your aim," whereupon he said:

Do you think you can tell the hour when a man goes out and no evil befall him or can warn of the time at which if one goes out harm will accrue? Whoever testifies to this falsifies the Quraan and becomes unmindful of Allah in achieving his desired objective and in warding off the undesirable. You cherish saying this so that he who acts on what you say should praise you rather than Allah because according to your misconception you have

---

-1- When Ameer al-Momineen decided to march towards Nahrawan to suppress the rising of the Kharijites, Afif bn Qays al-Kindi said to him, "This hour is not good. If you set out at this time. then instead of victory and success you will face defeat and vanquishment" But Ameer al-Momineen paid no heed to his view and ordered the army to march that very moment. In the result the Kharijites suffered such a clear defeat that out of their nine thousand combatants only nine individuals saved their lives by running away while the rest were killed.

Ameer al-Momineen has argued about astrology being wrong or incorrect in three ways, firstly, that if the view of an astrologer is accepted as correct it would mean falsification of the Quraan, because an astrologer claims to ascertain hidden things of the future by seeing the stars while the Quraan says:

Say: "None (either) in the heavens or in the earth knoweth the unseen save Allah..." (27:65)

Secondly that under his misconception the astrologer believes that he can know his benefit or harm through knowing the future. In that case he would be regardless of turning to Allah and seeking His help, while this indifference towards Allah and self-reliance is a sort of heresy and atheism, which puts an end to his hope in Allah. Thirdly, that if he succeeds in any objective, he would regard this success to be the result of his knowledge of astrology, as a result of which he would praise himself rather than Allah, and will expect that whomever he guides in this manner he too should be grateful to him rather than to Allah. These points do not apply to astrology to the extent it may be believed that the astrological findings are in the nature of effect of medicines which are subject to alteration at the will of Allah. The competence achieved by most of our religious scholars in astrology is correct in this very ground that they did not regard its findings as final.

guided him about the hour in which he would secure benefit and avoid harm.

Then Ameer al-Momineen advanced towards the people and said:

O People! Beware of learning the science of stars except that with which guidance is sought on land or sea, because it leads to divining and an astrologer is a diviner, while the diviner is like the sorcerer, the sorcerer is like the unbeliever and the unbeliever would be in Hell. Get forward in the name of Allah.

SERMONS 79

Short-comings of Women[1]

-1- Ameer al-Momineen delivered this sermon after the devastation created by the Battle of Jamal. Since the devastation resulting from this battle was the outcome of blindly following a woman's command, in this sermon he has described women's physical defects and their causes and effects. Thus their first weakness is that for a few days in every month they have to abstain from prayer and fasting, and this abstention from worship is a proof of their deficiency in Faith. Although the real meaning of Imaan (belief) is heart-felt testimony and inner conviction yet metaphorically it also applies to action and character. Since actions are the reflection of Belief they are also regarded as part of Belief. Thus, it is related from Imam Ali bn Mosa ar-Riza (p. b. u. t.) that:

Imaan (belief) is testimony at heart, admission by the tongue and action by the limbs.

The second weakness is that their natural propensities do not admit of full performance of their intelligence. Therefore, nature has given them the power of intelligence only in accordance with the scope of their activities which can guide them in pregnancy, delivery, child nursing, child care and house-hold affairs. On the basis of this weakness of mind and intelligence their evidence has not been accorded the status of man's evidence, as Allah says:

...then call to witness two witnesses from among your men and if there not be two men then (take) a man and two women, of those ye approve of the witnesses, so that should one of the two (women) forget the (second) one of the two may remind the other... (Quraan, 2:282)

The third weakness is that their share in inheritance is half of man's share in inheritance as the Quraan says:

Allah enjoineth you about your children. The male shall have the equal of the shares of two females...(4:11)

This shows woman's weakness because the reason for her share in inheritance being half is that the liability of her maintenance rests on man. When man's position is that of a

O ye peoples! Women are deficient in Faith, deficient in shares and deficient in intelligence. As regards the deficiency in their Faith, it is their abstention from prayers and fasting during their menstrual period. As regards deficiency in their intelligence it is because the evidence of two women is equal to that of one man. As for the deficiency of their shares that is because of their share in inheritance being half of men. So beware of the evils of women. Be on your guard even from those of them who are (reportedly) good. Do not obey them even in good things so that they may not attract you to evils.

SERMONS 80

Way of Preaching and Counselling

O people! abstinence is to shorten desires, to thank for bounties and to keep off prohibitions. If this is possible then (at least) the prohibitions should not overpower your patience. Allah has exhausted the excuse before you through clear, shining arguments and open, bright books.

---

maintainer and care taker the status of the weaker sex who is in need of maintenance and care-taking is evident.

After describing their natural weakness, Ameer al-Momineen points out the mischief of blindly following them and wrongly obeying them. He says that not to say of bad things but even if they say in regard to some good things it should not be done in a way that these should feel as if it is being done in pursuance of their wish, but rather in a way that they should realise that the good act has been performed because of its being good and that their pleasure or wish has nothing to do with it. If they have even the doubt that their pleasures has been kept in view in it they would slowly increase in their demands and would wish that they should be obeyed in all matters however evil, the inevitable consequence whereof will be destruction and ruin. Shaykh Mohammad Abdo writes about this view of Ameer al-Momineen as under:

Ameer al-Momineen has said a thing which is corroborated by experiences of centuries.

SERMONS 81

World and its People

In what way shall I describe this world whose beginning is grief and whose end is destruction?[1] The lawful actions performed here have to be

-1- "The beginning of the world is grief and its end is destruction" This sentence contains the same truth which the Quraan has presented in the verse:
Indeed We have created man (to dwell) amidst hardship. (90:4)
It is true that right from the narrow womb of the mother upto the vastness of the firmament the changes of human life do not come to an end. When man first tastes life he finds himself closed in such a dark prison where he can neither move the limbs nor change the sides. When he gets rid of this confinement and steps in this world he has to pass through innumerable troubles. In the beginning he can neither speak with the tongue so as to describe his difficulty or pain nor possesses energy in the limbs so as to accomplish his needs himself. Only his suppressed sobs and flowing tears express his needs and translate his grief and sorrow. When after the lapse of this period he enters the stage of learning and instruction, then on every step voices of admonition and abuse welcome him. All the time he seems frightened and terrified. When he is relieved of this period of subjugation he finds himself surrounded by the worries of family life and livelihood, where sometimes, there is clash with comrades in profession, sometimes collision with enemies, sometimes confrontation with vicissitudes of time, sometimes attack of ailments and sometimes shock of children, till old age approaches him with the tidings of helplessness and weakness, and eventually he bids farewell to this world with mortification and grief in the heart.
Thereafter Ameer al-Momineen says about this world, that in its lawful actions there is the question of reckoning and in its forbidden acts there are hardships of punishment, as a result of which even pleasant joys also produce bitterness in his palate. If there is plenty of wealth and money in this world then man finds himself in such a whirlpool (of worries) that he loses his joy and peace of mind. But if there is want and poverty, he is ever crying for wealth. He who hankers after this world there is no limit for his desires. If one wish is fulfilled the desire for fulfilment of another wish crops up. This world is like the reflection. If you run after it then it will itself run forward but if you leave it and run away from it then it follows you. In the same way, if a person does not run after the world, the world runs after him. The implication is that if a person breaks the clutches of greed and avarice and keeps aloof from undesirable hankering after the world, he too gets (pleasures of) the world and he does not remain deprived of it. Therefore, he who surveys this world from above its surface and takes lesson from its chances and happenings, and through its variation, and alterations gains knowledge about Allah's Might, Wisdom and Sagacity, Mercy, Clemency and Sustaining power, his eyes will gain real brightness and sight. On the other hand the person who is lost only in the colourfulness of the world and its

accounted for, while for the forbidden ones there is punishment. Whoever is rich here faces mischief and whoever is poor gets grief. One who hankers after it does not get it. If one keeps away from it then it advances towards him. If one sees through it, it would bestow him sight, but if one has his eye on it then it would blind him.

Sayyid Razi says: If a thinker thinks over this phrase of Ameer al-Momineen "waman absara biha bassarathu" (If one sees through it, it would bestow him sight) he would find thereunder very amazing meaning and far-reaching sense whose purpose cannot be appreciated and whose aim cannot be understood particularly when he joins it with Ameer al-Momineen's phrase "waman absara ilayha amathu" (If one, has his eye on it, them it would blind him) he would find the difference between "absara biha" and "absara laha, clear, bright, wonderful and shining.

SERMONS 82

Al-Gharra

This sermon is called the al-Gharra" and it is one of the most wonderful sermons of Ameer al-Momineen.

Praise be to Allah who is High above all else, and is Near (the creation) through His bounty. He is the Giver of all reward and distinction, and Dispeller of all calamities and hardships. I praise Him for His continuous mercy and His copious bounties.

I believe in Him as He is the First of all and He is Manifest. I seek guidance from Him as He is Near and is the Guide. I seek His succour as He is Mighty and Subduer. I depend upon Him as He is Sufficer and Supporter. And I stand witness that Mohammad (blessing of Allah be on him and his progeny) is His slave and His Prophet. He sent him for enforcement of His

---

decorations, he loses himself in the darkness of the world that is why Allah has forbidden to view the world thus:

And strain not thine eyes unto that which We have provided (different) parties of them, (of) the splendour of the life of this world, so that We may try them in it; for the provision of thy Lord is better and more abiding. (Quraan, 20:131)

commands, for exhausting His pleas and for presenting warnings (against eternal punishment).

Enjoining People To Piety

O creatures of Allah I advise you to have fear of Allah Who has furnished illustrations and Who has timed for you your lives. He has given you covering of dress[1] and He has scattered for you livelihood. He has surrounded you with His knowledge. He has ordained rewards. He has bestowed upon you vast bounties and extensive gifts. He has warned you through far reaching arguments, and He has counted you by numbers. He has fixed for you ages (to live) in this place of test and house of instruction.

Caution against this World

You are on test in this world and have to render account about it. Certainly this world is a dirty watering place and a muddy source of drinking.

Its appearance is attractive and its inside is destructive. It is a deception, a vanishing reflection and a bent pillar. When its despiser begins to like it and he who is not acquainted with it feels satisfied with it, then it raises and puts down its feet (in joy), entraps him in its trap, makes him the target of its arrows and puts round his neck the rope of death taking him to the narrow grave and fearful abode in order to show him his place of stay and the recompense of his acts. This goes on from generation to generation. Neither death stops from cutting them asunder nor do the survivors keep aloof from committing of sins.

-1- Allah has furnished every creature with natural dress, which is the means of protecting it from cold and heat. Thus, some animals are covered in feathers and some carry apparels of wool on their bodies. But the high degree of intelligence of man and the quality of shame and modesty in him demands distinction from other creatures. Consequently, to maintain this distinction he has been taught the ways of covering his body. It was this natural impulse that when Adam was made to give up his dress he began to cover his body with leaves. The Quraan says:

So when they tested (of) the tree their shameful things got displayed unto them and they began covering themselves with leaves of the garden ..." (Quraan, 7:22)

This was the punishment awarded for his committing what was better for him to omit. When removal of dress is punishment its putting on would be a favour, and since this is peculiar to man it has been particularly mentioned.

Death and Resurrection

They are emulating each other and proceeding in groups towards the final objective and the rendezvous of death, till when matters come to a close, the world dies and resurrection draws near. Allah[1] would take them out from the corners of the graves, the nests of birds. the dens of beasts and the centres of death. They hasten towards Him command and run towards the place fixed for their final return group by group, quiet, standing and arrayed in rows. They will be within Allah's sight and will hear every one who would call them.

They would be having the dress of helplessness and covering of submission and indignity. (At this time) contrivances would disappear, desires would be cut, hearts would sink quietly, voices would be curbed down, sweat would choke the throat, fear would increase and ears would resound with the thundering voice of the announcer calling towards the final judgement, award of recompense, striking of punishment and paying of reward.

-1- The intention is that Allah would resurrect all the dead, even though they had been eaten by beasts and been merged in their bodies. Its aim is to refute the view of the philosophers who hold that the resurrection of the non-existent is impossible and who do not therefore believe in the physical resurrection. Their argument briefly is that a thing which has lost existence by death cannot return to life. Consequently, after the destruction of this world the return of any of its beings to life is out of question. But this belief is not correct because dispersal of the parts does not mean its non-existence, so as to say that putting these parts together again would involve resurrection of the non-existent. On the other hand separated and dispersed parts continue to exist in some form or the other. Of course, in this connection this objection has some force that when every person is to be resurrected in his own form, then in case one person has eaten the other, then in such a case it would be impossible to resurrect either of them with his own constituent parts, since this would involve creating deficiency of parts in that who had eaten the other.

To this metaphysicians have replied that in everybody there are some constituents which are essential and others which are non-essential. The essential constituents remain constant from the beginning till end of life and suffer no change or alteration, and resurrection with regard to such constituents would not create any deficiency in the man who ate the other.

Limitations of Life

People have been created as a proof of (His) power, have been brought up with authority, they are made to die through pangs, and placed in graves where they turn into crumbs. Then they would be resurrected one by one, awarded their recompense and would have to account for their actions, each one separately. They had been allowed time to seek deliverance, had been shown the right path and had been allowed to live and seek favours, the darkness of doubts had been removed, and they had been let free in this period of life as a training place in order to make preparation for the race on the Day of Judgement, to search for the objective with thoughtfulness, to get time necessary to secure benefits and provide for the next place of stay.

No Happiness without Piety

How appropriate are these illustrations and effective admonitions provided they are received by pure hearts, open ears, firm views and sharp wits. Fear Allah like him who listened (good advice) and bowed before it, when he committed sin he admitted it, when he felt fear he acted virtuously, when he apprehended he hastened (towards good acts), when he believed he performed virtuous acts, when he was asked to take lesson (from the happenings of this world) he did take the lesson, when he was asked to desist he abstained (from evil), when he responded to the call (of Allah) he leaned (towards him), when he turned back (to evil) he repented, when he followed he almost imitated and when he was shown (the right path) he saw it.

Such a man was busy in search of truth and got rid (of the worldly evils) by running away. He collected provision (of good acts) for himself, purified his inner self, built for the next world, and took with himself provision for the day of his departure, keeping in view his journey, his requirement and the position of his need. He sent ahead of him for the abode of his stay (in the next world). O creatures of Allah, fear Allah keeping in view the reason why He created you and be afraid of Him to the extent He has advised you to do. Make yourself deserve what He has promised you, by having confidence in the truth of His promise and entertaining fear for the Day of Judgement.

Reminding People of Allah's Bounties

He has made for you ears to preserve what is important, eyes to have sight in place of blindness and limbs which consist of many (smaller) parts, whose curves are in proportion with the moulding of their shapes and lengths of their ages, and also bodies that are sustaining themselves and hearts that are busy in search of their food, besides other big bounties, obliging bestowings and fortresses of safety. He has fixed for you ages that are not known to you. He has retained for you remains of the past people for your instruction. Those people enjoyed themselves fully and were completely unhampered. Death overtook them before (satisfaction of) their desires, from which the hands of death separated them. They did not provide for themselves during health of their bodies, and did not take lesson during their youth.

Are these people who are in youth waiting for the back-bending old age, and those enjoying fresh health waiting for ailments, and these living persons looking for the hour of death? When the hour of departure would be close and the journey at hand, with pangs of grief and trouble, suffering of sorrows and suffocation of saliva, and the time would arrive for calling relations and friends for help and changing sides on the bed. Could then the near ones stop death, or the mourning women do any good? He would rather be left alone in the graveyard confined to the narrow corner of his grave.

His skin has been pierced all over by reptiles, and his freshness has been destroyed by these tribulations. Storms have removed his traces and calamities have obliterated even his signs. Fresh bodies have turned thin and withered and bones have become rotten. The spirits are burdened with the weight of sins and have become conscious of the unknown things. But now neither the good acts can be added to nor evil acts can be atoned for by repentance. Are you not sons, fathers, brothers and relations of these dead and are not to follow their footsteps and pass by their paths? But hearts are still unmoved, heedless of guidance and moving on wrong lines, as though the addressee is someone else, and as though the correct way is to amass worldly gains.

Preparation for the Day of Judgement

And know that you have to pass over the pathway (of Sirat) where steps waver, feet slip away and there are fearful dangers at every step. O creatures of Allah, fear Allah, like the fearing of wise man whom the thought (of next world) has turned away from other matters, fear (of Allah) has afflicted his body with trouble and pain, his engagement in the night prayer has turned even his short sleep into awakening, hope (of eternal recompense) keeps him thirsty in the day, abstention has curbed his desires, and remembrance of Allah is ever moving his tongue. He entertains fear before dangers. He avoids uneven ways in favour of clear ones. He follows the shortest route to secure his purpose, wishfulness does not twist his thinking and ambiguities do not blind his eyes. He enjoys deep sleep and passes his day happily because of the happiness of good tidings and pleasure of (eternal bounties).

He passes the pathway of this world in praiseworthy manner. He reaches the next world with virtues. He hastens (towards virtue) out of fear (for vice). He moves briskly during the short time (of life in this world). He devotes himself in seeking (eternal good), he runs away from evil. During today he is mindful of tomorrow, and keeps the future in his view. Certainly Paradise is the best reward and achievement, which hell is appropriate punishment and suffering. Allah is the best Avenger and Helper and the Quraan is the best argument and confronter.

Warning against Satan

I enjoin upon you fear of Allah Who has left no excuse against what He has warned, has exhausted argument (of guidance) about the (right) path He has shown. He has warned you of the enemy that steals into hearts and stealthily speaks into ears, and thereby misguides and brings about destruction, makes (false) promises and keeps under wrong impression, he represents evil sins in attractive shape, and shows as light even serious crimes. When he has deceived his comrades and exhausted the pledge he begins to find fault with what he presented as good, and considers serious what he had shown as light, and threatens from what he had shown as safe.

Creation of Man

Or look at man whom Allah has created in the dark wombs and layers of curtains from what was overflowing semen, then shapeless clot, then embryo, then suckling infant, then child and then fully grown up young man. Then He gave him heart with memory, tongue to talk and eye to see with, in order that he may take lesson (from whatever is around him) and understand it and follow the admonition and abstain from evil.

When he attained the normal growth and his structure gained its average development he fell in self-conceit and got perplexed. He drew bucketfuls of his desires, got immersed in fulfilling his wishes for pleasures of the world and his (sordid) aims. He did not fear any evil nor got frightened of any apprehension. He died infatuated with his vices. He spent his short life in rubbish pursuits. He earned no reward nor did he fulfil any obligation. Fatal illness overtook him while he was still in his enjoyments and perplexed him. He passed the night in wakefulness in the hardships of grief and pricking of pains and ailments in the presence of real brother, loving father, wailing mother, crying sister, while he himself was under maddening uneasiness, serious senselessness, fearful cries, suffocating pains, anguish of suffocating sufferings and the pangs of death.

Thereafter he was clad in the shroud while he remained quiet and thoroughly submissive to others. Then he was placed on planks in such a state that he had been down-trodden by hardships and thinned by ailments. The crowd of young men and helping brothers carried him to his house of loneliness where all connections of visitors are severed. Thereafter those who accompanied him went away and those who were wailing for him returned and then he was made to sit in his grave for terrifying questioning and slippery examination. The great calamity of that place is the hot water and entry into Hell, flames of eternal Fire and intensity of blazes. There is no resting period, no gap for ease, no power to intervene, no death to bring about solace and no sleep to make him forget pain. He rather lies under several kinds of deaths and moment-to-moment punishment. We seek refuge with Allah.

Lesson from those who passed away

O creatures of Allah! where are those who were allowed (long) ages to live and they enjoyed bounty. They were taught and they learnt; they were given time and they passed it in vain; they were kept healthy and they forgot (their duty). They were allowed long period (of life), were handsomely provided, were warned of grievous punishment and were promised big rewards. You should avoid sins that lead to destruction and vices that attract wrath (of Allah).

O people who possess eyes and ears and health and wealth! Is there any place of protection, any shelter of safety, or asylum or haven, or occasion to run away or to come back (to this world)? If not,

how are you then turned away" (Quraan, 6:95; 10:34; 35:3; 40:62)

and wither are you averting? By what things have you been deceived? Certainly, the share of every one of you from this earth is just a piece of land equal to his own stature and size where he would lie on his cheeks covered with dust. The present is an opportune moment for acting.

O creatures of Allah, since the neck is free from the loop, and spirit is also unfettered, now you have time for seeking guidance: you are in ease of body; you can assemble in crowds, the rest of life is before you; you have opportunity of acting by will; there is opportunity for repentance, and peaceful circumstances. (But you should act) before you are overtaken by narrow circumstances and distress, or fear and weakness, before the approach of the awaited death and before seizure by the Almighty, the Powerful.

Sayyid Razi says: It is related that when Ameer al-Momineen delivered this sermon people began to tremble, tears flowed from their eyes and their hearts were frightened. Some people call this sermon the Brilliant Sermon (al-Khotbatol-Gharra)

SERMONS 83

Amr bn al-Aas

I am surprised at the son of an-Nabigha that he says about me among the people of Syria (Sham) that I am a jester and that I am engaged in frolics and fun. He said wrong and spoke sinfully. Beware, the worst speech is what is untrue. He speaks and lies. He promises and breaks the promise. He begs and sticks, but when someone begs from him he withholds miserly. He betrays the pledge and ignores kinship.

When in a battle, he commands and admonishes but only uptil the swords do not come into action. When such a moment arrives his great trick is to turn naked[1] before his adversary. By Allah, surely the remembrance of death has kept me away from fun and play while obliviousness about the next world has prevented him from speaking truth. He has not sworn allegiance to Moaawiya without purpose; but has beforehand got him to agree that he will have to pay its price, and gave him an award for forsaking religion.

-1- Ameer al-Momineen here refers to the incident when the "Conqueror of Egypt" Amr bn Aas exhibited the feat of his courage by displaying his private parts. What happened was that when in the battlefield of Siffeen he and Ameer al-Momineen had an encounter, he rendered himself naked in order to ward off the blow of the sword. At this Ameer al-Momineen turned his face away and spared him his life. The famous Arab poet al-Farazdaq said about it:

There is no good in warding off trouble by ignominy as was done one day by Amr bn Aas by display of his private parts.

Even in this ignoble act Amr bn Aas had not the credit of doing it himself, but had rather followed another one who had preceded him, because the man who first adopted this device was Talha bn Abi-Talha who had saved his life in the battle of Ohod by becoming naked before Ameer al-Momineen, and so he showed this way to the others. Thus, besides Amr bn Aas this trick was played by Bishr bn Abi-Artat also to save himself from the sword of Ameer al-Momineen. When after the performance of this notable deed Bishr went to Moaawiya the latter recalled Amr bn Aas's act as precedent in order to remove this man's shamefulness and said "O Bishr, no matter. There is nothing to feel shameful about it in view of Amr bn Aas's precedent before you. "

SERMONS 84

Perfection of Allah and Counselling

I stand witness that there is no god but Allah, He is One and there is no partner with Him. He is the First, such that nothing was before Him. He is the Last, such that there is not limit for Him. Imagination cannot catch any of His qualities. Hearts cannot entertain belief about His nature. Analysis and division cannot be applied to Him. Eyes and hearts cannot compare Him.

O creatures of Allah! take lesson from useful items of instruction and shining indications. Be cautioned by effective items of warning. Get benefit from preaching and admonition. It is as though the claws of death are pressed in you, the connection of hope and desires has been cut asunder, hard affairs have befallen you and your march is towards the place where everyone has to go, namely death. Hence,

with every person there is a driver and a witness" (Quraan, 50:21).

The driver drives him towards resurrection while the witness furnishes evidence about his deeds.

Paradise

In Paradise there are high classes and different places of stay. Its boundary never ends. He who stays in it will never depart from it. He who is endowed with everlasting abode in it will not get old, and its resident will not face want.

SERMONS 85

Getting Ready for the next World by following Allah's Commandments

Allah knows hidden matters and is aware of inner feelings. He encompasses everything. He has control over everything and power over everything. Everyone of you should do whatever he has to do during his days of life before the approach of death, in his leisure before his occupation, and during the breathing of his breath before it is overtaken by suffocation, should provide for himself and his journey and should collect provision from his place of halt for his place of stay.

So remember Allah, O people, about what He has asked you in His Book to take care of, and about His rights that He has entrusted to you. Verily, Allah has not created you in vain nor left you unbridled nor left you alone in ignorance and gloom. He has defined what you should leave behind. taught you your acts, ordained your death, sent down to you "the Book (Quraan) explaining everything" (Quraan, 16:89) and made His Prophet live among you for a long time till He completed for him and for you the message sent through the Quraan namely the religion liked by Him, and clarified through him His good acts and evil acts, His prohibitions and His commands.

He placed before you His arguments and exhausted his excuses upon you. He put forth to you His promises and warned you of severe retribution. You should therefore make full atonement during your remaining days and let yourselves practice endurance in these days. These days are fewer as against the many days during which you have shown obliviousness and heedlessness towards admonition. Do not allow time to yourselves because it will put you on the path of wrong-doers and do not be easy-going because this will push you towards sinfulness.

O creatures of Allah! the best adviser for himself is he who is the most obedient to Allah, and the most deceiving for himself is he who is the most disobedient to Allah. Deceived is he who deceived his own self. Enviable is he whose Faith is safe. Fortunate is he who takes lesson from others, while unfortunate is he who fell victim to his desires. You should know that even the smallest hypocrisy is like believing in more than one God, and keeping company of people who follow their desires is the key to obliviousness from religion, and is the seat of Satan.

Be on your guard against falsehood because it is contrary to Faith. A truthful person is on the height of salvation and dignity, while the liar is on the edge of ignominy and degradation. Do not be jealous because jealousy eats away Faith just as fire eats away dried wood. Do not bear malice because, it is a scraper (of virtues). And know that desires make wit forgetful and make memory oblivious. You should falsify desire because it is a deception, and he who has desires is in deceit.

SERMONS 86

Faithful and Unfaithful Believers Qualities of a Faithful Believer

O creatures of Allah! the most beloved of Allah is he whom Allah has given power (to act) against his passions, so that his inner side is (submerged in) grief and the outer side is covered with fear. The lamp of guidance is burning in his heart. He has provided entertainment for the day that is to befall him. He regards what is distant to be near himself and takes the hard to be light. He looks at and perceives; he remembers (Allah) and enhances (the tempo of his) actions. He drinks sweet water to whose source his way has been made easy. So he drinks to satisfaction and takes the level path. He has put off the clothes of desires and got rid of worries except one worry peculiar to him. He is safe from misguidance and the company of people who follow their passions. He has become the key to the doors of guidance, and the lock for the doors of destruction.

He has seen his way and is walking on it. He knows his pillar (of guidance) and has crossed over his deep water. He has caught hold of the most reliable supports and the strongest ropes. He is on that level of conviction which is like the brightness of the sun. He has set himself for Allah, the Glorified, for performance of the most sublime acts of facing all that befalls him and taking every step needed for it. He is the lamp in darkness. He is the dispeller of all blindness, key to the obscure, remover of complexities, and a guide in vast deserts. When he speaks he makes you understand whereas when he remains silent then it is safe to do so. He did everything only for Allah and so Allah also made him His own. Consequently, he is like the mines of His faith and as a stump in His earth. He has enjoined upon himself (to follow) justice.

The first step of his justice is the rejection of desires from his heart. He describes right and acts according to it. There is no good which he has not aimed at nor any likely place (of virtue) of the Quraan. Therefore the Quraan is his guide and leader. He gets down when the Quraan puts down his weight and he settles where the Quraan settles him down.

Characteristics of an Unfaithful Believer

While the other (kind of) man is he who calls himself learned but he is not so. He has gleaned ignorance from the ignorant and misguidance from the misguided. He has set for the people a trap (made) of the ropes of deceit and untrue speech. He takes the Quraan according to his own views and right after his passions. He makes people feel safe from big sins and takes light the serious crimes. He says that he is waiting for (clarification of) doubts but he remains plunged therein, and that he keeps aloof from innovations but actually he is immersed in them. His shape is that of a man, but his heart is that of a beast. He does not know the door of guidance to follow nor the door of misguidance to keep aloof therefrom. These are living dead bodies.

The Descendants of the Holy Prophet (Etra)

So wither are you going to" (Quraan, 81:26) and "how are you then turned away?" (Quraan, 6:95; 10:34; 35:3; 40:62).

Ensigns (of guidance) are standing, indications (of virtue) are clear, and the minarets (of light) have been fixed. Where are you being taken astray and how are you groping while you have among you the descendants of the Prophet? They are the reins of Right, ensigns of Faith and tongues of truth. Accord to them the same good position as you accord to the Quraan, and come to them (for quenching the thirst of guidance) as the thirsty camels approach the water spring.

O people take this saying[1] of the last of the Prophets that he who dies from among us is not dead, and he who decays (after dying) from among

-1- This saying of the Prophet is a definite proof of the view that the life of any one from among the Ahlil-Bayt (Household of the Holy Prophet) does not come to an end and that apparent death makes no difference in their sense of living, although human intelligence is unable to comprehend the conditions and happenings of that life. There are many truths beyond this world of senses which human mind cannot yet understand. Who can

us does not really decay. Do not say what you do not understand, because most of the Right is in what you deny. Accept the argument of one against whom you have no argument. It is I. Did I not act before you on the greater thaqal (ath-thaqal al-akbar, i. e. the Quraan) and did I not retain among you the smaller thaqal (ath-thaqal al-asghar, i. e. the descendants of the Prophet).[1] I fixed among you the standard of faith, and I taught you the

---

say how in the narrow corner of the grave where it is not possible even to breathe, replies will be given to the questions of the angels Monkar and Nakeer? Similarly, what is the meaning of life of the martyrs in the cause of Allah, who have neither sense nor motion, can neither see nor hear? Although to us they appear to be dead, yet the Quraan testifies to their life.

And say not of those who are slain in the path of Allah that they are dead; Nay, (they are) living, but ye perceive not. (2:154)

At another place it says about their life:

Reckon not those who are slain in the way of Allah, to be dead; Nay! alive they are with their Lord being sustained. (3:169)

When restriction has been placed on mind and tongue even in respect of the common martyrs that they should not be called dead nor considered dead, how would not those individuals whose necks were reserved for sword and palate for poison be living for all times to come. About their bodies Ameer al-Momineen has said that by passage of time no signs of ageing or decay occur in them, but they remain in the same state in which they fell as martyrs. There should be nothing strange in it because dead bodies preserved through material means still exist. When it is possible to do so through material means will it be out of the Power of the Omnipotent Creator to preserve against change and decay the bodies of those upon whom He has bestowed the sense of everlasting life? Thus about the martyrs of Badr, the Holy Prophet said:

Shroud them even with their wounds and flowing blood because when they would rise on the Day of Judgement blood would be pushing out of their throats.

-1- "ath-thaqal al-Akbar" implies the Quraan and "ath-thaqal al-Asghar" means Ahlil-Bayt (the Household of the Holy Prophet) as in the Prophet's saying:

Verily, I am leaving among you (the) two precious things (of high estimation and of care)" the reference is to Quraan and Ahlil-Bayt.

There are several reasons for using this word Firstly, "thaqal" means the kit of a traveller, and since the kit is much in need, it is protected carefully. Secondly, it means a precious thing; and since this is of great importance, one is bound to follow the injunctions of the Quraan and the actions of Ahlil-Bayt. So they have been called "precious things. Since Allah has made arrangements for the protection of the Quraan and Ahlil-Bayt till doomsday so they have been called "thaqalayn. So the Prophet before leaving this world for the next, declared them to be his valuable possessions and ordered people to

limits of lawful and unlawful. I clothed you with the garments of safety with my justice and spread for you (the carpet of) virtue by my word and deed.

I showed you high manners through myself. Do not exercise your imagination about what the eye cannot see or the mind cannot conceive.

Bani-Omayya

Till people begin thinking that the world is attached to the Omayyads, would be showering its benefits on them, and lead them to its clear spring for watering, and that their whip and sword will not be removed from the people. Whoever thinks so is wrong. There are rather a few drops from the joys of life which they would suck for a while and then vomit out the whole of it.

SERMONS 87

Factions of Community

So now, certainly, Allah did not break the neck of any unruly tyrant in this world except after allowing him time and opportunity and did not join the broken bone of any people (omma) until He did not inflict calamity and

---

preserve them. Thirdly, then have been called "Thaqalayn" (precious things) in view of their purity and high value. Thus bn Hajar al-Haythami writes:

The Prophet has called the Quraan and his Descendants as "thaqalayn" (two precious things) because "thaqal" means a pure, chaste and preserved thing, and either of these two were really so, each of them is the treasure of Divine knowledge and a source of scholarly secrets and religious commandments. For that reason the Prophet desired the people to follow them and to stick to them and to secure knowledge from them. Among them the most deserving of attachment is the Imam and Scholar of the family of the Prophet namely Ali bn Abi-Talib (Allah may honour his face) because of his great insight and copiousness of knowledge which we have already described. (as-Sawaaiq al-Mohriqa, p.90)

Since the Prophet has with regard to apparent implication attributed the Quraan to Allah and the descendants to himself, therefore in keeping with the natural status the Quraan has been called the bigger weight while the descendants, the smaller weight. Otherwise from the point of view of being followed both are equal and from the point of view of utility in the development of character there can be no question in the status of the speaking party (the Ahlil-Bayt) being higher than the silent one (the Quraan).

distress upon them. Even less than what sufferings and misfortunes have yet to fall upon you or have already befallen you are enough for giving lessons. Every man with a heart is not intelligent, every ear does not listen and every eye does not see.

I wonder, and there is no reason why I should not wonder, about the faults of these groups who have introduced alterations in their religious pleas, who do not move on the footsteps of their Prophet nor follow the actions of the vicegerent. They do not believe in the unknown and do not avoid the evil. They act on the doubts and tread in (the way of) their passions. For them good is whatever they consider good and evil is whatever they consider evil. Their reliance for resolving distresses is on themselves. Their confidence in regard to dubious matters is on their own opinions as if every one of them is the Leader (Imam) of himself. Whatever he has decided himself he considers it to have been taken through reliable sources and strong factors.

SERMONS 88

Holy Prophet

Allah sent the Prophet when the mission of other Prophets had stopped and the peoples were in slumber for a long time. Evils were raising heads, all matters were under disruption and in flames of wars, while the world was devoid of brightness, and full of open deceitfulness. Its leaves had turned yellow and there was absence of hope about its fruits. While water had gone underground. The minarets of guidance had disappeared and signs of destruction had appeared. It was stern to its people and frowned in the face of its seeker. Its fruit was vice and its food was carcass. Its inner dress was fear and outer cover was sword.

So take lesson, O creatures of Allah, and recall that (evil doing) with which your fathers and brothers are entangled, and for which they have to account. By my life, your time is not much behind theirs, nor have long periods or centuries lapsed between you and them, nor are you much distant from when you were in their loins.

By Allah, whatever the Prophet told them, I am here telling you the same and whatever you hear today is not different from what they heard yesterday. The eyes that were opened for them and the hearts that were made for them at that time, just the same have been given to you at this time. By Allah, you have not been told anything that they did not know and you have not been given anything which they were deprived. Certainly you have been afflicted by a calamity (which is like a she-camel) whose nose-string is moving about and whose strap is loose So in whatever condition these deceitful people are should not deceive you, because it is just a long shadow whose term is fixed.

SERMONS 89

Allah's Attributes and some Advice

Praise be to Allah who is well-known without being seen, Who creates without pondering over, Who has ever been existent when there was no sky with domes, nor curtains with lofty doors, nor gloomy night, nor peaceful ocean, nor mountains with broad pathways, nor curved mountain roads, nor earth of spread floors, nor self-reliant creatures. He is the Originator of creation and their Master. He is the God of the creation and its feeder. The sun and the moon are steadily moving in pursuit of His will. They make every fresh thing old and every distant thing near.

He distributed their sustenance and has counted their deeds and acts, the number of their breaths, their concealed looks, and whatever is hidden in their bosoms. He knows their places of stay and places of last resort in the loins and wombs till they reach their end.

His punishment on enemies is harsh despite the extent of His Mercy, and His compassion on His friends is vast despite His harsh punishment. He overpowers one who wants to overcome Him, and destroys one who clashes with Him. He disgraces one who opposes Him and gains sway over one who bears Him hostility. He is sufficient for one who relies on Him. He gives one who asks Him. He repays one who lends to Him. He rewards one who thanks Him.

O creatures of Allah, weigh yourselves before you are weighed and assess yourselves before you are assessed. Breathe before suffocation of the throat. Be submissive before you are harshly driven. Know that if one does not help himself in acting as his own adviser and warner then no one else can (effectively) be his adviser or warner.

SERMONS 90

The Skeletons (al-Ashbaah) [1]

This sermon is known as the sermon of skeletons (Khotbatol-Ashbaah) and it holds one of the highest positions among the sermons of Ameer al-Momineen. Masada bn-Sadaqa has related from Imaam Jafar bn-Mohammad as-Saadiq (p.b.u.t.) Saying: "Ameer al-Momineen delivered this sermon from the pulpit of (the mosque of) Koofa when someone asked him "O Ameer al-Momineen! Describe Allah for us in such a way that we may imagine that we see him with eyes so that our love and knowledge may increase about him." Ameer al-Momineen became angry at this (request of the questioner) and ordered the Moslims to gather in the mosque. So many Moslims gathered in the mosque that the place was over-crowded. Then Ameer al-Momineen ascended the pulpit while he was still in a state of anger and his colour was changed. After he had praised Allah and extolled him and sought his blessings on the prophet he said:

Description Of Allah

Praise be to Allah whom refusal to give away and stinginess do not make rich and Whom munificence and generosity do not make poor, although everyone who gives away loses (to that extent) except He, and every miser is blamed for his niggardliness. He obliges through beneficial bounties and

---

-1- The name of this sermon is the Sermon of "al-Ashbaah. "Ashbaah" is the plural of shabah which means skeleton, since it contains description of angels and other kinds of beings it has been named by this name.
The ground for being angry on the questioner was that his request was unconnected with the obligations of sharia and beyond limits of human capacity.

plentiful gifts and grants. The whole creation is His dependants (in sustenance)[1]. He has guaranteed their livelihood and ordained their

---

-1- Allah is the Guarantor of sustenance and Provider of livelihood as He says:
No creature is there crawling on the earth, but its provision rests on Allah...(Quraan, 11:6)
But His being guarantor means that He has provided ways for everyone to live and earn livelihood, and has allowed every one equal shares in forests, mountains, rivers, mines and in the vast earth, and has given everyone the right to make use of them. His bounties are not confined to any single person, nor is the door of His sustenance closed to any one. Thus, Allah says:
All We do aid, these and (also) those out of the bounty of thy Lord; and the bounty of thy Lord is not confined. (Quraan, 17:20)
If someone does not secure these things through languor or ease and sits effortless it is not possible that livelihood would reach his door. Allah has laid the table with multifarious feeds but to get them it is necessary to extend the hand. He has deposited pearls in the bottom of the sea but it requires diving to get them out. He has filled the mountains with rubies and precious stones but they cannot be had without digging the stones. The earth contains treasures of growth but benefit cannot be drawn from them without sowing of seed. Heaps of edibles lie scattered on all four sides of the earth but they cannot be collected without the trouble of travelling. Thus, Allah says:
...Traverse ye then its broad sides, and eat ye of His provision ...(Quraan, 67:15)
Allah's providing livelihood does not mean that no effort is needed in searching livelihood or no going out of the house is required for it, and that livelihood should itself finds its way to the seeker. The meaning of His being the provider of livelihood is that He has given earth the property of growing, He has sent rain from clouds for germination, created fruits, vegetables and grains. All this is from Allah but securing them is connected with human effort. Whoever will strive will reap the benefits of his efforts, and whoever abstains from strife would face the consequences of his idleness and laziness. Accordingly Allah says:
And that man shall have nothing but what he striveth for. (Quraan, 53:39)
The order of universe hinges on the maxim 'sow and reap" It is wrong to expect germination without sowing, to hope for results without effort. Limbs and faculties have been given solely to be kept active. Thus, Allah addresses Mary and says:
And shake towards thee the trunk of the palm-tree, it will drop on thee dates fresh (and) ripe. Then eat and drink and refresh the eye... (Quraan, 19:25-26)
Allah provided the means for Mary's livelihood. He did not however pluck the dates from the tree and put them in her lap. This was because so far as production of food goes it is His concern. So he made the tree green, put fruits on it and ripened the fruits. But when the stage arrived for plucking them He did not intervene. He just recalled to Mary her job namely that she should now move her hand and get her food.
Again, if His providing the livelihood means that whatever is given is given by Him and whatever is received from Him, then whatever a man would earn and eat, and in whatever manner he would obtain it would be permissible for him, whether he obtains

sustenance. He has prepared the way for those who turn to Him and those who seek what is with Him. He is as generous about what He is asked as He is about that for which He is not asked. He is the First for whom there was no "before" so that there could be anything before Him. He is the Last for whom there is no "after" so that there could be anything after Him. He prevents the pupils of the eyes from seeing Him or perceiving Him. Time does not change over Him, so as to admit of any change of condition about Him. He is not in any place so as to allow Him movement (from one place to another).

If He gives away all that the mines of the mountains emit out or the gold, silver, pearls and cuttings of coral which the shells of the ocean vomit out, it would not affect his munificence, nor diminish the extent of what He has. (In fact) He would still have such treasures of bounty as would not decrease by the demands of the creatures, because He is that generous Being Whom the begging of beggars cannot make poor nor the pertinacity of beseechers make miser.

Attributes of Allah as Described in the Holy Quraan

Then look on questioner, be confined to those of His attributes which the Quraan had described and seek light from the effulgence of its guidance. Leave to Allah that knowledge which Satan has prompted you to seek and which neither the Quraan enjoins you to seek nor is there any trace of it in the actions or sayings of the Prophet and other leaders (Aimma) of guidance. This is the extreme limit of Allah's claim upon you. Know that

---

it by theft, bribery, oppression or violence, because it would mean Allah's act and the food would be that given by Him, wherein he would have no free will, and where anything is out of the limits of free action there is no question of permissible or forbidden for it, nor is there any liability to account for it. But when it is not actually so and there is the question of permissible and forbidden then it should have bearing on human actions, so that it could be questioned whether is was secured in lawful or unlawful manner. Of course, where He has not bestowed the power of seeking the livelihood, there He has taken upon Himself the responsibility to provide the livelihood. Consequently, He has managed for the feeding of the embryo in the mother's womb, and it reaches him there according to its needs and requirements. But when this very young life enters the wide world and picks up energy to move its limbs, then it cant get its food from the source without moving his lips (for sucking).

firm in knowledge are those who refrain from opening the curtains that lie against the unknown, and their acknowledgement of ignorance about the details of the hidden unknown prevents them from further probe. Allah praises them for their admission that they are unable to get knowledge not allowed to them. They do not go deep into the discussion of what is not enjoined upon them about knowing Him and they call it firmness. Be content with this and do not limit the Greatness of Allah after the measure of your own intelligence, of else you would be among the destroyed ones.

He is Powerful, such that when imagination shoots its arrows to comprehend the extremity of His power, and mind, making itself free of the dangers of evil thoughts, tries to find Him in the depth of His realm, and hearts long to grasp realities of His attributes and openings of intelligence penetrate beyond description in order to secure knowledge about His Being, crossing the dark pitfalls of the unknown and concentrating towards Him He would turn them back. They would return defeated admitting that the reality of His knowledge cannot be comprehended by such random efforts, nor can an iota of the sublimity of His Honour enter the understanding of thinkers.

Allah's Creation

He originated the creation without any example which He could follow and without any specimen prepared by any known creator that was before Him. He showed us the realm of His Might, and such wonders which speak of His Wisdom. The confession of the created things that their existence owes itself to Him made us realise that argument has been furnished about knowing Him (so that there is no excuse against it). The signs of His creative power and standard of His wisdom are fixed in the wonderful things He has created. Whatever He has created is an argument in His favour and a guide towards Him. Even a silent thing is a guide towards Him as though it speaks, and its guidance towards the Creator is clear.

(O Allah) I stand witness that he who likens Thee with the separateness of the limbs or with the joining of the extremities of his body did not acquaint his inner self with knowledge about Thee, and his heart did not secure conviction to the effect that there is no partner for Thee. It is as though he has not heard the (wrongful) followers disclaiming their false gods by saying:

By Allah, we were certainly in manifest error when we equalled you with the Lord of the worlds." (Quraan, 26:97-98).

They are wrong who liken Thee to their idols, and dress Thee with apparel of the creatures by their imagination, attribute to Thee parts of body by their own thinking and consider Thee after the creatures of various types, through the working of their intelligence. I stand witness that whoever equated Thee with anything out of Thy creation took a match for Thee, and whoever takes a match for Thee is an unbeliever, according to what is stated in Thy unambiguous verses and indicated by the evidence of Thy clear arguments. (I also stand witness that) Thou art that Allah who cannot be confined in (the fetters of) intelligence so as to admit change of condition by entering its imagination nor in the shackles of mind so as to become limited and an object of alterations.

Greatest Perfection In Allah's Creation

He has fixed limits for every thing He has created and made the limits firm, and He has fixed its working and made the working delicate. He has fixed its direction and it does not transgress the limits of its position nor fall short of reaching the end of its aim. It did not disobey when it was commanded to move at His will; and how could it do so when all matters are governed by His will. He is the Producer of varieties of things without exercise of imagination, without the urge of an impulse, hidden in Him, without (the benefit of) any experiment taken from the vicissitudes of time and without any partner who might have assisted Him in creating wonderful things.

Thus the creation was completed by His order and it bowed to His obedience and responded to His call. The laziness of any slug or the inertness of any excuse-finder did not prevent it from doing so. So He straightened the curves of the things and fixed their limits. With His power He created coherence in their contradictory parts and joined together the factors of similarity. Then He separated them in varieties which differ in limits, quantities, properties and shapes. All this is new creation. He made them firm and shaped them according as He wished and invented them.

Description of the Sky

He has arranged the depressions and elevations of the openings of the sky. He has joined the breadths of its breaches, and has joined them with one another. He has made easy the approach to its heights for those (angels) who come down with His commands and those (angels) who go up with the deeds of the creatures. He called it when it was yet (in the form of) vapour. At once the links of its joints joined up. Then Allah opened up its closed door and put the sentinels of meteors at its holes, and held them with His hands (i.e. power) from falling into the vastness of air.

He commanded it to remain stationary in obedience to His commands. He made its sun the bright indication for its day, and moon the gloomy indication for its night. He then put them in motion in their orbits and ordained their (pace of) movement in the stages of their paths in order to distinguish with their help between night and day, and in order that the reckoning of years and calculations may be known by their fixed movements. Then He hung in its vastness its sky and put therein its decoration consisting of small bright pearls and lamp-like stars. He shot at the over-hearers arrows of bright meteors. He put them in motion on their appointed routine and made them into fixed stars, moving stars, descending stars, ascending stars, ominous stars and lucky stars.

Description of Angels

Then Allah, the Glorified, created for inhabiting of His skies and populating the higher strata of his realm new (variety of) creatures namely the angels. With them He filled the openings of its cavities and populated with them the vastness of it circumference. In between the openings of these cavities there resounds the voices of angels glorifying Him in the enclosures of sublimity, (behind) curtains of concealment and in veils of His Greatness. And behind this resounding which deafens the ears there is the effulgence of light which defies the approach of sight to it, and consequently the sight stands, disappointed at its limitation.

He created them in different shapes and with diverse characteristics. They have wings. They glorify the sublimity of His Honour. They do not appropriate to themselves His skill that shows itself in creation. Nor do they claim they create anything in which He is unparalleled.

But they are rather honoured creatures who do not take precedence over Him in uttering anything, and they act according to His command." (Quraan, 21: 26-27).

He has made them the trustees of His revelation and sent them to Prophets as holders of His injunctions and prohibitions. He has immunised them against the waviness of doubts. Consequently no one among them goes astray from the path of His will. He has helped them with the benefits of succour and has covered their hearts with humility and peace. He has opened for them doors of submission to His Glories. He has fixed for them bright minarets as signs of His Oneness. The weights of sins do not burden them and the rotation of nights and days does not make them move. Doubts do not attack with arrows the firmness of their faith. Misgivings do not assault the bases of their beliefs. The spark of malice does not ignite among them. Amazement does not tarnish what knowledge of Him their hearts possess, or His greatness and awe of His glory that resides in their bosoms. Evil thoughts do not lean towards them to affect their imagination with their own rust.

Among them are those who are in the frame of heavy clouds, or in the height of lofty mountains, or in the gloom of over-powering darkness. And there are those whose feet have pierced the lowest boundaries of the earth. These feet are like white ensigns which have gone forth into the vast expanse of wind. Under them blows the light wind which retains them upto its last end.

Occupation in His worship has made them carefree, and realities of Faith have served as a link between them and His knowledge. Their belief in Him has made them concentrate on Him. They long from Him not from others. They have tasted the sweetness of His knowledge and have drunk from the satiating cup of His love. The roots of His fear have been implanted in the depth of their hearts. Consequently they have bent their straight backs through His worship. The length of the humility, and extreme nearness has not removed from them the rope of their fear.

They do not entertain pride so as to make much of their acts. Their humility before the glory of Allah does not allow them to esteem their own virtues. Languor does not affect them despite their long affliction. Their longings (for Him) do not lessen so that they might turn away from hope in (Allah) their Sustainer. The tips of their tongues do not get dry by constant prayers (to Allah). Engagements (in other matters) do not betake them so as to turn their (loud) voices for Him into faint ones. Their shoulders do not get displaced in the postures of worship. They do not move their necks (this and that way) for comfort in disobedience of His command. Follies of negligence do not act against their determination to strive, and the deceptions of desires do not overcome their courage.

They regard the Master of the Throne (Allah) as the store for the day of their need. Because of their love (for Him) they turn to Him even when others turn to the creatures. They do not reach the ending limit of His worship. Their passionate fondness for His worship does not turn them except to the springs of their own hearts, springs which are never devoid of His hope and His fear. Fear (of Allah) never leaves them so that they might slacken in their efforts, nor have temptations entrapped them so that they might prefer this light search over their (serious) effort.

They do not consider their past (virtuous) deeds as big, for if they had considered them big then fear would have wiped away hopes from their hearts. They did not differ (among themselves) about their Sustainer as a result of Satan's control over them. The vice of separation from one another did not disperse them. Rancour and mutual malice did not overpower them. Ways of wavering did not divide them. Differences of degree of courage did not render them into divisions. Thus they are devotees of faith. Neither crookedness (of mind), nor excess, nor lethargy nor languor breaks them from its rope. There is not the thinnest point in the skies but there is an angel over it in prostration (before Allah) or (busy) in quick performance (of His commands). By long worship of their Sustainer they increase their knowledge, and the honour of their Sustainer increases in their hearts.

Description of Earth and its Spreading on Water

Allah spread the earth on stormy and tumultuous waves and the depths of swollen seas, where waves clashed with each other and high surges leapt over one another. They emitted foam like the she-camel at the time of sexual excitement. So the tumult of the stormy water was subdued by the weight of the earth, when the earth pressed it with its chest its shooting agitation eased, and when the earth rolled on it with its shoulder bones the water meekly submitted. Thus after the tumult of its surges it became tame and overpowered, and an obedient prisoner of the shackles of disgrace, while the earth spread itself and became solid in the stormy depth of this water. (In this way) the earth put an end to the pride, self-conceit, high position and superiority of the water, and muzzled the intrepidity of its flow. Consequently it stopped after its stormy flow and settled down after its tumult.

When the excitement of water subsided under the earth's sides and under the weight of the high and lofty mountains placed on its shoulders, Allah flowed springs of water from its high tops and distributed them through plains and low places and moderated their movement by fixed rocks and high mountain tops. Then its trembling came to a standstill because of the penetration of mountains in (various) parts of its surface and their being fixed in its deep areas, and their standing on its plains. Then Allah created vastness between the earth and firmament, and provided blowing wind for its inhabitants. Then He directed its inhabitants to spread all over its convenient places. Thereafter He did not leave alone the barren tracts of the earth where high portions lacked in water-springs and where rivers could not find their way, but created floating clouds which enliven the unproductive areas and grow vegetation.

He made a big cloud by collecting together small clouds and when water collected in it and lightning began to flash on its sides and the flash continued under the white clouds as well as the heavy ones He sent it raining heavily. The cloud was hanging towards the earth and southerly winds were squeezing it into shedding its water like a she-camel bending down for milking. When the cloud prostrated itself on the ground and delivered all the water it carried on itself Allah grew vegetation on the plain earth and herbage on dry mountains. As a result, the earth felt pleased at being decorated with its gardens and wondered at her dress of soft vegetation and the ornaments of its blossoms. Allah made all this the means of sustenance for the people and feed for the beasts. He has opened up highways in its expanse and has established minarets (of guidance) for those who tread on its highways.

The Creation of Man and the Sending of the Prophet

When He has spread out the earth and enforced His commands He chose Adam (peace be upon him) as the best in His creation and made him the first of all creation. He made him to reside in Paradise and arranged for his eating in it, and also indicated from what He had prohibited him. He told him that proceeding towards it meant His disobedience and endangering his own position. But Adam did what he had been refrained from, just as Allah already knew beforehand. Consequently, Allah sent him down after (accepting) his repentance, to populate His earth with his progeny and to serve as a proof and plea for Him among his creatures.

Even when He made Adam die He did not leave them without one who would serve among them as proof and plea for His Godhead, and serve as the link between them and His knowledge, but He provided to them the proofs through His chosen Messengers and bearers of the trust of His Message, age after age till the process came to end with our Prophet

Mohammad — Allah may bless him and his descendants — and His pleas and warnings reached finality.

He ordained livelihoods[1] with plenty and with paucity. He distributed them narrowly as well as profusely. He did it with justice to test whomever

---

-1- In the management of the affairs of this world Allah has connected the sequence with the cause of human acts as a result of which the power of action in man does not remain idle, in the same way He had made these actions dependent on His own will, so man should not rely on his own power of action and forget the Creator. This is the issue of the will between two wills in the controversy of "free will or compulsion. Just as in the entire Universe nature's universal and sovereign law is in force, in the same way the production and distribution of food also is provided in a set manner under the dual force of Divine ordainment and human effort. And this is somewhere less and somewhere more depending on the proportion of human effort and the aim of Divine ordainment. Since He is the Creator of the means of livelihood, and the powers of seeking food have also been bestowed by Him, the paucity or plenty of livelihood has been attributed to Him because He has fixed different and separate measures for livelihood keeping in view the difference in efforts and actions and the good of the creatures. Somewhere there is poverty and somewhere affluence, somewhere distress and somewhere comfort, and some one is enjoying pleasure while some one else is suffering the hardships of want.
Quraan says:
...amplifieth He their sustenance unto whomsoever He willeth and straiteneth; Verily He knoweth all things. (Quraan, 42:12)
In sermon 23 Ameer al-Momineen has referred to this matter and said:
The Divine command descends from the sky towards the earth with whatever is ordained for every one, whether less or more, just like rain drops.
So just as there is a fixed process and manner for the benevolence of rain namely that vapours rise from the sea with the store of water, spread over in the sky in the shape of dark clouds and then ooze the water by drops till they form themselves in regular lines. They irrigate plains as well as high lands thoroughly and proceed onwards to collect in the low areas, so that the thirsty may drink it, animals may use it and dry lands may be watered from it. In the same way Allah has provided all the means of livelihood but His bounty follows a particular mode in which there is never a jot of deviation. Thus Allah says:
And there is not a thing but with Us are its treasures, and We do not send it down but in a known measure. (Quraan, 15:21)
If man's greed and avarice exceeds its bounds, then just as excess of rain ruins crops instead of growing and bringing them up, so the abundance of the article of livelihood and necessaries of life would make man oblivious of Allah and rouse him to revolt and unruliness. Consequently, Allah says:

He desired, with prosperity or with destitution, and to test through it the gratefulness or endurance of the rich and the poor. Then He coupled plenty with misfortunes of destitution, safety with the distresses of calamities and pleasures of enjoyment with pangs of grief. He created fixed ages and made them long or short and earlier or later, and ended them up with death. He had made death capable of pulling up the ropes of ages and cutting them asunder.

And should Allah amplify the sustenance unto his servants, they would certainly rebel in the earth, but He sendeth it down by measure as he willeth; Verily of His servants, He is All-aware, All-seeing. (Quraan, 42:27)

If He lessens the food then just as stoppage of rain makes the land arid and kills the animals, in the same way, by closure of the means of livelihood, human society would be destroyed and so there would remain no means of living and livelihood. Allah accordingly says:

Or who is that who can provide you with sustenance should He withhold His sustenance? ...(Quraan, 67:21)

Consequently, Allah, the Wise the Omniscient has put the organisation for livelihood on moderate and proportionate lines, and in order to emphasise the importance of livelihood and sustenance and to keep them correlated with each other has introduced differences in the distribution of livelihood. Sometimes, this difference and unequal distribution owes itself to the difference of human effort and sometimes it is the consequence of overall arrangement of the affairs of the Universe and Divine acts of wisdom and objectives. This is because, if by poverty and want He has tested the poor in endurance and patience, in affluence and wealth there is severe test of the rich by way of thanks-giving and gratifying the rights of others, namely whether the rich person gratifies the claims of the poor and the distressed, and whether he takes care of the destitute or not. Again, where there is wealth there would also be dangers of all sorts. Sometimes there would be danger to the wealth and property and sometimes fear of poverty and want.

Consequently, there would be many persons who would be more satisfied and happy for lack of wealth. For them this destitution and want would be far better than the wealth which might snatch away their comfort and peace. Moreover sometimes this very wealth which one holds dearer than life becomes the cause of loss of one's life. Further, it has also been seen that so long as wealth was lacking character was above reproach, life was unblemished, but the moment property and wealth changed into plenty the conduct worsened, character became faulty and there appeared the vice of drink, crowd of beauties and gathering of singing and music. In such a case the absence of wealth was a blessing. However, being ignorant of Allah's objectives, man cries out and being affected by transitory distress begins complaining but does not realise from how many vices which could have accrued owing to wealth he has remained aloof. Therefore, if wealth produces conveniences, poverty serves as a guard for the character.

He[1] knows the secrets of those who conceal them, the secret conversation of those who engage in it, the inner feelings of those who indulge in guesses, the established certainties, the inklings of the eyes, the inner contents of hearts and depths of the unknown. He also knows what can be heard only by bending the holes of the ears, the summer resorts of ants and winter abodes of the insects, resounding of the cries of wailing women and the sound of steps. He also knows the spots in the inner sheaths of leaves where fruits grow, the hiding places of beasts namely caves in mountains and valleys, the hiding holes of mosquitoes on the trunks of trees and their herbage, the sprouting points of leaves in the branches, the dripping points of semen passing through passages of loins, small rising clouds and the big giant ones, the drops of rain in the thick clouds, the particles of dust scattered by whirlwinds through their skirts,

---

-1- The eloquence with which Ameer al-Momineen has thrown light on Allah's attributes of knowledge and the sublime words in which he has pictured the all-engrossing quality of His knowledge cannot but impress the mind of the most die-hard opponent. Thus, bn-Abil-Hadeed has written:

If Aristotle, who believed that Allah is only aware of the universe and not of its particulars, had heard this speech, his heart too would have inclined, his hair would have stood on end and his thinking would have undergone a dramatic change. Do you not see the brightness, force, vehemence, sublimity, glory, seriousness and ripeness of this speech? Besides these qualities, there is sweetness, colourfulness, delicacy and smoothness in it. I have not found any utterance similar to it. Of course, if there is any utterance matching it, that can be the word of Allah only. And there is no wonder in it, because he is an off-shoot of the same tree (of the Prophet Ibraheem, who set up the Unity of Allah) , a distributory of the same river and a reflection of the same light. (Sharh Nahjol-Balagha, vol.7, pp.23-24)

Those who regard Allah to possess only over-all knowledge argue that since details undergo changes, to believe Him to have knowledge of the changing details would necessitate changes in His knowledge but since knowledge is the same as His Being, His Being would have to be regarded as the object of change the result of which would be that He would have to be taken as having come into existence. In this way He would lose the attribute of being from ever. This is a very deceptive fallacy because changes in the object of knowledge can lead to changes in the knower only when it is assumed that the knower does not already possess knowledge of these changes. But since all the forms of change and alteration are crystal clear before Him there is no reason that with the changes in the objects of knowledge He too should be regarded changeable, although really this change is confined to the object of knowledge and does not affect knowledge in itself.

the lines erased by rain floods, the movements of insects on sand-dunes, the nests of winged creatures on the cliffs of mountains and the singing of chattering birds in the gloom of their brooding places.

And He knows whatever has been treasured by mother-of-pearls, and covered under the waves of oceans, all that which is concealed under the darkness of night and all that on which the light of day is shining, as well as all that on which sometimes darkness prevails and sometimes light shines, the trace of every footstep, the feel of every movement, the echo of every sound, the motion of every lip, the abode of every living being, the weight of every particle, the sobs of every sobbing heart, and whatever is there on the earth like fruits of trees or falling leaf, or the settling place of semen, or the congealing of blood or clot and the developing of life and embryo.

On all this He suffers no trouble, and no impediment hampers Him in the preservation of what he created nor any languor or grief hinders Him from the enforcement of commands and management of the creatures. His knowledge penetrates through them and they are within His counting. His justice extends to all of them and His bounty encompasses them despite their falling short of what is due to Him.

O my Allah! thou deservest handsome description and the highest esteem. If wish is directed towards Thee, Thou art the best to be wished for. If hope is reposed in Thee, Thou art the Most Honoured to be hoped from. O my Allah! Thou hast bestowed on me such power that I do not praise any one other than Thee, and I do not eulogise any one save Thee. I do not direct my praise towards others who are sources of disappointment and centres of misgivings. Thou hast kept away my tongue from the praises of human beings and eulogies of the created and the sustained. O my Allah! every praiser has on whom he praises the right of reward and recompense. Certainly, I have turned to Thee with my eye at the treasures of Thy Mercy and stores of forgiveness.

O my Allah! here stands one who has singled Thee with Oneness that is Thy due and has not regarded any one deserving of these praises and eulogies except Thee. My want towards Thee is such that nothing except Thy generosity can cure its destitution, nor provide for its need except Thy obligation and Thy generosity. So do grant us in this place Thy will and make us free from stretching hands to anyone other than Thee.

Certainly, Thou art powerful over every thing." (Quraan, 66:8).

SERMONS 91

When people decided to swear Allegiance[1] to him after the murder of Othmaan

-1- When with the murder of Othmaan the seat of Caliphate became vacant, Moslims began to look at Ali (p.b.u.h.) whose peaceful conduct, adherence to principles, and political acumen had been witnessed by them to a great extent during this long period. Consequently, they rushed for swearing allegiance in the same way as a traveller who had lost his way and catches sight of the objective would have rushed towards it, as the historian at-Tabari (in at-Taareekh, vol.1, pp.3066, 3067, 3076) records:

People thronged on Ameer al-Momineen and said "We want to swear allegiance to you and you see what troubles are befalling Islam and how we are being tried about the near ones of the Prophet. "

But Ameer al-Momineen declined to accede to their request whereupon these people raised a hue and cry and began to shout loudly, "O Abol-Hasan, do you not witness the ruination of Islam or see the advancing flood of unruliness and mischief? Do you have no fear of Allah?" Even then Ameer al-Momineen showed no readiness to consent because he was noticing that the effects of the atmosphere that had come into being after the Prophet had overcome hearts and minds of the people, selfishness and lust for power had become rooted in them, their thinking affected by materialism and they had become habituated to treating government as the means for securing their ends. Now they would like to materialise the Divine Caliphate too and play with it. In these circumstances it would be impossible to change the mentalities or turn the direction of temperaments. In addition to these ideas he had also seen the end in view that these people should get further time to think over so that on frustration of their material ends hereafter they should not say that the allegiance had been sworn by them under a temporary expediency and that thought had not been given to it, just as Omar's idea was about the first Caliphate, which appears from his statement that:

Abi-Bakr's Caliphate came into being without thought but Allah saved us from its mischief. If anyone repeats such an affair you should kill him. (Saheeh Bokhaari, vol. 8, pp.210, 211; al-Mosnad, Ahmad bn Hambal, vol.1, p.55; at-Tabari, vol.1, p.1822; bn al-Athir, vol.2, p.327; bn Hishaam, vol.4, pp.308-309; bn Katheer, vol.5, p.246)

Leave me and seek some one else. We are facing a matter which has (several) faces and colours, which neither hearts can stand nor intelligence can accept. Clouds are hovering over the sky, and faces are not discernible. You should know that if I respond to you I would lead you as I know and would not care about whatever one may say or abuse. If you leave me then I am the same as you are. It is possible I would listen to and obey whomever you make in charge of your affairs. I am better for you as a counsellor than as chief.

SERMONS 92

Annihilation of the Kharijites, Mischief Mongering of Omayyads and Vastness of his own knowledge[1]

In short, when their insistence increased beyond limits, Ameer al-Momineen delivered this sermon wherein he clarified that "If you want me for your worldly ends, then I am not ready to serve as your instrument. Leave me and select someone else who may fulfil your ends. You have seen my past life that I am not prepared to follow anything except the Quraan and Sonna and would not give up this principle for securing power. If you select someone else I would pay regard to the laws of the state and the constitution as a peaceful citizen should do. I have not at any stage tried to disrupt the collective existence of the Moslims by inciting revolt. The same will happen now. Rather, just as keeping the common good in view I have hitherto been giving correct advice, I would not grudge doing the same. If you let me in the same position it would be better for your worldly ends, because in that case I wont have power in my hands so that I could stand in the way of your worldly affairs, and create an impediment against your hearts" wishes. However, if you are determined on swearing allegiance on my hand, bear in mind that if you frown or speak against me I would force you to tread on the path of right, and in the matter of the right I would not care for anyone. If you want to swear allegiance even at this, you can satisfy your wish. "

The impression Ameer al-Momineen had formed about these people is fully corroborated by later events. Consequently, when those who had sworn allegiance with worldly motives did not succeed in their objectives they broke away and rose against his government with baseless allegations.

-1- Ameer al-Momineen delivered this sermon after the battle of Nahrawan. In it, mischief imply the battles fought in Basra, Siffeen and Nahrawan because their nature was different from the battles of the Prophet. There the opposite party were the unbelievers while here the confrontation was with those who had veils of Islam on their faces. So people were hesitant to fight against Moslims, and asked why they should fight

So now, praise and eulogy be to Allah, O people, I have put out the eye of revolt. No one except me advanced towards it when its gloom was swelling and its madness was intense. Ask me before you miss me,[1] because, by Allah, who has my life in His hands, if you ask me anything

---

with those who recited the call to the prayers and offered the prayers. Thus, Khozayma bn Thabit al-Ansaari did not take part in the Battle of Siffeen till the falling of Ammaar bn Yaasir as martyr did not prove that the opposite party was rebellious. Similarly the presence of companions like Talha and az-Zobayr who were included in the "Foretold Ten" on the side of Aysha in Basra, and the prayer signs on foreheads of the Kharijites in Nahrawan and their prayers and worships were creating confusion in the minds. In these circumstances only those could have the courage to rise against them were aware of the secrets of their hearts and the reality of their faith. It was the peculiar perception of Ameer al-Momineen and his spiritual courage that he rose to oppose them, and testified the saying of the Holy Prophet:

You will fight after me with the breakers of allegiance (people of Jamal) , oppressors (people of Syria) and deviators (the Kharijites). (al-Mostadrak ala as-Saheehayn, al-Hakim, vol.3, p.139, 140; ad-Dorrol-Manthoor, vol.6, p.18; al-Isteeaab, vol.3, p.1117; Osdol-Ghaaba, vol.4 pp.32, 33; Taareekh Baghdad, vol.8, p.340; vol.13, pp.186, 187; at-Taareekh, bn Asakir, vol.5, p.41; at-Taareekh, bn Katheer, vol.7, pp.304, 305, 306; Majma az-Zawaaid, vol.7, p.238; vol.9, p.235; Sharh al-Mawaahib, vol.3, pp.316-317; Kanz al-Ommaal, vol.6, pp.72, 82, 88, 155, 319, 391, 392; vol.8, p.215)

1 After the Holy Prophet no one save Ameer al-Momineen could utter the challenge "Ask whatever you want to" bn Abdl-Barr in Jaami" Bayaan al-Ilm wa Fazlihi, vol.1 p.58 and in al-Isteeaab, vol.3, p.1103; bn al-Athir in Osdol-Ghaaba, vol.4, p.22; bn-Abil-Hadeed in Sharh Nahjol-Balagha, vol.7, p.46; as-Seyooti in Taareekh al-Kholafaa, p.171 and bn Hajar al-Haythami in as-Sawaaiq al-Mohriqa, p.76 have written that "None among the companions of the Holy Prophet ever said "Ask me whatever you want to" except Ali bn Abi-Talib" However, among other than the companions a few names do appear in history who did utter such a challenge, such as Ibraheem bn Hishaam al-Makhzoomi, Moqatil bn Solaymaan, Qatada bn Diama, Abdr-Rahmaan (bn al-Jawzi) and Mohammad bn Idrees ash-Shaafii etc. but everyone of them had to face disgrace and was forced to take back his challenge. This challenge can be urged only by him who knows the realities of the Universe and is aware of the happenings of the future. Ameer al-Momineen, the opener of the door of the Prophet's knowledge, as he was, was the only person who was never seen being unable to answer any question on any occasion, so much so that even Caliph Omar had to say that "I seek Allah's protection from the difficulty for the solution of which Ali would not be available" Similarly, the prophecies of Ameer al-Momineen made about the future proved true word by word and served as an index to his vast knowledge, whether they be about the devastation of Bani-Omayya or the rising of the Kharijites, the wars and destruction by the Tartars or the attacks of the English, the floods of Basra of the ruination of Koofa. In short, when these events are historical realities there is no reason why this challenge of Ameer al-Momineen should be wondered at.

between now and the Day of Judgement or about the group who would guide a hundred people and also misguide a hundred people I would tell you who is announcing its march, who is driving it in the front and who is driving it at the rear, the stages where its riding animals would stop for rest and the final place of stay, and who among them would be killed and who would die a natural death.

When I am dead, hard circumstances and distressing events would befall you, many persons in the position of asking questions would remain silent with cast down eye, while those in the position of replying would lose courage. This would be at a time when wars would descend upon you with all hardship and days would be so hard on you that you would feel them prolonged because of hardship till Allah would give victory to those remaining virtuous among you.

When mischief come they confuse (right with wrong) and when they clear away they leave a warning. They cannot be known at the time of approach but are recognised at the time of return. They blow like the blowing of winds, striking some cities and missing others.

Beware that the worst mischief for you in my view is the mischief of Bani-Omayya, because it is blind and also creates darkness. Its sway is general but its ill effects are for particular people. He who remains clear-sighted in it would be affected by distress, and he who remains blind in it would avoid the distress. By Allah. you will find Bani-Omayya after me worst people for yourselves, like the old unruly she-camel who bites with its mouth, beats with its fore-legs, kicks with its hind legs and refuses to be milked. They would remain over you till they would leave among you only those who benefit them or those who do not harm them. Their calamity would continue till your seeking help from them would become like the seeking of help by the slave from his master or of the follower from the leader.

Their mischief would come to you like evil eyed fear and pre-Islamic fragments, wherein there would be no minaret of guidance nor any sign (of salvation) to be seen. We Ahlil-Bayt (the Household of the Prophet) are free from this mischief and we are not among those who would engender it. Thereafter, Allah would dispel it from you like the removal of the skin (from flesh) through him who would humble them, drag them by necks, make them drink full cups (of hardships), not extend them anything but sword and not clothe them save with fear. At that time Quraysh would wish at the cost of the world and all its contents to find me even only once and just for the duration of the slaughter of a camel in order that I may accept from them (the whole of) that of which at present I am asking them only a part but they are not giving me.

SERMONS 93

Allah's Praise and Eulogy of the Prophets

Exalted is Allah Whom heights of daring cannot approach and fineness of intelligence cannot find. He is such First that there is no extremity for Him so that He be contained within it, nor is there an end for Him where would cease.

About the Prophets

Allah kept the Prophets in deposit in the best place of deposit and made them stay in the best place of stay. He moved them in succession from distinguished fore-fathers to chaste wombs. Whenever a predecessor from among them died the follower stood up for the cause of the religion of Allah.

The Holy Prophet and His Descendants (Etra)

Until this distinction of Allah, the Glorified, reached Mohammad — peace and blessing of Allah be upon him and his descendants. Allah brought him out from the most distinguished sources of origin and the most honourable places of planting, namely from the same (lineal) tree from which He brought forth other Prophets and from which He selected His trustees. Mohammad's descendants are the best descendants, his kinsmen the best of kin and his lineal tree the best of trees. It grew in esteem and rose in distinction. It has tall branches and unapproachable fruits.

He is the leader (Imam) of all who exercise fear (of Allah) and a light for those who seek guidance. He is a lamp whose flame is burning, a meteor whose light is shining and a flint whose spark is bright. His conduct is upright, his behaviour is guiding, his speech is decisive and his decision is just. Allah sent him after an interval from the previous Prophets when people had fallen into errors of action and ignorance. Allah may have mercy on you.

May Allah shower His mercy on you! Do act according to the clear signs, because the way is straight and leads to the house of safety while you are in the place of seeking Allah's favour, and have time and opportunity. The books (of your doings) are open and pens (of angels) are busy (to record your actions) while your bodies are healthy, tongues are free, repentance is accepted and deeds are accorded recognition.

SERMONS 94

People at the time of the Prophet's Proclamation and his Actions to do with the Dissemination of His Message

Allah sent the Prophet at a time when the people were going astray in perplexity and were moving here and there in mischief. Desires had deflected them and self-conceit had swerved them. Extreme ignorance had made them foolish. They were confounded by the unsteadiness of matters and the evils of ignorance. Then the Prophet — blessing of Allah be upon him and his descendants — did his best in giving them sincere advice, himself trod on the right path and called (them) towards wisdom and good counsel.

SERMONS 95

In Eulogy of the Holy Prophet

Praise be to Allah who is such First that nothing is before Him and such Last that there is nothing after Him. He is such Manifest that there is nothing above Him and such Hidden that there is nothing nearer than He.

The Holy Prophet

His place of stay is the best of all places and his origin the noblest of all origins in the mines of honour and the cradles of safety. Hearts of virtuous persons have been inclined towards him and the reins of eyes have been turned towards him. Through him Allah buried mutual rancour and put off the flames of revolt. Through him He gave them affection like brothers and separated those who were together (through unbelief). Through him He gave honour to the low and degraded honour (of unbelief). His speaking is clear and his silence is (indicative) like tongue.

SERMONS 96

Admonishing his own Companions[1]

-1- In the atmosphere that had been created soon after the Prophet the Ahlil-Bayt (members of his family) had no course except to remain secluded as a result of which world has remained ignorant of their real qualities and unacquainted with their teachings and attainments, and to belittle them and keeping them away from authority has been considered as the greatest service to Islam. If Othmaan's open misdeeds had not given a chance to the Moslims to wake up and open their eyes there would have been no question of allegiance to Ameer al-Momineen and temporal authority would have retained the same course as it had so far followed. But all those who could be named for the purpose had no courage to come forward because of their own shortcomings while Moaawiya was sitting in his capital away from the centre. In these circumstances there was none except Ameer al-Momineen who could be looked at. Consequently people's eyes hovered around him and the same common people who, following the direction of the wind, had been swearing allegiance to others jumped at him for swearing allegiance. Nevertheless, this allegiance was not on the count that they regarded his Caliphate as from Allah and him as an Imam (Divine Leader) to obey whom was obligatory. It was rather under their own principles which were known as democratic or consultative. However, there was one group who was swearing allegiance to him as a religious obligation regarding his Caliphate as determined by Allah. Otherwise, the majority regarded him a ruler like the other Caliphs, and as regards precedence, on the fourth position, or at the level of the common men after the three caliphs. Since the people, the army, and the civil servants had been impressed by the beliefs and actions of the previous rulers and immersed in their ways whenever they found anything against their liking they fretted and frowned, evaded war and were ready to rise in disobedience and revolt. Further, just as among those who fought in Jihaad with the Prophet there were some seekers of this world and others of the next world, in the same way here too there was

Although Allah gives time to the oppressor, His catch would not spare him. Allah watches him on the passage of his way and the position of that which suffocates the throats.By Allah in Whose power my life lies, these people (Moaawiya and his men) will overcome you not because they have a better right than you but because of their hastening towards the wrong with their leader and your slowness about my right (to be followed). People are afraid of the oppression of their rulers while I fear the oppression of my subjects.

I called you for war but you did not come. I warned you but you did not listen. I called you secretly as well as openly, but you did not respond. I gave you sincere counsel, but you did not accept it. Are you present like the absent, and slaves like masters? I recite before you points of wisdom but you turn away from them, and I advise you with far reaching advice but you disperse away from it. I rouse you for Jihaad against the people of revolt but before I come to the end of my speech, I see you disperse like the sons of Saba.[1] You return to your places and deceive one another by

---

no dearth of worldly men who were, in appearance, with Ameer al-Momineen but actually they had connections with Moaawiya who has promised some of them positions and had extended to others temptation of wealth. To hold them as Shiahs of Ameer al-Momineen and to blame Shiism for this reason is closing the eyes to facts, because the beliefs of these people would be the same as of those who regarded Ameer al-Momineen fourth in the series. bn-Abil-Hadeed throws light on the beliefs of these persons in clear words:

Whoever observes minutely the events during the period of Caliphate of Ameer al-Momineen would know that Ameer al-Momineen had been brought to bay because those who knew his real position were very few, and the swarming majority did not bear that belief about him which was obligatory to have. They gave precedence to the previous Caliphs over him and held that the criterion of precedence was Caliphate, and in this matter those coming later followed the predecessors, and argued that if the predecessors had not the knowledge that the previous Caliphs had precedence over Ameer al-Momineen they would not have preferred them to him. Rather, these people knew and took Ameer al-Momineen as a citizen and subject. Most of those who fought in his company did so on grounds of prestige or Arab partisanship, not on the ground of religion or belief. (Sharh Nahjol-Balagha, vol.7, p.72)

1 The progeny of Saba" bn Yashjob bn-Yarob bn Qahtaan is known as the tribe of Saba. When these people began to falsify prophets then to shake them Allah sent to them a flood of water by which their gardens were submerged and they left their houses and

your counsel. I straighten you in the morning but you are back to me in the evening as curved as the back of a bow. The straightener has become weary while those to be straightened have become incorrigible.

O those whose bodies are present but wits are absent, and whose wishes are scattered. Their rulers are on trial. Your leader obeys Allah but you disobeyed him while the leader of the people of Syria (Sham) disobeys Allah but they obey him. By Allah, I wish Moaawiya exchanges with me like Dinars with Dirhams, so that he takes from me ten of you and gives me one from them.

O people of Koofa, I have experienced in you three things and two others: you are deaf in spite of having ears, dumb in spite of speaking, and blind in spite of having eyes. You are neither true supporters in combat nor dependable brothers in distress. Your hands may be soiled with earth. O examples of those camels whose herdsman has disappeared, if they are collected together from one side they disperse from the other. By Allah, I see you in my imagination that if war becomes intense and action is in full swing you would run away from the son of Abi-Talib like the woman who becomes naked in the front. I am certainly on clear guidance from my Lord (Allah) and on the path of my Prophet and I am on the right path which I adhere to regularly.

The Household of the Holy Prophet

Look at the people of the Prophet's family. Adhere to their direction. Follow their footsteps because they would never let you out of guidance, and never throw you into destruction. If they sit down, you sit down, and if they rise up you rise up. Do not go ahead of them, as you would thereby go astray and go not lag behind of them as you would thereby be ruined.

I have seen the companions of the Prophet but I do not find anyone resembling them. They began the day with dust on the hair and face (in hardship of life) and passed the night in prostration and standing in

---

property to settle down in different cities. This proverb arose out of this event and it is now applied wherever people so disperse that there can be no hope of their joining together again.

prayers. Sometimes they put down their foreheads and sometimes their cheeks. With the recollection of their resurrection it seemed as though they stood on live coal. It seemed that in between their eyes there were signs like knees of goats, resulting from long prostrations. When Allah was mentioned their eyes flowed freely till their shirt collars were drenched. They trembled for fear of punishment and hope of reward as the tree trembles on the day of stormy wind.

SERMONS 97

Oppression of the Omayyads

By Allah, they would continue like this till there would be left no unlawful act before Allah but they would make it lawful and no pledge but they would break it, and till there would remain no house of bricks or of woollen tents but their oppression would enter it. Their bad dealings would make them wretched, till two groups of crying complainants would rise, one would cry for his religion and the other for this world and the help of one of you to one of them would be like the help of a slave to his master, namely when he is present he obeys him, but when the master is away he backbites him. The highest among you in distress would be he who bear best belief about Allah. If Allah grants you safety accept it, and if you are put in trouble endure it, because surely (good) result is for the God-fearing.

SERMONS 98

Abstinence of the World and Vicissitudes of Time

We praise Allah for what has happened and seek His succour in our affairs for what is yet to happen, and we beg Him for safety in the faith just as we beg Him for safety in our bodies.

O creatures of Allah! I advise you to keep away from this world which is (shortly) to leave you even though you do not like its departure, and which would make your bodies old even though you would like to keep them fresh. Your example and its example is like the travellers who travel some distance and then as though they traverse it quickly or they aimed at a sign and reached it at once. How short is the distance to the aim if one heads towards it and reaches it. And how short is the stage of one who has only a day which he cannot exceed while a swift driver is driving him in this world till he departs from it.

So do not hanker after worldly honour and its pride, and do not feel happy over its beauties and bounties nor wail over its damages and misfortunate because its honour and pride would end while its beauty and bounty would perish, and its damages and misfortunes would pass away. Every period in it has an end and every living being in it is to die. Is not there for you a warning in the relics of the predecessors and an eye opener and lesson in your fore-fathers, provided you understand?

Do you not see that your predecessors do not come back and the surviving followers do not remain? Do you not observe that the people of the world pass mornings and evenings in different conditions? Thus, (somewhere) the dead is wept for, someone is being condoled, someone is prostrate in distress, someone is enquiring about the sick, someone is passing his last breath, someone is hankering after the world while death is looking for him, someone is forgetful but he is not forgotten (by death), and on the footsteps of the predecessors walk the survivors.

Beware! At the time of committing evil deeds remember the destroyer of joys, the spoiler of pleasures, and the killer of desires (namely death). Seek assistance of Allah for fulfillment of His obligatory rights, and for (thanking Him) for His countless bounties and obligations.

SERMONS 99

The Holy Prophet and His Descendants

Praise be to Allah Who spreads His bounty throughout the creation, and extends His hand of generosity among them. We praise Him in all His affairs and seek His assistance for fulfillment of His rights. We stand witness that there is no god except He and that Mohammad

(p.b.u.h.a.h.p) is His slave and Prophet. He sent him to manifest His commands and speak about His remembrance. Consequently, he fulfilled it with trustworthiness, and he passed away while on the right path.
He left among us the standard of right. Whoever goes further from it goes out of Faith, whoever lags behind it is ruined. Whoever sticks to it would join (the right). Its guide is short of speech, slow of steps, and quick when he rises. When you have bent your necks before him and pointed towards him with your fingers his death would occur and would take him away. They would live after him as long as Allah wills, till Allah brings out for you one who would collect you together and fuse you after diffusion. Do not place expectations in one who does not[1] come forward and do not lose hope in one who is veiled, because it is possible that one of the two feet of the veiled one may slip while the other may remain sticking, till both return to position and stick.
Beware! The example of the descendant (Al) of Mohammad — peace and blessing of Allah be upon him and his descendants — is like that of stars in the sky. When one star sets another one rises. So you are in a position that Allah's blessings on you have been perfected and He has shown you what you used to wish for.

SERMONS 100

Vicissitudes of time

He (Allah) is the First before every first and the Last after every last. His Firstness necessitates that there is no (other) first before Him and His Lastness necessitates that there is no other last after Him. I do stand witness that there is no god but Allah both openly as well as secretly, with heart as well as with tongue.
O people, do not commit the crime of opposing me, do not be seduced into disobeying me and do not wink at each other with eyes when you

-1- The implication is that if for the time being your expectations are not being fulfilled, you should not be disappointed. It is possible matters may improve, the impediments in the way of improvement may be removed and matters may be settled as you wish.

hear me. By Allah, Who germinates the seed and blows the wind, whatever I convey to you is from the Prophet. Neither the conveyor (of Allah's message, i. e. the Prophet) lied nor the hearer misunderstood. Well, it is as though I see a misguided man[1] who is shouting in Syria (Sham) and has put his banners in the out-skirt of Koofa. When his mouth would be fully opened, his recalcitrance would become intense and his steps on earth would become heavy (and tyrannical) then the disorder (so created) would cut the people with its teeth and war would rage with (all) its waves, days would become severe and night full of toil. So when the crops grows and stands on stalks, its foam shoots forth and its lightning shines, the banners of misguiding rebellion would fire up and shoot forth like darkening night and surging sea. This and how many other storms would rend Koofa and gales would sweep over it, and shortly heads would clash with heads, the standing crop would be harvested and the harvest would be smashed.

SERMONS 101

Day of Judgement

That day would be such that Allah would collect on it the anteriors and the posteriors, to stand in obedience for exaction of accounts and for award of recompense for deeds. Sweat would flow upto their mouths like reins while the earth would be trembling under them. In the best condition among them would be he who has found a resting place for both his feet and an open place for his breath.

Future Troubles (Fitan)

The troubles are like a dark night. Horses would not stand for (facing) them nor would their banners turn back. They would approach in full reins and ready with saddles. Their leader would be driving them and the rider would be exerting (them). The trouble-mongers are a people whose

-1- Some people have taken this to refer to Moaawiya and others to Abdl-Malik bn Marwaan.

attacks are severe. Those who would fight them for the sake of Allah would be a people who are low in the estimation of the proud, unknown in the earth but well known on the sky. Woe to you O Basra, when an army of Allah's infliction would face upon you without (raising) dust of cries. Your inhabitants would then face bloody death and dire hunger.

SERMONS 102

Abstemiousness and fear of Allah

O people! look at the world like those who abstain from it, and turn away from it. By Allah, it would shortly turn out its inhabitants and cause grief to the happy and the safe. That which turns and goes away from it never returns and that which is likely to come about is not known or anticipated. Its joy is mingled with grief. Herein men's firmness inclines towards weakness and languidness. The majority of what pleases you here should not mislead you because that which would help you would be little.

Allah may shower His mercy on him who ponders and takes lesson thereby, and when he takes lesson he achieves enlightenment. Whatever is present in this world would shortly not exist, while whatever is to exist in the next world is already in existence. Every countable thing would pass away. Every anticipation should be taken to be coming up and every thing that is to come up should be taken as just near.

Attributes of a Learned Person

Learned is he who knows his worth. It is enough for a man to remain ignorant if he knows not his worth. Certainly, the most hated man with Allah is he whom Allah has left for his own self. He goes astray from the right path, and moves without a guide. If he is called to the plantation of this world he is active, but if he is called to the plantation of the next world he is slow. As though what he is active for is obligatory upon him whereas in whatever he is slow was not required of him.

Concerning Future Times

There would be a time wherein only a sleeping (inactive) believer would be safe (such that) if he is present he is not recognised but if he is absent he is not sought after. These are the lamps of guidance and banners of night journeys. They do not spread calumnies nor divulge secrets, nor slander. They are those for whom Allah would open the doors of His mercy and keeps off from them the hardships of His chastisement.

O people! a time will come to you when Islam would be capsized as a pot is capsized with all its contents. O people, Allah has protected you from that He might be hard on you but He has not spared you from being put on trial. Allah the Sublimest of all speakers has said:

Verily in this are signs and We do only try (the people)." (Quraan, 23:30)

Sayyid Razi says: As regards Ameer al-Momineen's words "kollo Momineen nuwama" (every sleeping believer), he implies thereby one who is talked of little and causes no evil. And the word "al-masayih" is the plural of "misyah. He is one who spreads trouble among people through evils and calumnies. And the word "al-mazayi" is the plural of "mizya. He is one who on hearing of an evil about some one spreads it and shouts about it. And "al-buzur" is the plural of "bazur. He is one who excels in foolishness and speaks rubbish.

SERMONS 103

People before the Proclamation of Prophethood and the Prophet's performance in Spreading the message

So now, certainly Allah deputised Mohammad (p.b.u.h.a.h.p) as the Prophet while no one among the Arabs read the Book nor claimed Prophethood or revelation. He had to fight those who disobeyed him in company with those who followed him, leading them towards their salvation and hastening with them lest death overtook them. When any weary person sighed or a distressed one stopped he stood at him till he got him his aim, except the worst in whom there was not virtue at all. Eventually he showed them their goal and carried them to their places (of deliverance). Consequently, their affairs moved on and their hand-mill began to rotate (i.e. position gained strength), their spears got straightened.

By Allah, I was among their rear-guard till they turned back on their sides and were flocked in their rope. I never showed weakness or lack of courage, nor did I betray or become languid. By Allah, I shall split the wrong till I extract right from its flanks.

Sayyid Razi says: I have quoted a selected part of this sermon before, but since I have found in the narration that this part differs from the previous one, more or less, I deemed it necessary to quote it again here.

SERMONS 104

In eulogy of the Holy Prophet

Then Allah deputised Mohammad (p.b.u.h.a.h.p) as a witness, giver of good tidings and warner, the best in the universe as a child and the most chaste as a grown up man, the purest of the purified in conduct, the most generous of those who are approached for generosity.

The Omayyads

This world did not appear sweet to you in its pleasures and you did not secure milk from its udders except after having met it when its nose-rein was trailing and its leather girth was loose. For certain people its unlawful items were like bent branches (laden with fruit) while its lawful items were far away, not available. By Allah, you would find it like a long shade upto a fixed time. So the earth is with you without let or hindrance and your hands in it are extended while the hands of the leaders are held away from you. Your swords are hanging over them while their swords are held away from you.

Beware that for every blood (that is shed) there is an avenger and for every right there is a claimant. The avenger for our blood is like the judge for his own claim, and it is Allah who is such that if one seeks Him, then He does not disappoint him, and one who runs away from Him cannot escape Him. I swear by Allah, O Bani-Omayya, shortly you will see it (i.e. your possession) in the hands of others and in the house of your enemy. Know that the best looking eye is that whose sight catches virtue and know that the best hearing ear is that which hears good advice and accepts it.

Functions of the Imaams

O people, secure light from the flame of lamps of the preacher who follows what he preaches and draw water from the spring which has been cleaned of dirt.

O creatures of Allah, do not rely on your ignorance, do not be obedient to your desires, because he who stays at this place is like one who stays on the brink of a bank undermined by water carrying ruin on his back from one portion to the other following his opinion which he changes (one after the other). He wants to make adhere what cannot adhere and to bring together what cannot keep together. So fear Allah and do not place your complaints before him who cannot redress your grievance, nor undo with his opinion what has been made obligatory for you.

Certainly, there is no obligation on the Imam except what has been devolved on him from Allah, namely to convey warnings, to exert in good advice, to revive the Sonna, to enforce penalties on those liable to them and to issue shares to the deserving. So hasten towards knowledge before its vegetation dries up and before you turn yourselves away from seeking knowledge from those who have it. Desist others from the unlawful and abstain from it yourself, because you have been commanded to abstain (yourself) before abstaining (others).

SERMONS 105

Islam: Most Bright of All Paths

Praise be to Allah who established Islam and made it easy for those who approach it and gave strength to its columns against any one who tries to overpower it. So Allah made it (a source of) peace for him who clings to it, safety for him who enters it, argument for him who speaks about it, witness for him who fights with its help, light for him who seeks light from it, understanding for him who provides it, sagacity for him who exerts, a sign (of guidance) for him who perceives, sight for him who resolves, lesson for him who seeks advice, salvation for him who testifies, confidence for him who trusts, pleasure for him who entrusts, and shield for him who endures.

It is the most bright of all paths, the clearest of all passages. It has dignified minarets, bright highways, burning laps, prestigious field of activity, and high objective. It has a collection of race horses. It is approached eagerly. Its riders are honourable. Testimony (of Allah, Prophet etc.) is its way, good deeds are its minarets, death is its extremity, this world is its race-course, the Day of Judgement is its horses and Paradise is its point of approach.

About The Holy Prophet

The Prophet lighted flames for the seeker and put bright signs for the impeded. So he is Thy trustworthy trustee, Thy witness on the Day of Judgement, Thy deputy as a blessing and Thy messenger of truth as mercy. My Allah distribute to him a share from Thy Justice and award him multiples of good by Thy bounty. My Allah heighten his construction over the constructions of others, honour him when he comes to Thee, dignify his position before Thee, give him honourable position, and award him glory and distinction, and bring us out (on the Day of Judgement) among his party, neither ashamed, nor repentant, nor deviators, nor pledge-breakers, nor strayers, nor misleaders. nor seduced.

Sayyid Razi says: This sermon had already appeared earlier but we have repeated it here because of the difference between the two versions.

Addressed To His Followers

By bounty of Allah over you, you have acquired a position where even your slave maids are honoured, your neighbours are treated well. Even he over whom you enjoy no distinction or obligation honours you. Even those people fear you who had no apprehension of attack from you or any authority over you. You now see pledges to Allah being broken but do not feel enraged although you fret and frown on the breaking of the traditions of your forefathers. Allah's matters have been coming to you, and going from and again coming back to you; but you have made over your place to wrong-doers and thrown towards them your responsibilities, and have placed Allah's affairs in their hands. They act in doubts and tread in (fulfillment of) desires. By Allah, even if they disperse you under every star Allah would surely collect you on the day that would be worst for them.

SERMONS 106

Describing the Days of Siffeen

I have seen your flight and your dispersal from the lines. You were surrounded by rude and low people and Bedouins of Syria (Sham), although you are the chiefs of Arabs and summit of distinction, and possess dignity as that of the high nose and big hump of the camel. The sigh of my bosom can subside only when I eventually see you surrounding them as they surrounded you, and see you dislodging them from their position as they dislodged you, killing them with arrows and striking them with spears so that their forward rows might fall on the rear ones just like the thirsty camels who have been turned away from their place of drink and removed from their water-points.

SERMONS 107

Vicissitudes of Time

Praise be to Allah Who is Manifest before His creation because of themselves. Who is apparent to their hearts because of clear proof; Who created without meditating, since meditating does not befit except one who has thinking organs while He has no thinking organ in Himself. His knowledge has split forth the inside of unknown secrets and covered the bottom of deep beliefs.

The Holy Prophet

Allah chose him from the lineal tree of prophets, from the flame of light, from the forehead of greatness, from the best part of the valley of al-Bathaa, from the lamps for darkness, and from the sources of wisdom.

The Prophet was like a roaming physician who has set ready his ointments and heated his instruments. He uses them wherever the need arises for curing blind hearts, deaf ears, and dumb tongues. He followed with his medicines the spots of negligence and places of perplexity.

Blaming Moslims

They (people) did not take light from the lights of his wisdom nor did they produce flame from the flint of sparkling knowledge. So in this matter they are like grazing cattle and hard stones. Nevertheless, hidden things have appeared for those who perceive, the face of right has become clear for the wanderer, the approaching moment has raised the veil from its face and signs have appeared for those who search for them.

What is the matter with me! I see you just bodies without spirits and spirits without bodies, devotees without good, traders without profits, wakeful but sleeping, present but unseen, seeing but blind, hearing but deaf and speaking but dumb.

I notice that misguidance has stood on its centre and spread (all round) through its off-shoots. It weighs you with its weights and confuses you with its measures. Its leader is an out-cast from the community. He persists on misguidance. So on that day none from among you would remain except as the sediment in a cooking pot or the dust left after dusting a bundle. It would scrape you as leather is scraped, and trample you as harvest is trampled, and pick out the believer as a bird picks out a big grain from the thin grain.

Where are these ways taking you, gloom misleading you, and falsehoods deceiving you? Whence are you brought and where are you driven? For every period there is a written document and everyone who is absent has to return. So listen to your godly leader and keep your hearts present. If he speaks to you be wakeful. The forerunner must speak truth to his people, should keep his wits together and maintain presence of mind. He has clarified to you the matter as the stitch-hole is cleared, and scraped it as the gum is scraped (from the twigs).

Nevertheless, now the wrong has set itself on its places and ignorance has ridden on its riding beasts. Unruliness has increased while the call for virtue is suppressed. Time has pounced upon like a devouring carnivore, and wrong is shouting like a camel after remaining silent. People have become brothers over ill-doings. have forsaken religion, are united in speaking lie but bear mutual hatred in the matter of truth.

When such is the case, the son would be a source of anger (instead of coolness of the eye to parents) and rain the cause of heat, the wicked would abound and the virtuous would diminish. The people of this time would be wolves, its rulers beasts, the middle class men gluttons and the poor (almost) dead. Truth would go down, falsehood would overflow, affection would be claimed with tongues but people would be quarrelsome at heart. Adultery would be the key to lineage while chastity would be rare and Islam would be worn overturned like the skin.

SERMONS 108

Might of Allah

Everything submits to Him and everything exists by Him. He is the satisfaction of every poor, dignity of the low, energy for the weak and shelter for the oppressed. Whoever speaks, He hears his speaking, and whoever keeps quiet, He knows his secret. On Him is the livelihood of everyone who lives, and to Him returns whoever dies.

(O Allah!) The eyes have not seen Thee so as to be aware of Thee, but Thou wert before the describers of Thy creation. Thou didst not create the creation on account of loneliness, nor didst make them work for gain. He whom Thou catchest cannot go farther than Thee, and he whom Thou holdest cannot escape Thee. He who disobeys Thee does not decrease Thy authority, and he who obeys Thee does not add to Thy Might. He who disagrees with Thy judgement cannot turn it, and he who turns away from Thy command cannot do without Thee. Every secret before Thee is open and for Thee every absent is present.

Thou art everlasting, there is no end to Thee. Thou art the highest aim, there is no escape from Thee, Thou art the promised (point of return) from which there is no deliverance except towards Thee. In Thy hand is the forelock of every creature and to Thee is the return of every living being. Glory to Thee! How great is Thy creation that we see, but how small is this greatness by the side of Thy Might. How awe-striking is Thy realm that we notice, but how humble is this against what is hidden from us out of Thy authority. How extensive are Thy bounties in this world, but how small are they against the bounties of the next world.

The Angels

Thou (O Allah) made angels reside in Thy skies and place them high above from Thy earth. They have the most knowledge about Thee and Thy whole creation, the most fearing from Thee, and the nearest to Thee. They never stayed in loins nor were retained in wombs. They were not created "from mean water (semen)" (Quraan, 32:8; 77:20). They were not dispersed by vicissitudes of time. They are on their places (distinct) from Thee and in their positions near Thee. Their desires are concentrated in Thee. Their worship for Thee is much. Their neglect from Thy command is little. If they witness what remains hidden about Thee they would regard their deeds as very little, they would criticise themselves and would realise that they did not worship Thee according to Thy right for being worshipped and did not obey Thee as Thou hast the right of being obeyed.

Bounties and Guidance of Allah, and those who are Ungrateful

Glorified art Thou, the Creator, the Worshipped, on account of Thy good trials of Thy creatures. Thou created a house (the Paradise) and provided in it for feasting, drinks, foods, spouses, servants, places, streams, plantations and fruits. Then Thou sent a messenger to invite towards it, but the people did not respond to the caller, and did not feel persuaded to what Thou persuaded them nor showed eagerness towards what Thou desired them to feel eager. They jumped on the carcass (of this world), earned shame by eating it and became united on loving it.

When one loves a thing it blinds him and sickens his heart. Then he sees but with a diseased eye, hears but with unhearing ears. Desires have cut asunder his wit, and the world has made his heart dead, while his mind is all longing for it. Consequently, he is a slave of it and of everyone who has any share in it. Wherever it turns, he turns towards it and wherever it proceeds, he proceeds towards it. He is not desisted by any desister from Allah, nor takes admonition from any preacher. He sees those who have been caught in neglect whence there is neither rescission nor reversion.

Death

Whatever they were ignoring has befallen them, separation from this world, from which they took themselves safe, has come to them and they have reached that in the next world which they had been promised. Whatever has befallen them cannot be described. Pangs of death and grief for losing (this world) have surrounded them. Consequently, their limbs become languid and their complexion changes. Then death increases its struggle over them.

In some one it stands in between him and his power of speaking although he lies among his people, looking with eyes, hearing with his ears, with full wits and intelligence. He then thinks over how he wasted his life and in what (activities) he passed his time. He recalls the wealth he collected when he had blinded himself in seeking it, and acquired it from fair and foul sources. Now the consequences of collecting it have overtaken him. He gets ready to leave it. It would remain for those who are behind him. They would enjoy it and benefit by it.

It would be an easy acquisition for others but a burden on his back, and the man cannot get rid of it. He would thereupon bite his hands with teeth out of shame for what was disclosed to him about his affairs at the time of his death. He would dislike what he coveted during the days of his life and would wish that he who envied him on account of it and felt jealous over him for it should have amassed it instead of he himself.

Death would go on affecting his body till his ears too would behave like his tongue (and lose functioning). So he would lie among his people, neither speaking with his tongue or hearing with his ears. He would be rotating his glance over their faces, watching the movements of their tongues, but not hearing their speaking. Then death would increase its sway over him, and his sight would be taken by death as the ears had been taken and the spirit would depart from his body. He would then become a carcass among his own people. They would feel loneliness from him and get away from near him. He would not join a mourner or respond to a caller. Then they would carry him to a small place in the ground and deliver him in it to (face) his deeds. They abandoned visiting him.

Day of Judgement

Till whatever is written as ordained approaches its end, the affairs complete their destined limits, the posteriors join the anteriors and whatever Allah wills takes place in the shape of resurrection of His creation. Then He would convulse the sky and split it. He would quake the earth and shake it. He would root out the mountains and scatter them. They would crush each other out of awe of His Glory and fear of His Dignity.

He would take out everyone who is in it. He would refresh them after they had been worn out and collect them after they had been separated. Then He would set them apart for questioning about the hidden deeds and secret acts. He would then divide them into two groups, rewarding one and punishing the other. As regards the obedient people He would reward them with His nearness and would keep them for ever in His house from where those who settle therein do not move out. Their position would not undergo change, fear would not overtake them, ailments would not befall them, dangers would not affect them and journey would not force them (from place to place).

As for people of sins, He would settle them in the worst place, would bind their hands with the necks, bind the forelocks with feet and would clothe them in shirts of tar and dresses cut out of flames. They would be in punishment whose heat would be severe, door would be closed on the inmates — in fire which is full of shouts and cries and rising flames and fearful voices. Its inmate does not move out of it. its prisoner cannot be released by ransom and its shackles cannot be cut. There is no fixed age for this house so that it might perish, nor period for its life that might pass away.

The Holy Prophet

He treated this world disdainfully and regarded it low. He held it contemptible and hated it. He realised that Allah kept it away from him with intention and spread it out for others by way of contempt. Therefore, he remained away from it by his heart, banished its recollection from his mind and wished that its attraction should remain hidden from his eye so that he should not acquire any clothing from it, or hope for staying in it. He conveyed from Allah the pleas (against committing sins), counselled his people as a warner (against Divine chastisement) and called (people) towards Paradise as a conveyor of good tidings.

Descendants of the Holy Prophet

We are the tree of Prophethood, staying place of (Divine) Message, descending place of angels, mines of knowledge and the sources of wisdom. Our supporter and lover awaits mercy while our enemy and he who hates us awaits wrath.

SERMONS 109

Pinnacles of Islam

The best means by which seekers of nearness to Allah, the Glorified, the Exalted, seek nearness, is the belief in Him and His Prophet, fighting in His cause, for it is the high pinnacle of Islam, and (to believe) in the kalimat al-Ikhlaas (the expression of Divine purification) for it is just nature and the establishment of prayer for it is (the basis of) community, payment of zakat (Islamic tax) for it is a compulsory obligation, fasting for the month of Ramazaan for it is the shield against chastisement, the performance of Haj of the House of Allah (i.e. Kaba) and its Omra (other than annual visit) for these two acts banish poverty and wash away sins, regard for kinship for it increases wealth and length of life, to giving alms secretly for it covers shortcomings, giving alms openly for it protects against a bad death and extending benefits (to people) for it saves from positions of disgrace.

Holy Quraan and Sonna

Go ahead with the remembrance of Allah for it is the best remembrance, and long for that which He has promised to the pious, for His promise is the most true promise. Tread the course of the Prophet for it is the most distinguished course. Follow the Sonna of the Prophet for it is the most right of all behaviours. Learn the Quraan for it is the fairest of discourses and understand it thoroughly for it is the best blossoming of hearts. Seek cure with its light for it is the cure for hearts. Recite it beautifully for it is the most beautiful narration. Certainly, a scholar who acts not according to his knowledge is like the off-headed ignorant who does not find relief from his ignorance, but on the learned the plea of Allah is greater and grief more incumbent, and he is more blameworthy before Allah.

SERMONS 110

Caution about this World

So now, certainly I frighten you from this world for it is sweet and green, surrounded by lusts, and liked for its immediate enjoyments. It excites wonder with small things, is ornamented with (false) hopes and decorated with deception. Its rejoicing does not last and its afflictions cannot be avoided. It is deceitful, harmful, changing, perishable, exhaustible, liable to destruction, eating away and destructive. When it reaches the extremity of desires of those who incline towards it and feel happy with it, the position is just what Allah, the Glorified, says (in the Quraan) :

...like the water which We send down from heaven, and the herbage of the earth mingleth with it, then it becometh dry stubble which the winds scatter; for Allah over all things hath power. (18:45)

No person gets rejoicing from this world but tears come to him after it, and no one gets its comforts in the front but he has to face hardships in the rear. No one receives the light rain of ease in it but the heavy rain of distress pours upon him. It is just worthy of this world that in the morning it supports a man but in the evening it does not recognise him. If one side of it is sweet and pleasant the other side is bitter and distressing.

No one secures enjoyment from its freshness but he has to face hardship from its calamities. No one would pass the evening under the wing of safety but that his morning would be under the feathers of the wing-tip of fear. It is deceitful, and all that is there in it is deception. It is perishable and all that is on it is to perish. There is no good in its provisions except in piety. Whoever takes little from it collects much of what would give him safety, while one who takes much from it takes much of what would ruin him. He would shortly depart from his collection. How many people relied on it but it distressed them; (how many) felt peaceful with it but it tumbled them down; how many were prestigious but it made them low and how many were proud but it made them disgraceful.

Its authority is changing. Its life is dirty. Its sweet water is bitter. Its sweetness is like myrrh. Its foods are poisons. Its means are weak. The living in it is exposed to death; the healthy in it is exposed to disease. Its realm is (liable to be) snatched away. The strong in it is (liable to be) defeated and the rich is (liable to be) afflicted with misfortune. The neighbour in it is (liable to be) plundered.

Are you not (residing) in the houses of those before you, who were of longer ages, better traces, had bigger desires, were more in numbers and had greater armies. How they devoted themselves to the world and how they showed preference to it! Then they left it without any provision that could convey them through, or the back (of a beast for riding) to carry them.

Did you get the news that the world was ever generous enough to present ransom for them, or gave them any support or afforded them good company? It rather inflicted them with troubles, made them languid with calamities, molested them with catastrophes, threw them down on their noses, trampled them under hoofs and helped the vicissitudes of time against them. You have observed its strangeness towards those who went near it, acquired it and appropriated it, till they depart from it for good.

Did it give them any provision other than starvation or make them stay in other than narrow places, or give them light other than gloom, or give them in the end anything other than repentance? Is this what you much ask for or remain satisfied with, or towards which you feel greedy? How bad is this abode for him who did not suspect it (to be so) and did not entertain fear from it?

You should know as you do know, that you have to leave it and depart from it. While in it, take lesson from those "who proclaimed "who is more powerful than we" (Quran, 41:15) but they were carried to their graves, though not as riders. They were then made to stay in the graves, but not as guests. Graves were made for them from the surface of the ground. Their shrouds were made from earth. Old bones were made their neighbor. They are neighbors who do not answer a caller nor ward off trouble, nor pay heed to a mourner.

If they get rain they do not feel happy, and if they face famine they do not get disappointed. They are together but each one apart. They are close together but do not see each other. They are near but do not meet. They are enduring and have no hatred. They are ignorant and their malice has died away. There is no fear of trouble from them and no hope of their warding off (troubles). They have exchanged the back (surface) of the earth with its stomach (interior), vastness with narrowness, family with loneliness, and light with darkness. They have come to it (this world) as they had left it with bare feet and naked bodies. They departed from it with their acts towards the continuing life and everlasting house as Allah has said:

...As We caused the first creation, so will We get it return. (It is) a promise binding Us, verily We were doing it. (Quran, 21:104)

SERMONS 111

Angel of death and Depart of Spirit

Do you feel when the Angel of Death enters a house, or do you see him when he takes out life of anyone? How does he take out the life of an embryo in the womb of his mother? Does he reach it through any part of her body or the spirit responded to his call with the permission of Allah? Or does he stay with him in the mother's interior? How can he who is unable to describe a creature like this, describe Allah?

SERMONS 112

World and People

I warn you of the world for it is the abode of the unsteady. It is not a house for foraging. It has decorated itself with deception and deceives with its decoration. It is a house, which is low before Allah. So He has mixed its lawful with its unlawful, its good with its evil, its life with its death, and its sweetness with its bitterness. Allah has not kept it clear for His lovers, nor has He been niggardly with it towards His foes. Its good is sparing. Its evil is ready at hand. Its collection would dwindle away. Its authority would be snatched away. Its habitation would face desolation. What is the good in a house, which falls down like fallen construction, or in an age, which expires as the provision exhausts, or in time which passes like walking?

Include whatever Allah has made obligatory on you in your demands. Ask from Him fulfillment of what He has asked you to do. Make your ears hear the call of death before you are called by death. Surely the hearts of the abstemious weep in this world even though they may (apparently) laugh, and their grief increases even though they may appear happy. Their hatred for themselves is much even though they may be envied for the subsistence they are allowed. Remembrance of death has disappeared from your hearts while false hopes are present in you. So this world has mastered you more than the next world, and the immediate end (of this world) has removed you away from the remote one (of the next life). You are brethren in the religion of Allah. Dirty natures and bad conscience have separated you. Consequently you do not bear burdens of each other nor advise each other, nor spend on each other, nor love each other.

What is your condition? You feel satisfied with what little you have secured from this world while much of the next world of which you have been deprived does not grieve you. The little of this world which you lose pains you so much so that it becomes apparent in your faces, and in the lack of your endurance over whatever is taken away from you; as though this world is your permanent abode, and as though its wealth would stay with you for good. Nothing prevents anyone among you to disclose to his comrade the shortcomings he is afraid of, except the fear that the comrade would also disclose to him similar defects. You have decided together on leaving the next world and loving this world. Your religion has become just licking with the tongue. It is like the work of one who has finished his job and secured satisfaction of his master.

SERMONS 113

Abstemiousness, Fear of Allah and importance of Providing for Next Life

Praise be to Him Who makes praise followed by bounty and bounty with gratefulness. We praise Him on His bounties as on His trials. We seek His help against these hearts which are slow to obey what they have been commended but quick towards what they have been desisted from. We seek His forgiveness from that which His knowledge covers and His document preserves — knowledge which does not leave anything and a document, which does not omit anything. We believe in Him like the belief of one who has seen the unknown and has attained the promised rewards — belief, the purity whereof keeps off from belief in partners of Allah, and whose conviction removes doubt.

We stand witness that there is no god but Allah, the One, Who has no partner for Him, and that Mohammad is His slave and His Prophet, Allah may bless him and his descendants. These two testimonies heighten the utterance and raise the act. The scale wherein they would be placed would not be light while the scale from which they are removed would not become heavy.

Enjoining People to Piety

O creatures of Allah! I advise you to have fear of Allah which is the provision (for the next world) and with it is (your) return. The provision would take you (to your destination) and the return would be successful. The best one, who is able to make people listen has called towards it and the best listener has listened to it. So the caller has proclaimed and the listener has listened and preserved.

O creations of Allah! certainly fear of Allah has saved the lovers of Allah from unlawful items and gave His dread to their hearts till their nights are passed in wakefulness and their noons in thirst. So they achieve comfort through trouble and copious watering through thirst. They regarded death to be near and therefore hastened towards (good) actions. They rejected their desires and so they kept death in their sight.

Then, this world is a place of destruction, tribulations, changes and lessons. As for destruction, the time has its bow pressed (to readiness) and its dart does not go amiss, its wound does not heal; it afflicts the living with death, the healthy with ailment and the safe with distress. It is an eater who is not satisfied and a drinker whose thirst is never quenched. As for tribulation, a man collects what he does not eat and builds wherein he does not live. Then he goes out to Allah without carrying the wealth or shifting the building.

As for its changes, you see a pitiable man becoming enviable and an enviable man becoming pitiable. This is because the wealth has gone and misfortune has come to him. As for its lessons, a man reaches near (realization of) his desires when (suddenly) the approach of his death cuts them; then neither the desire is achieved nor the desirer spared. Glory to Allah, how deceitful are its pleasures, how thirst-rousing its quenching and how sunny its shade. That which approaches (i.e. death) cannot be sent back, he who goes away does not return. Glory to Allah, how near is the living to the dead because he will meet him soon and how far is the dead from the living because he has gone away from him.

Certainly nothing is viler than evil except its punishment, and nothing is better than good except its reward. In this world everything that is heard is better than what is seen, while of everything of the next world that is seen is better than what is heard. So you should satisfy yourself by hearing rather than seeing and by the news of the unknown. You should know that what is little in this world but much in the next is better than what is much in this world but little in the next. In how many cases little is profitable while much causes loss.

Certainly that which you have been commanded to do is wider than what you have been refrained from, and what has been made lawful for you is more than what has been prohibited. Then give up what is less for what is much, and what is limited for what is vast. Allah has guaranteed your livelihood and has commanded you to act. Therefore, the pursuit of that which has been guaranteed to you should not get preference over that whose performance has been enjoined upon you.

But by Allah, most certainly the position is that doubt has overtaken and certainty has been shattered and it seems as if what has been guaranteed to you is obligatory on you and what was made obligatory on you has been taken away from you. So, hasten towards (good) actions and dread the suddenness of death, because the return of age cannot be hoped for, as the return of livelihood can be hoped for. Whatever is missed from livelihood today may be hoped tomorrow with increase, but whatever is lost from the age yesterday, its return cannot be expected today. Hope can be only for that which is to come, while about that which is passed there is only disappointment.

So "fear Allah as He ought to be feared and do not die until you are (true) Muslim." (Quran, 3:102)

SERMONS 114

Seeking rain

O my Allah! surely our mountains have dried up and our earth has become dusty. Our cattle are thirsty and are bewildered in their enclosures. They are moaning like the moaning of mothers for their (dead) sons. They are tired of going to their meadows and longing for their watering places. O my Allah! have mercy on the groan of the groaning and yearn of the yearning. O my Allah! have mercy on their bewilderment and their passages and their groaning in their yards.

O my Allah! we have come out to Thee when the years of drought have crowded over us like (a herd of) thin camels, and rain clouds have abandoned us. Thou art the hope for the afflicted and succor for the seeker. We call Thee when the people have lost hopes, cloud has been denied and cattle have died, that do not seize us for our deeds and do not catch us for our sins, and spread Thy mercy over us through raining clouds, rain-fed blossoming, amazing vegetation, and heavy down-pours with which all that was dead regains life and all that was lost returns.

O my Allah! give rain from Thee which should be life giving, satisfying, thorough, wide-scattered, purified, blissful, plentiful and invigorating. Its vegetation should be exuberant, its branches full of fruits and its leaves green. With it Thou reinvigorates the weak among Thy creatures and bringeth back to life the dead among Thy cities. O my Allah! give rain from Thee with which our high lands get covered with green herbage, streams get flowing, our sides grow green, our fruits thrive, our cattle prosper, our far-flung areas get watered and our dry areas get its benefit, with Thy vast blessing and immeasurable grant on Thy distressed universe and Thy untamed beasts. And pour upon us rain which is drenching, continuous and heavy; wherein one cycle of rain clashes with the other and one rain drop pushes another (into a continuous chain), its lightning should not be deceptive, its cheek not rainless, its white clouds not scattered and rain not light, so that the famine-stricken thrive with its abundant herbage and the drought stricken come to life with its bliss. Certainly, Thou pourest down rain after the people lose hopes and spreadest Thy mercy, since Thou art the Guardian, the praiseworthy.

Sayyid Razi says: The wonderful expressions of this sermon: Ameer al-Momineen's words "insahat jibaluna" means the mountains cracked on account of drought. It is said "insahaththawbu" when it is torn. It is also said "insahan-nabtu" or 'saha" or 'sawwaha" when vegetation withers and dries up.

His words "wa hamat dawabbuna" means became thirsty, as "huyam" means thirst.

His words "hadabirus-sinin". This is plural of "hidbar". It means the camel whom treading has made thin. So Ameer al-Momineen likened with such a camel the year in which drought had occurred. The Arab poet Zor-Romma has said: These thin camels remain in their places, facing hardships and move only when we take them to some dry area.

His words "wa la qazain rababuha. Here "al-Qaza" means small pieces of cloud scattered all round.

His words "wa la shaffanin zihaboha. It stands for "wa la zata shaffanin zihaboha" "ash-shaffan" means the cold wind and "az-zihab" means light rain. He omitted the world "zata" from here because of the listener's knowledge of it.

SERMONS 115

Troubles which would arise and the Day of judgment

Allah deputized him (the Prophet) as a caller towards Truth and a witness over the creatures. The Prophet conveyed the messages of Allah without being lazy and without any shortcoming, and he fought His enemies in the cause of Allah without being languid and without pleading excuses. He is the foremost of all who practice piety and the power of perception of all those who achieve guidance.

Complaining About His Men

If you know what I know of the unknown that is kept wrapped up from you certainly you would have gone out into the open weeping over your deeds and beating yourselves in grief and you would have abandoned your properties without any guard for it or any substitute over it. Everyone would then have cared for his own self without paying attention to anyone else. But you have forgotten what was recalled to you and felt safe from what you had been warned. Consequently, your ideas went astray and your affairs were dispersed.

I do long that Allah may cause separation between me and you and give me those who have a better right to be with me than you. By Allah, they are people of blissful ideas, enduring wisdom and true speech. They keep aloof from revolt. They trod forward on the path (of Allah) and ran on the high road. Consequently, they achieved the everlasting next life and easeful honors.

Beware! By Allah, a tall lad of swinging gait from Bani-Thaqeef would be placed over you. He would eat away your vegetation and melt your fat. So, O Abi-Wazaha, is that all?

Sayyid Razi says: "al-Wazaha" means "al-khonfosa" (dung-beetle)." In this sentence Ameer al-Momineen has referred to al-Hajjaj bn-Yoosof ath-Thaqafi and he had an incident with "al-Khonfosa ", which need not be related here.[1]

SERMONS 116

Rebuking misers

You spend no wealth in the cause of Him Who gave it, nor do you risk your lives for the sake of Him Who created them. You enjoy honor through

-1- The detail of this incident is that one day al-Hajjaj stood up for saying prayers when al-khunfusa" advanced towards him. al-Hajjaj held out his hand to stop him but he bit him whereby his hand got swollen and eventually he died of it.

bn-Abil-Hadeed has written that "al-Wazaha" means the dung that remains sticking to the tail of an animal, and this surname is intended to disgrace him.

Allah among His creatures, but you do not honor Allah among His creatures. You should derive lessons from your occupying the places of those who were before you and from the departure of your nearest brothers.

SERMONS 117

In Praise of his Faithful Companions

You are supporters of Truth and brethren in faith. You are the shield on the day of tribulation, and (my) trustees among the rest of the people. With your support I strike the runner away and hope for the obedience of him who advances forward. Therefore, extend to me support, which is free from deceit and pure from doubt because, by Allah, I am the most preferable of all for the people.

SERMONS 118

When he collected the people and exhorted them[1] to Jihad but they observed long silence

What is the matter with you? Have you become dumb?

A group of them replied: "o Ameer al-Momineen, if you go forth we shall be with you." Whereupon Ameer al-Momineen said:

What has happened to you? You may not be guided aright or shown the right path. Should in these circumstances I go forth? In fact, at this time one of the brave and the valorous among you whom I select should go out. It does not suit me to leave the army, the city, the public treasury, the

---

-1- When after the Battle of Siffeen, Moaawiya's forces began to attack various places in Ameer al-Momineen's area, he asked the Iraqis to check them but they declined on the plea that they would follow him if he himself came forward. Thereupon he delivered this sermon, and clarified his limitations, that if he himself went out it was impossible to run the affairs of the state, and that the enemy's attacks had already started on all sides. In these circumstances it was impolitic to keep the centre unguarded. But what could be hoped from those who changed the victory at Siffeen into defeat and opened the door for these attacks.

land revenue, the dispensation of justice among Muslims and looking after the demands of the claimants and to follow one contingent after the other moving here and there like a featherless arrow moving in the quiver.

I am the axis of the mill. It rotates on me while I remain in my position. As soon as I leave it the center of its rotation would be disturbed and its lower stone would also be disturbed. By Allah, this is a very bad advice. By Allah, if I had not been hoping for martyrdom by my meeting with the enemy — and my meeting with him has been ordained, I would have secured my carrier and went away from you and would not have sought you so long as North and South differed.

There is no benefit in the majority of your numbers because of lack of unity of your hearts. I have put you on the clear path whereon no one will perish except who perishes by himself. He who sticks to it would achieve Paradise and he who deviates goes to Hell.

SERMONS 119

Ahlil-Bayt and the Laws of Islam

By Allah, I have knowledge of the conveyance of messages, fulfillment of promises and of entire expressions. We, the people of the house (of the Prophet — Ahlil-Bayt) possess the doors of wisdom and light of governance. Beware that the paths of religion are one and its highways are straight. He who follows them achieves (the aim) and secures (the objective). And he who stood away from it went astray and incurred repentance.

Do act for the day for which provisions are stored, and when the intentions would be tested. If a person's own intelligence which is present with him does not help him, the wits (of others) which are remote from him are more unhelpful and those which are away from him more useless. Dread the fire whose flame is severe, whose hollow is deep, whose dress is iron and whose drink is bloody pus. Beware! The[1] good name of a man retained by Allah, the Sublime, among the people Is better than wealth inherited by those who would not praise him.

SERMONS 120

Reasons for objecting Arbitration first and giving order for it thereafter

A man from among the companions of Ameer al-Momineen stood up and said "O Ameer al-Momineen, you first stopped us from arbitration and thereafter gave order for it. We do not know which of these two was more appropriate." Ameer al-Momineen struck one hand over the other and said:

This is the reward of one who breaks pledge. By Allah, when I gave you my orders (namely) to abide by arbitration I had led you to an undesirable thing (namely war) in which Allah had ordained good. If you had been steadfast I would have guided you, if you had been bent I would have straightened you and if you had refused I would have rectified you. This was the surest way. But with whom and to whom. I wanted my treatment from you but you proved to be my disease, like the extractor of thorn with the thorn when he knows that the thorn bends towards itself.

-1- If a person gives away something in his life time then the recipient feels obliged to him. But if wealth is extracted by force then the extractor does not feel himself under his obligation, nor does he praise it. The same is the case of one who dies. His successors think that whatever he had left behind was their right and they should have received it. In this there is no obligation of his to be acknowledged. But if he had done some good act with this very wealth his name would have remained behind him and people would have praised him also.

A Persian couplet says:

Happy is he who is remembered well after himself, for nothing save the name remains after the man is dead.

My Allah, the physicians have despaired of this fatal ailment and water-drawers have become tired with the rope of this well. Where[1] are those who were invited to Islam and they accepted it? They read the Quran and decided according to it. They were exhorted to fight and they leapt (towards it) as she-camels leap towards their young. They took their swords out of the sheaths and went out into the world in groups and rows. Some of them perished and some survived. The good news of survival does not please them nor do they get condoled about the dead. Their eyes have turned white with weeping. Their bellies are emaciated because of fasting. Their lips are dry because of (constant) praying. Their color is pale because of wakefulness. Their faces bear the dust of God-fearing. These are my comrades who have departed. We should be justified if we feel eager for them and bite our hands in their separation.

Certainly, Satan has made his ways easy for you and wants to unfasten the knots of religion one by one and to cause division among you in place of unity. Keep away from his evil ideas and enchantments and accept good advice of one who offers it to you and preserve it in your minds.

-1- Although all those who fought under the banner of Ameer al-Momineen were called Shiahs of Ali, yet only those who had tears in their eyes, paleness on their faces, the Quraanic verses on their tongues, zeal of religion in their hearts, steadfastness in their feet, determination and courage in their spirits, and patience and endurance in their minds could in true sense he called Shiahs of Ali. These were the people in whose separation Ameer al-Momineen's feelings were coming out in the shape of sighs through the breath, while the flames of the fire of separation were consuming his heart and spirit. These were the people who leapt towards death like mad men and did not feel happy if they survived. Rather, their heart's slogan was as the Persian hemistich says:

We are ashamed why we have remained alive.

He who has even a slight brilliance of these qualities can alone be called the follower of the Descendants of the Prophet or the Shia of Ali, otherwise it would be a word which has lost its meaning and been bereft of its dignity through misuse. Thus tradition has it that Ameer al-Momineen saw a group of men at his door and enquired from Qanbar who they were and he answered they were his Shiahs. On hearing this Ameer al-Momineen had a frown on his forehead and said. "Why are they called Shiahs? They have no sign of Shiahs" Thereupon Qanbar enquired what were the signs of Shiahs and Ameer al-Momineen replied:

Their bellies are thin through hunger, their lips dry through thirst and their eyes bleared through weeping.

SERMONS 121

Addressing the Kharijites at their camp When they persisted in their rejecting the Arbitration

Were all of you[1] with us in Siffeen? They replied that some of them were but some of them were not. Ameer al-Momineen said:

Then you divide yourselves into two groups. One of those who were in Siffeen and other of those who were not present there, so that I may address each as I see suitable. Then he shouted to the people:

Stop talking and keep quiet to listen to what I say. Turn your hearts to me. Whomever we ask for evidence, he should give it according to his knowledge about it.

Then he had a long conversation with them during which he said:

When they had raised the Quran by way of deceit, craft, artifice and cheat, did you not say, "They are our brothers and our comrades in accepting Islam. They want us to cease fighting, and ask for protection through the Book of Allah, the Glorified. Our opinion is to agree with them and to end their troubles." Then I said to you "In this affair the outer side is Faith but the inner side is enmity. Its beginning is pity and the end is repentance. Consequently you should stick to your position, and remain steadfast on your path. You should press your teeth (to put all your might) in Jihad and should not pay heed to the shouts of the shouter[2]. If he is answered he would mislead, but if he is left (unanswered) he would be disgraced

But when this thing (Arbitration) was done I found that you agreed to it. By Allah, if I had refused it, it would not have been obligatory on me. Nor would Allah have laid its sin on me. And by Allah, not that I have accepted it, I alone am the rightful person who should be followed, for certainly the

---

-1- bn-Abil-Hadeed writes that this sermon comprises three parts which do not fit together, because Sayyid Razi selected some parts of Ameer al-Momineen's sermons and did not record other parts as a result of which the continuity of utterance was not maintained. Thus, one part ends at "if he is left unanswered he would be disgraced, the other at "and endurance at the pain of wound" and the third runs till the end of the sermon.

-2- This reference is to Moaawiya or Amr bn Aas.

Quran is with me. I never forsake it since I adopted its company. We have been with the Prophet in battles wherein those killed were fathers, sons, brothers and relations of one another. Nevertheless, every trouble and hardship just increased us in our belief, in our treading on the right path, in submission to (divine) command and in endurance of the pain of wounds.

We now had to fight our brethren in Islam because of entry into Islam of misguidance, crookedness, doubts and (wrong) interpretation. However, if we find any way by which Allah may collect us together in our disorder and by which we may come near each other in whatever common remains between us we would accept it and would give up everything else.

SERMONS 122

Supporting the weak and the low-spirited during the fighting on the battlefield of Siffeen

Whoever among you feels spiritedness of heart during the action and finds any of his comrades feeling disheartened should ward off (the enemies) from him just as he would do from himself, because of the superiority he enjoys over the other, for if Allah had willed He would have made the former also like him. Certainly death is a quick seeker. Neither does the steadfast escape it nor can the runner-away defy it. The best death is to be killed. By Allah in Whose hand (power) lies the life of the son of Abi-Talib, certainly a thousand strikings of the sword on me are easier to me than a death in bed which is not in obedience to Allah.

It is as if I see you uttering voices like the rustling sound of lizards! You do not seek your own claims nor do you defend against oppression. You have been let free on the path. He who rushes (into the battle) achieves salvation, while he who lags behind, hesitating, gets destruction.

SERMONS 123

Exhorting his Followers to Fight[1]

-1 -Ameer al-Momineen delivered this Sermon on the occasion of the battle of Siffeen. This battle was fought in the year 37 A.H. between Ameer al-Momineen and the Governor of Syria (Sham) , Moaawiya, for the so-called avenging for the killing of Caliph Othmaan. But in reality it was nothing more than Moaawiya who had been the Autonomous Governor of Syria from Caliph Omar's days not wanting to lose that position by swearing allegiance to Ameer al-Momineen but wanting to keep his authority intact by exploiting the killing of Caliph Othmaan, for later events proved that after securing the government he did not take any practical step to avenge Othmaan's blood, and never spoke, not even through omission, about the killers of Othmaan.

Although from the first day Ameer al-Momineen realised that war was inevitable, it was still necessary to exhaust all pleas. Therefore when on Monday the 12th Rajab, 36 A.H. he returned to Koofa after the battle of Jamal he sent Jareer bn Abdillah al-Bajali with a letter to Moaawiya at Damascus wherein he wrote that the mohaajiroon and the Ansaar had sworn allegiance to him and that he too should first swear him allegiance and thereafter place the case of Othmaan's killing before him so that he could pass verdict thereon according to the Quraan and Sonna. But Moaawiya detained Jareer on several pretexts and after consulting Amr bn Aas staged a revolt on the excuse of Othmaan's killing, and with the help of important persons of Syria convinced the ignorant people that the liability for Othmaan's life lay on Ali (p. b. u. h) and that he, with his conduct had encouraged the besiegers and had given them protection. Meanwhile he hung the blood-stained shirt of Othmaan and the amputated fingers of his wife Naila bnt al-Farafisa on the pulpit in the Central Mosque of Damascus around which seventy thousand Syrians cried and swore the pledge to avenge Othmaan's blood. When Moaawiya had roused the feelings of the Syrians to such an extent that they were determined to lay down their lives and be killed, he secured their allegiance on the cause of avenging Othmaan's blood and busied himself in equipping for the battle. Thereafter, he showed all this to Jareer and then sent him back mortified.

When Ameer al-Momineen learnt of these matters through Jareer bn Abdillah al-Bajali he was forced to rise against Moaawiya, and ordered Malik bn Habeeb al-Yarbooi to mobilise the forces in the valley of An-Nokhayla. Consequently, people from the suburbs of Koofa began arriving there in large numbers, till they exceeded eighty thousand. First of all, Ameer al-Momineen sent a vanguard contingent, eight thousand strong, under Ziyad bn Nadr al-Haarithi and another of four thousand strong under Shorayh bn Haani al-Haarithi towards Syria. After the departure of this vanguard contingent he himself set out for Syria at the head of the remaining army on Wednesday the 5th of Shawwal. When he was out of the boundary of Koofa he offered zohr (noon) prayer and after staying at Dayr bn-Mosa, Nahr (river) Nars, Qubbat Qubbin, Babil, Dayr Kab, Karbala, Sabat, Bahorasini, al-Anbaar and al-Jazira arrived at ar-Riqqa. The people of this place were in favour of Othmaan, and at this very place Simak bn Makhtama al-Asadi was putting up with his eight hundred men. These people had left Koofa to join Moaawiya after deserting Ameer al-Momineen; when they had seen Ameer al-Momineen's force they had dismantled the bridge over the River Euphrates so that Ameer al-Momineen's army should not cross over to the other side of the River. But at the threatening of Malik bn Haarith al-Ashtar an-Nakhaai they were frightened, and after consultations among themselves they put the bridge together again and Ameer al-Momineen passed over it with his army. When he alighted on the other side of the River he saw that Ziyad and Shorayh were also putting up there along with their men since both of them had adopted the land route. When, on reaching here, they found that Moaawiya was advancing with his armies towards the Euphrates and thinking that they would not be able to face him, they stopped there waiting for Ameer al-Momineen. When they had given the reason for their stopping there, Ameer al-Momineen accepted their plea and sent them forward. When they reached Sorar-Rum they found that Abol-Awar as-Solaami was camping there with his army. Both of them informed Ameer al-Momineen of this, whereupon he despatched Ma1ik bn Haarith al-Ashtar an-Nakhaai in their wake as the Officer in Command and cautioned him not to initiate the fighting but to try to counsel them and apprise them of the correct position as far as possible. In this way, on reaching there Malik al-Ashtar encamped a little distance away. Fighting could have commenced any moment, but he did not interfere with the other side nor did he take any step by which fighting could have been commenced. But Abol-Awar suddenly attacked them at night, whereupon they took their swords out of the sheaths and prepared to repulse them. Clashes between the two sides went on for sometime but in the end, taking benefit of the darkness of night Abol-Awar fled away. Since fighting had already commenced, soon after the appearance of dawn an Iraqi commander, Hashim bn Otba al-Mirqal az-Zohri, took his position in the battlefield. From the other side also a contingent came to face him, and the flames of fighting rose high. At last Malik al-Ashtar challenged Abol-Awar to fight him, but he did not dare to face him, and towards the evening Malik al-Ashtar went onwards with his men. The next day Ameer al-Momineen reached there with his force and set off for Siffeen with the vanguard contingent and other forces. Moaawiya had already reached there and had set up his bases. He had also placed a guard on the Euphrates and had occupied it. On reaching there Ameer al-Momineen sent him word to remove the guard from Euphrates, but he refused, whereupon the Iraqis took out their swords and in a courageous attack captured the Euphrates. When this stage was over Ameer al-Momineen sent Basheer bn Amr al-Ansaari, Saeed bn Qays al-Hamdani and Shabath bn Ribi at-Tameemi to Moaawiya to apprise him of the consequences of war and to make him agree to settlement and allegiance. But his reply was that they could not by any means let Othmaan's blood remain neglected, and that now the sword alone would arbitrate between them. Consequently in the month of Zil-Hijja 36 A.H. both the parties decided on war and warriors from each side came out into the field to face their adversary. Those who entered the battlefield from Ameer al-Momineen's side were: Hijr bn Adi al-Kindi, Shabath bn Ribi at-Tameemi, Khaalid bn Moammar, Ziyad bn Nadr al-Haarithi, Ziyad bn Khasaafa at-Taymi, Saeed bn Qays al-Hamdani, Qays bn Saad al-Ansaari

---

and Malik bn Haarith al-Ashtar an-Nakhaai while from the Syrians there were, Abdr-Rahmaan bn-Khaalid bn Waleed al-Makhzoomi, Abol-Awar as-Solaami, Habeeb bn Maslama al-Fihri, Abdillah bn Zil-Kala" al-Himyari, Obaydillah bn Omar bn-Khattaab, Sharhabeel bn Simt al-Kindi, and Hamza bn Malik al-Hamdani. When the month of Zil-Hijja came to end the fighting had to be stopped for Moharram, but from the first of Safar fighting was resumed and both parties arrayed themselves opposite each other, equipped with swords, spears and other weapons. On Ameer al-Momineen's side Malik al-Ashtar was in command of the horsemen and Ammaar bn Yaasir of the foot soldiers of Koofa while Sahl bn Honayf al-Ansaari was in command of the horsemen and Qays bn Saad of the foot soldiers of Basra. The banner of the army was given to Hashim bn Otba. In the army of the Syrians on the right hand contingent bn Zil-Kala" was in command, while on the left hand contingent Habeeb bn Maslama, on horsemen Amr bn Aas and on foot soldiers az-Zahhaak bn Qays al-Fihri were in command.

On the first day Malik bn Ashtar entered the battle-field with his men, and from the other side Habeeb bn Maslama came out with his men to face him and from both sides a fierce battle ensued. Throughout the day swords clashed with swords and spears with spears.

Next day, Hashim bn Otba came out with Ali's army and from the other side Abol-Awar with his footmen came to face him. When the two armies approached near to each other, horsemen fell upon horsemen and footmen upon footmen and continued attacking each other. and they endured with great patience and steadfastness.

On the third day, Ammaar bn Yaasir and Ziyad bn Nadr came out with horsemen and foot soldiers and from the other side Amr bn Aas came forward with a big force. Ziyad attacked the horsemen of the opposite side and Malik al-Ashtar attacked the foot soldiers so furiously that the enemy's men lost ground and, failing to offer resistance, returned to their camps.

On the fourth day Mohammad bn Hanafiyya appeared on the battle-field with his men. From the other side Obaydillah bn Omar came forward with the Syrian army and both the armies had a serious encounter.

On the fifth day Abdillah bn Abbas came forward and from the other side al-Waleed bn Oqba bn Abi-Moayd came to face him. Abdillah bn Abbas carried the assaults with great steadfastness and courage and gave such a brave fight that the enemy left the field in retreat.

On the sixth day Qays bn Saad al-Ansaari came forward with the army and to face him bn Zil-Kala" came out with his contingent, and such a severe fighting ensued that at every step bodies were seen falling and blood flowing like streams. At last the darkness of the night separated the two armies.

On the seventh day Malik al-Ashtar came out and to face him, Habeeb bn Maslama came forward with his men, and fighting raged till zohr (noon).

On the eighth day Ameer al-Momineen himself came out with the army and made such an assault that the entire battlefield quaked, and piercing through the ranks and warding off shots of arrows and spears he came and stood between both the lines. Then he challenged Moaawiya, whereupon the latter, along with Amr bn Aas, came a bit closer. Then Ameer al-Momineen said to him: "Come out and face me. Let whoever kills the other be the ruler" Whereupon Amr bn Aas said to Moaawiya: "Ali is right. Gather up a little courage and face him. Moaawiya replied: "I am not prepared to waste my life at your taunting" Saying this he went back. When Ameer al-Momineen saw him retreating he smiled and himself too returned. The daring with which Ameer al-Momineen led the attacks in Siffeen can only be called a miraculous feat. Thus, whenever he came out challenging in the battlefield, the enemy lines were dispersed into utter disarray and confusion, and even courageous combatants hesitated to appear against him. That is why on a few occasions he came onto the battlefield in changed dress so that the enemy should not recognise him and someone should be prepared to engage with him personally. Once Arar bn Adham came from the other side to engage with al-Abbas bn Rabeea al-Haarith bn Abdl-Mottalib. They remained engaged but neither could defeat the other, until al-Abbas chanced to see that a link of his adversary's armour was loose. With a swift stroke he entangled the point of his sword in it, and then with a quick jerk he cut through a few more links. Then with true aim he gave such a blow that his sword went straight into his bosom. Seeing this, people raised the call of takbir. Moaawiya was startled at this noise and on coming to know that Arar bn Adham had been slain he was much disturbed and shouted if there was anyone to take revenge for Arar bn Adham and kill al-Abbas, whereupon some tired swordsmen of the tribe of Lakhm came out challenging al-Abbas. Al-Abbas said he would come after taking his Chief's permission. Saying al-Abbas came to Ameer al-Momineen to seek permission. Ameer al-Momineen detained him, put on al-Abbas's dress. and riding on al-Abbas's horse entered the battlefield. Taking him to be al-Abbas, the Lakhms said 'so you have got your Chief's permission" In reply Ameer al-Momineen recited the following verse:

Permission (to fight) is given unto those upon whom war is made for they have been oppressed, and verily, to help them, Allah is Most Potent. (Quraan, 22:39)

Now one man came out from the other side shouting like an elephant, ran amok and assaulted Ameer al-Momineen, but he avoided the blow and then gave such a clean cut with his sword to the other's back that he was split into two. People thought the blow had gone without avail, but when his horse jumped his two separate parts fell on the ground. After him another man came out but he too was finished in the twinkling of an eye. Then Ameer al-Momineen challenged others but from the strokes of his sword the enemy came to know that it was Ameer al-Momineen in the dress of al-Abbas and so none dared come to face him.

On the ninth day the right wing was under the command of Abdillah bn Bodayl and the left wing under that of Abdillah bn Abbas. In the centre was Ameer al-Momineen himself. On the other side Habeeb bn Maslama commanded the Syrian army. When both the lines had come face to face with each other, the valiant soldiers drew out their swords and pounced upon one another like ferocious lions, and fighting raged on all sides. The banner of the right wing Ameer al-Momineen's army was revolving in the hands of Bani-Hamdan. Whenever anyone of them fell, martyred, someone else would pick up the banner. First of all Korayb bn Shorayh raised the banner, on his fall Sharhabeel bn Shorayh took it up, then Marthad bn Shorayh, then Hobayra bn Shorayh then Yarim bn Shorayh, then Somayr bn Shorayh and after the killing of all these six brothers the banner was taken up by Sofyaan, then Abd, then Korayb, the three sons of Zayd, who all fell martyred. After that the banner was lifted by two brothers (sons) of Basheer namely Omayr and al-Haarith and when they too fell martyred, Wahab bn Korayb took up the banner. On this day the enemy's greater attention was on the right wing and its assaults were so fierce that the men lost ground and began to retreat from the battlefield. Only three hundred men remained with the Officer in Command Abdillah bn Bodayl. On seeing this Ameer al-Momineen asked Malik al-Ashtar to call them back and challenge them as to where they were fleeing. "If the days of life are over they cannot avoid death by running away" Now the defeat of the right wing could not be without effect on the left wing, so Ameer al-Momineen turned to the left wing and advanced forward, forcing through the enemy lines, whereupon a slave of Bani-Omayya named Ahmar said to him, "Allah may make me die if I fail to slay you today" On hearing this Ameer al-Momineen's slave Kaysan leapt over him but was killed by him. When Ameer al-Momineen saw this he caught him by the skirt of his armour and, picking him up, threw him down so forcefully that all his joints were smashed, whereupon Imam Hasan (p.b.u.h.) and Mohammad bn Hanafiyya came forward and despatched him to Hell. Meanwhile, after having been called to Malik al-Ashtar and his having made them feel ashamed, the retreaters came back and again assaulted so steadfastly that pushing back the enemy they reached the place where Abdillah bn Bodayl was surrounded by the enemy. When he saw his own men he picked up courage and leapt towards Moaawiya's tent with drawn sword. Malik al-Ashtar tried to stop him but he could not, and, killing seven Syrians, he reached the tent of Moaawiya. When Moaawiya noticed him close by he ordered him to be stoned, as a result of which he was overpowered and the Syrians crowded over him and killed him. When Malik al-Ashtar saw this he proceeded forward with the combatants of Bani-Hamdan and Bani-Mazhij for an attack on Moaawiya, and began dispersing the contingent on guard around him. When, out of the five circles of his guards only one remained to be dispersed, Moaawiya put his foot in the stirrup of his horse in order to run away, but on someone's encouragement again stopped. On another side of the battlefield a tumult was raging from one end to the other by the swords of Ammaar bn Yaasir and Hashim bn Otba. From whatever side Ammaar passed, the companions (of the Holy Prophet) flocked around him and then made such a joint assault that destruction spread throughout the enemy lines. When Moaawiya saw them advancing he threw his fresh forces towards them. But he continued displaying the excellence of his bravery under the storm of swords and spears. At last Abol-Adiyah al-Johaani hit him with a spear from which he could not balance himself and then bn Hawiy (Jawn as-Saksiki) came forward and slew him. Ammaar bn Yaasir's death caused tumult in Moaawiya's ranks because about him they had heard the Holy Prophet (p.b.u.h.) having said "Ammaar will be killed at the hands of a rebellious party" Thus before he fell as martyr. Zol-Kala" had said to Amr bn Aas: "I see Ammaar on Ali's side; are we that rebellious party?" Amr bn Aas had assured him that eventually Ammaar would join them, but when he killed fighting on Ali's side the rebellious party stood exposed and no scope was left for any other interpretation. Nevertheless Moaawiya started telling the Syrians

Put the armored man forward and keep the unarmored one behind. Grit your teeth because this will make the swords skip off the skull, and dodge on the sides of the spears for it changes the direction of their blades. Close the eyes because it strengthens the spirit and gives peace to the heart. Kill the voices because this will keep off spiritlessness.

Do not let your banner bend down, nor leave it alone. Do not give it to anyone except the brave and the defenders of honor among you because they alone endure the befalling of troubles; they surround the banners and encircle them on both sides, their rear and their front. They do not

---

that: "We did not kill Ammaar, but Ali did it because he brought him to the battlefield" When Ameer al-Momineen heard this cunning sentence he remarked:

In that case the Holy Prophet (p.b.u.h.) killed Hamza as he had brought him to the battlefield of Ohod" Hashim bn Otba also fell in this conflict. He was killed by al-Haarith bn Monzir at-Tanokhi. After him the banner of the contingent was taken over by his son Abdillah.

When such fearless warriors were gone Ameer al-Momineen said to the warriors from the tribes of Hamdan and Rabeea: "To me you are like armour and spear. Get up and teach these rebels a lesson" Consequently, twelve thousand combatants of the tribes of Rabeea and Hamdan stood up, swords in hand. The banner was taken up by Hodayn bn Monzir. Entering the lines of the enemy, they used their swords in such a way that heads began to drop, bodies fell in huge heaps and on every side streams of blood flowed. And the assaults of these swordsmen knew no stopping till the day began to end with all its devastation and the gloom of eve set in, ushering in that fearful night which is known in history as the night of al-Harir, wherein the clashing of weapons, the hoofs of horses and the hue and cry of the Syrians created such notice that even voices reaching the ears could not be heard. On Ameer al-Momineen's side, his wrong-crushing slogans raised waves of courage and valour, and on the enemy's side they shook the hearts in their bosoms. The battle was at its zenith. The quivers of the bowmen had become empty. The stalks of the spears had been broken. Hand to hand fighting went on with swords only and dead bodies collected in heaps, till by morning the number of killed had exceeded thirty thousand.

On the tenth day Ameer al-Momineen's men showed the same morale. On the right wing Malik al-Ashtar held the command and on the left wing Abdillah bn Abbas. Aasaults went on like the assaults of new soldiers. Signs of defeat appeared on the Syrians, and they were about to leave the battlefield and run away, when five hundred Quraan were raised on spears changing the entire face of the battle. Moving swords stopped, the weapon of deceit was successful, and the way was clear for wrong to hold its sway.

In this battle forty-five thousand Syrians were killed while twenty-five thousand Iraqis fell as martyrs. (Kitaab Siffeen by Nasr bn Mozaahim al-Minqari d. 212 A.H. and at-Taareekh at-Tabari, vol.1, pp.3256-3349).

separate from them lest they give them over (to the enemy). They do not go ahead of them lest they leave them alone. Everyone should deal with his adversary and also help his comrade by his own life, and should not leave the adversary to his comrade lest both his own adversary and his comrade join against him.

By Allah, even if you run away from the sword of today you would not remain safe from the sword of the next world. You are the foremost among the Arabs and great figures. Certainly in running away there is the wrath of Allah, unceasing disgrace and lasting shame. And certainly a runner-away does not lengthen his life, nor does any thing come to intervene between him and his day (of death). Who is there to go towards Allah like the thirsty going to the water? Paradise lies under the edges of spears. Today the reputations (about the velour of warriors) will be tested. By Allah! I am more eager to meet them (in combat) than they are for (returning to) their houses. O my Allah! If they reject truth disperse their group, divide their words (opinion) and destroy them on account of their sins.

They will not budge from their stand till the continuous striking of spears causes piercings (of wounds) through which wind may pass, and the hitting of swords cuts through the skull, cleaves bones and breaks forearms and legs, till they are attacked by contingent after contingent and assaulted by detachments which are followed by reserves for support, till their cities are continuously assailed by force after force, and till the horses trample even the extreme ends of the lands, the tracks of their beast and their meadows.

Sayyid Razi says: "ad-daq" means trampling, e. g. "tadoqqol-khoyoolo bihawafiriha ardahom" (the horses trample the ground with their hoofs) nawahini ardihim" means lands opposite each other, it is said "manazilu bani fulanin tatanaharo" meaning the "houses of so-and-so are opposite each other. "

SERMONS 124

Kharijites and Arbitration

We did not name people the arbitrators but we named the Quran the arbitrator. The Quran is a book, covered, between two flaps, and it does not speak. It should therefore necessarily have an interpreter. Men alone can be such interpreters. When these people invited us to name the Quran as the arbitrator between us, we could not be the party turning away from the Book of Allah. Since Allah has said:

... And then if ye quarrel about anything refer it to Allah and the Prophet. (Quran, 4:59)

Reference to Allah means that we decide according to the Quran while reference to the Prophet means that we follow his Sunna. Now therefore, if arbitration were truly done through the Book of Allah (Quran). We would be the most rightful of all people for the Caliphate; or if it were done by the Sunna of the Holy Prophet (p.b.u.h.), we would be the most preferable of them.

Concerning your point why I allowed a time lag between myself and them with regard to the Arbitration, I did so in order that the ignorant may find out (the truth) and one who already knows may hold with it firmly. Possibly Allah may, as a result of this peace, improve the condition of these people, and they will not be caught by the throats and will not, before indication of the right, fall into rebellion as before. Certainly the best man before Allah is he who loves most to act according to right, even though it causes him hardship and grief rather than according to wrong, even though it gives him benefit and increase.

So, where are you being misled and from where have you been brought (to this state)? Be prepared to march to the people who have deviated from the right and do not see it, have been entangled in wrongdoing and are not corrected. They are away from the Book and turned from the (right) path. You are not trustworthy to rely upon, nor are you holders of honor to be adhered to. You are very bad in kindling the fire of fighting.

Woe to you! I had to bear a lot of worries from you. Some day I call you (to Jihad) and some day I speak to you in confidence, you are neither true free men at the time of call, nor trustworthy brothers at the time of speaking in confidence.

SERMONS 125

In reply to objections on Equal Distribution of Shares from Bayt al-Mal (the Muslim public treasury)

Do you command me that I should seek support by oppressing those over whom I have been placed? By Allah, I wont do so as long as the world goes on, and as long as one star leads another in the sky. Even if it were my property, I would have distributed it equally among them, then why not when the property is that of Allah. Beware; certainly that giving of wealth without any right for it is wastefulness and lavishness. It raises its doer in this world, but lowers him in the next world. It honors him before people, but disgraces him with Allah. If a man gives his property to those who have no right for it or do not deserve it, Allah deprives him of their gratefulness, and their love too would be for others. Then if he falls on bad days and needs their help, they would prove the worst comrades and ignoble friends.

SERMONS 126

Clarifying Confusion for Kharijites

If you do not stop believing that I have gone wrong and been misled, why do you consider that the common men among the followers of the Prophet Mohammad (p.b.u.h.a.h.p) have gone astray like me, and accuse them with my wrong, and hold them unbelievers on account of my sins. You are holding your swords on your shoulders and using them right and wrong. You are confusing those who have committed sins with those who have not. You know that the Prophet (p.b.u.h.) stoned the protected (married) adulterer, then he also said his burial prayer and allowed his successors to inherit from him. He killed the murderer and allowed his successors to inherit from him. He amputated (the hand of) the thief and whipped the unprotected (unmarried) adulterer, but thereafter allowed their shares from the booty, and they married Muslim women. Thus the Prophet (p.b.u.h.) took them to ask for their sins and also abided by Allah's commands about them, but did not disallow them their rights created by Islam, nor did he remove their names from its followers.

Certainly you are the most evil of all persons and are those whom Satan has put on his lines and thrown out into his wayless land. With regard to me, two categories of people will be ruined, namely he who loves me too much and the love takes him away from rightfulness, and he who hates me too much and the hatred takes him away from rightfulness. The best man with regard to me is he who is on the middle course. So be with him and be with the great majority (of Muslims) because Allah's hand (of protection) is on keeping unity. You should beware of division because the one isolated from the group is (a prey) to Satan just as the one isolated from the flock of sheep is (a prey) to the wolf.

Beware; whoever calls to this course, kill him, even though he may be under this headband of mine. Certainly the two arbitrators were appointed to revive what the Quran revives and to destroy what the Quran destroys. Revival means to unite on it (in a matter) and destruction means to divide on a matter. If the Quran drives us to them we should follow them, and if it drives them to us they should follow up. May you have no father! (Woe to you), I did not cause you any misfortune, nor have I deceived you in any matter, nor created any confusion. Your own group had unanimously suggested in favor of these two men and we bound them that they would not exceed the Quran but they deviated from it and abandoned the right although both of them were conversant with it. This wrong-doing was the dictate of their hearts and so they trod upon it, although we had stipulated that in arbitrating with justice and sticking to rightfulness they would avoid the evil of their own views and the mischief of their own verdict (but since this has happened the award is not acceptable to us).

SERMONS 127

Foreseeing Happenings in Basra

O Ahnaf! It is as though I see him advancing with an army, which has neither dust nor noise, nor rustling of reins, nor neighing of horses. They are trampling the ground with their feet as if they are the feet of ostriches.

Sayyid Razi says: Ameer al-Momineen pointed to the Chief of the Negroes, (Saahib az-Zanj).[1] Then Amir al -Momineen said:

Woe to you (the people of Basra's) inhabited streets and decorated houses which possess wings like the wings of vultures and trunks like the

---

-1- Ali bn Mohammad was born in the village of Warzanin in the suburbs of Ray and belonged to the Azariqa sect of the Kharijites. He claimed to be a Sayyid (descendant of the Holy Prophet) by showing himself the son of Mohammad bn Ahmad al-Mokhtafi bn Esaa bn Zayd bn Ali bn Hosayn bn Ali bn Abi-Talib, but the experts on lineality and biographers have not accepted his claim to being a Sayyid and have given his father's name as Mohammad bn Abd Ar-Raheem instead of Mohammad bn Ahmad. The former was from the tribe of Abdl-Qays and had been born of a Sindi maid-slave.

Ali bn Mohammad rose as an insurgent in 255 A.H. in the reign of al-Mohtadi Billah and associated with him the people from the suburbs of Basra on promise of money, wealth and freedom. He entered Basra on the 17th Shawwal, 255 A.H. killing and looting, and in only two days he put to death thirty thousand individuals, men, women and children, and displayed extreme oppression, bloodshed, savageness and ferocity. He dismantled houses, burnt mosques, and after continuous killing and devastation for fourteen years, was killed in the month of Safar, 270 A.H. in the reign of Mowaffaq Billah. Then people got rid of his devastating deeds.

Ameer al-Momineen's prophecy is one of those prophecies which throw light on his knowledge of the unknown. The details of his army given by Ameer al-Momineen namely that there would be neither neighing of horses nor rustling of weapons therein is a historical fact. The historian at-Tabari has written that when this man reached near al-Karkh (a sector of Baghdad) with the intention of insurrection, the people of that place welcomed him, and a man presented him a horse for which no rein could be found despite a search. At last he rode it using a rope for the rein. Similarly there were at that time only three swords in his force — one with himself, one with Ali bn Aban al-Mohallabi, and one with Mohammad bn Salm, but later they collected some more weapons by marauding.

trunks of elephants; they are the people from among whom if one is killed he is not mourned and if one is lost he is not searched for. I turn this world over on its face, value it only according to its (low) value, and look at it with an eye suitable to it.

Referring To The Mongols

I can see a people[1] whose faces are like shields covered with rough-scraped skins. They dress themselves in silken and woolen clothes and

---

1 This prophecy of Ameer al-Momineen is about the attack of the Tartars (Mongols) who were inhabitants of the Mongolian desert in the north west of Torkistaan. These semi-savage tribes lived by marauding, killing and devastating. They used to fight among themselves and attack neighbouring areas. Each tribe had a separate chief who was deemed responsible for their protection. Chingiz-Khan (Temojin) who was one of the ruling chiefs of these tribes and was very brave and courageous had risen to organise all their divided tribes into one, and, despite their opposition he succeeded in overpowering them through his might and sagacity. Collecting a large number under his banner he rose in 606 A.H. like a torrent and went on dominating cities and ruining populations till he conquered the area upto North China.

When his authority was established he offered his terms of settlement to Alaoddeen Khwarizm Shah, ruler of the neighbouring country of Torkistaan, and through a deputation concluded an agreement with him that the Tartar traders would be allowed to visit his country for trade and their life and property would not be subject to any harm. For some time they traded freely without fear but on one occasion Alaoddeen accused them of spying, seized their goods and had them killed by the Chief of Atrar. When Chingiz Khan learnt of the breach of the agreement and the killing of Tartar merchants his eyes cast forth flames and he began trembling with rage. He sent word to Alaoddeen to return the goods of the Tartar merchants and to hand over to him the ruler of Atrar. Alaoddeen, who was mad with power and authority, did not pay any heed, and acting short-sightedly killed even the plenipotentiary of Chingiz Khan. Now Chingiz Khan lost all patience and his eyes filled with blood. He rose with his sword in hand, and the Tartar warriors leapt towards Bokhaara on their speedy stallions. Alaoddeen came out with four hundred thousand combatants to face him but could not resist the incessant assaults of the Tartars, and having been vanquished only after a few attacks ran away to Nishaboor across the river Jaxartes (Sihon). The Tartars smashed Bokhaara and razed it to the ground. They pulled down schools and mosques, burning to ashes the houses and killing men and women without distinction. Next year they assaulted Samarqand and devastated it completely. After the flight of Alaoddeen, his son Jalaloddeen Khwarizm Shah had assumed the reins of government The Tartars chased him also, and for ten years he fled from one place to the other but did not fall in their hands. At last he crossed over the river out of the boundaries of his realm. During this time the Tartars did their utmost to ruin populated lands and to annihilate humanity. No city escaped their ruining and no populace could avoid their trampling. Wherever they went they upset the kingdom, overthrew governments, and in a short time established their authority over the northern portion of Asia.

When Chingiz Khan died in 622 A.H. his own son Ogedei Khan succeeded him. He searched out Jalaloddeen in 628 A.H. and killed him. After him Mongka Khan, the son of the other son of Chingiz Khan, occupied the throne. After Mongka Khan, Qubilai Khan succeeded to a part of the country and the control of Asia fell to the share of his brother Holakoo Khan. On the division of the whole realm among the grandsons of Chingiz Khan, Holakoo Khan was thinking of conquering Moslims areas when the Hanafite of Khoraasaan in enmity with the Shafiite invited him to attack Khoraasaan. He therefore led an assault on Khoraasaan, and the Hanafite, thinking themselves to be safe from the Tartars, opened the city gates for them. But the Tartars did not make any distinction between Hanafite and Shafiite and killed whoever fell to their hands. After killing most of its population they took it in occupation. These very differences between the Hanafite and the Shafiite opened for him the door of conquest upto Iraq. Consequently, after conquering Khoraasaan his courage increased and in 656 A.H. he marched on Baghdad with two hundred thousand Tartars. al-Mostasim Billah's army and the people of Baghdad jointly faced them, but it was not in their power to stop this torrent of calamity. The result was that the Tartars entered Baghdad on the day of Aashooraa carrying with them bloodshed and ruin. They remained busy in killing for forty days. Rivers of blood flowed in the streets and all the alleys were filled with dead bodies. Hundred of thousands of people were put to the sword while al-Mostasim Billah was trampled to death under foot. Only those people who hid themselves in wells or underground places and hid from their sight could survive. This was the devastation of Baghdad which shook the Abbasid Kingdom to its foundation, so that its flag could never fly thereafter.

Some historians have laid the blame of this ruin on bn al-Alqami (Abo-Talib, Mohammad bn Ahmad al-Baghdadi) , the minister of al-Mostasim Billah, by holding that, moved by the general masses of the Shiahs and the ruin of al-Karkh sector (of Baghdad) , he invited Holakoo Khan through the latter's minister, the great scholar Naasirodeen Mohammad bn Mohammad at-Toosi, to march on Baghdad. Even if it be so, it is not possible to ignore the historical fact that before this the Abbasid Caliph an-Naasir Lideenillah had initiated the move for the attack on the Moslim areas. When the Khwarizm Shahs declined to acknowledge the authority of the Caliphate he had sent word to Chingiz Khan to march on Khwarizm, from which the Tartars had understood that there was no unity and co-operation among the Moslims. Thereafter the Hanafite had sent for Holakoo Khan to crush the Shafiite as a consequence of which the Tartars secured control over Khoraasaan, and prepared the way to march towards Baghdad. In these circumstances to hold only bn al-Alqami responsible for the ruination of Baghdad and to ignore the move of an-Naasir Lideenillah and the dispute between the Hanafite and the Shafiite would be covering up the facts, when in fact the cause for the ruin of Baghdad was this very conquest of Khoraasaan, whose real movers were the Hanafite inhabitants of the place. It was by this conquest that Holakoo Khan had the courage to march on the centre of Islam; otherwise it cannot have been the result of a single individual's message that

hold dear excellent horses. Their killing and bloodshed shall take place freely till the wounded shall walk over the dead and the number of runners-away shall be less than those taken prisoner:

One of his companions said to him: O Ameer al-Momineen, you have been given knowledge of hidden things. Whereupon Ameer al-Momineen laughed and said to the man who belonged to the tribe of Bani-Kalb:

O brother of Kalb! This is not knowledge of hidden things (ilmol-ghayb);[1] these matters have been acquired from him (namely in Prophet) who knew them. As regard knowledge of hidden things, that means knowledge of the Day of Judgment, and the things covered by Allah in the verse.

Verily, Allah is He with Whom is the knowledge of the Hour... (Quran, 31:34)

Therefore, Allah alone knows what is there in the wombs, whether male or female, ugly or handsome, generous or miserly, mischievous or pious, and who will be the fuel for Hell and who will be in the company of the Prophets in Paradise. This is the knowledge of the hidden things, which is not known to anyone save Allah. All else is that whose knowledge Allah passed on to His Prophet and he passed it on to me, and prayed for me that my bosom may retain it and my ribs may hold it.

---

he assaulted an old capital like Baghdad, the awe of whose power and grandeur was seated in the hearts of a large part of the world.

1 To know hidden things on a personal level is one thing, while to be gifted by Allah with knowledge of any matter and to convey it to others is different. The knowledge of the future which the prophets and vicegerents possess is gained by them through Allah's teaching and informing. Allah alone has knowledge of events which are to happen in the future. Of course, He passes this knowledge on to whoever He wills. Thus He says:

(He alone is) the "Knower of the unseen, neither doth He reveal His secrets unto any (one else) save unto that one of the Messengers whom He chooseth..." (Quraan, 72:26-27)

In this way Ameer al-Momineen also received knowledge of the future through the instructions of the Prophet or inspiration from Allah, for which these words of Ameer al-Momineen stand evidence. Of course, sometimes it is not proper or expedient to disclose certain matters and they are allowed to remain under a veil. Then no one can be acquainted with them as Allah says:

Verily, Allah is He with Whom is the knowledge of the Hour and He sendeth down the rain, and knoweth He what is in the wombs; and knoweth not any soul what he shall earn the morrow, and knoweth not any soul in what lands he shall die: Verily Allah is All-knowing, All-aware. (Quraan, 31:34)

SERMONS128

Measures and Weights

O creatures of Allah! You and whatever you desire from this world are like guests with fixed period of stay, and like debtors called upon to pay. Life is getting short while (the records of) actions are being preserved. Many strivers are wasting (their efforts) and many of those who exert are heading towards harm. You are in a period when steps of virtue are moving backwards, steps of evil are moving forward and Satan is increasing his eagerness to ruin people. This is the time that his equipment is strong, his traps have been spread and his prey has become easy (to catch).

Cast your glance over people wherever you like, you will see either a poor man suffering from poverty, or a rich man ignoring Allah despite His bounty over him, or a miser increasing his wealth by trampling on Allah's obligations, or an unruly person closing his ears to all counsel. Where are your good people; where are your virtuous people? Where are your high-spirited men and generous men? Where are those of you who avoid deceit in their business and remain pure in their behavior? Have they not all departed from this ignoble, transitory and troublesome world? Have you not been left among people who are just like rubbish and so low that lips avoid mention of them and do not move even to condemn their low position.

… "Verily we are Allah's and verily unto Him shall we return." (Quran, 2:156)

Mischief has appeared and there is no one to oppose and change it, nor anyone to dissuade from it or desist from it. Do you, with these qualities, hope to secure abode in the purified neighborhood of Allah and to be regarded His staunch lovers? Alas! Allah cannot be deceived about His paradise and His will cannot be secured save by His obedience. Allah may curse those who advise good but they themselves avoid it, and those who desist others from evil but they themselves act upon it.

SERMONS 129

When Abo-Zar[1] was exiled to Ar-Rabaza

-1- Abo-Zarr al-Ghifaari's name was Jondab bn Jonaada. He was an inhabitant of Ar-Rabaza which was a small village on the east side of Madeena. When he heard about the proclamation of the Prophet, he came to Mecca and after making enquires saw the Prophet and accepted Islam whereupon the unbelievers of Quraysh gave him all sorts of troubles and inflicted pain after pain, but he remained steadfast. Among the acceptors of Islam he is the third, fourth or fifth. Along with this precedence in Islam his renunciation and piety was so high that the Prophet said:
Among my people Abo-Zarr is the like of Esaa (Jesus) son of Maryam (Mary) in renunciation and piety.
In the reign of Caliph Omar, Abo-Zarr left for Syria and during Othmaan's reign also remained there. He spent his days in counselling, preaching, acquainting people with the greatness of the members of the Prophet's family and guiding the people to the rightful path. The traces of Shiism now found in Syria and Jabal Amil (north of Lebanon) are the result of his preaching and activity and the fruit of seeds sown by him. The Governor of Syria, Moaawiya, did not like the conduct of Abo-Zarr and was much disgusted with his open criticism and mention of the money-making and other wrongful activities of Othmaan. But he could do nothing. At last he wrote to Othmaan that if he remained there any longer he would rouse the people against the Caliph. There should therefore be some remedy against this. On this, Othmaan wrote to him that Abo-Zarr should be seated on an unsaddled camel and dispatched to Madeena. The order was obeyed and Abo-Zarr was sent to Madeena. On reaching Madeena he resumed his preaching of righteousness and truth. He would recall to the people the days of the Holy Prophet and refrain them from displays of kingly pageantry, whereupon Othmaan was much perturbed and tried to restrict his speaking. One day he sent for him and said "I have come to know that you go about propagating that the Holy Prophet said that:
When Bani-Omayya will become thirty in number they will regard the cities of Allah as their property, His creatures their slaves and His religion the tool of their treachery. "
Abo-Zarr replied that he had heard the Prophet say so. Othmaan said that he was speaking a lie and enquired from those beside him if any one had heard this tradition and all replied in the negative. Abo-Zarr then said that enquiry should be made from Ameer al-Momineen Ali bn Abi-Talib (p.b.u.h.). He was sent for and asked about it. He said it was correct and Abo-Zarr was telling the truth. Othmaan enquired on what basis he gave evidence for the correctness of this tradition. Ameer al-Momineen replied that he had heard the Holy Prophet say that:
There is no speaker under the sky or over the earth more truthful than Abo-Zarr.

O Abo-Zar! You showed anger in the name of Allah therefore have hope in Him for whom you became angry. The people were afraid of you in the

---

Now Othmaan could do nothing. If he still held him to be liar it would mean falsification of the Prophet. He therefore kept quiet despite much perturbation, since he could not refute him. On the other side Abo-Zarr began speaking against the usurping of Moslims" property quite openly and whenever he saw Othmaan he would recite this verse:

And those who hoard up gold and silver and spend it not in Allah's way; announce thou unto them a painful chastisement. On the Day (of Judgement) when it shall be heated in the fire of hell, then shall be branded with it their foreheads and their sides and their backs; (saying unto them) "This is what ye hoarded up for yourselves, taste ye then what ye did hoard up" (Quraan, 9:34-35)

Othmaan promised him money but could not entrap this free man in his golden net, then resorted to repression but could not stop his truth-speaking tongue. At last he ordered him to leave and go to Ar-Rabaza and deputised Marwaan, son of the man (al-Hakam) exiled by the Prophet, to turn him out of Madeena. At the same time he issued the inhuman order that no one should speak to him nor see him off. But Ameer al-Momineen, Imam Hasan, Imam Hosayn, Aqeel bn Abi-Talib, Abdillah bn Jafar and Ammaar bn Yaasir did not pay any heed to this order and accompanied him to see him off, and Ameer al-Momineen uttered these sentences (i. e., the above sermon) on that occasion.

In Ar-Rabaza, Abo-Zarr had to put up with a very had life. It was here that his son Zarr and his wife died and the sheep and goats that he was keeping for his livelihood also died. Of his children only one daughter remained, who equally shared his starvation and troubles. When the means of subsistence were fully exhausted and day after day passed without food she said to Abo-Zarr: "Father, how long shall we go on like this. We should go somewhere in search of livelihood" Abo-Zarr took her with him and set off for the wilderness. He could not find even any foliage. At last he was tired and sat down at a certain place. Then he collected some sand and, putting his head on it, lay down. Soon he began gasping, his eyes rolled up and pangs of death gripped him.

When the daughter saw this condition she was perplexed and said "Father, if you die in this vast wilderness, how shall I manage for your burial quite alone" He replied, "Do not get upset. The Prophet told me that I shall die in helplessness and some Iraqis would arrange for my burial. After my death you put a sheet over me and then sit by the roadway and when some caravan passes that way tell them that the Prophet's companion Abo-Zarr has died" Consequently, after his death she went and sat by the roadside. After some time a caravan passed that way. It included Malik bn Haarith al-Ashtar an-Nakhaai, Hijr bn Adi at-Tai, Alqama bn Qays an-Nakhaai, Sasaa bn Soohan al-Abdi, al-Aswad bn Yazeed an-Nakhaai etc. who were all fourteen persons in number. When they heard about the passing away of Abo-Zarr they were shocked at his helpless death. They stopped their riding beasts and postponed the onward journey for his burial. Ma1ik al-Ashtar gave a sheet of cloth for his shroud. It was valued at four thousand Dirhams. After his funeral rites and burial they departed. This happened in the month of Zil-Hijja, 32 A.H.

matter of their (pleasure of this) world while you feared them for your faith. Then leave to them that for which they are afraid of you and get away from them taking away what you fear them about. How needy are they for what you dissuade them from and how heedless are you towards what they are denying you. You will shortly know who is the gainer tomorrow (on the Day of Judgment) and who is more enviable. Even if these skies and earth were closed to some individual and he feared Allah, then Allah would open them for him. Only rightfulness should attract you while wrongfulness should detract you. If you had accepted their worldly attractions they would have loved you and if you had shared in it they would have given you asylum.

SERMONS 130

Grounds for accepting Caliphate and the Qualities of a ruler and governor

O (people of) differing minds and divided hearts, whose bodies are present but wits are absent. I am leading you (amicably) towards truthfulness, but you run away from it like goats and sheep running away from the howling of a lion. How hard it is for me to uncover for you the secrets of justice, or to straighten the curve of truthfulness.

O my Allah! Thou knowest that what we did was not to seek power nor to acquire anything from the vanities of the world. We rather wanted to restore the signs of Thy religion and to usher prosperity into Thy cities so that the oppressed among Thy creatures might be safe and Thy forsaken commands might be established. O my Allah! I am the first who leaned (towards Thee) and who heard and responded (to the call of Islam). No one preceded me in prayer (salat) except the Prophet.

You certainly know that he who is in charge of honor, life, booty, (enforcement of) legal commandments and the leadership of the Muslims should not be a miser as his greed would aim at their wealth, nor be ignorant as he would then mislead them with his ignorance, nor be of rude behavior who would estrange them with his rudeness, nor should he deal unjustly with wealth thus preferring one group over another, nor should he accept a bribe while taking decisions, as he would forfeit (others) rights and hold them up without finality, nor should he ignore Sunna as he would ruin the people.

SERMONS 131

Death and Counseling

We praise Him for whatever He takes or gives or whatever He inflicts on us or tries us with. He is aware of all that is hidden and He sees all that is concealed. He knows all that breasts contain or eyes hide. We render evidence that there is no god except He and that Mohammad — peace be upon him and his progeny — has been chosen by Him and deputized by Him -evidence tendered both secretly and openly, by heart and by tongue. By Allah, certainly it is reality not fun, truth not falsehood. It is none else than death. Its caller is making himself heard and its dragsman is making haste. The majority of the people should not deceive you. You have seen those who lived before you, amassed wealth, feared poverty and felt safe from its (evil) consequences, the longevity of desires and the (apparent) distance from death. How, then, death overtook them, turned them out of their homelands and took them out of their places of safety. They were borne on coffins, people were busy about them one after another, carrying them on their shoulders and supporting them with their hands.

Did you not witness those who engaged in long-reaching desires, built strong buildings, amassed much wealth but their houses turned to graves and their collections turned into ruin. Their property devolved on the successors and their spouses on those who came after them. They cannot (now) add to their good acts nor invoke (Allah's) mercy in respect of evil acts. Therefore, whoever makes his heart habituated to fear Allah achieves a forward position and his action is successful. Prepare yourself for it and do all that you can for Paradise. Certainly this world has not been made a place of permanent stay for you. But it has been created as a pathway in order that you may take from it the provisions of your (good) actions for the permanent house (in Paradise). Be ready for departure from here and keep close your riding animals for setting off.

SERMONS 132

On the Glory of Allah

This world and the next have submitted to Him their reins, and the skies and earths have flung their keys towards Him. The thriving trees bow to Him in the morning and evening, and produce for Him flaming fire from their branches, and at His command, turn their own feed into ripe fruits.

The Holy Quran

The Book of Allah is among you. It speaks and its tongue does not falter. It is a house whose pillars do not fall down, and a power whose supporters are never routed.

The Holy Prophet

Allah deputized the Prophet after a gap from the previous prophets when there was much talk (among the people). With him Allah exhausted the series of prophets and ended the revelation. He then fought for Him those who were turning away from Him and were equating others with Him.

This World

Certainly this world is the end of the sight of the (mentally) blind who see nothing beyond it. The sight of a looker (who looks with the eye of his mind) pierces through and realizes that the (real) house is beyond this world. The looker therefore wants to get out of it while the blind wants to get into it. The looker collects provision from it (for the next world) while the blind collects provision for this very world.

You should know that a man gets satiated and wearied with everything except life, because he does not find for himself any pleasure in death. It is in the position of life for a dead heart, sight for the blind eye, hearing for the deaf ear, quenching for the thirsty and it contains complete sufficiency and safety.

The Book of Allah is that through which you see, you speak and you hear. Its one part speaks for the other part, and one part testifies to the other. It does not create differences about Allah nor does it mislead its own follower from (the path of) Allah. You are joined together in hatred of each other and in the growing of herbage on your filth (i.e., for covering inner dirt by good appearance outside). You are sincere with one another in your love of desires and bear enmity against each other in earning wealth. The evil spirit (Satan) has perplexed you and deceit has misled you. I seek the help of Allah for myself and you.

SERMONS 133

When Caliph Omar bn-Khattaab consulted[1] him about taking part in the march towards Rome Empire

---

-1- About Ameer al-Momineen, the strange position is adopted that on the one hand, it is said that he was ignorant of practical politics and unacquainted with ways of administration from which it is intended that the revolts created by the Omayyad's lust for power should be shown to be the outcome of Ameer al-Momineen's weak administration. On the other hand, much is made of the various occasions when the then Caliphs consulted Ameer al-Momineen in important affairs of State in the matter of wars with unbelievers. The aim in this is not to exhibit his correctness of thinking and judgement or deep sagacity but to show that there was unity and concord between him and the Caliphs so that attention should not be paid to the fact that in some matters they also differed and that mutual clashes had also occurred. History shows that Ameer al-Momineen did have differences of principles with the Caliphs and did not approve every step of theirs. In the sermon of ash-Shaqshaqiyya he has expressed in loud words his difference of opinion and anger about each regime. Nevertheless, this difference does not mean that correct guidance should be withheld in collective Islamic problems. Again, Ameer al-Momineen's character was so high that no one could imagine that he would ever evade giving counsel which concerned the common weal, or would give such counsel which would damage public interests. That is why, despite differences of principle, he was consulted. This throws light on the greatness of his character and the correctness of his thinking and judgement. Similarly, it is a prominent trait of the Holy Prophet's character that despite rejecting his claim to Prophethood the unbelievers acknowledged him the best trustee and could never doubt his trustworthiness. Rather, even during clashes of mutual opposition they entrusted to him their property without fear and never suspected that their property would be misappropriated. Similarly, Ameer al-Momineen was held to occupy so high a position of trust and confidence that friend

Allah has taken upon Himself for the followers of this religion the strengthening of boundaries and hiding of the secret places. Allah helped them when they were few and could not protect themselves. He is living and will not die. If you will your self proceed towards the enemy and clash with them and fall into some trouble, there will be no place of refuge for the Muslims other than their remote cities, nor any place they would return to. Therefore, you should send there an experienced man and send with him people of good performance who are well-intentioned. If Allah grants you victory, then this is what you want. If it were otherwise, you would serve as a support for the people and a returning place for the Muslims.

---

and foe both trusted in the correctness of his counsel. So, just as the Prophet's conduct shows his height of trustworthiness, and just as it cannot be inferred from it that there was mutual accord between him and the unbelievers, because trust has its own place while the clash of Islam and unbelief has another, in the same way, despite having differences with the Caliphs, Ameer al-Momineen was regarded as the protector of national and community interests and as the guardian of Islam's well-being and prosperity. Thus when national interests were involved he was consulted and he tendered his unbiased advice raising himself above personal ends and keeping in view the Prophet's tradition to the effect that "He who is consulted is a trustee" never allowed any dishonesty or duplicity to interfere. When on the occasion of the battle of Palestine, the Caliph Omar consulted him about his taking part in it himself, then, irrespective of whether or not his opinion would accord with Omar's feelings, he kept in view Islam's prestige and existence and counselled him to stay in his place and to send to the battlefront such a man who should be experienced and well-versed in the art of fighting, because the going of an inexperienced man would have damaged the established prestige of Islam and the awe in which the Moslims were held which had existed from the Prophet's days would have vanished. In fact, in the Caliph Omar's going there Ameer al-Momineen saw signs of defeat and vanquishment. He therefore found Islam's interest to lie in detaining him and indicated his view in the words that:
If you have to retreat from the battlefield, it would not be your personal defeat only, but the Moslims would lose heart by it and leave the battle-field and disperse here and there, because with the officer in command leaving the field the army too would lose ground. Furthermore, with the centre being without the Caliph there would be no hope of any further assistance from behind which could sustain courage of the combatants. "
This is that counsel which is put forth as a proof of mutual accord although this advice was tendered in view of Islam's prestige and life which was dearer to Ameer al-Momineen than any other interest. No particular individual's life was dear to him for which he might have advised against participation in the battle.

SERMONS 134

Addressing al-Mogheera bn-Akhnas[1] when he wanted to speak in support of Othmaan (bn "Affaan)

O son of the accursed and issueless, and of a tree which has neither root nor branch. Will you deal with me? By Allah, Allah will not grant victory to him whom you support, nor will he be able to stand up whom you raise. Get away from us. Allah may keep you away from your purpose. Then do whatever you like. Allah may not have mercy on you if you have pity on me.

SERMONS 135

Take revenge for the Oppressed from the Oppressor

Your allegiance to me was not without thinking,[2] nor is my and your position the same. I seek you for Allah's sake but you seek me for your own benefits. O people! support me despite your heart's desires. By Allah, I will take revenge for the oppressed from the oppressor and will put a string in the nose of the oppressor and drag him to the spring of truthfulness even though he may grudge it.

-1- al-Mogheera bn Akhnas ath-Thaqafi was among the well-wishers of Othmaan bn Affaan and the son of his paternal aunt. His brother Abo-l Hakam bn Akhnas was killed at the hands of Ameer al-Momineen in the battle of Ohod, because of which he bore malice against Ameer al-Momineen. His father was one of those people who accepted Islam at the time of the fall of Mecca but retained heresy and hypocrisy in heart. That is why Ameer al-Momineen called him accursed, and he called him issueless because he who has a son like al-Mogheera deserves to be called issueless.

2 Here Ameer al-Momineen points to the view of Omar bn Khattaab which he had on the allegiance of Abi-Bakr on the day of Saqeefa when he said "... let me clarify this to you that the allegiance with Abi-Bakr was a mistake and without thinking (faltah) but Allah saved us from its evil. Therefore, whoever (intends to) acts like this you must kill him..." (Saheeh Bokhaari, vol.8, p.211; as-Seera an-Nabawiyya, bn Hishaam, vol.4, pp.308309; at-Taareekh, at-Tabari, vol.1, p.1822; al-Kaamil, bn al-Athir, vol.2, p.327; at-Taareekh, bn Katheer, vol.5, pp.245246; al-Mosnad, Ahmad bn Hambal, vol.1, p.55; as-Seera al-Halabiyya, vol.3, pp.388, 392; al-Ansab, al-Balazoori, vol.5, p.15; at-Tamheed, al-Baqillaani, p.196; ash-Sharh, bn-Abil-Hadeed, vol.2, p.23)

SERMONS 136

Talha and az-Zobayr

By Allah, they did not find any disagreeable thing in me, nor did they do justice between me and themselves. Surely, they are now demanding a right which they have abandoned and blood which they have themselves shed. If I partook in it with them then they too have a share in it, but if they committed it without me the demand should be against them. The first step of their justice should be that they pass verdict against themselves. I have my intelligence with me.

I have never mixed matters nor have they appeared mixed to me. Certainly, this is the rebellious group in which there is the near one (az-Zobayr), the scorpion's venom (Aysha) and doubts which cast a veil (on facts). But the matter is clear, and the wrong has been shaken from its foundation. Its tongue has stopped uttering mischief. By Allah, I will prepare for them a cistern from which I alone will draw water. They will not be able to drink from it nor would they be able to drink from any other place.

You advanced towards me shouting "allegiance, allegiance" like she-camels having delivered newly born young ones leaping towards their young. I held back my hand but you pulled it towards you., I drew back my hand but you dragged it. O my Allah! these two have ignored my rights and did injustice to me. They both have broken allegiance to me, and roused people against me. Unfasten Thou what they have fastened, and do not make strong what they have woven. Show them the evil in what they aimed at and acted upon. Before fighting I asked them to be steadfast in allegiance and behaved with them with consideration but they belittled the blessing and refused (to adopt the course of) safety.

SERMONS 137

Foreseeing Events

He will direct desires towards (the path of) guidance while people will have turned guidance towards desires, and he will turn their views to the direction of the Quran while the people will have turned the Quran to their views.

(Before this Enjoiner of Good[1], matters will deteriorate) till war will rage among you with full force, showing forth its teeth, with udders full of sweet milk but with a sour tip. Beware, it will be tomorrow and the morrow will come soon with things which you do not know. The Man in power, not from this crowd, will take to task all those were formerly appointed for their ill deeds and the earth will pour forth its eternal treasures and fling before him easily her keys. He will show you the just way of behavior and revive the Quran and Sunna which have become lifeless (among people).

As if I see (him), he (the Enjoiner of Evil)[2] is shouting in Syria (Sham) and is extending his banners to the outskirts of Koofa. He is bent towards it like the biting of the she-camel. He has covered the ground with heads. His mouth is wide open and (the trampling of) his footsteps on the ground have become heavy. His advance is broad and his attacks are severe.

By Allah, he will disperse you throughout the earth till only a few of you remain, like kohl in the eye. You will continue like this till the Arabs return

---

-1 -This prophecy of Ameer al-Momineen is with regard to the appearance of the Twelfth Imam, Abol-Qaasim Mohammad bn Hasan al-Mahdi (p.b.u.h.).

2 This refers to Abdl-Malik bn Marwaan who came to power in Syria (Sham) after his father Marwaan bn Hakam and then after the killing of al-Mokhtaar bn Abi Obayd ath-Thaqafi in his encounter with Mosab bn Zobayr he proceeded towards Iraq. He clashed with Mosab's force at Maskin near Dayrol-Jathaliq in the outskirts of Koofa. After defeating him he made a victorious entry into Koofa and took allegiance from its inhabitants. Then he sent al-Hajjaj bn Yoosof ath-Thaqafi to Mecca to fight with Abdillah bn Zobayr. Consequently this man besieged Mecca and stoned it, and shed the blood of thousands of innocent persons like water. He killed bn az-Zobayr and hung his body on the gallows. He perpetrated such atrocities on the people that one shudders at the thought of them.

to their sense. You should therefore stick to established ways, clear signs and the early period which has the lasting virtues of the Prophethood. You should know that Satan makes his ways easy so that you may follow him on his heels.

SERMONS 138

On the occasion of the Consultative Committee (after the death of Omar bn-Khattaab)

No one preceded me in inviting people to truthfulness, in giving consideration to kinship and practicing generosity. So, hear my word and preserve what I say. Maybe you will see soon after today that over this matter swords will be drawn and pledges will be broken, so much so that some of you will become leaders of the people of misguidance and followers of people of ignorance.

SERMONS 139

Backbiting and Speaking ill of others[1]

-1 -The habit of fault finding and backbiting has become so common that even the feeling of its evilness has disappeared. And at present neither the high avoid it nor the low; neither the high position of the pulpit prevents it nor the sacredness of the mosque. Whenever a few companions sit together their topic of conversation and engaging interest is just to discuss the faults of their opponents with added colourisation, and to listen to them attentively. Although the fault finder is himself involved in the faults which he picks up in others, yet he does not like that his own faults should be exposed. In such a case, he should have consideration for similar feelings in others and should avoid searching for their faults and hurting their feelings. He should act after the proverb: "Do not do unto others what you do not want others to do unto you. "

Backbiting is defined as the exposure of the fault of a brother-in-faith with the intent to vilify him in such a way as to irritate him, whether it be by speaking, acting, implication or suggestion. Some people take backbiting to cover only that which is false or contrary to fact. According to them to relate what was seen or heard, exactly as it was, is not backbiting, and they say that they are not backbiting but only relating exactly what they saw or heard. But in fact backbiting is the name of this very relating of the facts, because if it is not factually correct it would be false accusation and wrong blame. It is related about the Prophet that he said:

Do you know what backbiting is?" People said "Allah and His Prophet know better" Then he said "Backbiting means that you say about your brother a thing which pains him" Someone said "But what if I say what is actually true about him?" The Prophet replied, "It is backbiting only when it is factually true, otherwise you would be accusing him falsely. "

There are many causes for indulging in backbiting, and because of this a man commits it sometimes knowingly and sometimes unknowingly. Abo-Hamid al-Ghazaali has recounted these causes in detail in his book Ehyaa-Oloom ad-Deen. A few of the important ones are:

1) To make fun of anyone or to make him appear abased.
2) To make people laugh and to display one's own jolliness and high spiritedness.
3) Expressing one's feelings under the influence of rage and anger.
4) To establish one's feelings under the influence of rage and anger.
5) To disprove one's connection or involvement in a matter; namely that a particular evil was not committed by oneself but by someone else.
6) To associate oneself with some group when in their company in order to avoid strangeness with them.
7) To belittle a person from whom it is feared that he will expose some fault of one's.
8) To defeat a competitor in the same calling.
9) To seek position in the audience of someone in power.
10) To express sorrow by saying it is sad that so-and-so has fallen in such and such a sin.
11) To express astonishment, for example, to say it is wonderful that so and so has done this.
12) To name the committer of an act when expressing anger over it.

However, in some cases fault finding or criticising does not fall under backbiting.

1) If the oppressed complains of the oppressor in order to seek redress, it is not backbiting. Allah says about it:
Loveth not Allah open utterance of evil in speech except by one who hath been wronged.. (Quraan, 4:148)
2) To relate anyone's fault while giving advice is no backbiting because dishonesty and duplicity is not permissible in counselling.
3) If in connection with seeking the requirements of a religious commandment the naming of a particular individual cannot be avoided, then to state the fault of such person to the extent necessary would not be backbiting.
4) To relate the misappropriation or dishonesty committed by someone with a view to saving a Moslim brother from harm would not be backbiting.
5) To relate the fault of someone before one who can prevent him from committing it is not backbiting.
6) Criticism and expression of opinion about a relater of traditions is not backbiting.

Those who do not commit sins and have been gifted with safety (from sins) should take pity on sinners and other disobedient people. Gratefulness should be mostly their indulgence and it should prevent them from (finding faults with) others. What about the backbiter who blames his brother and finds fault with him? Does he not remember that Allah has concealed the sins which he committed while they were bigger than his brother's sins pointed out by him? How can he vilify him about his sins when he has himself committed one like it? Even if he has not committed a similar sin he must have committed bigger ones. By Allah, even if he did not commit big sins but committed only small sins, his exposing the sins of people is itself a big sin.

O creature of Allah, do not be quick in exposition anyone's sin for he may be forgiven for it, and do not feel yourself safe even for a small sin because you may be punished for it. Therefore, every one of you who comes to know the faults of others should not expose them in view of what he knows about his own faults, and he should remain busy in thanks that he has been saved from what others have been indulging in.

---

7) If a person is well acquainted with someone's shortcoming, then to relate such a fault in order to define his personality, for example, describing a deaf, dumb, lame or handless person as thus, is not backbiting.

8) To describe any fault of a patient before a physician for purposes of treatment is not backbiting.

9) If someone claims wrong lineage then to expose his correct lineage is not backbiting.

10) If the life, property or honour of someone can be protected only by informing him of some fault, it would not be backbiting.

11) If two persons discuss a fault of another which is already known to both it would not be backbiting, although to avoid discussing it is better, since it is possible one of the two might have forgotten it.

12) To expose the evils of one who openly commits evils is not back-biting as the tradition runs:

There is no backbiting in the case of he who has torn away the veil of shamefulness. "

SERMONS140

Reliance on Heresy

O people! If a person knows his brother to be steadfast in faith and of correct ways he should not lend ear to what people may say about him. Sometimes the bowman shoots arrows but the arrow goes astray; similarly talk can be off the point. Its wrong perishes, while Allah is the Hearer and the Witness. There is nothing between truth and falsehood except four fingers.

Ameer al-Momineen was asked the meaning of this whereupon he closed his fingers together and put them between his ear and eye and said:

It is falsehood when you say "I have heard so," while it is truth when you say "have seen

SERMONS 141

Misplaced Generosity

He who shows generosity to those who have no claim to it or who are not fit for it would not earn anything except the praise of the ignoble and appreciation of bad persons, although as long she continues giving, the ignorant will say how generous his hand is, even though in the affairs of Allah he is a miser.

Therefore, to whosoever Allah gives wealth he should use it in extending good behavior to his kinsmen, in entertaining, in releasing prisoners and the afflicted; in giving to the poor and to debtors, and he should endure (the troubles arising out of) the fulfillment of rights (of others) and hardships in expectation of reward. Certainly, the achievement of these qualities is the height of greatness in this world and achievement of the distinctions of the next world; if Allah so wills.

SERMONS 142

Praying for Rain

Beware; the earth which bears you and the sky which overshadows you are obedient to their Sustainer (Allah). They have not been bestowing their blessings on you for any feeling of pity on you or inclination towards you, nor for any good which they expect from you, but they were commanded to bestow benefits on you and they are obeying, and were asked to maintain your good and so they are maintaining it.

Certainly, Allah tries his creatures in respect of their evil deeds by decreasing fruits, holding back blessings and closing the treasures of good, so that he who wishes to repent may repent, he who wishes to turn away (from evils) may turn away, he who wishes to recall (forgotten good) may recall, and he who wishes to abstain (from evil) may abstain. Allah, the Glorified, has made the seeking of (His) forgiveness a means for the pouring down of livelihood and mercy on the people as Allah has said:

...Seek ye the forgiveness of your Lord! Verily, He is the Most-forgiving, He will send (down) upon you the cloud raining in torrents, and help you with wealth and sons (children)..." (Quran, 17:10-12)

Allah may shower mercy on him who took up repentance, gave up sins and hastened (in performing good acts before) his death.

O my Allah! we have come out to Thee from under the curtains and coverings (of houses) when the beasts and children are crying, seeking Thy Mercy, hoping for the generosity of Thy bounty and fearing Thy chastisement and retribution. O my Allah! give us to drink from Thy rain and do not disappoint us, nor kill us by years (of drought) nor punish us for what the foolish among us have committed, O the Most Merciful of all.

O my Allah! we have come out to Thee to complain to Thee who is (already) not hidden from Thee, when the seven troubles have forced us, draughty famines have driven us, distressing wants have made us helpless and troublesome mischiefs have incessantly befallen us. O my Allah! we beseech Thee not to send us back disappointed nor to return us with down-cast eyes, nor to address us (harshly) for our sins, nor deal with us according to our deeds.

O my Allah! do pour on us Thy mercy, Thy blessing, Thy sustenance and Thy pity, and make us enjoy a drink which benefits us, quenches our thirst, produces green herbage with which all that was lost gets a growing and all that had withered comes to life again. It should bring about the benefit of freshness and plentifulness of ripe fruits. With it plains may be watered, rivers may begin flowing, plants may pick up foliage and prices may come down. Surely, Thou art powerful over whatever Thou willest.

SERMONS 143

Deputation of Prophets

Allah deputed prophets and distinguished them with His revelation. He made them as pleas for Him among His creation, so that there should not remain any excuse for people. He invited people to the right path through a truthful tongue. You should know that Allah fully knows creation. Not that He was not aware of what they concealed from among their hidden secrets and inner feelings, but in order to try them as to whom from among them performs good acts, so that there is reward in respect of good acts and chastisement in respect of evil acts.

Position of Ahlil-Bayt (The Household of the Holy Prophet)

Where are those who falsely and unjustly claimed that they are deeply versed in knowledge, as against us, although Allah raised us in position and kept them down, bestowed upon us knowledge but deprived them, and entered us (in the fortress of knowledge) but kept them out. With us guidance is to be sought and blindness (of misguidance) is to be changed into brightness. Surely Imams (divine leaders) will be from the Quraysh. They have been planted in this line through Hashim. It would not suit others nor would others be suitable as heads of affairs.

Those Who go against Ahlil-Bayt

They have adopted this world and abandoned the next world; left clean water and drunk stinking water. I can almost see their wicked one1 who committed unlawful acts, associated himself with them, befriended them and accorded with them till his hair grew gray and his nature acquired their tinge. He proceeded onward emitting foam like a torrential stream not caring whom he drowned, or, like fire in straw, without realizing what he burnt.

Where are the minds which seek light from the lamps of guidance, and the eyes which look at minarets of piety? Where are the hearts dedicated to Allah, and devoted to the obedience of Allah? They are all crowding towards worldly vanities and quarrelling over unlawful issues. The ensigns of Paradise and Hell have been raised for them but they have turned their faces away from Paradise and proceeded to Hell by dint of their performances. Allah called them but they showed dislike and ran away. When Satan called them they responded and proceeded (towards him).

SERMONS 144

This World

O people, you are, in this world, the target for the arrows of death. With every drinking there is choking and with every eating there is suffocation. You do not get any benefit in it except by foregoing another (benefit) and no one among you advances in age by a day except by the taking away of a day from his life. Nothing more is added to his eating unless it reduces what was there before. No mark appears for him unless a mark disappears. Nothing new comes into being unless the new becomes old. No new crop comes up unless a crop has been reaped. Those roots are gone whose off-shoots we are. How can an off-shoot live after the departure of its root?

-1- Here the reference is to Abdl-Malik bn Marwaan who committed extreme atrocities through his officer al-Hajjaj bn Yoosof ath-Thaqafi.

On Innovation (Bidaa)

No innovation is introduced unless one Sunna is forsaken, keep away from innovations and stick to the broad road. Surely the old tested ways are the best and the innovated ones are bad.

SERMONS 145

When Omar bn-Khattaab consulted him about taking part in the Battle of Persia.[1]

---

1 When some people advised Caliph Omar to partake in the battle of al-Qaadisiyya or Nahawand, he finding it against his personal inclination, thought it necessary to consult Ameer al-Momineen, so that if he advised against it he would plead before others that he had stayed back on Ameer al-Momineen's advice, but also if he advised partaking in the battle some other excuse would be found. However, unlike others, Ameer al-Momineen advised him to stay back. The other people had advised him to join in fighting, because the Holy Prophet did not send only others to fight but took part in it himself as well, keeping his close relations also with him. What Ameer al-Momineen had in view was that Omar's presence in the battle could not be beneficial to Islam, but rather his staying back would save the Moslims from dispersion.

Ameer al-Momineen's view that "the position of the head of government is that of the axis around which the system of the government rotates" is a point of principle and does not concern any particular personality. Whether the ruler is a Moslim or an unbeliever, just or despotic, virtuous or vicious, for the administration of the state his presence is a necessity, as Ameer al-Momineen has explained elsewhere at greater length:

The fact is that there is no escape for men from a ruler good or bad. Faithful persons perform (good) acts in his rule while the unfaithful enjoys (worldly) benefits in it. During the rule, Allah will carry everything to its end. Through the ruler tax is collected, the enemy is fought, roads are protected and the right of the weak is taken from the strong till the virtuous enjoy peace and are allowed protection from (the oppression of) the wicked. (Sermon 40)

The words which Ameer al-Momineen uttered in his advice are not indicative of any quality of Caliph Omar except his being the ruler. There is no doubt that he held worldly authority, irrespective of the question of whether it was secured in the right way or wrong way. And where there is authority there is centring of people's affairs. That is why Ameer al-Momineen said that if Omar would go out the Arabs would follow him in large numbers towards the battlefield, because when the ruler is on the march the people will not like to stay behind. The result of their going would be that city after city would become vacant, while the enemy will infer from their reaching the battlefield that the Islamic cities are lying vacant, and that if these people were repulsed no assistance would reach the Moslims from the centre. Again, if the ruler were killed the army would

In this matter, victory of defeat is not dependent on the smallness or greatness of forces. It is Allah's religion which He has raised above all faiths, and His army which He has mobilised and extended, till it has reached the point where it stands now, and has arrived its present positions. We hold a promise from Allah, and He will fulfil His promise and support His army.

The position of the head of government is that of the thread for beads, as it connects them and keeps them together. If the thread is broken, they will disperse and be lost, and will never come together again. The Arabs today, even though small in number are big because of Islam and strong because of unity. You should remain like the axis for them, and rotate the mill (of government) with (the help of) the Arabs, and be their root. Avoid battle, because if you leave this place the Arabs will attack you from all sides and directions till the unguarded places left behind by you will become more important than those before you.

If the Persians see you tomorrow they will say "He is the root (chief) of Arabia. If we do away with him we will be in peace." In this way this will heighten their eagerness against you and their keenness to aim at you. You say that they have set out to fight against the Moslims. Well, Allah detests their setting out more than you do, and He is more capable of

---

disperse automatically, because the ruler is as its foundation. When the foundation is shaken the walls cannot remain standing. The word "aslol-Arab" (the root chief) of Arabia has not been used by Ameer al-Momineen as his own but he has taken it from the Persians. Obviously in his capacity as the head of the State, Caliph Omar was, in their view, the chief of Arabia. Besides, the reference is to the country, not to Islam or Moslims, so that there is no suggestion of any importance for him from the Islamic point of view.

When Ameer al-Momineen pointed out to Caliph Omar that on his reaching there the Persians would aim at him, and that if he fell into their hands they would not spare him without killing, although such words would have touched the brave to the quick and would have heightened their spirits, Omar liked the advice to stay back and thought it better to keep himself away from the flames of battle. If this advice had not been in accord with his personal inclination he would not have received it so heartily and would have tried to argue that the administration of the country could be maintained by leaving a deputy. Again when other people had already advised him to go out, what was the need for consulting Ameer al-Momineen except to get an excuse to stay back.

preventing what He detests. As regards your idea about their (large) number, in the past we did not fight on the strength of large numbers but we fought on the basis of Allah's support and assistance.

SERMONS 146

Purpose of Deputation of the Holy Prophet and what happens when People go against Quraan

Allah deputed Mohammad (p.b.u.h.a.h.p) with Truth so that he may take out His people from the worship of idols towards His worship and from obeying Satan towards obeying Him and sent him with the Quraan which He explained and made strong, in order that the people may know their Sustainer (Allah) since they were ignorant of Him, may acknowledge Him since they were denying Him, and accept Him since they were refusing (to believe in) Him. Because He, the Glorified, revealed Himself to them through His Book without their having seen Him, by means of what He showed them out of His might and made them fear His sway. How He destroyed those whom He wished to destroy through His chastisement and ruined those whom He wished to ruin through His retribution!

On The Future

Certainly, a time will come upon you after me when nothing will be more concealed than rightfulness, nothing more apparent than wrongfulness and nothing more current than untruth against Allah and His Prophet. For the people of this period nothing will be more valueless than the Quraan being recited as it ought to be recited, nor anything more valuable than the Quraan being misplaced from its position. And in the towns nothing will be more hated than virtue, nor anything more acceptable than vice. The holders of the book will throw it away and its memorisers would forget it. In these days the Quraan and its people will be exiled and expelled. They will be companions keeping together on one path, but no one will offer them asylum. Consequently at this time the Quraan and its people will be among the people but not among them, will be with them but not with them, because misguidance cannot accord with guidance even though they may be together. The people will have united on division and will therefore have cut away from the community, as though they were the leaders of the Quraan and not the Quraan their leader. Nothing of it will be left with them except its name, and they will know nothing save its writing and its words. Before that, they will inflict hardships on the virtuous, naming the latter's truthful views about Allah false allegations, and enforcing for virtues the punishment of the vice.

Those before you passed away because of the lengthening of their desires and the forgetting of their death, till that promised event befell them about which excuses are turned down, repentance is denied and punishment and retribution is inflicted.

About Ahlil-Bayt

O people, he who seeks counsel from Allah secures guidance and he who adopts His word as guide is led towards what is more straight, because Allah's lover feels secure and His opponent feels afraid. It does not behove one who knows His greatness to assume greatness, but the greatness of those who know His greatness is that they should know before Him, and the safety for those who know what His power is lies in submitting to Him. Do not be scared away from the truth like the scaring of the healthy from the scabbed person, or the sound person from the sick.

You should know that you will never know guidance unless you know who has abandoned it, you will never abide by the pledges of the Quraan unless you know who has broken them, and will never cling to it unless you know who has forsaken it. Seek these things from those who own them because they are the life spring of knowledge and death of ignorance. They are the people whose commands will disclose to you their (extent of) knowledge, their silence will disclose their (capacity of) speaking and their outer appearance will disclose their inner self. They do not go against religion, and do not differ from one other about it, while it is among them a truthful witness and a silent speaker.

SERMONS 147

Talha and az-Zobayr and the People of Basra

Both of these two (Talha and az-Zobayr) wishes the Caliphate for himself, and is drawing towards himself as against the other fellow. They do not employ any connection for getting access to Allah nor proceed towards Him through any means. Both of them bear malice against the other. Shortly his veil over it will be uncovered. By Allah, if they achieve what they aim at, one of them will kill the other, and one will finish the other. The rebellious party has stood up. Where are the seekers of virtue; for the paths have already been determined and they have been given the news. For every misguidance there is a cause and for every break of pledge there is a misrepresentation. By Allah, I shall not be like him who listens to the voice of mourning, hears the man who brings news of death and also visits the mourner yet does not take lesson.

SERMONS 148

Before his Passing away (last will)

O people. Every one has to meet what he wishes to avoid by running away.[1] Death is the place to which life is driving. To run away from it means to catch it. How many days did I spend in searching for the secret of this matter, but Allah did not allow save its concealment. Alas! It is a treasured knowledge. As for my last will, it is that concerning Allah, do not believe in a partner for Him, and concerning Mohammad (p.b.u.h.a.h.p), do not disregard his Sonna. Keep these two pillars and burn these two lamps. Till you are not divided, no evil will come to you.[2] Every one of you

---

-1- This means that during all the time spent in the attempts that a man makes to avoid death and in the means he adopts for it, it is only the span of life that is shortened. As the time passes the objective of death approaches near, so much so that in one's attempt to seek life one meets death.

2 "wa khalakum zammun" (No evil will come to you). This sentence is used as a proverb. It was first employed by Qasir, slave of Jazima bn Malik al-Abrash.

has to bear his own burden. It has been kept light for the ignorant. Allah is Merciful. Faith is straight. The leader (Prophet) is the holder of knowledge. Yesterday I was with you; today I have become the object of a lesson for you, and tomorrow I shall leave you. Allah may forgive me and you.

If the foot remains firm in this slippery place, well and good. But if the foot slips, this is because we are under the shade of branches, the passing of the winds and the canopy of the clouds whose layers are dispersed in the sky, and whose traces disappeared[1] in the earth. I was your neighbour. My body kept you company for some days and shortly you will find just an empty body of mine which would be stationary after (all its) movement and silent after speech so that my calmness, the closing of my eyes, and the stillness of my limbs may provide you counsel, because it is more of a counsel for those who take a lesson (from it) than eloquent speech and a ready word. I am departing from you like one who is eager to meet (someone). Tomorrow you will look at my days, then my inner side will be disclosed to you and you will understand me after the vacation of my place and its occupation by someone else.

SERMONS 149

Coming Events and Hypocrites Activities

They took to the right and the left piercing through to the ways of evil and leaving the paths of guidance. Do not make haste for a matter which is to happen and is awaited, and do not wish for delay in what the morrow is to bring for you. For, how many people make haste for a matter, but when they get it they begin to wish they had not got it. How near is today to the dawning of tomorrow. O my people, this is the time for the occurrence of every promised event and the approach of things which you do not know. Whoever from among us will be during these days will move through them

-1-The intention is that when all these things die, how can those who inhabit them remain safe? Certainly they too, like every thing else, have to pass away some day or other. Then why should there be any wonder at my life coming to an end?

with a burning lamp and will tread on the footsteps of the virtuous, in order to unfasten knots, to free slaves, to divide the united and to unite the divided. He will be in concealment from people. The stalker will not find his footprints even though he pursues with his eye. Then a group of people will be sharpened like the sharpening of swords by the blacksmith. Their sight will be brightened by revelation, the (delicacies of) commentary will be put in their ears and they will be given drinks of wisdom, morning and evening.

Their period became long in order that they might complete (their position of) disgrace and deserve vicissitudes, till the end of the period was reached, and a group of people turned towards mischief and picked up their arms for fighting. The virtuous did not show any obligation to Allah but calmly endured, and did not feel elated for having engaged themselves in truthfulness. Eventually the period of trial came to an end according to what was ordained. Then they propagated their good views among others and sought nearness to Allah according to the command of their leader.

When Allah took the Prophet (to himself) a group of men went back on their tracks. The ways (of misguidance) ruined them and they placed trust in deceitful intriguers, showed consideration to other than kinsmen, abandoned the kin whom they had been ordered to love, and shifted the building from its strong foundation and built it in other than its (proper) place. They are the source of every shortcoming and the door of gropers in the dark. They were moving to and fro in amazement and lay intoxicated in the way of the people of the Pharaohs. They were either bent on this world and taking support on it or away from the faith and removed from it.

SERMONS 150

Advice against Disorder, Oppression and Unlawful Earning

I praise Allah and seek His help from (what led to the) punishment of Satan and his deceitful acts, and (I seek His) protection from Satan's traps and waylayings. I stand witness that there is no god but Allah and I stand witness that Mohammad is His slave and His Prophet (peace be upon him and his progeny) and his chosen and his selected one. Mohammad's (p.b.u.h.a.h.p) distinction cannot be paralleled nor can his loss be made good. Populated places were brightened through him when previously there was dark misguidance, overpowering ignorance and rude habits, and people regarded unlawful as lawful, humiliated the man of wisdom, passed lives when there were no prophets and died as unbelievers.

You, O people of Arabia, will be victims of calamities which have come near. You should avoid the intoxication of wealth, fear the disasters of chastisement, keep steadfast in the darkness and crookedness of mischief when its hidden nature discloses itself, its secrets become manifest and its axis and the pivot of its rotation gain strength. It begins in imperceptible stages but develops into great hideousness. Its youth is like the youth of an adolescent and its marks are like the marks of beating by stone.

Oppressors inherit it by (mutual) agreement. The first of them serves as a leader for the latter one and the latter one follows the first one. They vie with each other in (the matter of) this lowly world, and leap over this stinking carcass. Shortly the follower will denounce his connection with the leader, and the leader with the follower. They will disunite on account of mutual and curse one another when they meet. Then after this there will appear another arouser of mischief who will destroy ruined things. The heart will become wavering after being normal, men will be misled after safety, desires will multiply and become diversified and views will become confused.

Whoever proceeds towards this mischief will be ruined and whoever strives for it will be annihilated. They will be biting each other during it as the wild asses bite each other in the herd. The coils of the rope will be disturbed and the face of affairs will be blinded. During it sagacity will be on the ebb, and the oppressors will (get the opportunity to) speak. This mischief will smash the Bedouins with its hammers and crush them with its chest. In its dust the single marchers will be lost, and in its way the horsemen will be destroyed. It will approach with the bitterness of destiny and will give pure blood (instead of milk). It will breach the minarets of faith and shatter the ties of firm belief. The wise will run away from it while the wicked will foster it. It will thunder and flash (like lightning). It will create a severe disaster. In it kinship will be forsaken and Islam will be abandoned. He who declaims it will also be affected by it, and he who flees from it will (be forced to) stay in it.

Among them some will be unavenged martyrs and some will be stricken with fear and seek protection. They will be deceived by pledges and fraudulent belief. You should not become landmarks of mischiefs and signs of innovations but should adhere to that on which the rope of the community has been wound and on which the pillars of obedience have been founded. Proceed towards Allah as oppressed and do not proceed to Him as oppressors. Avoid the paths of Satan and the places of revolt. Do not put in your bellies unlawful morsels because you are facing Him Who has made disobedience unlawful for you, and made the path of obedience easy for you.

SERMONS 151

Allah and His Vicegerents[1]

-1- The first part of this sermon consists of important issues concerning the science of knowledge about Allah, wherein Ameer al-Momineen has thrown light on the matter that Allah is from ever and His attributes are the same as He Himself. When we cast a glance at creation, we see that for every movement there is a mover, from which every man of ordinary wisdom is compelled to conclude that no effect can appear without a cause, so much so, that even an infant a few days old, when his body is touched, feels in the depth of his consciousness that someone has touched him. He indicates it by opening his eyes or turning and looking. How then can the creation of the world and the system of all creation be arranged without a Creator or Organiser? Once it is necessary to believe in a Creator, then He should exist by Himself, because everything which has a beginning must have a centre of existence from which it should terminate. If that too needed a creator, there would be the question of whether this creator is also the creation of some other creator or exists by itself. Thus unless a Self-created Creator is believed in, who should be the cause of all causes, the mind will remain groping in the unending labyrinth of cause and effect, and never attain the idea of the last extremity of the series of creation. It would fall into the fallacy of circular arguing and would not reach any end. If the creator were taken to have created himself, then there would be (one of the two positions, namely) either he should be non-existent or existent. If he were not existent, then it would not be possible for something non-existent to create any existent being. If he were existent before creating himself, there would be no sense in coming into being again. Therefore it is necessary to believe that the Creator should be a Being not dependent on any other creator for His own existence, and everything else should be dependent on Him. This dependence of the entire creation is a proof that the existence of the Source of all creation is from ever and eternal. And since all beings other than He are subject to change, are dependent on position and place and are similar to one another in qualities and properties, and since similarity leads to plurality whereas unity has no like save itself, therefore nothing can be like Him. Even things called one cannot be reckoned after His Unity because He is One and Singular in every respect. He is free and pure from all those attributes which are found in body or matter because He is neither body, nor colour, nor shape, nor does He lie in any direction, nor is He bounded within some place or locality. Therefore, man cannot see or understand Him through his senses or feelings, because senses can know only those things which accord with the limitations of time, place and matter. To believe that He can be seen is to believe that He has body, but since He is not a body, and He does not exist through a body, and He does not lie in any direction or place, there is no question of His being seen. But His being unseen is not like that of subtle material bodies, due to whose delicacy the eye pierces through them and eyes remain unable to see them; as for example the wind in the vast firmament. But He is unseen by His very existence. Nevertheless, nothing is unseen for Him. He sees as well as hears, but is not dependent on instruments of seeing or hearing, because if He were in need of organs of the body for hearing and seeing He would be in need of external things for His perfection and would not be a perfect Being, whereas He should be perfect in all respects and no attribute of perfection should be apart from His Self. To believe in attributes separately from His Self would mean that there would be a self and a few attributes and the compound of the self and the attributes would be Allah. But a thing which is compounded is dependent on its parts and these parts must exist before their composition into the whole. When the parts exist from before, how can the whole be from ever and eternal because its existence is later than that of its parts. But Allah had the attributes of knowledge, power and sustaining even when nothing was existent, because none of His attributes were created in Him from outside, but His attributes are His Self and His Self is His attributes. Consequently, His knowledge does not depend on the object of knowledge existing first and then His knowledge, because His Self is prior to things coming into existence. Nor is it necessary for His power that there should first exist the object to be over-powered and then alone He would be called Powerful, because Powerful is that who has power equally for doing or abandoning and as such the existence of the object to be over-powered is not necessary. Similarly Sustainer means master. Just as He is the Master of the non-existent after its coming into

Praise be to Allah who is proof of His existence through His creation, of His being external through the newness of His creation, and through their mutual similarities of the fact that nothing is similar to Him. Senses cannot touch Him and curtains cannot veil Him, because of the difference between the Maker and the made, the Limiter and the limited and the Sustainer and the sustained.

He is One but not by the first in counting, is Creator but not through activity or labour, is Hearer but not by means of any physical organ, is Looker but not by a stretching of eyelids, is Witness but not by nearness, is Distinct but not by measurement of distance, is Manifest but not by seeing and is Hidden but not by subtlety (of body). He is Distinct from things because He overpowers them and exercises might over them, while things are distinct from Him because of their subjugation to Him and their turning towards Him.

He who describes Him limits Him. He who limits Him numbers Him. He who numbers Him rejects His eternity. He who said "how" sought a description for Him. He who said "where" bounded him. He is the Knower even though there be nothing to be known. He is the Sustainer even though there be nothing to be sustained. He is the Powerful even though there be nothing to be overpowered.

Divine Leaders (Imams)

The riser has risen, the sparkler has sparkled, the appearer has appeared and the curved has been straightened. Allah has replaced one people with another and one day with another. We awaited these changes as the famine-stricken await the rain. Certainly the Imams are the vicegerents of Allah over His creatures and they make the creatures know Allah. No one will enter Paradise except he who knows them and knows Him, and no one will enter Hell except he who denies them and denies Him.

Allah the Glorified, has distinguished you with Islam and has chosen you for it. This is because it is the name of safety and the collection of honour.

existence, in the same way He has power to bring it into existence from non-existence, namely if He so wills He may bestow existence upon it.

Allah the Glorified, chose its way and disclosed its pleas through open knowledge and secret maxims. Its (Quraan) wonders are not exhausted and its delicacies do not end. It contains blossoming bounties and lamps of darkness. (The doors of) virtues cannot be opened save with its keys, nor can gloom be dispelled save with its lamps. Allah has protected its inaccessible points (from enemies) and allowed grazing (to its followers) in its pastures. It contains cover (from the ailment of misguidance) for the seeker of cure and full support for the seeker of support.

SERMONS 152

The Negligent, Beasts, and Carnivores

He has been allowed time by Allah. He is falling into error along with negligent persons and goes early in the morning with sinners, without any road to lead or any Imam to guide.

At last when Allah will make clear to them the reward for their sins, and take them out from the veils of their neglectfulness they will proceed to what they were running away from, and run away from what they were proceeding to. They will not benefit from the wants they will satisfy or the desires they would fulfil.

I warn you and myself from this position. A man should derive benefit from his own self. Certainly, prudent is he who hears and ponders over it, who sees and observes and who benefits from instructive material and then treads on clear paths wherein he avoids falling into hollows and straying into pitfalls, and does not assist those who misguide him by turning away from truthfulness, changing his words, or fearing truth.

O my listener! Be cured from your intoxication, wake up from your slumber, decrease your hasty activity and ponder over what has come to you through the Holy Prophet, the Ommi[1] which is inevitable and inescapable. You should turn away from him who opposes him and leave

-1- The word "Ommi" has been used in the Holy Quraan with reference to the Holy Prophet in chapter 7:157-158. For better understanding of the word refer to the books of commentary on the Holy Quraan.

him and leave whatever he has adopted for himself. Put off your vanity, drop your haughtiness and recall your grave because your way passes over it. You will be dealt with as you deal with others, you will reap what you sow, and what you send today will meet you tomorrow. So provide for your future and send (some good acts) for your day (of reckoning). Fear, fear, O listener! Act, act, O careless! No one will warn you like him who knows.

One of the firm decisions of Allah in the Wise Reminder (Quraan) upon which He bestows reward or gives punishment, and through which He likes or dislikes is that it will not benefit a man, even though he exerts himself and acts sincerely if he leaves this world to meet Allah with one of these acts without repenting, namely that he believed in a partner with Allah during his obligatory worship, or appeased his own anger by killing an individual, or spoke about acts committed by others, or sought fulfillment of his needs from people by introducing an innovation in his religion, or met people with a double face, or moved among them with a double tongue. Understand this because an illustration is a guide for its like.

Beasts are concerned with their bellies. Carnivores are concerned with assaulting others. Women are concerned with the adornments of this ignoble life and the creation of mischief herein.[1] (On the other hand)

-1- The intention is to say that the cause of all mischief and evil is the passion to satisfy bodily needs and the passion to subdue. If a human being is subjugated by the passion to satisfy bodily needs and considers filling the stomach as his aim there will be no difference between him and a beast, because a beast too has no aim except to fill its belly. But if he is over-powered by the passion to subdue others and takes to killing and devastation there will be no difference between him and a carnivorous beast, because the latter's aim is also tearing and devouring. If both the passions are at work in him then he is like a woman, because in a woman both these passions act side by side and because of this she is extremely eager of adornment and is active in fanning mischief and disturbance. However, a true believer will never agree to adopt these habits as his mode of behaviour, rather he keeps his passions suppressed so that he neither allows pride and vanity to approach near him nor does he fan mischief or disturbance for fear of Allah.

bn-Abil-Hadeed has written that Ameer al-Momineen delivered this sermon at the time of marching towards Basra, and since the trouble of Basra was the result of a woman's

believers are humble, believers are admonishers and believers are afraid (of Allah).

SERMONS 153

Ahlil-Bayt and their Opposers

He who has an intelligent mind looks to his goal. He knows his low road as well as his high road. The caller has called. The shepherd has tended (his flocks). So respond to the caller and follow the shepherd.

They (the opposers) have entered the oceans of disturbance and have taken to innovations instead of the Sonna (the Prophet's holy deeds, utterances and his unspoken approvals), while the believers have sunk down, and the misguided and the liars are speaking. We are the near ones, companions, treasure holders and doors (to the Sonna). Houses are not entered save through their doors. Whoever enters them from other than the door is called a thief.

The delicacies of the Quraan are about them (Ahlil-Bayt, the descendants of the Prophet) and they are the treasurers of Allah. When they speak they speak the truth, but when they keep quiet no one can speak unless they speak. The forerunner should report correctly to his people, should retain his wits and should be one of the children (a man) of the next world, because he has come from there and would return to it.

The beginning of the action of one who sees with heart and acts with eyes it is to assess whether the action will go against him or for him. If it is for him he indulges in it, but if it is against him he keeps away from it. For, he who acts without knowledge is like one who treads without a path. Then his deviation from the path keeps him at a distance from his aim. And he who acts according to knowledge is like he who treads the clear path. Therefore, he who can see should see whether he should proceed or return.

---

instigation, Ameer al-Momineen has, after mentioning beasts and carnivore, held a woman also to possess such qualities. Thus the battle of Basra was the result of these qualities, whereby thousands of persons were involved in death and destruction.

You should also know that the outside (of every thing) has a similar inside. Of whatever the outside is good, its inside too is good, and whatever the outside is bad, its inside too is bad. The truthful Prophet (peace and blessing of Allah be upon him and his progeny) has said that: "Allah may love a man but hate his action, and may love the action but hate the man." You should also know that every action is like a vegetation, and a vegetation cannot do without water while waters are different. So where the water is good the plant is good and its fruits are sweet, whereas where the water is bad. the plant will also be bad and its fruits will be bitter.

SERMONS 154

Wonderful Creation of the Bat

Praise be to Allah who is such that it is not possible to describe the reality of knowledge about Him, since His greatness has restrained the intellects, and therefore they cannot find the way to approach the extremity of His realm. He is Allah, the True, the Manifester of Truth. He is more True and more Manifest than eyes can see. Intellects cannot comprehend Him by fixing limits for Him since in that case to Him would be attributed shape. Imagination cannot catch Him by fixing quantities for Him for in that case to Him would be attributed body. He created creatures without any example, and without the advice of a counsel, or the assistance of a helper. His creation was completed by His command, and bowed to His obedience. It responded (to Him) and did not defy (Him). It obeyed and did not resist.

An example of His delicate production, wonderful creation and deep sagacity which He has shown us is found in these bats which keep hidden in the daylight although daylight reveals everything else, and are mobile in the night although the night shuts up every other living being; and how their eyes get dazzled and cannot make use of the light of the sun so as to be guided in their movements and so as to reach their known places through the direction provided by the sun.

Allah has prevented them from moving in the brightness of the sun and confined them to their places of hiding instead of going out at the time of its shining. Consequently they keep their eyelids down in the day and treat night as a lamp and go with its help in search of their livelihood. The darkness of night does not obstruct their sight nor does the gloom of darkness prevent them from movement. As soon as the sun removes its veil and the light of morning appears, and the rays of its light enter upon the lizards in their holes, the bats pull down their eyelids on their eyes and live on what they had collected in the darkness of the night. Glorified is He who has made the night as day for them to seek livelihood and made the day for rest and stay.

He has given them wings of flesh with which, at the time of need they rise upwards for flying. They look like the ends of ears without feathers or bones. Of course, you can see the veins quite distinctly. They have two wings which are neither too thin so that they get turned in flying, nor too thick so that they prove heavy. When they fly, their young ones hold on to them and seek refuge with them, getting down when they get down and rising up when they rise. The young does not leave them till its limbs become strong, its wings can support it for rising up, and it begins to recognise its places of living and its interest. Glorified is He who creates everything without any previous sample by someone else.

SERMONS 155

Malice borne by Aysha and Warning the people of Basra

Whoever can at this time keep himself clinging to Allah should do so. If you follow me I shall certainly carry you, if Allah so wills, on the path of Paradise, even though it may be full of severe hardship and of bitter taste. As regards a certain woman,[1] she is in the grip of womanly views, and malice is boiling in her bosom like the furnace of the blacksmith. If she

-1 -There is no denying the fact that Aysha's behaviour towards Ameer al-Momineen was throughout inimical, and very often her heart's turbidity expressed itself on her face, and her hatred and dislike became quite apparent, so much so that if in connection with some affair Ameer al-Momineen's name came up a frown appeared on her forehead and she did not relish pronouncing it with her tongue. For example, when Obaydillah bn Abdillah bn Otba mentioned to Abdillah bn Abbas the narration by Aysha namely that "in his death-illness the Prophet, taking support on al-Fazl bn Abbas and another person, came to her (Aysha's) house" Abdillah bn Abbas said:

Do you know who this "other man" was?" He said "No" Then he said "Ali bn Abi-Talib, but she is averse to name him in a good context" (Ahmad bn Hambal, al-Mosnad, vol.6, pp.34, 228; bn Saad, at-Tabaqaat al-Kabeer, vol.2, part 2, p.29; at-Tabari, at-Taareekh, vol.1, pp.1800-1801; al-Balazoori, Ansab al-Ashraf, vol.1, pp.544-545; al-Bayhaqi, as-Sonan al-Kobra, vol.3, p.396).

One cause for this hatred and malice was the presence of Hazrat Fatima (p.b.u.h.) whose wholesome dignity and esteem pricked her heart like a thorn. Her jealousy towards the other wives (of the Prophet) did not allow her to let the Prophet love the daughter of his other wife to such a degree that he should stand on her approach, seat her in his own place, declare her most honourable of all the women of the world and bear such love towards her children as to call them his own sons. All these things pained her much and naturally her feelings on such an occasion were that if she had borne children they would have been the Prophet's sons and they would have been the pivot of the Prophet's affection instead of Imam Hasan and Imam Hosayn. But she was not gifted with any issue and she gratified her own desire to be a mother by adopting the surname Om-Abdillah (mother of the slave of Allah) after her sister's son. In short all these things created the passion of hatred in her heart, as a result of which she off and on complained to the Prophet against Hazrat Fatima but could not succeed in diverting the Prophet's attention from her. News about this mortification and estrangement also reached the ears of Abi-Bakr. That would only perturb him as he too could do nothing, except that his verbal sympathies were with his daughter. At last the Prophet left this world and the reins of Government fell into his hands. Now was the opportunity for him to avenge as best as he could and to perpetrate whatever violence he had in mind. Consequently the first step he took was that, in order to deprive Hazrat Fatima of inheritance, he denied the principle of inheritance in the case of the prophets and held that neither do the prophets inherit nor are they inherited from, but the property left by them escheats to the state. Fatima was so much affected that she gave up speaking to him and passed away from this world with these very feelings. Aysha did not even take the trouble to express any sorrow at her tragic death. Thus bn-Abil-Hadeed has written:

When Fatima expired, all the wives of the Prophet came to Bani-Hashim in condolence except Aysha. She did not come and showed herself sick and words from her reached Ali which displayed her joy. (Sharh Nahjol-Balagha, vol.9, p.198).

As long as she bore so much malice against Hazrat Fatima, how could Fatima's spouse be spared similar enmity and malice. Particularly when such events also occurred which worked like a fan and roused her feeling of hatred, such as the incident of "Ifk" when Ameer al-Momineen said to the Prophet: 'she is no better than the buckles of your shoe, leave her and divorce her away" On hearing this Aysha must have felt miserable in her

were called upon to deal with others as she is dealing with me she would not have done it. (As for me), even hereafter she will be allowed her original respect, while the reckoning (of her misdeeds) is an obligation on Allah.

---

bed, and must have developed the severest feeling of hatred against him. There were also moments when distinction was conferred on Ameer al-Momineen in preference to Abi-Bakr. For instance, in connection with the dispatch of the Quraanic verses on Baraa (innocence) , the Prophet removed Abi-Bakr from the job, recalled him and assigned it to Ameer al-Momineen saying that he had been commanded by Allah to take it himself or send it through a member of his family. Similarly the Prophet closed all the doors opening into the mosque including that of Abi-Bakr but allowed the door of Ameer al-Momineen's house to continue to open thereinto.

Aysha could not relish Ameer al-Momineen's distinction over her father, and whenever there was any occasion for such distinction she did her best to undo it. When in his last days the Prophet ordered the contingent under Osaama bn Zayd to march, and ordered Abi-Bakr and Omar also to go under his command, they received a message from the wives of the Prophet that his condition was serious and therefore the contingent should come back instead of proceeding further. This was because their far-reaching sight had realised that the only purpose in getting Madeena vacated by the mohaajiroon and the Ansaar could be that after the death of the Prophet no one should stand in Ameer al-Momineen's way and that he should get the caliphate without any trouble. On receipt of this message the contingent under Osaama came back. When the Prophet learnt this he again ordered Osaama to march with the contingent and even said "Allah may curse him who keeps away from the contingent" whereupon they again set off, but they were again called back till the Prophet's illness assumed serious proportions, but Osaama's contingent did not go out as it did not want to. After this Abi-Bakr was sent word through Bilaal that he should deputise the Prophet in leading the prayers in order to pave the way for his Caliphateship. Accordingly, keeping this in view he was first shown as the Prophet's caliph (deputy) in prayers and eventually was accepted as his caliph for all purposes. Thereafter matters were so contrived that Ameer al-Momineen could not get the Caliphate. However, after the reign of the third caliph circumstances took such a turn that people were obliged to swear allegiance at Ameer al-Momineen's hand. On this occasion Aysha was present in Mecca. When she learnt about Ameer al-Momineen's caliphate her eyes began emitting flames, and rage and anger perturbed her mind, and her hatred for Ameer al-Momineen assumed such seriousness that she rose against him on the excuse of avenging blood of the same man (Othmaan) whom she had herself proclaimed fit to be killed, and openly declared war as a result of which so much bloodshed occurred that the whole land of Basra was smeared with the blood of those killed, and the door of disunity was opened for good. (Sharh, bn-Abil-Hadeed, vol.9, pp.190-200).

This path is the lightest course and the brightest lamp. Guidance towards virtuous actions is sought through faith while guidance towards faith is achieved through virtuous actions. Knowledge is made to prosper through faith, and death is feared because of knowledge. This world come to an end with death, while the next world is secured (by virtuous actions) in this world. For people there is no escape from resurrection. They are heading for this last end in its appointed course.

They have got up from the resting places in their graves and have set off for the final objectives. Every house has its own people. They are not changed nor shifted from there. Commanding for good and refraining from evil are two characteristics of Allah, the Glorified. They can neither bring death near nor lessen sustenance.

You should adhere to the Book of Allah because it is the strong rope, a clear light, a benefiting cure, a quenching for thirst, protection for the adherent and deliverance for the attached. It does not curve so as to need straightening and does not deflect so as to be corrected. Frequency of its repetition and its falling on ears does not make it old. Whoever speaks according to it, speaks truth and whoever acts by it is forward (in action).

A man stood up and said: O Ameer al-Momineen, tell us about this disturbance and whether you enquired about it from the Holy Prophet.

Thereupon Ameer al-Momineen said:

When Allah, the Glorified sent down the verse:

Alif lam mim. What! Do people imagine that they will be let off on (their) saying: "We believe!" and they will not be tried? (Quraan, 29:1-2)

I came to know that the disturbance would not befall us so long as the Prophet (peace and blessing of Allah be upon him and his progeny) is among us. So I said "O Prophet of Allah, what is this disturbance of which Allah, the Sublime, has informed you?" and he replied "O Ali, my people will create trouble after me." I said "O Prophet of Allah, on the day of Ohod, when people had fallen martyrs and I was not among them, and this had been very annoying to me, did you not say to me "cheer up, as martyrdom is for you hereafter?" The Prophet replied "Yes it is so, but what about your enduring at present?" I said "O Prophet of Allah, this is not an occasion for endurance, but rather an occasion for cheering up and gratefulness." Then he said: "O Ali, people will fall into mischief through their wealth, will show obligation to Allah on account of their faith, will expect His mercy, will feel safe from His anger and regard His unlawful matters as lawful by raising false doubts and by their misguiding desires. They will then hold lawful (the use of) wine by calling it barley water, a bribe by calling it a gift, and taking of usurious interest by calling it sale." I said "O Prophet of Allah, how should I deal with them at the time, whether to hold them to have gone back in heresy or just in revolt." He said "in revolt

SERMONS 156

Urging People towards piety (Taqwa)

Praise be to Allah who made praise the Key for His remembrance, a means for increase of His bounty and a guide for His Attributes and Dignity.

O creatures of Allah! Time will deal with the survivors just as it dealt with those gone by. The time that has passed will not return and whatever there is in it will not stay for ever. Its later deeds are the same as the former ones. Its trouble try to excel one another. Its banners follow each other. It is as though you are attached to the last day which is driving you as rapidly as are driven the she camels which are dry for seven months. He who busies himself with things other than improvement of his own self becomes perplexed in darkness and entangled in ruination. His evil spirits immerse him deep in vices and make his bad actions appear handsome. Paradise is the end of those who are forward (in good acts) and Hell is the end of those who commit excesses.

Know O creatures of Allah! that piety is a strong house of protection while impiety is a weak house which does not protect its people, and does not give security to him who takes refuge therein. Know that the sting of sins is cut by piety and the final aim is achieved by conviction of belief.

O creatures of Allah! (fear) Allah, (fear) Allah, in the matter of your own selves, which are the most beloved and dear to you, because Allah has clarified to you the way of truthfulness and lighted its paths. So (you may choose) either ever-present misfortune or eternal happiness. You should therefore provide in these mortal days for the eternal days. You have been informed of the provision, ordered to march and told to make haste in setting off. You are like staying riders who do not know when they would be ordered to march on. Beware, what will he, who has been created for the next world, do with this world? What will a person do with wealth which he would shortly be deprived of while only its ill effects and reckoning would be left behind for him?

O creatures of Allah! the good which Allah has promised should not be abandoned and the evil from which He has refrained should not be coveted. O creatures of Allah! fear the day when actions will be reckoned; there will be much quaking and even children will get old.

Know, O creatures of Allah! that your own self is a guard over you; limbs are watchmen and truthful vigil-keepers who preserve (the record of) your actions and the numbers of your breaths. The gloom of the dark night cannot conceal you from them, nor can closed doors hide you from them. Surely tomorrow is close to today.

Today will depart with all that it has and tomorrow will come in its wake. It is as though every one of you has reached that place on earth where he would be alone, namely the location of his grave. So, what to say of the lonely house, the solitary place of staying and the solitary exile. It is as though the cry (of the Horn) has reached you, the Hour has overtaken you and you have come out (of your graves) for the passing of judgement. (The curtains of) falsehood have been removed from you and your excuses have become weak. The truth about you has been proved. All your matters have proceeded to their consequences. Therefore. you should (now) take counsel from examples, learn lessons from vicissitudes and take advantage of the warners.

SERMONS 157

Holy Prophet and Holy Quraan

Allah deputed the Prophet at a time when there had been no prophets for some time. People had been in slumber for a long time and the twist of the rope had loosened. The Prophet came with (a Book containing) testification to what (books) were already there and also with a light to be followed. It is the Quraan. If you ask it to speak it wont do so; but I will tell you about it. Know that it contains knowledge of what is to come about, stories of the past, cure for your ills and regulation for whatever faces you.

The Autocracy Of The Omayyads

At that time there will remain no house or tent but oppressors would inflict it with grief and inject sickness in it. On that day no one in the sky will listen to their excuse and no one on the earth will come to their help. You selected for the governance (caliphate) one who is not fit for it, and you raised him to a position which was not meant for him. Shortly Allah will take revenge from every one who has oppressed, food for food and drink for drink, namely (they will be given) colocynth for eating, myrrh and aloes for drinking, and fear for an inner and the sword for an outer covering.

They are nothing but carrier-beasts laden with sins and camels laden with evil deeds. I swear and again swear that the Omayyads will have to spit out the caliphate as phlegm is spat and thereafter they will never taste it nor relish its flavour so long as day and night rotate.

SERMONS 158

Good behaviour, and Ignoring People's Faults

I lived as a good neighbour to you and tried my best to look after you, and I freed you from the snare of humbleness and the fetters of oppression through my gratefulness for the little good (from your side) and closed my eyes to your many misdeeds which my eyes had observed and my body had witnessed.

SERMONS 159

Praise of Allah

Allah's verdict is judicious and full of wisdom. His pleasure implies protection and mercy. He decides with knowledge and forgives with forbearance.

O my Allah! Praise be to Thee for what Thou takest and givest and for that from which Thou curest or with which Thou afflictest; praise which is the most acceptable to Thee, the most like by Thee and the most dignified before Thee; praise which fills all Thy creation and reaches where Thou desirest; praise which is not veiled from Thee and does not end, and whose continuity does not cease.

Greatness Of Allah

We do not know the reality of Thy greatness except that we know that thou art Ever-living and Self-subsisting by Whom all things subsist. Drowsiness or sleep do not overtake Thee, vision does not reach Thee and sight does not grasp Thee. Thou seest the eyes and countest the ages. Thou holdest (people as slaves) by foreheads and feet. We see Thy creation and wonder over it because of Thy might, and describe it as (a result of) Thy great authority; whereas what is hidden from us, of which our sight has fallen short, which our intelligence has not attained, and between which and ourselves curtains of the unknown have been cast, is far greater.

He who frees his heart (from all other engagements) and exerts his thinking in order to know how Thou established Thy throne, how Thou created Thy creatures, how Thou suspended the air in Thy skies and how Thou spread Thy earth on the waves of water, his eyes would return tired, his intelligence defeated, his ears eager and his thinking awander.

Fear and Hope in Allah.

He claims according to his own thinking that he hopes from Allah. By Allah, the Great, he speaks a lie. The position is that his hope (in Allah) does not appear through his action although the hope of every one who hopes is known through his action. Every hope is so, except the hope in Allah, the Sublime, if it is impure; and every fear is established except the fear for Allah if it is unreal.

He hopes big things from Allah and small things from men but he gives to man (such consideration as) he does not give to Allah. What is the matter with Allah, glorified be His praise? He is accorded less (consideration) than what is given to His creatures. Do you ever fear to be false in your hope in Allah? Or do you not regard Him the centre of your hope? Similarly, if a man fears man he gives him (such consideration) out of his fear which he does not give to Allah. Thus, he has made his fear for men ready currency while his fear from the Creator is mere deferment or promise. This is the case of every one in whose eye this world appears big (and important) and in whose heart its position is great. He prefers it over Allah, so he inclines towards it, and becomes its devotee.

The Example of the Holy Prophet

Certainly, in the Prophet of Allah (peace and blessing of Allah be upon him and his progeny) was sufficient example for you and a proof concerning the vices of the world, its defects, the multitude of its disgraces and its evils, because its sides had been constrained for him, while its flanks had been spread for others; he was deprived of its milk and turned away from its adornments.

The Example of Prophet Moosa

If you want, I will, as a second example, relate to you concerning Moosa, the Interlocutor of Allah (p.b.u.h.) when he said: O Allah! I need whatever good Thou mayest grant me (Quraan, 28:24). By Allah, he asked Him only for bread to eat because he was used to eating the herbs of the earth, and the greenness of the herbs could be seen from the delicate skin of his belly due to his thinness and paucity of his flesh.

The Example of Prophet Dawood

If you desire I can give you a third example of Dawood (p.b.u.h.). He is the holder of the Psalms and the reciter among the people of Paradise. He used to prepare baskets of date palm leaves with his own hands and would say to his companions: "Which of you will help me by purchasing it?" He used to eat barley bread (bought) out of its price.

The Example of Esaa (Jesus)

If you desire I will tell you about Esaa (p.b.u.h.) son of Maryam (Mary). He used a stone for his pillow, put on coarse clothes and ate rough food. His condiment was hunger. His lamp at night was the moon. His shade during the winter was just the expanse of earth eastward and westward. His fruits and flowers were only what grows from the earth for the cattle. He had no wife to allure him, nor any son to give grief, nor wealth to deviate (his attention), nor greed to disgrace him. His two feet were his conveyance and his two hands his servant.

Following the Example of the Holy Prophet

You should follow your Prophet, the pure, the chaste, may Allah bless him and his descendants. In him is the example for the follower, and the consolation for the seeker of consolation. The most beloved person before Allah is he who follows His Prophet and who treads in his footsteps. He took the least (share) from this world and did not take a full glance at it. Of all the people of the world he was the least satiated and the most empty of stomach. The world was offered to him but he refused to accept it. When he knew that Allah, the Glorified, hated a thing, he too hated it; that Allah held a thing low, he too held it low; that Allah held a thing small, he too held it small. If we love what Allah and His Prophet hate and hold great what Allah and His prophet hold small that would be enough isolation from Allah and transgression of His commands.

The Prophet used to eat on the ground, and sat like a slave. He repaired his shoe with his hand, and patched his clothes with his hand. He would ride an unsaddled ass and would seat someone behind him. If there was a curtain on his door with pictures on it he would say to one of his wives "O such-and-such, take it away out of my sight because if I look at it I recall the world and its allurements." Thus, he removed his heart from this world and destroyed its remembrance from his mind. He loved that its allurements should remain hidden from his eye so that he should not secure good dress from it, should not regard it a place of stay and should not hope to live in it. Consequently, he removed it from his mind, let it go away from his heart and kept it hidden from his eyes. In the same way he who hates a thing should hate to look at it or to hear about it.

Certainly there was in the Prophet of Allah all that would apprise you of the evils of this world and its defects, namely that he remained hungry along with his chief companions, and despite his great nearness the allurements of the world remained remote from him. Now, one should see with one's intelligence whether Allah honoured Mohammad (the peace and blessings of Allah be upon him and his descendants) as a result of this or disgraced him. If he says that Allah disgraced him, he certainly lies and perpetrates a great untruth. If he says Allah honoured him, he should know that Allah dishonoured the others when He extended the (benefits of the) world for him but held them away from him who was the nearest to Him of all men.

Therefore, one should follow His Prophet, tread in his footsteps and enter through his entrance. Otherwise he will not be safe from ruin. Certainly, Allah made Mohammad (the peace and blessing of Allah be upon him and his descendants) a sign for the Day of Judgement. a conveyor of tidings for Paradise and a warner of retribution. He left this world hungry but entered upon the next world safe. He did not lay one stone upon another (to make a house) till he departed and responded to the call of Allah. How great is Allah's blessing in that He blessed us with the Prophet as a predecessor whom we follow and a leader behind whom we tread.

Following his Example

By Allah, I have been putting patches in my shirts so much that now I feel shy of the patcher. Someone asked me whether I would not put it off, but I said "Get away from me." Only in the morning do people (realised the advantage of and) speak highly of the night journey.

SERMONS 160

Deputation of the Holy Prophet

Allah deputed the Prophet with a sparkling light, a clear argument, an open path and a guiding book. His tribe is the best tribe and his lineal tree the best lineal tree whose branches are in good proportion and fruits hanging (in plenty). His birth-place was Mecca, and the place of his immigration Tayba (Madeena), from where his name rose high and his voice spread far and wide.

Allah sent him with a sufficing plea, a convincing discourse and a rectifying announcement. Through him Allah disclosed the ways that had been forsaken, and destroyed the innovations that had been introduced. Through him He explained the detailed commands. Now, whoever adopts a religion other than Islam, his misery is definite, his stick (of support) will be cracked, his fate will be serious, his end will be long grief and distressing punishment.

Drawing Lessons from this World

I trust in Allah, the trust of bending towards Him, and I seek His guidance for the way that leads to His Paradise and takes to the place of His pleasure. I advise you, O creatures of Allah, to exercise fear of Allah and to obey Him because it is salvation tomorrow and deliverance for ever. He warned (you of chastisement) and did so thoroughly. He persuaded (you towards virtues) and did so fully. He described this world, its cutting away from you, its decay and its shifting. Therefore, keep aloof from its attractions, because very little of it will accompany you. This house is the closest to the displeasure of Allah and the remotest from the pleasure of Allah.

So close your eyes, O creatures of Allah, from its worries and engagements, because you are sure about its separation and its changing conditions. Fear it like a sincere fearer and one who struggles hard, and take a lesson from what you have seen about the falling places of those before you, namely that their joints were made to vanish, their eyes and ears were destroyed, their honour and prestige disappeared and their pleasure and wealth came to an end. The nearness of their children changed into remoteness. The company of their spouses changed into separation with them. They do not boast over each other, nor do they beget children nor meet each other nor live as neighbours. Therefore, fear O creature of Allah, like the fear of one who has control over himself, who can check his passions and perceive with his wisdom. Surely, the matter is quite clear, the banner is standing, the course is level and the way is straight.

SERMONS 161

Reasons for Keeping himself away from the Caliphate

One Of Ameer al-Momineen's Companions (From Bani-Asad) Asked Him: "How Was It That Your Tribe (Quraysh) Deprived You Of This Position (Caliphate) Although You Deserved It Most." Then In Reply He Said:

O brother of Bani-Asad! Your girth is loose and you have put it on the wrong way. Nevertheless you enjoy in-law kinship and also the right to ask, and since you have asked, listen. As regards the oppression against us in this matter although we were the highest as regards descent and the strongest in relationship with the Messenger of Allah. It was a selfish act over which the hearts of people became greedy, although some people did not care for it. The Arbiter is Allah and to Him is the return on the Day of Judgement.

Now leave this story of devastation about which there is hue and cry all round[1]

-1- This is a hemistich from the couplet of the famous Arab poet Imriol-Qays al-Kindi. The second hemistich is:

And let me know the story of what happened to the riding camels

The incident behind this couplet is that when the father of Imriol-Qays namely Hijr bn Haarith was killed, he roamed about the various Arab tribes to avenge his father's life with their help. In this connection he stayed with a man of Jadila (tribe) but finding himself unsafe left that place, and stayed with Khaalid bn Saad an-Nabhani. In the

Come and look at the son of Abo-Sofyaan (Moaawiya). Time has made me laugh after weeping. No wonder, by Allah; what is this affair which surpasses all wonder and which has increased wrongfulness. These people have tried to put out the flame of Allah's light from His lamp and to close His fountain from its source. They mixed epidemic-producing water between me and themselves. If the trying hardships were removed from among us, I would take them on the course of truthfulness otherwise:

... So let not thy self go (in vain) in grief for them; verily Allah knoweth all that they do." (Quraan, 35:8)

SERMONS 162

Attributes of Allah

Praise be to Allah, Creator of people; He has spread the earth. He makes streams to flow and vegetation to grow on high lands. His primarity has no beginning, nor has His eternity any end. He is the First and from ever. He is the everlasting without limit. Foreheads bow before Him and lips

---

meantime a man of Jadila named Baith bn Howays drove away some of his camels. Imriol-Qays complained of this matter to his host and he asked him to send with him his she-camels then he would get back his camels. Consequently, Khaalid went to those people and asked them to return the camels of his guest which they had robbed. They said that he was neither a guest nor under his protection. Thereupon Khaalid swore that he was really his guest and showed them his she-camels that he had with him. They then agreed to return the camels. But actually instead of returning the camels they drove away the she-camels as well. One version is that they did return the camels to Khaalid but instead of handing them over to Imriol-Qays he kept them for himself. When Imriol-Qays came to know this he composed a few couplets out of which this is one. It means "now you leave the story of these camels which were robbed but now let me know about the she-camels snatched from my hands. "

Ameer al-Momineen's intention in quoting this verse as an illustration is that "Now that Moaawiya is at war, we should talk about and should leave the discussion about the devastation engendered by those who had usurped my rights. That time has gone away. Now is the time for grappling with the mischiefs of the hour. So discuss the event of the moment and do not start untimely strain" Ameer al-Momineen said this because the man had put the question to him at the time of the battle of Siffeen, when the battle was raging and bloodshed was in full swing.

declare His oneness. He determined the limits of things at the time of His creating them, keeping Himself away from any likeness.

Imagination cannot surmise Him within the limits of movements limbs or senses. It cannot be said about Him: "whence; and no time limit can be attributed to Him by saying "till. He is apparent, but it cannot be said "from what. He is hidden, but it cannot be said "in what. He is not a body which can die, nor is He veiled so as to be enclosed therein. He is not near to things by way of touch, nor is He remote from them by way of separation. The gazing of people's eyes is not hidden from Him, nor the repetition of words, nor the glimpse of hillocks, nor the tread of a footstep in the dark night or in the deep gloom, where the shining moon casts its light and the effulgent sun comes in its wake, through its setting and appearing again and again with the rotation of time and periods, by the approach of the advancing night or the passing away of the running day.

He precedes every extremity and limit, and every counting and numbering. He is far above what those whose regard is limited attribute to Him, such as the qualities of measure, having extremities, living in house and dwelling in abodes, because limits are meant for creation and are attributable only to other than Allah.

Allah, The Originator from Naught

He did not create things from eternal matter nor after ever-existing examples, but He created whatever He created and then He fixed limits thereto, and He shaped whatever He shaped and gave the best shape thereto. Nothing can disobey Him, but the obedience of something is of no benefit to Him. His knowledge about those who died in the past is the same as His knowledge about the remaining survivors, and His knowledge about whatever there is in the high skies is like His knowledge of whatever there is in the low earth.

Requirements of Life

O creature who has been equitably created and who has been nurtured and looked after in the darkness of wombs with multiple curtains. You were originated from the essence of clay (Quraan, 23:12) and placed in a still place for a known length (Quraan, 77:21-22) and an ordained time. You used to move in the womb of your mother as an embryo, neither responding to a call nor hearing any voice.

Then you were taken out from your place of stay to a place you had not seen, and you were not acquainted with the means of awaiting its benefits, or with who guided you to eke out your sustenance from the udder of your mother, and, when your were in need, appraised you of the location of what you required or aimed at. Alas! Certainly he who is unable to understand the qualities of a being with shape and limbs is the more unable to understand the qualities of the Creator and the more remote from appreciating Him through the limitations of creatures.

SERMONS 163

Dialogue with Othmaan (bn "Affaan)

When people went to Ameer al-Momineen in a deputation and complained to him through what they had to say against Othmaan, and requested him to speak to him on their behalf and to admonish him for their sake, he went to see him and said:[1]

-1- During the Caliphate of Othmaan when the Moslims were weary of the oppression of the Government and its officials collected in Madeena to complain to the senior companions of the Prophet, they came to Ameer al-Momineen in a peaceful manner and requested him to see Othmaan and advise him not to trample on the Moslims" rights and to put an end to the troubles which were proving the cause of the people's ruin, whereupon Ameer al-Momineen went to him and uttered these words.

In order to make the bitterness of the admonition palatable Ameer al-Momineen adopted that way of speech in the beginning which would create a sense of responsibility in the addressee and direct him towards his obligations. Thus, by mentioning his companionship of the Prophet, his personal position, and his kinship to the Prophet as against the two previous Caliphs, his intention was to make him realise his duties; in any case, this was obviously not an occasion for eulogising him, so that its later portion can be disregarded and the whole speech be regarded as an eulogy of his attainments, because from its very beginning it is evident that whatever Othmaan did, he did it wilfully, that nothing was done without his knowledge or his being informed, and that he could not be held unaccountable for it because of his being unaware of it. If the adoption of a line of action which made the whole Islamic world raise hue and cry in spite of his having being a companion of the Prophet, having heard his instructions, having seen his behaviour and having been acquainted with the commandments of Islam can be regarded as a distinction, then this taunt may also be regarded as praise. If that is not a distinction then this too cannot be called and eulogy. In fact, the words about which it is argued that they are in praise are enough to prove the seriousness of his crime, because a crime in ignorance and unawareness is not so serious as the weight given to the seriousness of the commission of a crime despite knowledge and awareness. Consequently a person who is unaware of the rise and fall of a road and stumbles in the dark night is excusable but a person who is aware of the rise and fall of the road and stumbled in broad day light is liable to be blamed. If on this occasion he is told that he has eyes and is also aware of the rise and fall of the way, it would not mean that his vastness of knowledge or the brightness of his eye-sight is being praised, but the intention would be that he did not notice the pitfalls despite his eyes, and did not walk properly, and that therefore for him, having or not having eyes is the same, and knowing or not knowing is equal.

In this connection great stress in laid on his being a son-in-law, namely that the Prophet married his two daughters Roqayya and Om-Kolthoom to him one after the other. Before taking this to be a distinction, the real nature of Othmaan's son-in-lawship should be seen. History shows that in this matter Othmaan did not enjoy the distinction of being the first, but before him Roqayya and Om-Kolthoom had been married to two sons of Abo-Lahab namely Otba and Otayba, but despite their being sons-in-law, they have not been included among people of position of pre-Prophethood period. How then can this be regarded as a source of position without any personal merit, when there is no authority about the importance of this relationship, nor was any importance attached to this matter in such a way that there might have been some competition between Othmaan and some other important personality in this regard and that his selection for it might have given him prominence, or that these two girls might have been shown to possess an important position in history, tradition or biography as a result of which this relationship could be given special importance and regarded as a distinction for him? If the marriage of these two daughters with Otba and Otayba in the pre-Prophethood period is held as lawful on the ground that marriage with unbelievers had not till then been made unlawful, then in Othmaan's case also the condition for lawfulness was his acceptance of Islam, there is no doubt that he had pronounced the kalima ash-Shahaadatayn (there is no god but Allah and Mohammad is His Messenger) and had accepted Islam outwardly. As such this marriage can be held a proof of his outward Islam, but no other honour can be proved through it. Again, it is also not agreed that these two were the real daughters of the Messenger of Allah, because there is one group which denies them to be his real daughters, and regards them as being the daughters of Khadeeja's sister Hala, or the daughters of her own previous husband. Thus, Abol-Qaasim al-Koofi (d. 352 A.H.) writes:

When the Messenger of Allah married Khadeeja, then some time thereafter Hala died leaving two daughters, one named Zaynab and the other named Roqayya and both of them were brought up by the Prophet and Khadeeja and they maintained them, and it

The people are behind me and they have made me an ambassador between you and themselves; but by Allah, I do not know what to say to you. I know nothing (in this matter) which you do not know, nor can I lead you to any matter of which you are not aware. You certainly know what we know, we have not come to know anything before you which we could

---

was the custom before Islam that a child was assigned to whoever brought him up" (al-Istighaatha, p.69)

bn Hishaam has written about the issues of Hazrat Khadeeja as follows:

Before marriage with the Prophet she was married to bn-Hala bn Malik. She delivered for him Hind bn Abi Hala and Zaynab bnt bn-Hala. Before marriage with bn-Hala she was married to Otayyiq bn Abdillah bn Amr bn Makhzoom and she delivered for him Abdillah and a daughter" (as-Seera an-Nabawiyya, vol.4, p.293)

This shows that of Hazrat Khadeeja had two daughters before being married to the Prophet and according to all appearance they would be called his daughters and those to whom they were married would be called his sons-in-law, but the position of this relationship would be the same as if those girls were his daughters. Therefore, before putting it forth as a matter for pride the real status of the daughters should be noted and a glance should be cast at Othmaan's conduct. In this connection, al-Bokhaari and other narrators (of traditions) and historians record this tradition as follows:

Anas bn Malik relates that: "We were present on the occasion of the burial of the Prophet's daughter Om-Kolthoom, while the Prophet was sitting beside her grave. I saw his eyes shedding tears. Then he said "Is there any one among you who has not committed a sin last night?" Abo-Talha (Zayd bn Sahl al-Ansaari) said "I, then the Prophet said "Then you get into the grave" consequently he got down into the grave.

The commentators said about "committed sin" that the Holy Prophet meant to say "one who had not had sexual intercourse" On this occasion the Holy Prophet unveiled the private life of Othmaan and prevented him from getting down into the grave, although it was a prominent merit of the Prophet's character that he did not disgrace or belittle any one by making public his private life, and despite of knowledge of others" shortcomings, ignored them; but in this case the filth was such that it was deemed necessary to disgrace him before the whole crowd.

Since Othmaan did not show any regard for the demise of his wife (Om-Kolthoom) nor was he moved or felt sorry (for this event) , and paid no heed to the cutting off his relationship with the Holy Prophet (for being his son-in-law) , he (Othmaan) had sexual intercourse on the same night, therefore the Holy Prophet deprived him of this right and honour. (Saheeh Bokhaari, vol.2, pp.100-101, 114; Ahmad bn Hambal, al-Mosnad, vol.3, pp.126, 228, 229, 270; al-Hakim, al-Mostadrak, vol.4, p.47; al-Bayhaqi, as-Sonan al-Kobra, vol.4, p.53; bn Saad, at-Tabaqaat al-Kabeer, vol.8, p.26; as-Sohayli, ar-Rawdal-Onof, vol.2, p.107; bn Hajar, al-Isaba, vol.4, p.489; Fath al-Bari, vol.3, p.122; al-Ayni, Omdatol-Qaari, vol.4, p.85; bn al-Athir, an-Nehaaya, vol.3, p.276; bn-Manzor, Lisaan al-Arab, vol.9, pp.280-281; az-Zabidi, Taaj al-Aroos, vol.6, p.220).

tell you; nor did we learn anything in secret which we should convey to you. You have seen as we have seen and you have heard as we have heard. You sat in the company of the Prophet of Allah as we did. (Abi-Bakr) bn-Abi-Quhaafa and (Omar) bn-Khattaab were no more responsible for acting righteously than you, since you are nearer than both of them to the Prophet of Allah through kinship, and you also hold relationship to him by marriage which they do not hold.

Then (fear) Allah, in your own self; for, by Allah, you are not being shown anything as if you are blind or being apprised of anything as if you are ignorant. The ways are clear while the banners of faith are fixed. You should know that among the creatures of Allah, the most distinguished person before Allah is the just Imam who has been guided (by Allah) and guides others. So, he stands by the recognised ways of the Prophet's behaviour and destroys unrecognised innovations. The (Prophet's) ways are clear and they have signs, while innovations are also clear and they too have signs. Certainly, the worst man before Allah is the oppressive Imam who has gone astray and through whom others go astray. He destroys the accepted Sonna and revives abandoned innovations. I heard the Messenger of Allah saying: "On the Day of Judgement the oppressive Imam will be brought without anyone to support him or anyone to advance excuses on his behalf, and then he will be thrown into Hell where he will rotate as the hand-mill rotates, then (eventually) he will be confined to its hollow

I swear to you by Allah that you should not be that Imam of the people who will be killed because it has been said that "An Imam of this people will be killed after which killing and fighting will be made open for them till the Day of Judgement, and he will confuse their matters and spread troubles over them. As a result, they will not discern truth from wrong. They will oscillate like waves and would be utterly misled." You should not behave as the carrying beast for Marwaan so that he may drag you wherever he likes, despite (your) seniority of age and length of life.

Then Othmaan said to Ameer al-Momineen: 'speak to the people to give me time until I redress their grievances." Ameer al-Momineen then said: So far as Madeena is concerned here is no question of time. As for remoter areas you can have the time needed for your order to reach there

SERMONS 164

Magnificence of The Creator in Birds

Allah has provided wonderful creations including the living, the lifeless, the stationary, and the moving. He has established such clear proofs for His delicate creative power and great might that minds bend down to Him in acknowledgement thereof and in submission to Him, and arguments about His Oneness strike our ears. He has created birds of various shapes which live in the burrows of the earth, in the openings of high passes and on the peaks of mountains.

They have different kinds of wings, and various characteristics. They are controlled by the rein of (Allah's) authority. They flutter with their wings in the expanse of the vast firmament and the open atmosphere. He brought them into existence from non-existence in strange external shapes, and composed them with joints and bones covered with flesh. He prevented some of them from flying easily in the sky because of their heavy bodies and allowed them to use their wings only close to the ground. He has set them in different colours by his delicate might and exquisite creative power.

Among them are those which are tinted with one hue and there is no other hue except the one in which they have been dyed. There are others which are tinted with one colour, and they have a neck ring of a different colour than that with which they are tinted.

The Peacock

The most amazing among them in its creation is the peacock, which Allah has created in the most symmetrical dimensions, and arranged its hues in the best arrangement with wings whose ends are interleaved together and whose tail is long. When it moves to its female it spreads out its folded tail and raises it up so as to cast a shade over its head, as if it were the sail of a boat being pulled by the sailor. It feels proud of its colours and swaggers with its movements. It copulates like the cocks. It leaps (on the female) for fecundation like lustful energetic men at the time of fighting. I am telling you all this from observation, unlike he who narrates on the basis of weak authority, as for example, the belief of some people that it fecundates the female by a tear which flows from its eyes and when it stops on the edges of the eyelids the female swallows it and lays its eggs thereby and not through fecundation by a male other than by means of this flowing tear. Even if they say this, it would be no amazing than (what they say about) the mutual feeding of the crows (for fecundation). You would imagine its feathers to be sticks made of silvers and the wonderful circles and sun-shaped feathers growing thereon to be of pure gold and pieces of green emerald. If you likened them to anything growing on land, you would say that it is a bouquet of flowers collected during every spring. If you likened them to cloths, they would be like printed apparels or amazing variegated cloths of Yemen. If you likened them to ornaments then they would be like gems of different colour with studded silver.

The peacock walks with vanity and pride, and throws open its tail and wings and laughs admiring the handsomeness of its dress and the hues of its necklace of gems. But when it casts its glance at its legs it cries loudly with a voice which indicates its call for help and displays its true grief, because its legs are thin like the legs of Indo-Persian cross-bred cocks. At the end of its shin there is a thin thorn and on the crown of its head there is a bunch of green variegated feathers. Its neck begins in the shape of a goblet and its stretch up to its belly is like the hair-dye of Yemen in colour or like silk cloth put on a polished mirror which looks as if it has been covered with a black veil, except that on account of its excessive lustre and extreme brightness it appears that a lush green colour has been mixed with it. Along the openings of its ears there is a line of shining bright daisy colour like the thin end of a pen. Whiteness shines on the black background. There is hardly a hue from which it has not taken a bit and improved it further by regular polish, lustre, silken brightness and brilliance. It is therefore like scattered blossoms which have not been seasoned by the rains of spring or the sun of the summer.

It also sheds its plumage and puts off its dress. They all fall away and grow again. They fall way from the feather stems like the falling of leaves from twigs, and then they begin to join together and grow till they return to the state that existed before their falling away. The new hues do not change from the previous ones, nor does any colour occur in other than its own place. If you carefully look at one hair from the hairs of its feather stems it would look like red rose, then emerald green and then golden yellow.

How can sharpness of intellect describe such a creation, or faculty of mind, or the utterances of describers manage to tell of it. Even its smallest parts have made it impossible for the imagination to pick them out or for tongues to describe them. Glorified is Allah who has disabled intellects from describing the creation which He placed openly before the eyes and which they see bounded, shaped, arranged and coloured. He also disabled tongues from briefly describing its qualities and also from expanding in its praise.

Great and Small Creation

Glorified is Allah who has assigned feet to small ants and gnats and also to those above them, the serpents and the elephants. He has made it obligatory upon Himself that no skeleton in which He infuses the spirit would move, but that death is its promised place and destruction its final end.

Sermon Describing Paradise

If you cast your mind's eye at what is described to you about Paradise, your heart would begin to hate the delicacies of this world that have been displayed here, namely its desires and its pleasures, and the beauties of its scenes, and you would be lost in the rustling of the trees whose roots lie hidden in the mounds of musk on the banks of the rivers in Paradise and in the attraction of the bunches of fresh pearls in the twigs and branches of those trees, and in the appearance of different fruits from under the cover of their leaves. These fruits can be picked without difficulty as they come down at the desire of their pickers. Pure honey and fermented wine will be handed round to those who settle down in the courtyards of its palaces.

They are a people whom honour has always followed till they were made to settle in the house of eternal abode, and they obtained rest from the movement of journeying. O listener! If you busy yourself in advancing towards these wonderful scenes which will rush towards you, then your heart will certainly die due to eagerness for them, and you will be prepared to seek the company of those in the graves straight away from my audience here and hasten towards them. Allah may, by His mercy, include us and you too among those who strive with their hearts for the abodes of the virtuous.

Note Explaining Some Of The Wonderful And Obscure Portions Of This Sermon

Sayyid Razi says: In Ameer al-Momineen's words "yaurru bimalaqihihi "al-arr" implies "copulation, e. g. when it is said "arrar-rajulu al-marata yaurruha, it means "He copulated with the woman

In his words "kaannahu qalu dariyyin anajahu nutiyyuhu "al-qal" means the sail of a boat" "dari" means belonging to Darin which is a small town on the coast from where scents are bought. And "anajahu" means "turned it. It is said "anajtonn-naqata — like nasartu — anajuha anjan" "When you turn the she-camel." And "an-nuti" means sailor. His words "daffatay jufunihi" means edges of the eyelids, since "ad-daffatan" means the two edges. His words "wa filazuz-zabarjadi: "al-filaz" is the plural of "al-filza" it means piece. His words "ka baisil-loloir-ratibi" "al-kibasa" means bunch of dates "al-asalij" means twigs. Its singular is "usluj.

SERMONS 165

Observing courtesy and kindness and keeping in and out of the same

The young among you should follow the elders while the elders should be kind to the young. Do not be like those rude people of the pre-Islamic (al-jahiliyya) period who did not exert themselves in religion nor use their intellects in the matter of Allah. They[1] are like the breaking of eggs in the nest of a dangerous bird, because their breaking looks bad, but keeping them intact would mean the production of dangerous young ones.

Autocracy and Oppression of the Omayyads and their fate

They will divide after their unity and scatter away from their centre. Some of them will stick to the branches, and bending down as the branches bend, until Allah, the Sublime, will collect them together for the day that will be worst for the Omayyads just as the scattered bits of clouds collect together in the autumn. Allah will create affection among them. Then He will make them into a strong mass like the mass of clouds. Then he will open doors for them to flow out from their starting place like the flood of the two gardens (of Saba) from which neither high rocks remained safe nor small hillocks, and its flow could be repulsed neither by strong mountains nor by high lands. Allah will scatter them in the low lands of valleys and then He will make them flow like streams throughout the earth, and through them He will arrange the taking of rights of one people by another people and make one people to stay in the houses of another people. By Allah, all their position and esteem will dissolve as fat dissolves on the fire.

The cause of tyranny

O people! If you had not evaded support of the truth and had not felt weakness from crushing wrong then he who was not your match would

-1- The implication is that the outer Islam of these people required that they should not be molested, but the consequence of sparing them in this way was that they would create mischief and rebellion.

not have aimed at you and he who overpowered you would not have overpowered you. But you roamed about the deserts (of disobedience) like Bani-Israaeel (Children of Israel). I swear by my life that after me your tribulations will increase several times, because you will have abandoned the truth behind your backs, severed your connection with your near ones and established relations with remote ones. Know that if you had followed him who was calling you (to guidance) he would have made you tread the ways of the Prophet, then you would have been spared the difficulties of misguidance, and you would have thrown away the crushing burden from your necks.

SERMONS 166

Fulfillment of Rights and Obligations, and advice to fear Allah in all matters.

Delivered at the beginning of his Caliphate

Allah, the Glorified, has sent down a guiding Book wherein He has explained virtue and vice. You should adopt the course of virtue whereby you will have guidance, and keep aloof from the direction of vice so that you remain on the right way. (Mind) the obligations (mind) the obligations. Fulfil them for Allah and they will take you to Paradise. Surely, Allah has made unlawful the things which are not unknown and made lawful the things which are without defect. He has declared paying regard to Moslims as the highest of all regards. He has placed the rights of Moslims in the same grade (of importance) as devotion (to Himself and His oneness). Therefore, a Moslim is one from whose tongue and hand every (other) Moslim is safe save in the matter of truth. It is not, therefore, lawful to molest a Moslim except when it is obligatory.

Hasten towards the most common matter which is peculiar to every one; and that is death. Certainly, people (who have already gone) are ahead of you while the hour (Day of Judgement) is driving you from behind. Remain light, in order that you may overtake them. Your backs are being awaited for the sake of the fronts. Fear Allah in the matter of His creatures and His cities because you will be questioned even about lands and beasts. Obey Allah and do not disobey Him. When you see virtue adopt it, and when you see vice avoid it.

SERMONS 167

In reply to the People's demand for avenging "Othmaan's blood

After Swearing Of Allegiance To Ameer al-Momineen, Some People From Among The Companions Of The Prophet Said To Him "You Should Punish The People Who Aasaulted Othmaan," Whereupon He Said:

O my brothers! I am not ignorant of what you know, but how do I have the power for it while those who assaulted him are in the height of their power. They have superiority over us, not we over them. They are now in the position that even your slaves have risen with them and Bedouin Arabs too have joined them. They are now among you and are harming you as they like. Do you see any way to be able to do what you aim at?

This demand is certainly that of the pre-Islamic (al-jahiliyya) period and these people have support behind them. When the matter is taken up, people will have different views about it. One group will think as you do, but another will not think as you think, and there will be still another group who will be neither this way nor that way. Be patient till people quieten down and hearts settle in their places so that rights can be achieved for people easily. Rest assured from me, and see what is given to you by me. Do not do anything which shatters your power, weakens your strength and engenders feebleness and disgrace. I shall control this affair as far as possible, but if I find it necessary the last treatment will, of course, be branding with a hot iron (through fighting).

SERMONS 168

When the People of Jamal set off for Basra

There is no doubt that Allah sent down the Prophet as a guide with an eloquent Book and a standing command. No one will be ruined by it except one who ruins himself. Certainly, only doubtful innovations cause ruin except those from which Allah may protect. In Allah's authority lies the safety of your affairs. Therefore, render Him such obedience as is neither blameworthy nor insincere. By Allah, you must do so, otherwise Allah will take away from you the power of Islam, and will never thereafter return it to you till it reverts to others.

Certainly, these people are in agreement in disliking my authority. I will carry on till I perceive disunity among you; because if, in spite of the unsoundness of their view, they succeed, the whole organisation of the Moslims will be shattered. They are hankering after this world out of jealousy against him on whom Allah has bestowed it. So they intend reverting the matters on their backs (pre-Islamic period), while on us it is obligatory, for your sake, to abide by the Book of Allah (Quraan), the Sublime, and the conduct of the Prophet of Allah, to stand by His rights and the revival of his Sonna.

SERMONS 169

In reply to a man[1] who came from Basra to enquire about his position vis-à-vis the People of Jamal

When Ameer al-Momineen approached Basra an Arab met him and spoke to him, as he had been sent to him by a group of people of Basra to enquire from him on their behalf position vis-à-vis the people of Jamal. Ameer al-Momineen explained to him his position with respect to them, from which he was convinced that Ameer al-Momineen was in the right. Then Ameer al-Momineen asked him to swear allegiance, but he replied "I am just a message carrier of a people and shall not do anything until I get back to them." Upon this Ameer al-Momineen said to him:

If those at your back send you as a forerunner to search out a rain-fed area for them, and you return to them and apprise them of greenery and water

-1- This man was known as Kolayb al-Jarmi.

but they disagree with you and go towards dry and barren land, what would you do then?

He said: I would leave them and go towards greenery and water. Ameer al-Momineen then said:

So then extend your hand.

This man related that: By Allah, by such a clear argument I could not refrain from swearing allegiance to Ameer al-Momineen.

SERMONS 170

When he decided to fight the enemy face to face at Siffeen

O my Allah! Sustainer of the high sky and the suspended firmament which Thou hast made a shelter for the night and the day, an orbit for the sun and the moon and a path for the rotating stars, and for populating it Thou hast created a group of Thy angels who do not get weary of worshipping Thee. O Sustainer of this earth which Thou hast made an abode for people and a place for the movement of insects and beasts and countless other creatures seen and unseen. O Sustainer of strong mountains which Thou hast made as pegs for the earth and (a means of) support for people. If Thou givest us victory over our enemy, save us from excesses and keep us on the straight path of truth. But if Thou givest them victory over us, then grant us martyrdom and save us from mischief.

Where are those who protect honour, and those self-respecting persons who defend respectable persons in the time of hardship? Shame is behind you while Paradise is in front of you.

SERMONS 171

Consultative committee and the Battle of Jamal

Praise be to Allah from whose view one sky does not conceal another sky nor one earth another earth.

Consultative Committee after the Death of Omar bn-Khattaab

Someone[1] said to me "O son of Abi-Talib, you are eager for the caliphate." Then I told him:

Rather, you are, by Allah, more greedy, although more remote, while I am more suited as well as nearer. I have demanded it as my right, while you are intervening between me and it, and you are turning my face from it." When I knocked at his ears with arguments among the crowd of those present he was startled as if he was stunned not knowing what reply to give me about it.

O my Allah! I seek Thy succor against the Quraysh and those who are assisting them, because they are denying me (the rights of) kinship, have lowered my high position, and are united in opposing me in the matter (of the caliphate) which is my right, and then they said "Know that the rightful thing is that you have it and also that you may leave it[2]

-1- On the occasion of the Consultative Committee Saad bn Abi Waqqas repeated to Ameer al-Momineen what Caliph Omar had said in his last hours namely that "O Ali, you are very greedy for the position of caliphate" and Ali replied that, "He who demands his own right cannot be called greedy; rather greedy is he who prevents the securing of the right and tries to grab it despite being unfit for it

There is no doubt that Ameer al-Momineen considered the Caliphate to be his right, and demanded his right. The demand for a right does not dispel a right so that it may be put forth as an excuse for not assigning him the caliphate, and the demand may be held as a mark of greed. Even if it was greed, who was not involved in this greed? Was not the pull between the mohaajiroon and the Ansaar the mutual struggle between the members of the Consultative Committee and the mischief mongering of Talha and az-Zobayr the product of this very greed. If Ameer al-Momineen had been greedy for this position, he would have stood for it, closing his eyes to the consequences and results, when Abbas (uncle of the Prophet) and Abo-Sofyaan pressed him for (accepting) allegiance, and when, after the third Caliph people thronged to him for (swearing) allegiance, he should have accepted their offer without paying any attention to the deteriorated conditions. But at no time did Ameer al-Momineen take any step which could prove that he wanted the Caliphate for the sake of caliphate, but rather his demand for the caliphate was only with the object that its features should not be altered and the religion should not become the victim of others" desires, not that he should enjoy the pleasures of life which could be attributed to greed.

2 Explaining the meaning, bn-Abil-Hadeed writes that Ameer al-Momineen's intention was to say:

They (the Quraysh and those who are assisting them) were not only content to keep me away from my right over the caliphate which they have usurped (from me) , but rather

Describing The People of Jamal

They (Talha, az-Zobayr and their supporters) came out dragging the wife of the Messenger of Allah (the peace and blessing of Allah be upon him and his descendants) just as a maid-slave is dragged for sale. They took her to Basra where those two (Talha and az-Zobayr) put their own women in their houses but exposed the wife of the Messenger of Allah to themselves and to others in the army in which there was not a single individual who had not offered me his obedience and sworn to me allegiance quite obediently, without any compulsion.

Here in Basra they approached my governor and treasurers of the public treasury and its other inhabitants. They killed some of them in captivity and others by treachery. By Allah, even if they had wilfully killed only one individual from among the Moslims without any fault, it would have been lawful for me to kill the whole of this army because they were present in it but did not disagree with it nor prevented it by tongue or hand, not to say that they killed from among the Moslims a number equal to that with which they had marched on them.

SERMONS 172

On Eligibility for the Caliphate

The Prophet is the trustee of Allah's revelation, the Last of His Prophets. the giver of tidings of His mercy and the warner for His chastisement.

O people. the most rightful of all persons for this matter (namely the caliphate) is he who is most competent among them to maintain it, and he who knows best Allah's commands about it. If any mischief is created by a mischief-monger, he will be called upon to repent. If he refuses. he

---

claimed that it was their right whether to give it to me or prevent me from the same; and that I have no right to argue with them.

Furthermore, the intention (of Ameer al-Momineen) is that:

If they had not said that it is right to keep away from the caliphate, it would have been easy to endure it because this would have, at least, showed their admitting my right although they were not prepared to concede it. (Sharh Nahjol-Balagha, vol.9, p.306)

will be fought. By my life,[1] if the question of Imaama was not to be decided unless all the people were present, then there would be no such case. But those who agreed about it imposed the decision on those who were absent, so much so that he who was present could not dissent and the one who was absent could not choose (any one else). Know that I shall fight two persons — one who claims what is not his and the other who ignores what is obligatory upon him.

The Need for Sagacity in Fighting against Moslims

O creatures of Allah! I advise you to have fear of Allah because it is the best advice to be mutually given by persons, and the best of all things before Allah. The door of war has been opened between you and the other Moslims. And this banner will be borne only by him who is a man of sight, of endurance and of knowledge of the position of rightfulness.

---

1 When the people collected in the Saqeefa of Bani-Saaida in connection with the election, even those who were not present there were made to follow the decision taken there, and the principle was adopted that those present at the election had no right to reconsider the matter or to break the allegiance and those not present could do nothing but acquiesce in the agreed decision. But when the people of Madeena swore allegiance at the hands of Ameer al-Momineen, the Governor of Syria (Moaawiya) refused to follow suit on the ground that since he was not present on the occasion he was not bound to abide by it, whereupon Ameer al-Momineen gave a reply in this sermon on the basis of these accepted and agreed principles and conditions which had been established among these people and had become incontrovertible namely that: "When the people of Madeena and the Ansaar and the mohaajiroon have sworn allegiance on my hand, Moaawiya had no right to keep aloof from it on the ground that he was not present on the occasions nor were Talha and az-Zobayr entitled to break the pledge after swearing allegiance

On this occasion, Ameer al-Momineen did not argue on the strength of any saying of the Prophet which would serve as his final say about the caliphate, because the grounds for refusal in his case was in respect of the modus operandi of the principle of election. Therefore, in keeping with the requirements of the situation a reply based on the agreed principles of the adversary could alone quieten him. Even if he had argued on the strength of the Prophet's command it would have been subjected to various interpretations and the matter would have been prolonged instead of being settled. Again Ameer al-Momineen had seen that soon after the death of the Prophet all his sayings and commands had been set aside. Therefore, how after the lapse of a long time, could one be expected to accept it when habit had been established to follow one's free will against the Prophet's sayings.

Therefore, you should go ahead with what you are ordered and desist from what you are refrained. Do not make haste in any matter till you have clarified it. For in the case of every matter which you dislike we have a right to change it.

Behaviour of this World with its Adherents

Know that this world which you have started to covet and in which you are interested, and which sometimes enrages you and sometimes pleases you is not your (permanent) abode, nor the place of your stay for which you might have been created, nor one to which you have been invited. Know that it will not last for you nor will you live along with it. If anything out of this world deceives you (into attraction), its evils warn you too. You should give up (the objects of) its deceits in favour of (the objects of) its warning and (the objects of) its attractions in favour of (the objects of) its terrors. And while here in it, advance towards that house to which you have been called, and turn away your hearts from the world. None of you should cry like a maid slave over anything which she has been deprived of. Seek the perfection of Allah's bounty over you by endurance in obedience to Allah and in guarding what He has asked you to guard, namely His Book. Know that the loss of anything of this world will not harm you, if you have guarded the principles of your religion. Know also that after the loss of your religion nothing of this world for which you have cared will benefit you. May Allah carry our hearts and your hearts towards the right and may He grant us and you endurance.

SERMONS 173

When he received the news that Talha and az-Zobayr had already left for Basra to fight against him

As for me, I would never be frightened of fighting or be made to fear striking because I am satisfied with Allah's promise of support to me. By Allah, Talha has hastened with drawn sword to avenge Othmaan's blood for fear lest the demand for Othmaan's blood be made against himself, because the people's idea in this matter is about him, and, in fact, he was the most anxious among them for his killing. Therefore, he has tried to create misunderstanding by collecting forces in order to confuse the matter and to create doubt.

By Allah. he did not act in either of three ways about Othmaan. If the son of Affaan (Othmaan) was in the wrong, as Talha believed, it is necessary for him to support those who killed[1] him or to keep away from his supporters. If Othmaan was the victim of oppression. then Talha should have been among those who were keeping (the assaulters) away from him or were advancing pleas on his behalf. If he was in doubt about these two alternatives, then it was incumbent upon him to leave him (Othmaan) and retire aside and leave the men with him (to deal with him as they wished). But he adopted none of these three ways, and came out with a thing in which there is no good, and his excuses are not acceptable.

SERMONS 174

Warning to Neglectful People

O people who are (negligent of Allah but) not neglected (by Allah), and those who miss (doing good acts) but are to be caught. How is it that I see you becoming removed from Allah and becoming interested in others? You are like the camel whom the grazer drives to a disease-stricken pasture and a disastrous watering place. They are like beasts who are fed in order to be slaughtered, but they do not know what is intended for them. When they are treated well they think that day to be their whole life, and eating their full to be their aim.

By Allah, if I wish, I can tell every one of you from where he has come, where he has to go and all his affairs, but I fear lest you abandon the Messenger of Allah — peace and blessing of Allah be upon him and his

-1- It means that if Talha considered Othmaan an oppressor, then after his assassination, instead of getting ready to avenge his blood, he should have supported his killers and justified their action. It is not the intention that in the case of Othmaan being in the wrong Talha should have supported the attackers because he was already supporting and encouraging them.

progeny — in my favour. I shall certainly convey these things to the selected ones who will remain safe from that fear. By Allah, Who deputed the Prophet with Right and distinguished him over creation. I do not speak save the truth. He (the Prophet) informed me of all this and also about the death of every one who dies, the salvation of every one who is granted salvation, and the consequences of this matter (the caliphate). He left nothing (that could) pass into my head without putting it in my ear and telling me about it.[1]

-1- Those who drink from the springs of revelation and divine inspiration see things hidden behind the curtains of the unknown and the events which will occur in the future in the same way as objects can be seen with the eyes, and this does not conflict with the saying of Allah that:
Say: "None (either) in the heavens or in the earth knoweth the unseen save Allah..." (Quraan, 27:65)
because this verse contains the negation of personal knowledge of the unknown, but not the negation of knowledge which is required by the prophets and holy persons through divine inspiration, by virtue of which they make prophesies about the future and unveil many events and happenings. Several verses of the Quraan support this view such as:
When the Prophet confided unto one of his wives a matter, but when she divulged it (unto others) and Allah apprised him thereof, he made known a part of it and avoided a part; so when he informed her of it, said she: "Who informed thee of this?" He said "Informed me, the All-knowing, the All-aware" (Quraan, 66:3)
These are of the tidings of the unseen which We reveal unto thee (O" Our Prophet Mohammad) ...(Quraan, 11:49)
Therefore, it is incorrect to argue in support of the view that if it is said that the prophets and holy persons possess knowledge of the unknown it would imply duality in the divine attributes. It would have implied duality if it were said that someone other than Allah has personal knowledge of the unknown. When it is not so and the knowledge possessed by the Prophets and Imams is that given by Allah it has no connection with duality. If duality should mean what is alleged, what would be the position of Esaa's assertion related in the Quraan namely:
... Out of clay will I make for you like the figure of a bird, and I will breathe into it, and it shall become a flying bird by Allah's permission; and I shall heal the blind and the leper and will rise the dead to life by Allah 's permission; and I will declare to you what ye eat and what ye store up in your houses... (Quraan, 3:49)
If it is believed that Esaa (Jesus) could create and bestow life with Allah's permission does it mean that he was Allah's partner in the attributes of creation and revival? If this is not so then how can it be held that if Allah gives someone the knowledge of the unknown it implies that he has been taken to be His partner in His attributes, and how can one extol

one's belief in the oneness of Allah by holding that the knowledge of the unknown implies duality.

No one can deny the fact that some people either see in dreams certain things which have yet to occur in the future, or that things can be read through interpretation of the dream, while during a dream neither do the senses function nor do the powers of understanding and comprehension co-operate. Therefore, if some events become known to some people in wakefulness why should there be amazement over it and what are the grounds for rejecting it, when it stands to reason that things possible in dreams are also possible in wakefulness. Thus, bn Maytham al-Bahraani has written that it is possible to achieve all this, because in a dream the spirit becomes free from looking after the body and is removed from bodily connections; as a result of this it perceives such hidden realities which could not be seen because of the obstruction of the body. In the same way those perfect beings who pay no heed to bodily matters, and turn with all the attention of spirit and heart towards the centre of knowledge can see those realities and secrets which the ordinary eyes are unable to discern. Therefore, keeping in view the spiritual greatness of Ahlil-Bayt (members of the Prophet's family) it should not appear strange that they were aware of events which were going to occur in future. bn Khaldoon has written:

When thaumaturgic feats are performed by others what do you think about those who were distinguished in knowledge and honesty and were a mirror of the Prophet's traits, while the consideration Allah had for their noble root (namely the Prophet) is a proof of the high performances of his chaste off-shoots (Ahlil-Bayt). Consequently many events about knowledge of the unknown are related about Ahlil-Bayt which are not related about others." (al-Moqaddama, p.23).

In this way there is no cause for wonder over Ameer al-Momineen's claim since he was brought up by the Prophet and was a pupil of Allah's school. Of course, those whose knowledge does not extend beyond the limits of physical objectivity and whose means of learning are confined to the bodily senses refuse to believe in the knowledge about the paths of divine cognisance and reality. If this kind of claim were unique and were heard only from over Ameer al-Momlneen then minds could have wavered and temperaments could have hesitated in accepting it, but if the Quraan records even such a claim of Esaa (Jesus) that — "I can tell you what you eat or drink or store in your houses" then why should there be hesitation over Ameer al-Momineen's claim, when it is agreed that Ameer al-Momineen had succeeded to all the attainments and distinctions of the Prophet and it cannot be contended that the Prophet did not know what Esaa (Jesus) knew. Thus, if the successor of the Prophet advances such a claim, why should it be rejected, particularly as this vastness of knowledge of Ameer al-Momineen is the best evidence and proof for the Prophet's knowledge and perfection and a living miracle of his truthfulness.

In this connection, it is amazing that even having knowledge of events Ameer al-Momineen did not, through any of his words or deeds, indicate that he knew them. Thus, commenting of the extraordinary importance of this claim, Sayyid bn Taawoos writes:

An amazing aspect of this claim is that despite the fact that Ameer al-Momineen was aware of conditions and events, yet he observed such conduct by way of his words and deeds that one who saw him could not believe that he knew the secrets and unknown acts of others, because the wise agree that if a person knows what event is likely to take place or what step his comrade is going to take, or if the hidden secrets of people are known to him, then the effects of such knowledge would appear through his movements and the expressions of his face. But the man who, in spite of knowing everything, behaves in a way as though he is unaware and knows nothing, then his personality is a miracle and a combination of contradictions

At this stage, the question arises as to why Ameer al-Momineen did not act upon the dictates of his secret knowledge. The reply to this is that the commands of the sharia are based on apparent conditions. Otherwise secret knowledge is a kind of miracle and power which Allah grants to His prophets and Imams. Although the prophets and Imams possess this power always, they cannot make use of it at any time unless and until by the permission of Allah and on the proper occasion. For example, the verse quoted above about Esaa (Jesus) which tells that he had the power to give life, to heal the blind and declare what one ate and stored in his house, etc., he (Jesus) did not used to practise this power on every thing or every corpse or everyone who met him. He used to practise this power only by the permission of Allah and on the proper occasion.

If prophets and other divines acted on the basis of their secret knowledge it would have meant serious dislocation and disturbance in the affairs of the people. For example, if a prophet or divine, on the basis of his secret knowledge, punishes a condemnable man by killing him, there would be great commotion and agitation among those who see it on the ground that he killed an innocent man. That is why Allah has not permitted the basing of conclusions on secret knowledge save in a few special cases, and has enjoined the following of observable factors. Thus, despite his being aware of the hypocrisy of some of the hypocrites, the Prophet extended to them the treatment that should be extended to a Moslim.

Now, there can be no scope for the objection that if Ameer al-Momineen knew secret matters then why did he not act according to them because it has been shown that he was not obliged to act according to the requirements of his secret knowledge. Of course, where conditions so required he did disclose some matters for the purposes of preaching, admonishing, giving good tidings (of reward) or warning (against punishment) , so that future events could be fore-closed. For example, Imam Jafar as-Saadiq (p.b.u.h.) informed Yahya bn Zayd that if he went out he would be killed. bn Khaldoon writes in this connection:

It has been authentically related from Imam Jafar as-Saadiq that he used to apprise some of his relations of the events to befall them. For example, he warned his cousin Yahya bn Zayd of being killed but he disobeyed him and went out and was killed in Jozajan" (al-Moqaddama, p.233).

Nevertheless, where there was apprehension that minds would get worried it was not at all disclosed. That is why in this sermon Ameer al-Momineen avoided more details, in view of the fear that people would begin to regard him higher than the Prophet. Despite

O people! By Allah, I do not impel you to any obedience unless I practise it before you and do not restrain you from any disobedience unless I desist from it before you.

SERMONS 175

Preaching

(O creatures!) Seek benefit from the sayings of Allah, be admonished of Allah and accept the advice of Allah because Allah has left no excuse for you by providing clear guidance, has put before you the plea and clarified for you what acts He likes and what acts He hates, so that you may follow the one and avoid the other. The Prophet of Allah used to say "Paradise is surrounded by unpleasant things while Hell is surrounded by desires

You should know that every obedience to Allah is unpleasant in appearance while every disobedience to Allah has the appearance of enjoyment. Allah may have mercy on the person who kept aloof from his desire and uprooted the appetite of his heart, because this heart has far-reaching aims and it goes on pursuing disobedience through desires.

You should know, O creatures of Allah, that a believer should be distrustful of his heart every morning and evening. He should always blame it (for shortcomings) and ask it to add to (its good acts). You should behave like those who have gone before you and the precedents in front of you. They left this world like a traveller and covered it as distance is covered.

The greatness of the holy Quraan

And know that this Quraan is an adviser who never deceives, a leader who never misleads and a narrator who never speaks a lie. No one will sit beside this Quraan but that when he rises he will achieve one addition or one diminution — addition in his guidance or elimination in his (spiritual) blindness. You should also know that no one will need anything after (guidance from) the Quraan and no one will be free from want before

all this people did go astray about Esaa (Jesus) , and in the same way about Ameer al-Momineen also they began to say all sorts of things and were misled into resorting to exaggeration.

(guidance from) the Quraan. Therefore, seek cure from it for your ailments and seek its assistance in your distresses. It contains a cure for the biggest diseases, namely unbelief, hypocrisy, revolt and misguidance. Pray to Allah through it and turn to Allah with its love. Do not ask the people through it. There is nothing like it through which the people should turn to Allah, the Sublime.

Know that it is an interceder and its intercession will be accepted. It is a speaker who is testified. For whoever the Quraan intercedes on the Day of Judgement, its intercession for him would be accepted. He about whom the Quraan speaks ill on the Day of Judgement shall testify to it. On the Day of Judgement an announcer will announce “Beware. every sower of a crop is in distress except the sowers of the Quraan.” Therefore, you should be among the sowers of the Quraan and its followers. Make it your guide towards Allah. Seek its advice for yourselves, do not trust your views against it. and regard your desires in the matter of the Quraan as deceitful.

Good deeds and Bad deeds

Action! action! Then (look at) the end; the end, and (remain) steadfast; steadfast. Thereafter (exercise) endurance, endurance, and piety, piety. You have an objective. Proceed towards your objective. You have a sign. Take guidance from your sign. Islam has an objective. Proceed towards its objective. Proceed towards Allah’s by fulfilling His rights which He has enjoined upon you. He has clearly stated His demands for you. I am a witness for you and shall plead excuses on your behalf on the Day of Judgement.

Beware! what had been ordained has occurred and that which had been destined has come into play. I am speaking to you with the promise and pleas of Allah.

Allah the Sublime, has said:

Verily, those who say: Our Lord is Allah! and persevere aright, the angels descend upon them (saying): “Fear Ye not, nor be grieved, and receive the glad tidings of the Garden which Ye were promised.” (Quraan, 41:30)

You have said "Our Lord is Allah." Then keep steadfast to His Book, to the way of His command and to the virtuous course of His worship. Thereafter do not go out of it, do not introduce innovations in it, and do not turn away from it, because those who go away from this course will be cut off from (the mercy of) Allah on the Day of Judgement.

Beware from destroying your manners and changing them, maintaining one tongue. A man should control his tongue because the tongue is obstinate with its master. By Allah, I do not find that fear of Allah benefits a man who practises it unless he controls his tongue. Certainly the tongue of a believer is at the back of his heart while the heart of a hypocrite is at the back of his tongue; because, when a believer intends to say anything, he thinks it over in his mind. If it is good he discloses it, but if it is bad he lets it remain concealed. While a hypocrite speaks whatever comes to his tongue, without knowing what is in his favour and what goes against him. The Prophet of Allah — peace and blessing of Allah be upon him and his descendants — said: "The belief of a person cannot be firm unless his heart is firm, and his heart cannot be firm unless his tongue is firm." So whoever of you can manage to meet Allah, the Sublime, in such a position that his hands are unsmeared with the blood of Moslims and their property and his tongue is safe from exposing them, he should do so.

Following the Sonna and refraining from innovation

Know, O creatures of Allah, that a believer should regard lawful this year what he regarded lawful in the previous year, and should consider unlawful this year what he considered unlawful in the previous year. Certainly people's innovation cannot make lawful for you what has been declared unlawful; rather, lawful is that which Allah has made lawful and unlawful is that which Allah has made unlawful. You have already tested the matters and tried them; you have been preached by those before you. Illustrations have been drawn for you and you have been called to clear fact. Only a deaf man can remain deaf to all this, and only a blind man can remain blind to all this.

He whom Allah does not allow benefit from trials and experience cannot benefit from preaching. He will be faced with losses from in front, so that he will approve what is bad and disapprove what is good. People are of two categories — the follower of the sharia (religious laws), and the follower of the innovations to whom Allah has not given any testimony by way of Sonna or the light of any plea.

Guidance from the holy Quraan

Allah the Glorified, has not counselled anyone on the lines of this Quraan, for it is the strong rope of Allah and His trustworthy means. It contains the blossoming of the heart and springs of knowledge. For the heart there is no other gloss than the Quraan although those who remembered it have passed away while those who forgot or pretended to have forgotten it have remained. If you see any good give your support to it, but if you see evil evade it, because the Messenger of Allah used to say: "O son of Adam, do good and evade evil; by doing so you will be treading correctly

Categories of oppression

Know that injustice is of three kinds — one, the injustice that will not be forgiven, another, that will not be left unquestioned, and another that will be forgiven without being questioned. The injustice that will not be forgiven is duality of Allah. Allah has said: "Verily Allah forgiveth not that (anything) be associated with Him ..." (Quraan, 4:48, 116). The injustice that will be forgiven is the injustice a man does to himself by committing small sins; and the injustice that will not be left unquestioned is the injustice of men against other men. The retribution in such a case is severe. It is not wounding with knives, nor striking with whips, but it is so severe that all these things are small against it. You should therefore avoid change in the matter of Allah's religion for your unity in respect of a right which you dislike is better than your scattering away in respect of a wrong that you like. Certainly, Allah the Glorified has not given any person, whether among the dead or among those who survive, any good from separation.

O people, blessed is the man whose own shortcomings keep him away from (looking into) the shortcomings of others, and also blessed is the man who is confined to his house, eats his meal, buries himself in obeying his Allah. and weeps over his sins, so that he is engaged in himself and people are in safety from him.

SERMONS 176

The two arbiters (after the Battle of Siffeen)

Your party had decided to select two persons, and so we took their pledge that they would act according to the Quraan and would not commit excess, that their tongues should be with it and that their hearts should follow it. But they deviated from it, abandoned what was right although they had it before their eyes. Wrong-doing was their desire, and going astray was their behaviour. Although we had settled with them to decide with justice. to act according to the light and without the interference of their evil views and wrong judgement. Now that they have abandoned the course of right and have come out with just the opposite of what was settled, we have strong ground (to reject their verdict).

SERMONS 177

Praise of Allah, transience of this World, and causes of the decline of Allah's blessings.

Delivered At The Beginning Of His Caliphate After The Killing Of Othmaan

One condition does not prevent Him from (getting into) another condition, time does not change Him, place does not locate him and the tongue does not describe Him. The number of drops of water, of stars in the sky, or of currents of winds in the air are not unknown to Him, nor the movements of ants on rocks, or the resting place of grubs in the dark night. He knows the places where leaves fall, and the secret movements of the pupils of the eyes.

I stand witness that there is no god but Allah, Who has no parallel, Who is not doubted, Whose religion is not denied and Whose creativeness is not questioned. My witnessing is like that of a man whose intention is free, whose conscience is clear, whose belief is pure and whose loads (of good actions) are heavy. I also stand witness that Mohammad — the peace and blessings of Allah be upon him and his progeny — is His slave and His Messenger, chosen from His creations, selected for detailing His realities, picked for His selected honours and chosen for His esteemed messages. Through him the signs of guidance have been lighted and the gloom of blindness (misguidance) has been dispelled.

O people, surely this world deceives him who longs for it and who is attracted towards it. It does not behave niggardly with him who aspires for it and overpowers him who overpowers it. By Allah, no people are deprived of the lively pleasures of life after enjoying them, except as a result of sins committed by them, because certainly Allah is not unjust to His creatures. Even then, when calamities descend upon people and pleasures depart from them, they turn towards Allah with true intention and the feeling in their hearts that He will return them everything that has fled from them and cure all their ills.

I fear about you lest you fall into ignorance (that prevailed before the appearance of the Prophet). In the past there were certain matters in which you were deflected, and in my view you were not worthy of admiration; but if your previous position could be returned to you then you would become virtuous. I can only strive; but if I were to speak I would (only) say may Allah forgive your past actions.

SERMONS 178

In reply to a question about seeing Allah

Zilib Al-Yamani Asked Ameer al-Momineen Whether He Had Seen Allah, When He Replied "Do I Worship One Whom I Have Not Seen?" Then He Enquired "How Have You Seen Him?" Then Ameer al-Momineen Replied:

Eyes do not see Him face to face, but hearts perceive Him through the realities of belief. He is near to things but not (physically) contiguous. He is far from them but not (physically) separate. He is a speaker, but not with reflection. He intends, but not with preparation. He moulds, but not with (the assistance of) limbs. He is subtle but cannot be attributed with being concealed. He is great but cannot be attributed with haughtiness. He sees but cannot be attributed with the sense (of sight). He is Merciful but cannot be attributed with weakness of heart. Faces feel low before His greatness and hearts tremble out of fear of Him.

SERMONS 179

Condemning his disobedient men

I praise Allah for whatever matter He ordained and whatever action He destines and for my trial with you, O group of people who do not obey when I order and do not respond when I call you. If you are at ease you engage in (conceited) conversation, but if you are faced with battle you show weakness. If people agree on one Imam you taunt each other. If you are faced with an arduous matter you turn away from it. May others have no father (woe to your enemy!) what are you waiting for in the matter of your assistance and for fighting for your rights? For you there is either death or disgrace. By Allah, if my day (of death) comes. and it is sure to come, it will cause separation between me and you although I am sick of your company and feel lonely with you.

May Allah deal with you! Is there no religion which may unite you nor sense of shamefulness that may sharpen you? Is it not strange that Moaawiya calls out to some rude low people and they follow him without any support or grant, but when I call you, although you are the successors of Islam and the (worthy) survivors of the people, with support and distributed grants you scatter away from me and oppose me? Truly, there is nothing between me to you which I like and you also like it, or with which I am angry and you may also unite against it. What I love most is death. I have taught you the Quraan, clarified to you arguments, apprised you of what you were ignorant and made you swallow what you were spitting out. Even a blind man would have been able to see, and he who was sleeping would have been awakened. How ignorant of Allah is their leader Moaawiya and their instructor bn-an-Nabigha.[1]

SERMONS 180

The group who decided to join the Kharijites

Ameer al-Momineen Sent One Of His Men To Bring Him News About A Group Of The Army Of Koofa Who Had Decided To Join The Kharijites But Were Afraid Of Him.[2] When The Man Came Back Ameer al-Momineen Said To Him:

-1- "an-Nabigha" is the surname of Layla bnt Harmala al-Anaziyya, mother of Amr bn Aas. The reason for attributing him to his mother is her common reputation in the matter. When Arwa bnt al-Haarith bn Abdl-Mottalib went to Moaawiya, during the conversation, when Amr bn Aas intervened, she said to him: "O son of an-Nabigha, you too dare speak, although your mother was known publicly and was a singer of Mecca. That is why five persons claimed you (as a son) , and when she was asked she admitted that five people had visited her and that you should be regarded as the son of him you resembled most. You must have resembled al-Aas bn Wail and therefore you came to be known as his son These five persons were (1) al-Aas bn Wail, (2) Abo-Lahab, (3) Omayya bn Khalaf, (4) Hishaam bn Mogheera, and (5) Abo-Sofyaan bn Harb. (bn Abd Rabbih, Iqd al-Fareed, vol.2, p.120; bn Tayfor, Balaghat an-Nisaa, p.27; bn Hijja, Thamarat al-Awraq, vol.1, p.132; Safwat, Jamharat khutab al-Arab, vol.2, p.363; bn-Abil-Hadeed, vol.6, pp.283-285, 291; al-Halabi, as-Seera vol.1, p.46).

-2- A man of the tribe Bani-Najiyya named al-Khirrit bn Rasheed an-Naji was on Ameer al-Momineen's side in the battle of Siffeen, but after Arbitration he became rebellious, and, coming to Ameer al-Momineen with thirty persons, said "By Allah, I Will no more obey your command, nor offer prayers behind you, and shall leave you tomorrow" Whereupon Ameer al-Momineen said "You should first take into account the grounds underlying this Arbitration and discuss it with me. If you are satisfied, you do as you will" He said he would come the next day to discuss the matter. Ameer al-Momineen then cautioned him, "Look, on going from here do not get mislead by others and do not adopt any other course. If you have the will to understand, I will get you out of this wrong path and put you on the course of guidance" After this conversation he went away, but his countenance indicated he was bent on revolt, and would not see reason by any means. And so it happened. He stuck to his point and on reaching his place he said to his tribesmen, "When we are determined to abandon Ameer al-Momineen there is no use

Are They Satisfied And Staying Or Feeling Weak And Going Astray? The Man Replied "They Have Gone Away, O Ameer al-Momineen." Then Ameer al-Momineen Said:

May Allah's mercy remain away from them as in the case of Thamood. Know that when the spears are hurled towards them and the swords are struck at their heads they will repent of their doings. Surely today Satan has scattered them and tomorrow he will disclaim any connection with them, and will leave them. Their departing from guidance, returning to misguidance and blindness, turning away from truth and falling into wrong is enough (for their chastisement).

SERMONS 181

Creatures and Attributes of Allah

It has been related by Nawf al-Bikali that Ameer al-Momineen Ali (p.b.u.h.) delivered this sermon at Koofa standing on a stone which Jada bn-Hobayra al-Makhzomi had placed for him. Ameer al-Momineen had a woollen apparel on his body, the belt of his sword was made of leaves, and the sandals on his feet too were of palm leaves. His forehead had a hardened spot like that a camel (on its knee, due to many and long prostrations).

Praise be to Allah to Whom is the return of all creation and the end of all matters. We render Him praise for the greatness of His generosity, the charity of His proofs, the increase of His bounty and His favours, — praise

---

going to him. We should do what we have decided to do" On this occasion Abdillah bn Qayn al Azdi also went to them to enquire, but when he came to know the position he asked Modrik bn Rayyan an-Naji to speak to him and to apprise him of the ruinous consequence of this rebellion, whereupon Modrik assured him that this man would not be allowed to take any step. Consequently, Abdillah came back satisfied and related the whole matter before Ameer al-Momineen on returning the next day. Ameer al-Momineen said "Let us see what happens when he comes" But when the appointed hour passed and he did not turn up Ameer al-Momineen asked Abdillah to go and see what the matter was and what was the cause for the delay. On reaching there Abdillah found that all of them had left. When he returned to Ameer al-Momineen he spoke as in this sermon.

The fate that befell al-Khirrit bn Rasheed an-Naji has been stated under Sermon 44.

which may fulfil His right, repay His thanks, take (us) near His reward and be productive of increase in His kindness. We seek His help like one who is hopeful of His bounty, desirous of His benefit, and confident of His warding off (calamities), who acknowledges His gifts and is obedient to Him in word and deed. We believe in Him like him who reposes hope in Him with conviction, inclines to Him as a believer, humbles himself before Him obediently, believes in His oneness exclusively, regards Him great, acknowledging His dignity, and seeks refuge with Him with inclination and exertion.

Allah the Glorified has not been born so that someone could be (His) partner in glory. Nor has He begotten anyone so as to be inherited from after dying. Time and period have not preceded Him. Increase and decrease do not occur to Him. But He has manifested Himself to our understanding through our having observed His strong control and firm decree. Among the proofs of His creation is the creation of the skies which are fastened without pillars and stand without support. He called them and they responded obediently and humbly without being lazy or loathsome. If they had not acknowledged His Godhead and obeyed Him He would not have made them the place for His throne, the abode of His angels and the destination for the rising up of the pure utterances and the righteous deeds of the creatures.

He has made the stars in the skies by way of signs by which travellers wandering the various routes of the earth may be guided. The gloom of the dark curtains of the night does not prevent the flame of their light, nor do the veils of blackish nights have the power to turn back the light of the moon when it spreads in the skies. Glory be to Allah from Whom neither the blackness of dark dusk or of gloomy night (falling) in the low parts of the earth or on high dim mountains is hidden, nor the thundering of clouds on the horizons of the skies, nor the sparking of lightning in the clouds, nor the falling of leaves blown away from their falling places by the winds of hurricanes or by downpour from the sky. He knows where the drops fall and where they stay, where the grubs leave their trails or where they drag themselves, what livelihood would suffice the mosquitoes and what a female bears in its womb.

Praise be to Allah Who exists from before the coming into existence of the seat, the throne, the sky, the earth, the jinn or human being. He cannot be perceived by imagination nor measured by understanding. He who begs from Him does not divert Him (from others), nor does giving away cause Him diminution. He does not see by means of an eye, nor can He be confined to a place. He cannot be said to have companions. He does not create with (the help of) limbs. He cannot be perceived by senses. He cannot be thought of after the people.

It is He who spoke to Moosa clearly and showed him His great signs without the use of bodily parts, the organ of speech or the uvula. O you who exert yourself in describing Allah if you are serious then (first try to) describe Gabriel, Michael or the host of angels who are close (to Allah) in the receptacles of sublimity; but their heads are bent downwards and their wits are perplexed as to how to assign limits (of definition) to the Highest Creator. This is because those things can only be perceived through qualities which have shape and parts and which succumb to death after reaching the end of their times. There is no god but He. He has lighted every darkness with His effulgence and has darkened every light with the darkness (of death).

Learning from Past People

I advise you, creatures of Allah, to practise fear of Allah Who gave you good clothing and bestowed an abundance of sustenance on you. If there was anyone who could secure a ladder to everlasting life or a way to avoid death it was Solaymaan bn-Dawood (p.b.u.h.) who was given control over the domain of the jinn and men along with Prophethood and great position (before Allah), but when he finished what was his due in food (of this world) and exhausted his (fixed) time the bow of destruction shot him with arrow of death. His houses became vacant and his habitations became empty. Another group of people inherited them. Certainly, the by-gone centuries have a lesson for you.

Where are the Amalekites[1] and the sons of Amalekites? Where are the Pharaohs?[2] Where are the people of the cities of Rass[1] who killed the

---

-1- History shows that very often the ruin and destruction of peoples has been due to their oppression and open wickedness and profligacy. Consequently, communities which had extended their sway over all the corners of the populated world and had flown their flags in the East and West of the globe disappeared from the surface of the earth like a wrong word, on disclosure of their vicious actions and evil doings.

Amalekites: Ancient nomadic tribe, or collection of tribes, described in the Old Testament as relentless enemies of Israel, even though they were closely related to Ephraim, one of the twelve tribes of Israel. Their name derives from Amalek, who is celebrated in Arabian tradition but cannot be identified. The district over which they ranged was south of Jodah and probably extended into northern Arabia. The Amalekites harassed the Hebrews during their exodus out of Egypt and attacked them at Rephidim (near Mt. Sinai) , where they were defeated by Joshua. They also filled out the ranks of the nomadic raiders defeated by Gideon and were condemned to annihilation by Samuel. The Amalekites, whose final defeat occurred in the time of Hezekia, were the object of a perpetual curse. (The New Encyclopaedia Britannica Micropaedia, vol.1, p.288, ed.1973-1974; also see for further reference The Encyclopaedia Americana, International Edition vol.1, p.651, ed.1975).

-2- Pharaoh: Hebrew form of the Egyptian per-o (the great house) , signifying the royal palace, an epithet applied in the New Kingdom and after, as a title of respect, to the Egyptian king himself. In the 22nd dynasty the title was added to the king's personal name. In official documents the full titulary of the Egyptian king contained five names. The first and oldest identified him as the incarnation of the falcon god, Horees; it was often written inside a square called Serekh, depicting the facade of the archaic palace. The second name, "two ladies, placed him under the protection of Nekhbet and Buto, the vulture and uraeus (snake) goddesses of Upper and Lower Egypt; the third, "golden Horees, signified perhaps originally "Horees victorious over his enemies" The last two names, written within a ring or cartouche, are generally referred to as the praenomen and nomen, and were the ones most commonly used; the praenomen and nomen, and were the ones most commonly used; the praenomen, preceded by the hieroglyph meaning "King of Upper and Lower Egypt" usually contained a reference to the king's Unique relationship with the sun god, Re, while the fifth, or nomen, was preceded by the hieroglyph for 'son of Re, " or by that for "Lord of the two lands" The last name was given him at birth, the rest at his coronation. (The New Encyclopaedia Britannica Micropaedia, vol.vii, p.927, ed.1973-1974; also see for further reference The Encyclopaedia Americana, International Edition, vol.21, p.707, ed.1975).

Among the Pharaohs was the Pharaoh of the days of Prophet Mosa. His pride, egotism, insolence and haughtiness were such that by making the claim "I am your sublime God" he deemed himself to be holding sway over all other powers of the world, and was under the misunderstanding that no power could wrest the realm and government from his hands. The Quraan has narrated his claim of "I and no one else" in the following words:

prophets, destroyed the traditions of the divine messengers and revived the traditions of the despots? Where are those who advanced with armies, defeated thousands, mobilised forces and populated cities?

About The Imam Al-Mahdi

He will be wearing the armour of wisdom, which he will have secured with all its conditions, such as full attention towards it, its (complete) knowledge and exclusive devotion to it. For him it is like a thing which he had lost and which he was then seeking, or a need which he was trying to fulfil. If Islam is in trouble he will feel forlorn like a traveller and like a (tired) camel beating the end of its tail and with its neck flattened on the ground. He is the last of Allah's proofs and one of the vicegerents of His prophets.

Then Ameer al-Momineen continued:

On The Method Of His Ruling, And Grief Over The Martyrdom Of His Companions

O people! I have divulged to you advice which the prophets used to preach before their peoples, and I have conveyed to you what the vicegerents (of the prophets) conveyed to those coming after them. I tried to train you with my whip but you could not be straightened. I drove you with

---

And proclaimed Pharaoh unto his people, "O my people! is not the kingdom of Egypt mine? And these rivers flow below me; What! behold ye not? (43:51)

But when his empire came near the end it was destroyed in a few moments. Neither his position and servants could come in the way of its destruction nor could the vastness of his realm prevent it. Rather, the waves of the very streams which he was extremely proud to possess, wrapped him in and dispatched his spirit to Hell throwing the body on the bank to serve as a lesson for the whole of creation.

1 The people of the cities of ar-Rass: In the same way the people of ar-Rass were killed and destroyed for disregarding the preaching and call of a prophet, and for revolt and disobedience. About them the Quraan says:

And the (tribes of) Ad and Thamood and the inhabitants of ar-Rass, and generations between them, in great number. And unto each of them We did give examples and every one (of them) We did destroy with utter extermination. (25:38, 39)

Belied (also) those before them the people of Noah and the dwellers of ar-Rass and Thamood; And Ad and Pharaoh, and the brethren of Lot; And the dwellers of the Wood and the people of Tobba; all belied the apostles, so was proved true My promise (of the doom) (50:12-14)

admonition but you did not acquire proper behaviour. May Allah deal with you! Do you want an Imam other than me to take you on the (right) path, and show you the correct way?

Beware, the things in this world which were forward have become things of the past, and those of which were behind are going ahead. The virtuous people of Allah have made up their minds to leave and they have purchased, with a little perishable (pleasure) of this world, a lot of such (reward) in the next world that will remain. What loss did our brothers whose blood was shed in Siffeen suffer by not being alive today? Only that they are not suffering choking on swallowings and not drinking turbid water. By Allah, surely they have met Allah and He has bestowed upon them their rewards and He has lodged them in safe houses after their (having suffered) fear.

Where are my brethren who took the (right) path and trod in rightness. Where is Ammaar?[1]

-1- Ammaar bn Yaasir bn Amir al-Ansi al-Mazhiji al Makhzoomi (a confederate of Bani-Makhzoom) was one of the earliest converts to Islam, and the first Moslim to build a mosque in his own house in which he used to worship Allah (at-Tabaqaat, vol.3, Part 1, p.178; Osdol-Ghaaba, vol.4, p.46; bn Katheer, at-Taareekh, vol.7, p.311).

Ammaar accepted Islam along with his father Yasir and his mother Somayya. They suffered great tortures by the Quraysh, due to their conversion to Islam, to such an extent that Ammaar lost his parents; and they were the first martyrs man and woman in Islam.

Ammaar was among those who immigrated to Abysinia, and the earliest immigrants (mohaajiroon) to Madeena. He was present in the battle of Badr and all other battles as well as places of assembly by the Moslims during the lifetime of the Holy Prophet; and he showed his might and favour in all Islamic struggles in the best way.

Many traditions are narrated from the Holy Prophet about Ammaar regarding his virtues, outstanding traits and his glorious deeds, such as the tradition which Aysha and other have narrated that the Holy Prophet himself had said that Ammaar was filled with faith from the crown of his head to the soles of his feet. (bn Maaja, as-Sonan, vol.1, p.65; Abo-Noaym, Hilyatol-Awliyaa, vol.1, p.139; al-Haytami, Majma az-Zawaaid, vol.9, p.295; al-Isteeaab, vol.3, p.1137; al-Isaba, vol.2, p.512)

In another tradition the Holy Prophet said about Ammaar:

Ammaar is with the truth and the truth is with Ammaar. He turns wherever the truth turns. Ammaar is as near to me as an eye is near to the nose. Alas! a rebellious group will kill him. (at-Tabaqaat, vol.3, part 1, p.187; al-Mostadrak, vol.3, p.392; bn Hishaam, as-Seera, vol.2, p.143; bn Katheer, at-Taareekh, vol.7, pp.268-270)

Also in the decisive and widely known tradition which al-Bokhaari (in Saheeh, vol.8, pp.185-186) , at-Tirmizi (in al-Jaami" as-Saheeh, vol.5, p.669); Ahmad bn Hambal (in al-Mosnad, vol.2, pp.161, 164, 206; vol.3, pp.5, 22, 28, 91; vol.4, pp.197, 199, vol.5 pp.215, 306, 307; vol.6, pp.289, 300, 311, 315) , and all the narrators of Islamic traditions and historians transmitted through twenty-five Companions that the Holy Prophet said about Ammaar:

Alas! a rebellious group which swerves from the truth will murder Ammaar. Ammaar will be calling them towards Paradise and they will be calling him towards Hell. His killer and those who strip him of arms and clothing will be in Hell.

bn Hajar al-Asqalani (in Tahzeeb at-Tahzeeb, vol.7, p.409; al-Isaba, vol.2, p.512) and as-Seyooti (in al-Khasaais al-Kobra, vol.2, p.140) say: "The narration of this (above mentioned) tradition is motawaatir (i.e. narrated successively by so many people that no doubt can be entertained about its authenticity)

bn Abdl-Barr (in al-Isteeaab, vol.3, p.1140) says:

The narration followed uninterrupted succession from the Holy Prophet, that he said "A rebellious group will murder Ammaar" and this is a prophecy of the Prophet's secret knowledge and the sign of his Prophethood. This tradition is among the most authentic and the most rightly ascribed traditions.

After the death of the Holy Prophet, Ammaar was one of the closest adherents and best supporters of Ameer al-Momineen during the reign of the first three Caliphs. During the caliphate of Othmaan when the Moslim protested (to Othmaan) against his policy on the distribution of the Public Treasury (Baytol-Mal) Othmaan said in a public assembly that, "the money which as in the treasury was sacred and belonged to Allah, and that he (as being the successor of the Prophet) had the right to dispose of them as he thought fit. "He (Othmaan) threatened and cursed all who presumed to censure or murmur at what he said. Upon this, Ammaar bn Yaasir boldly declared his disapprobation and began to charge him with his invcterate propensity to ignore the Interests of the general public; accused him with reviving the heathenish customs abolished by the Prophet. Whereupon Othmaan commanded him to be beaten and immediately some of the Omayyads, the kindred of the Caliph fell upon the venerable Ammaar, and the Caliph himself kicking him with his shoes (on his feet) on Ammaar's testicles, and afflicted him with hernia. Ammaar became unconscious for three days, and he was taken care of by Om-al-Momineen Om-Salama in her own house. (al-Balazoori, Ansab al-Ashraf, vol.5, pp.48, 54, 88; bn-Abil-Hadeed, vol.3, pp.47-52; al-Imaama was-Siyasa, vol.1, pp.35-36; al-Iqd al-Fareed, vol.4, p.307; at-Tabaqaat, vol.3, Part 1, p.185; Taareekh al-Khamees, vol.2, p.271)

When Ameer al-Momineen became Caliph, Ammaar was one of his most sincere supporters. He participated fully in all social, political and military activities during this period, especially in the first battle (the battle of Jamal) and the second one (the battle of Siffeen).

However, Ammaar was martyred on 9th Safar 37 A.H. in the battle of Siffeen when a he was over ninety years of age. On the day Ammaar bn Yaasir achieved martyrdom, he turned his face to the sky and said:

O" my Allah! surely Thou art aware that if I know that Thy wish is that I should plunge myself into this River (the Euphrates) and be drowned, I will do it. O" my Allah! surely Thou knowest that if I knew that Thou would be pleased if I put my scimitar on my chest (to hit my heart) and pressed it so hard that it came out of my back, I would do it. O" my Allah! I do not think there is anything more pleasant to Thee than fighting with this sinful group, and if knew that any action were more pleasant to Thee I would do it.

Abo-Abdr-Rahmaan as-Solaami narrates:

We were present with Ameer al-Momineen at Siffeen where I saw Ammaar bn Yaasir was not turning his face towards any side, nor valleys (wadis of the land) of Siffeen but the companions of the Holy Prophet were following him as if he was a sign for them. Then I heard Ammaar say to Hashim bn "Otba (al-Mirqal): "O Hashim! rush into enemy's ranks, paradise is under sword!

Today I meet beloved one, Mohammad and his party

Then he said "By Allah, if they put us to flight (and pursue us) to the date-palms of Hajar (a town in Bahrain, Persian Gulf i. e., if they pursue us along all the Arabian desert nevertheless) we know surely that we are right and they are wrong. "

Then he (Ammaar) continued (addressing the enemies) :

We struck you to (believe in) its (Holy Quraan) revelation; And today we strike you to (believe in) its interpretation; Such strike as to remove heads from their resting places; And to make the friend forget his sincere friend; Until the truth returns to its (right) path."

The narrator says: "I did not see the Holy Prophet's companions killed at any time as many as they were killed on this day

Then Ammaar spurred his horse, entered the battlefield and began fighting. He persistently chased the enemy, made attack after attack, and raised challenging slogans till at last a group of mean-spirited Syrians surrounded him on all sides, and a man named Abol-Ghadiya al-Johari (al-Fazari) inflicted such a wound upon him that he could not bear it, and returned to his camp. He asked for water. A tumbler of milk was brought to him. When Ammaar looked at the tumbler he said "The Messenger of Allah had said the right thing" People asked him what he meant by these words. He said "The Messenger of Allah informed me that the last sustenance for me in this world would be milk" Then he took that tumbler of milk in his hands, drank the milk and surrendered his life to Allah, the Almighty. When Ameer al-Momineen came to know of his death, he came to Ammaar's side, put his (Ammaar's) head on his own lap, and recited the following elegy to mourn his death:

Surely any Moslim who is not distressed at the murder of the son of Yasir, and is not be afflicted by this grievous misfortune does not have true faith.

May Allah show His mercy to Ammaar the day he embraced Islam, may Allah show His mercy to Ammaar the day he was killed, and may Allah show His mercy to Ammaar the day he is raised to life.

Certainly, I found Ammaar (on such level) that three companions of the Holy Prophet could not be named unless he was the fourth, and four of them could not be mentioned unless he was the fifth.

There was none among the Holy Prophet's companions who doubted that not only was Paradise once or twice compulsorily bestowed upon Ammaar, but that he gained his claim to it (a number of times). May Paradise give enjoyment to Ammaar.

Certainly, it was said (by the Holy Prophet) 'surely, Ammaar is with the truth and the truth is with Ammaar. He turns wherever the truth turns. His killer will be in hell

Then Ameer al-Momineen stepped forward and offered funeral prayers for him, and then with his own hands, he buried him with his clothes.

Ammaar's death caused a good deal of commotion in the ranks of Moaawiya too, because there were a large number of prominent people fighting from his side under the impression created in their minds that he was fighting Ameer al-Momineen for a right cause. These people were aware of the saying of the Holy Prophet that Ammaar would be killed by a group who would be on the wrong side. When they observed that Ammaar had been killed by Moaawiya's army, they became convinced that they were on the wrong side and that Ameer al-Momineen was definitely on the right. This agitation thus caused among the leaders as well as the rank and file of Moaawiya's army, was quelled by him with the argument that it was Ameer al-Momineen who brought Ammaar to the battlefield and therefore it was he who was responsible for his death. When Moaawiya's argument was mentioned before Ameer al-Momineen he said it was as though the Prophet was responsible for killing Hamza as he brought him to the battle of Ohod. (at-Tabari, at-Taareekh, vol.1, pp.3316-3322; vol.3, pp.2314-2319; bn Saad, at-Tabaqaat, vol.3, Part 1, pp.176-189; bn al-Athir, al-Kaamil, vol.3, pp.308-312; bn Katheer, at-Taareekh, vol.7, pp, 267-272; al-Minqari, Siffeen, pp.320-345; bn Abdl-Barr, al-Isteeaab, vol.3, pp.1135-1140; vol.4, p.1725; bn al-Athir, Osdol-Ghaaba, vol.4, pp.43-47; vol.5, p.267; bn-Abil-Hadeed, Sharh Nahjol-Balagha, vol.5, pp.252-258; vol.8, pp.10-28; vol.10, pp.102-107, al-Hakim, al-Mostadrak, vol.3, pp.384-394; bn Abd Rabbih, al-Iqd al-Fareed, vol.4, pp.340-343; al-Masoodi, Morooj az-Zahab, vol.2, pp.381-382, al-Haytami, Majma az-Zawaaid, vol.7, pp.238-244; vol.9, pp.291-298; al-Balazoori, Ansab al-Ashraf (Biography of Ameer al-Momineen) , pp.310-319.

Where is bn-at-Tayyihan?[1] Where is Zosh-Shahaadatayn?[2] And where are others like them[1] from among their comrades who had pledged

---

-1- Abol-Haytham (Malik) bn Tayyihan al-Ansaari was one of the twelve chiefs (Naqeeb of Ansaar) who attended the fair and met at al-Aqaba — in the first Aqaba and among those who attended in the second Aqaba — where he gave the Holy Prophet the "pledge of Islam. He was present in the battle of Badr and all other battles as well as places of assembly by the Moslims during the lifetime of the Holy Prophet. He was also among the sincere supporters of Ameer al-Momineen and he attended the battle of Jamal as well as Siffeen where he was martyred. (al-Isteeaab, vol.4, p.1773; Siffeen, p.365; Osdol-Ghaaba, vol.4, p.274; vol.5, p.318; al-Isaba, vol.3, p.341; vol.4, pp.312-313; bn-Abil-Hadeed, vol.10, pp.107-108; Ansab al-Ashraf, p.319).

-2- Khozayma bn Thabit al-Ansaari. He is known as Zosh-Shahaadatayn because the Holy Prophet considered his evidence equivalent to the evidence of two witnesses He was present in the battle of Badr, and other battles as well as in the places of assembly of the Moslims during the lifetime of the Holy Prophet. He is counted among the earliest of those who showed their adherence to Ameer al-Momineen and he was also present in the battle of Jamal and Siffeen. Abdr-Rahmaan bn Abi-Layla narrated that he saw a man in the battle of Siffeen fighting the enemy valiantly and when he protested against his action, the man said:

I am Khozayma bn Thabit al-Ansaari, I have heard the Holy Prophet saying "Fight, fight, by the side of Ali" (al-Khateeb al-Baghdadi, Mowazih awham al-jam wat-Tafreeq, vol.1, p.277).

Khozayma was martyred in the battle of Siffeen soon after the martyrdom of Ammaar bn Yaasir.

Sayf bn Omar al-Osayydi (the well known liar) has fabricated another Khozayma, and claimed that the one who was martyred in the battle of Siffeen was this one and not the one with the surname of "Zosh-Shahaadatayn. at-Tabari has quoted this fabricated story from Sayf either intentionally or otherwise, and through him this story has affected some other historians who quoted from at-Tabari or relied on him. (For further reference, see al-Askari, Khamsoon wa miah sahabi mokhtalaq one hundred and fifty fabricated companions, vol.2, pp.175-189).

After having denied this story bn-Abil-Hadeed adds (in Sharh Nahjol-Balagha, vol.10, pp.109-110) that:

Furthermore, what is the need for those who to defend Ameer al-Momineen to make a boast of abundance with Khozayma, Abol-Haytham, Ammaar and others. If people treat this man (Ameer al-Momineen) with justice and look at him with healthy eyes they will certainly realise that should he be alone (on one side) and the people all together (on the other side) fighting him, he will be in the truth and all the rest will be in the wrong. (at-Tabaqaat, vol.3, Part 1, pp.185, 188; al-Mostadrak, vol.3, pp.385, 397; Osdol-Ghaaba, vol.2, p.114; vol.4, p.47; al-Isteeaab, vol.2, p.448; at-Tabari, vol.3, pp.2316, 2319, 2401; al-Kaamil, vol.3, p.325; Siffeen, pp.363, 398; Ansab al-Ashraf, pp.313-314).

themselves to death and whose (severed) heads were taken to the wicked enemy.

Then Ameer al-Momineen wiped his hand over his auspicious, honoured beard and wept for a long time, then he continued:

O! my brothers. who recited the Quraan and strengthened it, thought over their obligation and fulfilled it, revived the Sonna and destroyed innovation. When they were called to Jihaad they responded and trusted in their leader then followed him.

Then Ameer al-Momineen shouted at the top of his voice:

al-Jihaad, al-Jihaad (fighting, fighting), O creatures of Allah! By Allah, I am mobilising the army today. He who desires to proceed towards Allah should come forward.

-1- Among the people who were present in the battle of Jamal on the side of Ameer al-Momineen there were one hundred and thirty Badries (those who participated in the battle of Badr with the Holy Prophet) and seven hundred of those who were present in the "pledge of ar-Rizwaan" (Bayator-Rizwaan) which took place under a tree. (az-Zahabi, Taareekh al-Islam, vol.2, p.171; Khaleefa bn Khayyat, at-Taareekh vol.1, p.164). Those who were killed in the battle of Jamal from the side of Ameer al-Momineen numbered some five hundred (some said that the number of martyrs were more than that). But on the side of the people of Jamal twenty thousand were killed. (al-Iqd al-Fareed, vol.4, p.326).

Among those who were present in the battle of Siffeen on the side of Ameer al-Momineen, there were eighty Badries and eight hundred of those who gave the Holy Prophet the "pledge of ar-Rizwaan" (al-Mostadrak, vol.3, p.104 al-Isteeaab, vol.3, p.1138; al-Isaba, vol.2, p.389; at-Taareekh, al-Yaqoobi, vol.2, p.188).

On the side of Moaawiya forty-five thousand were killed, and on the side of Ameer al-Momineen twenty-five thousand. Among these martyrs (of Ameer al-Momineen) there were twenty-five or twenty-six Badries and sixty-three or three hundred and three of the people of the "pledge of ar-Rizwaan. (Siffeen, p.558; al-Isteeaab, vol.2, p.389, Ansab al-Ashraf, p.322; bn-Abil-Hadeed, vol.10, p.104; Abol-Fidaa vol.1, p.175, bn al-Wardi, at-Taareekh, vol.1, p.240; bn Katheer, vol.7, p.275; Taareekh al-Khamees, vol.2, p.277)

Besides the distinguished and eminent companions of Ameer al-Momineen like Ammaar, Zosh-Shahaadatayn and bn at-Tayyihan, who lay martyred in Siffeen were: -

i. Hashim bn Otba bn Abi Waqqas al-Mirqal was killed on the same day when Ammaar was martyred. He was the bearer of the standard of Ameer al-Momineen's army on that day.

ii. Abdillah bn Bodayl bn Warqa al-Khozai was sometimes the right wing Commander of Ameer al-Momineen's army and sometimes the infantry Commander.

Nawf says: Then Ameer al-Momineen put Hosayn (p.b.u.h.) over (a force of) ten thousand, Qays bn-Saad (mercy of Allah be upon him) over ten thousand, Abo-Ayyoob al-Ansaari over ten thousand, and others over different numbers, intending to return to Siffeen, but Friday did not appear again and the accursed bn-Moljam (may Allah curse him) killed him. Consequently, the armies came back and were left like sheep who had lost their shepherd while wolves were snatching them away from all sides.

SERMONS 182

Praise of Allah for his bounties

Praise be to Allah Who is recognised without being seen and Who creates without trouble. He created the creation with His Might, and receives the devotion of rulers by virtue of His dignity. He exercises superiority over great men through His generosity. It is He who made His creation to populate the world and sent towards the jinn and human beings His messengers to unveil it for them, to warn them of its harm, to present to them its examples, to show them its defects and to place before them a whole collection of matters containing lessons about the changings of health and sickness in this world, its lawful things and unlawful things and all that Allah has ordained for the obedient and the disobedient, namely, Paradise and Hell and honour and disgrace. I extend my praise to His Being as He desires His creation to praise Him. He has fixed for everything a measure, for every measure a time limit, and for every time limit a document.

About The Greatness And Importance Of The Holy Quraan

The Quraan orders as well as refrains, remains silent and also speaks. It is the proof of Allah before His creation. He has taken from them a pledge (to act) upon it. He has perfected its effulgence, and completed through it His religion. He let the Prophet leave this world when he had conveyed to the people all His commands of guidance through the Quraan. You should therefore regard Allah great as he has held Himself great, because He has not concealed anything of His religion from you, nor has He left out anything which He likes or which He dislikes, but He made for it a clear emblem (of guidance) and a definite sign which either refrains from it or calls towards it. His pleasure is the same for all time to come.

You should know that He will not be pleased with you for anything for which He was displeased with those before you, and He will not be displeased with you for anything for which He was pleased with those before you. You are treading on a clear path, and are speaking the same as the people before you had spoken. Allah is enough for your needs in this world. He has persuaded you to remain thankful, and has made it obligatory on you to mention Him with your tongues.

Warning Against Punishment On The Day Of Judgement

He has advised you to exercise fear and has made it the highest point of His pleasure and all that He requires from His creatures. You should therefore fear Allah, who is such that you are as though just in front of Him, and your forelocks are in His grip, and your change of position is in His control. If you conceal a matter, He will know of it. If you disclose a matter, He will record it. For this He has appointed honoured guards (angels) who do not omit any rightful matter nor include anything incorrect. You should know that whoever fears Allah, He would make for him a way to get out of troubles and (grant him) a light (to help him) out of darkness. He will ever keep him in whatever condition) he wishes, and will make him stay in a position of honour near Himself, in the house which He has made for Himself. The shade of this house is His house is His throne, its light is His effulgence, its visitors are His angels and its companions are His prophets.

Therefore, hasten towards the place of return and go ahead of (your) deaths (by collecting provision for the next world). Shortly, the expectations of the people will be cut short and death will overtake them while the door of repentance will be closed for them. You are still in a place to which those who were before you have been wishing to return. In this world, which is not your house, you are just a traveller in motion.

You have been given the call to leave from here, and you have been ordered to collect provision while you are here. You should know that this thin skin cannot tolerate the Fire (of Hell). So, have pity on yourselves because you have already tried it in the tribulations of the world.

Have you ever seen the crying of a person who has been pricked with a thorn or who bleeds due to stumbling or whom hot sand has burnt? How would he feel when he is between two frying pans of Hell with stones all round with Satan as his companion? Do you know that when Maalik (the guard-in-charge of Hell) is angry with the fire, its parts begin to clash with each other (in rage), and, when he scolds it, it leaps between the doors of Hell crying on account of his scolding.

O you old and big whom old age has made hoary, how will you feel when rings of fire will touch the bones of your neck, and handcuffs hold so hard that they eat away the flesh of the forearms? (Fear) Allah! Allah! O crowd of men, while you are in good health before sickness (grips you) and you are in ease before straitness (overtakes you). You should try for the release of your necks before their mortgage is foreclosed, your eyes, thin down bellies, use your feet, spend your money, take your bodies and spend them over yourselves, and do not be niggardly about them, because Allah the Glorified, has said:

...if you help (in the way) of Allah, He will(also) help you, and will set firm your feet. (Quraan, 47:7)

And He, the Sublime has said:

Who is he who would loan unto Allah a goodly loan? so that He may double it for him, and for him shall be a noble recompense. (Quraan, 57:11)

He does not seek your support because of any weakness, nor does He demand a loan from you because of shortage. He seeks your help, although He possesses all the armies of the skies and the earth and He is strong and wise. He seeks a loan from you, although He owns the treasures of the skies and the earth and He is rich and praiseworthy. (Rather) He intends to try you as to which of you performs good acts. You should therefore be quick in performance of (good) acts so that your way be with His neighbours in His abode; He made His Prophet's companions of these neighbours and made the angels to visit them. He has honoured their ears so that the sound of Hell fire may never reach them, and He has afforded protection to their bodies from weariness and fatigue...

...that is the grace of Allah, He bestoweth it upon whomsoever He willeth; and Allah is the Lord of Mighty Grace. (Quraan, 57:21)

I say you are hearing. I seek Allah's help for myself and yourselves. He is enough for me and He is the best dispenser.

SERMONS 183

On hearing Kharijite "al-Borj bn-Moshir at-Taii" raising the slogan "command behoves only Allah

Keep quite, may Allah make you ugly, O you with broken tooth. Certainly, by Allah, when truth became manifest even then your personality was weak and your voice was lose. But when wrong began to shout loudly you again sprouted up like the horns of a kid.

SERMONS 184

Praise of Allah and His Wonderful Creatures

Praise be to Allah. He is such that senses cannot perceive Him, place cannot contain Him, eyes cannot see Him and veils cannot cover Him. He proves His eternity by the coming into existence of His creation, and (also) by originating His creation (He proves) His existence, and by their (mutual) similarity He proves that there is nothing similar to Him. He is true in His promise. He is too high to be unjust to His creatures. He stands by equity among His creation and practices justice over them in His commands. He provides evidence through the creation of things of His being from ever, through their marks of incapability of His power, and through their powerlessness against death of His eternity.

He is One, but not by counting. He is everlasting without, any limit. He is existent without any support. Minds admit of Him without (any activity of the) senses. Things which can be seen stand witness to Him without confronting Him. Imagination cannot encompass Him. He manifests Himself to the imagination with his help for the imagination, and refuses to be imagined by the imagination. He has made imagination the arbiter (in this matter). He is not big in the sense that volume is vast and so His body is also big. Nor is He great in the sense that His limits should extend to the utmost and so His frame be extensive. But He is big in position and great in authority.

The Holy Prophet

I stand witness that Mohammad is His slave, His chosen Prophet and His responsible trustee — may Allah bless him and his descendants. Allah sent him with undeniable proofs, a clear success and open paths. So he conveyed the message declaring the truth with it. He led the people on the (correct) highway, established signs of guidance and minarets of light, and made Islam's ropes strong and its knots firm.

Creation of Animal Species

Had they pondered over the greatness of His power and the vastness of His bounty they would have returned to the right path and feared the punishment of the Fire; but hearts are sick and eyes are impure. Do they not see the small things He has created, how He strengthened their system and opened for them hearing and sight and made for them bones and skins? Look at the ant with its small body and delicate form. It can hardly be seen in the corner of the eye, nor by the perception of the imagination — how it moves on the earth and leaps at its livelihood. It carries the grain to its hole and deposits it in its place of stay. It collects during the summer for its winter, and during strength for the period of its weakness. Its livelihood is guaranteed, and it is fed according to fitness. Allah, the Kind, does not forget it and (Allah the Giver) does not deprive it, even though it may be in dry stone or fixed rocks.

If you have thought about its digestive tracts in its high and low parts, the carapace of its belly, and its eyes and its ears in its head you would be amazed at its creation and you would feel difficulty in describing it. Exalted is He who made it stand on its legs and erected it on its pillars (of limbs). No other originator took part with Him in its origination and no one having power assisted Him in its creation. If you tread on the paths of your imagination and reach its extremity it will not lead you anywhere except that the Originator of the ant is the same as He who is the Originator of the date-palm, because everything has (the same) delicacy and detail, and every living being has little difference.

Creation of Universe

In His creation, the big, the delicate, the heavy, the light, the strong, the weak are all equal.[1] So is the sky, the air, the winds and the water. Therefore, you look at the sun, moon, vegetation, plants, water, stone, the difference of this night and day, the springing of the streams, the large number of the mountains, the height of their peaks, the diversity of languages and the variety of tongues. Then woe be to him who disbelieves in the Ordainer and denies the Ruler. They believe that they are like grass for which there is no cultivator nor any maker for their diverse shapes. They have not relied on any argument for what they assert, nor on any research for what they have heard. Can there be any construction without a Constructor, or any offence without an offender.

Creation of the Locust

If you wish you can tell about the locust (as well). Allah gave it two red eyes, lighted for them two moon — like pupils, made for it small ears,

---

-1- The meaning is that if the smallest thing in creation is examined it will be found to contain all that which is found in the biggest creatures, and each will exhibit the same reflection of natures, workmanship and performance, and the ratio of each to Allah's might and power will be the same, whether it be as small as an ant or as big as a date palm. Is it not that making a small thing is easy for Him while the making of a big thing is difficult for Him, because the diversity of colour, volume and quantity is just based on the dictates of His sagacity and expediency, but as regards creation itself there is no difference among them. Therefore, this uniformity of creation is a proof of the oneness and unity of the Creator.

opened for it a suitable mouth and gave it keen sense, gave it two teeth to cut with and two sickle-like feet to grip with. The farmers are afraid of it in the matter of crops since they cannot drive it away even though they may join together. The locust attacks the fields and satisfies its desires (of hunger) from them although its body is not equal to a thin finger.

Glory Of Allah

Glorified is Allah before Whom every one in the skies or the earth bows in prostration willingly or unwillingly, submits to Him by placing his cheeks and face (in the dust), drops before Him (in obedience) peacefully and humbly, and hands over to Him full control in fear and apprehension.

The birds are bound by His commands. He knows the number of their feathers and their breaths. He has made their feet to stand on water and on land. He has ordained their livelihoods. He knows their species: this is the crow, this is the eagle, this is the pigeon and this is the ostrich. He called out every bird with its name (while creating it) and provided it with its livelihood. He created heavy clouds and produced from them heavy rain and spread it on various lands. He drenched the earth after its dryness and grew vegetation from it after its barrenness.

SERMONS 185

Oneness of Allah

This sermon contains principles of knowledge which no other sermon contains.

He who assigns to Him (different) conditions does not believe in His oneness, nor does he who likens Him grasp His reality. He who illustrates Him does not signify Him. He who points at Him and imagines Him does not mean Him. Everything that is known through itself has been created, and everything that exists by virtue of other things is the effect (of a cause). He works but not with the help of instruments. He fixes measures but not with the activity of thinking. He is rich but not by acquisition.

Times do not keep company with Him, and implements do not help Him. His Being precedes times. His Existence precedes non-existence and His eternity precedes beginning. By His creating the senses it is known that He has no senses. By the contraries in various matters it is known that He has no contrary, and by the similarity between things it is known that there is nothing similar to Him. He has made light the contrary of darkness, brightness that of gloom, dryness that of moisture and heat that of cold. He produces affection among inimical things.

He fuses together diverse things, brings near remote things and separates things which are joined together. He is not confined by limits, nor counted by numbers. Material parts can surround things of their own kind, and organs can point out things similar to themselves. The word[1] "monzo" (i.e. since) disproves their eternity, the word "qad" (that denotes nearness of time of occurrence), disproves their being from ever and the word "lawla" (if it were not) keep them remote from perfection.

Through them the Creator manifests Himself to the intelligence, and through them He is guarded from the sight of the eyes.

Stillness and motion do not occur in Him, and how can that thing occur in Him which He has Himself made to occur, and how can a thing revert to Him which He first created, and how can a thing appear in Him which He first brought to appearance. If it had not been so, His Self would have become subject to diversity, His Being would have become divisible (into parts), and His reality would have been prevented from being deemed Eternal. If there was a front to Him there would have been a rear also for Him. He would need completing only if shortage befell Him. In that case

---

-1- The meaning is that the sense for which the words "monzu, "qad" and "lawla" have been formed is opposed to the attributes of "Ever, "Eternal" and "Perfect. Therefore, their application to anything would prove that they have come into existence from non-existence and are imperfect. For example, "monzu" is used to denote time as is "qad wujida monzu kaza" (this thing is found since so-and-so). Here a time limit has been stated, and anything for which a limit of time can be described cannot exist from ever or for ever. The word "qad" shows (indicating the present perfect tense) the immediate past. This sense also can apply to a thing which is limited in time. The word "lawla" is used to denote the negation of something in another thing, as "ma ahsanahu wa akmalahu lawla annahu kaza" (how handsome and perfect it would be if it were so-and-so). Therefore, the thing for which this word is used would be in need of others in handsomeness and perfection, and would remain deficient by itself.

signs of the created would appear in Him, and He would become a sign (leading to other objects) instead of signs leading to Him. Through the might of His abstention (from affectedness) He is far above being affected by things which effect others.

He is that which does not change or vanish. The process of setting does not behove Him. He has not begotten any one lest He be regarded as having been born. He has not been begotten otherwise He would be contained within limits. He is too High to have sons. He is too purified to contact women. Imagination cannot reach Him so as to assign Him quantity. Understanding cannot think of Him so as to give him shape. Senses do not perceive Him so as to feel Him. Hands cannot touch Him so as to rub against Him. He does not change into any condition. He does not pass from one state to another. Nights and days do not turn Him old. Light and darkness do not alter Him.

It cannot be said that He has a limit or extremity, or end or termination; nor do things control Him so as to raise Him or lower Him, nor does anything carry Him so as to bend Him or keep Him erect. He is not inside things nor outside them. He conveys news, but not with the tongue or voice. He listens, but not with the holes of the ears or the organs of hearing. He says, but does not utter words. He remembers, but does not memorise. He determines, but not by exercising His mind. He loves and approves without any sentimentality (of heart). He hates and feels angry without any painstaking. When He intends to create someone He says "Be" and there he is, but not through a voice that strikes (the ears) is that call heard. His speech is an act of His creation. His like never existed before this. If had been eternal it would have been the second god.

It cannot be said that He came into being after He had not been in existence because in that case the attributes of the created things would be assigned to Him and there would remain no difference between them and Him, and He would have no distinction over them. Thus, the Creator and the created would become equal and the initiator and the initiated would be on the same level. He created (the whole of) creation without any example made by someone else, and He did not secure the assistance of any one out of His creation for creating it.

He created the earth and suspended it without being busy, retained it without support, made it stand without legs, raised it without pillars, protected it against bendings and curvings and defended it against crumbling and splitting (into parts). He fixed mountains on it like stumps, solidified its rocks, caused its streams to flow and opened wide its valleys. Whatever He made did not suffer from any flow, and whatever He strengthened did not show any weakness.

He manifests Himself over the earth with His authority and greatness. He is aware of its inside through his knowledge and understanding. He has power over every thing in the earth by virtue of His sublimity and dignity. Nothing from the earth that he may ask for defies Him, nor does it oppose Him so as to overpower Him. No swift-footed creature can run away from Him so as to surpass Him. He is not needy towards any possessing person so that he should feed Him. All things bow to Him and are humble before His greatness. They cannot flee away from His authority to someone else in order to escape His benefit or His harm. There is no parallel for Him who may match Him and no one like Him so as to equal Him.

He will destroy the earth after its existence, till all that exists on it will become non-existent. But the extinction of the world after its creation is no stranger than its first formation and invention. How could it be? Even if all the animals of the earth, whether birds or beasts, stabled cattle or pasturing ones, of different origins and species, dull people and sagacious men — all jointly try to create (even) a mosquito they are not able to bring it into being and do not understand what is the way to its creation. Their wits are bewildered and wandering. Their powers fall short and fail, and return disappointed and tired, knowing that they are defeated and admitting their inability to produce it, also realising that they are too weak (even) to destroy it.

Surely, after the extinction of the world, Allah the Glorified will remain alone with nothing else beside Him. He will be, after its extinction, as He was before its production: without time or place or moment or period. At this moment, period and time will not exist, and years and hours will disappear. There will be nothing except Allah, the One, the All-powerful. To Him is the return of all matters. Its initial creation was not in its power; and the prevention of its extinction was (also) not in its power. If it had the power to prevent it, it would have existed for ever. When He made anything of the world, the making of it did not cause Him any difficulty, and the creation of anything which He created and formed did not fatigue Him. He did not create it to heighten His authority nor for fear of loss or harm, nor to seek its help against an overwhelming foe, nor to guard against any avenging opponent with its help, nor for the extension of His domain by its help, nor for boasting (over largeness of His possession) against a partner, nor because He felt lonely and desired to seek its company.

Then after its creation He will destroy it, but not because any worry has overcome Him in its upkeep and administration, nor for any pleasure that will accrue to Him, nor for the cumbrousness of anything over Him. The length of its life does not weary Him so as to induce Him to its quick destruction. But Allah, the Glorified, has maintained it with His kindness, kept it intact with His command and perfected it with His power. Then after its destruction, He will resuscitate it, but not for any need of His own towards it, nor to seek the assistance of any of its things against it, nor to change over from the condition of loneliness to that of company, nor from the condition of ignorance and blindness to that of knowledge and search, nor from paucity and need towards needlessness and plenty, nor from disgrace and lowliness towards honour and prestige.

SERMONS 186

Vicissitudes of Time (the mischiefs that are to occur and the absence of lawful ways of livelihood)

May my father and my mother be sacrificed for those few whose names are well-known in the sky and not known on the earth. Beware, you should expect what is to befall you such as adversity in your affairs, severance of relations and the rising up of inferior people. This will happen when the blow of a sword will be easier for a believer than to secure one Dirham lawfully. This will happen[1] when the reward of the beggar is more than that of the giver. This will be when you are intoxicated, not by drinking, but with wealth and plenty, you are swearing without compulsion and are speaking lies without compulsion. This will be when troubles hurt you as the saddle hurts the hump of the camel. How long will these tribulations be and how distant the hope (for deliverance from them)?

O people, throw away the reins of the horses who carry on their backs the weight of your hands (i.e. sins), do not cut away from your chief (Imam) otherwise you will blame yourself for your own doings. Do not jump in the fire which is in flames in front of you; keep away from its courses and leave the middle way for it. Because, by my life, the believer will die in its flames, and others will remain safe in it.

I am among you like a lamp in the darkness. Whoever enters by it will be lit from it. So listen O men, preserve it and remain attentive with the ears of your hearts so that you may understand.

SERMONS 187

Allah's Favours

I advise you, O people, to fear Allah and to praise Him profusely for His favours to you and His reward for you and His obligations on you. See how

---

-1- In that period the reward of the beggar who takes will be higher than that of the giver because the ways of earning livelihood of the rich will be unlawful, and whatever he will donate of it, its purpose will be showing himself, hypocrisy and seeking fame, for which he will not be entitled to any reward, while the poor who take it by force of their poverty and helplessness, and to spend it in the right manner, will deserve more reward and recompense.

The commentator, bn-Abil-Hadeed has written another meaning of it also, namely if the beggar does not take the wealth from the rich and it remains with him he will spend it on unlawful matters and enjoyments, and since his taking it from him prevents him from using it in unlawful manner; therefore, for this prevention of evil, the beggar will deserve more reward and recompense. (Sharh Nahjol-Balagha, vol.13, p.97)

He chose you for favours and dealt with you with mercy. You sinned openly; He kept you covered. You behaved in a way to incur His punishment, but He gave you more time.

Persons Facing Death

I also advise you to remember death and to lessen your heedlessness towards it. Why should you be heedless of Him Who is not heedless of you? Why expect from him (i.e., the angel of death) who will not give you time? The dead whom you have been watching suffice as preachers. They were carried to their graves, not riding themselves, and were placed in them but not of their own accord. It seems as if they never lived in this world and as if the next world had always been their abode. They have made lonely the place where they were living, and are now living where they used to feel lonely. They remained busy about what they had to leave, and did not care for where they were to go. Now they cannot remove themselves from evil, nor add to their virtues They were attached to the world and it deceived them. They trusted it and it overturned them.

Transience Of This World

May Allah have pity on you. You should therefore hasten towards (the preparation of) houses which you have been commanded to populate, and towards which you have been called and invited. Seek the completion of Allah's favours on you by exercising endurance in His obedience and abstention from His disobedience, because tomorrow is close to today. How fast are the hours of the day, how fast are the days in the month, how fast are the months in the years and how fast the years in a life.

SERMONS 188

Steadfast and Transient Belief

One belief is that which is firm and steadfast in hearts, and one is that which remains temporarily in the heart and the breast up to a certain time. If you were to acquit (yourself) before any person, you should wait till death approaches him, for that is the time limit for being acquitted.

And immigration stands as its original position. Allah has no need towards him who secretly accepts belief or him who openly does so. Immigration will not apply to any one unless he recognises the proof (of Allah) on the earth. Whoever recognises him and acknowledges him would be a mohaajir (immigrant). Istidaf (i.e. freedom from the obligation of immigration) does not apply to him whom the proof (of Allah) reaches and he hears it and his heart preserves it.[1]

The Challenge: "Ask me before you miss me"

Certainly, our case is difficult and complicated. No one can bear it except a believer whose heart Allah has tried with belief. Our traditions will not be preserved except by trustworthy hearts and (men of) solid understanding. O people! ask me before you miss me, because certainly I am acquainted with the passages of the sky more than the passages of the earth,[2] and before that mischief springs upon its feet which would trample even the nose string and destroy the wits of the people.

-1- This is the interpretation of the word "mohaajir" and "mustazaf" as mentioned in the Holy Quraan:

Verily those whom the angels take away (at death) while they are unjust to their (own) selves (in sin) , they (the angels) shall ask (the sinning souls): "In what state were ye? " They shall reply, "Weakened (mustazaf — and oppressed) were we in the land; " They (angels) will say "Was not the land of Allah vast (enough) for you to immigrate therein? " So these (are those) whose refuge shall be Hell; and what a bad resort it is. Except the (really) weakened ones from among the men and the women and the children, who have not in their power the means (to escape from the unbelievers) and nor do they find the (right) way. So these, may be, Allah will pardon them; and Allah is the Clement, the Oft-forgiving. (4:97-99)

The meaning of Ameer al-Momineen here is that hijra (immigration) was not only obligatory during the lifetime of the Holy Prophet, but it is a permanent obligation. This immigration is even now obligatory for attaining the proof of Allah and the true religion. Therefore, if one has attained the proof of Allah and believed in it, even if he is in midst of the unbelievers of his locality, he is not duty bound to immigrate.

The "mustazaf" (weakened) is one who is living among the unbelievers and is far from being informed of the proofs of Allah, and at the same time he is unable to immigrate in order to attain the proofs of Allah.

2 Some people have explained this saying of Ameer al-Momineen to mean that by the passages of the earth he means matters of the world and by passages of the sky matters of religious law and that Ameer al-Momineen intends to say that he knows the matters

SERMONS 189

Fear of Allah and Love of Ahlil-Bayt

---

of religious law and commandments more than the worldly matters. Thus, bn Maytham al-Bahraani writes (in Sharh Nahjol-Balagha, vol.4, pp.200-201) :

It is related from Allama al-Wabari, that he said that Ameer al-Momineen's intention is to say that the scope of his religious knowledge is larger than his knowledge about matters of the world.

But taking the context into account, this explanation cannot be held to be correct because this sentence (which is the subject of explanation) has been used as the cause of the sentence "Ask me before you miss me, and after it, is the prophesy about revolt. In between these two the occurrence of the sentence that "I know religious matters more than worldly matters, makes the whole utterance quite uncounted, because Ameer al-Momineen's challenge to ask whatever one likes is not confined to matters of religious law only so this sentence could be held as its cause. Then, after that, the prophesy of the rising up of the revolt has nothing to do with matters of religious law, so that it could be put forth as a proof of more knowledge of religious matters. To ignore the clear import of the words and to interpret them in a way which does not suit the occasion, does not exhibit a correct spirit, when from the context also the same meaning accrues which the words openly convey. Thus, it is to give a warning about the Omayyad's mischief that Ameer al-Momineen uttered the words: "Ask me whatever you like; because I know the paths and courses of divine destiny more than the passages of the earth. So, even if you ask me about matters which are recorded in the "preserved tablet" and concern divine destiny I can tell you, and a serious mischief is to rise against me in those matters in which you should have doubt, because my eyes are more acquainted with those ethereal lines which concern the occurrence of events and mischiefs than, with what I know about live appearing on the earth. The occurrence of this mischief is as certain as an object seen with eyes. You should therefore ask me its details and the way to keep safe from it, so that you may be able to manage your defence when the times comes" This meaning is supported by the successive sayings of Ameer al-Momineen which he uttered in connection with the unknown, and to which the future testified. Thus, bn-Abil-Hadeed comments on this claim of Ameer al-Momineen as follows:

Ameer al-Momineen's claim is also supported by his sayings about future events which he uttered not once or a hundred times but continuously and successively, from which there remains no doubt that whatever he spoke was on the basis of knowledge and certainly and not in the way of chance. (Sharh Nahjol-Balagha, vol.13, p.106)

In connection with this saying of Ameer al-Momineen it has already been shown and explained (in Sermon 92, Foot-note No. 2) that no one else dared advance such a claim, and those who made such a claim had to face only disgrace and humility. About the prophecies made by Ameer al-Momineen see bn-Abil-Hadeed, Sharh Nahjol-Balagha, vol.7, pp.47-51; al-Qazi Noorollah al-Marashi, Ihqaaq al-Haqq (New ed.) , vol.8, pp.87-182.

I praise Him out of gratefulness for His reward, and I seek His assistance in fulfilling His rights. He has a strong army. His dignity is grand. I stand witness that Mohammad — peace and blessing of Allah be upon him and his progeny — is His slave and His Prophet. He called (people) to His obedience and overpowered His enemies by fighting for the sake of His religion. People's joining together to falsify him and their attempt to extinguish His light did not prevent him from it.

You should therefore exercise fear of Allah because it has a rope whose twist is strong and its pinnacle is lofty and invulnerable. Hasten toward death in its pangs (by doing good acts) and be prepared for it before its approach, because the ultimate end is the Day of Judgement. This is enough preaching for one who understands and enough of a lesson for one who does not know. What idea do you have, before reaching that end, of the narrowness of grave, the hardship of loneliness, fear of the passage towards the next world, the pangs of fear, the shifting of ribs here and there (due to narrowing of the grave), the deafness of ears, the darkness of the grave, fear of the promised punishment, the closing of the receptacle of the grave and the laying of stones?

Therefore, (fear) Allah, (fear) Allah, O creatures of Allah, because the world is behaving with you in the usual way and you and the Day of Judgement are in the same rope (close to each other). As though it has come with its signs, has approached with its pleas and has made you stand in its way; and as though it has come forward with all its quakings and has settled down with its chest on the ground while the world has parted from its people and has turned them out of its lap. It was like a day that has passed or a month that has gone by. Its new things have become old and the fat ones have become thin.

They are in a narrow place, in very complicated affairs and in a fire whose pain is sharp, cries are loud, flames are rising, sound is trembling, burning is severe, abatement is remote; its fuel is burning, its threats are fearful, its hollows are hidden, its sides are dark, its vessels are aflame, and everything about it is abominable.

And shall be conveyed those who feared (the wrath of) their Lord, in companies unto the garden... (Quraan. 39:73)

They are safe from chastisement, away from punishment, and kept aloof from fire. Their abode will be peaceful and they will be pleased with their longing and their place of stay. These are the people whose acts in this world were chaste, their eyes were tearful, their nights in this world were like days because of fearing and seeking forgiveness, and their days were like nights because of feeling of loneliness and separation. Therefore, Allah made Paradise the place of their (eventual) return and a reward in recompense.... They were most eligible and suitable for it ..." (Quraan, 48:26) in the eternal domain and everlasting favours.

Therefore, O creatures of Allah, pay regard to all that by being regardful of which one will succeed and by ignoring which one will incur loss, and hasten towards your death by means of your (good) acts, because you are bound by what you have done in the past and you have to your credit only what (good acts) you have sent forward. (Behave in such a way) as though the feared event (death) has come upon you, so that you cannot return (to do good acts) nor can you be cleared of evil acts. Allah may prompt us and you for His obedience and obedience of His Prophet, and forgive us and you by His great mercy.

Stick to the earth, keep patient in trials, do not move your hands and swords after the liking of your tongues, and do not make haste in matters in which Allah has not asked for haste because any one of you who dies in his bed while he had knowledge of the rights of Allah and the rights of His Prophet and members of the Prophet's house, will die as martyr. His reward is incumbent on Allah. He is also eligible to the recompense of what good acts he has intended to do, since his intention takes the place of drawing his sword. Certainly, for every thing there is a time and a limit.

SERMONS 190

Praise and Fear of Allah

Praise be to Allah Whose praise is wide-spread, Whose army is over-powering and Whose dignity is grand. I praise Him for His successive favours and His great gifts. His forbearance is high so that He forgives and is just in whatever He decides. He knows what is going on and what has already passed. He crafted all creation by His knowledge and produced it by His intelligence without limitation, without learning, without following the example of any intelligent producer, without committing any mistake and without the availability of any group (for help); I stand witness that Mohammad — the peace and blessing of Allah be upon him and his descendants — is His slave and His messenger whom He deputed (at a time) when people were collecting in the abyss and moving in bewilderment. The reins of destruction were dragging them, and the locks of malice lay fixed on their hearts.

World and its People

I advise you, O creature of Allah, that you should have fear of Allah because it is a right of Allah over you and it creates your right over Allah, and that you should seek Allah's help in it, and its help in (meeting) Allah. Certainly, for today fear of Allah is a protection and a shield, and for tomorrow (the Day of Judgement) it is the road to Paradise. Its way is clear and he who treads it is the gainer. Whoever holds it, guards it. It has presented itself to the people who have already passed and to those coming from behind, because they will need it tomorrow (on the Day of Judgement) when Allah will revive His creation again, take back what He has given and take account of what He has bestowed. How few will be those who accept it and practise it as it ought to be practised. They will be very few in number, and they are the people who correspond to the description given by Allah, the Glorified, when He says:

...And very few of My creatures are grateful! (Quraan. 34:13)

Therefore, hasten with your ears towards it and intensify your efforts for it. Make it a substitute for all your past (short-comings) to take their place as a successor, and make it your supporter against every opponent. Turn your sleep into wakefulness by its help, and pass your days with it. Make it the equipment of your hearts, wash your sins with it, treat your ailments with it and hasten towards your death with it. Take a lesson from him who neglects it, so that others who follow it should not take a lesson from you (i.e., from your neglecting it). Beware, therefore; you should take care of it and should take care of yourselves through it.

Keep away from this world and proceed towards the next world infatuatedly. Do not regard humble he whom fear Allah has given a high position, and do not accord a high position to him whom this world has given a high position. Do not keep your eyes on the shining clouds of the world, do not listen to him who speaks of it, do not respond to him who calls towards it, do not seek light from its glare, and do not die in its precious things, because its brightness is deceitful, its words are false, its wealth is liable to be looted, and its precious thing are to be taken away.

Beware, this world attracts and then turns away. It is stubborn, refusing to go ahead. It speaks lies and misappropriates. It disowns and is ungrateful. It is malicious and abandons (its lovers). It attracts but causes trouble. Its condition is changing, its step shaking, its honour disgrace, its seriousness jest, and its height lowliness. It is a place of plunder and pillage, and ruin and destruction. Its people are ready with their feet to drive, to overtake and to depart. Its routes are bewildering, its exits are baffling, and its schemes end in disappointment. Consequently, strongholds betray them, houses throw them out and cunning fails them. Some of them are like hocked camel, some like butchered meat, some like severed limbs, some like spilt blood, some are biting their hands (in pain) some are rubbing their palms (in remorse), some are holding their cheeks on their hands (in anxiety), some are cursing their own views and some are retreating from their determination. But the time for action has gone away and the hour of calamity has approached, while (there was no longer) the time to escape (Quraan, 38:3). Alas! Alas! what has been lost is lost! what has gone is gone! The world has passed in its usual manner. So wept not on them the heavens and the earth nor were they respited. (Quraan, 44:29)

SERMONS 191

"al-Qaaseeaa" Disparagement (against Shaytan)

It comprises disparagement of Satan (Eblees) for his vanity and his refusing to prostrate before Adam (p.b.u.h.), and his being the first to display bigotry and to act through vanity; it comprises a warning to people treading in Satan's path

Praise be to Allah who wears the apparel of Honour and Dignity and has chosen them for Himself instead of for His creation. He has made them inaccessible and unlawful for others. He has selected them for His own great self, and has hurled a curse on him who contests with Him concerning them.

Allah's Trial and Vanity of Eblees

Then He put His angels on trial concerning these attributes in order to distinguish those who are modest from those who are vain. Therefore, Allah, who is aware of whatever is hidden in the hearts and whatever lies behind the unseen said:

...Verily I am about to create man from clay," And when I have completed and have breathed into him of My spirit, then fall ye prostrating in obeisance unto him. And did fall prostrating in obeisance the angels all together, Save Eblees ..." (Quraan. 38:71-74)

His vanity stood in his way. Consequently, he felt proud over Adam by virtue of his creation and boasted over him on account of his origin. Thus, this enemy of Allah is the leader of those who boast, and the fore-runner of the vain. It is he who laid the foundation of factionalism, quarrelled with Allah about the robe of greatness, put on the dress of haughtiness and took off the covering of humility. Do you not see how Allah made him low on account of his vanity and humiliated him for his feigning to be high? He discarded him in this world and provided for him burning fire in the next world.

If Allah had wanted to create Adam from a light whose glare would have dazzled the eyes, whose handsomeness would have amazed the wits and whose smell would have caught the breath, He could have done so; and if He had done so, people would have bowed to him in humility and the trial of the angels through him would have become easier. But Allah, the Glorified, tries His creatures by means of those things whose real nature they do not know in order to distinguish (good and bad) for them through the trial, and to remove vanity from them and keep them and keep them aloof from pride and self-admiration.

You should take a lesson from what Allah did with Satan; namely He nullified his great acts and extensive efforts on account of the vanity of one moment, although Satan had worshipped Allah for six thousand years — whether by the reckoning of this world or of the next world is not known. Who now can remain safe from Allah after Satan by committing a similar disobedience? None at all. Allah, the Glorified, cannot let a human being enter Paradise if he does the same thing for which Allah turned out from it an angel. His command for the inhabitants in the sky and of the earth is the same. There is no friendship between Allah and any individual out of His creation so as to give him license for an undesirable thing which He has held unlawful for all the worlds.

Warning against Satan

Therefore, you should fear lest Satan infects you with his disease, or leads you astray through his call, or marches on you with his horsemen and footmen, because, by my life, he has put the arrow in the bow for you, has stretched the bow strongly, and has aimed at you from a nearby position, and: He (Satan) said:

My Lord! because Thou hast left me to stray, certainly will I adorn unto them the path of error, and certainly will I cause them all to go astray." (Quraan, 15:39)

Although he (Satan) had said so only by guessing about the unknown future and by wrong conjecturing, yet the sons of vanity, the brothers of haughtiness and the horsemen of pride and intolerance proved him to be true, so much so that when disobedient persons from among you bowed before him, and his greed about you gained strength; and what was a hidden secret turned into a clear fact, he spread his full control over you and marched with his forces towards you.

Then they pushed you into the hollows of disgrace, threw you into the whirlpools of slaughter, and trampled you, wounding you by striking your eyes with spears, cutting your throats, tearing your nostrils, breaking your limbs and taking you in ropes of control towards the fire already prepared. In this way he became more harmful to your religion and a greater kindler of flames (of mischief) about your worldly matters than the enemies against whom you showed open opposition and against whom you marched your forces.

You should therefore spend all your force against him, and all your efforts against him, because, by Allah, he boasted over your (i.e., Adam's) origin, questioned your position and spoke lightly of your lineage. He advanced on you with his army, and brought his footmen towards your path. They are chasing you from every place, and they are hitting you at every finger joint. You are not able to defend by any means, nor can you repulse them by any determination. You are in the thick of disgrace, the ring of straitness, the field of death and the way of distress.

You should therefore put out the fires of haughtiness and the flames of intolerance that are hidden in your hearts. This vanity can exist in a Moslim only by the machinations of Satan, his haughtiness, mischief and whisperings. Make up your mind to have humility over your heads, to trample self-pride under your feet and to cast off vanity from your necks. Adopt humility as the weapon between you and your enemy, Satan and his forces. He certainly has, from every people, fighters, helpers, footmen and horsemen. Do not be like him who feigned superiority over the son of his own mother without any distinction given to him by Allah except the feeling of envy which his feeling of greatness created in him and the fire of anger that vanity kindled in his heart. Satan blew into his nose his own vanity, after which Allah gave him remorse and made him responsible for the sins of all killers up to the Day of Judgement.

Caution against Vanity and Boasting about Ignorance

Beware! you strove hard in revolting and created mischief on the earth in open opposition to Allah and in challenging the believers over fighting. (You should fear) Allah! Allah! in feeling proud of your vanity and boasting over ignorance, because this is the root of enmity and the design of Satan wherewith he has been deceiving past people and bygone ages, with the result that they fell into the gloom of his ignorance and the hollows of his misguidance, submitting to his driving and accepting his leadership. In this matter the hearts of all the people were similar, and centuries passed by, one after the other, in just the same way, and there was vanity with which chests were tightened.

Caution against Obeying Haughty Leaders and Elders

Beware! beware of obeying your leaders and elders who felt proud of their achievements and boasted about their lineage. They hurled the (liability for) things on Allah and quarrelled with Allah in what He did with them, contesting His decree and disputing His favours. Certainly, they are the main foundation of obstinacy, the chief pillars of mischief and the swords of pre-Islamic boasting over forefathers. Therefore, fear Allah, do not become antagonistic to His favours on you, nor jealous of His bounty over you[1] and do not obey the claimants (of Islam) whose dirty water you drink along with your clean one, whose ailments you mix with your healthiness and whose wrongs you allow to enter into your rightful matters.

They are the foundation of vice and the linings of disobedience. Satan has made them carriers of misguidance and the soldiers with whom he attacks men. They are interpreters through whom he speaks in order to steal

---

-1- The intention is that "you should not create conditions by which you may be deprived of Allah's favours, like the jealous who aims at harming him of whom he is jealous

away your wits, enter into your eyes and blow into your ears. In this way he makes you the victim of his arrows, the treading ground of his footsteps and source of strength for his hands. Take instruction from how he brought Allah's wrath, violence, chastisement and punishment on those who were vain among the past people. Take admonition from their lying on their cheeks and falling on their sides, and seek Allah's protection from the dangers of vanity, as you seek His protection from calamities.

Humbleness of Holy Prophet

Certainly. if Allah were to allow anyone to indulge in pride He would have allowed it to his selected prophets and vicegerents. But Allah, the Sublime, disliked vanity for them and liked humbleness for them. Therefore, they laid their cheeks on the ground, smeared their faces with dust, bent themselves down for the believers and remained humble people. Allah tried them with hunger, afflicted them with difficulty, tested them with fear, and upset them with troubles. Therefore, do not regard wealth and progeny the criterion for Allah's pleasure and displeasure, as you are not aware of the chances of mischief and trials during richness and power as Allah, the Glorified, the Sublime, has said:

What! Think they that what We aid them with of wealth and children, We are hastening unto them the good things? Nay! they (only) perceive not. (Quraan, 23:55-56)

Certainly, Allah the Glorified, tries His creatures who are vain about themselves through His beloved persons who are humble in their eyes. When Moosa son of Emraan went to Pharaoh along with his brother Haroon (Aaron) wearing (coarse) shirts of wool and holding sticks in their hands, they guaranteed him retention of his country and continuity of his honour if he submitted; but he said: "Do you not wonder at these two men guaranteeing me the continuity of my honour and the retention of my country although you see their poverty and lowliness. Otherwise, why do they not have gold bangles on their wrists?" He said so feeling proud of his gold and collected possessions, and considering wool and its cloth as nothing.

When Allah, the Glorified, deputed His prophets, if He had wished to open for them treasures and mines of gold and (surround them with) planted gardens and to collect around them birds of the skies and beasts of the earth, He could have done so. If He had done so then there would have been no trial, nor recompense and no tidings (about the affairs of the next world). Those who accepted (His message) could not be given the recompense falling due after trial and the believers could not deserve the reward for good acts, and all these words[1] would not have retained their meanings. But Allah, the Glorified, makes His Prophets firm in their determination and gives them weakness of appearance as seen from the eyes, along with contentment that fills the hearts and eyes resulting from care-freeness, and with want that pains the eyes and ears.

If the prophets possessed authority that could not be assaulted, or honour that could not be damaged or domain towards which the necks of people would turn and the saddles of mounts could be set, it would have been very easy for people to seek lessons and quite difficult to feel vanity. They would have then accepted belief out of fear felt by them or inclination attracting them, and the intention of them all would have been the same, although their actions would have been different. Therefore, Allah, the Glorified decided that people should follow His prophets, acknowledge His books, remain humble before His face, obey His command and accept His obedience with sincerity in which there should not be an iota of anything else; and as the trial and tribulation would be stiffer the reward and recompense too should be larger.

Holy Kaba

-1- The intention is to say that if belief is accepted under force of awe and fear and worship is offered under the influence of power and authority then neither will it be belief in the true sense nor worship in real spirit. This is because belief is the name of inner testimony and heart-felt conviction. The conviction produced by force and compulsion can be only verbal but not heart-felt. Similarly, worship is the name of open acknowledgement of one's position of servitude. Worship which is devoid of the feeling of servitude or the sense of devotion and which is performed only in view of authority or fear cannot be real worship. Therefore, such belief and such worship would not present their correct connotation.

Do you not see that Allah, the Glorified, has tried all the people among those who came before, beginning with Adam, upto the last ones in this world with stones which yield neither benefit nor harm, which neither see nor hear. He made those stones into His sacred house which He made a standby for the people. He placed it in the most rugged stony part of the earth and on a highland with least soil thereon, among the most narrow valleys between rough mountains. soft sandy plains, springs of scanty water and scattered habitants, where neither camels nor horses nor cows and sheep can prosper.

Then He commanded Adam and his sons to turn their attention towards it. In this way it became the centre of their journey in seeking pastures and the rendezvous for meeting of their carrier-beasts, so that human spirits hasten towards it from distant waterless deserts, deep and low lying valleys and scattered islands in the seas. They shake their shoulders in humbleness, recite the slogan of having reached His audience, march with swift feet, and have dishevelled hair and dusted faces. They throw their pieces of cloth on their backs, they have marred the beauty of their faces by leaving the hair uncut as a matter of great test, severe tribulation, open trial, and extreme refining. Allah has made it a means to His mercy and an approach to His Paradise.

If Allah, the Glorified, had placed His sacred House and His great signs among plantations, streams, soft and level plains, plenty of trees, an abundance of fruits, a thick population, close habitats, golden wheat, lush gardens, green land, watered plains, thriving orchards and crowded streets, the amount of recompense would have decreased because of the lightness of the trial. If the foundation on which the House is borne and the stones with which it has been raised had been of green emerald and red rubies, and there had been brightness and effulgence, then this would have lessened the action of doubts in the breasts, would have dismissed the effect of Satan's activity from the hearts, and would have stopped the surging of misgivings in people. But Allah tries His creatures by means of different troubles, wants them to render worship through hardships and involves them in distresses, all in order to extract out vanity from their hearts, to settle down humbleness in their spirits and to make all this an open door for His favours and an easy means for His forgiveness (for their sins).

Caution against Rebellion and Oppressiveness

(Fear) Allah! Allah! from the immediate consequence of rebellion (to accrue in this world), and the eventual consequence of weighty oppressiveness (to accrue in the next world), and from the evil result of vanity, because it is the great trap of Satan and his big deceit which enters the hearts of the people like a fatal poison. It never goes waste, nor misses anyone — neither the learned because of his knowledge, nor the destitute[1] in his rags. This is the thing against which Allah has protected His creatures who are believers by means of prayers, and alms-giving, and suffering the hardship of fasting in the days in which it has been made obligatory, in order to give their limbs peacefulness, to cast fear in their eyes, to make their spirits humble, to give their hearts humility and to remove haughtiness from them. All this is achieved through the covering of their delicate cheeks with dust in humility, prostrating their main limbs on the ground in humbleness, and retracting of their bellies so as to reach to their backs due to fasting by way of lowliness (before Allah), besides giving all sorts of products of the earth to the needy and the destitute by way of alms.

Look what there is in these acts by way of curbing the appearance of pride and suppressing the traces of vanity. I cast my glance and noticed that no one in the world, except you, feels vanity for anything without a cause which may appeal to the ignorant, or a reason which may cling to the

---

-1- The reason for specifying the learned and the poor is that the learned has the light of learning to lead him, which the destitution of the poor may deny to him. In spite of this, both the learned and the poor fall into his deceit.

Then how can the ignorant save himself from his clutches, and how can the rich who has all the means to get into wrong ways, defend himself against him.

Nay! Verily man is wont to rebel!

As the deemeth himself needless!

minds of the foolish, because you feel vanity for something for which no reason is discernible, nor any ground.

As for Satan, he felt proud over Adam because of his origin and taunted at him about his creation, since he said "I am of fire while you are of clay." In the same way the rich among the prosperous communities have been feeling vanity because of their riches, as (Allah) said:

And said they: "We are more (than you) in wealth and in children, and we shall not be chastised." (Quraan, 34:35)

Enthusiasm for Attractive Manners, Respectable Position

In case you cannot avoid vanity, your vanity should be for good qualities, praiseworthy acts, and admirable matters with which the dignified and noble chiefs of the Arab families distinguished themselves, as attractive manners, high thinking, respectable position and good performances. You too should show vanity in praiseworthy habits like the protection of the neighbour, the fulfillment of agreements, obedience to the virtuous, opposition to the haughty, extending generosity to others, abstention from rebellion, keeping aloof from blood-shed, doing justice to people, suppressing anger and avoiding trouble on the earth. You should also fear what calamities befell peoples before you on account of their evil deeds and detestable actions. Remember, during good or bad circumstances, what happened to them, and be cautious that you do not become like them.

After you have thought over both the conditions of these people, attach yourself to everything with which their position became honourable, on account of which enemies remained away from them through which safety spread over them, by reason of which riches bowed before them and as a result of which distinction connected itself with their rope. These things were abstention from division, sticking to unity, calling each other to it and advising each other about it. You avoid everything which broke their backbone and weakened their power, such as malice in the heart, hatred in the chest, turning away (from each other's help) and withholding the hand from one another's assistance.

Think about the condition of people from among the believers who passed before you. What distresses and trials they were in! Were they not the most over-burdened among all the people and in the most straitened circumstances in the whole world? The Pharaohs took them as slaves. They inflicted on them the worst punishments and bitter sufferings. They continuously remained in this state of ruinous disgrace and severe subjugation. They found no method for escape and no way for protection. Till when Allah, the Glorified, noticed that they were enduring troubles in His love and bearing distresses out of fear for Him, He provided escape from the distress of trials. So, He changed their disgrace into honour and fear into safety. Consequently, they became ruling kings and conspicuous leaders. and Allah's favours over them reached limits to which their own wishes had not reached.

Look, how they were when their groups were united, their views were unanimous, their hearts were moderate, their hands used to help one another, their swords were intended for assisting one another, their eyes were sharp and their aims were the same. Did they not become masters of the corners of the earth and rulers over the neck of all the worlds? Thereafter, also see what happened to them towards the end when division overtook them, unity became fractured, and differences arose between their words and their hearts. They divided into various groups and were scattered fighting among themselves. Then Allah took away from them the apparel of His honour and deprived them of the prosperity produced by His favours. Only their stories have remained among you for the guidance of those who may learn the lesson from them.

You should take a lesson from the fate of the progeny of Ismaaeel, the children of Isaac and the children of Israel. How similar are their affairs and how akin are their examples. In connection with the details of their division and disunity, think of the days when Kisras of Persia and the

Caesars of Rome had become their masters[1]. They turned them out from the pastures of their lands the rivers of Iraq and the fertility of the world,

-1- If a glance is cast at the rise and fall and events and happenings of the past people this fact will shine like daylight that the rise and fall of communities is not the result of luck or change, but that, to a great extent, it is affected by their acts and deeds. And of whatever type those deeds are, their results and consequences are in accord with them. Consequently, the stories and events of past people openly reflect that the result of oppression and evil deeds has always been ruin and destruction, while the consequence of virtuous action and peaceful living was always good luck and success. Since time and people make no difference, if the same conditions appear again and the same actions are repeated the same results must accrue which had appeared in the earlier set of circumstances, because the accrual of the results of good or bad actions is sure and certain like the properties and effects of everything. It this were not so it would not be possible to kindle hope in the minds of the oppressed and the afflicted by presenting to them past events and their effects, nor could the oppressors and tyrants be warned of the ill-effects of their deeds, on the ground that it was not necessary that the same would accrue now as had accrued earlier. But it is the universality of causality which makes past events the object of a lesson for posterity. Consequently, it was for this purpose that Ameer al-Momineen provoked thinking and consideration and mentioned the various events of Bani-Ismaaeel, Bani-Ishaaq and Bani-Israaeel and their affliction at the hands of the kings of Persia and Rome.

The progeny of Ismaaeel, the elder son of Ibraheem (Abraham) , is called Bani-Ismaaeel while the progeny of his younger son Isaac is called Bani-Ishaaq which later continued to divide into various off-shoots and acquired different names. Their original abode was at Canaan in Palestine, where Ibraheem had settled after the immigration from the plains of the Euphrates and the Tigris. His son Ismaaeel had settled in the Hijaaz, where Ibraheem had left him and his mother Hajar (Hagar). Ismaaeel married Sayyida bnt-Miqdaad a woman of the tribe of Jorhom which also inhabited this very area. His progeny sprang from her and spread throughout the world. The other son of Ibraheem namely Ishaaq remained in Canaan. His son was Yaqoob (Jacob/Israel) who married Liya the daughter of his mother's brother and after her death married his other daughter. Both of them bore him progeny which is known as Bani-Israaeel. One of his sons was Yoosof (Joseph) , who reached the neighbouring country, Egypt, through an accident, and, after suffering slavery and imprisonment, eventually became the ruler and occupier of the throne.

After this change, he sent for all his relations and kith and kin and in this way Egypt became the abode of Bani-Israaeel. For some time they lived there in peace and safety, and led a life of respect and esteem, but by and by the locals began to view them with disdain and hatred and made them the target of all sorts of tyrannies, so much so that they used to kill their children and retained their women as slave-maids, as a result of which their determination and courage was trampled and their spirit of freedom was completely subdued. At last, conditions changed and the period of their troubles came to an end, after four hundred years of the shackles of slavery; when Allah sent Mosa to deliver them from the oppression of the Pharaoh. Mosa set off with them to leave Egypt, but in order to destroy the Pharaoh, Allah turned them towards the Nile where there was all flood in front, and on the rear the huge forces of the Pharaoh. This bewildered them much, but Allah commanded Mosa to enter the river without fear. Thus, when he went forward, there appeared in the river not only one but several courses to pass through and Mosa crossed to the other side of the river along with Bani-Israaeel. Pharaoh was closely following. When he saw them passing he too advanced with his arm but when they reached the middle of the stream the still water began moving and, engulfing Pharaoh and his army in its waves, finished them. About them the Quraan says:

And (remember ye) when We delivered you from Pharaoh's people who afflicted you with grievous torment, slaying your sons and by letting your women alive, and in that was a great trial from your Lord. (2:49)

However, when, after leaving the boundaries of Egypt, they entered their motherland Palestine, they established their own state and began to live in freedom, and Allah changed their lowliness and disgrace into the greatness and sublimity of rule and power. In this connection, Allah says:

And made We inheritors the people who were deemed weak (to inherit) the eastern parts of the earth and the western parts of it, which we had blessed therein (with fertility) and the good word of thy Lord was fulfilled in the children of Israel for what they did endure; and destroyed We, what Pharaoh and his people had wrought, and what shade they did make. (Quraan, 7:137)

On occupying the throne of rule and regaining prosperity and peacefulness, Bani-Israaeel forgot all the ignominies and disgraces of the period of slavery, and instead of being thankful to Allah for the favours granted by Him they took to rebellion and revolt. Consequently, they shamelessly indulged in vices and misconduct and partook in mischiefs and evil deeds to the maximum, made lawful things unlawful and unlawful things lawful by false excuses and disobeyed the prophets who tried to preach and correct them under the command of Allah, and even killed them. The natural consequence of their vicious activities was that they were caught in punishment for their deeds. Consequently, Nebuchadnezzar, who was ruling in Babylon (Iraq) in 600 B. C., rose to march against Syria and Palestine and killed seventy thousand Bani-Israaeel with his blood-thirsty swords, devastated their towns, drove away the survivors with him like sheep and goats and threw them in the abyss of ignominy by turning them into slaves.

Although after this ruination there seemed no way for them to regain position and power, yet nature gave them still another chance to recover. When Nebuchadnezzar died and power came in the hands of Belshazzar he started all sorts of oppression on the people. Being disgusted with this, they sent word to the ruler of Persia that they were tired of enduring the oppression of their ruler and that he should rescue them from him, and free them from the oppression of Belshazzar. Cyrus the Great, who was a just and upright ruler, rose up in response to this request and, with the co-operation of the local population, overturned the government, as a consequence of which the yoke of slavery on Bani-Israaeel's necks was also removed, and they were allowed to return to Palestine.

towards thorny forests, the passages of (hot) winds and hardships in livelihood. In this way they turned them into just herders of camels. Their houses were the worst in the world and their places of stay were the most drought-stricken. There was not one voice towards which they could turn

---

Thus, after seventy years of subjugation they again set foot in their homeland and took over the reins of government. If they had taken their lesson from the past events they would not have committed the same evils as a consequence of which they had to suffer slavery; but the mental constitution of this community was such that whenever they achieved prosperity and freedom from care they lost themselves in the intoxication of riches and in the enjoyment of pleasure, mocked the laws of religion, derided the prophets and even killing them did not mean anything serious to them. Thus, when their ruler Herod at the request of his sweetheart, beheaded the Prophet Yahya (John) and presented his head to her, none of them raised any voice against this brutality or was affected by it in any manner. This was the state of their unruliness and fierceness when Esaa made his appearance. He stopped them from evil deeds and exhorted them to adopt good habits, but they opposed him too and gave him troubles of various sorts, so much so that they tried to end his life. However, Allah foiled all their devices and made Esaa safe against their approach. When their disobedience reached this stage and their capacity to accept guidance was completely wiped out, fate decided to ruin them and made full arrangements for their annihilation and destruction. The ruler of Roma (Byzantia) Vespasianus sent his son Titus to attack Syria, he laid siege round Jerusalem, demolished the houses and broke down the walls of the Synagogue as a result of which thousand of Bani-Israaeel left their houses and became scattered abroad, while thousands died of hunger; and those who remained were put to sword. Most of them settled in Hijaaz, but because of their rejecting Prophet Mohammad (p.b.u.h.a.h.p) their unity was so disturbed that they could never again converge on any one centre of honour and could never regain a life of prestige and dignity in place of disgrace and ignominy.

In the same way the ruler of Persia made serious attacks on Arabia and subjugated the inhabitants of those places. Thus, Shapoor bn Hormoz, at the age of sixteen, took with him four thousand combatants and attacked Arabs who resided within the boundaries of Persia and then advanced towards Bahrain, Qateef and Hajar and ruined Bani-Tameem, Bani-Bakr bn Wail and Bani-Abdl-Qays and cut through the shoulders of seventy thousand Arabs, after which his nickname became "Zol-Aktaf" (the shoulderer). He forced the Arabs that they should live in tents built of hair, should grow long hair on their heads, should not wear white clothes and should ride unsaddled horses. Then he settled twelve thousand people of Isfahaan and other cities of Persia in the area between Iraq and Syria. In this way he drove the inhabitants of those places from fertile lands to waterless forests which had neither any of the conveniences of life nor means of livelihood, and for long these people remained the victims of other's oppression due to their own disunity and division. At last, Allah deputed the Prophet and raised them out of disgrace to the highest pinnacle of progress and sublimity.

for protection, nor any shade of affection on whose strength they could repose trust.

Their condition was full of distress. Their hands were scattered. Their majority was divided. They were in great anguish and under layers of ignorance. They buried their daughters alive, worshipped idols, disregarded kinship and practised robbery.

Now, look at the various favours of Allah upon them, that He deputed towards them a prophet who got them to pledge their obedience to him and made them unite at his call. (Look) how (Allah's) bounty spread the wings of its favours over them and flowed for them streams of its blessing, and the whole community became wrapped in blissful prosperity. Consequently, they were submerged under its bounty and enjoyed its lush life. Their affairs were settled under the protection of a powerful ruler, and circumstances offered them overpowering honour, and all things became easy for them under the auspices of a strong country. They became rulers over the world and kings in the (various) parts of the earth. They became masters of those who were formerly their masters, and began issuing commands over those who used to command them. They were so strong that neither did their spears need testing nor did their weapons have any flaw.

Condemning His People

Beware! You have shaken your hands loose from the rope of obedience, and broken the divine fort around you by (resorting to) pre-Islamic rules. Certainly, it is a great blessing of Allah, the Glorified, that He has engendered among them unity through the cord of affection in whose shade they walk and take shelter. This is a blessing whose value no one in the whole world realises, because it is more valuable than any price and higher than any wealth.

You should know that you have again reverted to the position of the Bedouin Arabs after immigration (to Islam), and have become different parties after having been once united. You do not possess anything of Islam except its name, and know nothing of belief save its show. You say

"The Fire" Yes. but no shameful position," as if you would throw down Islam on its face in order to defame its honour and break its pledge (for brotherhood) which Allah gave you as a sacred trust on His earth and (a source of) peace among the people. Be sure that if you incline towards anything other than Islam. the unbelievers will fight you. Then there will be neither Gabriel nor Michael, neither mohaajiroon nor Ansaar to help you, but only the clashing of swords, till Allah settles the matter for you.

Certainly, there are examples before you of Allah's wrath, punishment, days of tribulations and happenings. Therefore, do not disregard His promises, ignoring His punishment, making light His wrath and not expecting His violence, because Allah, the Glorified, did not curse the past ages except because they had left off asking others to do good acts and refraining them from bad acts. In fact Allah cursed the foolish for committing sins and the wise because they gave up refraining others from evils. Beware! You have broken the shackles of Islam, have transgressed happenings. Therefore, do not disregard His pr

His High Position and Wonderful Deeds in Islam

Beware! surely Allah has commanded me to fight those who revolt, or who break the pledge, or create trouble on the earth. As regards pledge-breakers, I have fought them, as regards deviators from truth, I have waged holy war against them, and as regards those who have gone out of the faith, I have put them in (serious) disgrace.[1] As for Satan of the pit,[1] he too has been dealt with by me through the loud cry with which the scream

---

-1- Ameer al-Momineen, Abo-Ayyoob al-Ansaari, Jabir bn Abdillah al-Ansaari, Abdillah bn-Masood, Ammaar bn Yaasir, Abo-Saeed al-Khodri and Abdillah bn Abbas narrated that the Holy Prophet commanded Ali bn Abi-Talib to fight those who are pledge-breakers (nakitheen) , deviators from truth (qasiteen) and those who have left the faith (mariqeen). (al-Mostadrak, vol.3, p.139; al-Isteeaab, vol.3, p.1117; Osdol-Ghaaba, vol.3, pp.32-33; ad-Dorrol-Manthoor, vol.6, p.18; al-Khasaais al-Kobra, vol.2, p.138; Majma az-Zawaaid, vol.5, p.186; vol.6, p.235; vol.7, p.238; Kanz al-Ommaal, vol.6, pp.72, 82, 88, 155, 215, 319, 391, 392; Taareekh Baghdad, vol.8, p.340; vol.13, pp.186-187; at-Taareekh, bn Asakir, vol.5, p.41; at-Taareekh, bn Katheer, vol.7 pp.304-306; ar-Riyaaz an-Nazira, vol.2, p.240; Sharh al-Mawahibil-Ladonniyya, vol.3, pp.316-317; Mowazih al-Awham, vol.1, p.386).

bn-Abil-Hadeed says: "It has been proved (by right ascription) from the Holy Prophet that he said to Ali (p.b.u.h.) :

You will fight after me those who are pledge-breakers, deviators from truth and those who have gone out of the faith.

The pledge-breakers were the people of Jamal, because they broke their allegiance with him. The deviators from truth were the people of Syria (Sham) at Siffeen. Those who have gone out of the faith were the Kharijites at an-Nahrawan. Regarding these three groups, Allah says (about the first one) :

Verily, those who swear their fealty unto thee do but swear fealty unto Allah; the hand of Allah is above their hands; so whosoever violateth his oath, doth violate it only to the hurt of his (own) self; ... (Quraan, 48:10)

(About the second group) Allah says:

And as for the deviators, they shall be for the hell, a fuel. (Quraan, 72:15) "

Concerning the third group, bn-Abil-Hadeed has referred to the following tradition (hadeeth) that al-Bokhaari (in as-Saheeh, vol.4, pp.166-167, 243) , Moslim (in as-Saheeh, vol.3, pp.109-117) , at-Tirmizi (in al-Jaami" as-Saheeh, vol.4, p.481) , bn Maaja (in as-Sonan, vol.i, pp.59-62) , an-Nasaaee (in as-Sonan, vol.3, pp.65-66) , Malik bn Anas (in al-Mowatta, pp.204-205) , ad-Darqotni (in as-Sonan, vol.3, pp.131-132) , ad-Darimi (in as-Sonan, vol.2, p.133) , Abo-Dawood (in as-Sonan, vol.4, pp.241-246) , al-Hakim (in al-Mostadrak, vol.2, pp.145-154; vol.4, p.531) , Ahmad bn Hambal (in al-Mosnad, vol.1, pp.88, 140, 147; vol.3, pp.56, 65) and al-Bayhaqi (in as-Sonan al-Kobra, vol.8, pp.170-171) have narrated through a group of the companions of the Holy Prophet that he said about Zol-Khowaysira (the surname for Zoth-Thodayya Horqus bn Zohayr at-Tameemi, the chief of the Kharijites) :

From this very person's posterity there will arise people who will recite the Quraan, but it will not go beyond their throat, they will kill their followers of Islam and will spare the idol-worshippers. They will glance through the teaching of Islam as hurriedly as the arrow passes through its prey. If I were to ever find them I would kill them like Ad.

Then bn-Abil-Hadeed continues:

of his heart and shaking of his chest was also heard. Only a small portion of the rebels has remained. If Allah allows me one more chance over them I will annihilate them except a few remnants that may remain scattered in the suburb of the cities.

Even in my boyhood I had lowered the chest of (the famous men) of Arabia, and broken the horn points (i.e., defeated the chiefs) of the tribes of Rabeea and Mozar. Certainly, you know my position of close kinship and special relationship with the Prophet of Allah — peace and blessing of Allah be upon him and his descendants. When I was only a child he took charge of me. He used to press me to his chest and lay me beside him in his bed, bring his body close to mine and make me smell his smell. He used to chew something and then feed me with it. He found no lie in my speaking, nor weakness in any act.

From the time of his weaning, Allah had put a mighty angel with him to take him along the path of high character and good behaviour through day and night, while I used to follow him like a young camel following in the footprints of its mother. Every day he would show me in the form of a banner some of his high traits and commanded me to follow it. Every year he used to go in seclusion to the hill of Hira, where I saw him but no one else saw him. In those days Islam did not exist in any house except that of the Prophet of Allah — peace and blessing of Allah be upon him and his descendants — and Khadeeja, while I was the third after these two. I used

---

This is the sign for his (Holy Prophet's) Prophethood and his prophecy of the secret knowledge. (Sharh Nahjol-Balagha, vol.13, p.183)

1 By "Satan of the pit" the reference is to Zoth-Thodayya who was killed in Nahrawan by the stroke of lightning from the sky, and there was no need to kill him by sword. The Holy Prophet had foretold his death. Therefore, after the annihilation of the Kharijites at Nahrawan, Ameer al-Momineen came out in search, but could not find his body anywhere. In the meantime, ar-Rayyan bn Sabira saw forty to fifty bodies in a pit on the bank of the canal. When they were taken out the body of Zoth-Thodayya was also found among them. He was called Zoth-Thodayya because of a mass of flesh on his shoulder. When Ameer al-Momineen saw his body he said "Allah is Great, neither I spoke lie nor was I told wrong" (bn-Abil-Hadeed, vol.13, pp.183-184; at-Tabari, vol.1, pp.3383-3384; bn al-Athir vol.3, p.348)

to see and watch the effulgence of divine revelation and message, and breathed the scent of Prophethood.

When the revelation descended on the Prophet of Allah — peace and blessing of Allah be upon him and his descendants — I heard the moan of Satan. I said "O Prophet of Allah, what is this moan?" and he replied "This is Satan who has lost all hope of being worshipped. O Ali, you see all that I see and you hear all that I hear, except that you are not a Prophet, but you are a vicegerent and you are surely on (the path of) virtue

I was with him when a party of the Quraysh came to him and said to him "O Mohammad, you have made a big claim which none of your fore-fathers or those of your family have made. We ask you one thing; if you give us an answer to it and show it to us, we will believe that you are a prophet and a messenger, but if you cannot do it, we will know that you are a sorcerer and a liar

The Messenger of Allah said: "What do you ask for?" They said: "Ask this tree to move for us, even with its roots, and stop before you." The Prophet said "Verily, Allah has power over everything. If Allah does it for you, will you then believe and stand witness to the truth?" They said "Yes. Then he said "I shall show you whatever you want, but I know that you wont bend towards virtue, and there are among you those who will be thrown into the pit, and those who will form parties (against me)." Then the Holy Prophet said: "O tree, if you do believe in Allah and the Day of Judgement, and know that I am the Prophet of Allah, come up with your roots and stand before me with the permission of Allah." By Him who deputed the Prophet with truth, the tree did remove itself with its root and came with a great humming sound and a flapping like the flapping of the wings of birds, till it stopped before the Messenger of Allah while some of its twigs came down onto my shoulders, and I was on the right side of the Holy Prophet.

When the people saw this they said by way of pride and vanity "Now you order half of it to come to you and the other half of it remain (in its place)." The Holy Prophet ordered the tree to do the same. Then half of the tree advanced towards him in an amazing manner and with greater humming. It was about to touch the Prophet of Allah. Then they said, disbelieving and revolting "Ask this half to get back to its other half and be as it was." The Prophet ordered it and it returned. Then I said "O Prophet of Allah, I am the first to believe in you and to acknowledge that the tree did what it did just now with the command of Allah, the Sublime, in testimony to your Prophethood and to heighten your word. Upon this all the people shouted "Rather a sorcerer, a liar; it is wonderful sorcery, he is very adept in it. Only a man like this (pointing to me) can stand testimony to you in your affairs

Certainly, I belong to the group of people who care not for the reproach of anybody in matters concerning Allah. Their countenance is the countenance of the truthful and their speech is the speech of the virtuous. They are wakeful during the nights (in devotion to Allah), and over beacons (of guidance) in the day. They hold fast to the rope of the Quraan. revive the traditions of Allah and of His Prophet. They do not boast nor indulge in self conceit, nor misappropriate, nor create mischief. Their hearts are in Paradise while their bodies are busy in (good) acts.

SERMONS 192

Qualities of the God-fearing, the effect of Preaching on minds amenable to it, etc.

It is related that a companion of Ameer al-Momineen called Homam[1] who was a man devoted to worship said to him "O Ameer al-Momineen, describe to me the pious man in such a way as though I see them." Ameer al-Momineen avoided the reply and said,

O Homam, fear Allah and perform good acts because "verily, Allah is with those who guard (themselves against evil), and those who do good (to others)" (Quraan, 16:128).

-1- According to bn-Abil-Hadeed this is Homaam bn Shorayh but Allama Majlisi says that apparently this is Homaam bn Obada.

Homam was not satisfied with this and pushed him to speak. Thereupon, Ameer al-Momineen praised Allah and extolled him and sought his blessings on the holy prophet and then spoke:

Now then, Allah the Glorified, the Sublime, created (the things of) creation. He created them without any need for their obedience or being safe from their sinning, because the sin of anyone who sins does not harm Him nor does the obedience of anyone who obeys Him benefit Him. He has distributed among them their livelihood, and has assigned them their positions in the world.

Thus, the God-fearing, in it are the people of distinction. Their speech is to the point, their dress is moderate and their gait is humble. They keep their eyes closed to what Allah has made unlawful for them, and they put their ears to that knowledge which is beneficial to them. They remain in the time of trials as though they remain in comfort. If there had not been fixed periods (of life) ordained for each, their spirits would not have remained in their bodies even for the twinkling of an eye because of (their) eagerness for the reward and fear of chastisement. The greatness of the Creator is seated in their heart, and, so, everything else appears small in their eyes. Thus to them Paradise is as though they see it and are enjoying its favours. To them, Hell is also as if they see it and are suffering punishment in it.

Their hearts are grieved, they are protected against evils, their bodies are thin, their needs are scanty, and their souls are chaste. They endured (hardship) for a short while, and in consequence they secured comfort for a long time. It is a beneficial transaction that Allah made easy for them. The world aimed at them, but they did not aim at it. It captured them, but they freed themselves from it by a ransom.

During a night they are upstanding on their feet reading portions of the Quraan and reciting it in a well-measured way, creating through it grief for themselves and seeking by it the cure for their ailments. If they come across a verse creating eagerness (for Paradise) they pursue it avidly, and their spirits turn towards it eagerly, and they feel as if it is in front of them.

And when they come across a verse which contains fear (of Hell) they bend the ears of their hearts towards it, and feel as though the sound of Hell and its cries are reaching their ears. They bend themselves from their backs, prostrate themselves on their foreheads, their palms, their knees and their toes, and beseech Allah, the Sublime, for their deliverance. During the day they are enduring, learned, virtuous and God-fearing. Fear (of Allah) has made them thin like arrows. If any one looks at them he believes they are sick, although they are not sick, and he says that they have gone mad. In fact, great concern (i.e., fear) has made them mad.

They are not satisfied with their meagre good acts, and do not regard their major acts as great. They always blame themselves and are afraid of their deeds. When anyone of them is spoken of highly, he says: "I know myself better than others, and my Lord knows me better than I know. O Allah do not deal with me according to what they say, and make me better than they think of me and forgive me (those shortcomings) which they do not know

The peculiarity of anyone of them is that you will see that he has strength in religion, determination along with leniency, faith with conviction, eagerness in (seeking) knowledge in forbearance, moderation in riches, devotion in worship, gracefulness in starvation, endurance in hardship, desire for the lawful, pleasure in guidance and hatred from greed. He performs virtuous deeds but still feels afraid. In the evening he is anxious to offer thanks (to Allah). In the morning his anxiety is to remember (Allah). He passes the night in fear and rises in the morning in joy — fear lest night is passed in forgetfulness, and joy over the favour and mercy received by him. If his self refuses to endure a thing which it does not like he does not grant its request towards what it likes. The coolness of his eye lies in what is to last for ever, while from the things (of this world) that will not last he keeps aloof. He transfuses knowledge with forbearance, and speech with action.

You will see his hopes simple, his shortcomings few, his heart fearing, his spirit contented, his meal small and simple, his religion safe, his desires dead and his anger suppressed. Good alone is expected from him. Evil from him is not to be feared. Even if he is found among those who forget (Allah) he is counted among those who remember (Him), but if he is among the rememberers he is not counted among the forgetful. He forgives him who is unjust to him, and he gives to him who deprives him. He behaves well with him who behaves ill with him.

Indecent speech is far from him, his utterance is lenient, his evils are non-existent his virtues are ever present, his good is ahead and mischief has turned its face (from him). He is dignified during calamities, patient in distresses, and thankful during ease. He does not commit excess over him whom he hates, and does not commit sin for the sake of him whom he loves. He admits truth before evidence is brought against him. He does not misappropriate what is placed in his custody, and does not forget what he is required to remember. He does not call others bad names, he does not cause harm to his neighbour, he does not feel happy at others misfortunes, he does not enter into wrong and does not go out of right.

If he is silent his silence does not grieve him, if he laughs he does not raise his voice, and if he is wronged he endures till Allah takes revenge on his behalf. His own self is in distress because of him, while the people are in ease from him. He puts himself in hardship for the sake of his next life, and makes people feel safe from himself. His keeping away from others is by way of asceticism and purification, and his nearness to those to whom he is near is by way of leniency and mercifulness. His keeping away is not by way of vanity or feeling of greatness, nor his nearness by way of deceit and cheating.

It is related that Homam passed into a deep swoon and then expired. Then Ameer al-Momineen said:

Verily, by Allah I had this fear about him.

Then he added:

Effective advises produce such effects on receptive minds.

Someone[1] said to him: O Ameer al-Momineen, how is it you do not receive such an effect? Ameer al-Momineen replied:

Woe to you. For death there is a fixed hour which cannot be exceeded, and a cause which does not change. Now look, never repeat such talk which Satan had put on your tongue.

SERMONS 193

Deputation of the Holy Prophet. Animosity of Arab Tribes. Position of Hypocrites

We praise Allah for the succour He has given us in carrying out His obedience and in preventing us from disobedience, and we ask Him to complete His favours (to us) and to make us hold on to His rope. We stand witness that Mohammad is His slave and His Messenger. He entered every hardship in search of Allah's pleasure and endured for its sake every grief. His near relations changed themselves for him and those who were remote from him (in relationship) united against him. The Arabs let loose the reins (of their horses to quicken their march) against him, and struck the bellies of their carriers to (rouse them) in fighting against him, so much so that enemies came to his threshold from the remotest places and most distant areas.

I advise you, O creatures of Allah, to fear Allah and I warn you of the hypocrites, because they are themselves misguided and misguide others, and they have slipped and make others slip too. They change into many colours, and adopt various ways. They support you with all sorts of supports, and lay in waiting for you at every lookout. Their hearts are diseased while their faces are clean. They walk stealthily and tread like the approach of sickness (over the body). Their words speak of cure, but their acts are like incurable diseases. They are jealous of ease, intensify distress, and destroy hopes. Their victims are found lying down on every path,

-1-This man was Abdillah bn Kawwa" who was in the fore-front of the Kharijite movement and was a great opponent of Ameer al-Momineen.

while they have means to approach every heart and they have (false) tears for every grief.

They eulogise each other and expect reward from each other. When they ask something they insist on it, if they reprove (any one) they disgrace (him), and if they pass verdict they commit excess. They have adopted for every truth a wrong way, for every erect thing a bender, for every living being a killer, for every (closed) door a key and for every night a lamp. They covet, but with despair, in order to maintain with it their markets, and to popularise their handsome merchandise. When they speak they create doubts. When they describe they exaggerate. First they offer easy paths but (afterwards) they make them narrow. In short, they are the party of Satan and the stings of fire.

Satan hath gained hold on them, so he maketh them forget the remembrance of Allah; they are Satan's Party; Beware! verily, the party of Satan are the losers. (Quraan, 58:19)

SERMONS 194

Fear of Allah and Details about the Day of Judgement

Praise be to Allah who has displayed such effects of His authority and the glory of His sublimity through the wonders of His might that they dazzle the pupils of the eyes and prevent the minds from appreciating the reality of His attributes. I stand witness that there is no god but Allah by virtue of belief, certainty, sincerity and conviction. I also stand witness that Mohammad is His slave and His Prophet whom He deputed when the signs of guidance were obliterated and the ways of religion were desolate. So, he threw open the truth, gave advice to the people, guided them towards righteousness and ordered them to be moderate. May Allah bless him and his descendants.

Know, O creatures of Allah, that He has not created you for nought and has not left you free. He knows the extent of His favours over you and the quantity of His bounty towards you. Therefore, ask Him for success and for the attainment of aims. Beg before Him and seek His generosity. No curtain hides you from Him, nor is any door closed before you against Him. He is at every place, in every moment and every instance. He is with every man and jinn. Giving does not create any breach in Him. Gifting does not cause Him diminution. A beggar cannot exhaust Him and paying (to others) cannot take Him to the end.

One person cannot turn His attention from another, one voice does not detract Him from another voice, and one grant of favour does not prevent Him from refusing another favour. Anger does not prevent Him from mercy, mercy does not prevent Him from punishing; His concealment does not hide His manifestness and His manifestness does not prevent Him from concealment. He is near and at the same time distant. He is high and at the same time low. He is manifest and also concealed. He is concealed yet well-known. He lends but is not lent anything. He has not created (the things of) creation after devising, nor did He take their assistance on account of fatigue.

I advise you, O creatures of Allah, to have fear of Allah, for it is the rein and the mainstay (of religion). Hold fast to its salient points, keep hold of its realities. It will take you to abodes of easiness, places of comfort, fortresses of safety and houses of honour on the Day (of Judgement) when eyes will be wide open, (Quraan, 14:42), when there will be darkness all round, when small groups of camels pregnant for ten months will be allowed free grazing, and when the Horn will be blown, then every living being will die, every voice will become dumb the high mountains and hard rocks will crumble (to pieces) so that their hard stones will turn into moving sand and their bases will become level. (On that day) there will be no interceder to intercede and no relation to ward off (trouble), and no excuse will be of avail.

SERMONS 195

World at the time of the Proclamation of Prophethood. Transience of this World and the state of its inhabitants

Allah deputed the Prophet when no sign of guidance existed, no beacon was giving light and no passage was clear.

I advise you, O creatures of Allah, to have fear of Allah, and I warn you of this world which is a house from which departure is inevitable and a place of discomfort. He who lives in it has to depart, and he who stays here has to leave it. It is drifting with its people like a boat whom severe winds dash (here and there) in the deep sea. Some of them get drowned and die, while some of them escape on the surface of the waves, where winds push them with their currents and carry them towards their dangers. So, whatever is drowned cannot be restored, and whatever escapes is on the way to destruction.

O creatures of Allah, you should know now that you have to perform (good) acts, because (at present) your tongues are free, your bodies are healthy, your limbs have movement, the area of your coming and going is vast and the course of your running is wide; before the loss of opportunity or the approach of death. Take death's approach as an accomplished fact and do not think it will come (hereafter).

SERMONS 196

Attachment to the Holy Prophet. Performance of His Funeral Rites.

Those companions of Mohammad — the peace and blessing of Allah be upon him and his descendants — who were the custodians (of divine messages) know that I never disobeyed Allah or His Messenger[1] — the

-1- bn-Abil-Hadeed has written (in Sharh Nahjol-Balagha, vol.10, pp.180-183) that Ameer al-Momineen's saying that he never disobeyed the commands of the Prophet is a sort of taunt to those who felt no hesitation in rejecting the Prophet's commands and sometimes even checked him. For example, when, at the time of the peace of al-

peace and blessing of Allah be upon him and his descendants — at all, and by virtue of the courage[1] with which Allah honoured me I supported him

---

Hodaybiyya, the Prophet was agreeable to negotiate peace with the unbelievers among the Quraysh, one of the companions became so enraged that he expressed doubts about the Prophethood of the Prophet whereupon Abi-Bakr had to say:

Woe be to you! Keep clinging to him. He is certainly Allah's Messenger and He will not ruin him.

The introduction to the oath, "inna, and the word of emphasis "lam" which are used here to create conviction about the Prophethood shows that the addressee had gone farther than mere doubt, because these words of emphasis are employed only when the stage of denial has been reached. However, if belief required absence of doubt, the presence of doubt must imply defect in the belief, as Allah says:

The believers are only those who believe in Allah and His Messenger, they doubt not thereafter, ... (Quraan, 49:15)

Similarly, when the Prophet intended to say the funeral prayers of Obayy bn Salool the same companion said to him, "How do you intend to seek forgiveness for this Chief of hypocrites? " And he even drew away the Prophet by catching the skirt (of his shirt). Then the Prophet had to say, "No act of mine is beside the command of Allah. In the same way the Prophet's command to accompany the force of Osaama bn Zayd was ignored. The greatest of all these insolences was displayed in connection with the Prophet's intention to write down his advice as to when such a blame was laid against the Prophet which proves an absence of belief in the commands of the sharia, and creates a doubt about each command as to whether it is based on divine revelation or (Allah may forbid) just the result of mental disorder.

1 Who can deny that the ever-successful lion of Allah, Ali bn Abi-Talib (p.b.u.h.) shielded the Prophet on every critical occasion and performed the duty of protecting him by dint of the courage and valour gifted to him by Allah. The first occasion of risking his life was when the unbelievers from the Quraysh decided finally to kill the Prophet and Ali slept on his bed surrounded by enemies and under the direct peril of swords, whereby the enemies were not able to succeed in their aims. Then, in those battles where the enemies used to attack the Prophet together and where the feet of even the reputed heroes could not stand firm, Ameer al-Momineen remained steadfast with the banner (of Islam) in his hand. Abdl-Barr and al-Hakim writes about it:

bn Abbas says that Ali had four qualities which no one else possessed. Firstly, he was the first among Arabs and non-Arabs to have said prayers with the Messenger of Allah. Secondly, he always had the banner of Islam in his hand in every battle. Thirdly, when people ran away from the Prophet, Ali remained with him; and fourthly it was he who gave the Prophet his funeral ablution and laid him in his grave. (al-Isteeaab, vol.3, p.1090; al-Mostadrak ala as-Saheehayn vol.3, p.111)

A study of the holy wars of Islam fought in the Prophet's days leaves no doubt that, except for the battle of Tabook in which Ameer al-Momineen did not partake, all other battles bear testimony to his fine performance and all the successes are due to his valour.

with my life on occasions when even the brave turned away and feet remained behind (instead of proceeding forward).

When the Prophet — the peace and blessing of Allah be upon him and his descendants — died his head was on my chest, and his (last) breath blew over my palms and I passed it over my face. I performed his (funeral) ablution, may Allah bless him and his descendants, and the angels helped me. The house and the courtyard were full of them. One party of them was descending and the other was ascending. My ears continually caught their humming voice, as they invoked Allah's blessing on him, till we buried him in his grave. Thus, who can have greater rights with him than I during his life or after his death? Therefore depend on your intelligence and make your intentions pure in fighting your enemy, because I swear by Him who is such that there is no god but He, that I am on the path of truth and that they (the enemy) are on the misleading path of wrong. You hear what I say; and I seek Allah's forgiveness for myself and for you.

Thus, in the battle of Badr seventy unbelievers were killed, half of whom were killed by Ali's sword. In the battle of Ohod, when victory changed into defeat as a result of the Moslims engaging themselves in the collection of booty, and they fled away under the sudden attack of the enemy, Ameer al-Momineen remained steadfast, taking Jihaad to be a religious obligation, and displayed such conspicuous performance in support and defence of the Prophet that the Prophet too acknowledged it and also the Angel. Again, in the battle of the Trench (al-Khandaq) , the Prophet was accompanied by three thousand combatants, but none dared face Amr bn Abdawid. At last, Ameer al-Momineen killed him and saved the Moslims from ignominy. In the battle of Honayn, the Moslims were proud of their number because they were ten thousand while the unbelievers were only four thousand, but here too they leapt onto the booty, as a consequence of which the unbelievers gained the opportunity, and pounced upon them. Bewildered with this sudden attack the Moslims fled away as the Holy Quraan says:

Most certainly did Allah help you in many (battle) fields, and on the day of Honayn, when made you vain your great number, but they availed you nothing, and was straitened the earth against you with all its extensiveness, then ye turned back in retreat. (9:25)

On this occasion also, Ameer al-Momineen was steady like a rock, and eventually, with Allah's support, victory was achieved.

SERMONS 197

Allah's Attribute of Omniscience

Allah knows the cries of the beasts in the forest, the sins of the people in seclusion, the movements of the fishes in the deep seas and the rising of the water by tempestuous winds. I stand witness that Mohammad is the choice of Allah, the conveyor of His revelation and the messenger of His mercy.

Advantages of fear of Allah

Now then, I advise you to fear Allah, Who created you for the first time; towards Him is your return, with Him lies the success of your aims, at Him terminate (all) your desires, towards Him runs your path of right and He is the aim of your fears (for seeking protection). Certainly, fear of Allah is the medicine for your hearts, sight for the blindness of your spirits, the cure for the ailments of your bodies, the rectifier of the evils of your breasts, the purifier of the pollution of your minds, the light of the darkness of your eyes, the consolation for the fear of your heart and the brightness for the gloom of your ignorance.

Therefore, make obedience to Allah the way of your life and not only your outside covering, make it your inner habit instead of only outer routine, subtle enough to enter through your ribs (up to the heart), the guide for all your affairs, the watering place for your getting down (on the Day of Judgement), the interceder for the achievement of your aims, asylum for the day of your fear, the lamp of the interior of your graves, company for your long loneliness, and deliverance from the troubles of your abodes. Certainly, obedience to Allah is a protection against encircling calamities. expected dangers and the flames of burning fires.

Therefore, whoever entertains fear of Allah, troubles remain away from him after having been near, affairs become sweet after their bitterness, waves (of troubles) recede from him after having crowded over him, difficulties become easy for him after occurring, generosity rains fast over him after there had been famine, mercy bends over him after it had been loath, the favours (of Allah) spring forth on him after they had been dried, and blessing descends over him in showers after being scanty. So, fear Allah Who benefits you with His good advice, preaches to you through His Messenger, and obliges you with His favours. Devote yourselves to His worship, and acquit yourselves of the obligation of obeying Him.

Islam

This Islam is the religion which Allah has chosen for Himself, developed it before His eyes, preferred it as the best among His creations, established its pillars on His love. He has disgraced other religions by giving honour to it. He has humiliated all communities before its sublimity; He has humbled its enemies with His kindness and made its opponents lonely by according it His support. He has smashed the pillars of misguidance with its columns. He has quenched the thirst of the thirsty from its cisterns, and filled the cisterns through those who draw its water.

He made Islam such that its constituent parts cannot break, its links cannot separate, its construction cannot fall, its columns cannot decay, its plant cannot be uprooted, its time does not end, its laws do not expire, its twigs cannot be cut, its parts do not become narrow, its ease does not change into difficulty, its clarity is not affected by gloom, its straightness does not acquire curvature, its wood has no crookedness, its vast paths have no narrowness, its lamp knows no putting off and its sweetness has no bitterness.

It consists of columns whose bases Allah has fixed in truthfulness and whose foundation He has strengthened, and of sources whose streams are ever full of water and of lamps, whose flames are full of light, and of beacons with whose help travellers get guidance, and of signs through which a way is found to its highways and of watering places which provide water to those who come to them. Allah has placed in Islam the height of His pleasure, the pinnacle of His pillars and the prominence of His obedience. Before Allah, therefore, its columns are strong, its construction is lofty, its proofs are bright, its fires are aflame, its authority is strong, its beacons are high and its destruction is difficult. You should therefore honour it, follow it, fulfil its obligations and accord the position due to it.

The Holy Prophet

Then, Allah, the Glorified, deputed Mohammad — the peace and blessing of Allah be upon him and his descendants — with truth at a time when the destruction of the world was near and the next life was at hand, when its brightness was turning into gloom after shining, it had become troublesome for its inhabitants, its surface had become rough, and its decay had approached near. This was during the exhaustion of its life at the approach of signs (of its decay), the ruin of its inhabitants, the breaking of its links, the dispersal of its affairs, the decay of its signs, the divulging of its secret matters and the shortening of its length. Allah made him responsible for conveying His message and (a means of) honour for his people, a period of bloom for the men of his days, a source of dignity for the supporters and an honour for his helpers.

The holy Quraan

Then, Allah sent to him the Book as a light whose flames cannot be extinguished, a lamp whose gleam does not die, a sea whose depth cannot be sounded, a way whose direction does not mislead, a ray whose light does not darken, a separator (of good from evil) whose arguments do not weaken, a clarifier whose foundations cannot be dismantled, a cure which leaves no apprehension for disease, an honour whose supporters are not defeated, and a truth whose helpers are not abandoned. Therefore, it is the mine of belief and its centre, the source of knowledge and its oceans, the plantation of justice and its pools, the foundation stone of Islam and its construction, the valleys of truth and its plains, an ocean which those who draw water cannot empty, springs which those who draw water cannot dry up, a watering place which those who come to take water cannot exhaust, a staging place in moving towards which travellers do not get lost, signs which no treader fails to see and a highland which those who approach it cannot surpass it.

Allah has made it a quencher of the thirst of the learned, a bloom for the hearts of religious jurists, a highway for the ways of the righteous, a cure after which there is no ailment, an effulgence with which there is no darkness, a rope whose grip is strong, a stronghold whose top is invulnerable, an honour for him who loves it, a peace for him who enters it, a guidance for him who follows it, an excuse for him who adopts it, an argument for him who argues with it, a witness for him who quarrels with it, a success for him who argues with it, a carrier of burden for him who seeks the way, a shield for him who arms himself (against misguidance), a knowledge for him who listens carefully, worthy story for him who relates it and a final verdict of him who passes judgements.

SERMONS 198

Prayer, Zakat and Fulfillment of Trust

Pledge yourself with prayer and remain steady on it; offer prayer as much as possible and seek nearness (of Allah) through it, because it is, (imposed) upon the believers as (a) timed ordinance (Quraan 4:103). Have you not heard the reply of the people of Hell when they were asked: What hath brought you into the hell? They shall say: We were not of those who offered the regular prayers (to Allah)! (Quraan, 74:42-43). Certainly, prayer drops out sins like the dropping of leaves (of trees), and removes them as ropes are removed from the necks of cattle. The Messenger of Allah — the peace and blessing of Allah he upon him and his descendants — likened it to a hot bath situated at the door of a person who bathes in it five times a day. Will then any dirt remain on him?

Its obligation is recognised by those believers whom neither the adornment of property nor the coolness of the eyes produced by children can turn away from it. Allah, the Glorified, says:

Men whom neither merchandise nor any sale diverteth from the remembrance of Allah and constancy in prayer and paying the poor-rate ..." (Quraan. 24:37)

Even after receiving assurance of Paradise, the Messenger of Allah — peace and blessing of Allah be upon him and his descendants — used to exert himself for prayers because of Allah, the Glorified's command:

And enjoin prayer on thy followers, and adhere thou steadily unto it, ..." (Quraan, 20:132).

Then the Holy Prophet used to enjoin his followers to prayer and exert himself for it.

Islamic tax (zakat)

Then, Islamic tax has been laid down along with prayer as a sacrifice (to be offered) by the people of Islam. Whoever pays it by way of purifying his spirit, it serves as a purifier for him and a protection and shield against fire (of Hell). No one therefore (who pays it) should feel attached to it afterwards, nor should feel grieved over it. Whoever pays it without the intention of purifying his heart expects through it more than its due. He is certainly ignorant of the Sonna, he is allowed no reward for it, his action goes to waste and his repentance is excessive.

Fulfillment of Trust

Then, as regards fulfillment of trust, whoever does not pay attention to it will be disappointed. It was placed before the strong skies, vast earths and high mountains but none of them was found to be stronger. vaster, or higher than it. If anything could be unapproachable because of height, vastness, power or strength they would have been unapproachable, but they felt afraid of the evil consequences (of failure in fulfilling a trust) and noticed what a weaker being did not realise it, and this was man:

... Verily he was (proved) unjust, ignorant." (Quraan, 33:72)

Surely, Allah, the Glorified, the Sublime, nothing is hidden from Him of whatever people do in their nights or days. He knows all the details, and His knowledge covers them. Your limbs are a witness, the organs of your body constitute an army (against yourself), your inner self serves Him as eyes (to watch your sins), and your loneliness is open to Him.

SERMONS 199

Treason and Treachery of Moaawiya and the fate of those guilty of treason

By Allah,[1] Moaawiya is not more cunning than I am, but he deceives and commits evil deeds. Had I not been hateful of deceit I would have been

-1- People who are ignorant of religion and ethics free from the shackles of religious law and unaware of the conception of punishment and reward find no paucity of excuses and means for the achievement of their objects. They can find ways of success at every stage; but when the dictates of humanity, or Islam, or the limitations imposed by ethics and religious law act as impediments, the chances of devising and finding means become narrow, and the possibility of action becomes restricted. Moaawiya's influence and control was the result of these devices and ways in following which he knew no impediment nor any obstacle of what is lawful or unlawful, nor did fear of the Day of Judgement prevent him from acting fearlessly. As Allama ar-Ragheeb al-Isfahaani while taking account of his characters writes:

His aim always was to achieve his object whether lawful or unlawful. He did not care for religion nor did he ever think of divine chastisement. Thus, in order to maintain his power he resorted to mis-statements and concoctions, practised all sorts of deceits and contrivances. When he saw that success was not possible without entangling Ameer al-Momineen in war he roused Talha and az-Zobayr against him. When success could not be achieved by this means he instigated the Syrians and brought about the civil war of Siffeen. And when his rebellious position had become known by the killing of Ammaar, he at once duped the people by saying that Ali was responsible for killing him as he had brought him into the battlefield; and on another occasion he interpreted the words "rebellious party" occurring in the saying of the Prophet to mean "avenging party" intending to prove that Ammaar would be killed by the group that would seek revenge of Othmaan's blood, although the next portion of this saying namely "he will call them towards Paradise while they will call him to Hell, " does not leave any scope for interpretation. When there was no hope of victory even by these cunning means, he contrived to raise the Quraan on spears, although in his view neither the Quraan nor its commandments carried any weight. If he had really aimed at a decision by the Quraan, he should have put this demand before the commencement of the battle, and when it became known to him that the decision had been secured by Amr bn Aas by deceiving Abo-Mosa al-Ashari, and that it did not have even a remote connection with the Quraan, he should not have accepted it and should have punished Amr bn Aas for this cunning, or at least should have warned and rebuked him. But on the contrary, his performance was much appreciated and in reward he was made the Governor of Egypt

In contrast to this Ameer al-Momineen's conduct was a high specimen of religious law and ethics. He kept in view the requirements of truth and righteousness even in adverse

the most cunning of all men. But (the fact is that) every deceit is a sin and every sin is disobedience (of Allah), and every deceitful person will have a banner by which he will be recognised on the Day of Judgement. By Allah, I cannot be made forgetful by strategy, nor can I be overpowered by hardships.

---

circumstances and did not allow his chaste life to be tarnished by the views of deceit and contrivance. If he wished he could face cunning by cunning, and Moaawiya's shameful activities could have been answered by similar activities. For example, when he put a guard on the Euphrates and stopped the supply of its water (to Ameer al-Momineen's men) , then the supply of water could have been cut from them also on the grounds that since they had occupied the Euphrates it was lawful to retaliate, and in this way they could be overpowered by weakening their fighting power. But Ameer al-Momineen could never tarnish his hands with such an inhuman act which was not permitted by any law or code of ethics, although common people regard such acts against the enemy as lawful and call this duplicity of character for achievement of success, a stroke of policy and administrative ability. But Ameer al-Momineen could never think of strengthening his power by fraud or duplicity of behaviour on any occasion. Thus when people advised him to retain the officers of the days of Othmaan in their position and to befriend Talha and az-Zobayr by assigning them governorship of Koofa and Basra, and make use of Moaawiya's ability in administration by giving him the government of Syria, Ameer al-Momineen rejected the advice and preferred the commandments of religious law over worldly expediency, and openly declared about Moaawiya as follows:

If I allow Moaawiya to retain what he already has I would be one "who taketh those who lead (people) astray, as helpers" (Quraan, 18:51). Those who look at apparent successes do not care to find out by what means the success has been achieved. They support anyone whom they see succeeding by means of cunning ways and deceitful means and begin to regard him an administrator, intelligent, a politician, intellectually brilliant and so on, while he who does not deploy cunning and fraudulent methods owing to his adherence to Islamic commandments and divine instructions and prefers failure to success secured through wrong methods is regarded as ignorant of politics and weak in foresight. They do not feel it necessary to think what difficulties and impediments exist in the way of a person who adheres to principles and laws which prevent him from proceeding forward even after approaching near success

SERMONS 200

One should not be afraid of the scarcity of those who tread on the right path

O people, do not wonder at the small number of those who follow the right path, because people throng only round the table (of this world) whose edibles are few but whose hunger is insatiable.

O people, certainly, what gathers people together (in categories) is (their) agreement (to good or bad) and (their) disagreement, for only one individual killed the camel of Thamood[1] but Allah held all of them in

---

-1- Thamood, in ancient Arabia, a tribe or group of tribes, seems to have been prominent from about the 4th Century B. C. to the first half of the 7th Century A. D. Their place of stay and homeland was at a place lying on the way between the Hijaaz and Syria called the Valley of al-Qura and bore this name because it consisted of several townships. Allah deputed for their guidance and directions the Prophet Saalih who preached to them as Allah relates in his story:

And unto (the people of) Thamood (We did send) their brother Saalih, he said:

O my people! worship ye Allah (alone). Ye have no god other than Him; indeed came unto you a clear proof from your Lord; this is the She-camel of Allah (which) unto you is a sign, so leave it (free) to pasture in Allah's earth and touch her not with any harm, or ye shall be seized with a painful chastisement. And remember when He made you successors after the (people) Ad and settled you in the earth, ye build mansions on its plain and hew the mountains into dwellings. So remember ye the bounties of Allah, and see ye not evil in the earth, making mischief" Saeed the chiefs of those who were puffed up with pride among his people to those who were reckoned weak, to those who believed from among them; "Know ye that Saalih is sent by his Lord? " Saeed they: "Verily, in what he hath been sent with, we are believers" Saeed those who were puffed up with pride; "Verily we, in that which ye believe are disbelievers" They hamstrung the She-camel and rebelled against the command of their Lord, and they said "O Saalih! bring us what thou didst, threaten us with, if thou art of the apostles" Then seized them (unawares) the earthquake, so became they in their dwellings, motionless (dead). Then he turned away from them and said "O my people! Indeed I did deliver unto you the message of my Lord, and did admonish you, but ye love not the admonishers" (Quraan, 7:73-79).

(The people of) Thamood belied the warners, and said they: "What! a single man, from among us! and we to follow him? Verily then we shall be astray and in distress. It is that (the duty of) reminding hath been bestowed on him (alone) , of all the (people) among us? Nay! he is a great liar, an insolent one! " 'soon they shall know on the morrow, (as to) who is the liar, the insolent one! (O" Our Apostle Saalih!) verily We are going to send

punishment because all of them joined him by their acquiescing in their consenting to it. Thus, Allah, the Glorified. has said:

Then they hamstrung her, and turned (themselves) regretful. (Quraan, 26:157).

Then their land declined by sinking (into the earth) as the spike of a plough pierces unploughed weak land. O people, he who treads the clear path (of guidance) reaches the spring of water, and whoever abandons it strays into waterless desert.

SERMONS 201

On the Occasion of the Burial of Sayyidat an-Nisaa Fatima (p.b.u.h.) While addressing the Holy Prophet at His grave

O Prophet of Allah, peace be upon you from me and from your daughter who has come to you and who has hastened to meet you. O Prophet of Allah, my patience about your chosen (daughter) has been exhausted, and my power of endurance has weakened, except that I have ground for consolation in having endured the great hardship and heart-rending event of your separation. I laid you down in your grave when your last breath had passed (when your head was) between my neck and chest.

... Verily we are Allah's and verily unto Him shall we return. (Quraan 2:156)

Now. the trust has been returned and what had been given has been taken back. As to my grief, it knows no bounds, and as to my nights. they will remain sleepless till Allah chooses for me the house in which you are now residing.

---

the She-camel as a trial for them; so watch them and be patient. And (thou O" Saalih!) make them aware (beforehand) that the water is (to be) divided between them; and every drinking share shall be witnessed (on it)" But they called their companions, then he pursued (her) and hamstrung (her). How (great) was My chastisement and My warning? Verily sent We upon them a single (violent) blast, and they were (all) like the dry stubble used by a fencer in a fence. (Quraan, 54:23-31).

Certainly, your daughter would apprise you of the joining together of your[1] Omma (people) for oppressing her. You ask her in detail and get all the news about the position. This has happened when a long time had not elapsed and your remembrance had not disappeared. My salam (salutation) be on you both, the salam of a grief stricken not a disgusted or hateful person; for if I go away it is not because I am weary (of you), and if I stay it is not due to lack of belief in what Allah has promised the endurers.

SERMONS 202

Transience of this World, and importance of Collecting Provisions for the Next World

O people, certainly this world is a passage while the next world is a place of permanent abode. So, take from the passage (all that you can) for the permanent abode. Do not tear away your curtain before Him Who is aware of your secrets. Take away from this world your hearts before your bodies go out of it, because herein you have been put on trial, and you have been created for the other world. When a man dies people ask what

---

-1-The treatment meted out to the daughter of the Prophet after his death was extremely painful and sad. Although Sayyidat an-Nisaa Fatima (p.b.u.h.) did not live in this world more than a few months after the death of the Prophet yet even this short period has a long tale of grief and woe (about her). In this connection, the first scene that strikes the eyes is that arrangements for the funeral rites of the Prophet had not yet been made when the contest for power started in the Saqeefa of Bani-Saaida. Naturally, their leaving the body of the Prophet (without burial) must have injured Sayyidat an-Nisaa" Fatima's grief-stricken heart when she saw that those who had claimed love and attachment (with the Prophet) during his life became so engrossed in their machinations for power that instead of consoling his only daughter they did not even know when the Prophet was given a funeral ablution and when he was buried, and the way they condoled her was that they crowded at her house with material to set fire to it and tried to secure allegiance by force with all the display of oppression, compulsion and violence. All these excesses were with a view to so obliterate the prestigious position of this house that it might not regain its lost prestige on any occasion. With this aim in view, in order to crush her economic position, her claim for (the estate of) Fadak was turned down by dubbing it as false, the effect of which was that Sayyidat an-Nisaa" Fatima (p.b.u.h.) made the dying will that none of them should attend her funeral.

(property) he has left while the angels ask what (good actions) he has sent forward. May Allah bless you; send forward something, it will be a loan for you, and do not leave everything behind, for that would be a burden on you.

SERMONS 203

Warning his Companions about the dangers of the Day of Judgement

May Allah have mercy on you! Provide yourselves for the journey because the call for departure has been announced. Regard your stay in the world as very short, and return (to Allah) with the best provision that is with you, because surely, in front of you lies a valley, difficult to climb, and places of stay full of fear and dangers. You have to reach there and stay in them. And know that the eyes of death are approaching towards you. It is as though you are (already) in its talons and it has struck itself against you. Difficult affairs and distressing dangers have crushed you into it. You should therefore cut away all the attachments of this world and assist yourselves with the provision of Allah's fear.

Sayyid Razi says: A part of this saying has been quoted before through another narration.

SERMONS 204

In reply to Talha and az-Zobayr's Complainment for not consulting them in the affairs (of state)

Both of you frown over a small matter and leave aside big ones. Can you tell me of anything wherein you have a right of which I have deprived you or a share which was due to you and which I have held away from you, or any Moslim who has laid any claim before me and I have been unable to decide it or been ignorant of it, or committed a mistake about it?

By Allah, I had no liking for the caliphate nor any interest in government, but you yourselves invited me to it and prepared me for it. When the caliphate came to me, I kept the Book of Allah in my view and all that Allah had put therein for us, and all that according to which He has commanded us to take decisions; and I followed it, and also acted on whatever the Prophet — may Allah bless him and his descendants — had laid down as his Sonna. In this matter I did not need your advice or the advice of anyone else, nor has there been any order of which I was ignorant so that I ought to have consulted you or my Moslim brethren. If it were so I would not have turned away from you or from others.

As regards your reference to the question of equality (in distribution of shares from the Moslim common fund), this is a matter in which I have not taken a decision by my own opinion, nor have I done it by my caprice. But I found, and you too (must have) found, that whatever the Prophet — may Allah bless him and his descendants — brought had been finalised. Therefore, I felt no need to turn towards you about a share which had been determined by Allah and in which His verdict has been passed. By Allah, in this matter, therefore, you two or anyone else can have no favour from me. May Allah keep our hearts and your hearts in righteousness, and may He grant us and you endurance.

May Allah have mercy on the person who, when he sees the truth, supports it, when he sees the wrong, rejects it, and who helps the truth against him who is on the wrong.

SERMONS 205

On hearings some of his men abusing the Syrians during the Battle of Siffeen

I dislike you starting to abuse them, but if you describe their deeds and recount their situations that would be a better mode of speaking and a more convincing way of arguing. Instead of abusing them you should say "O Allah! save our blood and their blood, produce reconciliation between us and them, and lead them out of their misguidance so that he who is ignorant of the truth may know it, and he who inclines towards rebellion and revolt may turn away from it

SERMONS 206

On Imam Hasan when he saw him proceeding rapidly to fight in the Battle of Siffeen

Hold back this young man on my behalf, lest he causes my ruin, because I am loath to send these two (meaning al-Hasan and al-Hosayn) towards death, lest the descending line of the Prophet — may Allah bless him and his descendants — is cut away by their death.

Sayyid Razi says: Ameer al-Momineen's words "amliku anni hazal-ghulam" (i.e. "Hold back this young man on my behalf) represents the highest and the most eloquent form of expression.

SERMONS 207

When his army was on the verge of Mutiny in connection with Arbitration,[1]

-1- When the surviving forces of the Syrians lost ground and were ready to run away from the field Moaawiya changed the whole phase of the battle by using the Quraan as his instrument of strategy, and succeeded in creating such a division among the Iraqis that, despite Ameer al-Momineen's efforts at counselling, they were not prepared to take any forward step, but insisted on stopping the war, whereupon Ameer al-Momineen too had to agree to arbitration. Among these people some had actually been duped and believed that they were being asked to abide by the Quraan but there were others who had become weary of the long period of war and had lost courage. Then people got a good opportunity to stop the war, and so they cried hoarse for its postponement. There were others who had accompanied Ameer al-Momineen because of his temporal authority but did not support him by heart, nor did they aim at victory for him. There were some people who had expectations with Moaawiya, and had started attaching hopes to him for this, while there were some who were, from the very beginning, in league with him. In these circumstances and with this type of the army it was really due to Ameer al-Momineen's political ability and competence of military control and administration that he carried the war up to this stage, and if Moaawiya had not adopted this trick there could have been no doubt in Ameer al-Momineen's victory because the military power of the Syrian forces had been exhausted and defeat was hovering over its head. In this connection, bn-Abil-Hadeed writes:

Malik al-Ashtar had reached Moaawiya and grabbed him by the neck. The entire might of the Syrians had been smashed. Only so much movement was discernible in them as

O people, matters between me and you went as I wished till war exhausted you. By Allah, it has overtaken some of you and left others, and has completely weakened your enemy. Till yesterday I was giving orders but today I am being given orders, and till yesterday I was dissuading people (from wrong acts) but today I am being dissuaded. You have now shown liking to live in this world, and it is not for me to bring you to what you dislike.

SERMONS 208

When he went to enquire about the Health of his Companion al-Alaa bn-Ziyad al-Haarithi and when he noticed the vastness of his house

What will you do with this vast house in this world, although you need this house more in the next world. If you want to take it to the next world you could entertain in it guests and be regardful of kinship and discharge all (your) obligations according to their accrual. In this way you will be able to take it to the next world.

Then al-Ala" said to him: O Ameer al-Momineen, I want to complain to you about my brother Aasim bn-Ziyad. Ameer al-Momineen enquired:

What is the matter with him?

al-Ala" said: He has put on a woollen coat and cut himself away from the world. Ameer al-Momineen said:

Present him to me.

When he came, Ameer al-Momineen said:

O enemy of yourself. Certainly, the evil (Satan) has misguided you. Do you feel no pity for your wife and your children? Do you believe that if you use those things which Allah has made lawful for you, He will dislike you? You are too unimportant for Allah to do so.

---

remains in the tail of a lizard which is killed, but the tail continues hopping right and left. (Sharh Nahjol-Balagha, vol.11, pp.30-31)

He said: O Ameer al-Momineen, you also put on coarse dress and eat rough food. Then he replied:

Woe be to you, I am not like you. Certainly, Allah, the Sublime, has made it obligatory on true leaders that they should maintain themselves at the level of low people so that the poor do not cry over their poverty.[1]

-1- From ancient days asceticism and the abandonment of worldly attachments has been regarded as a means of purification of the spirit and important for the character. Consequently, those who wished to lead a life of abstemiousness and meditation used to go out of the cities and towns to stay in forests and caves in the mountains and stay there concentrating on Allah according to their own conception. They would eat only if a casual traveller or the inhabitant of nearby dwellings gave them anything to eat, otherwise they remained contented with the fruits of wild trees and the water of the streams, and thus they passed their life. This way of worship commenced in a way that was forced by the oppression and hardships of rulers. Certain people left their houses and, in order to avoid their grip, hid themselves in some wilderness or cave in a mountain, engaging themselves in worship of and devotion to Allah. Later on, this forced asceticism acquired a voluntary form and people began to retire to caves and hollows of their own volition. Thus it became an accepted way that whoever aimed at spiritual development retired to some corner after severing himself from all worldly ties. This method remained in vogue for centuries and even now some traces of this way of worship are found among the Buddhists and the Christians.

The moderate views of Islam do not, however, accord with the monastic life, because for attaining spiritual development it does not advocate the abandonment of worldly enjoyments and successes, nor does it view with approbation that a Moslim should leave his house and fellow men and busy himself in formal worship, hiding in some corner. The conception of worship in Islam is not confined to a few particular rites, but it regards the earning of one's livelihood through lawful means, mutual sympathy and good behaviour, and co-operation and assistance also to be important constituents of worship. If an individual ignores worldly rights and obligations and does not fulfil his responsibility towards his wife and children, nor occupies himself in efforts to earn a livelihood, but all the time stays in meditation, he ruins his life and does not fulfil the purpose of living. If this were Allah's aim, what would have the need for creating and populating the world when there was already a category of creatures who were all the time engaged in worshipping and adoration.

Nature has made man to stand on the cross-roads at which the midway is the centre of guidance. If he deviates from this point of moderateness even a bit, this way or that way, there is shear misguidance for him. That midway is that he should neither bend towards this world to such an extent as to ignore the next life, devoting himself entirely to this one, nor should he abstain from this world so as not to have any connection with anything of it, confining himself to some corner leaving everything else. Since Allah has created man in this world he should follow the code of life for living in this world, and should partake of the comforts and pleasures bestowed by Allah within moderate limits. The eating and using of things made lawful by Allah is not against Allah's worship, but rather Allah has created these things for the very purpose that they should be taken advantage of. That is why those who were the chosen of Allah lived in this world with others and ate and drank like others. They did not feel the need to turn their faces away from the people of the world, and to adopt the wilderness or the caves of mountains as their abodes, or to live in distant spots. On the other hand they remembered Allah, remained disentangled from worldly affairs, and did not forget death despite the pleasures and comforts of life.

The life of asceticism sometimes produces such evils as ruin the next life also as well as this one, and such an individual proves to be the true picture of "the looser in this life as well as the next" When natural impulses are not satisfied in the lawful and legal way the mind turns into a centre of evil-ideas and becomes incapable of performing worship with peace and concentration; and sometimes passions so overcome the ascetic that breaking all moral fetters, he devotes himself completely to their satisfaction and consequently falls in an abyss of ruin for which it is impossible to extract himself. That is why religious law accords a greater position to the worship performed by a family man than that by a non-family man, because the former can exercise mental peace and concentration in the worship and rituals.

Individuals who put on the cloak of Sofism and make a loud show of their spiritual greatness are cut off from the path of Islam and are ignorant of its wide teachings. They have been misled by Satan and, relying on their self-formed conceptions, tread wrongful paths. Eventually their misguidance becomes so serious that they begin to regard their leaders as having attained such a level that their word is as the word of Allah and their act is as the act of Allah. Sometimes they regard themselves beyond all the bounds and limitations of religious law and consider every evil act to be lawful for them. This deviation from faith and irreligiousness is named Sofism (complete devotion to Allah). Its unlawful principles are called "at-tariqah" (ways of achieving communion with Allah) and the followers of this cult are known as Sofis. First of all Abo-Hashim al-Koofi and Shami adopted this nickname. He was of Omayyad descent and a fatalist (believing that man is bound to act as pre-ordained by Allah). The reason for giving him this name was that, in order to make a show of his asceticism and fear for Allah, he put on a woollen cloak. Later on this nickname became common and various grounds were put forth as the basis of this name. For example, one ground is that "Sofi" has three letters, 'sad, "waw" and "fa" 'sad" stands for 'sabr" (endurance) , 'sidq" (truthfulness) and 'safa" (purity of heart); "waw" stands for "wudd" (love) , "wird" (repeating Allah's name) and "wafa" (faithfulness to Allah) , and "fa" stands for "fard" (unity) , "faqr" (destitution) and "fana" (death or absorption in Allah's Self). The second view is that it has been derived from "as-Soffah, which was a platform near the Prophet's mosque which had a covering of date-palm leaves. Those who stayed there were called Ashaabos-Soffah (people of the platform). The third view is that the name of the progenitor of an Arab tribe was Soffah, and this tribe performed the duties of serving the pilgrims and the Kaba, and it is with

reference to their connection with this tribe that these people were called Sofis. This group is divided among various sects but the basic sects are seven only.
1) al-Wahdatiyya (unitarian): This sect believes in the oneness of all existence. Its belief is that everything of this world is Allah, so much so that they assign to even polluted things the same godly position. They liken Allah with the river and the waves rising in it, and argue that the waves which sometimes rise and sometimes fall have no separate existence other than the river, but their existence is exactly the existence of the river. Therefore, nothing can be separated from its own existence.
2) al-Ittihadiyya (the unitists): They believe that they have united with Allah and Allah has united with them. They liken Allah with fire and themselves with iron that lies in the fire and acquires its form and property.
3) al-Holooliyya (the formists): Their belief is that Allah takes the form of those who claim to know Him and the perfect ones, and their bodies are places of His stay. In this way, they are seemingly men but really Allah.
4) al-Wasiliyya (the combiners): This sect considers itself to have combined with Allah. Their belief is that the laws of the sharia are a means of development of human personality and character, and that when the human self combines with Allah it no more needs perfection or development. Consequently, for the "wasilin, worship and ritual become useless, because they hold that when truth and reality is achieved sharia remains of no avail. Therefore, they can do anything and they cannot be questioned.
5) az-Zarraqiyya (the revellers): This sect regards vocal and instrumental music as worship, and earns the pleasures of this world through a show of asceticism and begging from door to door. They are ever engaged in relating concocted stories of miraculous performances of their leaders to over-awe the common people.
6) al-Oshshaqiyya (the lovers): The theory of this sect is that apparency is the means to reality, meaning that carnal love is the means to achieve love of Allah. That is, in order to reach the stage of Allah's love it is necessary to have love with some human beauty. But the love which they regard as love for Allah is just the product of mental disorder through which the lover inclines to one individual with all his attention and his final aim is to have access to the beloved. This love can lead to the way of evil and vice, but it has no connection with the love of Allah.
A Persian couplet says:
The truth of the fact is that carnal love is like a jinn and a jinn cannot give you guidance.
7) at-Talqiniyya (the encounterers): According to this sect, the reading of religious sciences and books of scholarship is thoroughly unlawful. Rather, the position that is achieved by an hour of spiritual effort of the Sofis cannot be achieved by seventy years of reading books.
According to Shia Olamaa" all these sects are on the wrong path and out of the fold of Islam. In this connection, numerous sayings of the Imams are related. In this sermon also Ameer al-Momineen has regarded the severance of Asim bn Ziyad from this world as the mischief of Satan, and he forcefully dissuaded him from adopting that course. (For further study, see Sharh Nahjol-Balagha, al-Haj Mirza Habeebollah al-Khoi, vol.13, pp.132-417; vol.14, pp.2-22).

SERMONS 209

Causes of difference in the traditions and categories of the Relators of traditions

Someone[1] asked Ameer al-Momineen about concocted traditions and contradictory sayings of the prophet current among the people, whereupon he said:

Certainly what is current among the people is both right and wrong, true and false, repealing and repealed, general and particular, definite and indefinite, exact and surmised. Even during the Prophet's days false sayings had been attributed to him, so much so that he had to say during his sermon that "Whoever attributes falsehoods to me makes his abode in Hell." Those who relate traditions are of four categories,[2] no more.

-1- This was Solaym bn Qays al-Hilaali who was one of the relaters of traditions through Ameer al-Momineen.

2 In this sermon Ameer al-Momineen has divided the traditionists into four categories. The first category is that of a man concocts a tradition and attributes it to the Prophet. Traditions were in fact falsified and attributed to him, and this process continued, with the result that numerous novel traditions came into being. This is a fact which cannot be denied but if anyone does deny it his basis would be not knowledge or sagacity by oratory or argumentative necessity. Thus, once, Alam al-Hodaa (Ensign of Guidance) Sayyid al-Mortaza had a chance of meeting the Sonni "Olamaa" (scholars) in confrontation and on this occasion Sayyid al-Mortaza proved by historical facts that the traditions related about the merits of the great companions are concocted and counterfeit. On this, the (Sonni) "Olamaa" argued that it was impossible that someone should dare speak a lie against the Prophet and prepare a tradition himself and attribute it to him. Sayyid al-Mortaza said there is a tradition of the Prophet that:

A lot of false things will be attributed to me after my death and whoever speaks a lie against me would be preparing his abode in Hell. (al-Bokhaari, vol.1, p.38; vol.2, p.102; vol.4, p.207; vol.8, p.54; Moslim, vol.8, p.229; Abo-Dawood, vol.3, pp.319-320; at-Tirmizi, vol.4, p.524; vol.5, pp.35-36, 40, 199, 634; bn Maaja, vol.1, pp.13-15)

If you regard this tradition as true then you should agree that false things have been attributed to the Prophet, but if you regard it false, this would prove our point. However, these were people whose hearts were full of hypocrisy and who used to prepare traditions of their own accord in order to create mischief and dispersion in religion and to misguide Moslims of weak convictions. They remained mixed with them as they used to do during the lifetime of the Prophet; and just as they remained busy in activities of mischief and destruction in those days, in the same way, even after the Prophet, they were not unmindful of deforming the teachings of Islam and metamorphosing its features. Rather, in the days of the Prophet they were always afraid lest he unveiled them and put them to shame, but after the Prophet their hypocritical activities increased and they attributed false things to the Prophet without demur for their own personal ends, and those who heard them believed in them because of their status as companions of the Prophet, thinking that whatever they said was correct and whatever they gave out was true. Afterwards also, the belief that all the companions are correct put a stopper on their tongues, as a result of which they were taken to be above criticism, questioning, discussion and censure. Besides, their conspicuous performance had made them prominent in the eyes of the government, and also because of this it needed courage and daring to speak against them. This is proved by Ameer al-Momineen's words:

These people gained positions with the leaders of misguidance and callers towards Hell, through falsehood and slanderings. So, they put them in high posts and made them officers over the heads of the people.

Along with the destruction of Islam, the hypocrites also aimed at amassing wealth, and they were doing so freely by claiming to be Moslims, because of which they did not want to remove the veil of Islam (from their faces) and to come out openly, but they wanted to continue their Satanic activities under the garb of Islam and engaged themselves in its basic destruction and spreading of division and dispersal by concocting traditions. In this connection, bn-Abil-Hadeed has written:

When they were left free they too left many things. When people observed silence about them they also observed silence about Islam, but they continued their underground activities such as the fabrication of falsehoods to which Ameer al-Momineen has alluded, because a lot of untrue matters had been mixed with the traditions by the group of people of wrong beliefs, while some of them also aimed at extolling some particular party with whom they had other worldly aims as well.

On the expiry of this period, when Moaawiya took over the leadership of religion and occupied the throne of temporal authority, he opened an official department for the fabrication of false traditions, and ordered his officers to fabricate and popularise traditions in disparagement of the Ahlil-Bayt (the Household of the Holy Prophet) and in extolment of Othmaan and the Omayyads, and announced rewards and grants of land for this work. Consequently, a lot of traditions about self-made distinctions gained entry in the books of traditions. Thus, Abol-Hasan al-Madaini has written in his book al-Ahdath and bn-Abil-Hadeed has quoted it, namely:

Moaawiya wrote to his officers that they should take special care of those who were adherents of Othmaan, his well-wishers and lovers and to award high positions, precedence and honour to those who related traditions about his merits and distinctions, and to convey to him whatever is so related by any person, along with his name, the name of his father and the name of his tribe. They did accordingly and heaped up traditions about the merits and distinctions of Othmaan because Moaawiya used to award them rewards, clothes, grants and lands.

When the fabricated traditions about the merits of Othmaan had been spread throughout the realm, with the idea that the position of the earlier Caliphs should not remain low, Moaawiya wrote to his officers:

As soon as you receive this order of mine you should call upon the people to prepare traditions about the distinctions of the companions and other caliphs also, and take care that if any Moslim relates any tradition about Abo-Toraab (Ali) you should prepare a similar tradition about the companions to contradict it because this gives me great pleasure and cools my eyes, and it weakens the position of Abo-Toraab and his partymen. and is more severe to them than the merits and distinctions of Othmaan.

When his letters were read to the people, a large number of such traditions were related extolling the companions that are all fabricated with no truth at all. (Sharh Nahjol-Balagha, vol.11, pp.43-47)

In this connection Abo-Abdillah Ibraheem bn Mohammad bn Arafa known as Niftawayh (244/858-323/935) who was one of the prominent scholars and traditionists has written, and bn-Abil-Hadeed has quoted him, that:

Most of the false traditions about the merits of the companions were fabricated during the days of Moaawiya in order to gain position in his audience because his view was that in this way he could disgrace Bani-Hashim and render them low. (ibid.)

After that, fabrication of traditions became a habit, the world seekers made it a means of securing position with kings and nobles and to amass wealth. For example, Ghiyath bn Ibraheem an-Nakhaai (2nd cent. A.H.) fabricated a tradition about the flight of pigeons, in order to please al-Mahdi bn Mansoor (the Abbasid Caliph) and to secure position near him. (Taareekh Baghdad, vol.12, pp.323-327; Mizan al-itidal, vol.3) pp.337-338; Lisaan al-Mizan, vol.4, p.422). Abo-Saeed al-Madaini and others made it a means of livelihood. The limit was reached when the al-Karramiyya and some of the al-Motasawwifa gave the ruling that the fabrication of traditions for the prevention of sin or for persuasion towards obedience was lawful. Consequently, in connection with persuading and dissuading, traditions were fabricated quite freely, and this was not regarded against the religious law or morality. Rather, this work was generally done by those who bore the appearance of asceticism or fear of Allah and who passed their nights in praying and days in filling their registers with false traditions. An idea about the number of these fabricated traditions can be had from the fact that out of six hundred thousand traditions al-Bokhaari selected only two thousand seven hundred and sixty-one traditions, (Taareekh Baghdad, vol.2, p.8; al-Irshaad as-sari, vol.1, p.28; Sifatos-Safwa, vol.4, p.143). Moslim thought fit for selection only four thousand out of three hundred thousand (Taareekh Baghdad, vol.13, p.101; al-Montazam, vol.5, p.32; Tabaqaat al-Hoffaz, vol.2, pp.151, 157; Wafayat al-Ayan, vol.5, p.194). Abo-Dawood took four thousand and eight hundred out of five hundred thousand (Taareekh Baghdad, vol.9, p.57; Tabaqaat al-Hoffaz, vol.2, p.154; al-Montazam, vol.5, p.97; Wafayat al-Ayan, vol.2, p.404) , and Ahmad bn Hambal took thirty thousand out of nearly on million traditions (Taareekh Baghdad, vol.4, p.419-420; Tabaqaat al-Hoffaz, vol.2, p.17; Wafayat al-Ayan, vol.1, p.64; Tahzeeb at-Tahzeeb, vol.1, p.74). But when this selection is studied some traditions which come across can, in no circumstances, be attributed to the Prophet. The result is that a group of considerable number has cropped up among Moslims who, in view of these (so-called) authoritative collections and true traditions, completely reject the evidentiary value of the traditions, (For further reference see al-Ghadeer, vol.5, pp.208-378).

The second category of relaters of traditions are those who, without appreciating the occasion or context, related whatever they could recollect, right or wrong. Thus, in al-Bokhaari (vol.2, pp.100-102; vol.5, p.98); Moslim (vol.3, pp.41-45); at-Tirmizi (vol.3, pp.327-329); an-Nasaaee (vol.4, p.18); bn Maaja (vol.1, pp.508-509); Malik bn Anas (al-Mowatta" vol.1, p.234); ash-Shaafii (Ikhtilaafil-Hadeeth, on the side lines of "al-Om, vol.7, p.266); Abo-Dawood (vol.3, p.194); Ahmad bn Hambal (vol.1, pp.41, 42) and al-Bayhaqi (vol.4, pp.72-74) in the chapter entitled "weeping over the dead" it is stated that when Caliph Omar was wounded Sohayb came weeping to him, then Omar said:

O" Sohayb, you weep over me, while the Prophet had said that the dead person is punished if his people weep over him.

When after the death of Caliph Omar this was mentioned to Aysha, she said "May Allah have mercy on Omar. The Messenger of Allah did not say that weeping of relations causes punishment on the dead. but he said that the punishment of an unbeliever increases if his people weep over him" After this Aysha said that according to the Holy Quraan no person has to bear the burden of another, so how could the burden of those who weep be put on the dead. After this the following verse was quoted by Aysha:

...And no bearer of burden shall bear the burden of another; (Quraan, 6:164; 17:15; 35:18; 39:7; 53:38).

The wife of the Holy Prophet Aysha relates that once the Prophet passed by a Jewish woman over whom her people were weeping. The Prophet then remarked, "Her people are weeping over her but she is undergoing punishment in the grave

The third category of the relaters of traditions is of those who heard some repealed traditions from the Prophet but could not get any chance to hear the repealing traditions which he could relate to others. An example of a repealing tradition is the saying of the Prophet which also contains a reference to the repealed tradition, namely: "I had disallowed you to visit graves, but now you can visit them" (Moslim, vol.3, p.65; at-Tirmizi, vol.3, p.370; Abo-Dawood, vol.3, pp.218, 332; an-Nasaaee, vol.4, p.89; bn Maaja, vol.1, pp.500-501; Malik bn Anas, vol.2, p.485; Ahmad bn Hambal, vol.1, pp.145, 452; vol.3, pp.38, 63, 66, 237, 350; vol.5, pp.350, 355, 356, 357, 359, 361; al-Hakim, al-Mostadrak, vol.1, pp.374-376; and al-Bayhaqi, vol.4, pp.76-77). Herein the permission to visit graves has repealed the previous restriction on it. Now, those who heard only the repealed tradition continued acting according to it.

The fourth category of relaters of traditions is of those who were fully aware of the principles of justice, possessed intelligence and sagacity, knew the occasion when a tradition was first uttered (by the Prophet) and were also acquainted with the repealing and the repealed traditions, the particular and the general, and the timely and the absolute. They avoided falsehood and fabrication. Whatever they heard remained preserved in their memory, and they conveyed it with exactness to others. It is they whose traditions are the precious possession of Islam, free from fraud and counterfeit and worthy of being trusted and acted upon. That collection of traditions which has been

1st: Lying Hypocrites

The hypocrite is a person who makes a show of faith and adopts the appearance of a Moslim; he does not hesitate in sinning nor does he keep aloof from vice; he wilfully attributes false things against the Messenger of Allah — may Allah bless him and his descendants. If people knew that he was a hypocrite and a liar, they would not accept anything from him and would not confirm what he says.

Rather they say that he is the companion of the Prophet, has met him, heard (his sayings) from him and acquired (knowledge) from him. They therefore accept what he says. Allah too had warned you well about the hypocrites and described them fully to you. They have continued after the Holy Prophet. They gained positions with the leaders of misguidance and callers towards Hell through falsehoods and slanderings. So, they put them in high posts and made them officers over the heads of the people,

---

conveyed through trustworthy bosoms like that of Ameer al-Momineen and has remained free from cutting, curtailing, alteration or change particularly present Islam in its true form. The position of Ameer al-Momineen in Islamic knowledge has been most certainly proved through the following traditions narrated from the Holy Prophet such as:

Ameer al-Momineen, Jabir bn Abdillah, bn Abbas and Abdillah bn Omar have narrated from the Holy Prophet that he said:

I am the city of knowledge and Ali is its door. He who wants to acquire (my) knowledge should come through its door. (al-Mostadrak, vol.3, pp.126-127; al-Isteeaab, vol.3, p.1102; Osdol-Ghaaba, vol.4, p.22; Taareekh Baghdad, vol.2, p.377; vol.4, p.348; vol.7, p.172; vol.11, pp.48-50; Tazkirat al-Hoffaz; vol.4, p.28; Majma az-Zawaaid, vol.9, p.114; Tahzeeb at-Tahzeeb, vol.6, p.320; vol.7, p.337; Lisaan al-Mizan, vol.2, pp.122-123; Taareekh al-Kholafaa, p.170; Kanz al-Ommaal, vol.6, pp.152, 156, 401; Omdatol-Qaari, vol.7, p.631; Sharh al-Mawaahib al-Ladonniyya, vol.3, p.143).

Ameer al-Momineen and bn Abbas have also narrated from the Holy Prophet that:

I am the store-house of wisdom and Ali is its door. He who wants to acquire wisdom should come through its door. (Hilyatol-Awliyaa, vol.1, p.64; Masabeeh as-Sonna, vol.2, p.275; Taareekh Baghdad, vol.11, p.204; Kanz al-Ommaal, vol.6, p.401; ar-Riyaaz an-Nazira, vol.2, p.193).

If only people could take the Prophet's blessings through these sources of knowledge. But it is a tragic chapter of history that although traditions are accepted through the Kharijites and enemies of the Prophet's family, whenever the series of relaters includes the name of any individual from among the Prophet's family there is hesitation in accepting the tradition.

and amassed wealth through them. People are always with the rulers and after this world, except those to whom Allah affords protection. This is the first of the four categories.

2nd: The Mistaken

Then there is the individual who heard (a saying) from the Holy Prophet but did not memorise it as it was, but surmised it. He does not lie wilfully. Now, he carries the saying with him and relates it, acts upon it and claims that: "I heard it from the Messenger of Allah." If the Moslims come to know that he has committed a mistake in it, they will not accept it from him, and if he himself knows that he is on the wrong he will give it up.

3rd: The Ignorant

The third man is he who heard the Prophet ordering to do a thing and later the Prophet refrained the people from doing it, but this man did not know it, or he heard the Prophet refraining people from a thing and later he allowed it, but this man did not know it. In this way he retained in his mind what had been repealed, and did not retain the repealing tradition. If he knew that it had been repealed he would reject it, or if the Moslims knew, when they heard it from him, that it had been repealed they would reject it.

4th: The Truthful

The last, namely the fourth man, is he who does not speak a lie against Allah or against His Prophet. He hates falsehood out of fear for Allah and respect for the Messenger of Allah, and does not commit mistakes, but retains (in his mind) exactly what he heard (from the Prophet), and he relates it as he heard it without adding anything or omitting anything. He heard the repealing tradition, he retained it and acted upon it, and he heard the repealed tradition and rejected it. He also understands the particular and the general, and he knows the definite and indefinite, and gives everything its due position.

The sayings of the Prophet used to be of two types. One was particular and the other common. Sometimes a man would hear him but he would not know what Allah, the Glorified, meant by it or what the Messenger of

Allah meant by it. In this way the listener carries it and memorises it without knowing its meaning and its real intention, or what was its reason. Among the companions of the Messenger of Allah all were not in the habit of putting him questions and ask him the meanings, indeed they always wished that some Bedouin or stranger might come and ask him (peace be upon him) so that they would also listen. Whenever any such thing came before me, I asked him about its meaning and preserved it. These are the reasons and grounds of differences among the people in their traditions.

SERMONS 210

Greatness of Universe Creation

It is through the strength of Allah's greatness and His subtle power of innovation that He made solid dry earth out of the water of the fathomless, compact and dashing ocean. Then He made from it layers and separated them into seven skies after they had been joined together. So, they became stationary at His command and stopped at the limit fixed by Him. He so made the earth that it is born by deep blue, surrounded and suspended water which is obedient to His command and has submitted to His awe while its flow has stopped due to fear of Him.

He also created high hills, rocks of stones and lofty mountains. He put them in their positions and made them remain stationary. Their peaks rose into the air while their roots remained in the water. In this way He raised the mountains above the plains and fixed their foundations in the vast expanse wherever they stood. He made their peaks high and made their bodies lofty. He made them like pillars for the earth and fixed them in it like pegs. Consequently, the earth became stationary; otherwise it might bend with its inhabitants or sink inwards with its burden, or shift from its positions.

Therefore, glorified is He who stopped it after the flowing of its waters and solidified it after the watery state of its sides. In this way He made it a cradle for His creatures and spread it for them in the form of a floor over the deep ocean which is stationary and does not move and is fixed and does not flow. Severe winds move it here and there and clouds draw up water from it.

Verily in this there is a lesson unto him who feareth (Allah) (Quraan, 79:26)

SERMONS 211

Those who give up supporting right

O my Allah! whoever listens to our utterance which is just and which seeks the prosperity of religion and the worldly life and does not seek mischief, but rejects it after listening, then he certainly turns away from Thy support and desists from strengthening Thy religion. We make Thee a witness over him and Thou art the greatest of all witnesses, and we make all those who inhabit Thy earth and Thy skies witness over him. Thereafter, Thou alone can make us needless of his support and question him for his sin.

SERMONS 212

Sublimity of Allah and Eulogy of the Prophet

Praise be to Allah who is above all similarity to the creatures, is above the words of describers, who displays the wonders of His management for the on-lookers, is hidden from the imagination of thinkers by virtue of the greatness of His glory, has knowledge without acquiring it, adding to it or drawing it (from someone), and Who is the ordainer of all matters without reflecting or thinking. He is such that gloom does not concern Him, nor does He seek light from brightness, night does not overtake Him nor does the day pass over Him (so as to affect Him in any manner). His comprehension (of things) is not through eyes and His knowledge is not dependent on being informed.

Allah deputised the Prophet with light, and accorded him the highest precedence in selection. Through him Allah united those who were divided, overpowered the powerful, overcame difficulties and levelled rugged ground, and thus removed misguidance from right and left.

SERMONS 213

Prophet's Nobility of Descent

I stand witness that He is just and does justice, He is the arbiter Who decides (between right and wrong). I also stand witness that Mohammad is His slave. His Messenger and the Chief of His creatures. Whenever Allah divided the line of descent, He put him in the better one, and therefore, no evil-doer ever shared with him nor was any vicious person his partner. Beware! surely Allah, the Glorified, has provided for virtue those who are suited to it, for truth pillars (that support it), and for obedience protection (against deviation). In every matter of obedience you will find Allah, the Glorified's succour that will speak through tongues and accord firmness to hearts. It has sufficiency for those who seek sufficiency, and a cure for those who seek cure.

The characteristics of the virtuous whose guidance must be followed

Know that, certainly, those creatures of Allah who preserve His knowledge offer protection to those things which He desires to be protected and make His springs flow (for the benefit of others). They contact each other with friendliness and meet each other with affection. They drink water from cups that quench the thirst and return from the watering places fully satiated. Misgiving does not affect them and backbiting does not gain ground with them. In this way Allah has tied their nature with good manners. Because of this they love each other and meet each other. They have become superior, like seeds which are selected by taking some and throwing away others. This selection has distinguished them and the process of choosing has purified them.

Therefore, man should secure honour by adopting these qualities. He should fear the day of Doom before it arrives, and he should appreciate the shortness of his life and the shortness of his sojourn in the place of stay which has only to last for his change over to the next place. He should therefore do something for his change over and for the known stages of his departure. Blessed be he who possesses a virtuous heart, who obeys one who guides him, desists from him who takes to ruin, catches the path of safety with the help of him who provides him light (of guidance) and by obeying the leader who commands him, hastens towards guidance before its doors are closed, gets open the door of repentance and removes the (stain of) sins. He has certainly been put on the right path and guided towards the straight road.

SERMONS 214

Prayer He often Recited

Praise be to Allah! Who made me such that I have not died nor am I sick, nor have my veins been infected with disease, nor have I been hauled up for my evil acts, nor am I without progeny, nor have I forsaken my religion, nor do I disbelieve in my Lord, nor do I feel strangeness with my faith, nor is my intelligence affected, nor have I been punished with the punishment of peoples before me. I am a slave in Thy possession, I have been guilty of excesses over myself. Thou hast exhausted Thy pleas over me and I have no plea (before Thee). I have no power to take except what Thou givest me, and I cannot evade except what Thou savest me from.

O my Allah! I seek Thy protection from becoming destitute despite Thy riches, from being misguided despite Thy guidance, from being molested in Thy realm and from being humiliated while authority rests with Thee.

O my Allah! let my spirit be the first of those good objects that Thou takest from me and the first trust out of Thy favours held in trust with me.

O my Allah! we seek Thy protection from turning away from Thy command or revolting against Thy religion, or being led away by our desires instead of by guidance that comes from Thee.

SERMONS 215

Mutual Rights of the Ruler and the Ruled

Delivered at the battle of Siffeen

So now, Allah, the Glorified, has, by placing me over your affairs, created my right over you, and you too have a right over me like mine over you. A right is very vast in description but very narrow in equitability of action. It does not accrue to any person unless it accrues against him also, and right does not accrue against a person unless it also accrues in his favour. If there is any right which is only in favour of a person with no (corresponding) right accruing against him it is solely for Allah, the Glorified, and not for His creatures by virtue of His might over His creatures and by virtue of the justice permeating all His decrees. Of course, He the Glorified, has created His right over creatures that they should worship Him, and has laid upon Himself (the obligation of) their reward equal to several times the recompense as a mark of His bounty and the generosity that He is capable of.

Then, from His rights, He, the Glorified, created certain rights for certain people against others. He made them so as to equate with one another. Some of these rights produce other rights. Some rights are such that they do not accrue except with others. The greatest of these rights that Allah, the Glorified, has made obligatory is the right of the ruler over the ruled and the right of the ruled over the ruler. This is an obligation which Allah, the Glorified, has placed on each other. He has made it the basis of their (mutual) affection, and an honour for their religion. Consequently, the ruled cannot prosper unless the rulers are sound, while the rulers cannot be sound unless the ruled are steadfast.

If the ruled fulfil the rights of the ruler and the ruler fulfils their rights, then right attains the position of honour among them, the ways of religion become established, signs of justice become fixed and the Sonna gains currency.

In this way time will improve, the continuance of government will be expected, and the aims of the enemies will be frustrated. But if the ruled gain sway over the ruler, or the ruler oppresses the ruled, then difference crops up in every word, signs of oppression appear, mischief enters religion and the ways of the Sonna are forsaken. Then desires are acted upon, the commands (of religion) are discarded, diseases of the spirit become numerous and there is no hesitation in disregarding even great rights, nor in committing big wrongs. In such circumstances, the virtuous are humiliated while the vicious are honoured, and there are serious chastisements from Allah, the Glorified, onto the people.

You should therefore counsel each other (for the fulfillment of your obligations) and co-operate with each other. However extremely eager a person may be to secure the pleasure of Allah, and however fully he strives for it, he cannot discharge (his obligation for) obedience to Allah, the Glorified, as is really due to Him, and it is an obligatory right of Allah over the people that they should advise each other to the best of their ability and co-operate with each other for the establishment of truth among them. No person, however great his position in the matter of truth, and however advanced his distinction in religion may be, is above co-operation in connection with the obligations placed on him by Allah. Again, no man, however small he may be regarded by others, and however humble he may appear before eyes, is too low to co-operate or to be afforded co-operation in this matter.

One of Ameer al-Momineen's companions replied to him by a long speech wherein he praised him much and mentioned his own listening to him and obeying him, whereupon Ameer al-Momineen said:

If a man in his mind regards Allah's glory as being high and believes in his heart that Allah's position is sublime, then it is his right that on account of the greatness of these things he should regard all other things small. Among such persons he on whom Allah's bounty is great and Allah's favours are kind has a greater obligation, because Allah's bounty over any person does not increase without an increase in Allah's right over him.

In the view of virtuous people, the worst position of rulers is that it may be thought about them that they love glory, and their affairs may be taken to be based on pride. I would really hate that it may occur to your mind that I love high praises or to hear eulogies. By the grace of Allah I am not like this. Even If I had loved to be mentioned like this, I would have given it up in submissiveness before Allah, the Glorified, rather than accept greatness and sublimity to which He is more entitled. Generally, people feel pleased at praise after good performances; but do not mention for me handsome praise for the obligations I have discharged towards Allah and towards you, because of (my) fear about those obligations which I have not discharged and for issuing injunctions which could not be avoided, and do not address me in the manner despots are addressed.

Do not evade me as the people of passion are (to be) evaded, do not meet me with flattery and do not think that I shall take it ill if a true thing is said to me, because the person who feels disgusted when truth is said to him or a just matter is placed before him would find it more difficult to act upon them. Therefore, do not abstain from saying a truth or pointing out a matter of justice because I do not regard myself above erring.[1] I do not

-1- That the innocence of angels is different from the innocence of man needs no detailed discussion. The innocence of angels means that they do not possess the impulse to sin, but the innocence of man means that, although he has human frailties and passions, yet he possesses a peculiar power to resist them and he is not over-powered by them so as to commit sins. This very ability is called innocence and it prevents the rising up of personal passions and impulses. Ameer al-Momineen's saying that "I do not regard myself above erring" refers to those human dictates and passions, and his saying that "Allah helps me in avoiding "errors" refers to innocence. The same tone is found in the Quraan in the words of Prophet Yoosof that:

I exculpate not myself, verily (one's) self is wont to bid (him to) evil, except such as my Lord hath had mercy on; verily my Lord is Oft-forgiving, All-merciful. (12:53)

Just as in this verse, because of the existence of exception, its first part cannot be used to argue against his innocence, similarly, due to the existence of the exception "but that Allah helps me in avoiding errors" in Ameer al-Momineen's saying, its first part cannot be used to argue against his innocence, otherwise the Prophet's innocence too will have to be rejected. In the same way, the last sentence of this sermon should not be taken to mean that before the proclamation of Prophethood he had been under the influence of pre-Islamic beliefs, and that just as others had been unbelievers he too might have been

escape erring in my actions but that Allah helps me (in avoiding errors) in matters in which He is more powerful than I. Certainly, I and you are slaves owned by Allah, other than Whom there is no Lord except Him. He owns our selves which we do not own. He took us from where we were towards what means prosperity to us. He altered our straying into guidance and gave us intelligence after blindness.

SERMONS 216

Excesses of the Quraysh

O my Allah! I beseech Thee to take revenge on the Quraysh and those who are assisting them, for they have cut asunder my kinship and over-turned my cup and have joined together to contest a right to which I was entitled more than anyone else. They said to me: "If you get your right, that will be just, but if you are denied the right, that too will be just. Endure it with sadness or kill yourself in grief." I looked around but found no one to shield me, protect me or help me except the members of my family. I refrained from flinging them into death and therefore closed my eyes despite the dust, kept swallowing saliva despite (the suffocation of) grief and endured pangs of anger although it was more bitter than colocynth and more grievous than the bite of knives.

---

in darkness and misguidance, because from his very birth Ameer al-Momineen was brought-up by the Prophet and the effect of his training and up-bringing permeated him. It cannot therefore be imagined that he who had from infancy trod in the foot-prints of the Prophet would deviate from guidance even for a moment. Thus, al-Masoodi has written:

Ameer al-Momineen never believed in any other god than Allah so that there could be the question of his accepting Islam. He rather followed the Prophet in all his actions and (virtually) initiated him, and in this very state he attained majority. (Morooj az-Zahab, vol.2, p.3).

Here, by those whom Allah led from darkness into guidance, the reference is to the persons whom Ameer al-Momineen was addressing. bn-Abil-Hadeed writes in this connection:

The reference here is not to his own self because he had never been an unbeliever so as to have accepted Islam after that, but in these words he is referring to those group of people whom he was addressing. (Sharh Nahjol-Balagha, vol.11, p.108)

Sayyid Razi says: This utterance of Ameer al-Momineen has already appeared in an earlier Sermon (171), but I have repeated it here because of the difference of versions.

Those who went to Basra to fight him

They marched on my officers and the custodians of the public treasury which is still under my control and on the people of a metropolis, all of whom were obedient to me and were in allegiance to me. They created division among them, instigated their party against me and attacked my followers. They killed a group of them by treachery, while another group took up swords against them and fought with the swords till they met Allah as adherents to truth.

SERMONS 217

On passing by the corpses of Talha bn-Obaydillah and Abdr-Rahmaan bn-Attab bn-Asad who were both killed in the Battle of Jamal

Abo-Mohammad (Talha) lies here away from his own place. By Allah, I did not like that the Quraysh should lie killed under the stars. I have avenged myself with the descendants of Abd Manaf, but the chief persons of Bani-Jonaah[1] have escaped me. They had stretched their necks towards a matter for which they were not suited, and therefore their necks were broken before they reached the goal.

SERMONS 218

Qualities of the God-Fearing and the Pious

He (the believer) kept his mind alive and killed (the desires of) his heart till his body became thin, his bulk turned light and an effulgence of extreme

-1- In the battle of Jamal a group of Bani-Jomah was with Aysha, but the chief men of this group fled away from the battle-field. Some of them were: Abdillah at-Taweel bn Safwan, Yahya bn Hakim, Amir bn-Masood and Ayyoob bn Habeeb. From this group (Bani-Jomah) only two persons were killed.

brightness shone for him. It lighted the way for him and took him on the (right) path. Different doors led him to the door of safety and the place of (his permanent) stay. His feet, balancing his body became fixed in the position of safety and comfort, because he kept his heart (in good acts) and pleased his Allah.

SERMONS 219

Engage (your) vying in exuberance, until ye come to the graves. (Quraan, 102:1-2)[1]

After reciting this Quraanic verse, Ameer al-Momineen said:

How distant (from achievement) is their aim, how neglectful are these visitors and how difficult is the affair. They have not taken lessons from things which are full of lessons, but they took them from far off places. Do they boast on the dead bodies of their fore-fathers, or do they regard the number of dead persons as a ground for feeling boastful of their number? They want to revive the bodies that have become spiritless and the movements that have ceased. They are more entitled to be a source of lesson than a source of pride. They are more suitable for being a source of humility than of honour.

They looked at them with weak-sighted eyes and descended into the hollow of ignorance. If they had asked about them from the dilapidated houses and empty courtyards, they would have said that they went into the earth in the state of misguidance and you too are heading ignorantly towards them. You trample their skulls, want to raise constructions on their corpses, you graze what they have left and live in houses which they

---

-1- The genesis of the descending of this verse is that the tribes of Bani-Abd Manaf and Bani-Sahm began to boast against each other over the abundance of their wealth and the number of their tribesmen, and in order to prove they had a greater number each one began to include their dead as well, whereupon this verse was revealed to the effect that abundance of riches and majority in numbers has made you so forgetful that you count the dead also with the living. This verse is also taken to mean that abundance of riches and progeny has made you forgetful till you reached the graves, but the utterance of Ameer al-Momineen supports the first meaning.

have vacated. The days (that lie) between them and you are also bemoaning you and reciting elegies over you.

They are your fore-runners in reaching the goal and have arrived at the watering places before you. They had positions of honour and plenty of pride. They were rulers and holders of positions. Now they have gone into the interstice where earth covers them from above and is eating their flesh and drinking their blood. They lie in the hollows of their graves lifeless, no more growing, and hidden, not to be found. The approach of dangers does not frighten them, and the adversity of circumstances does not grieve them. They do not mind earthquakes, nor do they pay heed to thunders. They are gone and not expected back. They are existent but unseen. They were united but are now dispersed. They were friendly and are now separated.

Their accounts are unknown and their houses are silent, not because of length of time or distance of place, but because they have been made to drink the cup (of death) which has changed their speech into dumbness, their hearing into deafness and their movements into stillness. It seems as though they are fallen in slumber. They are neighbours not feeling affection for each other, or friends who do not meet each other. The bonds of their knowing each other have been worn out and the connections of their friendship have been cut asunder. Everyone of them is therefore alone although they are a group, and they are strangers, even though friends. They are unaware of morning after a night and of evening after a day. The night or the day when they departed has become ever existent for them.[1] They found the dangers of their placed of stay more serious than they had apprehended, and they witnessed that its signs were greater than they had guessed. The two objectives (namely paradise

---

-1- This means that for him he who dies in the day it is always day whereas for him who dies in the night the darkness of night never dispels, because they are at a place where there is no turning of the moon and the sun and no rotation of the nights and the days. The same meaning has been expressed by a poet like this:
There is sure to be a day without a night,
Or a night that would come without a day.

and hell) have been stretched for them upto a point beyond the reach of fear or hope. Had they been able to speak they would have become dumb to describe what they witnessed or saw.

Even though their traces have been wiped out and their news has stopped (circulating), eyes are capable of drawing a lesson, as they looked at them, ears of intelligence heard them and they spoke without uttering words. So, they said that handsome faces have been destroyed and delicate bodies have been smeared with earth. We have put on a worn-out shroud. The narrowness of the grave has overwhelmed us and strangeness has spread among us. Our silent abodes have been ruined. The beauty of our bodies has disappeared. Our known features have become hateful. Our stay in the places of strangeness has become long. We do not get relief from pain, nor widening from narrowness.

Now. if you portray them in your mind, or if the curtains concealing them are removed from them for you, in this state when their ears have lost their power and turned deaf, their eyes have been filled with dust and sunk down, their tongues which were very active have been cut into pieces, their hearts which were ever wakeful have become motionless in their chests, in every limb of theirs a peculiar decay has occurred which has deformed it, and has paved the way for calamity towards it, all these lie powerless, with no hand to help them and no heart to grieve over them, (then) you would certainly notice the grief of (their) hearts and the dirt of (their) eyes.

Every trouble of theirs is such that its position does not change and the distress does not clear away. How many a prestigious body and amazing beauty the earth has swallowed, although when in the world he enjoyed abundant pleasures and was nurtured in honour. He clung to enjoyments (even) in the hour of grief. If distress befell him he sought refuge in consolation (derived) through the pleasures of life and playing and games. He was laughing at the world while the world was laughing at him because of his life full of forgetfulness. Then time trampled him like thorns, the days weakened his energy and death began to look at him from near. Then he was overtaken by a grief which he had never felt, and ailments appeared in place of the health he had previously possessed.

He then turned to that with which the physician had made him familiar, namely suppressing the hot (diseases) with cold (medicines) and curing the cold with hot doses, but the cold things did nothing save aggravate the hot ailments, while the hot ones did nothing except increasing the coldness, nor did he acquire temperateness in his constitution but rather every ailment of his increased till his physicians became helpless, his attendants grew loathsome and his own people felt disgusted from describing his disease, avoided answering those who enquired about him and quarrelled in front of him about the serious news which they were concealing from him. Thus, someone would say "his condition is what it is" and would console them with hopes of his recovery, while another one would advocate patience on missing him, recalling to them the calamities that had befallen the earlier generations.

In this state when he was getting ready to depart from the world and leave his beloved ones, such a serious choking overtook him that his senses became bewildered and the dampness of his tongue dried up. Now, there was many an important question whose reply he knew about he could not utter it, and many a voice that was painful for his heart that he heard but remained (unmoved) as though he was deaf the voice of either and elder whom he used to respect or of a younger whom he used to caress. The pangs of death are too hideous to be covered by description or to be appreciated by the hearts of the people in this world.

SERMONS 220

"... Therein declare glory unto him in the mornings and the evenings; men whom neither merchandise nor any sale diverteth from the remembrance of Allah and constancy in prayer and paying the poor-rate; they fear the day when the hearts and eyes shall writhe of the anguish. (Quraan, 24:36-37)

After reciting this Quraanic verse, Ameer al-Momineen said:

Certainly, Allah, the Glorified, the Sublime, has made His remembrance the light for hearts which hear with its help despite deafness, see with its help despite blindness and become submissive with its help despite unruliness.

In all the periods and times when there were no prophets, there have been persons with whom Allah, precious are His bounties, whispered through their wits and spoke through their minds. With the help of the bright awakening of their ears, eyes and hearts they keep reminding others of the remembrance of the days of Allah and making others feel fear for Him like guide-points in wildernesses. Whoever adopts the middle way, they praise his ways and give him the tidings of deliverance, but whoever goes right and left they vilify his ways and frighten him with ruin. In this way, they served as lamps in these darknesses and guides through these doubts.

There are some people devoted to the remembrance (of Allah) who have adopted it in place of worldly matters so that commerce or trade does not turn them away from it. They pass their life in it. They speak into the ears of neglectful persons warning against matters held unlawful by Allah, they order them to practise justice and themselves keep practising it, and they refrain them from the unlawful and themselves refrain from it. It is as though they have finished the journey of this world towards the next world and have beheld what lies beyond it. Consequently, they have become acquainted with all that befell them in the interstice during their long stay therein, and the Day of Judgement fulfils its promises for them. Therefore, they removed the curtain from these things for the people of the world, till it was as though they were seeing what people did not see and were hearing what people did not hear.

If you picture them in your mind in their admirable positions and well-known sittings, when they have opened the records of their actions and are prepared to render an account of themselves in respect of the small as well as the big things they were ordered to do but they failed to do, or were ordered to refrain from but they indulged therein, and they realised the weight of their burden (of bad acts) on their backs, and they felt too weak to bear them, then they wept bitterly and spoke to each other wile still crying and bewailing to Allah in repentance and acknowledgement (of their shortcomings), you would find them to be emblems of guidance and lamps in darkness, angels would be surrounding them, peace would be descending upon them, the doors of the sky would be opened for them and positions of honour would be assigned to them in the place of which Allah had informed them. Therefore, He has appreciated their actions and praised their position. They call Him and breathe in the air of forgiveness, they are ever needy of His bounty and remain humble before His greatness, the length of their grief has pained their hearts, and the length of weeping their eves. They knock at every door of inclination towards Allah. They ask Him Whom generosity does not make destitute and from Whom those who approach Him do not get disappointed.

Therefore, take account of yourself for your own sake because the account of others will be taken by one other than you.

SERMONS 221

O thou man! What hath beguiled thee from thy lord, the most gracious one. (Quraan, 82:6)

After reciting this Quraanic verse, Ameer al-Momineen said:

The addressee (in this verse) is devoid of argument and his excuse is most deceptive. He is detaining himself in ignorance.

O man! what has emboldened you to (commit) sins, what had deceived you about your Allah and what has made you satisfied with the destruction of yourself. Is there no cure for your ailment or no awakening from your sleep? Do you not have pity on yourself as you have on others? Generally, when you see anyone exposed to the heat of the sun you cover him with shade, or if you see anyone afflicted with grief that pains his body you weep out of pity for him. What has then made you patient over your own disease, what has made you firm in your own afflictions, and what has consoled you from weeping over yourself although your life is the most precious of all lives to you, and why does not the fear of an ailment that may befall you in the night keep you wakeful although you lie on the way to Allah's wrath due to your sins?

You should cure the disease of languor in your heart by determination, and the sleep of neglectfulness in your eyes by wakefulness. Be obedient to Allah, and love His remembrance, and picture to yourself that you are running away while He is approaching you. He is calling you to His forgiveness and concealing your faults with His kindness, while you are fleeing away from Him towards others. Certainly, Great is Allah the powerful, Who is so generous, and how humble and weak are you and still so bold to commit His disobedience although you live in His protection and undergo changes of life in the expanse of His kindness. He does not refuse you His kindness and does not remove His protection from you. In fact, you have not been without His kindness even for a moment, whether it be a favour that He conferred upon you or a sin of yours that He has concealed or a calamity that He has warded off from you. What is your idea about Him if you had obeyed Him? By Allah, if this had been the case with two persons equal in power and matching in might (one being inattentive and the other showering favours upon you) then you would have been the first to adjudge yourself to be of bad behaviour and evil deeds.

I truthfully say that the world has not deceived you but you have had yourself deceived by it. The world had opened to you the curtains and divulged to you (everything) equally. And in all that it foretold you about the troubles befalling your bodies and the decay in your power, it has been too true and faithful in promise, and did not speak a lie to you or deceive you. There are many who advise you about it but they are blamed, and speak the truth about it but they are opposed. If you understand the world by means of dilapidated houses and forlorn abodes, then with your good understanding and far reaching power of drawing lessons you will find it like one who is kind over you and cautious about you. It is good abode for him who does not like it as an abode, and a good place of stay for him who does not regard it a permanent home for stay.

Only those who run away from this world today will be regarded virtuous tomorrow. When the earthquake occurs, the Day of Resurrection approaches with all its severities, the people of every worshipping place cling to it, all the devotees cling to the object of their devotion and all the followers cling to their leader. Then on that day even the opening of an eye in the air and the sound of a footstep on the ground will be assigned its due through His Justice and His Equity. On that day many an argument will prove void and a contention for excuses will stand rejected.

Therefore, you should now adopt for yourself the course with which your excuse may hold good and your plea may be proved. Take from the transient things of this world that which will stay for you (in the next world), provide for your journey, keep (your) gaze on the brightness of deliverance and keep ready the saddles (for setting off).

SERMONS 222

Keeping aloof from Oppression and Misappropriation.

By Allah, I would rather pass a night in wakefulness on the thorns of as-Sadan (a plant having sharp prickles) or be driven in chains as a prisoner than meet Allah and His Messenger on the Day of Judgement as an oppressor over any person or a usurper of anything out of worldly wealth. And how can I oppress any one for (the sake of a life) that is fast moving towards destruction and is to remain under the earth for a long time.

Aqeel's Condition of Poverty and Destitution

By Allah, I certainly saw (my brother) Aqeel fallen in destitution and he asked me a sa" (about three kilograms in weight) out of your (share of) wheat, and I also saw his children with dishevelled hair and a dusty countenance due to starvation, as though their faces had been blackened by indigo. He came to me several times and repeated his request to me again and again. I heard him, and he thought I would sell my faith to him and follow his tread leaving my own way. Then I (just) heated a piece of iron and took it near his body so that he might take a lesson from it, then he cried as a person in protracted illness cries with pain and he was about to get burnt with its branding. Then I said to him "Moaning women may moan over you, O Aqeel. Do you cry on account of this (heated) iron which has been made by a man for fun while you are driving me towards the fire which Allah, the Powerful, has prepared for (a manifestation of) His wrath? Should you cry from pain, but I should not cry from the flames?"

A stranger incident than this is that a man[1] came to us in the night; with a closed flask full of honey paste but I disliked it as though it was the saliva of a serpent or its vomit. I asked him whether it was a reward, or zakat (poor-tax) or charity, for these are forbidden to us members of the Prophet's family. He said it was neither this nor that but a present. Then I said "Childless women may weep over you. Have you come to deviate me from the religion of Allah, or are you mad, or have you been overpowered by some jinn, or are you speaking without senses? "

By Allah, even if I am given all the domains of the seven (stars) with all that exists under the skies in order that I may disobey Allah to the extent of snatching one grain of barley from an ant I would not do it. For me your world is lighter than the leaf in the mouth of a locust that is chewing it. What has Ali to do with bounties that will pass away and pleasures that will not last? We do seek protection of Allah from the slip of wisdom and the evils of mistakes, and from Him we seek succour.

SERMONS 223

A Supplication

O my Allah! preserve (the grace of) my face with easiness of life and do not disgrace my countenance with destitution, lest I may have to beg a livelihood from those who beg from Thee, try to seek the favour of Thy evil creatures, engage myself in praising those who give to me, and be

-1- It was al-Ashath bn Qays.

tempted in abusing those who do not give to me, although behind all these Thou art the master of giving and denying.
... Verily Thou over all things, art the All-powerful. (Quraan, 66:8)

SERMONS 224

Transience of the World and the Helplessness of those in graves

This is a house surrounded by calamities and well-known for deceitfulness. Its conditions do not last and those who inhabit it do not remain safe. Its conditions are variable and its ways changing. Life in it is blameworthy and safety in it is non-existent. Yet its people are targets; it strikes them with its arrows and destroys them through death.
Know, O creatures of Allah, that, certainly, you and all the things of this world that you have are (treading) on the lines of those (who were) before you. They were of longer ages, had more populated houses and were of more lasting traces. Their voices have become silent, their movements have become stationary, their bodies have become rotten, their houses have become empty and their traces have been obliterated. Their magnificent places and spread-out carpets were changed to stones, laid-in-blocks and cave-like dug out graves whose very foundation is based on ruins and whose construction has been made with soil. Their positions are contiguous, but those settled in them are like far flung strangers. They are among the people of their area but feel lonely, and they are free from work but still engaged (in activity). They feel no attachment with homelands nor do they keep contact among themselves like neighbours despite nearness of neighbourhood and priority of abodes. And how can they meet each other when decay has ground them with its chest, and stones and earth have eaten them.
It is as though you too have gone where they have gone, the same sleeping place has caught you and the same place has detained you. What will then be your position when your affairs reach their end and graves are turned upside down (to throw out the dead) ?

There shall every soul realise what it hath sent before, and they shall be brought back to Allah, their true Lord, and what they did fabricate (the false deities) will vanish (away) from them. (Quraan, 10:30)

SERMONS 220

A Supplication

O my Allah! Thou art the most attached to Thy lovers and the most ready to assist those who trust in Thee. Thou seest them in their concealments, knowest whatever is in their consciences, and art aware of the extent of their intelligence. Consequently, their secrets are open to Thee and their hearts are eager from Thee. If loneliness bores them, Thy remembrance gives them solace. If distresses befall them, they beseech Thy protection, because they know that the reins of affairs are in Thy hands, and that their movements depend upon Thy commands.

O my Allah! if I am unable to express my request or cannot see my needs, then guide me towards my betterment and take my betterment and take my heart towards the correct goal. This is not against (the mode of) Thy guidance nor anything new against Thy ways of support.

O my Allah! deal with me through Thy forgiveness and do not deal with me according to Thy justice.

SERMONS 226

About a Companion who passed away from this World before the Occurrence of Troubles

May Allah reward such and such man[1] who straightened the curve, cured the disease, abandoned mischief and established the Sonna. He departed

-1- bn-Abil-Hadeed has written (in Sharh Nahjol-Balagha, vol.14, pp.3-4) that the reference here is to the second Caliph Omar, and that these sentences have been uttered in his praise as indicated by the word “Omar” written under the word ‘such and such” in Sayyid Razi’s own hand in the manuscript of Nahjol-Balagha written by him. This is bn-Abil-Hadeed’s statement, but it is to be seen that if Sayyid Razi had written the word

---

"Omar" by way of explanation it should have existed, as other explanations by him have remained, in those versions which have been copied from his manuscript. Even now there exists in al-Mosil (Iraq) university the oldest copy of Nahjol-Balagha written by the famous calligraphist Yaqoot al-Mostasimi; but no one has afforded any clue to this explanation of Sayyid Razi. Even if the view of bn-Abil-Hadeed is accepted it would be deemed to represent the personal opinion of Sayyid Razi which may serve as a supplementary argument in support of an original argument but this personal view cannot be assigned any regular importance.

It is strange that two and a half centuries after Sayyid Razi namely in the seventh century A.H., bn Abil Hadeed makes the statement that the reference here is to Caliph Omar and that Sayyid Razi himself had so indicated, as a result of which some other annotators also followed the same line, but the contemporaries of Sayyid Razi who wrote about Nahjol-Balagha have given no such indication in their writings although as contemporaries they should have had better information about Sayyid Razi's writing. Thus, Allama Ali bn Naasir who was a contemporary of Sayyid Razi and wrote an annotation of Nahjol-Balagha under the name of Alam Nahjol-Balagha writes in connection with this sermon:

Ameer al-Momineen has praised one of his own companions for his good conduct. He had died before the troubles that arose after the death of the Prophet of Allah.

This is supported by the annotations of Nahjol-Balagha written by Allama Qutboddeen ar-Rawandi (d. 573 A.H.). bn-Abil-Hadeed (vol.14, p.4) and bn Maytham al-Bahraani (in Sharh Nahjol-Balagha, vol.4, p.97) have quoted his following view.

By this Ameer al-Momineen refers to one of his own companions who died before the mischief and disruption that occurred following the death of the Prophet of Allah.

Allama al-Haj al-Mirza Habeebollah al-Khoi is of the opinion that the person is Malik bn Haarith al-Ashtar on the ground that after the assassination of Malik the situation of the Moslim community was such as Ameer al-Momineen explains in this sermon.

al-Khoi adds that:

Ameer al-Momineen has praised Malik repeatedly such as in his letter to the people of Egypt sent through Malik when he was made the governor of that place, and like his utterances when the news of Maalik's assassination reached him, he said "Malik! who is Malik? If Malik was a stone, he was hard and solid; if he was a rock, he was a great rock which had no parallel. Women have become barren to give birth to such as Malik" Ameer al-Momineen had even expressed in some of his utterances that, "Malik was to me as I was to the Holy Prophet" Therefore, one who possesses such a position certainly deserves such attributes and even beyond that. (Sharh Nahjol-Balagha, vol.14, pp.374-375)

If these words had been about Caliph Omar and there was some trustworthiness about it bn-Abil-Hadeed would have recorded the authority or tradition and it would have existed in history and been known among the people. But here nothing is found to prove the statement except a few self-concocted events. Thus about the pronouns in the words "khayraha" and 'sharraha" he takes them to refer to the caliphate and writes that these words can apply only to one who enjoys power and authority because without authority it is impossible to establish the Sonna or prevent innovation. This is the gist of the argument he has advanced on this occasion; although there is no proof to establish that the antecedent of this pronoun is the caliphate. It can rather refer to the world (when Ameer al-Momineen says, "He achieved good of this world and remained safe from its evils) and that would be in accord with the context. Again, to regard authority as a condition for the safeguarding of people's interest and the propagation of the Sonna means to close the door to prompting others to good and dissuading them from evil, although Allah has assigned this duty to a group of the people without the condition of authority:

And that there should be among you a group who call (mankind) unto virtue and enjoin what is good and forbid wrong; and these are they who shall be successful. (Quraan, 3:104)

Similarly it is related from the Prophet:

So long as people go on prompting for good and dissuading from evil and assisting each other in virtue and piety they will remain in righteousness.

Again, Ameer al-Momineen, in the course of a will, says in general terms:

Establish the pillars of the Unity of Allah and the Sonna, and keep both these lamps aflame.

In these sayings there is no hint that this obligation cannot be discharged without authority. Facts also tell us that (despite army and force, and power and authority) the rulers and kings could not prevent evil or propagate virtue to the extent to which some unknown godly persons were able to inculcate moral values by imprinting their morality on heart and minds, although they were not backed by any army or force and they did not have any equipment save destitution. No doubt authority and control can bend heads down before it, but it is not necessary that it should also pave the way for virtue in hearts. History shows that most of the rulers destroyed the features of Islam. Islam's existence and progress has been possible by the efforts of those helpless persons who possessed nothing save poverty and discomfiture.

If it is insisted that the reference here should only be to a ruler, then why should it not be taken to mean a companion of Ameer al-Momineen who had been the head of a Province such as Salmaan al-Farisi for whose burial Ameer al-Momineen went to al-Madain; and it is not implausible that Ameer al-Momineen might have uttered these words after his burial by way of comments on his life and way of governance. However, to believe that they are about Caliph Omar is without any proof. In the end, bn-Abil-Hadeed has quoted the following statements of (the historian) at-Tabari in proof of his hypothesis:

It is related from al-Mogheera bn Shoba that when Caliph Omar died bn-Abi-Hathmah said crying "O Omar, you were the man who straightened the curve, removed ills, destroyed mischief, revived the Sonna, remained chaste and departed without entangling in evils" (According to at-Tabari) al-Mogheera related that "When Omar was buried I came to Ali and I wanted to hear something from him about Omar. So, on my arrival Ameer al-Momineen came out in this state that was wrapped in one cloth after bathing and was jerking the hair of his head and beard and he had no doubt that the Caliphate would come to him. On this occasion he said "May Allah have mercy on Omar.

bn-Abi-Hathmah has correctly said that he enjoyed the good of the Caliphate and remained safe from its evils. By Allah, she did not say it herself but was made to say so" (at-Tabari, vol.1, p.2763; bn-Abil-Hadeed, vol.12, p.5; bn Katheer, vol.7, p.140)
The relater of this event is al-Mogheera bn Shoba whose adultery with Om-Jameel, the Caliph Omar's saving him from the penalty despite the evidence, and his openly abusing Ameer al-Momineen in Koofa under Moaawiya's behest are admitted facts of history. On this ground what weight his statements can carry is quite clear. From the factual point of view also, this story cannot be accepted. Al-Mogheera's statement that Ameer al-Momineen had no doubt about his Caliphate is against the facts. What were the factors from which he made this guess when the actual facts were to the contrary. If the caliphate was certain for any one, it was Othmaan. Thus, at the Consultative Committee Abdr-Rahmaan bn Awf said to Ameer al-Momineen: "O Ali! do not create a situation against yourself for I have observed and consulted the people and they all want Othmaan" (at-Tabari, vol.1, p.2786; bn al-Athir, vol.3, p.71; Abol-Fida, vol.1, p.166)
Consequently, Ameer al-Momineen was sure not to get the caliphate as has already been stated on the authority of at-Tabari's History, under the sermon of the Camel's Foam (ash-Shaqshaqiyya) , namely that on seeing the names of the members of the Consultative Committee, Ameer al-Momineen had said to al-Abbas bn Abdl-Mottalib that the caliphate could not be given to anyone except Othmaan since all the powers had been given to Abdr-Rahmaan bn Awf and he was Othmaan's brother-in-law (sister's husband) and Saad bn Abi Waqqas was a relative and tribesman of Abdr-Rahmaan. These two would join in giving the caliphate to him.
At this stage, the question arises as to what the reason was that actuated al-Mogheera to prompt Ameer al-Momineen to say something about Omar. If he knew that Ameer al-Momineen had good ideas about Omar, he should have also known his impression; but if he thought that Ameer al-Momineen did not entertain good ideas about him then the purpose of his asking Ameer al-Momineen would be none other than that whatever he may say he would, by exposing it, create an atmosphere against him and make the members of the Consultative Committee suspicious of him. The views of the members of the Consultative Committee are well understood from the very fact that by putting the condition of following the conduct of the first two Caliphs in electing the caliph they had shown their adherence to them. In these circumstances when al-Mogheera tried to play this trick Ameer al-Momineen said just by way of relating a fact that Omar achieved the good (of this world) and remained safe from its evil. This sentence has no connection with praise or eulogy. Omar did in his days enjoy all kinds of advantages while his period was free from the mischiefs that cropped up later. After recording this statement bn-Abil-Hadeed writes:
From this event the belief gains strength that in this utterance the allusion is towards Omar.
If the utterance means the word uttered by Bn-Abi-Hathmah about which Ameer al-Momineen has said that they are not her own heart's voice but she was made to utter them, then doubtlessly the reference is to Omar, but the view that these words were uttered by Ameer al-Momineen in praise of Omar is not at all established. Rather, from

(from this world) with untarnished clothes and little shortcomings. He achieved good (of this world) and remained safe from its evils. He offered Allah's obedience and feared Him as He deserved. He went away and left the people in dividing ways wherein the misled cannot obtain guidance and the guided cannot attain certainty.

SERMONS 227

Allegiance to Him for the Caliphate

(A similar sermon in somewhat different version has already appeared earlier.)

You drew out my hand towards you for allegiance but I held it back and you stretched it but I contracted it. Then you crowed over me as the thirsty camels crowd on the watering cisterns on their being taken there, so much so that shoes were torn, shoulder-cloths fell away and the weak got trampled, and the happiness of people on their allegiance to me was so manifested that small children felt joyful, the old staggered (up to me) for it, the sick too reached for it helter skelter and young girls ran for it without veils.

---

this tradition it is evidently shown that these words were uttered by Bn-Abi-Hathmah. Allah alone knows on what ground the words of Bn-Abi-Hathmah are quoted and then it is daringly argued that these words were uttered by Ameer al-Momineen about Omar. It seems Ameer al-Momineen had uttered these words about someone on some occasion, then Bn-Abi-Hathmah used similar words on Omar's death and then even Ameer al-Momineen's words were taken to be in praise of Omar. Otherwise, no mind except a mad one can argue that the words uttered by Bn-Abi-Hathmah should be deemed a ground to hold that Ameer al-Momineen said these words in praise of Omar. Can it be expected, after (a glance at) the sermon of the Camel's Foam, that Ameer al-Momineen might have uttered these words. Again, it is worth consideration that if these words had been uttered by Ameer al-Momineen on Omar's death, then at the Consultative Committee when he refused to follow the conduct of the (first) two Caliphs it should have been said to him that only the other day he has said that Omar had established the Sonna and banished innovations, so that when his conduct was in accord with the Sonna what was the sense in accepting the Sonna but refusing to follow his conduct.

SERMONS 228

An Account of those who remain Apprehensive of Death and adopt Abstemiousness

Certainly, fear of Allah is the key to guidance, provision for the next world, freedom from every slavery and deliverance from all ruin. With its help the seeker succeeds and he who makes for safety escapes and achieves his aims.

Perform (good) acts while such acts are being raised (in value), repentance can be of benefit, prayer can be heard, conditions are peaceful and the pens (of the two angels) are in motion (to record the actions). Hasten towards (virtuous) actions before the change of age (to oldness), lingering illness or snatching death (overtakes you). Certainly, death will end your enjoyments, mar your pleasures and remove your objectives. It is an unwanted visitor, an invincible adversary and an unaccounting killer. Its ropes have entrapped you, its evils have surrounded you, its arrowheads have aimed at you, its sway over you is great, its oppression on you is continuous and the chance of its missing you is remote.

Very soon you will be overwhelmed with the gloom of its shades, the severity of its illness, the darkness of its distresses, the nonsense utterances of its pangs, the grief of its destruction, the darkness of its encompassment and the unwholesomeness of its taste. It will seem as if it has come to you all of a sudden, silenced those who were whispering to you, separated your group, destroyed your doings, devastated your houses and altered your successors to distribute your estate among the chief relatives, who did not give you any benefit, or the grieved near ones who could not protect (you), or those rejoicers who did not lament (you). Therefore, it is upon you to strive, make effort, equip yourself, get ready and provide yourself from the place of provision. And let not the life of this world deceive you as it deceived those before you among the past people and by-gone periods — those who extracted its milk, benefited from its neglectfulness, passed a long time and turned its new things into old (by living long). Their abodes turned into graves and their wealth into inheritable estate. They do not know who came to them (at their graves); do not pay heed to those who weep over them, and do not respond to those who call them. Therefore, beware of this world as it is treacherous, deceitful and cheating, it gives and takes back, covers with clothes and uncovers. Its pleasure does not last, its hardship does not end and its calamity does not stop.

About Ascetics

They are from among the people of this world but are not its people, because they remain in it as though they do not belong to it. They act herein on what they observe and hasten here in (to avoid) what they fear. Their bodies move among the people of the next world. They see that the people of this world attach importance to the death of their bodies but they themselves attach more importance to the death of the hearts of those who are living.

SERMONS 229

Holy Prophet

Ameer al-Momineen delivered this sermon at Ziqar on his way to Basra, and the historian al-Waaqidi has mentioned it (in Kitaab al-Jamal).

The Prophet manifested whatever he was commanded and conveyed the messages of his Lord. Consequently, Allah repaired through him the cracks, joined through him the slits and created (through him) affection among kin although they bore intense enmity in (their) chests and deep-seated rancour in (their) hearts.

SERMONS 230

When Abdillah bn-Zamaa asked him for some money (from the public treasury)

This money is not for me nor for you, but it is the collective property of the Moslims and the acquisition of their swords. If you had taken part with them in their fighting you would have a share equal to theirs, otherwise the earning of their hands cannot be for other than their mouths.

SERMONS 231

On Jada bn-Hobayra al-Makhzomi's[1] inability to deliver a sermon.

Know that the tongue is a part of a man's body. If the man desists, speech will not co-operate with him and when he dilates, speech will not give him time to stop. Certainly, we are the masters of speaking. Its veins are fixed in us and its branches are hanging over us.

Know that — may Allah have mercy on you — you are living at a time when those who speak about right are few, when tongues are loath to utter the truth and those who stick to the right are humiliated. The people of this time are engaged in disobedience. Their youths are wicked, their old men are sinful, their learned men are hypocrites, and their speakers are sycophants. Their youngs do not respect their elders, and their rich men do not support the destitute.

SERMONS 232

Causes for difference in the features and traits of People

Zilib al-Yamami has related from Ahmad bn-Qutayba, and he from Abdillah bn-Yazeed and he from Maalik bn-Dihyah who said "We were with Ameer al-Momineen when discussion arose about the differences of men (in features and conduct) and then Ameer al-Momineen said:

-1- Once Ameer al-Momineen asked his nephew (sister's son) Jadah bn Hobayra al-Makhzoomi to deliver a sermon, but when he rose for speaking his tongue faltered and he could utter nothing, whereupon Ameer al-Momineen ascended the pulpit to speak and delivered a long sermon out of which a few sentences have been recorded here by Sayyid Razi.

They differ among themselves because of the sources[1] of their clay (from which they have been created). This is because they are either from saltish

-1- Ameer al-Momineen has ascribed the differences in features and characters of people to the differences in the clay from which they are created and according to which their features are shaped and the skeletons of their characters are formed. Therefore, to the extent that their clay of origin is akin, their mental and imaginative tendencies too will be similar and to the extent by which they differ, there will be a difference in their inclinations and tendencies. By origins of a thing are meant those things on which its coming into existence depends, but they should not be its cause. The word "tin" is the plural of "tinah" which means origin or basis. Here "tinah" means semen which after passing through various stages of development emerges in the human shape. Its origin means those constituents from which those items are created which help in the formation of semen. Thus, by saltish, sweet, soft or hard soil the reference is to these elementary constituents. Since those elementary constituents carry different properties the semen growing out of them will also bear different characteristics and propensities which will (eventually) show forth in the differences in features and conduct of those borne in it.

bn-Abil-Hadeed has written (in Sharh Nahjol-Balagha, vol.13, p.19) that "origins of tinah" implies those preservative factors which are different in their properties as Plato and other philosophers have held. The reason for calling them "origins of tinah" is that they serve as an asylum for the human body and prevent the elements from diffusion. Just as the existence of a thing hinges on its basis, in the same way the existence of this body which is made up of elements depends on preservative factors. So long as the preservative factor exists the body is also safe from disruption and disintegration and the elements too are immune to diffusion and dispersal. When it leaves the body the elements also get dispersed.

According to this explanation Ameer al-Momineen's words would mean that Allah has created different original factors among whom some are vicious and some are virtuous, some are weak and some are strong, and every person will act according to his original factor. If there is similarity in the inclinations of two persons it is because their original factor are similar, and if their tendencies differ it is because their original factors do not have any similarity. But this conclusion is not correct because Ameer al-Momineen's words do not only refer to differences in conduct and behaviour but also of features and shape and the differences of features and shape cannot be the result of differences in original factors.

In any case, whether the original factors are the cause of differences in features and conduct or the elementary constituents are the cause, these words appear to lead to the negation of volition and to prove the compulsion (of destiny) in human actions, because if man's capacity for thinking and acting is dependent on "tinah" then he would be compelled to behave himself in a fixed way on account of which he would neither deserve praise for good acts nor be held blame worthy for bad habits. But this hypothesis is incorrect because it is well established that just as Allah knows everything in creation

soil or sweet soil or from rugged earth or soft earth. They, resemble each other on the basis of the affinity of their soil and differ according to its difference. Therefore, sometimes a person of handsome features is weak in intelligence, a tall statured person is of low courage, a virtuous person is ugly in appearance, a short statured person is far-sighted, a good-natured person has an evil trait, a person of perplexed heart has bewildering mind and a sharp-tongued person has a wakeful heart.

SERMONS 233

When he was busy in the funeral ablution (Ghosl) of the Holy Prophet and shrouding him

May my father and my mother shed their lives for you. O Messenger of Allah! With your death the process of Prophethood, revelation and heavenly messages has stopped, which had not stopped at the death of others (prophets). Your position with us (members of your family) is so special that your grief has become a source of consolation (to us) as against the grief of all others; your grief is also common so that all Moslims share it equally. If you had not ordered endurance and prevented us from bewailing, we would have produced a store of tears and even then the pain would not have subsided, and this grief would not have ended, and they would have been too little of our grief for you. But this (death) is a matter that cannot be reversed nor is it possible to repulse it. May my father and my mother die for you; do remember us with Allah and take care of us.

---

after its coming into being, in the same way He knew it before its creation. Thus, He knew what actions man would perform of his free will and what he would leave. Therefore, Allah gave him capacity to act according to his free will, and created him from a suitable "tinah. This tinah is not the cause of his actions so as to snatch away from him his free will but the meaning of creating from suitable tinah is that Allah does not by force stand in man's way but allows him to tread the path he wants to tread of his own free will.

SERMONS 234

His own condition after the Prophet's immigration till his meeting with Him[1]

-1- Since the commencement of Prophethood, the Prophet remained in Mecca for thirteen years. For him, this period was of the severest oppression and destitution. The unbelievers of the Quraysh had closed all the doors of livelihood upon him, and had left no deficiency in inflicting hardships upon him, so much so that in order to take his life they began contriving how to do away with him. Forty of their nobles assembled in the hall of audience (Dar an-Nadwa) for consultation, and decided that one individual should be picked out from every tribe and they should jointly attack him. In this way, Bani-Hashim would not dare to face all the tribes, and the matter would quieten down on the payment of blood price. To give a practical shape to this scheme, these people sat in ambush near the house of the Prophet on the night of the first of Rabi" al-Awwal, so that when the prophet slept in his bed he would be attacked. On this side the preparation for killing him was complete, and on the other side Allah informed him of all the intrigues of the Quraysh unbelievers and commanded him to make Ali (p.b.u.h.) sleep on his bed and himself to immigrate to Madeena. The Prophet sent for Ali (p.b.u.h.) and disclosing to him his plan, said "Ali, you lie on my bed" Ameer al-Momineen enquired: "O Messenger of Allah, will your life be saved by my sleeping here?" The Prophet said "Yes" Hearing this Ameer al-Momineen performed a prostration in thanks-giving and, exposing himself fully to the danger, lay on the Prophet's bed while the Prophet left from the rear door. The Quraysh unbelievers were peeping and getting ready for the attack but Abo-Lahab said "It is not proper to attack in the night because there are women and children also in the house. When morning dawns you attack him, but keep watch during night that he should not move anywhere" Consequently, they kept their eyes on the bed throughout the night and soon, on the appearance of the dawn, proceeded forward stealthily. Hearing the sound of their footsteps, Ameer al-Momineen removed the covering from his face and stood up. The Quraysh gazed at him with stretched eyes as to whether it was an illusion or fact. After making sure that it was Ali they enquired, "Where is Mohammad?" and Ali replied, "Did you entrust him to me, that now you are asking me?" They had no reply to this. Men ran to chase him but found footprints only up to the cave of Thawr. Beyond that there were neither footprints nor any sign of hiding in the cave. They came back bewildered while the Prophet after staying in the cave for three days left for Madeena. Ameer al-Momineen passed these three days in Mecca, returned to the people their properties lying in trust with the Prophet and set off towards Madeena to join the Prophet. Upto al-Araj which is a place between Mecca and Madeena, he kept getting news about the Prophet and he continued his anxious march in his search till he met the Prophet at Quba on the twelfth of Rabi" al-Awwal, and entered Madeena with him. (at-Tabari, at-Tafseer, vol.9, pp.148-151; at-Taareekh, vol.1, pp.1232-1234; bn Saad, at-Tabaqaat, vol.1, Part 1, pp.153-154; bn Hishaam, as-Seera, vol.2, pp.124-128; bn al-Athir,

I began following the path adopted by the Prophet and treading on the lines of his remembrance till I reached al-Araj.

Sayyid Razi says: Ameer al-Momineen's words "faatau zikrahu" constitute the highest forms of brevity and eloquence. He means to say that he was being given news about the Prophet from the commencement of his setting out till he reached this place, and he has expressed this sense in this wonderful expression.

SERMONS 235

Collecting Provision for the Next World and Performing Good Acts before Death

Perform (good) acts while you are still in the vastness of life, the books are open (for recording of actions), repentance is allowed, the runner away (from Allah) is being called and the sinner is being given hope (of forgiveness) before the (light of) action is put off, time expires, life ends, the door for repentance is closed and angels ascend to the sky.

Therefore a man should derive benefit from himself for himself, from the living for the dead, from the mortal, for the lasting and from the departer for the stayer. A man should fear Allah while he is given age to live upto his death, and is allowed time to act. A man should control his self by the rein and hold it with its bridle, thus by the rein he should prevent it from disobedience towards Allah, and by the bridle he should lead it towards obedience to Allah.

Osdol-Ghaaba, vol.4, p.25; al-Kaamil, vol.2, pp.101-104; bn Katheer, at-Tafseer, vol.2, pp.302-303; at-Taareekh, vol.3, pp.180-181; bn-Abil-Hadeed, vol.13, pp.303-306; as-Seyooti, ad-Dorrol-Manthoor, vol.3, pp.179-180; Allama Majlisi, Bihar al-Anwar, vol.19, pp.28-103).

SERMONS 236

The two arbitrators (Abo-Moosa al-Ashari and Amr bn al-Aas) and Disparagement of the People of Syria (ash-sham)

Rude, low people and mean slaves. They have been collected from all sides and picked up from every pack. They need to be taught the tenets (of Islam), disciplined, instructed, trained, supervised and led by the hand. They are neither mohaajiroon (immigrants from Mecca), nor Ansaar (helpers of Madeena) nor those who made their dwellings in the abode (in Madeena) and in belief.

Look! They have chosen for themselves one who is nearest of all of them to what they desire, while you have chosen one who is nearest to what you dislike. You may certainly recall that the other day Abdillah bn-Qays (Abo-Moosa) was saying: "It is a mischief, therefore, cut away your bow-string and sheathe your swords." If he was right (in what he said) then he was wrong in marching (with us) without being forced, but if he was lying then he should be viewed with suspicion. Therefore, send Abdillah bn-Abbas to face Amr bn al-As. Make use of these days and surround the borders of Islam. Do you not see that your cities are being attacked and your prowess is being aimed at?

SERMONS 237

Members of the Prophet's Family

They are life for knowledge and death for ignorance. Their forbearance tells you of their knowledge, and their silence of the wisdom of their speaking. They do not go against right nor do they differ (among themselves) about it. They are the pillars of Islam and the asylums of (its) protection. With them right has returned to its position and wrong has left its place and its tongue is severed from its root. They have understood the religion attentively and carefully, not by mere heresy or from relaters, because the relaters of knowledge are many but its understanders are few.

SERMONS 238

When Othmaan bn-Affaan sent word through Abdillah bn-Abbas that he should leave for Yanboo

When Othmaan bn-Affaan was surrounded, Abdillah bn-Abbas brought a letter to Ameer al-Momineen from Othmaan in which he expressed the desire that Ameer al-Momineen should leave for his estate Yanboo" so that the proposal that was being mooted out for him to become caliph should subside. Othmaan had this request earlier also. Upon this Ameer al-Momineen said to bn-Abbas:

O bn-Abbas! Othmaan just wants to treat me like the water-drawing camel so that I may go forward and backward with the bucket. Once he sent me word that I should go out then sent me word that I should come back. Now, again he sends me word that I should go out. By Allah, I continued protecting him till I feared lest I become a sinner.

SERMONS 239

Exhorting his men to Jihaad and asking them to refrain from seeking ease

Allah seeks you to thank Him and assigns to you His affairs. He has allowed time in the limited field (of life) so that you may vie with each other in seeking the reward (of Paradise). Therefore, tight up your girdles and wrap up the skirts. High courage and dinners do not go together. Sleep causes weakness in the big affairs of the day and (its) darkness obliterates the memories of courage.

Selections from the writings of our master Ameer al-Momineen, Ali bn Abi-Taalib and his letters to his enemies, and the governors of his provinces, including selections of his letters of appointment to his administrative officers, and his injunctions to members of his family and his companions

letters

Selaction From the Writings of our Master of Ameer al-Momineen Ali bn Abi-Talib (Peace be Upon him) And his Letters to the Enemies, and the Governors of his Provinces, including Letters of Appointments to his Administrative Officer, And his Injections to Members of Family and Companions.

Nahj ALBALAAGHA

Peak of Eloquence

1- To the people of Koofa at the time of his march from Madeena to Basra[1]

-1- bn-Maytham writes (in Sharh Nahjol-Balagha, vol.4, p.338) that when on hearing about the mischief-mongering of Talha and az-Zobayr, Ameer al-Momineen set off for Basra, he sent this letter to the people of Koofa through Imaam al-Hasan and Ammaar bn-Yaasir from al-Maa" al-Azb, while bn-Abil-Hadeed has written (in Sharh Nahjol-Balagha, vol.14, pp.8,16; at-Tabari, vol.1, p.3139; and bn-Atheer, vol.3 p.223) that when Ameer al-Momineen camped at Ar-Rabaza, he sent this letter through Mohammad bn-Jafar bn-Abi-Talib and Mohammad bn-Abi-Bakr. In this letter Ameer al-Momineen has clearly thrown light on the point that the assassination of Othmaan was the result of the efforts of Aysha, Talha and az-Zobayr, and that it was they who took a prominent part in it. In fact, Aysha went beyond her bounds and exposed his shortcomings in public meetings and ordered that he should be killed. Thus, ash-Shaykh Mohammad Abdo has written:

Once Othmaan was on the pulpit when Om-al-Momineen Aysha took out the shoes and the shirt of the Prophet (may Allah bless him and his descendants) from under her veil and said: "These are the shoes of the Messenger of Allah and his shirt, not yet decayed while you have altered his religion and changed his Sonna." Upon this, hot words followed between them when she said "Kill this Nathal," symbolising him as a long bearded Jew (of that name). (Nahjol-Balagha, printed in Egypt, vol.2, p.3; also see Ansab al-Ashraaf, vol.5, p.88; Abol-Fidaa, vol.1, p.172).

People were already displeased with Othmaan, so this event increased their boldness and they surrounded him so that he might mend his ways or abdicate from the caliphate. In these circumstances, there was serious apprehension that if he did not accept either of the two alternatives he would be killed. All this was observed by Aysha, but she paid no heed to it and, leaving him in the siege, decided to leave for Mecca, although on this occasion Marwaan bn-Hakam and Attab bn-Asid did say to her "If you postpone your departure it is possible his life may be saved and this crowd may disperse" whereupon she said that she had decided to go for Haj (pilgrimage) and that that could not be changed. Then Marwaan recited this couplet by way of a proverb:

Qays set fire to my cities, and when they came into flames he slipped away saving himself clear of it.

Similarly, Talha and az-Zobayr were (also) in rage against him and they were ever forward in fanning this fire and intensifying the opposition. From this angle they were, to a great extent, taking part in his assassination and responsible for his blood. Other people also knew them in this perspective and regarded them as his murderers, while their supporters too were not able to offer any explanation (for absolving them). Thus, bn-Qutayba writes that when al-Mogheera bn-Shoba met Aysha at Awtas he asked her:

O Om-al-Momineen, where are you bound for." She replied "I am going to Basra." He inquired for what purpose and she replied "To avenge Othmaan blood." He said "But his assassins are with you." Then he turned to Marwaan and enquired where he was going.

From the servant of Allah, Ali, the Commander of the faithful, to the people of Koofa who are foremost among the supporters and chiefs of the Arabs.

Now, I am apprising you of what befell Othmaan so (correctly) that its hearing may be like its seeing. People criticised him, and I was the only man from among the mohaajiroon (immigrants) who asked him to seek to satisfy (the Muslims)most and to offend them the least. As for Talha and az-Zobayr, their lightest step about him was hard and their softest voice was strong. Aysha too was in a rage with him. Consequently, a group overpowered him and killed him. Then, people swore allegiance to me, not by force or compulsion, but obediently and out of free will.

You should know that Madeena has been vacated by residents and they have abandoned it. It is boiling like a huge cooking pot and rebellion is fixed on its axis moving with full force. So, hasten towards your amir (commander) and proceed forward to fight your enemy, if so wills Allah to Whom belongs Might and Majesty.

2- To the people of Koofa after the victory of Basra

May Allah reward you, townsmen (of Koofa), on behalf of a member of your Prophet's family, with the best reward that He bestows on those who act in obedience to Him, and on those who thank Him for His bounties. Surely, you heard (me) and obeyed, and when you were called you promptly responded.

He replied that he too was going to Basra. He enquired the purpose and the reply was "to avenge Othmaan's blood." Then he said "Othmaan's assassins are with you. These Talha and az-Zobayr have killed him." (al-Imaama was-Siyaasa, vol.1, p.60)

In any case, when, after laying the blame on Ameer al-Momineen, this group who had killed Othmaan reached Basra, Ameer al-Momineen also rose to quell this mischief and wrote this letter to the people of Koofa to seek their support. Upon this their combatants and warriors rose in large numbers and enlisted in his army. They faced the enemy with full courage which Ameer al-Momineen also acknowledged. Thus, the letter hereafter is in acknowledgement of this very fact.

3- To Shorayh bn al-Haarith al-Kindi (his Judge at Koofa).

It is related that Shorayh bn d-Haarith (al-Kindi) who was Amir al-Momineen's Qaazi (judge) at Koofa during his tenure, purchased a house for eighty Dinars. When it became known to amir al-Momineen he sent for him:

I have come to know that you have purchased a house for eighty Dinars, and that you have written a document for it and put witnessing on it.

Shorayh replied: Yes, Amir al-Momineen, it is so. Amir al-Momineen cast an angry look at him and said to him:

O Shorayh, beware, shortly one body (the angel of death) will come to you who will not look at the document, nor question you about your evidence but take you out of it far away and deposit you in your grave quite alone. Look! O Shorayh, if you have purchased this house from money other than yours or paid the price from unlawful source, you have incurred loss of this world as well as of the next. If you had come to me at the time of purchase I would gave written for you a document on this paper and then you would have liked to purchase the house even for one Dirham, not to speak of more. That document is this:

This is about a purchase made by a humble slave (of Allah) from another slave ready to depart (for the next world). He has purchased a house out of houses of deceit in the area of mortals and the place of those liable to perish.

This house has four boundaries as follows: The first boundary is contiguous to sources of calamities; the second boundary adjoins the sources of distress; the third boundary adjoins devastating desire; and the fourth boundary adjoins deceitful Shaitan and towards this opens the door of this house. This house has been purchased by one who has been waylaid by desires from one who is being driven by death at the price of leaving the honour of contentment and entering into the humility of want and submissiveness. If the purchaser encounters some (evil) consequences of this transaction then it is for him who dismantles the bodies of monarchs snatches the lives of despots, destroys the domain of

Pharaoh like Kisras,[1] Caesars,[2] Tobbas[3] and Himyars[4] and all those who amass wealth upon wealth and go on increasing it, build high houses and decorate them and collect treasures and preserve them, as they claimed according to their own thinking, for children to take them to the place of accounting and judgement and the position of reward and punishment. When the verdict will be passed those who stood on falsehood would then be the losers. (Quraan, 40:78)

This document is witnessed by intelligence when it is free from the shackles of desire and away from the adornments of this world.

-1- Kisraa, is the Arabicised form of "Khosroo" which means a King whose domain of rule extends to a vast area. This was the title of the rulers of Iran.

-2- Caesar, was the title of the rulers of Rome, which in Latin means that child whose mother dies before delivery and who is extracted by cutting open her body. Since among the Kings of Rome, Augustus was born like this he was known by this name and after that this word was adopted as the title of every ruler.

-3- Tobba, is an appellation of each of the Kings of Yemen who possessed Himyar and Hazramawt. Their names have been mentioned in the Holy Quraan in chaps. 44:37 and 50:14.

-4- Himyar, originally, an important tribe in the ancient Sabaean kingdom of south-western Arabia; later the powerful rulers of much of southern Arabia from c.115 BC to c.AD 525. The Himyarites were concentrated in the area known as Zor- Raydan (later called Qatabaan) on the coast of present-day Yemen; thus they were probably aided in the overthrow of their Sabaean kinsmen by the discovery of a sea route from Egypt to India, which deprived the inland Sabaean kingdom of its former importance as a centre for overland trade. The Himyarites inherited the Sabaean language and culture, and from their capital at Zafar their power at times extended eastward as far as the Persian Gulf and northward into the Arabian Desert. At the beginning of the 4th century AD the Himyar capital was moved northward to Sanaa, and later in that century both Christianity and Judaism gained firm footholds in the area. Internal disorders and changing trade routes caused the kingdom to decline, and in 525, after several unsuccessful attempts, Abysinian invaders finally crushed the Himyarites. A Himyar appeal to Persia for aid led to Persian control in 575. (The New Encyclopaedia Britannica (Micropaedia), vol.5, p.49, ed. 1973-1974).

4- To one of his Army Officers

If they[1] return to the umbrella of obedience then this is all that we want. But if the condition of these people points out towards disruption and disobedience then, taking with you those who obey you, rush upon those who disobey you, and while you have those with you who follow you do not worry about those who hold back from you, because the absence of a half-hearted man is better than his presence, and his sitting down is better than his rising up.

5- To al-Ashath bn Qays al-Kindi, the Governor of Azarbaijaan (Iran)[2]

Certainly, your assignment is not a morsel for you, but it is a trust round your neck, and you have been charged with the protection (of the people)

-1- When Othmaan bn-Honayf, the Governor of Basra informed Ameer al-Momineen of the arrival of Talha and az-Zobayr in Basra and of their intentions, Ameer al-Momineen wrote this letter to him, wherein he has instructed him that in case the enemy was bent of fighting, when facing him he should not enlist on his side those who on the one hand showed consideration for the personalities of Aysha, Talha and az-Zobayr and who on the other hand had agreed to fight against them merely by persuasion, because such people could not be expected to fight steadfastly nor could they be depended upon. Rather, such people would try to dishearten others too. Therefore, it was only good to leave aside such people.

-2- When Ameer al-Momineen was free from the battle of Jamal, he wrote to al-Ashath bn-Qays (al-Kindi) who had been the Governor of Azarbaijaan from the days of Othmaan, to send the revenue and levies of his province. But since he had fears about the future of his position and assignment, he intended to swallow all this money like other officers of Othmaan. Therefore, when this letter reached him he sent for his chief associates and after mentioning this letter to them said: "I fear that this money will be taken away from me; I therefore intend to join Moaawiya." Whereupon those people said that it was a matter of shame to leave kith and kin and seek refuge with Moaawiya. Consequently, on the advice of these people he postponed his idea to run away but did not agree to part with the money. On getting this information Ameer al-Momineen sent Hijr bn-Adi al-Kindi to bring him to Koofa. He persuaded him and brought him to Koofa. On reaching there his kit was found to contain four hundred thousand Dirhams out of which Ameer al-Momineen left thirty thousand for him and deposited the rest in the public treasury.

on behalf of your superiors. It is not for you to be oppressive towards the ruled, nor to risk yourself save on strong grounds. You have in your hand s the funds which is the property of Allah, to Whom belongs Might and Majesty, and you hold its charge till you pass it on to me. Probably, I will not be one of the bad rulers for you, and that is an end to the matter.

6- To Moaawiya bn Abi-Sofyaan

Verily, those who swore allegiance to Abo-Bakr "Omar and "Othmaan have sworn allegiance[1] to me on the same basis on which they swore

-1- When all the people of Madeena unanimously swore allegiance to Ameer al-Momineen, Moaawiya refused to acquiesce apprehending danger for his own power, and in order to contest Ameer al-Momineen's caliphate he concocted the excuse that it had not been agreed to unanimously and that therefore after cancelling it there should be another general election, although the caliphate from which (the process of) election was started was the result of a timely situation. There was no question of the common vote therein so that it could be called the result of the people's election. However, it was imposed on the people and assumed to be their verdict. From then it became a principle that whomever the nobles of Madeena elected would be deemed to represent the entire world of Islam and no person would be allowed to question it, whether he was present at the time of election or not. In any case, after the establishment of the principle, Moaawiya had no right to propose a re-election nor to refuse allegiance when he had in practice recognised these caliphates which, it was alleged, had been settled by the important people of Madeena. That is why when he held this election to be invalid and refused allegiance, Ameer al-Momineen pointed out to him the (recognised) way of election and demolished his argument. It was a method known as arguing with the adversary on the basis of his wrong premises so as to demolish his argument, since Ameer al-Momineen never at any state regarded consultation (with chiefs) or the common vote to be the criterion of validity of the caliphate. Otherwise, in connection with the caliphate about which it is alleged that they were based on the unanimity of the mohaajiroon and the Ansaar, he would have regarded that unanimity of vote as a good authority and held them as valid; but his refusal for allegiance in the very first period, which cannot be denied by anyone, is a proof of the fact that he did not regard these self-concocted methods as the criterion of (validity of) the caliphate. That is why at all times he continued pressing his own case for the caliphate, which was also established on the basis of the Prophet's saying and deeds. However, to place it before Moaawiya meant opening the door to questions and answers. He therefore attempted to convince him with his own premises and beliefs so that there could be no scope for interpretation or for confusing the matter, in fact Moaawiya's real aim was to prolong the matter so that at some point his own authority might get support.

allegiance to them. (On this basis) he who was present has no choice (to consider), and he who was absent has no right to reject; and consultation is confined to the mohaajiroon and the Ansaar. If they agree on an individual and take him to be Caliph it will be deemed to mean Allah's pleasure. If any one keeps away by way of objection or innovation they will return him to the position from where he kept away. If he refuses they will fight him for following a course other than that of the believers and Allah will put him back from where he had run away. By my life, O Moaawiya, if you see with your brain without any passion you will find me the most innocent of all in respect of "Othmaan's blood and you will surely know that I was in seclusion from him, unless you conceal what is quite open to you. Then you may commit an outrage (on me) as you like and that is an end to the matter.

7- To Moaawiya bn Abi-Sofyaan

I have received from you the packet of unconnected advises and the embellished letter. You have written it because of your misguidance, and despatched it because of lack of wisdom. This is the letter of a man who has neither light to show him the way nor a leader to guide him on the right path. Passion prompted him and he responded to it. Misguidance led him and he followed it. Consequently, he began to speak nonsense and became recklessly astray.

Because allegiance is once and for all. It is not open to reconsidered nor is there any scope for fresh proceedings of election. He who remains out of it is deemed to be critical of Islam while he who prevaricates upon it is a hypocrite.

8- To Jareer bn Abdillah al-Bajali when he sent him to Moaawiya (and there was delay in his return)

Now then, when you receive this letter of mine ask Moaawiya to take a final decision and to follow a determined course. Then ask him to choose either war that exiles him from home or ignoble peace. If he chooses war leave him alone, but if he chooses peace secure his allegiance; and that is an end to the matter.

9- To Moaawiya bn Abi-Sofyaan[1]

-1- When the Messenger of Allah (may Allah bless him and his descendants) was commanded (by Allah) to call people to (believe in) the Unity of Allah, the powers of unbelief and disobedience stood up to block the way of Truthfulness and the tribes of Quraysh decided to quell this voice through pressure and force. The love of their idols was so staunch in the hearts of these unbelievers that they were not prepared to hear a single word against them. The idea of one God was enough to rouse their passions. In addition, they were made to hear such epithets about their gods that gave them no better position than lifeless stones. When they saw their principles and beliefs in danger they prepared themselves to trouble the Prophet and got ready to try every means to that end. They adopted such pain-inflicting devices (against the Prophet) that it was impossible for him to step out of his house. Those who had accepted Islam in this period too had to face continuous tribulations. For example, these adherents of belief were often laid prostrate on the ground under the sun and beaten with straps and stones till they lost their senses. When the atrocities of the Quraysh rose to this extent the Prophet permitted them to leave Mecca and immigrate towards Abysinia, in the fifth year of his call to Prophethood. The Quraysh followed them there as well, but the ruler of Abysinia refused to hand them over to them, and by his fairness and justice did not allow any trouble to befall them.

On the other side the Prophet's preaching was continuing and the magnetism and influence of Truth was producing its effect. People were impressed by his teachings and personality and coming into his fold as a result of which the Quraysh felt much perturbed and tried to stop this increasing influence and power. When they could not do anything they decided to sever all connections with Bani-Hashim and Bani-Abd al-Mottalib, to have no social contacts with them and to have no transactions with them, so that they might be forced to give up supporting the Prophet and then they would deal with him as they wished. Consequently, they concluded a mutual agreement about it and a document was written on the subject and kept in deposit. After this agreement, although the locality was the same and the inhabitants too were the same yet for Bani-Hashim every nook and corner became strange and well-known faces turned as if they had never known each other. All of them turned their faces and stopped mutual meeting and contacts. In these circumstances, there was also apprehension that the Prophet might be attacked suddenly in a valley outside the city. For this reason, they were forced to take refuge in a place called 'shib (quarter) of Abi-Talib." At this stage those Bani-Hashim who had not yet accepted Islam shared these privations on account of lineal unity and offered defence at the hour of need, while those who had accepted Islam like Hamza and Abi-Taalib, were active in protecting the Prophet by way of a religious obligation. In particular, Abi-Taalib had given up all his personal ease and comfort. He spent his days in

Our people (the Quraysh) decided to kill our Prophet and to annihilate our root. They created worries for us, behaved with us harshly, denied us ease of life, exposed us to fear, forced us to fake refuge in a rugged mountain and ignited for us the flames of war.

Allah then gave us determination to protect His religion and defend His honour. The believers among us expected (heavenly) reward from it, and the unbelievers among us gave their support because of kinship. Those who accepted Islam from among the Quraysh were away from the

---

consoling the Prophet and his nights in changing his bed, in this way, that if the Prophet used a bed one night the next night Ali was made to sleep in it, so that in case someone attacked, then Ali should suffer the brunt.

This was a period of great privation and trouble for Bani-Hashim. If they could get leaves of trees to eat that was enough, otherwise they had to starve. After the lapse of three years in these hardships Mohair bn-Abi-Omayya (whose mother was Atika bnt Abd al-Mottalib), Hishaam bn-Amr bn-Rabeea (who had family relationship with Bani-Hashim through his mother), al-Motim bn-Aadil bn-Nawfal bn-Abd-Manaaf, Abol-Bakhtari al-Aas bn-Hishaam bn-Mogheera and Zamaa bn-Aswad bn-Mottalib proposed that this agreement should be abrogated. For a discussion of this issue, the Chiefs among the Quraysh assembled in the Kaba. No decision has yet been taken when Abi-Taalib also came out of the Valley and joined them. He said to them "My nephew Mohammad has told me that the paper on which this agreement was written has been eaten by white-ants and nothing in it has remained save the name of Allah. So, you should send for the document and see it. If he is correct then you should give up animosity to him; and if he is wrong I am ready to hand him over to you." Consequently, the document was sent for and seen. It was a fact that except the words "with Your name, O my Allah" which was written on the top of all documents in those days the rest of it had been eaten away by white-ants. Seeing this al-Motim bn-Aadil tore off the writing and thus this agreement was abrogated. At last Bani-Hashim got rid of the life of oppression and helplessness; but even after this there was no change in the unbelievers" behaviour towards the Prophet; rather they were so keen in their enmity and malice against him that they started thinking of taking his life, as a consequence of which the great event of hijra (immigration of the Holy Prophet from Mecca to Madeena) took place. Although on this occasion Abi-Talib was no longer alive, Ali represented him by lying down on the Prophet's bed, because it was the lesson taught by Abi-Taalib through which he managed to protect the Holy Prophet's life.

Although these events were not unknown to Moaawiya yet by recounting to him the deeds of his predecessors, the intention was to awaken his malicious spirit. Therefore, his attention has been drawn to the hardships inflicted (on the Holy Prophet and his adherents) by the Quraysh and especially Bani-Abd Shams so that he might see the conduct of each of the followers of truth and the followers of wrong and realise whether he himself was treading on the right path or just following his forefathers.

distresses in which we were involved either because of a pledge that protected them or because of the tribe that would rise to support them. They were therefore safe from killing. The way with the Prophet (may Allah bless him and his descendants) was that when fighting became fierce and people began to loose ground he would send forward members of his family and through them protect his companions from the attacks of swords and spears. In this way "Obayda bn-Haarith was killed on the day of Badr, Hamza (bn Abd al-Mottalib) on the day of Ohod and Jafar (bn Abi-Talib) on the day of Mota. One more person, whom I can name if I wish, desired to seek martyrdom as they did; but their deaths approached, while his death had not yet approached.

How strange it is that I am being grouped with him who never evinced briskness of pace like me nor had he to his credit any achievement like mine unless he claims something of which I do not know and which I think Allah too does not know. In any case, all praise belongs to Allah.

As regards your request to hand over to you the murderers of "Othmaan. I have thought over this matter and I do not find their handing over to you or to someone else possible for me. By my life, if you do not give up your wrong ways and disruptive acts you will surely know them. They will shortly be seeking you and ell not five you the trouble of seeking them in land, sea, mountains or plain. But this search will be painful for you and their visit will not give you happiness. Peace be on those who deserve it.

10- To Moaawiya bn Abi-Sofyaan

What will you do when the coverings of this world in which you are wrapped are removed from you. The world attracted you with its embellishment and deceived you with its pleasure. It called you and you responded to it. It led you and you followed it. It commanded you and you obeyed it. Shortly an informer will inform you of things against which there will be no shield (to protect you). Therefore. Keep off from this affair, take heed of the accounting (on the Day of Judgement), get ready for death that will soon overtake you and do not give your ears to those who have gone astray. If you do not do so I shall recall to you whatever you have forgotten, because you are a man living in ease and luxury[1]. Shaitan has taken you in his clutches, has secured his wishes in you and has taken complete control of you like your soul and blood.

O Moaawiya, when were you all protectors of the ruled and guardians of the affairs of the people? Without any forward step or conspicuous distinction? We seek Allah's protection against the befalling of previous misfortunes, and I warn you lest you continue being deceived by desires and your appearance becomes different from your inner self.

You have called me to war. Better to leave the people on one side, come out to me and spare both the parties from fighting so that it may be known who of us has a rusted heart, and covered eyes. I am Abol-Hasan who killed your grandfather[2] your brother[3] and your uncle[4] by cutting them to pieces on the day of Badr. The same sword is with me and I meet my adversary with the same heart. I have not altered the religion nor put up any new prophet. I am surely (treading) on that very highway which you had willingly forsaken (in the beginning) and then adopted per force. You think you have come out seeking to revenge "Othmaan's blood. Certainly, you know how "Othmaan's blood was shed. If you want to avenge it, avenge it there. It is as though I see that when war is cutting you with its teeth you cry like camels crying under a heavy load. And it is as though I see your party bewildered by the incessant striking of swords, occurrence of death and falling of bodies after bodies. Calling me towards the Quran[5]

-1- This is in reference to the verse:

We sent no warner into any city except its man who lived at ease said "We disbelieve in the Message you have been sent with." (Quraan, 34:34)

-2- Otba bn-Rabeea.

-3- Hanzala bn-Abi-Sofyaan.

-4- al-Waleed bn-Otba.

-5- This prophecy of Ameer al-Momineen is about the battle of Siffeen. Herein he has depicted the whole picture in very few words. Thus, on one side Moaawiya was bewildered on account of the attacks of the Iraqis and was thinking to run away, and on the other, his army was crying under the constant onslaught of death, and, eventually, although they would themselves be either unbelievers, deniers of truth or breakers of allegiance after swearing it.

11- To the Contingent sent to confront the enemy[1]

---

when there was no way of escape, they raised the Quraan on spears and shouted for peace. By this device, the remaining persons saved their lives.
This prophecy" as bn-Abil-Hadeed al-Motazili says "is either true prophetic keen eye of Ameer al-Momineen which is really a significant power, or it is an information through knowledge of the unknown (ilmol-ghayb) which is too most significant and wonderful. However, both cases are in the state of extreme significance and wonderfulness.
bn Abil-Hadeed has further quoted the same prophecy from other letters of Ameer al-Momineen to Moaawiya. (Sharh Nahjol-Balagha, vol.15, pp.83-85)
This prophecy cannot be attributed to imagination, guessing or the drawing of inference from events, nor can these details be ascertained by wit or far-reaching intelligence. Only he can disclose them whose source of information is either the Prophet's own revelation-bearing tongue or Divine inspiration.
-1- When Ameer al-Momineen put Ziyad bn-an-Nadr al-Haarithi and Shorayh bn-Ham al-Haarithi in command of contingents of eight thousand and four thousand strong at the camp of an-Nokhayla and ordered them to advance towards Syria (ash-Sham), some dispute arose between them about their ranks, of which they apprised Ameer al-Momineen and wrote letters of complaints about each other. In reply, Ameer al-Momineen wrote to them that when they marched jointly the command of the whole force would be with Ziyad bn-an-Nazr al-Haarithi and when they marched separately each would be in command of the force over which he had been placed.
In this letter Ameer al-Momineen also wrote for them certain instructions. Here Sayyid Razi has taken down only the portion containing the instructions. These instructions are not only useful as concerns the strategies of fighting of those days, but their utility and importance in bringing out the principles of fighting in these days also is undeniable. These instructions are that at the time of encounter with the enemy the forces should be encamped on the tops of mountains and turns of rivers, because in this way the low areas of the rivers would serve as trenches and the peaks of mountains as the walls of the fortress and thus it would be possible to feel secure and face the enemy from the other side. Secondly, that the attack should be from one side or at the most from two sides, because by distribution of the entire force on several fronts weakness would inevitably arise. Thirdly, that the watchers should be put in position on the tops of high ground and the peaks of mountains so that they may give warning before the attack. Sometimes it happens that instead of attacking from the expected side the enemy attacks from a different side. Therefore, if watchers are in position in high places they will detect the enemy from the cloud of dust seen from a distance.
To clarify the useful aspect of these instructions bn-Abil-Hadeed has recorded (in vol.15, p.91) a historical incident that when Qahtaba (bn Shibeeb at-Taai) encamped in a village

When you proceed towards the enemy or he proceeds towards you, the position of your force should be on the approaches high ground or on the edges of mountains or the bends of rivers, so that it may serve you as help and a place to return to. Your encounter should be from one side or two sides. Place watchers on the peaks of mountains and the raised sides of the high ground so that the enemy may not approach you from any place, whether of danger or safety. And know that the vanguard of an army serves as their eyes, and the eyes of the vanguard are their informers. Beware of dispersal. When you halt do so together and when you move you should move together. When night comes fix your spears in a circle and do not sleep except for dosing or napping.

12- To Maqil bn Qays ar-Riyahi when dispatched to Syria as the head of a vanguard contingent three thousand strong

---

after leaving Khoraasaan, he and Khaalid bn-Barmak went and sat on the top of a nearby hill. No sooner had they sat down than Khaalid noticed flocks of deer coming running from the forest. On seeing this he said to Qahtaba "O commander, get up and announce to the army that they should at once fall in line and take up arms." Hearing this, Qahtaba was startled and stood up but looking hither and thither said "I do not see the enemy's men anywhere." He replied "O Amir, this is not the time that should be lost in conversation. You see these deer which are proceeding towards the people, leaving their abodes. This means that the army of the enemy is marching from their rear" Consequently, he ordered his army to get ready. As soon as the army got ready the noise of horses" hoofs was heard and within moments the enemy was on them. Since they had prepared themselves for defence in time, they defended themselves against the enemy thoroughly. Now, if Khaalid had not been at such a height and had not acted with such sagacity, the enemy would have attacked them unawares and annihilated them. Fourthly, that the reconnaissance should be spread here and there, so that they can be aware of the movements and intentions of the enemy, and thereby foil his plans. Fifthly, that when the army camps it should camp together and when it moves it should move together so that the enemy does not attack you in a state of dispersal and overpower you easily. Sixthly, that at night the guard should be formed by fixing spears in a circle in the ground so that if the enemy attacks in the night, it is possible to prepare for defence by taking up arms at once and if the enemy showers arrows that too can be defied. Seventhly, that deep sleep should be avoided lest you remain unaware of the enemy's approach and he succeed in attacking you before you get ready.

Fear Allah before Whom attendance is inevitable, and with other than Whom there is no meeting. Do not fight except with those who fight you. Travel in the two cool periods (i.e., morning and evening). Let the men have a midday sleep. March easily and do not travel during the early night for Allah has made it for resting and has ordained it for staying, nor for journeying. Therefore, give rest to your body in the night and let your carrier-beasts also rest. When you are sure that morning has appeared and when dawn has dawned, commence your journey with Allah's blessings. If and when you face the enemy stand in the midst of your comrades. Do not get too near the foe like one who wants to commence the fighting, nor remain too distant like one who is afraid of action, till you receive my orders. Hatred for them should not lead you to fight before inviting them (to guidance) and exhausting your pleas before them.

13- To 2 of His Army Officers

I have placed Malik[1] bn-Haarith al-Ashtar in command over you and over all those under you. Therefore, follow his commands and take him as the armour and shield for yourselves, because he is one of those from whom I have no fear of weakness nor any mistake, nor laziness where haste is more appropriate, nor haste where slackness is expected of him.

-1- When Ameer al-Momineen sent a vanguard contingent twelve thousand strong under Ziyad bn-an-Nadr al-Haarith and Shorayh. bn-Hani al-Haarith to Syria, on the way, near Soor ar-Room, they encountered with Abol-Awar (Amr bn-Solaymaan) as-Solaami who was camping there with a contingent of the Syrians. Both of them informed Ameer al-Momineen of this through al-Haarith bn-Jomhaan al-Jofi, whereupon he sent Malik bn-Haarith al-Ashtar as the Officer-in-command and wrote this letter to inform them. The brief but comprehensive words in which Ameer al-Momineen has mentioned Malik al-Ashtar in this letter gives an indication of his intelligence, sagacity, courage, daring, expanse and versatility in the art of war and his personal greatness and importance.

14- To the Army before the encounter with the enemy at Siffeen[1]

-1- The responsibility for the war and fighting that took place between Ameer al-Momineen and Moaawiya lies solely on Moaawiya because he brought about the war by laying the wrong blame for Othmaan's blood on Ameer al-Momineen, although the real facts about the causes of Othmaan's killing and by whom he was killed were not unknown to him. But since there was no way for him to achieve his end save by creating an occasion for war, he entered into war to retain his authority which was evidently offensive and which cannot by any means be considered as permissible, because revolt and rebellion against the rightful Imaam is unlawful according to the general consensus of Muslims. Thus, Abd Zakariyya Yahya bn-Sharaf an-Nawawi (631/1233-676/1277) writes:
Do not fight against those in authority in matters of governance, nor raise objections against them except when you observe them committing things which you know are definitely against Islam. If you see them doing such things regard it bad for them and speak the truth wherever you may be, but rising against them or fighting is prohibited by the consensus of Muslims (Sharh Saheeh Moslim, vol.2, p.125. In agreement with this view, see also, al-Qazi Abi-Bakr Mohammad bn-at-Tayyib al-Baqillaani (338/950-403/1013), the Asharite great scholar, in at-Tamheed, p.186; and Sadoddeen Masood bn-Omar at-Taftazani 1712/1312-793/1390| in Sharh al-Maqaasid, vol.2, p.272).
Mohammad bn-Abdl-Kareem ash-Shahristani writes:
Whoever rises against the true Imaam, by the unanimity of opinion of the (Muslim) community, is known as a Kharijite, the deviator. The same is the case of rising, during the days of the companions, against the rightful Imaams, or even after them against those who followed them in virtue. (al-Milal wan-Nehal, vol.1, p.114)
There is no doubt that Moaawiya's action was the result of uprising and revolt, and to take up arms for the purpose of stopping the advance of the one who revolts is not to be regarded as being against any code of peacefulness or peace-loving. Rather, it is a natural right of the oppressed; and if he is deprived of this right then there will remain no way of preventing oppression and tyranny or of safeguarding rights in the world. That is why Allah has permitted taking up arms against rebels. Thus, Allah says:
And if two parties of the believers fall into a quarrel (among themselves), restore ye peace between them two; but if one of the two transgresseth against the other, (then) fight ye (all against) that which transgresseth until it complieth with the command of Allah; and if it complieth then restore ye peace between the two with justice, and act ye justly; Verily, Allah loveth the just ones. (Quraan, 49:9)
It was the first plea to which Ameer al-Momineen pointed out by saying "By the Grace of Allah you are in the right," but even after exhaustion of this plea he prevented his army from taking the initiative in fighting, because he wished that the initiative should not be from his side and that he should take up the sword only in defence. Consequently, when all his effort for peace and tranquillity proved futile and the enemy took the step towards war, this was the second argument in their favour, after which Ameer al-Momineen could

Do not fight them unless they initiate the fighting, because, by the grace of Allah, you are in the right and to leave them till they begin fighting will be another point from your side against them. If, by the will of Allah, the enemy is defeated then do not kill the runner away, do not strike a helpless person, do not finish off the wounded, and do not inflict pain on women even though they may attack your honour with filthy words and abuse your officers, because they are weak in character, mind and intelligence. We have been ordered to desist from them although they

---

not be blamed for getting ready to fight, nor accused of aggressive action. It was rather an obligation to stop oppression and tyranny that he had to discharge and which Allah has permitted in plain words. Thus, Allah's command is that:

And fight in the cause of Allah (against) those who fight you but be not aggressive; for verily Allah loveth not the aggressors. (Quraan, 2:190)

Besides, fighting against Ameer al-Momineen means fighting against the Prophet, as the Prophet's saying "O Ali, your peace is my peace and your war is my war" (bn al-Maghaazili, al-Manaaqib, p.5; bn-Abil-Hadeed, vol.18, p.24). In this way whatever punishment should be for fighting against the Prophet should be for Fighting against Ameer al-Momineen. For him who wages war against the Prophet, Allah has laid down the following punishment.

To recompense of those who war against Allah and His Apostle, and strive in the land, spreading mischief (therein), is only that they be slain or crucified or their hands and their feet should be cut off, from the opposite sides, or be banished from the land; This for them shall be the disgrace in this world, and for them, in the hereafter, shall be a great torment. (Quraan, 5:33)

Apart from this, the instructions that Ameer al-Momineen issued in connection with the war, namely that no runner away or wounded should be molested, are so high from the moral point of view that they can be regarded as a sublime specimen of moral values and the high standard of Islamic fighting. Then, these instructions were not confined to mere words but Ameer al-Momineen followed them to the letter, and ordered others also to follow them strictly. He did not, on any occasion, tolerate the chasing of a runner away, attack the helpless or molest women, in fact, on the battlefield of Jamal, where the command of the opposite force was with a woman, he did not change his principle. After the defeat and vanquishment of the foe he gave proof of his high character and sent Aysha to Madeena under guard. Had there been someone other than Ameer al-Momineen he would have proposed the same punishment as that which ought to be awarded for such a step! Thus, bn-Abil-Hadeed has written:

What she did with Ameer al-Momineen, if she had done the same with (Caliph) Omar and had spread rebellion against him among the people, he would, after securing victory over her, have killed her and cut her into pieces, but Ameer al-Momineen was very fore-bearing and large-hearted. (Sharh Nahjol-Balagha, vol.17, p.254)

may be unbelievers. Even in pre-Islamic (al-jaahiliyya) period if a man struck a woman with a stone or a stick he was rebuked along with his posteriors after him.

15- Invocation when he used to face the enemy

O my Allah! Hearts are getting drawn to You, necks are stretching (towards You), eyes are fixed (on You), steps are in motion and bodies have turned lean. O my Allah! Hidden animosity has become manifest and the pots of malice are boiling.

O my Allah! We complain to You of the absence of our Prophet, the numerousness of our enemy and the diffusion of our passions.

O Lord! Decide between us and between our people with truth, and You are the Best of Deciders. (Quran, 7:89)

16- Instruction he used to give to his followers at the time of battle

The retreat after which return is intended and the withdrawal after which attack is in view should not make you unhappy. Do justice with the swords (allow your swords to do their duties). Keep ready a place for the falling of bodies (of your foe); prepare yourselves for hurling strong spears and striking swords with full force, and keep your voices down as that keeps off cowardice.

By Him Who broke open the seed (for growing) and created living beings, they had not accepted Islam but they had secured safety (by verbally professing it) and had hidden their misbelief. Consequently, when they found helpers for their misbelief they disclosed it.

17- In reply to a letter from Moaawiya[1]

-1- During the battle of Siffeen, Moaawiya thought of again demanding the province of Syria from Ameer al-Momineen and to play such a trick as to succeed in his designs. In this connection, he consulted Amr bn-Aas. But the latter did not agree with this idea and said "O Moaawiya, think a little, what effect will this writing of yours have on Ali? How can he fall in this trap by your persuasion." On this Moaawiya said "We are all descendants of Abd Manaf. What difference is there between Ali and me that he may score over me and I may not succeed in deceiving him?" Amr bn-Aas said "If you think so, then write and see (the outcome)." Moaawiya therefore wrote a letter to Ameer al-Momineen wherein he made a demand for Syria and also wrote: "We are descendants of Abd Manaf. There is no distinction of one over the other among us." Then, Ameer al-Momineen wrote this letter in reply and mentioning his own predecessors along with those of Moaawiya disproved his contention of equality. Although the origin of both was the same and the paternal chain of both joined at Abd Manaf, the progeny of Abd Shams was the source of all evil in morality and character and was involved in heresy and vice whereas the house of Hashim was the worshipper of one God and kept aloof from idolatry. If the branches growing out of the same root bear both flowers as well as thorns, then both cannot be deemed equal. Consequently, it does not need any detailed explanation to show that Omayya and Hashim, Harb and Abd al-Mottalib and Abi Sofyaan and Abi Talib were not match of each other from any angle. This is not denied by any historian nor by any biographer. In fact, after this reply even Moaawiya did not dare refute it, because the fact could be concealed that after Abd Manaf it was Hashim alone who possessed conspicuous prestige among the Quraysh, and the most important positions with relation to the Kaba namely siqaaya (i.e., the superintendence of the water-supply, especially with a view to the needs of pilgrims) and rifaada (provisioning of pilgrims) was assigned to him. As such, at the time of Haj, caravan after caravan used to come and stay with him and he was such a generous host to them that those who partook of his generosity and benevolence would praise him for long thereafter.

The worthy son of this very large-hearted and courageous father was Abd al-Mottalib whose name was Shayba and surname was Sayyidol-Bat-haa (the Chief of the Valley of Mecca). He was the successor to the destinction of Abraham's line and owner of the greatness and chiefdom of Quraysh. The high courage and far-sightedness showed by him before Abraham is a shining star of the family of Abd Manaf. Abd Manaf was a pearl and Abd al-Mottalib was the lustre of the pearl.

Abdl-Mottalib's son was Abi-Taalib whose lap served as the cradle for Abdillah's orphan child and the training place of the Prophet. He brought up the Prophet in his care, and shielded him against his enemies. To compare Abi-Sofyaan, Harb and Omayya with them or to regard them as their matches is the same as to close one's eyes to the lustre of light and to regard it as darkness.

After recounting this genealogical difference the next point of distinction that Ameer al-Momineen has described is that he himself is a mohaajir (immigrant from Mecca) while

Moaawiya is a Taleeq (i.e., one of those whom the Prophet had spared on the day of fall of Mecca). Therefore, when the Prophet entered Mecca victorious he enquired from the Quraysh how they thought he would deal with them, and all said that being a generous son of a generous father they expected only good from him, whereupon the Prophet said "Go away, you have all been spared." That is "you did deserve to be detained as slaves but as a mark of obligation you have been left free." These spared ones included Moaawiya and Abi-Sofyaan also. Thus, bn-Abil-Hadeed and ash-Shaykh Mohammad Abdo have recorded the following note in their annotations to this letter "Abi-Sofyaan and Moaawiya both were among the spared ones." (bn Abil-Hadeed, vol.17, p.119; Abdo, vol.3, p.17)

The third point of distinction is that Ameer al-Momineen's lineage is pure and clear and there is no doubtful point anywhere. As against this, for Moaawiya he has used to the word "laseeq. Men of letters have given laseeq to mean "One who is attributed to other than his father." In this connection, the first doubt that is entertained about Omayya is whether he was the son of Abd Shams or only his slave who began to be known as his son because of having been brought up by him. Thus, al-Allama al-Majlisi has related from Kaamil al-Bahaai that:

Omayya was a Byzantine slave of Abd Shams. When he found him intelligent and sagacious he freed him and adopted him as his son, as a result of which he began to be called Omayya son of Abd Shams, as Zayd (bn al-Haaritha) was called Zayd bn-Mohammad before the verse was revealed (to prohibit it). (Bihaar al-Anwaar, 1st ed., vol.8, p.383)

The second doubt in the Omayyad lineage is whether Harb who is known as the son of Omayya was really his son or a slave brought up by him. In this connection, bn-Abil-Hadeed has quoted from Abol-Faraj al-Isbahaani's book that:

Moaawiya enquired from the lineage expert Daghfal (bn Hanzala) whether he had seen Abdl-Mottalib and he replied in the affirmative. He further enquired how he found him and Daghfal replied "He was prestigious, handsome and a man of open forehead, while his face bore the brightness of Prophethood." Then, Moaawiya enquired whether he had seen Omayya bn-Abd Shams also, and he replied that he had seen him too. He enquired how he found him and he replied "Weak bodied, bent stature and blind in the eyes. In front of him was his slave Zakwaan who led here and there." Moaawiya said it was his son Abi-Amr (Harb) whereupon he said "You say so but the Quraysh only know that he was his slave." (al-Afghani, vol.1, p.12; Sharh Nahjol-Balagha, vol.17, pp.231-232)

In this connection, the third doubt is about Moaawiya himself. Thus bn-Abil-Hadeed has written that:

Moaawiya's mother Hind led a life of vileness and immorality. az-Zamakhshari (Abol-Qaasim Mahmood bn-Omar 1467/1075-538/1144) has written in his book Rabiol-Abraar that Moaawiya's parentage was traced back to four persons who were: Mosaafir bn-Abi-Amr, Omaara bn-Waleed bn-Mogheera, al-Abbaas bn-Abdl-Mottalib and as-Sabaah (a singer for Omaara). (Sharh Nahjol-Balagha, vol.1, p.336)

The fourth point of distinction that Ameer al-Momineen has stated is that he himself was the devotee of right while Moaawiya was the devotee of wrong and this fact needs no

As for your demand to me to (hand over) Syria, I cannot give you today what I denied you yesterday. As regards your saying that the war has eaten up Arabia save its last breath, you should know that he whom right has eaten up goes to Paradise and he whom wrong has eaten up goes to Hell. As for our equality in (the art of) war and in (numbers of) men, certainly you cannot be more penetrating in doubtfulness (of belief) than I am in certainty (of belief), and the people of Syria are not more greedy for this world than the people of Iraq are for the next world.

As for your saying that both of us are sons of Abd Manaf, it is no doubt so, but Omayya cannot be like Hashim, nor Harb like Abd al-Mottalib, nor can Abu Sofyaan be like Abu Talib. The Mohaajir (immigrant) cannot be a match for him who was set free (on the day of fall of Mecca), nor can one of pure descent be a match for him who has been adopted, nor the pursuer of truth be a match of the adherent to wrong, nor a believer be a match for a hypocrite. How bad are the successors who go on following their predecessors who have fallen in the fire of Hell!

Besides that, we also have the distinction of Prophethood among us, by virtue of which we subdued the strong and raised up the downtrodden. When Allah made Arabia enter (the fold of His religion, and the people submitted to it willingly or unwillingly, you were among those who entered the religion either from greed or from fear, at a time when those who had gone first had preceded and the first mohaajiroon had acquired their (peculiar) distinction.

Now, do not allow Shaitan have a share with you nor let him have his sway over you; and that is an end to the matter.

---

proof, for the whole life of Moaawiya was spent in suppressing right and hankering after wrong. No where is his step seen advancing towards right.

The fifth distinction that Ameer al-Momineen has mentioned is that he himself was a believer whereas Moaawiya was a mischief-monger and a hypocrite. Just as there can be no doubt about Ameer al-Momineen's belief, there can be no doubt about Moaawiya's mischief-mongering and hypocrisy. Thus, Ameer al-Momineen has exposed his hypocrisy in the earlier writing in these words. These people had not accepted Islam but they had secured safety by verbally professing it and had hidden their misbelief. Consequently, when they found helpers for their mischief they disclosed it.

18- To Abdillah bn al-Abbas, his Governor of Basra

You should know that Basra is the place where Shaitan descends and mischiefs happen. Keep the people of this place pleased with good treatment and remove the knots of fear from their hearts.

I have come to know of your strictness with Bani-Tameem[1] and your harshness over them. Bani-Tameem are those that if one star sets another one rises for them. They were never exceeded in (the art of) war in pre-Islamic times or after Islam. They have a special kinship with us and a particular relationship. We shall be rewarded if we pay heed to the kinship and be deemed sinful if we disregard it. O Abol-Abbas, may Allah have mercy on you, keep yourself restrained in whatever you say or do, good or bad about your people, as we are both partners in this (responsibility). Prove yourself according to my good impressions about you, and do not prove my opinion (about you) wrong; and that is an end to the matter.

19- To One of His Officers

Now, the cultivators[2] (dahaaqin, plural of dihqaan) of your city have complained of your strictness, hard heartedness, humiliating treatment

---

-1- When Talha and az-Zobayr reached Basra it was Bani-Tameem who took active part in the movement to avenge Othmaan's blood and were foremost in fanning this mischief. Therefore, when Abdillah bn-Abbaas took over as the Governor of Basra, in view of their breach of faith and animosity, he thought they deserved harsh treatment and was to some extent severe with them. But in this tribe there were also a few sincere followers of Ameer al-Momineen. When they saw this behaviour of bn-Abbaas with their tribe they sent a letter to Ameer al-Momineen through Jaariya bn-Qadaama wherein they complained of bn-Abbaas's harsh treatment. Thereupon, Ameer al-Momineen wrote this letter to bn-Abbaas in which he instructed him to change his ways and to behave well with them, and has drawn his attention to the kinship existing between Bani-Hashim and Bani-Tameem. That kinship was this that Bani-Hashim and Bani-Tameem join the lineal line at Ilyaas bn-Mozar because Hashim is the descendant of Modrikah bn-Ilyaas, while Tameem is the descendant of Taabikhah bn-Ilyaas.

-2- These people were Magians (majoos). That is why the treatment of Ameer al-Momineen's officer with them was not the same as with Muslims. Disgusted with this they wrote a letter of complaint to Ameer al-Momineen and spoke of the Officer's and harshness. I thought over it and found that since they are unbelievers they cannot be brought near nor kept away or treated severely because of the pledge with them. Behave with them in between strictness and softness and adopt for them a mingling or remoteness and aloofness with nearness and closeness if Allah so wills.

20- To Ziyad bn Abeeh, the deputy governor of Abdillah bn al-Abbas in Basra

I truthfully swear by Allah that if I come to know that you have misappropriated the funds of the Muslims, small or big; I shall inflict upon you such punishment, which will leave you empty, handed. heavy backed and humiliated; and that is an end to the matter.

21- To Ziyad bn Abeeh, the deputy governor of Abdillah bn al-Abbas in Basra

Give up lavishness and be moderate. Every day remember the coming day. Hold back from the funds what you need and send forward the balance for the day of your need.

Do you expect that Allah may give you the reward of the humble while you yourself remain vain in His view? And do you covet that He may give you the reward of those practising charity while you enjoy comforts and deny them to the weak and the widows? Certainly, a man is awarded according as he acts and meets what he has sent forward; and that is an end to the matter.

---

harshness. In reply, Ameer al-Momineen wrote to his officer that he should meet out treatment to them in which there should be neither harshness nor such leniency which they may exploit to create mischief because if they are let loose they get involved in machinations against the government and disturb the country's administration by creating one mischief or the other, while a wholly repressive policy cannot be justified because they are counted among the subjects and their rights as such cannot be ignored.

22- To Abdillah bn al-Abbas, his GOVERNOR in Basra

Abdillah bn al-Abbas used to say "apart from the prophet's sayings" I did not derive greater benefit from any saying than this one:
Let it be known to you that sometimes a man gets pleased at securing a thing which he was not going to miss at all and gets displeased at missing a thing which he would not in any case get. Your pleasure should be about what you secure in respect of your next life and your grief should be for what you miss in respect thereof. Do not be much pleased on what you secure from this world, nor get extremely grieved over what you miss out of it. Your worry should be about what is to come after death.

23- Will made shortly before his death when he had been fatally wounded by a blow from the sword of Abdr-Rahmaan bn Moljam (Curse of Allah upon him)

I enjoin upon you as my dying wish not to regard anything by way of partner with Allah, not to disregard the Sonna of Mohammad (may Allah bless him and his descendants), establish these two pillars and light these two lamps. You will then be free from evil. Yesterday I was your companion and today I am (just) a lesson for you, while tomorrow I shall be leaving you. If I survive I shall be the master of my blood (to avenge or not to avenge it), and if I die then death is a promised event. If I forgive, it is for me a means of nearness (to Allah) and for you a good act. Therefore, do forgive. What! Love you not that Allah should forgive you? (Quran, 24:22)
By Allah, this sudden death is not an event that I dislike, nor is it an accident that I hate. I am just like a night traveller who reaches the spring (in the morning) or like or seeker who secures (his aim):And whatever is with Allah is the best for the righteous ones. (Quran, 3:198)
Sayyid Razi says: A part of this utterance has already appeared in the sermons but it was found necessary to record it again, because of some additional matter.

24- Will as to how his property should be dealt with

He wrote it on return from Siffeen.

This is what Ali bn-Abi-Talib, the slave of Allah has laid down about his property, in pursuance of seeking Allah's pleasure so that He may by virtue of it give him entry into Paradise and accord him peace.

It will be administered by Hasan bn-Ali. He will take from it a suitable portion for his livelihood and spend it on charity. If something happens to Hasan, and if Hosayn survives he will administer it after Hasan, and deal with it accordingly. In the charitable estate of the two sons of Fatima they have the same rights as the all (other) sons of Ali. I have laid down the (functions of) administration of the two sons of Fatima in order to seek the pleasure of Allah and nearness to the Messenger of Allah (may Allah bless him and his descendants) with due regard for his honour and consideration of his kinship.

It is obligatory on him who administers it that he retains the estate as it is, and spends the usufruct as he has been ordered and instructed. He should not sell the seedlings in the plantations of these villages till the land changes its face by turning them into plants. As for those of my slave girls who where under me, if any one of them has a child or is pregnant, she will be retained for the sake of the child and will form part of his share. If the child dies and she survives, then she is free, bondage is removed from her and liberty is given to her.[1]

-1- The life of Ameer al-Momineen was that of a labourer or a cultivator. He worked in fields of other persons, cultivated barren and untilled lands, providing means of irrigating them, made them cultivable and planted orchards therein. Since these lands were cultivated by him they were his property but he never paid heed to property, and, declaring them a trust, gave up his proprietorship; but in consideration of the Prophet's kinship he assigned the management rights of this trust to Imaam Hasan and Imaam Hosayn one after the other. Yet he did not tolerate any additional rights for them but like other children gave them merely the right to take from it only for their livelihood, while the balance he ordered to be spent for the common good of the Muslims and for charitable purposes. Thus, bn-Abil-Hadeed writes:

Sayyid Razi says: In this will in Amir al-Momineen's phrase "alla yabi a min nakhliha wadiyyatan, the word "wadiyyah" means seedling of date-palm and its plural is "wadiyy. And his words "hatta tushkila arduha ghirasan, is one of the most eloquent form of expression and it means that when a number of date plants grow on the land then he who had seen it before the growth would regard it as a different land.

25- Instruction to whoever he appointed for the collection of zakat and charities

ash-Sharif says: We have recorded a few portions of it here to show that he always erected the pillars of right and created examples of justice in all matters, small or big, delicate or serious.

Move on with the fear of Allah Who is One and has no partner. Do not frighten any Muslim. Do not pass over his lands so as to make him feel unhappy. Do not take from him more than Allah's share in his property. When you go to a tribe, you should get down at their watering place instead of entering their houses. Then proceed towards them with peace and dignity till you stand among them. Then salute them and do not be remiss in greeting them, then say to them "O servants of Allah, the vicegerent of Allah and His caliph has sent me to you to collect from you Allah's share in your properties. Is there anything of His share in your properties? If so, give it to His vicegerent. "

If someone among them says "No, then do not repeat the demand. If someone speaks to you in the affirmative, then go with him without frightening him. threatening him, pressuring him or oppressing him. Take what he gives you such as gold or silver (coins). If he has cattle or camels do not enter upon them save with his permission, because their major

---

Everyone knows that in Madeena, Yanboo and Sowayqa, Ameer al-Momineen had dug several springs from under the land and brought under cultivation many barren and uncultivable lands. Thereafter, he gave up rights over them and declared them as trusts for the Muslims. When he left the world, nothing was owned by him. (Sharh Nahjol-Balagha, vol.15, p.146)

part is his. Therefore, when you get there do not enter upon them like one who has full control over them or in a violent manner. Do not scare any animal, do not tease anyone and do not let the owner feel grieved about anyone.

Divide the property into two parts and let the owner choose one. When he has chosen do not object to it. Then divide the remaining into two parts and let him choose one and when he has chosen do not raise any objection. Continue like this till only that much remains, which is enough to satisfy Allah's dues. Then take Allah's due from it. If he disputes your action allow his views, then mix the two (separated) parts and repeat what you had done before till you take Allah's due from his property. Do not take an old, decrepit broken-limbed, sick or unsound animal. Do not entrust the animals (for custody) except to one whom you trust to take care of Muslims" property till he hands it over to their chief who will distribute it. Do not entrust it to anyone except he who is a well-wisher, God-fearing, trustworthy and watchful, and who is not harsh on Muslims" property, nor makes them run too much, nor tires them, nor labours them. Then send to us all that you have collected and we shall deal with it as Allah has ordered.

When your trustee takes over (the animal) tell him that he should not separate the she-camel from its young and should not milk all its milk because that would affect its young, and also that he should not exert it in riding. In this matter, he should behave justly between it and all its companions. He should allow rest to camels (who are tired), and drive with ease those whose hoofs have been rubbed off. When you pass a water spring stay the camels there for drinking and do not take them away from vegetated land to barren paths. He should allow them rest now and then. and give them time near water and grass. In this way, when they reach us by leave of Allah, they will be fat with plenty of marrow and would not be fatigued or distressed. We will then distribute them according to the (commands of) the Book of Allah and the Sonna of His Prophet (peace be upon him and his progeny). Certainly, this will be a great source of reward for you and a means to secure guidance, if Allah so wills.

26- Instruction to one of his officers whom he sent for the collection of zakat and charities

He (Amir al-Momineen) ordered him to fear Allah in his secret matters and hidden actions, where there is no witness except He and no one watches save He. He also orders him that whatever he does in obedience to Allah openly should not be different from what he does secretly. He whose hidden position is not different from his open position, and whose action is not different from his words, has discharged his obligation and his worship is pure.

He also ordered him that he should not harass them, should not be harsh on them and should not turn away from them because of superiority of official position over them, because they are brethren in faith and help in the recovery of levies.

Certainly, you have a fixed share and a known right in this levy, and there are others sharers who are poor, weak and starving. We shall discharge your rights. So, you should discharge their rights. If you do not do so you will have the largest number of enemies on the Day of Judgement. How wretched is the man whose enemies in the view of Allah are the needy. the destitute, the beggars, the turned away, the indebted and (penniless) travellers. He who treats the trust lightly and indulges in treachery and does not keep himself and his faith untarnished by it has certainly secured humiliation in this world, and his humiliation and disgrace in the next world will be greater. Surely, the greatest treachery is the treachery against the Muslim community, and the most ugly deceit is the deceit towards the Muslim leaders; and that is an end to the matter.

27- Instruction to Mohammad bn Abi Bakr (may Allah be pleased with him), when he appointed him as the governor of Egypt

Behave humbly with the people, keep yourself lenient. meet them large-heartedly, accord them equal treatment so that the big should not expect injustice from you in their favour and the low should not be despondent of your justice to them. Allah, the Sublime, will certainly question you, O community of His creatures, about your actions, small or big, open or concealed. If He punishes you it is because you have been oppressive, and if He forgives. then it is because He is the Most Generous.

Know, O creatures of Allah, that the God-fearing have shared the joys of this transient world as well as the next coming world, for they shared with the people of this world in their worldly matters while their people did not share with them in the matters of the next world. They lived in this world in the best manner of living and ate the choicest food and consequently they enjoyed herein all that the people with ease of life enjoyed, and secured from it what the haughty and the vain secured. Then, they departed from it after taking provision enough to take them to the end of their journey and after doing a profitable transaction. They tasted the pleasure of renouncing the world in this world, and they firmly believed that on the coming day in their next life they would be neighbours of Allah, where their call would not be repulsed nor would their share of pleasure be small.

Therefore, O creatures of Allah, be afraid of death and its measures and keep ready all that is needed for it. It will come as a big event and a great affair, either as a good in which there will never be any evil, or an evil in which there will never be any good. Who is nearer to Paradise than he who works towards it, and who is nearer to Hell than he who works for it? You are being chased by death. If you stop, it will catch you, and if you run away from it, it will grip you. It is more attached to you than your reflection. Death is tied to your forelocks while the world is being wrapped up from behind you. Therefore, fear the Fire whose hollow is deep, whose flames are severe and whose punishment is novel. It is a place wherein there is no mercy. No call is heard in it. No pain is healed in it. If it is possible for you to have severe fear of Allah and to rest hope in Him, then do both these things because every individual can have hope in His Lord to the extent of his fear of His Lord. Certainly, the most hopeful person with Allah is he who fears Him most.

O Mohammad bn-Abi Bakr, know that I have given you charge of Egypt, which is my biggest force. So you are duty-bound to oppose your passions and serve as a shield against your religion even though you may get only an hour in the world; and do not enrage Allah for pleasing others because (Allah) is such that He may take the place of others, but others cannot take the place of Allah. Say prayers at the appointed time. Do not say it earlier for the sake of (available) leisure nor delay it on account of pre-occupation. Remember that every act of yours is dependent on your prayer.

The leader of guidance and the leader of destruction cannot be equal, nor the friend of the Prophet and the enemy of the Prophet. The Messenger of Allah (p.b.u.h.a.h.p.) has told me that: "In respect of my people I am afraid neither of a believer nor of an unbeliever. As for the believer Allah will afford him protection because of his belief and as for the unbeliever, Allah will humiliate him because of his unbelief. But I am afraid about every one of you who is hypocrite in his heart and learned of speech. He speaks what you hold good but does what you dislike.

28- In reply to Moaawiya,

It is one of his most elegant writings

Now, your letter[1] has reached me wherein you recall that Allah chose Mohammad (p.b.u.h.a.h.p.) for His religion and helped him through those

-1- This letter of Ameer al-Momineen's is in reply to Moaawiya's letter which he sent to Koofa through Abi-Omaama al-Baahili, and it also contains replies to some points which Moaawiya had written in the letter sent through Abi-Muslim al-Khawlaani.

In Abi-Omaama's letter, Moaawiya had mentioned the deputation of the Prophet and his ascension to the position of revelation and wrote in such a manner as though it was a matter not known to or not understood by Ameer al-Momineen and that he was in need of being informed and told of it. This i5 just like a stranger who may draw the map of a house for the guidance of those who dwell in it and apprise them of things already known to them. That is why Ameer al-Momineen has compared him to the man who carried dates to Hajar which was itself noted for abundant growth of dates.

This is a proverb employed when someone beings to tell a person matters which he already knows better. The basis of this proverb is that a man of Hajar, which is a town near Bahrain (Persian Gulf), went to Basra to sell goods and make purchases. After finishing the sale, he looked about the market to make his purchases and found nothing cheaper than dates. He therefore decided to purchase dates, and when he reached Hajar with his load of dates their plenty and cheapness there did not leave him any alternative but to store them so as to sell them later when their price had risen. The price however continued to fall day by day till all of them became rotten leaving to him nothing except their stones. In short, after referring to the Prophet's ascensions to Prophethood, Moaawiya recounted the distinction and merits of the three Caliphs according to his view and wrote:

The most distinguished among the companions and the most high ranking in the view of the Muslims was the first Caliph who collected all the Muslims under one voice, removed their disunity and fought those who were forsaking Islam. After him is the second Caliph who won victories, founded cities and humiliated the unbelievers. Then comes the third Caliph who was the victim of oppression. He propagated religion and spread the word of Allah far and wide. (Siffeen, al-Minqari, pp.8587; al-Iqd al-fareed, vol.4, pp.334-335; Sharh Nahjol-Balagha, vol.15, p.186)

Moaawiya's purpose behind in bringing up these pointless warblings was to injure Ameer al-Momineen's feelings and to rouse his temper so as to make him produce such words through his tongue or pen which would so disparage the caliphs that he would instigate the people of Syria and Iraq against him by exploiting them. In fact, he had already set it in the minds of these people that Ameer al-Momineen had instigated the people against Othmaan, had got Talha and az-Zobayr killed, had turned Aysha out from her house and had shed the blood of thousands of Muslims. Being unaware of the real facts they were convinced of these baseless allegations, yet to strengthen the opposition, he thought it advisable to make them believe that Ameer al-Momineen did not recognise the achievements of the three caliphs and bore enmity and malice towards them, and to produce Ameer al-Momineen's writing in evidence, and also to use it for rousing the people of Iraq, because their majority was much impressed with the environment created by the caliphs and with their greatness. But Ameer al-Momineen guessed his intention and gave him such a reply which put a knot in his tongue and which he could not dare show to anyone. So, Ameer al-Momineen exposed his lowness by referring to his enmity towards Islam and his accepting subjugation under force, and advised him to keep within his bounds, and warned him against fixing grades of distinction among those mohaajiroon who were in any case superior to him in so far as they had been the preceders in hijra (immigration from Mecca). Whereas since Moaawiya himself was only one of those whose life had been spared (on the day of fall of Mecca), he had not the remotest connection with the mohaajiroon. Consequently, in the matter under discussion Ameer al-Momineen has put Moaawiya's position as that of a false arrow among real arrows. This is a proverb which is employed when a man boasts over persons with whom he has no connection. As regards his statement that so-and-so is greater in distinction, Ameer al-Momineen has, by using the word "you think, shown that it is his personal opinion which has not the remotest connection with fact, because this word is used when a false or unreal statement is made.

After refuting this claim of being the most distinguished, Ameer al-Momineen has referred to these qualities and distinctions of Bani-Hashim which show conspicuously the high degree of their attainments. Thus, the people who took part in Jihaad with the Prophet and secured martyrdom attained high positions but the distinction that fell to Hamza by virtue of his high performance was not secured by anyone else. The Prophet gave him the title of Master of the Martyrs and said his funeral prayer fourteen times whereby the number of takbeer (Allaho Akbar) rose to seventy. Similarly, in various battles the hands of the fighters were cut off. For example, in the battle of Badr, the hands of Khobab bn-Isaaf al-Ansaari and Maaz bn-Jabal and in the battle of Ohod those of Amr bn-Jamooh as-Salami and Obayd (Atik) bn-at-Tayyihan (brother of Abol-Haytham at-Tayyihan) were cut off, but when in the battle of Mota the hands of Jafar bn-Abi-Talib were cut off, the Prophet singled him out by naming him "the flier in Paradise" and the "two-winged. After recounting the peculiar achievements of Bani-Hasidim, Ameer al-Momineen has referred to his own attainments with which the histories and traditions are replete and which could not be tarnished with doubts and misgivings. Thus, traditionsists like Ahmad bn-Hambal (164/780 -241/855), Ahmad bn-Ali an-Nisaai (215/830-303/915) and others say that:

The number of traditions that have been related through reliable sources in regard to the distinctions of Ali bn-Abi-Talib have not been related about any other companion of the Prophet. (al-Mostadrak, vol.3, p.107; al-Isteeaab, vol.3, p.1115; Tabaqaat, vol.1, p.319; al-Kaamil, vol.3, p.399; Tahzeeb at-Tahzeeb, vol.7, p.339; Fath al-Baari, vol.7, p.57)

An important distinction out of these particular distinctions of Ahlil-Bayt (the Household of the Holy Prophet) is the one to which Ameer al-Momineen has referred in these words that "We are the direct recipients of Allah's favours while others receive favours from us. This is the height of distinction that even the highest personality cannot reach its sublimity and every other distinction looks small before it. Acknowledging the greatness and supremacy of this sentence, bn-Abil-Hadeed writes:

Ameer al-Momineen intends to convey that we are not under obligation of any person since Allah has bestowed all blessings on us directly, there being no intermediary between us and Allah, while all other people are under our obligation and protection, being the intermediary between them and Allah, the Glorified; this is a high position indeed. Its apparent meaning is what the words show but its real sense is that the Ahlil-Bayt are the obedient servants of Allah and the people must be their obedient followers. (Sharh Nahjol-Balagha, vol.15, p.194)

Now, since these people are the first recipients of the bounties of Allah and the source of bounties for the rest of the people, no one from among the people can be compared with them, nor can anyone be regarded as their equal on the basis of social contacts with them, much less than those individuals who were in direct contrast to the attainments and characteristics of these people, and used to oppose truth and right on every occasion. Ameer al-Momineen places both the sides of the picture before Moaawiya and says:

The Prophet was from us while your father Abi-Sofyaan was foremost in opposing him. Hamza was from us and the Prophet gave him the title of "Lion of Allah" while your maternal grandfather, Otba-bn-Rabeea was proud of being the "lion of swearers (against the Prophet).

When in the battle of Badr, Hamza and Otba bn-Rabeea came face to face, Hamza said "I am Hamza son of Abdl-Mottalib; I am the lion of Allah and the lion of His Prophet," whereupon Otba said "I am the lion of swearers (against the Prophet)." In another version, the word "Asadol-Ahlaaf" has been recorded. The meaning is that he was the Chief of the allying parties. The story of swearing is that when Bani-Abd Manaf acquired a distinct position among the Arab tribes they thought they should take over from Bani-Abd-Daar the offices relating to the Kaba and to depose them from these offices. In this connection, Band Abd Manaf allied with themselves the tribes of Bani-Asad bn-Abdl-Ozzaa, Bani-Taym, Bani-Zohra and Band al-Haarith, and concluded an agreement with them. In order to solemnise this agreement they drenched their hands in teeb (perfume) and swore that they would help each other. For this reason, these tribes were called: "Tribes of sworn chaste parties. On the other side the tribes of Bani-Abd-Dar, Bani-Makhzoom, Bani-Sahm and Bani-Adi also swore that they would resist Bani-Abd-Manaf and their allies. These tribes are called the "allies. Otba has deemed himself the head of the allying parties. Some commentators have taken the word Asadol-Ahlaaf to mean Abi Sofyaan, because he made different tribes swear against the Prophet in the battle of the Trench, while some commentators take it to mean Asad-bn-Abdl-Ozzaa, but this interpretation does not carry weight because here Ameer al-Momineen is addressing Moaawiya and this interpretation does not hit Moaawiya since Bani-Abd Manaf were a party to this alliance. Then Ameer al-Momineen says "they have among themselves the masters of the youth of Paradise. Referring to the Prophet's saying "Hasan and Hosayn are the masters of the youth of Paradise, while the boys of the other side are in Hell. This reference is to the sons of Oqba bn-Abi-Moayd, about whom the Prophet has said "For you and your sons is Hell. Then Ameer al-Momineen says that among them is the chief of all the women of the worlds, namely Faatimatoz-Zahraa (p.b.u.h.), while in the other party is the bearer of the wood which refers to Om-Jameel, the sister of Abi-Sofyaan. This woman used to spread thorns in the path of the Prophet. She has been mentioned in the Quraan along with Abi-Lahab, in these words:

In the Name of Allah, the Beneficent, the Merciful

May perish both the hands of Abi Lahab, may perish (he himself); Shall avail him not his wealth nor what he earneth; Soon shall he burn in the flaming fire; And his wife, the bearer of the firewood; Upon her neck shall be a halter of twisted rope. (Quraan, 111)

companions who helped him. Strange things about you have remained concealed (by the irony of fate) from us, since you have started telling us of Allah's trials for us and His bounties to us through our Prophet. In this matter, you are like the person who carries dates to Hajar, or who challenges his own master to a duel in archery.

You think that so-and-so are the most distinguished persons in Islam. You have said such a thing which if it be true, you have nothing to do with it, but if it be not so, then its defect will not affect you. And what are you to do with the question of who is better and who is worse, or who is the ruler and who is the ruled. What have the freed ones and their sons to do with distinguishing between the first mohaajiroon and determining their position or defining their ranks. What a pity! the sound of an arrow is being produced by what is not a real arrow, and he against whom the judgement is to be passed is sitting in judgement. O man, why do you not see your own lameness and remain within bounds, and why do not you realise the shortness of your measure and stay back where destiny has placed you. You have no concern with the defeat of the defeated or the victory of the victor.

You are wandering in bewilderment and straying from the right path. Do you not realise it? I am not giving you any news: I am just recounting Allah's bounty, namely that a number of people from among the mohaajiroon (immigrants from Mecca) and Ansaar (helpers) fell as martyrs in the way of Allah the Sublime, and that each of them is distinguished (on that account), but when one of us secured martyrdom he was named the Chief of all martyrs, and the Messenger of Allah (p.b.u.h.a.h.p.) gave him the peculiar honour of saying seventy takbir (Allaho Akbar) during his funeral prayer. Do you not know that a number of people lost their hands in the way of Allah, and that everyone is distinguished (on that account), but when the same thing occurred to one of us he was given the name "the flier in Paradise; and "the two winged. If Allah had not forbidden self-praise, the writer would have mentioned numerous distinctions which the believer knows full well and which the ears of hearers do not wish to forget.

Better leave those whose arrows miss the mark. We are the direct recipients of our Lord's favours while others receive favours from us after that. In spite of our old established honour and our well-known superiority over your people, we did not stay away from mixing with you and married and got married (among you) like equals although you were not so. And how could you be so when (the position is that) among us is the Prophet while among you is the opposer, among us is the lion of Allah while among you is the lion of the opposing groups, among us are the two masters of the youth of Paradise[1] while among you are the children of Hell among us is the choicest of all the women of the worlds[2] while among you is the

-1- It is narrated from Ameer al-Momineen, Omar bn-Khattaab, Hozayfa bn-Yaman, Abi Said al-Khodri, Abi-Horayra, etc., that the Holy Prophet (may Allah bless him and his descendants) said:

Verily, Fatima is the Supreme Lady of the women of Paradise, and Hasan and Hosayn are the two Supreme Youth of Paradise. But their father (Ali) is Superior to them. (al-Jaami as-Saheeh, at-Tirmizi, vol.5, pp.656,661; al-Mosnad, Ahmad bn-Hambal, vol.3, pp.3,62,64,82; vol.5, pp.391,392; as-Sonan, bn-Maaja, vol.1, p.56; al-Mostadrak, al-Haakim, vol.3, p.167; Majma" az-Zawaaid, vol.9, pp.183,184,201; Kanz al-Ommaal, al-Mottaqi, vol.13, pp.127,128; al-Isteeaab, vol.4, p.1895; Osdol-Ghaaba, vol.5, p.574; Taareekh Baghdad, vol.1, p.140; vol.6, p.372; vol.10, p.230; at-Taareekh, bn-Aasaakir, vol.7, p.365).

2 It is narrated from "Imran bn-Hosayn and Abo-Thalaba al-Khoshni that the Holy Prophet (p.b.u.h.a.h.p.) said to Fatima (p.b.u.h.):

O my little daughter, are you not satisfied that you are verily the Supreme Lady of all women in the worlds?" She said "O father, then what about Maryam (Mary) daughter of Emraan?" He said "She was the Supreme Lady of her age, and you are the Supreme Lady of your age. Truly, by Allah, I married you to one who is the Master in this world and the hereafter. No one hates him save a hypocrite." (Hilyatol-Awliyaa, vol.2, p.92; al-Isteeaab, vol.4, p.1895; al-Isaaba, vol.4, p.275)

Also, Aysha narrated that the Holy Prophet (p.b.u.h.a.h.p.) said:

O Fatima, will you not be satisfied to be the Supreme Lady of the women of the worlds (or) to be the Supreme Lady of all women of this Omma (community) or of the women believers? (as-Saheeh, al-Bokhaari, vol.8, p.79; as-Saheeh, Moslim, vol.7, pp.142-144; as-Sonan, bn-Maaja, vol.1, p.518; al-Mosnad, Ahmad bn-Hambal, vol.6, p.282; al-Mostadrak "ala as-Saheehayn, al-Haakim, vol.3, p.156)

bearer of firewood, any many more distinctions on our side and shortcomings on your side.

Our Islam is well-known and our (greatness in the) pre-Islamic period too cannot be denied. Whatever remains has been mentioned in the words of Allah the Glorified, the Sublime:

. And blood relations have the better claim in respect of one to the other, according to the Book of Allah. (Quran, 33 :6)

He (Allah) the Sublime, also says:

Verily, of men the nearest to Abraham are surely those who followed him and this (Our) Prophet (Mohammad) and those who believe; and verily, Allah, is the Guardian of the faithful. (Quran, 3:68)

Thus, we are superior firstly because of kinship and secondly because of obedience. When at Saqeefa (of Bani-Saaida) the mohaajiroon contended kinship with the Messenger of Allah (p.b.u.h.a.h.p.) against the Ansaar, they scored over them. If that success was based on kinship then the right would be ours better than yours. Otherwise, the Ansaar's contention stands.

You think that I have been jealous of every caliph and have revolted against them. Even if this be so, it is not an offence against you and therefore no explanation is due to you.

This is a matter for which no blame comes to you.

You have said that I was dragged like a camel with a nose string to swear allegiance (to Abo-Bakr at Saqeefa). By the Eternal Allah, you had intended to revile me but you have praised me, and to humiliate me but have yourself been humiliated. What humiliation does it mean for a Muslim to be the victim of oppression so long as he does not entertain any doubt in his religion, nor any misgiving in his firm belief! This argument of mine is intended for others, but I have stated it to you only in so far as it was appropriate.

Then you have recalled my position vis-à-vis "Othmaan, and in this matter an answer is due to you because of your kinship with him. So (now tell me), which of us was more inimical towards Othmaan and who did more to bring about his killing; or who offered him his support but he made him sit down and stopped him; or who was he whom he called for help but who turned his face from him and drew his death near him till his fate overtook him? No, no; by Allah:

Indeed knoweth Allah those who hinder others among you and those who say unto their brethren "Come here unto us, and they come not to fight but a little. (Quran, 33 :18)

I am not going to offer my excuse for reproving him for (some of his innovations, for if my good counsel and guidance to him was a sin then very often a person who is blamed has no sin and sometimes the only reward a counsellor[1] reaps is suspicion (of evil). I desired naught but reform what I am able to (do); and my guidance is not but with Allah; On Him (alone) do I rely, and unto Him (alone) do I turn. (Quran, 11:88)

You have mentioned that for me and for my followers you have only the sword. This makes even a weeping person laugh. Did you ever see the descendants of Abd al-Mottalib running away from battle, or being frightened by swords "Wait a little till Hamal[2] joins the battle" shortly, then he whom you are seeking will seek you and he whom you think to be far away will approach near you. I am (shortly) speeding towards you with a force of mohaajiroon and Ansaar and those who follow them in virtue. Their number will be great and their dust will spread all round. They will

---

-1- The meaning is that the person who goes too far in counselling others will be thought to have his personal ends in so doing, even though his counsel may well be based on sincerity of intention and selflessness. This line is used as a proverb on such occasions. The whole couplet runs as follows:

How often a good counsel I offered you, but sometimes the only reward a counsellor reaps is suspicion.

-2- This line is of Hamal bn-Badr. The full couplet runs thus:

Wait a bit till Hamal reaches the battlefield; How pretty is death when is comes.

The story behind it is that Malik bn-Zohayr threatened Hamal bn-Badr with battle and in reply he recited this couplet and then attacked Malik and killed him. When Maalik's brother saw this, he killed Hamal and his brother Hozayfa in revenge. Then, he described this in his following couplet:

I appeased my heart by killing Hamal bn-Badr and my sword appeased me by killing Hozayfa.

be wearing their shrouds and their most coveted desire is to meet Allah. They will be accompanied by the descendants of those who took part in the battle of Badr, and they will have Hashemite swords whose cut you have already seen in the case of your brother, maternal uncle, your grandfather and your kinsmen. Nor are they far distant from the unjust ones. (Quran, 11:83)

29- To the people of Basra

Whatever disunity and schism you have is not hidden to you. I have forgiven your wrong-doers and held back my sword from those who ran away. I received everyone who came to me from among you. If devastating matters and wrong and silly views are prompting you to break the pledge with me and to oppose me then (listen) I have kept ready my horses and put saddles (on my riding camels), and if you force me to advance towards you I shall come down in such a manner that before it the battle of Jamal too would appear like the last licking of the tongue. At the same time I know the high position of the obedient among you and the right of the sincere without confusing the sinless with the offenders or the faithful with the pledge-breakers.

30- To Moaawiya bn Abi-Sofyaan

Fear Allah regarding what you have amassed and find out your true right therein, and turn to understand for what you will not be excused on the grounds of ignorance. Certainly, for (following the path of) obedience there are clear signs, shining ways, straight highways and a fixed aim. The shrewd proceed towards them while the mean turn away from them. Whoever turns his face from them deviates from the right and gropes in bewilderment. Allah takes away His bounty from him and afflicts him with His chastisement. Therefore, beware of yourself. Allah has already shown you your way and the end where your affairs will terminate. You are speeding towards the aim of loss and the position of unbelief. Your ego has pushed you towards evil, thrown you into misguidance, conveyed you to destruction and created difficulties in your way.

31- Commandment for al-Hasan bn Ali[1] (his son—peace be upon them), when he encamped at al-Haazireen on his way back from Siffeen

From the father who is (shortly) to die, who acknowledges the hardships of the times, who has turned away from life, who has submitted himself to the (calamities of) time, who realises the evils of the worlds who is living in the abodes of the dead and is due to depart from them any day; to the son who yearns for what is not to be achieved, who is treading the path of those who have died, who is the victim of ailments, who is entangled in the (worries of the) days, who is a target of hardships, a slave of the world, a trader of its deception, a debtor of wishes, a prisoner of mortality, an ally of worries, a neighbour of griefs, a victim of distresses, who has been overpowered by desires, and who is a successor of the dead.

Now (you should know that) what I have learnt from the turning away of this world from me, the onslaught of time over me and the advancing of the next world towards me is enough to prevent me from remembering anyone except myself and from thinking beyond myself. But when I

-1- bn-Maytham al-Bahraani (vol.5, p.2) has quoted Abi-Jafar bn-Babawayh al-Qummi to have stated that Ameer al-Momineen wrote this piece of advice in the name of his son Mohammad bn-Hanafiyya, while al-Allama Sayyid Razi has written that its addressee is Imaam al-Hasan (p.b.u.h.). But the fact is that Ameer al-Momineen wrote another piece of advice to bn-Hanafiyya in brief which included a part of the same which he wrote to al-Imaam al-Hasan. (Kashf al-Mahajjah, bn-Taawoos, pp.157-159; al-Behaar, vol.77, pp.196-198)

In any case, whether the addressee is al-Imaam al-Hasan or Mohammad bn-Hanafiyya, this manifesto of the Imaam is a lesson of guidance to action in which the ways of success and achievement can be opened and the straying caravans of mankind can tread the path of guidance. It contains principles of correcting the matters of this world and the next, creating the sense of morality and improving economic and social matters whose like cannot be produced by the epitomes of scholars and philosophers. Its truthful preachings are a strong incentive for recalling to humanity the lessons it has forgotten, reviving the dead lines of social dealings and raising the standards of morality.

confined myself to my own worries leaving the worries of others, my intelligence saved me and protected me from my desires. It clarified to me my affairs and led me to seriousness wherein there was no trickery and truth, which was not tarnished by falsehood. Here, I found you a part of myself, rather I found you my whole, so much so that if anything befell you, it was as though it befell me and if death came to you it was as though it came to me. Consequently, your affairs meant to me what my own matters meant to me. So. I have written this piece of advice (to you) as an instrument of seeking help through it, whether I remain alive for you or cease to exist.

I advise you to fear Allah, O my child, to abide by His commands, to fill your heart with remembrance of Him and to cling to hope from Him. No connection is more reliable than the connection between you and Allah provided you take hold of it. Enliven your heart with preaching, kill it by renunciation, energise it with firm belief, enlighten it with wisdom, humiliate it by recalling death, make it believe in mortality, make it see the misfortunes of this world, make it fear the authority of the time and the severity of some changes during the nights and the days, place before it the events of past people, recall to it what befell those who were before you and walk among their cities and ruins, then see what they did and from what they have gone away and where they have gone and stayed. You will find that they departed from (their) friends and remain in loneliness. Shortly, you too will be like one of them. Therefore, plan for your place of stay and do not sell your next life with this world.

Give up discussing what you do not know and speaking about what does not concern you. Keep off the track from which you fear to go astray because refraining (from moving) when there is fear of straying is better than embarking on dangers. Ask others to do good; you will thus be among the good doers. Desist others from evil with your action as well as your speech and keep off, to the best of your ability, from he who commits it. Struggle for Allah as is His due; and the reviling of a reviler should not deter you in matters of Allah. Leap into dangers for the sake of right wherever it be. Acquire insight into religious law. Habituate yourself to endure hardships since the best trait of character is endurance in matters of right. In all your affairs resign yourself to your Allah, because you will thus be resigning yourself to a secure shelter and a strong protector. Your should ask only from your Lord because in His hand is all the giving and depriving. Seek good (from Allah) as much as you can. Understand my advice and do not turn away from it, because the best saying is that which benefits. Know that there is no good in that knowledge which does not benefit, and if knowledge is not made use of then its acquisition is not justified.

O my child, when I noticed that I was of goodly age and noticed that I was increasing in weakness I hastened with my will for you and wrote down salient points of it lest death overtook me before I divulged to you what I have in my heart, or lest my wit be affected as my body has been affected, or the forces of passions or the mischiefs of the world overtake you making you like a stubborn camel. Certainly, the heart of a young man is like uncultivated land. It accepts whatever is strewn on it. So, I hastened to mould you properly before your heart hardened up and your mind became occupied, so that you might be ready to accept through your intelligence the results of the experience of others and be saved from going through these experiences yourself. In this way, you would avoid the hardship of seeking them and the difficulties of experimenting. Thus, you are getting to know what we had experienced and even those things are becoming clear to you, which we might have missed.

O my child, even though I have not reached the age which those before me have, yet I looked into their behaviour and thought over events of their lives. I walked among their ruins till I was as one of them. In fact, by virtue of those of their affairs that have become known to me it is as though I have lived with them from the first to the last. I have therefore been able to discern the impure from the clean and the benefit from the harm.

I have selected for you the choicest of those matters and collected for you their good points and have kept away from you their useless points. Since I feel for you affairs as a living father should feel and I aim at giving you training, I thought it should be at a time when you are advancing in age and new on the stage of the world, possessing upright intention and clean heart and that I should being with the teaching of the Book of Allah, to Whom belongs Might and Majesty, and its interpretation, the laws of Islam and its commands, its lawful matters and unlawful matters and that I should not go beyond these for you. Then I feared lest you should get confused as other people had been confused on account of their passions and (different) views. Therefore, in spite of my dislike for you being so warned, I thought it better for me to make this position strong rather than leave you in a position where I do not regard you safe from falling into destruction. I hoped that Allah would help you in your straight-forwardness and guide you in your resoluteness. Consequently, I wrote this piece of my will for you.

Know O my child, that what I love most for you to adopt from my will is to fear Allah, to confine yourself to what Allah has made obligatory on you, and to follow the actions of your forefathers and the virtuous people of your household, because they did not fall short in seeing for themselves what you will see for yourself, and they did about their affairs as you would like to think (about your affairs). Thereafter, their thinking led them to discharge the obligations they came to know of and to desist from what they were not required to do. If your heart does not accept this without acquiring knowledge as they acquired it, then your search should first be by way of understanding and learning and not by falling into doubts or getting entangled in quarrels.

And before you probe into this, you should begin by seeking your Allah's help and turning to Him for competence and keeping aloof from everything that throws you into doubt or flings you towards misguidance. When you have made sure that your heart is clean and humble and your thoughts have come together and you have only one thought which is about this matter, when you will see what I have explained to you; but if you have not been able to achieve that peace of observation and thinking which you would like to have, then know that you are only stamping the ground like a blind she-camel and falling into darkness while a seeker of religion should not grope in the dark or create confusion. It is better to avoid this.

Appreciate my advice, O my child, and know that He Who is the Master of death is also the Master of life, that the Creator causes death as well; that He Who destroys is also the restorer of life and that He Who inflicts disease is also the curer. This world continues in the way Allah has made it with regard to its pleasures, trials, rewards on the Day of Judgement and all that He wishes and you do not know. If anything of this advice is not understood by you then attribute it to your ignorance of it, because when you were first born you were born ignorant. Thereafter, you acquired knowledge. There are many matters of which you are ignorant and in which your sight first wonders and your eye wonders then after this you see them. Therefore, cling to Him Who created you, fed you and put you in order. Your worship should be for Him, your eagerness should be towards Him and your fear should be of Him.

Know O my child, that no one received messages from Allah, the Glorified, as the Prophet (may Allah bless him and his progeny) did. Therefore, regard him as your forerunner and leader towards deliverance. Certainly, I shall spare no effort in giving you advice and surely even if you try, you cannot acquire that insight for your welfare as I have for you.

Know O my child, that if there had been a partner with your Lord, his messengers too should have come to you and you would have seen signs of his authority and power and you should have known his deeds and qualities. But He is only One God as He has described Himself. No one can dispute with Him in His authority. He is from ever and will be for ever. He is before all things without any beginning. He will remain after all things without any end. He is far too great to have His divinity proved by the encompassing heart or eye. When you have understood this then you should do what is done by him who is like you by way of his low position, his lack of authority, his increasing incapability, and his great need of his Lord for seeking His obedience, fearing His chastisement and apprehending His anger, because He does not command you save for virtue and does not refrain you save from evil.

O my child, I have informed you about the world, its condition, its decay and its passing away and I have informed you of the next world and of what has been provided in it for its people. I have recounted to you parables about it so that you may draw instruction from them and act upon them. The example of those who have understood the world is like those travellers who, being disgusted with drought stricken places set off for greenery and a fruitful place. Then they endure difficulties on the way, separation from friends, hardships of the journey and unwholesome food in order to reach their fields of plenty and place of stay. Consequently, they do not feel any pain in all this and do not regard any expenditure to be waste. Nothing is more loveable to them than what takes them near their goal and carries them closer to their place of stay. (Against this), the example of those who are deceived by this world is like the people who were in a green place but they became disgusted with it and went to a drought-stricken place. Therefore, for them nothing is more detestable or abominable than to leave the place where they were to go to a place, which they will reach unexpectedly and for which they are heading.

O my child, make yourself the measure (for dealings) between you and others. Thus, you should desire for others what you desire for yourself and hate for others what you hate for yourself. Do not oppress as you do not like to be oppressed. Do good to others as you would like good to be done to you. Regard bad for yourself whatever you regard bad for others. Accept that (treatment) from others, which you would like others to accept from you. Do not talk about what you do not know even though what you know be very little. Do not say to others what you do not like to be said to you.

Know that self-admiration is contrary to propriety (of action) and is a calamity for the mind. Therefore, increase your striving and do not become a treasurer for (wealth to be inherited by) others. When you have been guided on the right path humble yourself before Allah as much as you can.

Know that in front of you lies a road of long distance and severe hardship and that you cannot avoid seeking it. Take your requirements of provision keeping the burden light. Do not load your back beyond your power lest its weight become a mischief for you. Whenever you come across a needy person who can carry for you your provision to hand it back to you on the Day of Judgement when you will need it, then accept him as good opportunity and get him to carry it. Put in that provision as much as you are able to, for it is likely that if you may need him (afterwards), you may not get hold of him. If a person is willing to borrow from you in the days of your affluence to pay it back to you at the time of your need then make use of this opportunity. Know that in front of you lies an impassable valley where-in the light-burdened man will be in a better condition than the heavy-burden one, and the slow-paced would be in a worse condition than the swift-paced. Your terminating point at the other end of this passage will necessarily be either Paradise or Hell. Therefore, reconnoitre for yourself before alighting, and prepare the place before getting down, because after death there can be no preparation nor return to this world.

Know that He Who owns the treasuries of the heavens and of the earth has permitted you to pray to Him and has promised you acceptance of the prayer. He has commanded you to beg from Him in order that He may give you and to seek His mercy in order that He may have mercy on you. He has not placed anything between you and Him that may veil Him from you. He has not required you to get a mediator for you to Him, and if you err, He has not prevented you from repentance. He does not hasten with punishment. He does not taunt you for repenting, nor does He humiliate you when humiliation is more appropriate for you. He has not been harsh in accepting repentance. He does not severely question you about your sins. He does not disappoint you of His mercy. Rather He regards abstention from sin as a virtue. He counts your one sin as one while He counts your one virtue as ten.

He has opened for you the door of repentance. Therefore, whenever you call Him He hears your call, and whenever you whisper to Him He knows the whispers. You place before Him your needs, unveil yourself before Him, complain to Him of your worries, beseech Him to remove your troubles, seek His help in your affairs and ask from the treasuries of His mercy that which no one else has power to give, namely length of life, health of body and increase in sustenance. Then He has placed the keys of His treasuries in your hands in the sense that He has shown you the way to ask Him.

Therefore, wherever you wish, open the doors of His favour with prayer. and let the abundant rains of His mercy fall on you. Delay in acceptance of the prayer should not disappoint you because the grant of prayer is according to the measure of (your) intention. Sometimes acceptance (of prayer) is delayed with a view to its being a source of greater reward to the asker and of better gifts to the expectant. Sometimes you ask for a thing but it is not given to you, and a better thing is given to you later or a thing is taken away from you for some greater good of yours, because sometimes you ask for a thing which contains ruin for your religion if it is given to you. Therefore, your request should be for things whose beauty should be lasting and whose burden should remain away from you. As for wealth it will not last for you nor will you live for it.

O my child, know that you have been created for the next world, not for this world, for destruction (in this world) not for lasting, and for dying not for living. You are in a place, which does not belong to you, a house for making preparations and a passage towards the next world. You are being chased by death from which the runner-away cannot escape, as it would surely overtake him. So, be on guard against it least it overtakes you at a time when you are in a sinful state and you are thinking of repenting but it creates obstruction between you and repentance. In such a case you will ruin yourself.

O my child, remember death very much and the place where you have to go suddenly and reach after death, so that when it comes you are already on your guard against it and have prepared yourself for it and it does not come to you all of a sudden and surprise you. Beware, lest you become deceived by the leanings of the people towards worldly attraction and their rushing upon it. Allah has warned you about it and the world has informed you of its mortal character and unveiled to you its evils.

Surely, those (who go) after it are like barking dogs or devouring carnivore who hate each other. The stronger among them eat away the weaker and the big among them tramples over the small. Some are like tied cattle and some like untied cattle who have lost their wits and are running in unknown directions. They are flocks of calamities wandering in rugged valleys. There is no herdsman to detain them nor any tenderer to take them to grazing. The world has put them on the track of blindness and taken away their eyes from the beacons of guidance. They have therefore been perplexed in its bewilderings and sunk in its pleasures. They took it as a god so it played with them. They too played with it and forgot what is beyond it.

Darkness is disappearing gradually. Now it is as though travellers have got down and the hasteners will soon meet. Know, O my child, that everyone who is riding on the carriage of night and day is being carried by them even though he may be stationary, and he is covering the distance even though he is staying and resting.

Know with certainty that you cannot achieve your desire and cannot exceed your destined life. You are on the track of those before you. Therefore, be humble in seeking and moderate in earning because often seeking leads to deprivation. Every seeker of livelihood does not get it, nor is everyone who is moderate in seeking deprived. Keep yourself away from every low thing even though they may take you to your desired aims, because you will not get any return for your own respect which you spend. Do not be the slave of others for Allah had made you free. There is no good in good which is achieved through evil and no good in comfort that is achieved through (disgracing) hardship.

Beware lest bearers of greed should carry you and make you descend down to the springs of destruction. If you can manage that there be no wealthy person between yourself and Allah, do so, because in any case you will find what is for you and get your share. A little received directly from Allah the Glorified, is more dignified than that which is more but is received through (the obligation of) His creatures, although (really) all is from Allah.

It is easier to rectify what you miss by silence than to secure what you lose by speaking. Whatever is in a pot can be retained by closing the lid. I should prefer you to retain what is in your hands rather to seek what is in other's hands. Bitterness of disappointment is better than seeking from people. Manual labour with chastity is better than the riches of a vicious life. A man is the best guard of his own secrets. Often a man strives for that harms him. He who speaks much speaks nonsense. Whoever ponders perceives. Associate with people of virtue; you will become one of them. Keep aloof from people of vice; you will remain safe from them. The worst food is that which is unlawful. Oppressing the weak is the worst oppression.

Where leniency is unsuitable, harshness is lenience. Often cure is illness and illness is cure. Often the ill-wisher gives correct advice while the well-wisher cheats. Do not depend upon hopes because hopes are the mainstay of fools. It is wise to preserve one's experience. Your best experience is that which teaches you a lesson. Make use of leisure before it changes into (the hour of) grief. Every seeker does not achieve (what he seeks); and every departer does not return. To lose provision and to earn evil for the Day of Judgement means ruin. Every matter has a consequence. What is destined for you will shortly come to you. A trader undertakes a risk. Often a small quantity is more beneficial than a large quantity. There is no good in an ignoble helper, nor in a suspicious friend. Be compliant with the world as long as it is in your grip. Do not put yourself to risk as regards anything in expectation for more than that. Beware lest the feeling of enmity should overpower you.

Bear yourself towards your brother in such a way that if he disregards kinship you keep to it; when he turns away be kind to him and draw near to him; when he withholds spend for him; when he goes away approach him; when he is harsh be lenient; when he commits wrong think of (his) excuse for it, so much so as though you are a slave of him and he is the benevolent master over you. But take care that this should not be done inappropriately, and that you should not behave so with an undeserving person. Do not take me enemy of your friend as a friend because you will thus antagonise your friend. Give true advice to your brother, be it good or bitter. Swallow your anger because I did not find a sweeter thing than it in the end, and nothing more pleasant in consequence. Be lenient to him who is harsh to you for it is likely that he will shortly become lenient to you. Treat your enemy with favours, because this is sweeter of the two successes (the success of revenge and the success of doing favour).

If you intend to cut yourself off from a friend leave some scope for him from your side by which he may resume friendship if it so occurs to him some day. If anyone has a good idea about you prove it to be true. Do not disregard the interests of your brother depending upon your terms with him, for he is not your brother if you disregard his interests. Your household should not become the most miserable people through you. Do not lean towards him who turns away from you. Your brother should not be more firm in his disregard of kinship than you in paying regard to it, and you should exceed in doing good to him than is evil to you. Do not feel too much the oppression of a person who oppresses you, because he is only busy in harming himself and benefiting you. The reward of him who pleases you is not that you displease him.

Know O my child, that livelihood is of two kinds-a livelihood that you seek and a livelihood that seeks you, which is such that if you do not reach it, it will come to you. How bad it is to bend down at the time of need and to be harsh in riches. You should have from this world only that with which you can adorn your permanent abode. If you cry over what has gone out of your hands then also cry for what has not at all come to you. Infer about what has not yet happened from what has already happened, because occurrences are ever similar. Do not be like those whom preaching does not benefit unless you inflict pain on them, because the wise take instruction from teaching while beasts learn only from beating.

Ward off from yourself the onslaught of worries by firmness of endurance and purity of belief. He who gives up moderation commits excess. A companion is like a relation. A friend is he whose absence also proves the friendship. Passion is a partner of distress. Often the near ones are remoter than the distant ones, and often the distant ones are nearer than the near ones. A stranger is he who has no friend. He who transgresses right narrows his own passage. He who stays in his position remains constant upon it. The most trustworthy intermediary is that which you adopt between yourself and Allah the Glorified. He who does not care for your interests is your enemy. When greed leads to ruin deprivation is an achievement. Not every defect can be reviewed, and not every opportunity recurs.

Often a person with eyes misses the track while a blind person finds the correct path. Delay an evil because you will be able to hasten it whenever you desire. The disregard of kinship of the ignorant is equal to the regard for kinship of the wise. Whoever takes the world to be safe, it will betray him. Whoever regards the world as great, it will humiliate him. Every one who shoots does not hit. When authority changes the time changes too. Consult the friend before adopting a course and the neighbour before taking a house. Beware, lest you mention in your speech what may rouse laughter even though you may be relating it from others.

Do not consult women because their view is weak and their determination is unstable. Cover their eyes by keeping them under the veil because strictness of veiling keeps them for long. Their coming out is not worse than your allowing an unreliable man to visit them. If you can manage that they should not know anyone other than you, do so. Do not allow a woman matters other than those about herself, because a woman is a flower not an administrator. Do not pay her regard beyond herself. Do not encourage her to intercede for others. Do not show suspicion out of place, because this leads a correct woman to evil and a chaste woman to deflection.

For everyone among your servants fix a work for which you may hold him responsible. In this way, they will not fling the work one over the other. Respect your kinsmen because they are your wings with which you fly, the origin towards which you return and your hands with which you attack. Place your religion and your world at Allah's disposal and beg Him to ordain the best for you in respect of the near and the far, this world and the next; and that is an end to the matter.

32- To Moaawiya bn Abi-Sofyaan

You have ruined a large group of people whom you have deceived by your misguidance, and have flung them into the currents of your sea where darkness has covered them and misgivings toss them about. As a result they have strayed from the right path and turned on their backs.

They turned their backs and pushed forward except those wise ones who came back because they left you after understanding you and ran towards Allah away from your assistance when you put them to troubles and deviated them from the middle path. Therefore, O Moaawiya, fear Allah about yourself and take away your rein from Shaitan, since this world is shortly to be cut off from you and the next world is near you; and that is an end to the matter.

33- To Qutham bn al-Abbas, his governor of Mecca

My spy in the West has written[1] to me telling me that some people of Syria have been sent for Hajj who are blind of heart, deaf of ears and devoid of

-1- Moaawiya sent some men in the garb of pilgrims to Mecca in order to create sensation in the peaceful atmosphere of the place, by taking common men into their confidence, by a show of piety and God-fearing and then convincing them that Ali bn-Abi-Talib has instigated the people against Othmaan and in the end succeeded in getting him killed. In

eyesight. They confound the truth with vanity, obey men in disobeying Allah, claim the milk of the world in the name of religion, and trade in the pleasures of this world by forsaking the rewards of the virtuous and the God-fearing. No one achieves good except he who acts for it, and no one is awarded the recompense of evil except he who commits it. Therefore, behave yourself in your duties like an intelligent, experienced, well-wishing and wise man who follows his superior and is obedient to his Imam. You should avoid what you may have to explain. Do not rise up in riches nor lose courage in distress; and that is an end to the matter.

34- To Mohammad bn Abi Bakr on coming to know that he had taken over the position of Maalik al-Ashtar as governor of Egypt after the latter had died on his way to Egypt

I have come to know of your anger at the position of al-Ashtar in your place, but I did not do so because of any shortcoming on your part or to get you to increase your efforts, but when I had taken away what was under your authority I would have placed you at a position which would have been less exacting and more attractive to you.

The man whom I have made Governor of Egypt was my well-wisher, and very harsh and vengeful towards our enemies. May Allah have mercy on him, as he has finished his days and met his death. I am quite pleased with him. May Allah too accord him His pleasure, and multiply his reward. Now get ready for your enemy and act according to your intelligence. Prepare for fighting him who fights you and calling to the path of Allah. Seek Allah's help exceedingly. If Allah wills He will assist you in what worries you and help you with what befalls you.

---

this way, they were to hold him responsible for the killing of Othmaan and to turn the people against him, and also to incline the people towards him (Moaawiya) by mentioning the greatness of his character, the sublimity of his manners and stories of his generosity. But when the men whom Ameer al-Momineen had put on the job gave him the information, he wrote this letter to Qutham bn-Abbaas to keep an eye on their movements and to put a stop to their mischief-mongerings.

35- To Abdillah bn al-Abbas after Mohammad bn Abi Bakr had been killed

Now then, Egypt has been conquered and Mohammad bn-Abi-Bakr, may Allah have mercy on him, has been martyred. We seek his reward from Allah. He was a son who was a well-wisher, a hard worker, a sharp sword and a bastion of defence. I had roused the people to join him and ordered them to reach him to help before this incident. I called to them secretly as well as openly repeatedly. Some of them came half-heartedly, some put up false excuses and some sat away leaving me. I ask Allah the Sublime, to give me early relief from them, for by Allah, had I not been yearning to meet the enemy for martyrdom and not prepared myself for death, I would not have liked to be with these people for a single day nor ever to face the enemy with them.

36- To his brother Aqeel Abi-Talib[1], in reply to his letter which contained a reference to the army he had sent to some enemy

I had sent towards him a large army of Muslims. When he came to know of it he fled away and retreated repenting. They met him on the way when the sun was about to set. They grappled for a while like nothing. It was about an hour and then he rescued himself half-dead as he had almost

-1- When after arbitration Moaawiya started a campaign of killing and devastation, he sent a force of four thousand under az-Zahhaak bn-Qays al-Fihri to attack Ameer al-Momineen's cities. When Ameer al-Momineen came to know of his activities he roused the people of Koofa to put up a defence, but they began to offer lame excuses. At last Hijr bn-Adi al-Kindi rose with a force of four thousand men and, chasing the enemy, overtook him at Tadmor. The two parties had only a few grappings when darkness came in and az-Zahhaak fled away under its cover. This was the time when Aqeel bn-Abi-Talib had come to Mecca for Omra. When he came to know that after attacking al-Heera, az-Zahhaak had escaped alive and that the people of Koofa were afraid of war and all their activities had come to a stop, he sent a letter to Ameer al-Momineen through Abdr-Rahmaan bn-Obayd al-Azdi offering his help. In reply to that Ameer al-Momineen wrote this letter wherein he complains of the behaviour of the people of Koofa and mentions the flight of az-Zahhaak.

been taken by the neck and only the last breath had remained in him. In this way, he escaped in a panic.

Leave the Quraysh in their rushing into misguidance, their galloping in disunity and their leaping over destruction. They have joined together to fight me as they had joined to fight the Messenger of Allah (p.b.u.h.a.h.p.) before me. I wish the Quraysh will get the reward of their treatment of me. For they disregarded by kinship and deprived me of the power due to me from the son of my mother (i.e., the Holy Prophet).

As for your enquiry about my opinion to fight till I die, I am in favour of fighting those who regard fighting lawful. The crowd of men around me does not give me strength nor does their dispersal from me cause any loneliness. Surely, do not consider the son of your father weak or afraid, even though all people have forsaken him, bow down submissively before injustice or hand over his reins into the hand of the puller, or allow his back to be used by the rider to sit upon. But he is as the man of Bani-Saalim has said:

If yon enquire how I am, then listen that I am enduring and strong against the vicissitudes of time. I do not allow myself to be grieved lest the foe feels joyed and the friend feels sorry.

37- To Moaawiya bn Abi-Sofyaan

Glory be to Allah! How staunchly you cling to innovated passions and painful bewilderment along with ignoring the facts and rejecting strong reasons which are liked by Allah and serve as pleas for the people. As regards your prolonging the question of "Othmaan's[1] murder the position

---

-1- There is no question of denying that Moaawiya claimed to help Othmaan after he had been killed, although when he was surrounded and clamoured for his help by writing letter after letter Moaawiya never budged an inch. However, just to make a show he had sent a contingent towards Madeena under Yazeed-bn-Asad al-Qasri, but had ordered it to remain in waiting in the valley of Zoo-Khoshob near Madeena. Eventually, Othmaan was murdered and he went back with his contingent.
No doubt Moaawiya wished Othmaan to be killed so that he should create confusion in the name of his blood and through these disturbances clear the way for allegiance to

is that you helped "Othmaan when it was really your own help while you forsook him when he was in need of help; and that is an end to the matter.

38- To the people of Egypt when he appointed Maalik al-Ashtar as their governor

From the slave of Allah Ali, Ameer al-Momineen to the people who became wrathful for the sake of Allah when He was disobeyed on His earth and His rights were ignored and oppression had spread its coverings over the virtuous as well as the vicious, on the local as well as the foreigner. Consequently, no good was acted upon nor any evil was avoided.

Now, I have sent to you a man from among the servants of Allah who allows himself no sleep in days of danger, nor does he shrink from the enemy at critical moments. He is severer on the wicked than a blazing fire. He is Malik bn-Haarith, our brother from (the tribe of) Mazhij. Therefore, listen to him and obey his orders that accord with right, because he is a sword among the swords of Allah, whose edge is not dull and which does not miss its victim. If he orders you to advance, advance, and if he orders you to stay, stay, because he surely neither advances or attacks nor puts anyone backward or forward save with my command. I have preferred him for you rather than for myself because of his being your will-wisher and (because of) the severity of his harshness over your enemies.

39- To Amr bn al-Aas

You have surely made your religion subservient to the worldly seekings of a man whose misguidance is not a concealed affair and whose veil has been torn away. He mars an honourable man with his company and befools those who keep his society. You are following in his footsteps and seeking his favours like the dog that follows the lion looking at his paws and waiting for whatever remnants of his prey fall down to him. In this

---

himself (as Caliph). That is why he neither helped him when he was surrounded nor thought it necessary to trace the murderers of Othmaan after securing power.

way, you have ruined your world as well as the next life, although if you had stuck to the right, you would have got what you were after. If Allah grants me power over you and Bn Abi Sofyaan (Moaawiya), I shall award you both recompense of what you have done, but if you escape and survive then hereafter there is only evil for you both; and that is an end to the matter.

40- To one of his officers

Now, I have come to know such a thing about you that if you have done so then you have displeased your Lord, disobeyed your Imam and betrayed your trust.

I have come to know that you have razed the ground and taken away whatever was under your feet and devoured whatever was in your hands. Send me your account and know that the accounting to Allah will be severer than that to the people; and that is an end to the matter.

41- To one of his officers

Now, I had made you a partner in my trust, and made you my chief man. And for me no other person from my kinsmen was more trustworthy than you in the matter of sympathising with me, assisting and respecting my trusts. But when you saw that time had attacked your cousin, the enemy had waged war, the trust of the people was being humiliated, and the whole community was trackless and disunited, you turned your back against your cousin and forsook him when others forsook him, you abandoned him when others abandoned him, and you betrayed him when others betrayed him. Thus, you showed no sympathy to your cousin, nor discharged the trust.

It seems as if you do not want (to please) Allah by your Jihad, and as if you do not stand upon a clear sign from your Lord, and as if you have been playing tricks with this Omma (Muslim community) to earn (the pleasure of) this world and watching for the moment of their neglectfulness to usurp their share of the wealth. As soon as it was possible for you to misappropriate the Omma's trust, you hastened to turn around and attack (them), and made a swift leap to snatch away whatever you could from their property meant for their widows and their orphans as a wolf snatches a wounded and helpless goat. Then, you happily loaded it off to the Hijaaz without feeling guilty for having appropriated it. Allah's woe be to your ill-wishers; it was as though you were sending to your family what you had inherited from your father and mother.

Glory be to Allah! Do you not believe in the Day of Judgement, or do you not fear the exaction of account? 07 you who were counted by us among the men possessed of mind, how can you enjoy food and drink when you know that you are eating the unlawful and drinking the unlawful. You are purchasing slave-maids and wedding women with the money of the orphans, the poor, the believers and the participants in jihad to whom Allah had dedicated this money and through whom He had strengthened these cities. Fear Allah and return to these people their properties. If you do not do so and Allah grants me power over you I shall excuse myself before Allah about you and strike you with my sword with which I did not strike anyone but that he went to Hell.

By Allah, even if Hasan and Hosayn had done what you did there would have been no leniency with me for them and they could not have won their way with me till I had recovered from them the right and destroyed the wrong produced by their unjust action. I swear by Allah, the Lord of all beings, that I would not be pleased to regard their money which you have appropriated as lawful for me and to leave it to my successors by way of inheritance. Mind yourself and consider for a while as though you had reached the end of life and had been buried under the earth. Then your actions will be presented before you in the place where the oppressor cries Alas" while he who wasted his life yearns for return (to the world), but time was none to escape. (Quran, 38:3)

42- To Omar bn Abi Salama al-Makhzoomi (foster son of the holy prophet from Om al-Momineen, Om Salama) who was his governor of Bahrain, but whom he removed and replaced by an-Nomaan bn Ajlaan Az-Zorqi

Now, I have posted an-Nomaan bn-Ajlaan Az-Zorqi at Bahrain and have released you from that position without anything bad from you nor reproach on you, because you managed the governorship well and discharged the obligations. Therefore, proceed to me when you are neither suspected nor rebuked, neither blamed nor guilty. I have just intended to proceed towards the recalcitrant of Syria and desired that you should be with me because you are among those on whom I rely in fighting the enemy and erecting the pillars of religion. if Allah wills.

43- To Masqala bn Hobayra ash-Shaybani, the governor of Ardasheer Khorra (Iran)

I have come to know concerning you a matter which if you have done it you have displeased your Allah and disobeyed your Imam. You are distributing among the Arabs (Bedouins) of your kin who tend towards you the property of the Muslims which they collected by dint of their spears and horses and on which their blood was shed. By Allah Who germinated the seed and created living beings, if this is true you will be humbled in my view and you will become light in weight. Therefore, do not treat lightly the obligations of your Lord and do not reform your world by ruining your religion, since then you will be among losers by the way of (your) actions.

Know that the right of those Muslims who are around you and those who are around me in this property is equal. For that reason they come to me and take from it.

44- To Ziyad bn Abeeh when he had come to know that Moaawiya had written to Ziyad to deceive him and to attach him to himself in kinship

I have learnt that Moaawiya has written to you to deceive your wit and blunt your sharpness. You should be on guard against him because he is the Shaitan who approaches a believer from the front and from the back, from the right and from the left, to catch him suddenly in the hour of his carelessness and overcome his intelligence.

In the days of Omar bn-Khattaab, Abu Sofyaan[1] happened to utter a thoughtless point which was an evil suggestion of Shaitan, from which neither kinship is established nor entitlement to succession occurs. He who relies on it is like the uninvited guest to a drink-party or like the dangling cup (tied to a saddle).

Sayyid Razi says: When Ziyad read this letter he said, (By Allah he has testified to it.) This point remained in his mind till Moaawiya claimed him (as his brother by his father).

-1- Caliph Omar sent Ziyad to Yemen for some encounter. When he returned after finishing the job he addressed a gathering which included Ameer al-Momineen, Omar, Amr bn-Aas and Abo-Sofyaan. Impressed with the speech Amr bn-Aas said:

What a good man! Had he been from the Quraysh he would have led the whole of Arabia with his stick." Whereupon Abo-Sofyaan said "He is from the Quraysh as I know who is his father." Amr bn-Aas enquired "Who was his father?" Abo-Sofyaan said "It is 1." History also conclusively holds that Ziyad's mother Somayya, who was the slave-maid of al-Haarith bn-Kalda and was married to a slave named Obayd, used to lead an immoral life in a quarter of at-Taaif known as Haaratol-Baghaaya, and immoral men used to visit her. Once Abi-Sofyaan also got to her through Abi-Maryam as-Salooli. As a result Ziyad was born. When Amr bn-Aas heard this from Abi-Sofyaan, he asked why he had not declared it. Abi-Sofyaan pointed to Omar and said that he was afraid of him, otherwise he would have declared him his own son. Although he would not have dared to do this, when Moaawiya acquired power he started correspondence with him because Moaawiya was in need of such persons who were intelligent and cunning and expert in machinations. In any case, when Ameer al-Momineen got information about this correspondence he wrote this letter to Ziyad wherein he warned him against Moaawiya so that he should not fall in the trap. But he did fall in his trap and joined Moaawiya and the latter declared him his brother by attaching him in his kin, although the Prophet had declared.

The child goes to the (lawful) husband while the adulterer gets stones.

Ameer al-Momineen's word (al-waaghil) means the man who joins the drinking group so as to drink with them, but he is not one of them. He is therefore constantly turned out and pushed off. As for the words (an-nawtol-mozabzab), it is a wooden cup or a bowl or the like attached to the saddle of the rider so that it dangles when the rider drives the beast or quickens its pace.

45- To Othmaan bn Honayf al-Ansaari, his governor of Basra, when he came to know that the people of that place had invited him to a banquet and he had attended

O Bn Honayf, I have come to know that a young man of Basra invited you to a feast and you leapt towards it. Foods of different colours were being chosen for you and big bowls were being given to you. I never thought that you would accept the feast of a people who turn out the beggars and invite the rich. Look at the morsels you take, leave out that about which you are in doubt and take that about which you are sure that it has been secured lawfully.

Remember that every follower has a leader whom he follows and from the effulgence of whose knowledge he takes light. Realise that your Imam has contented himself with two shabby pieces of cloth out of the (comforts of the) world and two loaves for his meal. Certainly, you cannot do so but at least support me in piety, exertion, chastity and uprightness, because, by Allah, I have not treasured any gold out of your world nor amassed plentiful wealth nor collected any clothes other than the two shabby sheets.

Of course, all that we had in our possession under this sky was Fadak, but a group of people felt greedy for it and the other party withheld themselves from it. Allah is, after all, the best arbiter. What shall I do: Fadak[1], or no Fadak, while tomorrow this body is to go into the grave in

-1- Fadak was a green fertile village near Madeena in the Hijaaz and it also had a fortress called ash-Shomrookh. (Mojam al-Boldaan, vol.4, p.238; Mojam Mostajam, al-Bakri, vol.3, p.1015; ar-Rawz al-Mitar, al-Himyari, p.437; Wafa al-Wafaa, vol.4, p.1280). Fadak belonged to the Jews and in the year 7 A.H. its ownership went from them to the Prophet under the terms of a settlement for peace. The reason for this settlement was that when after the fall of Khaybar the Jews realised the real power of the Muslims, their martial aspirations were lowered, and noting that the Prophet had spared some Jews on their seeking protection, they also sent a message of peace to the Prophet and expressed their wish that Fadak might be taken from them and their area should not be made a battlefield. Consequently, the Prophet accepted their request and allowed them an amnesty, and this land became his personal property wherein no one else had any interest, nor could there be any such interest; because the Muslims have a share only in those properties which they might have acquired as booty after Jihaad, while the property acquired without Jihaad is called "fay" and the Prophet alone is entitled to it. No other person has a share in it. Thus, Allah says:

And whatever hath Allah bestowed on His Apostle from them, ye pricked not against it any horse or a camel, but Allah granteth authority unto His apostles against whomsoever He willeth; And Allah over all things is All-powerful.(Quraan, 59:6)

No one has ever disputed the fact that Fadak was secured without battle. It was therefore the Prophet's personal property to which no one else had any title. The Historians write:

Fadak was personal to the Prophet as the Muslims did not use their horses or camels for it. (at Taareekh, at-Tabari, vol.1, pp.1582-1583,1589; al-Kaamil, bn-Athir, vol.2, pp.224-225; as-Seera, bn-Hishaam, vol.3, p.368; at-Taareekh, bn-Khaldoon, vol.2, part 2, p.40; Taareekh al-Khamees, ad-Diyaar Bakri, vol.2, p.58; as-Seera al-Halabiyya, vol.3, p.50)

The historian and geographical scholar Ahmad bn-Yahya al-Balazoori (d. 279/892) writes:

Fadak was the personal property of the Prophet as the Muslims had not used their horses or camels for it. (Fat-hol-Boldaan, vol.1, p.33)

Omar bn-Khattaab had himself regarded Fadak as the unshared property of the Holy Prophet when he declared:

The property of Bani-an-Nadir was among that which Allah has bestowed on His Messenger; against them neither horses nor camels were pricked but they belonged to the Messenger of Allah especially. (as-Saheeh, al-Bokhaari, vol.4, p.46; vol.7, p.82; vol.9, pp.121-122 as-Saheeh, Muslim, vol.5, p.151; as-Sonan, Abi-Dawood, vol.3, pp.139-141; as-Sonan, an-Nasal, vol.7, p.132; al-Mosnad, Ahmad bn-Hambal, vol.1, pp.25,48,60,208; as-Sonan al-Kobraa, al-Bayhaqi, vol.6, pp.296-299)

It is also proved in the accepted way that the Prophet had in his lifetime given this land (Fadak) to Fatima as a gift. It is narrated through al-Bazzar, Abi-Yala, bn-Abi-Hatim, bn-Mardowayh and others from Abi Said al-Khodri and through bn-Mardowayh from Abdillah bn-Abbaas that when the verse:

And give to the near of kin his due..." (Quraan, 17:26) was revealed the Holy Prophet called Fatima and gifted Fadak to her. (ad-Dorr al-Manthoor, as-Seyooti, vol.4, p.177; Majma" az-Zawaaid, al-Haythami, vol.7, p.46; Kanz al-Ommaal, al-Mottaqi, vol.3, p.439; Rooh al-Maani, al-Aaloosi, vol.15, p.62)

When Abi-Bakr assumed power then in view of some benefits of State he turned out Fatima from Fadak and took it from her possession. Thus, the historians write:

Certainly, Abi-Bakr snatched Fadak from Fatima (p.b.u.h.) (Sharh Nahjol-Balagha, bn-Abil-Hadeed, vol.16, p.219; Wafa al-Wafaa, as-Samhoodi, vol.3, p.I000; as-Sawaaiq al-Mohriqa, bn-Hajar, p.32)

Fatima raised a voice against it. Protesting to Abi-Bakr, she said "You have taken over possession of Fadak although the Prophet had gifted it to me during his life-time. On this Abi-Bakr asked her to produce witness of the gift. Consequently, Ameer al-Momineen and Om-Ayman gave evidence in her favour. (Om-Ayman was the freed bond maid and the dry nurse of the Holy Prophet. She was the mother of Osaama bn-Zayd bn-Haaritha. The Holy Prophet used to say "Om-Ayman is my mother after my mother. al-Mostadrak, vol.4, p.63; at-Tabari, vol.3, p.3460; al-Isteeaab, vol.4, p.1793; Osdol-Ghaaba, vol.5, p.567) The Holy Prophet bore witness that she is among the people of Paradise. bn Saad, vol.8, p.192; al-Isaaba, vol.4, p.4321). But this evidence was held inadmissible by Abi-Bakr and Fatima's claim was rejected as being based on false statement. About this al-Balazoori writes:

Fatima said to Abi-Bakr "The Messenger of Allah had apportioned Fadak to me. Therefore, give it to me." Then he asked her for another witness than Om-Ayman, saying "O daughter of the Prophet, you know that evidence is not admissible except by two men or one man and two women.

After these facts there remains no possibility of denying that Fadak was the personal property of the Prophet and that he had completed its gifting to her by handing over possession in his lifetime. But Abi-Bakr took over its possession and dislodged her from it. In this connection, he rejected the evidence of Ali and Om-Ayman on the ground that the requirement of evidence was not completed by the evidence of one man and one woman. Besides them, Imaam Hasan and Imaam Hosayn gave evidence in support of Fatima, but their evidence was rejected too on the ground that the evidence of the offspring and minors was not acceptable in favour of their parents. Then Rabah., the slave of the Holy Prophet was also produced as a witness in support of the claim of Fatima but he was rejected too. (Fotoohol-Boldaan, al-Balazoori, vol.1, p.35; at-Taareekh, al-Yaqoobi, vol.3, p.195; Morooj az-Zahab, al-Masoodi, vol.3, p.237; al-Awaail, Abi-Hilaal al-Askari, p.209; Wafa al-Wafaa, vol.3, pp.9g9,1000-1001; Mojam al-Boldaan, Yaqoot al-Hamwi, vol.4, p.239; Shar8, bn-Abil-Hadeed, vol.16, pp.216,219-220,274; al-Mohallab, bn-Hazm, vol.6, p.507; as-Seera al-Halabiyya, vol.3, p.361; at-Tafseer, al-Fakhr ar-Raazi, vol.29, p.284).

At this stage the question arises that when Fatima's possession over Fadak is admitted as Ameer al-Momineen has also clarified in this letter by saying "We had Fadak in our possession," what was the sense in asking Fatima to produce evidence in support of her claim, because the onus of proof does not lie on the person in possession. The onus of proof lies on the person filing a counter claim because possession itself constitutes a proof. As such it was on Abi-Bakr to produce a proof of the lawfulness of his taking over the land, and in the case of his being unable to do so Fatima's possession would mean a proof for her lawful ownership. As such it would be wrong to ask her to produce some more proof or evidence.

It is strange that when other claims of this nature came before Abi-Bakr he allowed them in favour of the claimant merely on the basis of the claim, and the claimant is neither asked to furnish proof of his claim nor to produce witnesses. In this connection, the traditionalists write:
It is related from Jabir bn-Abdillah al-Ansaari that he said that the Messenger of Allah had said that when the booty from Bahrain arrived he would allow him such and such out of it, but the booty did not arrive till the Prophet's death. When it arrived in the days of Abi-Bakr he went to him and Abi-Bakr made the announcement that whoever had a claim against the Messenger of Allah or to whomever he had made a promise should come for his claim. So I went to him and told him that the Prophet had promised to give me such and such property out of the booty from Bahrain whereupon he gave me all that. (as-Saheeh, al-Bokhaari, vol.3, pp.119,209,236; vol.4, p.110; vol.5, p.218; as-Saheeh, Muslim, vol.7, pp.75-76; al-Jaami as-Saheeh at-Tirmizi, vol.5, p.129; al-Mosnad, Ahmad bn-Hambal, vol.3, pp.307-308; at-Tabaqaat al-Kabeer, bn-Said, vol.2, part 2, pp.88-89).
In the annotations of this tradition, Shihabud-1)7n Ahmad bn-Ali (bn Hajar) al-Asqalani ash-Shaafii 1773/1372-852/1449) and Badroddeen Mahmood bn-Ahmad al-Ayni al-Hanafi 1762/1361-855il451) have written:
This tradition leads to the conclusion that the evidence of one just companion can also be admitted as full evidence even though it may be in his own favour, because Abi-Bakr did not ask Jabir to produce any witness in proof of his claim. (Fat-hol-Baari fee Sharh Saheeh al-Bokhaari, vol.5, p.380; Omdatol-Qaari fee Sharh Saheeh al-Bokhaari, vol.12, p.121)
If it was lawful to allow property to Jabir on the basis of good impression without calling for witness or evidence then what stopped allowing Fatima's claim on the basis of similar good impression. If good impression could exist in the case of Jabir to such an effect that he would not benefit by speaking a lie, then why should there not be the good belief about Fatima that she would not attribute a false saying to the Prophet just for a piece of land. Firstly, her admitted truthfulness and honesty was enough for holding her truthful in her claim and the evidence of Ali and Om-Ayman in her favour was also available besides other evidences. It has been said that the claim could not be decided in favour of Fatima on the basis of these two witnesses because the Holy Quraan lays down the principle of evidence that:
...then call to witness two witnesses from among your men and if there not be two men, then (take) a man and two women,... (Quraan, 2:282)
If this principle is universal and general then it should be taken into regard on every occasion, but on some occasion it is found not to have been followed; for example, when an Arab had a dispute with the Prophet about a camel, Khozayma bn-Thabit al-Ansaari gave evidence in favour of the Prophet and this one evidence was deemed to be equal to two, because there was no doubt in the honesty and truthfulness of the individual in whose favour the evidence was led. It was for this reason that the Holy Prophet granted him the title of Zosh-Shahaadatayn (i.e., one whose evidence is equivalent to the evidence of two witnesses). (al-Bokhaari, vol.4, p.24; vol.6, p.146; Abi-Dawood, vol.3,

p.308; an-Nesaai, vol.7, p.302; Ahmad bn-Hambal, vol.5, pp.188,189,216; al-Isteeaab, vol. 2, p.448; Osdol-Ghaaba, vol.2, p.114; al-Isaaba, vol.1, pp.425-426; al-Mosannaf, as-Sanani, vol.8, pp.366-368).

Consequently, neither was the generality of the verse about evidence affected by this action nor was it deemed to be against the cannons of evidence. So, if here in view of the Prophet's truthfulness one evidence in his favour was deemed to be equal to two, then could not the evidence of Ali and Om-Ayman be regarded enough for Fatima in view of her moral greatness and truthfulness? Besides, this verse does not show that there can be no other way of establishing a claim other than these two ways. In this connection, al-Qazi Noorollah al-Marashi at-Tostari (956/1549- 019/1610) has written in Ihqaaq al-Haqq, chapter on al-Mataain:

The view of the objector that by Om-Ayman's evidence the requirement of evidence remains incomplete is wrong, on the grounds that from certain traditions it is seen that it is lawful to give a decision on the basis of one witness and it does not necessarily mean that the injunction of the Quraan has been violated, because this verse means that a decision can be given on the strength of the evidence of two men or one man and two women, and that their evidence is enough. From this it does not appear that if there are some other grounds besides evidence of witnesses that are unacceptable, and that verdict cannot be given on its basis, unless it is argued that this is the only sense of the verse. But since every sense is not final argument, this sense can be brushed aside, particularly because the tradition clearly points to a contrary sense, and ignoring the sense does not necessarily mean violation of the verse. Secondly, the verse allows a choice between the evidence of two men or of one man and two women. If by virtue of the tradition a third choice is added namely that a verdict can be passed by means of other evidence as well, then how does it necessitate that the Quraanic verse should stand violated?

In any case, from this reply it is clear that a claimant is not obliged to produce the evidence of two men or one man and two women in support of the claim because if there is one witness and the claimant swears on oath, then he can be taken to have legitimacy in his claim and a decision can be given in his favour. In this connection, it has been narrated by more than twelve companions of the Holy Prophet that:

The Messenger of Allah used to decide cases on the strength of one witness and the taking of oath.

It has been explained by some companions (of the Prophet) and some scholars of jurisprudence that this decision is specially related to rights, property and transactions; and this decision was practised by the three Caliphs, Abi-Bakr, Omar and Othmaan. (Muslim, vol.5, p.128; Abi-Dawood, vol.3, pp.308-309; at-Tirmizi, vol.3, pp.627- 629; bn-Maaja, vol.2, p.793; Ahmad bn-Hambal, vol.1, pp.248,315,323; vol.3, p.305; vol.5, p.285; Malik bn-Anas, al-Mowtta, vol.2, pp.721-725; al-Bayhaqi, as-Sonan al-Kobraa, vol.10, pp.167-176; as-Sonan, ad-Darqutni, vol.4, pp.212-215; Majma" az-Zawaaid, vol.4, p.202; Kanz al-Ommaal, vol.7, p.13)

When decisions were passed on the strength of one witness and swearing, then even if in Abi-Bakr's view the requirement of evidence was incomplete, he should have asked her to swear and given the judgement in her favour. But here the very object was to tarnish the truthfulness of Fatima so that in future the question of her testimony should not arise.

However, when Fatima's claim was rejected in this manner and Fadak was not accepted as the Prophet's gift to her, she claimed it on the basis of inheritance saying:

If you do not agree that the Prophet had gifted it to me, you cannot at least deny that Fadak and the revenues of Khaybar as well as the lands around Madeena were the Prophet's personal properties, and I am his only successor." But she was deprived of her inheritance on the basis of a tradition related by Abi-Bakr himself that the Holy Prophet said "We prophets have no successors and whatever we leave behind constitutes charity." (al-Bokhaari, vol.4, p.96; vol.5, pp.25-26,115,117; vol.8, p.185; Muslim, vol.5, pp.153-155; at-Tirmizi, vol.4, pp.157-158; Abi-Dawood, vol.3, pp 142-143; an-Nesaai, vol.7, p.132; Ahmad bn-Hambal, vol.1, pp.4,6,9,10; al-Bayhaqi, vol.6, p.300; bn-Saad, vol.2, part 2, pp.86-87; at-Tabari, vol.1, p.1825; Taareekh al-Khamees, vol.2, pp.173-174). Besides Abi-Bakr no one else had knowledge of this saying which was shown to be a tradition of the Prophet nor had anyone from among the companions heard it. Thus, Jalaloddeen Abdr-Rahmaan bn-Abi-Bakr as-Seyooti ash-Shaafii (849/ 5-91 lJ1505) and Shihaboddeen Ahmad bn-Mohammad (bn Hajar) al-Haytami ash-Shaafii (909/1504-974/1567) have written:

After the death of the Prophet there was a difference of view about the inheritance and no one had any information in this matter. Then, Abi-Bakr said that he had heard the Messenger of Allah saying that: "We prophets leave no successors and whatever we leave behind constitutes charity. (Taareekh al-Kholafaa, p.73; as-Sawaaiq al-Mohriqa, p.19)

The mind refuses to believe that the Prophet should not tell those individuals who could be deemed his successors that they would not inherit, and inform a third party who had not the remotest kinship that there would be no successor to him. Then this story was made public only when the case for Fadak had been filed in his court and he himself constituted the contesting party. In such circumstances how can his presenting in his own support a tradition which no one else had heard be deemed permissible. If it is argued that this tradition should be relied upon in view of the greatness of position of Abi-Bakr, then why cannot Fatima's claim to the gift be relied upon because of her honesty and truthfulness, more so when the evidence of Ameer al-Momineen and Om-Ayman as well as others was also in her favour. If necessity was felt to call more evidence in her case, then evidence can also be called for about this tradition, particularly, since this tradition hits against the general instructions of the Quraan on succession. How can a tradition which is weak in the manner of its relating and altered and is questioned on the basis of facts be deemed to particularise a generality of the Quraanic injunction on succession, because the question of the inheritance of the prophets is clearly mentioned in the Quraan. Thus, Allah says:

And Solaymaan inherited Dawood... (Quraan, 27:16)

At another place it is stated through the words of Prophet Zakariyya:

...So grant me from yourself an heir, who shall inherit me and inherit from the family of Jacob... (Quraan, 19:5-6)

In these verses succession refers to succession in estate and to take it in its figurative meaning of succession in prophetic knowledge would not only be obtuse but also against facts, because knowledge and Prophethood are not objects of succession, nor do they posses the quality of transmission through inheritance, for in that case all the progeny of the prophets would have been prophets. There is no sense in making a distinction that the progeny of some prophets may inherit Prophethood while others should remain deprived of it. It is strange that the theory of transmission of Prophethood through inheritance is propagated by those who have always laid the objection against the Shiahs that they regard the Imaama and the caliphate as an object of inheritance and confined to one family only. Will not Prophethood become an object of inheritance by taking succession in this verse to mean succession to the Prophethood?

If in Abi-Bakr's view by virtue of this tradition there could be no successor of the Prophet then where was this tradition when a document had been written admitting Fatima's claim for succession? Thus, Nooroddeen Ali bn-Ibraheem al-Halabi ash-Shaafii (975/1567-1044/1635) quoting from Shamsoddeen Yoosof (Sibt bn-Jawz7) al-Hanafi 581/1185-654/1256) narrated:

Abi-Bakr was on the pulpit when Fatima came to him and said "O Abi-Bakr, the Quraan should allow your daughter to inherit you but I am not to inherit my father!" Abi-Bakr started weeping and alighted from the pulpit. Then he wrote for her about Fadak. At that time Omar arrived and enquired what it was. Abi-Bakr replied "It is a document I have written for Fatima about her inheritance from her father." Omar said "What will you spend on the Muslims while the Arabs are waging was against you, as you see?" Then, Omar took the document and tore it. (as-Seera al-Halabiyya, vol.3, pp.361-362)

Every sensible person who remarks this behaviour can easily reach the conclusion that this tradition is concocted and wrong, and was fabricated only to secure possession over Fadak and other inheritances. Consequently, Fatima refused to accept it and expressed her anger in this way that she made a will about Abi-Bakr and Omar that the two should not join in her funeral prayer. Aysha narrated:

Fatima (p.b.u.h.), the daughter of the Holy Prophet (p.b.u.h.a.h.p.) sent for Abi-Bakr (after he became Caliph after the death of the Holy Prophet) claiming from him her inheritance left by the Messenger of Allah from what Allah had bestowed (especially) upon him at Madeena and Fadak and what was left from one-fifth (khums) of the income (annually received) from Khaybar..., Abi-Bakr refused to hand over anything from it to Fatima. Then, Fatima became angry with Abi-Bakr and forsook him and did not talk to him until the end of her life... When she died, her husband, Ali bn-Abi-Talib buried her at night. He did not inform Abi-Bakr about her death and offered the funeral prayer over her himself... (al-Bokhaari, vol.5, p.177; vol.8, p.185; Muslim, vol.5, pp.153-155; al-Bayhaqi, vol.4, p.29; vol.6, pp.300-301; bn-Saad, vol.2, part 2, p.86; Ahmad bn-Hambal, vol.1, p.9; at-Tabari, vol.1, p.1825; bn-Katheer, at-Taareekh, vol.5, pp.285-286; bn-Abil-Hadeed, vol.6, p.46 and Wafa al-Wafaa, vol.3, p.995)

In this connection, Om-Jafar, the daughter of Mohammad bn-Jafar, narrated about the request of Fatima (p.b.u.h.) to Asma" bnt Omays near her death that:

When I die, I want you and Ali to wash me, and do not allow anyone to go in to me (in my house).

When she died Aysha came to enter, Asmaa told her "Do not enter." Aysha complained to Abi-Bakr (her father) saying "This Khathamiyya (a woman from the tribe of Katham, i.e. Asma) intervenes between us and the daughter of the Messenger of Allah..." Then, Abi-Bakr came and stood at the door and said "O Asmaa!, what makes you prevent the wives of the Prophet from entering in to the daughter of the Messenger of Allah?" Asma" replied "She had herself ordered me not to allow anyone to enter into her..." Abi-Bakr said "Do what she has ordered you." (Hilyatol-Awliyaa, vol.2, p.43; as-Sonan al-Kobra, vol.3, p.396; vol.4, p.334; Ansaab al-Ashraaf vol.1, p.405; al-Isteeaab, vol.4, pp.1897-1898; Osdol-Ghaaba, vol.5, p.524; al-Isaaba, vol.4, pp.378-379)

Fatima (p.b.u.h.) had also made a request to Ameer al-Momineen Ali that she must be buried at night and that no one should come to her, that Abi-Bakr and Omar should not be notified about her death and burial, and that Abi-Bakr should not be allowed to say the prayer over her body.

When she died, Ali washed and buried her in the quietness of the night, not notifying Abi-Bakr and Omar. So, these two were not aware of her burial.

Mohammad bn-Omar al-Waqidi (130/747-207/823) said:

It has been proved to us that Ali (p.b.u.h.) performed her funeral prayer and buried her by night, accompanied by al-Abbas (bn Abdl-Mottalib) and (his son) al-Fazl, and did not notify anyone.

It was for this reason that the burial place of Fatima (p.b.u.h.) was hidden and unknown, and no one is sure about it. (al-Mostadrak, vol.3, pp.162-163; al-Mosannaf, vol.4, p.141; Ansaab al-Ashraaf, vol.1, pp.402,405; al-Isteeaab, vol.4, p.1898; Osdol-Ghaaba, vol.5, pp.524-525; al-Isaaba, vol.4, pp.379-380; at-Tabari, vol.3, pp.2435- 2436; bn-Saad, vol.8, pp.19-20; Wafa" al-wafa, vol.3, pp.901-902,904,905; bn-Abil-Hadeed, vol.16, pp.279-281)

To attribute this displeasure of Fatima to sentiments and thereby to lower its importance does not evince a correct sentiment, because if this displeasure had been the result of sentiments then Ameer al-Momineen would have stopped her from this misplaced displeasure, but no history shows that Ameer al-Momineen took this displeasure to be misplaced. Besides, how could her displeasure be the result of personal feelings or sentiments since her pleasure or displeasure always accord with Allah's will. The Prophet's following saying is a proof of this:

O Fatima, surely Allah is enraged in your rage and is pleased in your pleasure. (al-Mostadrak, vol.3, p.153; Osdol-Ghaaba, vol.5, p.522; al-Isaaba, vol.4, p.366; Tahzeeb at-Tahzeeb, vol.12, p.441; al-Khasaais al-Kobraa vol.2, p.265; Kanz al-Ommaal, vol.13, p.96; vol.16, p.280; Majma" az-Zawaaid, vol.9, p.203)

A short history of Fadak after the death of Fatima

The motive which causes us to pursue the history of Fadak and to extract the continuation of events after it for a period of three centuries from the texts of historical books is to clarify three questions:-
a. The rule of annulment of inheritance from prophets made by the Holy Prophet, in other words, that the property of the Holy Prophet is a part of the public treasury and belongs to all Muslims. This was claimed by the first caliph Abi-Bakr, and was rejected by his successors, both by next the two caliphs (Omar and Othmaan) and by the Omayyads and the Abbaasids. We must consider that the lawfulness and rightfulness of their caliphate depended upon the correctness and lawfulness of the caliphate of the first Caliph and his actions.
b. Ameer al-Momineen (Ali-p.b.u.h.) and the descendants of Fatima never had any hesitation regarding the rightfulness and justifiability of their claim. They insisted and confirmed that Fatima (p.b.u.h.) had always been right and that Abi-Bakr's claim had always been rejected, and they did not yield to the false claim.
c. Whenever one of the Caliphs made a decision to put into effect Allah's command, in regard to Fadak, to observe justice and equity, and to restore the right to the entitled one in conformity with Islamic rules, he used to return back the Fadak to the descendants of Fatima (p.b.u.h.) and to hand it over to them.
1. Omar bn-Khattaab was the most harsh person in keeping Fatima (p.b.u.h.) from Fadak and her inheritance as he himself confessed:
When the Messenger of Allah died I came along with Abi-Bakr to Ali bn-Abi-Talib and said "What do you say about what has been left by the Messenger of Allah?" He replied "We have the most rights with the Holy Prophet." I (Omar) said "Even those properties of Khaybar?" He said "Yes, even those of Khaybar." I said "Even those of Fadak?" He replied "Yes, even those of Fadak." Then, I said "By Allah, we say no, even if you cut our necks with saws." (Majma" az-Zawaaid, vol.9, pp.39-40)
As it has been mentioned before, Omar then took the document of Fadak and tore it up. But when Omar became Caliph (13/634-23/644) he gave back the Fadak to inheritors of the Holy Prophet. Yaqoot al-Hamwi (S74/1178-626/1229), the famous historian and geographer, following the event of Fadak said:
...Then, when Omar bn-Khattaab became caliph and gained victories and the Muslims had secured abundant wealth (i.e. the public treasury satisfied the Caliphate's needs) he made his judgement contrary to that of his predecessor, and that was to give it (Fadak) back to the Prophet's heirs. At that time Ali bn-Abi-Talib and Abbaas bn-Abdl-Mottalib disputed Fadak.
Ali said that Holy Prophet (p.b.u.h.a.h.p.) had bestowed it on Fatima during his lifetime. Abbaas denied this and used to say "This was in the possession of the Holy Prophet (p.b.u.h.a.h.p.) and I am sharing with his heirs." They were disputing this among each other and asked Omar to settle the case. He refused to judge between them and said "Both of you are more conscious and aware to your problem; but I only give it to you..." (Mojam al-Boldaan, vol.4, pp.238- 239; Wafa al-Wafaa, vol.3, p.999; Tahzeeb al-Logha, vol.10, p.124; Lisaan al-Arab, vol.10, p.473; Taajol-Aroos, vol.7, p.166)

The reason that Omar and Abi-Bakr were trying to seize Fadak was an economic and political reason, not merely a religious one as the previous episode shows, for when the economic and political condition of the caliphate improved, and there was no need of the income obtained from Fadak, Omar's judgement changed also.
The last part of this historic event has been inserted afterwards to demonstrate the matter of inheritance by the brother of the deceased or the paternal uncle of the deceased when he has no sons. This problem is a matter of dispute between Islamic sects. The judicial and jurisprudencial discussion is separate from our goal. We are only discussing the matter historically.
Abbaas had no claim in this case because he had not shown that he had a share in this property nor did his descendants consider it to be among their own assets even when they had became caliphs and were reigning. They owned this estate either in their position as caliphs, or they used to return it to the descendants of Fatima when they had decided to be just governors.
2. When Othmaan bn-Affaan became caliph after the death of Omar (23/644- 35/656) he granted Fadak to Marwaan bn-Hakam, his cousin (as-Sonan al-Kobraa, vol.6, p.301; Wafa al-Wafaa, vol.3, p.1000; bn-Abil-Hadeed, vol.1, p.198), and this was one of the causes of vindictive feelings among the Muslims towards Othmaan (al-Maarif, bn-Qutayba,, p.195; al-Iqd al-fareed, vol.4, pp.283,435; at-Taareekh, Abol-Fida, vol.1, p.168; at-Taareekh, bn-Wardi, vol.1, p.204) which ended in the revolt against him and his murder. "While previously Fatima used to claim it, sometimes as her inheritance and sometimes as a gift (from her father) she was driven away from it (Fadak)" as bn-Abil-Hadeed said. (Sharh Nahjol-Balagha). In this way Fadak fell into the possession of Marwaan. He used to sell its crops and products for at least ten thousand Dinars per year, and if in some years its income decreased this drop was not very pronounced. This was its usual profit until the time of the caliphate of Omar bn-Abdl-Azeez (in 100/718). (bn Saad, vol.5, pp.286,287; Sobh al-Asha, vol.4, p.291)
3. When Moaawiya bn-Abi-Sofyaan became caliph (41/661-60/680) he became a partner with Marwaan and others in Fadak. He allotted one third to Marwaan and one third to Amr bn-Othmaan bn-Affaan and one third to his son Yazeed. This was after the death of Hasan bn-Ali (p.b.u.h.). "To make angry the progeny of the Holy Prophet" al-Yaqoobi states: (at-Taareekh, vol.2, p.199)
It was in the possession of the three above mentioned persons until Marwaan became caliph (64/684-65/685) and he completely took over possession of it. Then he donated it to his two sons, Abdl-Malik and Abdl-Azeez. Then Abdl-Azeez donated his share to his son (Omar bn-Abdl-Azeez).
4. When Omar bn-Abdl-Azeez became caliph (99/717-101/720) he delivered a lecture and mentioned that: "Verily, Fadak was among the things that Allah had bestowed on His Messenger, and no horse, nor camel was pricked against it..." and mentioned the case of Fadak during the past caliphates until he said: "Then Marwaan gave it (Fadak) to my father and to Abdl-Maalik. It became mine and al-Waleed's and Solaymaan's (two sons of Abdl-Maalik). When al-Waleed became caliph (86/705-96/715) I asked him for his share and he gave it to me. I asked also for Solaymaan's share and he gave it to me.

Then I gathered the three parts and I possess no property more preferable to me than this. Be witness that I returned it to its original state." He wrote this to his governor of Madeena (Abi-Bakr bn-Mohammad bn-Amr bn-Hazm) and ordered him to carry out what he had declared in the speech he delivered. Then Fadak came into the possession of the children of Fatima. "This was the first removal of oppression by returning it (Fadak) to the children of Ali." (al-Awaail, Abi-Hilaal al-Askari, p.209). They possessed it during the reign of this caliph.

5. When Yazeed bn-Abdl-Malik became caliph (101/720-105f724) he seized Fadak and they (the children of Ali) were dispossessed. It fell into the possession of the Bani-Marwaan as it had been previously. They passed it from hand to hand until their caliphate expired and passed away to the Bani al-Abbaas.

6. When Abol-Abbaas Abdillah as-Saffaah became the first caliph of the Abbaasid dynasty (132/749-136/754) he gave back Fadak to the children of Fatima and submitted it to Abdillah bn-Hasan bn-Hasan-bn-Ali bn-Abi-Talib.

7. When Abi- Jafar Abdillah al-Mansoor ad-Dawaaniqi (136/754-158/775) became caliph, he seized Fadak from the children of al-Hasan.

8. When Mohammad al-Mahdi bn-Mansoor became caliph (158/775-169/785) he returned Fadak to the children of Fatima.

9. The Moosa al-Haadi bn-Mahdi (169/785-170/786) and his brother Haroon ar-Rasheed (170/786-193/809) seized it from the descendants of Fatima and it was in the possession of Bani-al-Abbaas until the time that al-Mamoon became caliph (193/813- 218/833).

10. al-Mamoon al-Abbaasi gave it back to the descendants of Fatima (210/826). It is narrated through al-Mahdi bn-Saabiq that:

al-Mamoon one day sat to hear the complaints of the people and to judge in cases. The first utter of complaint which he received caused him to weep when he looked at it. He asked where the attorney of Faatima daughter of the Holy Prophet was? An old man stood up and came forth, arguing with him about Fadak and al-Mamoon also argued with him until he overcame al-Mamoon (al-Awaail, p.209)

al-Mamoon summoned the Islamic jurisprudents (al-Foqahaa) and interrogated them about the claim of the Bani-Fatima. They narrated to al-Mamoon that the Holy Prophet gifted Fadak to Fatima and that after the death of the Holy Prophet, Faatima demanded Abi Bakr to return Fadak to her. He asked her to bring witnesses to her claim regarding this gift. She brought Ali, al-Hasan, al-Hosayn and Om-Ayman as her witnesses. They witnessed the case in her favour. Abi-Bakr rejected their witness. Then al-Mamoon asked the Islamic jurisprudents: "What is your view about Om-Ayman?" They replied "She is a woman to whom the Holy Prophet bore witness that she is an inhabitant of Paradise." al-Mamoon disputed at length with them and forced them to accept the argument by proofs till they confessed that Ali, al-Hasan, al-Hosayn and Om-Ayman had witnessed only the truth. When they unanimously accepted this matter, he restored Fadak to the descendants of Fatima. (Taareekh, al-Yaqoobi, vol.3, pp.195-196)

Then al-Mamoon ordered that the estate (of Fadak) should be registered among the property (of the descendants of Fatima) and it was registered and al-Mamoon signed it. Then he wrote a letter to his governor in Madeena named Qutham bn-Jafar as follows:

Know that Ameer al-Momineen, in exercise of the authority vested upon him by the divine religion as the Caliph, successor and the kinsman of the Holy Prophet has considered himself more deserving to follow the precedent of the Holy Prophet (Sonnaton-Nabi and to carry out his commands. And (the chief is more entitled) to restore to the rightful persons any endowment gifted by the Holy Prophet or thing which the Holy Prophet had gifted to someone. The success and safeguard of Ameer al-Momineen is by Allah and he is particularly anxious to act in a way which will win the pleasure of the Almighty Allah for him.

Verily, the Holy Prophet had gifted the estate of Fadak to his daughter Fatima (p.b.u.h.). He had transferred its ownership to her. It is a clear and established fact. None of the kindred of the Holy Prophet have any difference of view. Fatima always claimed that which was more deserving (to be justified) than the person (Abi-Bakr) whose word was accepted. Ameer al-Momineen considers it right and proper to restore Fadak to the heirs of Fatima. He would hereby win nearness to Almighty Allah by establishing His justice and right. It would win the appreciation of the Holy Prophet by carrying into effect his commandments. Ameer al-Momineen has commanded that this restoration of Fadak should duly be registered. The commands should be transmitted to all the officials.

Then, if, as it was, a custom to proclaim on every Haj gathering (every year), following the death of the Holy Prophet, that anyone to whom the Holy Prophet had promised (the donation) of a gift or a present, should come forward, his statement will be accepted and the promise will be fulfilled. Certainly, Fatima (p.b.u.h.) had a superior right to have her statements accepted in the matter of the gifting of Fadak by the Holy Prophet (may Allah bless him and his descendants) to her.

Verily, Ameer al-Momineen has commanded his slave Mobaarak at-Tabari to restore Fadak to the descendants of Fatima the daughter of the Holy Prophet with all its borders, its rights and all slaves attached thereto, cereal crops and other things.

The same has been restored to Mohammad bn-Yahya bn-Hasan bn-Zayd bn-Ali bn-Hosayn bn-Abi-Talib and Mohammad bn-Abdillah bn-Hasan bn-Ali bn-Hosayn bn-Ali bn-Abi-Talib.

Ameer al-Momineen has appointed the two of them as the agents representing the owners of the lands-the heirs of Faatima. Know then this is the view of Ameer al-Momineen and that Allah has inspired him to obey the order of Allah and to win His pleasure and the pleasure of the Holy Prophet. Let also your subordinates know this. Behave towards Mohammad bn-Yahya and Mohammad bn-Abdillah in the same manner as you used to behave towards Mobaarak at.-Tabari. Help them both to everything which has to do with its flourishing and prosperity and its improvement in abundance of cereals by Allah's will; and that is an end to the matter.

This is written this Wednesday, two nights past Zol-Qida, the year 210 (15/2/826).

11. During the period of al-Mamoon's caliphate Fadak was in the possession of Fatima's descendants, and this continued during the caliphate of al-Motasim (218/833-227/842) and al-Waathiq (227/842-232/847).

12. When Jafar al-Motawakkil became caliph (232/847-247/861), the one among them who was marked as an arch enemy of the progeny of the Holy Prophet both of those

whose darkness its traces will be destroyed and (even) news of it will disappear. It is a pit that, even if its width is widened or the hands of the digger make it broad and open, the stones and clods of clay will narrow it and the falling earth will close its aperture. I try to keep myself engaged in

---

alive and of those dead, gave the order to recapture Fadak from the descendants of Fatima. (He seized it and granted it to Harmala al-Hajjam or the Cupper), and after the death of al-Hajjam he granted it to al-Baazyaar or the Falconer, a native of Tabarastaan. (Kashf al-Ghomma, vol.2, pp.121-122; al-Bihar, (1st ed.), vol.8, p.108; Safeena al-Bihaar, vol.2, p.351). Abd Hilaal al-Askari mentioned that his name was Abdillah bn-Omar al-Baazyaar and added:

And there were in it (Fadak) eleven date-palm trees which the Holy Prophet had planted by his own hands. The descendants of Abi-Talib used to gather these dates. When pilgrims (al-Haj), entered Madeena they donated the dates to them. Through this they received a considerable return. This news reached al-Motawakkil. He ordered Abdillah bn-Omar to cut up the fruits and to squeeze the juice from them. Abdillah bn-Omar sent a man named Bishr bn-Omayya ath-Thaqafi who squeezed the fruits. It was reported that he made it into wine. It had not reached Basra (on its way to the Caliph) before it decayed and al-Motawakkil was killed." (al-Awaail, p.209).

13. When al-Motawakkil was killed and al-Montasir (his son) succeeded him (247/861-248/862) he gave the order to restore Fadak to the descendants of Hasan and Hosayn and delivered the donations of Abi-Talib to them and this was in 248/862.

(Ref. for Nos. 3-13- Fotooh al-Boldaan, vol.1, pp.33-38; Mojam al-Boldaan, vol.4, pp. 238-240; at-Taareekh, al-Yaqoobi, vol.2, p.199; vol.3, pp.48, 195-196; al-Kaamil, bn-Atheer, vol.2, pp.224-225; vol.3, pp.457,497; vol.5, p.63; vol.7, p.116; al-Iqd al-fareed, vol.4, pp.216,283,435; Wafa al-Wafa, vol.3, pp.999-1000; at-Tabaqaat al-Kabeer, vol.5, pp.286-287; Taareekh al-Kholafaa, pp.231-232,356; Moroojoz-Zahab, vol.4, p.82; Seera Omar bn-Abdl-Azeez, bn-Jawzi, p.110; Sobh al-Asha, vol. 4, p.291; Jamharat Rasaail al-Arab, vol.2, pp.331-332; vol.3, pp.509-510; "Alaam an-Nesaa, vol.3, pp.1211-1212; bn-Abil-Hadeed, vol.16, pp.277-278; al-Awaail, p.209; Kashf al-Ghomma, vol.2, pp.120-122; al-Bi8dr, vol.8, pp.107-108)

14. It seemed that Fadak was recaptured from the descendants of Fatima after the death of al-Montasir (248-862), because Abol-Hasan, Ali bn-Esaa al-Arbeeli (d. 692/1293) mentioned "al-Motazid (279/892-289/902) returned Fadak to the descendants of Fatima. Then he mentioned that al-Moqtafi (289-902-295/908) seized it from them. It is said also that al-Moqtadir (295/908-320/932) returned it to them (the descendants of Fatima)." (Kashf al-Ghomma, vol.2, p.122; al-Bihaar, vol.8, p.108; Safeena, vol.2, p.351).

15. And after this long period of recapturing and restoration, Fadak was returned to the possession of the usurpers and their heirs as it seems, no further mention was made in history and the curtain fell.

Is it (then that) the judgement of (the times of pagan) ignorance they desire? And who (else) can be better than Allah to judge for a people of assured faith. (Quraan, 5:50)

piety so that one the day of great fear it will be peaceful and steady in slippery places.

If I wished I could have taken the way leading towards (worldly pleasures like) pure honey, fine wheat and silk clothes but it cannot be that my passions lead me and greed take me to choosing good meals while in the Hijaaz or in Yamama there may be people who have no hope of getting bread or who do not have a full meal. Shall I lie with a satiated belly while around me there may be hungry bellies and thirsty livers? Or shall I be as the poet has said?

It is enough for you to have a disease that you lie with your belly full while around you people may be badly yearning for dried leather.

Shall I be content with being called Ameer al-Momineen" (The Commander of the Believers), although I do not share with the people the hardships of the world? Or shall I be an example for them in the distresses of life? I have not been created to keep myself busy in eating good foods like the tied animal whose only worry is his fodder or like a loose animal whose activity is to swallow. It fills its belly with its feed and forgets the purpose behind it. Shall I be left uncontrolled to pasture freely, or draw the rope of misguidance or roam aimlessly in the paths of bewilderment?

I see as if one of you would say that if this is what the son of Abi-Talib eats then weakness must have made him unfit to fight his foes and encounter the brave. Remember that the tree of the forest is the best of timber, while green twigs have soft bark, and the wild bushes are very strong for burning and slow in dying off. My relation with the Messenger of Allah is that of one branch with another, or of the wrist with the forearm. By Allah, if the Arabs join together to fight me I will not run away from them and if I get the opportunity I will hasten to catch them by their necks. I shall surely strive to relieve the earth of this man of perverse mind and uncouth body, till the bits of earth are removed from the grain.

Get away from me. O world. Your rein is on your own shoulders as I have released myself from your ditches, removed myself of your snares and avoided walking into your slippery places. Where are those whom you have deceived by your jokes? Where are those communities whom you have enticed with your embellishments? They are all confined to graves and hidden in burial places. By Allah, if you had been a visible personality and a body capable of feeling, I would have awarded you the penalties fixed by Allah because of the people whom you received through desires and the communities whom you threw into destruction and the rulers whom you consigned to ruin and drove to places of distress after which there is neither going nor returning. Indeed whoever stepped on your slippery place slipped, whoever rode your waves was drowned, and whoever evaded your snares received inward support. He who keeps himself safe from you does not worry even though his affairs may be straitened and the world to him is like a day which is near expiring.

Get away from me, for, by Allah, I do not bow before you so that you may humiliate me, nor do I let loose the reins for you so that you may drive me away. I swear by Allah an oath wherein I, except the will of Allah, that I shall so train myself that it will feel joyed if it gets one loaf for eating, and be content with only salt to season it. I shall let my eyes empty themselves of tears like the stream whose water has flown away. Should Ali eat whatever he has and fall asleep like the cattle who fill their stomachs from the pasture land and lie down, or as the goats (who) graze, eat the green grass and go into their pen! His eyes may die if he, after long years, follows loose cattle and pasturing animals.

Blessed is he who discharges his obligations towards Allah and endures his hardships, allows himself no sleep in the night but when sleep overpowers him lies down on the ground using his hand as a pillow, along with those who keep their eyes wakeful in fear of the Day of Judgement, whose bodies are ever away from beds, whose lips are humming in remembrance of Allah and whose sins have been erased through their prolonged beseechings for forgiveness. They are the parry of Allah; Be it known, verily the party of Allah alone shall be the successful one (Quran, 58:22). Therefore, O Bn Honayf, fear Allah and be content with your own loaves so that you may escape Hell.

46- To one of his officers

Now, you are surely one of those whose help I take in establishing religion and with whose help I break the haughtiness of the sinful and guard critical boundaries. You should seek Allah's help in whatever causes you anxiety. Add a little harshness to the mixture of leniency and remain lenient where leniency is more appropriate. Adopt harshness when you cannot do without harshness. Bend your wings (in humbleness) before the subjects. Meet them with your face broad and keep yourself lenient (in behaviour) with them. Treat them equally in looking at them with half eyes or full eyes, in signalling and in greeting so that the great should not expect transgression on your part and the weak should not lose hope in your justice; and that is an end to the matter.

47- Will for Imam Hasan and Imam Hosayn (Peace be upon them) when Abdr-Rahmaan bn Moljam (Curse of Allah be upon him) struck him fatally with a sword

I advise you (both) to fear Allah and that you should not hanker after the (pleasures of this) world even though it may run after you. Do not be sorry for anything of this world that you have been denied. Speak the truth and act (in expectation) for reward. Be an enemy of the oppressor and helper of the oppressed.

I advise you (both) and all my children and members of my family and everyone whom my writing reaches, to fear Allah, to keep your affairs in order, and to maintain good relations among yourselves for I have heard your grand-father (the Holy Prophet -p.b.u.h.a.h.p.) saying, Improvement of mutual differences is better than general prayers and fastings

(Fear) Allah (and) keep Allah in view in the matter of orphans. So do not allow them to starve and they should not be ruined in your presence.

(Fear) Allah (and) keep Allah in view in the matter of your neighbours, because they were the subject of the Prophet's advice. He went on advising in their favour till we thought he would allow them a share in inheritance.

(Fear) Allah (and) keep Allah in view in the matter of the Quran. No one should excel you in acting upon it. (Fear) Allah (and) keep Allah in view in the matter of prayer, because it is the pillar of your religion.

(Fear) Allah (and) keep Allah in view in the matter of your Lord's House (Kaba). Do not forsake it so long as you live, because if it is abandoned you will not be spared.

(Fear) Allah (and) keep Allah in view in the matter of jihad with the help of your property, lives and tongues in the way of Allah.

You should keep to a respect for kinship and spending for others. Avoid turning away from one another and severing mutual relations. Do not give up bidding for good and forbidding from evil lest the mischievous gain positions over you, and then if you will pray, the prayers will not be granted.

Then he said:

O sons of Abd al-Mottalib, certainly I do not wish to see you plunging harshly into the blood of Muslims shouting Ameer al-Momineen has been killed" Beware, do not kill on account of me except my killer.

Wait till I die by his (Bn Moljam's) existing stroke. Then strike him one stroke for his stroke and do not dismember the limbs of the man, for I have heard the Messenger of Allah (p.b.u.h.a.h.p.) saying Avoid cutting limbs even though it may be a rabid dog

48- To Moaawiya bn Abi-Sofyaan

Surely, revolt and falsehood abase a man in his religious as well as worldly matters and manifest his shortcomings before his critic. You know that you cannot catch what is destined to remain away from you. Many people had aims other than right (ones) and began to swear by Allah (that they will attain their goal) but He falsified them. Therefore, fear the Day when happy is he who made his end happy (by good actions) while repentant is he who allowed Shaitan to lead him and did not resist him. You called us to a settlement through the Quran although you were not a man of the Quran, and we responded to the Quran through its judgement, and not to you; and that is an end to the matter.

49- To Moaawiya bn Abi-Sofyaan

So now, this world turns away from the next one. He who is devoted to it achieves nothing from it except that it increases his greed and coveting for it. He who is devoted to it is not satisfied with what he gets from it because of what he has not got. Eventually, there is separation from what has been amassed, and a breaking of what has been strengthened. If you take a lesson from the past you can be safe in the future; and that is an end to the matter.

50- To the officers of his army

From the servant of Allah, Ali, Ameer al-Momineen to the Officer-in-charge of garrisons:

Now, it is obligatory on an officer that the distinction he achieves, or the wealth with which he has been exclusively endowed, should not make him change his behaviour towards those under him, and that the riches Allah has bestowed on him should increase him in nearness to his people and kindness over his brethren.

Beware, that it is obligatory for you on me that I should not keep anything secret from you except during war, nor should I decide any matter without consulting you except the commands of religion. nor should I ignore the fulfillment of any of your rights nor desist till I discharge it fully, and that for me all of you should be equal in rights. When I have done all this, it becomes obligatory on you to thank Allah for this bounty and to obey me, and you should not hold back when called, nor shirk good acts, and you should face hardships for the sake of right. If you do not remain steadfast in this, there will be no one more humiliated in my view than the one among you who has deviated, and then I will increase the punishment for him, wherein no one will get any concession from me. Take this (pledge) from your (subordinate) officers and accord to them such behaviour from your side by which Allah may improve your matters; and that is an end to the matter.

51- To his collectors of (land) tax

From the servant of Allah Ali, Ameer al-Momineen to the tax collectors:

So now, he who does not fear where he is going, does not send forward for himself that which could protect him. You should know that the obligations laid on you are few, while their reward is much. Even if there had been no fear of punishment for revolt and disobedience, which Allah has prohibited, the reward in keeping aloof from it would be enough (incentive) to abstain from going after it. Behave yourselves justly with the people and act with endurance with regard to their needs, because you are the treasurers of the people, representatives of the community and the ambassadors of the Imams.

Do not deprive anyone of his needs and do not prevent him from (securing) his requirements. For the collection of tax (kharaaj) from the people do not sell their winter or summer clothes, nor cattle with which they work, nor slaves. Do not whip anyone for the sake of one Dirham. Do not touch the property of any person whether he be one who prays (a Muslim) or a protected unbeliever, unless you find a horse or weapons used for attack against Muslims, because it is not proper for the Muslims to leave these things in the hands of the enemies of Islam to enable them to have power over Islam.

Do not deny good counsel to yourself, good behaviour to the army, succour to the subjects and strength to the religion of Allah. Strive in the way of Allah as is obligatory on you, because Allah the Glorified, desires us and you to be thankful to Him as best as we can and that we should help Him to the best of our power. And there is no power save with Allah, the All-high, the All-glorious.

52- To the governors of various places concerning prayers

Now, say the zohr (noon) prayers with the people when the shade of the wall of the goats" pen is equal to the wall. Say the "asr (afternoon) prayers with them when the sun is still shining in a portion of the day enough for covering the distance of two farsakhs (about six miles). Say the maghrib (sunset) prayers when he who is fasting ends the fast and the pilgrim rushes (from Arafaat) to Mina. Say the "isha" (night) prayers with them when twilight disappears and upto one third of the night. Say the (early) morning prayers with them when a man can recognise the face of his companion. Say the prayers with the people as the weakest of them would do and do not be a source of trouble to them.

53- Document[1] of instruction for Maalik al-Ashtar an-Nakhaai, when the position of Mohammad bn Abi Bakr, had become

-1- This document, which deserves to be called the constitution of Islamic policy, was prepared by the person who was the greatest scholar of Divine law and acted upon it more than anyone else. From the study of Ameer al-Momineen's way of governance in these pages it can be concluded that his aim was only the enforcement of Divine law and the improvement of social conditions, and not to disrupt public security or to fill treasures by plunder, or to strive to extend the country's boundaries by fair means or foul. Worldly governments generally adopt such constitutions which cater to their utmost benefit and try to change every law which is against that aim or is injurious for their objective. But every article of this constitution serves as a custodian of common interests and protector of collective organisation. Its enforcement has no touch of selfishness or any iota of self-interest. It contains such basic principles of the fulfilment of Allah's obligations, the protection of human rights without distinction of religion or community, the care of the destitute and the poor and the provision of succour to the low and the down-trodden from which full guidance can be had for the propagation of right and justice, the establishment of peace and security, and the prosperity and well-being of the people.

Ameer al-Momineen wrote this instrument for Malik bn-Haarith al-Ashtar when he was appointed the Governor of Egypt in 38 A.H.. Malik al-Ashtar was one of the chief companions of Ameer al-Momineen. He had shown great endurance and steadfastness and perfect confidence and trust in Ameer al-Momineen. He had attained the utmost nearness and attachment to him by moulding his conduct and character after the conduct and character of Ameer al-Momineen. This can be gauged by Ameer al-Momineen's words:

Malik was to me as I was to the Messenger of Allah" (bn Abil-Hadeed, vol.15, p.98; al-Alaam, vol.6, p.131). Malik al-Ashtar too, actuated by selfless feelings of service, took a very active part in military encounters and proved himself to be Ameer al-Momineen's arm in all battles and encounters. He showed such feats of courage and daring that his bravery was acknowledged throughout Arabia. Along with this bravery he was also conspicuous in endurance and forbearing. In this connection, Warraam bn-Abi-Firaas an-Nakhaai has written that once Malik was passing through the market of Koofa with the dress and turban made of gunny-cloth when a shopkeeper finding him in this condition and clothing, he threw some rotten leaves upon him, but he did not at all mind this dirty behaviour, nor did he even look at him. Rather, he quietly stepped forward. Then someone said to this shopkeeper "Do you know to whom you have been so insolent?" He replied that he did not know who he was, whereupon he said that it was Malik al-Ashtar, the companion of Ameer al-Momineen. Hearing this, he lost his senses and at once ran behind him to seek pardon for this insolence and humiliating treatment.

While in his search he reached a mosque where Malik was offering prayers. When he finished the prayers this man went forward and fell on his feet and begged pardon with great pertinacity and weeping. Malik raised the man's beard up and said "By Allah, I have come to the mosque to pray to Allah to forgive you. I myself had pardoned you that very moment, and I hope Allah too will pardon you." (Tanbeehol-khawaatir wa Nuzhatusn-Nawaazir, vol.1, p.2; al-Bihaar, vol.42, p.157). This is the forgiveness and tolerance of a warrior at who name courage trembled, and whose swordsmanship was acknowledged by the brave men of Arabia. And this is the real sign of bravery that a man should exercise self-control during bitterness of anger and rage and endure hardships with patience and calmness. In this connection, Ameer al-Momineen's saying is that "The bravest of men is he who over-powers his passions.

However, besides these characteristics and qualities, he had a perfect aptitude for organisation and administration. Thus, when the Othmaani (al-Othmaaniyya) party began to spread the germs of destruction in Egypt and tried to upset the law and order of the country by mischief and revolt then Ameer al-Momineen removed Mohammad bn-Abi-Bakr from the governship and decided to appoint Malik al-Ashtar in his place, although at that time he was posted as the Governor of Naasibeen. However, Ameer al-Momineen sent him word that he should name someone as his deputy and come to Ameer al-Momineen. On receipt of this order Malik al-Ashtar appointed Shibeeb bn-Amir al-Azdi in his place and himself came to Ameer al-Momineen. Ameer al-Momineen gave him a warrant of appointment and sent him off to Egypt, and also sent a written order to Egyptians to obey him. When Moaawiya got the news of Malik al-Ashtar's appointment through his spies he was perplexed because he had promised Amr bn-Aas that he would give him the governship of Egypt in reward of his services and he had hoped that Amr bn-Aas would easily defeat Mohammad bn-Abi-Bakr and wrest the power from him, but could not imagine conquering Egypt by defeating Malik al-Ashtar. He therefore decided to do away with him before he took over the charge. For this he arranged with a landlord of the city of al-Arish (or al-Qulzom) that when Malik passed through al-Arish on his way to Egypt he should kill him by some device or other and in reward for this the revenue of

precarious, and he had appointed al-Ashtar as the governor of Egypt and the surrounding areas

This is the longest document and contains the greatest number of beautiful sayings.

In the Name of Allah, the Compassionate, the Merciful

This is what Allah's servant Ali, Ameer al-Momineen, has ordered Malik bn-Haarith al-Ashtar in his instrument (of appointment) for him when he made him Governor of Egypt for the collection of its revenues, fighting against its enemies, seeking the good of its people and making its cities prosperous.

He has ordered him to fear Allah, to prefer obedience to Him, and to follow what He has commanded in His Book (Quraan) out of His obligatory and elective commands, without following which one cannot achieve virtue, nor (can one) be evil save by opposing them and ignoring them, and to help Allah the Glorified, with his heart, hand and tongue, because

---

his estate would be written off. So, when Malik al-Ashtar reached al-Arish with retinue and force the chief of al-Arish gave him a good ovation and insisted on having Malik as his guest. Malik agreed and stayed at his place. When he finished the meal the host gave him some syrup of honey to drink in which he had mixed with poison. Soon after drinking it the poison began to show its effect and before the eyes of everyone this great warrior known for his swordsmanship and for putting the rows of the enemy to flight calmly went into the embrace of death.

When Moaawiya got news of his success of this device he was overjoyed and shouted in merriment "Oh, honey is also an army of Allah, and then said during a speech:

Ali bn-Abi-Talib had two right hand men. One was chopped off on the day of Siffeen and he was "Ammaar bn-Yasir, and the second has been severed now and he is Malik al-Ashtar.

But when the news of Maalik's assassination reached Ameer al-Momineen, he was highly grieved and sorrowful, then he said:

Malik! who is Malik? If Malik was a stone, he was hard and solid; if he was a rock, he was a great rock which had no parallel. It seems his death has made me also lifeless. I swear by Allah that his death made the Syrians joyous and insulted the Iraqis.

Then he continued:

Women have become barren to give birth to such as Malik. (a!-Tabari, vol.1, pp.3392-3395; bn-Atheer, vol.3, pp.352-353; al-Yaqoobi, vol.2, p.194; at-Isteeaab, vol.3, p.1366; bn-Abil-Hadeed, vol.6, pp.74-77; bn-Katheer, vol.7, pp.313-314; Abol-Fida, vol.1, p.179).

Allah whose name is Sublime takes the responsibility for helping him who helps Him, and for protecting him who gives Him support.

He also orders him to break his heart off from passions, and to restrain it at the time of their increase, because the heart leads towards evil unless Allah has mercy.

Qualifications of a governor and his responsibilities

Then, know O Malik that I have sent you to an area where there have been governments before you, both just as well as oppressive. People will now watch your dealings as you used to watch the dealings of the rulers before you, and they (people) will criticise you as you criticised them (rulers). Surely, the virtuous are known by the reputation that Allah circulates for them through the tongues of His creatures. Therefore, the best collection with you should be the collection of good deeds. So, control your passions and check your heart from doing what is not lawful for you, because checking the heart means detaining it just half way between what it likes and dislikes.

Habituate your heart to mercy for the subjects and to affection and kindness for them. Do not stand over them like greedy beasts who feel it is enough to devour them, since they are of two kinds, either your brother in religion or one like you in creation. They will commit slips and encounter mistakes. They may act wrongly, wilfully or by neglect. So, extend to them your forgiveness and pardon, in the same way as you would like Allah to extend His forgiveness and pardon to you, because you are over them and your responsible Commander (Imam) is over you while Allah is over him who has appointed you. He (Allah) has sought you to manage their affairs and has tried you through them.

Do not set yourself to fight Allah because you have no power before His power and you cannot do without His pardon and mercy. Do not repent of forgiving or be merciful in punishing. Do not act hastily during anger if you can find way out of it. Do not say:

I have been given authority, I should be obeyed when I order" because it engenders confusion in the heart, weakens the religion and takes one near ruin. If the authority in which you are placed produces pride or vanity in you then look at the greatness of the realm of Allah over you and His might the like of which might you do not even possess over yourself. This will curb your haughtiness, cure you of your high temper and bring back to you your wisdom which had gone away from you.

Beware of comparing yourself to Allah in His greatness or likening yourself to Him in His power, for Allah humiliates every claimant of power and disgraces every one who is haughty.

Do justice for Allah and do justice towards the people, as against yourself, your near ones and those of your subjects for whom you have a liking, because if you do not do so you will be oppressive, and when a person oppresses the creatures of Allah then, instead of His creatures, Allah becomes his opponent, and when Allah is the opponent of a person He tramples his plea; and we will remain in the position of being at war with Allah until he gives it up and repents. Nothing is more inductive of the reversal of Allah's bounty or for the hastening of His retribution than continuance in oppression, because Allah hears the prayer of the oppressed and is on the look out for the oppressors.

Ruling should be in favour of the people as a whole

The way most coveted by you should be that which is the most equitable for the right, the most universal by way of justice, and the most comprehensive with regard to the agreement among those under you, because the disagreement among the common people sweeps away the arguments of the chiefs can be disregarded when compared with the agreement of the common people. No one among those under you is more burdensome to the ruler in the comfort of life, less helpful in distress, more disliking of equitable treatment, more tricky in asking favours, less thankful at the time of giving, less appreciative of reasons at the time of refusal and weaker in endurance at the time of the discomforts of life than the chiefs. It is the common people of the community who are the pillars of the religion, the power of the Muslims and the defence against the enemies. Your leanings should therefore be towards them and your inclination with them.

The one among the people under you who is furthest from you and the worst of them in your view should be he who is the most inquisitive of the shortcomings of the people, because people do have short-comings and the ruler is the most appropriate person to cover them. Do not disclose whatever of it is hidden from you because your obligation is to correct what is manifest to you, while Allah will deal with whatever is hidden from you. Therefore, cover shortcomings so far as you can; Allah would cover those of your shortcomings which you should like to remain under cover from your subjects. Unfasten every knot of hatred in the people and cut away from yourself the cause of every enmity. Feign ignorance from what is not clear to you. Do not hasten to second a backbiter, because a backbiter is a cheat although he looks like those who wish well.

Counsellors

Do not include among those you consult a miser who would keep you back from being generous and caution you against destitution, nor a coward who would make you feel too weak for your affairs, nor a greedy person who would make beautiful to you the collection of wealth by evil ways. This is because although miserliness, cowardice and greed are different qualities, yet they are common in having an incorrect idea about Allah.

The worst minister for you is he who has been a minister for mischievous persons before you, and who joined them in sins. Therefore, he should not be your chief man, because they are abettors of sinners and brothers of the oppressors. You can find good substitutes for them who will be like them in their views and influence, while not being like them in sins and vices. They have never assisted an oppressor in his oppression or a sinner in his sin. They will give you the least trouble and the best support. They will be most considerate towards you and the least inclined towards others. Therefore, make them your chief companions in privacy as well as in public.

Then, more preferable among them for you should be those who openly speak better truths before you and who support you least in those of your actions which Allah does not approve in His friends, even though they may be according to your wishes. Associate yourself with God-fearing and truthful people; then educate them, so that they should not praise you or please you by reason of an action you did not perform, because and excess of praise produces pride and drives you near haughtiness.

The virtuous and the vicious should not be in equal position before you because this means dissuasion of the virtuous from virtue and persuasion of the vicious to vice. Keep everyone in the position which is his. You should know that the most conducive thing for the good impression of the ruler on his subjects is that he should extend good behaviour towards them, lighten their hardships, and avoid putting them to unbearable troubles. You should therefore, in this way follow a course by which you will leave a good impression with your subjects, because such good ideas will relieve you of great worries. Certainly, the most appropriate for good impression of you is he to whom your behaviour has not been good.

Do not discontinue the good lives in which the earlier people of this community had been acting, by virtue of which there was general unity and through which the subjects prospered. Do not innovate any line of action which injures these earlier ways because (in that case) the reward for those who had established those ways will continue, but the burden for discontinuing them will be on you. Keep on increasing your conversations with the scholars and discussions with the wise to stabilise the prosperity of the areas under you, and to continue with that in which the earlier people had remained steadfast.

Classes of people

Know that the people consist of classes who prosper only with the help of one another, and they are not independent of one another. Among them are the army of Allah, then the secretarial workers of the common people and the chiefs, then the dispensers of justice, then those engaged in law and order, then the payers of head tax (Jizya) and land tax (kharaaj) from the protected unbelievers and the common Muslims, then there are the traders and the men of industry and then the lowest class of the needy and the destitute. Allah has fixed the share of every one of them and laid down His precepts about the limits of each in His Book (Quraan) and the Sonna of His Prophet by way of a settlement which is preserved with us.

Now the army is, by the will of Allah, the fortress of the subjects, the ornament of the ruler, the strength of the religion and the means of peace. The subjects cannot exist without them while the army can be maintained only by the funds fixed by Allah in the revenues, through which they acquire the strength to fight the enemies, on which they depend for their prosperity, and with which they meet their needs. These two classes cannot exist without the third class namely the judges, the executives and the secretaries who pass judgements about contracts, collect revenues and are depended upon in special and general matters.

And these classes cannot exist except with the traders and men of industry, who provide necessities for them, establish markets and make it possible for others not to do all this with their own hands. Then is the lowest class of the needy and the destitute support of and help for whom is an obligation, and everyone of them has (a share in) livelihood in the name of Allah. Everyone of them has a right on the ruler according to what is needed for his prosperity. The ruler cannot acquit himself of the obligations laid on him by Allah in this matter except by striving and seeking help from Allah and by training himself to adhere to the right and by enduring on that account all that is light or hard.

1. The Army

Put in command of your forces the man who in your view is the best well-wisher of Allah, His Prophet and your Imam. The chastest of them in heart and the highest of them in endurance is he who is slow in getting enraged, accepts excuses, is kind to the weak and is strict with the strong; violence should not raise his temper and weakness should not keep him sitting.

Also associate with considerate people from high families, virtuous houses and decent traditions, then people of courage, valour, generosity and benevolence, because they are repositories of honour and springs of virtues. Strive for their matters as the parents strive for their child. Do not regard anything that you do to strengthen them as big nor consider anything that you have agreed to do for them as little (so as to give it up), even though it may be small, because this will make them your well-wishers and create a good impression of you. Do not neglect to attend to their small matters, confining yourself to their important matters, because your small favours will also be of benefit to them while the important ones are such that they cannot ignore them.

That commander of the army should have such a position before you that he renders help to them equitably and spends from his money on them and on those of their families who remain behind so that all their worries converge on the one worry for fighting the enemy. Your kindness to them will turn their hearts to you. The most pleasant thing for the rulers is the establishment of justice in their areas and the manifestation of the love of their subjects, but the subjects" love manifests itself only when their hearts are clean. Their good wishes prove correct only when they surround their commanders (to protect them). Do not regard their positions to be a burden over them and do not keep watching for the end of their tenure. Therefore, be broad-minded in regard to their desires, continue praising them and recounting the good deeds of those who have shown such deeds, because the mention of good actions shakes the brave and rouses the weak, if Allah so wills.

Appreciate the performance of every one of them, do not attribute the performance of one to the other, and do not minimise the reward below the level of the performance. The high position of a man should not lead you to regard his small deeds as big, nor should the low position of a man make you regard his big deeds as small.

Refer to Allah and His Prophet the affairs which worry you and matters which appear confusing to you, because, addressing the people whom Allah the Sublime, wishes to guide, He said:

O you who believe! Obey Allah and obey the Prophet and those vested with authority from among you; and then if you quarrel about anything refer it to Allah and the Prophet if you believe in Allah and in the Last Day (of Judgement). (Quraan, 4:59)

Referring to Allah means to act according to what is clear in His Book and referring to the Prophet means to follow his unanimously agreed Sonna in regard to which there are no differences.

2. The Chief Judge

For the settlement of disputes among people, select him who is the most distinguished of your subjects in your view. The cases (coming before him) should not vex him, disputation should not enrage him, he should not insist on any wrong point, and should not grudge accepting the truth when he perceives it; he should not lean towards greed and should not content himself with a cursory understanding (of a matter) without going thoroughly into it. He should be most ready to stop (to ponder) on doubtful points, most regardful of arguments, least disgusted at the quarrel of litigants, most patient at probing into matters and most fearless at the time of passing judgement. Praise should not make him vain and elation should not make him lean (to any side). Such people are very few. Then, very often check his decisions and allow him so much money (as remuneration) that he has no excuse worth hearing (for not being honest) and there remains no occasion for him to go to others for his needs. Give him that rank in your audience for which no one else among your chiefs aspires, so that he remains safe from the harm of those around you. You should have a piercing eye in this matter because this religion has formerly been a prisoner in the hands of vicious persons when action was taken according to passion, and worldly wealth was sought.

3. Executive Officers

Thereafter, look into the affairs of your executives. Give them appointment after tests and do not appoint them according to partiality or favouritism, because these two things constitute sources of injustice and unfairness. Select among them those who are people of experience and modesty, hailing from virtuous houses, having been previously in Islam, because such persons possess high manners and untarnished honour. They are the least inclined towards greed and always have their eyes on the ends of matters.

Give them an abundant livelihood (by way of salary) because this gives them the strength to maintain themselves in order and not to have an eye upon the funds in their custody, and it would be an argument against them if they disobeyed your orders or misappropriated your trust. You should also check their activities and have people who report on them who should be truthful and faithful, because your watching their actions secretly will urge them to preserve trust with and to be kind to the people. Be careful of assistants. If any one of them extends his hands towards misappropriation and the reports of your reporters reaching you confirm it, that should be regarded enough evidence. You should then inflict corporal punishment on him and recover what he has misappropriated. You should put him in a place of disgrace, blacklist him with (the charge of) misappropriation and make him wear the necklace of shame for his offence.

4. The Administration of Revenues

Look after the revenue (kharaaj or land tax) affairs in such a way that those engaged in it remain prosperous because in their prosperity lies the prosperity of all others. The others cannot prosper without them, because all people are dependent on revenue and its payers. You should also keep an eye on the cultivation of the land more than on the collection of revenue because revenue cannot be had without cultivation and whoever asks for revenue without cultivation, ruins the area and brings death to the people. His rule will not last only a moment.

If they complain of the heaviness (of the revenue) or of diseases, or dearth of water, or excess of water or of a change in the condition of the land either due to flood or to drought, you should remit the revenue to the extent that you hope will improve their position. The remission granted by you for the removal of distress from them should not be grudged by you, because it is an investment which they will return to you in the shape of the prosperity of your country and the progress of your domain in addition to earning their praise and happiness for meeting out justice to them. You can depend upon their strength because of the investment made by you in them through catering to their convenience, and can have confidence in them because of the justice extended to them by being kind to them. After that, circumstances may so turn that you may have ask for their assistance, when they will bear it happily, for prosperity is capable of bearing whatever you load on it. The ruin of the land is caused by the poverty of the cultivators, while the cultivators become poor when the officers concentrate on the collection (of money), having little hope for continuance (in their posts) and deriving no benefit from objects of warning.

5. The Clerical Establishment

Then you should take care of your secretarial workers. Put the best of them in charge of your affairs. Entrust those of your letters which contain your policies and secrets to him who possesses the best character, who is not elated by honours, lest he dares speak against you in common audiences. He should also not be negligent in presenting the communications of your officers before you and issuing correct replies to them on your behalf and in matters of your receipts and payments. He should not make any damaging agreement on your behalf and should not fail in repudiating an agreement against you. He should not be ignorant of the extent of his own position in matters because he who is ignorant of his own position is (even) more ignorant of the position of others.

Your selection of these people should not be on the basis of your understanding (of them), confidence and your good impression, because people catch the ideas of the officers through affectation and personal service and there is nothing in it which is like well-wishing or trustfulness. You should rather test them by what they did under the virtuous people before you. Take a decision in favour of one who has a good name among the common people and is the most renowned in trustworthiness, because this will be a proof of your regard for Allah and for him on whose behalf you have been appointed to this position (namely your Imam). Establish one chief for every department of work. He should not be incapable of big matters, and a rush of work should not perplex him. Whenever there is a defect in your secretaries which you overlook, then you will be held responsible for it.

6. Traders and Industrialists

Now take some advice about traders and industrialists. Give them good counsel whether they be settled (shop-keepers) or traders or physical labourers because they are sources of profit and the means of the provision of useful articles. They bring them from distant and far-flung areas throughout the land and sea, plains or mountains, from where people cannot come and to where they do not dare to go, for they are peaceful and there is no fear of revolt from them, and they are quite without fear of treason.

Look after their affairs before yourself or wherever they may be in your area. Know, along with this, that most of them are very narrow-minded, and awfully avaricious. They hoard goods for profiteering and fix high prices for goods. This is a source of harm to the people and a blot on the officers in charge. Stop people from hoarding, because the Messenger of Allah (p.b.u.h.a.h.p.) has prohibited it. The sale should be smooth, with correct weights and prices, not harmful to either party, the seller or the purchaser; whoever commits hoarding after you prohibit it, give him exemplary but not excessive punishment.

7. The Lowest Class

(Fear) Allah and keep Allah in view in respect of the lowest class, consisting of those who have few means: the poor, the destitute, the penniless and the disabled; because in this class are both the discontented and those who beg. Take care for the sake of Allah of His obligations towards them for which He has made you responsible. Fix for them a share from the public funds and a share from the crops of lands taken over as booty for Islam in every area, because in it the remote ones have the same shares as the near ones. All these people are those whose rights have been placed in your charge. Therefore, a luxurious life should not keep you away from them. You cannot be excused for ignoring small matters because you were deciding big problems. Consequently. do not be unmindful of them, nor turn your face from them out of vanity.

Take care of the affairs of those of them who do not approach you because they are of unsightly appearance or those whom people regard as low. Appoint for them some trusted people who are God-fearing and humble. They should inform you of these people's conditions. Then deal with them with a sense of responsibility to Allah on the day you will meet Him, because of all the subjects these people are the most deserving of equitable treatment, while for others also you should fulfil their rights so as to render account to Allah.

Take care of the orphans and the aged who have no means (for livelihood) nor are they ready for begging. This is heavy on the officers; in fact, every right is heavy. Allah lightens it for those who seek the next world and so they endure (hardships) upon themselves and trust on the truthfulness of Allah's promise to them. And fix a time for complainants wherein you make yourself free for them, and sit for them in common audience and feel humble therein for the sake of Allah who created you. (On that occasion) you should keep away your army and your assistants such as the guards and the police so that anyone who like to speak may speak to you without fear, because I have heard the Messenger of Allah (p.b.u.h.a.h.p.) say in more than one place. "The people among whom the right of the weak is not secured from the strong without fear will never achieve purity" Tolerate their awkwardness and inability to speak. Keep away from you narrowness and haughtiness; Allah would, on this account, spread over you the skirts of His mercy and assign the reward of His obedience for you. Whatever you given give it joyfully, but when you refuse, do it handsomely and with excuses.

Then there are certain matters which you cannot avoid performing yourself. For example, replying to your officers when your secretaries are unable to do so, or disposing of the complaints of the people when your assistants shirk them. Finish every day the work meant for it, because every day has its own work. Keep for yourself the better and greater portion of these periods for the worship of Allah, although all these items are for Allah provided the intention is pure and the subjects prosper thereby.

Communion with Allah

The particular thing by which you should purify your religion for Allah should be the fulfillment of those obligations which are especially for Him. Therefore, devote to Allah some of your physical activity during the night and the day, and whatever (worship) you perform for seeking nearness to Allah should be complete, without defect or deficiency, whatsoever physical exertion it may involve. When you lead the prayers for the people it should be neither (too long as to be) boring nor (too short as to be) wasteful, because among the people there are the sick as well as those who have needs of their own. When the Messenger of Allah (p.b.u.h.a.h.p.) sent me to Yemen I enquired how I should offer prayers with them and he replied "Say the prayers as the weakest of them would say, and be considerate to the believers."

Behaviour and action of a Ruler

Then, do not keep yourself secluded from the people for a long time, because the seclusion of those in authority from the subjects is a kind of narrow-sightedness and causes ignorance about their affairs. Seclusion from them also prevents them from the knowledge of those things which they do not know and as a result they begin to regard big matters as small and small matters as big, good matters as bad and bad matters as good, while the truth becomes confused with falsehood. After all, a governor is a human being and cannot have knowledge of things which people keep hidden from him.

No writ is big on the face of truth to differentiate its various expressions from falsehood. Then you can be one of two kinds of men. Either you may be generous in granting rights; and then why this hiding in spite of (your) discharging the obligations and good acts that you perform? Or you are a victim of stinginess; in that case people will soon give up asking you since they will lose hope of generous treatment from you. In spite of that there are many needs of the people towards you which do not involve any hardship on you, such as the complaint against oppression or the request for justice in a matter.

Further, a governor has favourites and people of easy access to him. They misappropriate things, are high-handed and do not observe justice in matters. You should destroy the root of evil in the people by cutting away the causes of these defects. Do not make any land grants to your hangers on or supporters. They should not expect from you the possession of land which may cause harm to adjoining people over the question of irrigation or common services whose burden the grantees place on others. In this way, the benefit will be rather theirs than yours, and the blame will lie on you in this world and the next.

Allow rights to whomsoever it is due, whether near you or far from you. In this matter, you should be enduring and watchful even though it may involve your relations and favourites, and keep in view the reward of that which appears burdensome on you because its reward is handsome.

If the subjects suspect you of high-handedness, explain to them your position openly and remove their suspicion with your explanation, because this would mean exercise for your soul and consideration to the subjects while this explanation will secure your aim of keeping them firm in truth.

Do not reject peace to which your enemy may call you and wherein there is the pleasure of Allah, because peace brings rest to your army and relief from your worries and safety for your country. But after peace there is great apprehension from the enemy because often the enemy offers peace to benefit by your negligence. Therefore, be cautious and do not act by a wishfulness in this matter.

If you conclude an agreement between yourself and your enemy or enter into a pledge with him then fulfil your agreement and discharge your pledge faithfully. Place yourself as a shield against whatever you have pledged because among the obligations of Allah there is nothing on which people are more strongly united despite the difference of their ideas and variation of their views than respect for fulfilling pledges. Besides Muslims, even unbelievers have abided by agreements because they realised the dangers which would come in the wake of violation (thereof). Therefore, do not deceive your enemy, because no one can offend Allah save the ignorant and the wicked. Allah made His agreement and pledged the sign of security which He has spread over His creatures through His mercy and an asylum in which they stay in His protection and seek the benefit of nearness to Him. Therefore, there should be no deceit, cunning or duplicity in it.

Do not enter into an agreement which may admit of different interpretations and do not change the interpretation of vague words after the conclusion and confirmation (of the agreement). If an agreement of Allah involves you in hardship do not seek its repudiation without justification, because the bearing of hardships through which you expect relief and a handsome result is better than a violation whose consequence you fear, and that you fear that you will be called upon by Allah to account for it and you will not be able to seek forgiveness for it in this world or the next.

You should avoid shedding blood without justification, because nothing is more inviting of Divine retribution, greater in (evil) consequence, and more effective in the decline of prosperity and cutting short of life than the shedding of blood without justification. On the Day of Judgement Allah the Glorified, would commence giving His judgement among the people with the cases of bloodshed committed by them. Therefore, do not strengthen your authority by shedding prohibited blood because this will weaken and lower the authority, moreover destroy it and shift it. You cannot offer any excuse before Allah or before me for wilful killing because there must be the question or revenge in it. If you are involved in it be error and you exceed in the use of your whip or sword, or are hard in inflicting punishment, as sometimes even a blow by the fist or a smaller stroke causes death, then the haughtiness of your authority should not prevent you from paying the blood price to the successors of the killed person.

You should avoid self-admiration, having reliance in what appears good in yourself and love of exaggerated praise, because this is one of the most reliable opportunities for Shaytan to obliterate the good deeds of the virtuous.

Avoid showing (the existence of) obligation on your subjects for having done good to them or praising your own actions or making promises and then breaking them, because showing (the existence of) obligation destroys good, self-praise takes away the light of truth, and breaking promises earns the hatred of Allah and of the people. Allah the Glorified, says:

Most hateful is it unto Allah that you say what you (yourselves) do (it) nor. (Quraan 61:3)

Avoid haste in matters before their time, slowness at their proper time, insistence on them when the propriety of action is not known or weakens when it becomes clear. Assign every matter its proper place and do every job at the appropriate time.

Do not appropriate to yourself that in which the people have an equal share, nor be regardless of matters which have come to light with the excuse that you are accountable for others. Shortly, the curtains of all matters will be raised from your view and you will be required to render redress to the oppressed. Have control over (your) sense of prestige, any outburst of anger, the might of your arm and the sharpness of your tongue. Guard against all this by avoiding haste and by delaying severe action till your anger subsides and you gain your self-control. You cannot withhold yourself from this unless you bear in mind that you have to return to Allah.

It is necessary for you to recall how matters went with those who preceded you, be it a government or a great tradition or a precedent of our Prophet (may Allah bless him and his descendants) or the obligatory commands contained in the Book of Allah. Then you should follow them as you have seen us acting upon them and should exert yourself in following that I have enjoined upon you in this document in which I have exhausted my pleas on you, so that if your heart advances towards its passions you may have no plea in its support.

I ask Allah through the extent of His mercy and the greatness of His power of giving a good inclination that He may prompt me and you to advance a clear plea before Him and His creatures in a manner that may attract His pleasure along with handsome praise among the people, good effect in the country, an increase in prosperity and a heightening of honour; and that He may allow me and you to die a death of virtue and martyrdom. Surely, we have to return to Him. Peace be on the Messenger of Allah-may Allah show His blessings and plentiful salutation on him and his pure and chaste descendants; and that is an end to the matter.

54- To Talha and az-Zobayr though Emraan bn al-Hosayn al-Khozaai[1].

-1- "Imran bn-Hosayn al-Khozaai was a high ranking companion distinguished in learning and achievements and very cautious in relating traditions. He accepted Islam in the year of Khaybar and participated in Jihaad with the Prophet. Was honoured with the judicial position at Koofa and died at Basra in 52 A.H.

One of the genuine traditions related by "Imran bn-Hosayn about Ameer al-Momineen is:

The Messenger of Allah raised and sent an army under the command of Ali bn-Abi-Talib. From the chomps (one-fifth) received by him Ali set aside a slave girl for himself. This was distasteful to some of his men and four of them decided to complain of this to the Prophet (p.b.u.h.a.h.p.). On their return they approached the Prophet, and one of them stood up and said:

O Messenger of Allah! Do you not see that Ali did so and so?" The Prophet turned away his face from him. Another man stood up and made the same complaint and the Prophet turned away his face from him. Still another man stood up and repeated what his two colleagues had said and met the same reaction. Then the fourth man stood up and spoke like his predecessors. The Prophet (p.b.u.h.a.h.p.) then turned to them with signs of anger on his face and said: "What do you want me to do to Ali? (repeating thrice). Surely,

Abu Jafar al-Iskaafi has mentioned this in his "Kitaab al-Maqaamaat" on the excellent qualities (Manaaqib) of Ameer al-Momineen (peace be upon him).

Now, both of you know, although you conceal it, that I did not approach the people till they approached me, and I did not ask them to swear allegiance to me till they themselves swore allegiance to me, and both of you were among those who approached me and swore me allegiance. Certainly, the common people did not swear me allegiance under any force put on them or for any money given to them. If you two swore allegiance to me obediently, come back and offer repentance to Allah soon, but if you swore allegiance to me reluctantly, you have certainly given me cause for action, by showing your obedience and concealing your disobedience[1]. By my life, you were not more entitled than other mohaajiroon to conceal and hide the matter. Your refusing allegiance before entering into it would have been easier than getting out of it after having accepted it.

You have indicated that I killed "Othmaan; then let someone from among the people of Madeena who supported neither me nor you decide the matter between me and you. Then one of us shall face (the command of law) according to (their) involvement. You should give up your way now, when the great question before you is only one of shame, before you face

---

Ali is from me and I am from him, and after me he is the Master of all the believers." (al-JAmias-saet8, at-Tirmizi, vol.5, p.632; al-Masnad, Ahmad bn-Hambal, vol.4, pp.437438; al-Masnad, Abi-Dawood at-Tayalisi, p.111; al-Mostadrak, al-Haakim, vol.3, pp.110-111; Hilyatol-Awliyaa, Abi Noaym, vol.6, p.294; Taareekh al-Islaam, az-Zahabi, vol.2, p.196; at-Taareekh, bn-Katheer, vol.7, p.345; Osdol-Ghaaba, bn-Athir, vol.4, p.27, al-Isaaba, bn-Hajar, vol.2, p.509)

-1- That is you are men of riches and means having a large tribe and community. What is the need to you to do for this double dealing of concealing the real feelings of the heart, showing obedience and swearing allegiance loathsomely and unwillingly. Of course, if someone else, who was weak and helpless, said that he was obliged to swear allegiance, his point could be accepted to some extent. But when no one else has expressed his helplessness in the matter, why did this helplessness befall you so that you now regard your swearing of allegiance to be the result of your helplessness.

the question of shame coupled with the Hell-fire; and that is and end to the matter.

55- To Moaawiya bn Abi-Sofyaan

Now, Allah, the Glorified, has made this world for what is to come hereafter, and put its inhabitants to trial as to which of you is good in action, and we have not been created for this world, nor ordered to strive for it, but we have been made to stay in it to stand trial therein. So, Allah has tried me with you and tried you with me. He has therefore made either of us a plea for the other.

Now, you have leapt on the world by a wrong interpretation of the Quraan, and wanted me to account for what neither my hand nor tongue was responsible, but you and the Syrians put the blame on me, and your scholar incited against me the ignorant and one who is sitting incited the one who is standing. You should fear Allah about yourself and not allow Shaytan to lead you. Turn your face towards the next world because that is our path and your path, and fear that Allah may not entangle you in any sudden infliction which may destroy the root as well as cut away the branches. I swear to you by Allah an oath which will not be broken that if destiny brings me and you together I shall steadfastly hold before you:

Until Allah judges between us, and He is the Best of the judges. (Quraan, 7:87)

56- Document of instruction to Shorayh bn Hani al-Mazhiji when he placed him at the head of the vanguard preceding towards Syria

Fear Allah every morning and evening and remain apprehensive about yourself of this deceitful world and do not regard it safe in any case. Know that if for fear of some evil you do not refrain yourself from things which you love, then passions will fling you into a lot of harm. Therefore, be for yourself a refrainer and protector, and for your anger a suppresser and killer.

57- To the people of Koofa at the time of his march from Madeena to Basra

Now, I have come out of my city either as an oppressor or as the oppressed, either as a rebel or one against whom rebellion has been committed. In any case, to whomsoever this letter of mine reaches, I appeal to him in the name of Allah that he should come to me and if I am in the right he should help me; but if I am in the wrong then he should try to get me to the right according to his view.

58- To the people of various localities describing what took place between him and the people of Siffeen

The whole thing began thus that we and the Syrians met in an encounter although we believe in one and the same Allah and the same Prophet, and our message in Islam is the same. We did not want them to add anything in the belief in Allah or in acknowledging His Messenger (may Allah bless him and his descendants) nor did they want us to add any such thing. In fact, there was complete unity except that we differed on the question of "Othmaan's blood while we were uninvolved in it. We suggested to them to appease the situation by calming the temporary irritation and pacifying the people till matters settled down and stabilised when we would gain strength to put matters right.

They however said that they would settle it by war. Thus, they refused our offer and consequently war spread its wings and came to stay. Its flames rose and became strong. When the war had bitten us as well as them and pierced its talons into us as well as them, they accepted what we had proposed to them. So, we agreed to what they suggested and hastened to meet their request. In this way, the plea became clear to them and no excuse was left to them. Now, whoever among them adheres to this will be saved by Allah from ruin, and whoever shows obstinacy and insistence (on wrong) is the reverser whose heart has been blinded by Allah and evils will encircle his head.

59- To al-Aswad bn Qotba, the governor of Holwaan

Now, if the actions of a governor follow the passions he will be greatly hampered in justice. AD the people should be equal in right before you, because injustice cannot be a substitute for justice. Avoid that thing the like of which you would not like for yourself. Exert yourself in what Allah has made obligatory on you, hoping for His reward and fearing His chastisement.

Know that this world is the place of trial. Whoever hare wastes any hour of his time will repent it on the Day of Judgement, and nothing can ever make you too satisfied as not to need right. One of the rights on you is that you should protect yourself (from sins) and look after the subjects to your best. The benefit that will come to you from this will be greater than that which will accrue (to people) through you; and that is an to the matter.

60- To the officers through whose jurisdiction the army passed

From the servant of Allah A11, Ameer al-Momineen to all the collectors of revenue and officers of the realm through whose area the army passes.

Now, I have sent an army that will pass by you, if Allah wills. I have instructed them about what Allah has made obligatory on them, namely that they should avoid molestation and evade harm. I hold myself clear before you and those (unbelievers) who are under your protection from any annoyance committed by the army except when one is compelled by hunger and there is no other way of satisfying it. If anyone of them takes anything through force you should punish him. None of you should be silly enough to obstruct them or intervene in matters which we have allowed them by way of exception. I am myself within the army. So, refer to me their high-handedness, and any hardship which is caused by them and which you cannot avert except through Allah and through me. I shall then avert it with the help of Allah, if He so wills.

61- To Komayl bn Ziyad an-Nakhaai, the governor of Heet expressing displeasure on his inability to prevent the enemy forces that passed through his area from marauding

Now, the neglecting by a man of what he has been made responsible for and doing what is to be done by others is a manifest weakness and a ruinous sight. Certainly, your advance on the people of Qirqeesiya, and your leaving the arsenals over which we had set you, without anyone to protect them or to repulse the enemy force, savoured of shattered thinking. In this way, you served like a bridge for the enemy who came marauding on your allies while your arms were weak, you had no awe around you; you could not prevent the enemy from advancing; you could not break his might; you could not defend the people of your area and you could not discharge functions on behalf of your Imam.

62- To the people of Egypt sent through Malik al-Ashtar when he was made the governor of that place

Now, Allah the Glorified, deputed Mohammad (may Allah bless him and his descendants) as a warner for all the worlds and a witness for all the prophets. When the Prophet expired, the Muslims quarrelled about power after him. By Allah, it never occurred to me, and I never imagined, that after the Prophet the Arabs would snatch away the caliphate from his Ahlil-Bayt (the members of his house), nor that they would take it away from me after him, but I suddenly noticed people surrounding the man to swear him allegiance.[1]

-1- The Prophet's declarations about Ameer al-Momineen that "This is my brother, my vicegerent and my caliph among you, and while returning from his farewell Haj at Ghadeer Khom that "For whosoever I am the master, Ali is his master" had settled the issue of his own replacement and succession after which there was no need at all for any new election, nor could it be imagined that the people of Madeena would feel the need for an election. But some power-thirsty individuals so ignored these clear injunctions as if their ears had never been acquainted with them, and considered the election so necessary, that, leaving the burial rites of the Prophet, they assembled in the Saqeefa of

I therefore withheld my hand till I saw that many people were reverting from Islam and trying to destroy the religion of Mohammad (may Allah bless him and his descendants). I then feared that if I did not protect Islam and its people and there occurred in it a breach or destruction, it would mean a greater blow to me than the loss of power over you which was, in any case, to last for a few days of which everything would pass away as the mirage passes away, or as the cloud scuds away. Therefore, in these happenings I rose till wrong was destroyed and disappeared, and religion attained peace and safety.

By Allah, if I had encountered them alone and they had been so numerous as to fill the earth to the brim, I would not have worried or become perplexed. I am clear in myself and possess conviction from Allah about their misguidance and my guidance. I am hopeful and expectant that I will meet Allah and get His good reward. But I am worried that silly and wicked people will control the affairs of the entire community, with the result that they will grab the funds of Allah as their own property and make His people slaves[1], fight with the virtuous, and ally with the sinful. Indeed,

---

Bani-Saaida and elected Abi-Bakr as Caliph with a show of democracy. This was a very critical moment for Ameer al-Momineen. On one side some interested persons declared that he should take up arms and on the other hand he noticed that those Arabs who had accepted Islam by dint of its military strength were leaving it and Mosaylama bn-Thomaama al-Hanafi the liar (al-Kazzaab) and Tulayha bn-Khowaylid al-Asadi (the liar) were throwing tribe after tribe into misguidance. In these circumstances, if there had been a civil was and the Muslims had fought against the Muslims, the forces of heresy and hypocrisy would have joined together and swept Islam off the surface of the globe. Therefore, Ameer al-Momineen preferred to keep quiet rather than to fight, and, with the purpose of maintaining the solidarity of Islam, confined himself to protesting peacefully rather than taking up arms. This was because formal power was not so dear to him as the good and prosperity of the community. For stopping the machinations of the hypocrites and defeating the aims of the mischief-mongers there was no other course but that he should not fan the flames of war by giving up his own claim. This was such a big act for the preservation of Islamic polity that it is acknowledged by all the sects of Islam.

-1- This refers to the saying of the Holy Prophet about the children of Omayya and the children of Abi al-Aas bn-Omayya (the grandfather of Othmaan bn-Affaan and the

there is among them he who drank (wine) unlawfully[1] and was whipped by way of punishment fixed by Islam, and there is he who did not accept Islam until he had secured financial gain through it.[2] If this had not been so I would not have insisted on gathering you, reprehending you,

dynasty of Marwaan's caliphs) as related by Abu-Zarr al-Ghifaari that the Holy Prophet said:

When the number of Bani (children of) Omayya reaches forty men they will make Allah's people their slaves, grab Allah's funds as their own property and make the Book of Allah a cause of corruption. (al-Mostadrak, vol.4, p.479; Kanz al-Ommaal, vol.11, p.149).

About the children of Abi al-Aas it is related by Abi-Zarr, Abi Saeed al-Khodri, bn-Abbaas, Abi-Horayra and others that the Holy Prophet said:

When the number of Bani-(children of) Abi al-Aas reaches thirty men, they will grab the funds of Allah as their own property, make Allah's people their slaves and make the religion of Allah a cause of corruption. (al-Mosnad, Ahmad bn-Hambal, vol.3, p.80; al-Mostadrak, al-Haakim, vol.4, p.480; al-Mataalib al-Aaleeya, bn-Hajar, vol.4, p.332; Majma" az-Zawaaid, al-Haytami, vol.5, pp.241,243; Kanz al-Ommaal, al-Mottaqi, vol.11, pp.148,149,351,354).

The history of Islam (after the death of the Holy Prophet) has enough evidence to prove this prophecy of the Holy Prophet; and the fear of Ameer al-Momineen for the Muslim community was based on this reason.

1 The man who drank wine was al-Waleed bn-Oqba bn-Abi-Moayd. He was of the same mother as Caliph Othmaan and his Governor of Koofa. al-Waleed on an occasion in a state of intoxication led the morning prayers in the Central mosque of Koofa with four units (rakah) instead of the usual two as prescribed by the Holy Prophet. The congregation, which consisted of several pious persons like bn-Masood, was much incensed and still more irritated when, finishing the four units, al-Waleed said:

What a pleasant morning! I would like to extent the prayers further if you consent.

Repeated complains had already been made to the Caliph against al-Waleed on account of his debauchery, but as often dismissed. People now reproached Othmaan for not listening to their grievances, and favouring such a scoundrel. By chance they succeeded in taking off the signet ring from the hand of the Governor while he lay senseless from the effects of a debauch, and carried it off to Madeena. Still the caliph was slow and hesitated to enforce punishment upon his Governor (of the same mother); giving cause to be himself reproachfully accused of ignoring the law; though at last he was persuaded to have al-Waleed scourged with forty strokes. He was consequently deposed from his office. Saad bn-Aas, a cousin of Othmaan was appointed to take his place, and this was a matter of great reproach against Othmaan. (Ansab al-Ashraaf, al-Balazoori, vol. 5, pp.33-35; al-Aghaani, Ab0/-Faraj al-Isbahaani, vol.4, pp.174-187; al-Isfi6ab, vol.4, pp.1554-1557; Osdol-Ghaaba, vol.5, pp.91-92; at-Tabari, vol.1, pp.2843-2850; bn-Atheer, vol.3, pp.105-107; bn-Abil-Hadeed, vol.17, pp.227-245)

-2- The man who accepted Islam after securing financial gain was Moaawiya who was adhering to Islam only for worldly benefits.

mobilising you and urging you (for jihad but if you refuse and show weakness I will leave you.

Do you not see that the boundaries of your cities have diminished, your populated areas have been conquered, your possessions have been snatched away and your cities and lands have been attacked. May Allah have mercy on you, get up to fight your enemy and do not remain confined to the earth, otherwise you will face oppression and suffer ignominy and your fate will be the worst. The warrior should be wakeful because of he sleeps the enemy does not sleep; and that is an end to the matter.

63- To Abu Moosa al-Ashari, the governor of Koofa when he learned that he was dissuading the people of Koofa from joining in the battle of Jamal when he had called them to fight along with him

From the servant of Allah, Ameer al-Momineen to Abdillah bn-Qays:

Now, I have come to know of words uttered by you which go in your favour as well as against you[1]. So, when my messenger reaches you prepare yourself and get ready, come out of your den and call those who are with you. Then, if you are convinced of the truth get up but if you feel

-1- When Ameer al-Momineen had the idea of suppressing the revolt of the people of Basra he sent this letter through Imaam al-Hasan to Abi-Moosa (Abdillah bn-Qays) al-Ashari, who had been appointed Governor of Koofa by Othmaan, wherein he has scolded him for his duplicity and contradictory behaviour and attempted to persuade him to Jihaad, because on one side he used to say that Ameer al-Momineen was the true Imaam and allegiance to him was right and on the other he said that to support him in fighting against the Muslims was not right; but it was a mischief and it was necessary to keep off this mischief. Thus, Ameer al-Momineen has referred to this contradictory view by the words "hawa loka waalayka" (which go in your favour as well as against you). The intention is that when Ameer al-Momineen is the rightful Imaam how can fighting his enemy with him be wrong? And if fighting on his side is wrong then what is the meaning of his being the rightful Imaam.

In any case, in spite of his dissuading from fighting, the people of Koofa came out in large number to join Ameer al-Momineen's army and took full part in the battle, giving such a defeat to the people of Basra that they never again dared to revolt.

cowardice go away. By Allah, you will be caught wherever you may be and you will not be spared till you are completely upset and everything about you is scattered and till you are shaken from your seat. Then, you will fear from your front as you do from the rear.

What you hope is not a light matter, but it is serious calamity. We have to ride its camels, overcome its difficulties and level its mountains. Set your mind in order, take a grip on your affairs and acquire your (lot and your) share. If you do not like it then go away to where neither you are welcome nor can you escape from it. It is better that you be left alone and lie sleeping. Then no one will enquire where is so-and-so. By Allah, this is the case of right with the rightful person and we do not care what the heretics do; and that is an end to the matter.

64- In reply to Moaawiya

Now then, certainly, we and you were on amiable terms as you say but difference arose between us and you the other day, when we accepted belief (Emaan) and you rejected it. Today the position is that we are steadfast (in the belief) but you are creating mischief. Those of you who accepted Islam did so reluctantly and that too when all the chief men had accepted Islam and joined the Messenger of Allah (may Allah bless him and his descendants).

You have stated that I killed Talha and az-Zobayr, forced Aysha out of her house and adopted residence between the two cities (Koofa and Basra).[1]

-1- Moaawiya had written a letter to Ameer al-Momineen in which after recalling mutual unity and amicability he laid on him the blame of killing Talha and az-Zobayr and ousting Aysha from her house and objected to his adopting Koofa as his seat of government in place of Madeena. In the end, he grave a threat of war and said that he was about to come out with a force of mohaajiroon and Ansaar to fight. Ameer al-Momineen wrote this letter in reply to him, wherein commenting on Moaawiya's claim for unity he says that: "There might have been unity between you and us but with the advent of Islam such a gulf has developed between the two that it is not possible to bridge it, and such a separation has occurred which cannot be removed. This was because we responded to the call of the Prophet and hastened towards Islam but your position was that you were still in the state of unbelief and ignorance whereby we and you came to adopt separate ways. But when Islam secured stability and the chief of Arabs entered its fold you too were obliged to, and secured protection of your lives by putting the covering of Islam on your faces, but continued secretly to fan the mischief intended to shatter its foundations. Since we had accepted Islam of our own free will and pleasure we adhered to the right path and at no stage did any faltering occur in our steadfastness. Therefore, your acceptance of Islam too could not make us agree with your views.

As regards Moaawiya's accusation that Ameer al-Momineen engineered the killing of Talha and az-Zobayr; then even if this blame is admitted as true, is it not a fact that they had openly revolted against Ameer al-Momineen and had risen for war after breaking the allegiance. Therefore, if they were killed in connection with the revolt their blood would be wasted and no blame would lie on the killer, because the penalty for him who revolts against the rightful Imaam is death, and fighting against him in permissible, without doubt. The fact however, is that this accusation has no reality because Talha was killed by a man of his own party. Thus, the historians write:

Marwaan bn-Hakam shot Talha with an arrow and turning to Aban bn-Othmaan said:

We have killed a killer of your father and relieved you of revenge." (bn Saad, vol.3, part 1, p.159; bn-Atheer, vol.3, p.244; al-Isteeaab, vol.2, pp.769769; Osdol-Ghaaba vol.3, pp.60,61; al-Isaaba, vol.2, p.230; Tahzeeb, at-Tahzeeb, vol.5, p.21).

As for az-Zobayr, he was killed by Amr bn-Jermooz on his way back from Basra, and there was no prompting by Ameer al-Momineen in it. Similarly, Aysha herself came out of her house as the head of this rebellious group while Ameer al-Momineen counselled her several times to realise her position and not to step out of her bounds but these things had no effect on her.

Of the same type was his criticism that Ameer al-Momineen left Madeena and adopted Koofa as the seat of his government because Madeena turns out bad people from itself and throws away dirt. The reply to it is only this that Moaawiya himself too always retained Syria as his capital keeping away from Madeena.

In this way, what right can he have to object to Ameer al-Momineen changing his seat. Ameer al-Momineen left Madeena because of those rebellions which had cropped up from all sides. To suppress them only the selection of such a place as capital from where military assistance could be mobilised at any time could be useful. Thus, Ameer al-Momineen had seen on the occasion of the battle of Jamal that a great majority of the people of Koofa had supported him and that therefore by making it a base for the army, defence against the enemy could be easily managed, while Madeena was not appropriate for military mobilisation or for supplies.

Lastly, as for Moaawiya's threat that he would march with mohaajireen and Ansaar, Ameer al-Momineen gave a reply to this point in a very subtle way, namely that "How would you bring mohaajireen now since the door for Hijra was closed the day when your brother Yazeed bn-Abi-Sofyaan was taken prisoner." This man was taken prisoner on the day of the fall of Mecca and there is no question of) hijra after the fall of Mecca so as to enable anyone to be called a mohaajir because of the Prophet's saying:

There is no hijra after the victory over Mecca.

These are matters with which you have no concern nor do they involve anything against you. Therefore, no explanation about them is due to you. You also state that you are coming to me with a party of mohaajiroon and Ansaar, but hijra came to an end on the day your brother was taken prisoner. If you are in a hurry, then wait a bit as I may come to meet you and that would be more befitting as that would mean that Allah has appointed me to punish you. But if you come to me it would be as the poet of Bani-Asad said:

They are advancing against summer winds which are hurling stones on them in the highlands and lowlands.

(Remember) I have still the sword with which I dispatched your grandfather, your mother's brother and your brother to one and the same place. By Allah, I know what you are. Your heart is sheathed and your intelligence is weak. It is better to say that you have ascended to where you view a bad scene which is against you, not in your favour, because you are searching a thing lost by someone else, you are tending someone else's cattle and you are hankering after a thing which is not yours nor have you any attachment with it. How remote are your words from your actions, and how closely you resemble your paternal and maternal uncles who were led by their wickedness and love for wrong to oppose Mohammad (may Allah bless him and his descendants) and in consequence they were killed as you know. They could not put up a defence against the calamity and could not protect their place of safety from the striking of swords which abound in the battle and which do not show weakness.

You have said a lot about killing of "Othmaan. You first join what the people have joined (i.e., allegiance) then seek a verdict about (the accused people) from me and I shall settle the matter between you and them according to the Book of Allah, the Sublime. But what you are aiming at is just the fake nipple given to a child in the first days of stopping of nursing. Peace be on those who deserve it.

65- To Moaawiya bn Abi-Sofyaan

Now, this is the time[1] that you should derive benefit by observing a clear view of the main matters, because you have been treading in the path of your forefathers in making wrong claims, spreading false and untrue notions, claiming for yourself what is far above you and demanding what is not meant for you, because you want to run away from right and to revolt against what is more fastened to your flesh and blood namely what has been heard by the depth of your ears and has filled your chest. And after forsaking right there remains nothing except clear misguidance, and after disregarding a (clear) statement there is nothing except confusion. You should therefore guard (yourself) against doubts and its ill-effects of confusion, because for a long time mischief has spread its veils and its gloom has blinded your eyes.

I have received your letter which is full of uncouth utterances which weaken the cause of peace and nonsensical expressions which have not been prepared with knowledge and forbearance. By reason of these

-1- At the end of the battle of the Kharijites, Moaawiya wrote a letter to Ameer al-Momineen wherein, as usual, he indulged in mud-throwing. In reply, Ameer al-Momineen wrote this letter in which he has tried to draw Moaawiya's attention to the clear facts about this very battle of the Kharijites, because this battle took place in accordance with the prophecy of the Prophet while Ameer al-Momineen himself too had said before the battle that besides the people of Jamal and Siffeen he had to fight against one more group and they were the "deviators" from the religion, namely the Kharijites, The occurrence of this battle and the killing of the man with breasts (Zoth-Thodayya) was a clear proof of Ameer al-Momineen being in the right. If Moaawiya had not been obsessed with self-advertisement and lust for conquests, and had not shut his eyes against the right like his forefathers Abi Sofyaan and his brother Otba he would have seen right and come on its path. But compelled by his natural inclination he always evaded right and truth and kept himself blind to those sayings of the Prophet which threw light on Ameer al-Momineen's Imaama and vicegerency. Because of being with the Prophet in the farewell pilgrimage the Prophet's saying:

Of whomsoever I am the master "A1I is his master" was not hidden from him, and neither was the Prophet's saying that:

O Ali you are to me as Haroon was to Moosa, because of his presence on the occasion of the battle of Tabook. In spite of all this, he passed his life in concealing right and encouraging wrong. This was not due to any misunderstanding but it was his lust for power that kept prompting him to suppress and trample truth and justice.

things you have become like one who is sinking in a marsh or groping in a dark place. You have raised yourself to a position which is difficult to approach and devoid of any signs (to guide) Even the royal kite cannot reach it. It is parallel to the Ayyooq (the star Capella), in height.

May Allah forbid that you be in charge of people's affairs after my assuming authority as Caliph, or that I issue an edict or document granting you authority over any one of them. Therefore, from now onwards you guard yourself and be watchful, because if you recalcitrate till the people of Allah (are forced to) rush upon you, then matters will be closed for you and whatever can be accepted from you today will not be accepted then; and that is an end to the matter.

66- to Abdillah bn al-Abbas (this letter has already been included with a different version)

And then, sometimes a person feels joyful about a thing which he was not to miss in any case and feels grieved for a thing which was not to come to him at all. Therefore, you should not regard the attainment of pleasure and the satisfaction of the desire for revenge as the best favour of this world, but it should be the putting off of the (flame of) wrong and the revival of right. Your pleasure should be for what (good acts) you have sent forward; your grief should be for what you are leaving behind; and your worry should be about what is to befall after death.

67- to Qutham bn al-Abbas, his governor of Mecca

Now, make arrangements for Haj by the people, remind them of the days (to be devoted to) Allah. Sit for giving them audience morning and evening. Explain the law to the seeker, teach the ignorant and discuss with the learned. There should be no intermediary between you and the people except your tongue, and no guard save your own face. Do not prevent any needy person from meeting you, because if the needy is returned unsatisfied from your door in the first instance then even doing it thereafter will not bring you praise.

See what has been collected with you of the funds of Allah (in the public treasury) and spend it over the persons with families, the distressed, the starving and the naked, at your end. Then, send the remaining to us for distribution to those who are on this side.
Ask the people of Mecca not to charge rent from lodgers, because Allah, the Glorified, says that:
alike; for the dweller therein as well as the stranger" (Quraan, 22:25).
al-akif" (the dweller) here means he who is living there while "al-baadee" (the stranger) means he who is not among the people of Mecca, comes for Haj from outside. May Allah grant us and you promptitude for seeking His love (by doing good acts); and that is an end to the matter.

68- to Salmaan Farisi- before Ameer al-Momineen's caliphate

Now, the example of the world is like that of a snake which is soft in touch but whose poison is fatal. Therefore, keep yourself aloof from whatever appears good to you because of its short stay with you. Do not worry for it because of your conviction that it will leave you and that its circumstances are vicissitudes. When you feel most attracted towards it, shun it most, because whenever someone is assured of happiness in it, it throws him into danger; or when he feels secure in it, the world alters his security into fear; and that is an end to the matter.

69- to al-Haarith (bn Abdillah, al-Awar) al-Hamdani

Adhere to the rope of the Quraan and seek instructions from it. Regard its lawful as lawful and its unlawful as unlawful. Testify the right that has been in the past. Take lesson for the present condition of this world from the past (condition), because its one phase resembles the other, and its end is to meet its beginning, and the whole of it is to change and depart. Regard the name of Allah as too great to mention Him, save in the matter of right. Remember more often death, and (what is to come) after death. Do not long for death except on a reliable condition.

Avoid every action which the doer likes for his own self but dislikes for the Muslims in general. Avoid every such action which is performed in secret and from which shame is felt in the open. Also avoid that action about which if the doer is questioned he himself regards it bad or offers excuses for it. Do not expose your honour to be treated as the subject of people's discussions. Do not relate to the people all that you hear, for that would amount to falsehood. Do not contest all that the people relate to you for that would mean ignorance. Kill your anger and forgive when you have power (to punish). Show forbearance in the moment of rage, and pardon in spite of authority; the eventual end will then be in your favour. Seek good out of every favour that Allah has bestowed on you, and do not waste any favour of Allah over you. The effect of Allah's favours over you should be visible on you.

Know that the most distinguished among the believers is he who is the most forward of them in spending from himself, his family and his property, because whatever good you send forward will remain in store for you and the benefit of whatever you keep behind will be derived by others. Avoid the company of the person whose opinion is unsound and whose action is detestable, because a man is judged after his companion. Live in big cities because they are collective centres of the Muslims. Avoid places of neglectfulness and wickedness and places where there are paucity of supporters for the obedience of Allah. Confine your thinking to matters which are helpful to you. Do not sit in the marketing centres because they are the meeting places of Shaytan, and targets of mischiefs. Frequently look at those over whom you enjoy superiority because this is a way of giving thanks.

Do not undertake a journey on Friday until you have attended the prayers, except when you are going in the way of Allah, or in an excusable matter. Obey Allah in all your affairs because Allah's obedience has precedence over all other things. Deceive your heart into worshipping, persuade it and do not force it. Engage it (in worshipping) when it is free and merry, except as regards the obligations enjoined upon you, for they should not be neglected and must be performed at the five times. Be on guard lest death comes down upon you while you have fled away from your Lord in search of worldly pleasure. Avoid the company of the wicked because vice adjoins vice. Regard Allah as great, and love His lovers. Keep off anger because it is one large army from Shaytan's armies; and that is an end to the matter.

70- To Sahl bn Honayf al-Ansaari, his governor of Madeena about certain persons in Madeena who had gone over to Moaawiya

Now, I have come to know that certain persons from your side are stealthily going over to Moaawiya. Do not feel sorry for their numbers so lost to you or for their help of which you are deprived. It is enough that they have gone into misguidance and you have been relieved of them. They are running away from guidance and truth and advancing towards blindness and ignorance. They are seekers of this world and are proceeding to it and are leaping towards it. They have known justice, seen it, heard it and appreciated it. They have realised that here, to us, all men are equal in the matter of right. Therefore, they ran away to selfishness and partiality. Let them remain remote and far away.

By Allah, surely they have not gone away from oppression and joined justice. In this matter, we only desire Allah to resolve for us its hardships and to level for us its unevenness, if Allah wills; and that is an end to the matter.

71- to al-Monzir bn Jarood al-Abdi who had misappropriated certain things given into his administrative charge.

Now, the good behaviour of your father deceived me about you and I thought that you would follow his way and tread in his path. But according to what has reached me about you, you are not giving up following your passions and are not retaining any provision for the next world. You are making this world by ruining your next life, and doing good to your kinsmen by cutting yourself off from religion.

If what has reached me about you is correct, then the camel of your family and the strap of your shoe is better than yourself. A man with qualities like yours is not fit to close a hole in the ground, nor for performing any deed, nor for increasing his position, nor for taking him as a partner in any trust, nor for trusting him against misappropriation. Therefore, proceed to me as soon as this letter of mine reaches you if Allah so wills.

Sayyid Razi says: al-Monzir bn-Jarood al-Abdi is he about whom Ameer al-Momineen (peace be upon him) said that :

He looks very often at his shoulders, feels proud in his garments (appearance) and usually blows away (dust) from his shoes.

72- to Abdillah al-Abbas

Now, you cannot go farther than the limit of your life, nor can you be given a livelihood which is not for you. Remember that this life consists of two days — a day for you and a day against you, and that the world is a house (changing) authorities. Whatever in it is for you will come to you despite your weakness; and whatever in it turns against you cannot be brought back despite your strength.

73- To Moaawiya bn Abi-Sofyaan

Now, (in) exchanging replies and listening to your letters my view has been weak and my intelligence has been erring. When you refer your demands to me and expect me to send you written replies, you are like one who is in deep slumber while his dreams contradict him, or one who stands perplexed and overwhelmed, not knowing whether whatever comes to him is for him or against him. You are not such a man but he is (to some extent) like you (as you are worse than him). I swear by Allah that, had it not been for (my) giving you time, you would have faced from me catastrophe that would have crushed the bones and removed the flesh.

Know that Shaytan has prevented you from turning to good actions and listening to the words of counsels. Peace be upon those who deserve it

74- document written by Ameer al-Momineen as a protocol between the tribes of Rabeea and the people of Yemen. Taken from the writing of Hishaam bn (Mohammad) al-Kalbi.

This indenture contains what the people of Yemen, including the townsmen and nomads, and the tribes of Rabeea, including the townsmen and nomads, have agreed upon: that they will adhere to the Book of Allah, will call to it and order according to it and will respond to whoever calls to it and orders according to it They will not sell it for any price nor accept any alternative for it. They will join hands against anyone who opposes it and abandons it. They will help one another. Their voice will be one. They will not break their pledge on account of the rebuke of a rebuker the wrath of an angry person the humiliating treatment of one group to the other, or the use of abusive terms by one party against the other.

75- To Moaawiya, soon he was sworn in

(Mohammad bn Omar) al-Waqidi has mentioned this in his "Kitaab al-Jamal

From the servant of Allah, Ali Ameer al-Momineen to Moaawiya son of Abu Sofyaan:

Now, you are aware of my excuses before you people and my shunning you till that happened which was inevitable and which could not be prevented. The story is long and much is to be said. What was to pass has passed and what was to come has come. Therefore, secure (my) allegiance from those who are with you and come in a deputation of your people to me; and that is an end to the matter.

76- Instruction to Abdillah bn al-Abbas at the time of his appointment as his governor of Basra

Meet people with a broad face, allow them free audience and pass generous orders Avoid anger because it is a augury of Shaytan Remember that whatever takes you near Allah takes you away from the Fire (of Hell), and whatever takes you away from Allah takes you near the Fire.

77- Instruction to Abdillah bn al-Abbas, at the time of his being deputed to confront the Kharijites

Do not argue with them by the Quraan because the Quraan has many faces You would say your own and they would say their own; but argue with them by the Sonna, because they cannot find escape from it.

78- In Reply to Abi Moosa al-Ashari's letter regarding the two arbitrators.

Saeed bn Yahya al-Omawi has mentioned this in his "Kitaab al-Maghaazi Certainly, many people have turned away from many a (lasting) benefit (of the next life), for they bent towards the world and spoke with passions I have been struck with wonder in this matter, upon which people who are self-conceited have agreed I am providing a cure for their wound but I fear lest it develops into a clot of blood (and becomes incurable). Remember that no person is more covetous than I for the unity of the Omma of Mohammad (may Allah bless him and his descendants) and their solidarity. I seek through it good reward and an honourable place to return to.

I shall fulfil what I have pledged upon myself even though you may go back from the sound position that existed when you left me last, because wretched is he who is denied the benefit of wisdom and experience. I feel enraged if anyone speaks wrong, or if I should worsen a matter which Allah has kept sound. Therefore, leave out what you do not understand, because wicked people will be conveying to you vicious things; and that is an end to the matter.

79- To the army officers when he became caliph

Now, what ruined those before you was that they denied people their rights and then they had to purchase them (by bribes), and they led the people to wrong and they followed it.

Sayings

Selaction From the Saying and Preachings of Ameer al-Momineen Ali bn Abi-Talib (Peace be Upon him) Including his Replies to Questions, and Mazims made for Various Purposes

Nahj ALBALAAGHA

Peak of Eloquence

1 During civil disturbance be like an adolescent camel[1] who has neither a back strong enough for riding nor udders for milking.

2 He who adopts greed as a habit devalues himself; he who discloses his hardship agrees to humiliation; and he who allows his tongue to overpower his soul debases the soul.

3 Miserliness is shame; cowardice is a defect; poverty disables an intelligent man from arguing his case; and a destitute person is a stranger in his home town.

4 Incapability is a catastrophe; endurance is bravery; abstinence is riches; self-restraint is a shield (against sin); and the best companion is submission-(to Allah's will).

5 Knowledge is a venerable estate; good manners are new dresses; and thinking is clear mirror.

6 The bosom of the wise is the safe of his secrets; cheerfulness is the bond of friendship; effective forbearance is the grave of short-comings.

It is narrated that Ameer al-Momineen said in expressing this meaning that:

Mutual reconciliation is the covering for shortcomings; and he who admires himself attracts many opponents against him.[2]

-1- "laboon" means a milk camel and "ibnul-labun" means its two year old young. In this age the young is neither suitable for riding nor does it has udders which could be milked. It is called "ibnul-labun" because in this period of two years its mother bears another young and begins yielding milk again.

The intention is that during civil disturbance or trouble a man should behave in such a manner that he may be regarded of no consequence and ignored. No need should be felt for his participation in either party. This is because during mischief only dissociation can save from molestation. Of course, when the clash is between right and wrong it is not permissible to keep aloof nor can it be called civil disturbance: but on such occasions it is obligatory to rise up for the support of right and suppression of wrong. For example, during the battles of Jamal and Siffeen it was obligatory to support the right and to fight against the wrong.

-2- In the last phrase, Ameer al-Momineen has described the consequences and effects resulting from self-admiration namely that it creates the feeling of hatred and humiliation-against others. Thus, the man who manifests his greatness by every pretext in order to make himself conspicuous is never regarded with esteem. People being to

7 Charity is an effective cure, and the actions of people in their present life will be before their eyes in the next life.[1]

8 How wonderful is man that he speaks with fat, talks with a piece of flesh, hears with a bone and breathes through a hole.

9 When this world advances towards anyone (with its favours) it attributes to him other's good; and when it turns away from him it deprives him of his own good.[2]

10 Meet people in such a manner that if you die they should weep for you and if you live they should long for you.[3]

---

despise him because of his mental condition in seeking self-conspicuity and are not prepared to accord him the worth which he relay has, much less to regard him as he himself thinks to be.

-1- This saying comprises of two phrases:-

The first sentence relates to charity and Ameer al-Momineen has described it as an effective cure, because when a man helps the poor and the destitute by alms they pray for his health and recovery from the depth of their hearts and therefore their prayer is granted and brings him cure. In this connection, there is the saying of the Holy Prophet that "Cure your sick by charity.

The second sentence relates to the disclosure of actions on the Day of Judgement, namely that the good and bad deeds which a person performs in this world cannot be perceived by human senses because of the veil of material elements but on the Day of Judgement when material curtains will be lifted they will so appear before the eyes that there will be no possibility of denial by anyone, Thus, Allah has said:

On that day shall come out people (from their graves) in (scattered) groups, to be shown their own deeds. Then he who has done an atom-weight of good shall see it. And he who has done an atom-weight of evil shall see it. (Quraan, 99:6-8)

-2- The meaning is that when a man's fortune is helpful and the world is favourable to him then people describe his performances with exaggeration and give credit to him for others" actions as well, while if a man loses the favour of the world and the clouds of ill-luck and misfortune engulf him, they ignore his virtues and do not at all tolerate even to recall his name.

They are friends of him whom the world favours and the toes of him whom the world hits.

3 To the person who behaves with others with benignity and mannerliness, people extend their hand of co-operation, they honour and respect him and shed tears after his death. Therefore, a person should lead such an agreeable life that no one should have any complaint against him, nor should any harm be caused by him to anyone so that during life he should attract others and after death too he should be remembered in good words.

11 When you gain power over your adversary pardon him by way of thanks for being able to overpower him.[1]

12 The most helpless of all men is he who cannot find a few brothers during his life, but still more helpless is he who finds such a brother but loses him.[2]

13 When you get (only) small favours do not push them away through lack of gratefulness.

14 He who is abandoned by near ones is dear to remote ones.

15 Every mischief monger cannot even be reproved.[3]

16 All matters are subject to destiny, so much so that sometimes death results from effort.

17 Ameer al-Momineen, peace be upon him, was asked to explain the saying of the Messenger of Allah that: Banish your old age (by hair-dye) and do not acquire resemblance to the Jews. Ameer al-Momineen replied:

-1- The occasion for pardon and forgiveness is when there is power to take revenge. But when there is no such power, then pardon is just the result of helplessness, for which there is no credit. However, to practise pardon despite having power and the ability to avenge is the essence of human distinction and an expression of thanks to Allah for bestowing this power, because the feeling of gratefulness necessitates that man should bow before Allah in humbleness and humiliation by which the delicate feeling of pity and kindness will arise in his heart and the rising flames of rage and anger will cool down after which there will be no urge to take revenge under the effect of which he would use his power and capability to satisfy his anger instead of using it properly.

-2- It is not difficult to attract by good manners and cheerfulness and to befriend them by sweet speech because no physical exertion or mental worry is required for this; and after making friends it is still easier to maintain the friendship and good relations because for making friends some effort or other is needed while for maintaining it no difficulty is to be surmounted. Therefore, no one can be more wretched than the man who cannot even retain a thing which could be retained just by keeping away a frown from the face. The intention is that a man should meet everyone with good manners and cheerfulness so that people may like to associate with him and extend a hand of friendship towards him.

-3- Ameer al-Momineen uttered this sentence when Saad bn-Abi Waqqas, Mohammad bn-Maslama and Abdillah bn-Omar refused to support him against the people of Jamal. He means to say that these people are so against me that neither have my words any effects on them nor do I need to reproof, rebuke or correct them.

The Prophet (p.b.u.h.a.h.p.) said this at a time when the religion was confined to a few, but now that its expanse has widened and it is firmly settled everyone is free in his action.[1]

18 Ameer al-Momineen, peace be upon him, said about those who avoided fighting on his side:

They abandoned right but did not support wrong.[2]

19 He who gallops with loose rein collides with death.

20 Forgive the shortcomings of considerate people because when they fall into error Allah raises them up.

21 The consequence of fear is disappointment and of bashfulness is frustration. Opportunity passes away like the cloud. Therefore, make use of good opportunities.[3]

-1- The intention is that since in the beginning of Islam the number of Muslims was limited it was necessary to keep them distinct from the Jews in order to maintain their collective entity, so the Prophet ordered the use of hair-dye which was not in use among the Jews. Besides, it was also the aim that when facing the enemy the people should not appear old in age and weak.

-2- This saying is about those who claimed to be neutrals, such as Abdillah bn-Omar, Saad bn-Abi-Waqqas Abi-Moosa al-Ashari, al-Ahnaf bn-Qays, Mohammad bn-Maslama, Osaama bn-Zayd and Anas bn-Malik, etc. No doubt these people did not openly support wrong but not to support right is also a kind of support of wrong. Therefore, they will be counted among the opponents of right.

-3- However bad a thing may be regarded among the people and however it may be looked down upon, if it is not really bad then to feel bashful about it is quite foolish, because it will often cause deprival from things which are the source of successes and achievements in this as well as the next world. For example, if a man fears lest people may regard him to be ignorant and therefore feels bashful in asking an important and necessary issue then this misplaced bashfulness would result in his being deprived of knowledge. Therefore, no sane person should feel bashful about making enquiries. Thus, an old man who was learning despite old age was asked whether he did not feel ashamed of learning in old age and he replied: "I do not feel shame for ignorance during old age, then how can I feel shame for learning in old age." Of course, to feel shame in doing things which are really bad and mischievous is the essence of humanity and nobility; for instance, those immoral acts which are bad according to religion, intelligence and ethics. In any case, the first kind of bashfulness is bad and the second one is good. In this connection, the Holy Prophet's saying is that:

Bashfulness is of two kinds, bashfulness of intelligence and bashfulness of foolishness. The bashfulness of intelligence is knowledge whereas the bashfulness of foolishness is ignorance.

22 We have a right. If it is allowed to us well and good, otherwise, we will ride on the hind of the camel (like lowly people) even though the night journey may be long.

Sayyid Razi says: This is a very fine and eloquent expression. It means that if we are not allowed our right we will be regarded humble. This sense comes out from this expression because on the rear part of the camel only slaves, prisoners or other people of this type used to ride.[1]

23 He whose deeds accord (him) a back position cannot be given a front position because of his lineage.

24 To render relief to the grief-stricken and to provide comfort in hardship means the atonement of great sins.

25 O son of Adam, when you see that your Lord, the Glorified, bestows His favours on you while you are disobeying Him, you should fear Him.[2]

-1- The sense of the interpretation written by Sayyid Razi is that Ameer al-Momineen intends to say that if our right, that lies with others in our position, as with the Imaam whom it is obligatory to obey, is acknowledged and we are given the chance of worldly rule well and good, otherwise, we will have to bear all sorts of hardships and ignominies and we shall be compelled to live this life of ignominy and humiliation for a long time.

Some commentators have stated a different meaning than this, namely that: "If our position is belittled and put aside, and others are given precedence over us, we shall bear it patiently and agree to remain behind" and this is what is meant by riding on the hind part of the camel, because the person who rides on the hind part is on the rear while the person who sits on its back is in the fore. Some people take it to mean that if we are allowed our right we will accept it but if it is not given we shall not behave like the rider who gives over the rein of his animal into the hands of some other person who is free to take him wherever he likes but we shall stick to out right even though a long time may elapse and not surrender to the usurpers.

-2- When a person goes on receiving favours despite sinfulness he develops the misunderstanding that Allah is pleased with him and that this is the result of His pleasure, because increase in favours arises out of gratefulness and in the event of ungratefulness the bestowal of favours stops, as Allah says:

And when declared your Lord: "If you be grateful, I will increase (My favours) to you, and if you be ungrateful, verily My torment is indeed severe." (Quraan, 14:7)

Nevertheless, continuous bestowal of favours, despite disobedience and ungratefulness, cannot be the result of Allah's pleasure, nor can it be said that in this way Allah has put him under the misconception that he should regard this exuberance of favours as the result of Allah's pleasure because when he knows that he is a sinner and disobedient and is committing sins and vices, knowing them to be sins and vices, then there are no

26 Whenever a person conceals a thing in his heart it manifests itself through unintentional words from his tongue and (in) the expressions of his face.[1]

27 Keep walking in your sickness as long as you can.[2]

28 The best abstemiousness is to conceal it.

29 When you are running away from the world and death is approaching, there is no question of delay in the encounter.

30 Fear! Fear! By Allah, He has hidden your sins so much so as though He has forgiven.

FAITH, UNBELIEF, DOUBT AND THEIR SUPPORTS

31 Ameer al-Momineen, peace be upon him, was asked about faith when he said:

Faith stands on four supports: on endurance. conviction, justice and jihad (fighting in the way of Allah).

Endurance again has four aspects: eagerness, fear, abstention (from the world) and anticipation (of death). So, whoever is eager for Paradise will ignore the passions; whoever fears the Fire (of Hell) will refrain from

---

grounds for misconception on his part by assuming Allah's pleasure and consent. He should rather think that this is a sort of trial and respite for when his sinfulness and high-handedness reaches its zenith he will be caught all at once. Therefore, in such a case he should keep waiting as to when Allah's favours are taken away from him and he is punished with deprival and discomfiture.

-1- The things which a man wants to conceal from others do come out through his tongue sometime or another, and his effort at concealment is unsuccessful. This is because although the far-sighted mind desires to keep them concealed yet sometimes it gets entangled in some more important matter and becomes careless on this score when the concealed thing comes out in words through his tongue. When the mind becomes attentive, it is not possible to undo the matter just as an arrow cannot be got back after shooting. Even if this is not the case and mind is fully cautious and attentive, the thing cannot remain concealed because the lines of the face are indicative of mental feelings and reflect the heart's emotions, and consequently redness of face can easily point out to the sense of shame, and its yellowness fear.

-2- The intention is that as long as sickness does not become serious do not give it importance, because by giving importance the feelings get effected and the illness increases. Therefore, continued activity and regarding oneself well dispels sickness and also prevents the power of resistance from getting weak, and keeps up its psychological power, while the psychological power curbs small ailments by itself, provided it is not forced to give up resistance by the surrendering the imagination to the ailment.

prohibited acts; whoever abstains from the world takes hardships lightly; and whoever anticipates death will hasten towards good deeds.

Conviction also has four aspects: prudent perception, intelligence and understanding, drawing lessons from instructive things and following the precedents of past people. So, whoever perceives with prudence, wise knowledge will be manifest to him, and to whomsoever wise knowledge becomes manifest he appreciates instructive objects, and whoever appreciates instructive objects he is just like past people.

Justice also has four aspects: keen understanding, deep knowledge, a good power of decision and firm forbearance. Therefore, whoever understands comes to acquire depth of knowledge; whoever acquires depth of knowledge drinks from the spring of judgement; and whoever exercises forbearance never commits evil actions in his affairs and leads a praiseworthy life among the people.

Jihad also has four aspects: to ask others to do good, to keep away others from doing evil, to fight (in the way of Allah) sincerely and firmly on all occasions, and to detest the vicious. So, whoever asks others to do good provides strength to the believers; whoever desists others from evil humiliates the unbelievers; whoever fights sincerely on all occasions discharges all his obligations; and whoever detests the vicious and becomes angry for the sake of Allah, then Allah will be angry in favour of him and will keep him pleased on the Day of Judgement.

Unbelief stands on four supports: hankering after whims, mutual quarrelling, deviation from the truth, and dissension. So, whoever hankers after whims does not incline towards right; whoever quarrels much on account of ignorance remains permanently blinded from the right; whoever deviates from truth, for him good becomes evil and evil becomes good and he remains intoxicated with misguidance; and whoever makes a breach (with Allah and His Messenger), his path becomes difficult, his affairs become complicated and his way of escape becomes narrow.

Doubt has also four aspects: unreasonableness, fear, wavering and undue submission to every thing. So, he who adopts unreasonableness as his way, for him there is no dawn after the night; he who is afraid of what befalls him has to run on his heels; he who wavers in doubt Shayaateen trample him under their feet; and he who submits to the destruction of this and the next world succumbs to it.

Sayyid Razi says: We have left out the remaining portion of this saying for fear of length and for being outside the purpose of this chapter.

32 The doer of good is better than the good itself, and the doer of evil is worse than the evil itself.

33 Be generous but not extravagant; be thrifty but not miserly.

34 The best of riches is the abandonment of desires.

35 If someone is quick in saying about people what they dislike, they speak about him that about which they have no knowledge.

36 Whoever prolongs his desire ruins his actions.

37 Once Ameer al-Momineen, peace be upon him, was proceeding towards Syria when the countrymen of al-Anbaar met him. Seeing him they began to walk on foot and then ran in front of him. He enquired why they were doing so and they replied that this was the way they respected their chiefs. Then he said:

By Allah, this does not benefit your chiefs. You are belabouring yourself in this world and earning misery for the next world by it. How harmful is the labour in whose wake there is punishment and how profitable is the case with which there is deliverance from the Fire (of Hell).

38 Ameer al-Momineen, peace be upon him, said to his son a1-Hasan:

O my son, learn four things and (a further) four things from me. Nothing will harm you if you practise them. That the richest of riches is intelligence; the biggest destitution is foolishness; the wildest wildness is vanity and the best achievement is goodness of the moral character.

O my son, you should avoid making friends with a fool because he may intend to benefit you but may harm you; you should avoid making friends with a miser because he will run away from you when you need him most; you should avoid making friends with a sinful person because he will sell you for nought; and you should avoid making friends with a liar because he is like a mirage, making you feel far things near and near things far.

39 Supererogatory worship cannot bring about nearness to Allah if it hampers the obligatory.

40 The tongue of the wise man is behind his heart, and the heart of the fool is behind his tongue.

Sayyid Razi says: This sentence has a special and beautiful meaning. It means that the wise man does not speak with his tongue except after consulting his mind and exercising his imagination, but the fool quickly utters whatever comes to his tongue without thinking. In this way, the tongue of the wise man follows his heart while the heart of the fool follows his tongue.

41 This very sense has been related from Ameer al-Momineen, peace be upon him, in a different version as follows:

The heart of a fool is in his mouth while the tongue of the wise man is in his heart.

The meaning of both the saying (40 and 41) is the same.

42 Ameer al-Momineen, peace be upon him, said to one of his companions during his sickness:

May Allah make your illness a means for writing off your sins, because there is no reward for sickness but that it erases sins and makes them fall like (dried) leaves. Reward lies in saying by the tongue and doing something with the hands and feet. Certainly, Allah, the Glorified. admits into Paradise by virtue of truthfulness of intention and chastity of heart to whomsoever He wishes from among His creatures.

Sayyid Razi says: Ameer al-Momineen is right in saying that there is no reward for sickness as such because compensation is admissible in respect of the acts of Allah, the Sublime, towards His creatures such as grief, illness and the like, whereas reward and recompense becomes admissible against actions by the creature. This is the difference between the two and Ameer al-Momineen has clarified it through his lustrous knowledge and sound view.

43 Ameer al-Momineen, peace be upon him, said About Khabab bn-Aratt[1]
May Allah have mercy on Khobab bn-Aratt since he accepted Islam willingly, immigrated (from Mecca) obediently, remained content with what sufficed him, was pleased with Allah and lived the life of a mojaahid (holy soldier).

44 Blessed is the person who kept in mind the next life, acted so as to be able to render account. remained content with what sufficed him and remained pleased with Allah

45 Even if I strike the nose of a believer with this, my sword, for hating me he will not hate me. and even if I pile all the wealth of the world before a hypocrite (Muslim) for loving me he will not love me. This is because it is a verdict pronounced by the tongue of the revered Prophet, may Allah bless him and his descendants, as he said:
O Ali, a believer will never hate you and a hypocrite (Muslim) will never love you.[2]

-1- Khabbab bn-Aratt was a distinguished companion of the Holy Prophet and was one of the early mohaajiroon (immigrants). He suffered various sorts of hardships at the hands of the Quraysh. He was made to stand in the scorching sun, and to lie on fire but he did not for any reason abandon the side of the Holy Prophet. He accompanied the Holy Prophet in Badr and other battles. He supported Ameer al-Momineen in Siffeen and Nahrawan. He had left Madeena and settled in Koofa. Thus, he died here in 39 A.H. at the age of 73, Ameer al-Momineen led his funeral prayer and he was buried outside Koofa. Ameer al-Momineen uttered these mercy-invoking words standing on his grave.
2 This is one of the authentic traditions (Ahaadeeth) of the Holy Prophet whose authenticity the scholars of traditions had never doubted. It was narrated by certain companions of the Holy Prophet such as Abdillah bn-Abbaas "Imran bn-Hosayn, Om al-Momineen Om-Salama and others, such as Ameer al-Momineen himself, also narrated that:
By Him Who split the seed and created the soul, verily the Messenger of Allah, peace be upon him and his progeny, gave me a promise that no one but a (true) believer will love me, and none but a hypocrite will hate me (Saheeh, Muslim, vol.1, p.60; Muslim, in his book, regards the love of Ali as an ingredient of (Emaan) or faith and one of its signs; and the hatred of Ali as the sign of dissemblance) al-Jaami as-Saheeh,vol.5, pp.635,643; as-Sonan, bn-Maaja, vol.1, p.55; as-Sonan, an-Nesaai, vol.8, pp.115-116,117; al-Mosnad, Ahmad bn-Hambal, vol.1, pp.84,95,128; vol.6, p.292; Ilaal al-Hadeeth, Abi-Haatim, vol.2, p.400; Hilyatol-Awliyaa, Abi-Noaym, vol.4, p.185; Jaami al-Osool, bn-Atheer, vol.9, p.473; Majma" az-Zawaaid, vol.9, p.133; Manaaqib Ali bn-Abi-Talib, bn-Maghaazili, pp.190-195;

46 The sin that displeases you is better in the view of Allah than the virtue which makes you proud.[1]

47 The worth of a man is according to his courage, his truthfulness is according to his balance of temper, his valour is according to his self-respect and his chasteness is according to his sense of shame.

48 Victory is by determination; determination is by turning over of thoughts, and thoughts are formed by guarding secrets.

49 Fear the attack of a noble person when he is hungry, and that of an ignoble person when he is satiated.[2]

50 The hearts of the people are like wild beasts. Whoever tames them, they would pounce upon him.[3]

---

al-Isteeaab, vol.3, p.1100; Osdol-Ghaaba, vol.4, p.26; al-Isaaba, vol.2, p.509; T4rlDth Baghdad, vol.2, p.255; vol.8, p.417; vol.14, p.426; at-Taareekh, bn-Katheer, vol.7, p.354)

It was in this way that the companions of the Holy Prophet used to test the faith (Emaan) or hypocrisy (nifaaq) of the Muslims through their love or hatred towards Ameer al-Momineen, as is related from Abi-Zarr al-Ghifaari, Abu-Saeed al-Khodri, Abdillah bn-Masood and Jabir bn-Abdillah that:

We (the companions of the Holy Prophet) used to distinguish the hypocrites by their hatred of Ali bn-Abi-Talib. (at-Tirmizi, vol.5, p.635; al-Mostadrak, vol.3, p.129; Hilyatol-Awliyaa, vol.6, p.294; Majma az-Zawaaid, vol.9, pp.132-133; Jaami al-Osool, vol.9, p.473; ad-Dorr al-Manthoor, vol.6, pp.66-67; Taareekh Baghdad, vol.13, p.153; ar-Riyaaz an-Nazira, vol.2, pp.214-215; al-Isteeaab vol.3, p.1110; Osdol-Ghaaba, vol.4, pp.29-30)

-1- The person who feels ashamed and repentant after committing sin and offers repentance before Allah remains safe from the penalty of that sin and deserves the reward of repentance: while the person who after doing a virtuous deed begins to feel superiority over others, and being proud of his virtues thinks that he has no apprehension whatever, destroys his virtue and remains deprived of the reward of the virtuous deed. Obviously, he who has erased the blot of his sin by repentance will be better than he who has ruined his action by being proud of it, and having not repented of it either.

-2- The meaning is that a man of prestige and esteem never tolerates humiliation or disgrace. If his honour is assailed he will leap like a hungry lion and break away the shackles of humiliation. If a low and narrow minded person is raised beyond his name he would not be able to contain himself but, regarding himself very high, will assail other's position.

-3- This saying confirms the theory that by nature human hearts love wildness and that the feeling of love and affection in them is an acquired attribute. Consequently, when the factors and causes of love and affection crop up they get tamed but when these factors disappear or the feelings of hatred are created against them, the people return

51 So long as your position is good, your defects will remain covered.

52 The most capable of pardoning is he who is the most powerful to punish.

53 Generosity is that which is by one's own initiative, because giving on being asked is either out of self-respect or to avoid rebuke.

54 There is no wealth like wisdom, no destitution like ignorance, no inheritance like refinement and no support like consultation.

55 Patience is of two kinds, patience over what pains you, and patience against what you covet.

56 With wealth a strange land is a homeland, while with destitution even a homeland is a strange land.[1]

57 Contentment is wealth that does not diminish.[2]

Sayyid Razi says: This saying has also been related from the Prophet, may Allah bless him and his descendants.

58 Wealth is the fountain head of passions.

59 Whoever warns you is like one who gives you good tidings.

60 The tongue is a beast; if it is let loose, it devours.

61 Woman is a scorpion whose grip is sweet.

---

to wildness, and thereafter they return to the path of love and affection with great difficulty.

Do nor tease the heart because it is a wind bird. If once it flies away from the roof it would come down with great difficulty.

-1- A person who has wealth and riches will get friends and acquaintances wherever he may be and therefore he will not feel strange in a foreign land; but if he is poor and destitute he will have no friends even in his homeland because people do not like to make friends with the poor and the destitute, or to extend relations with them. He is therefore, a stranger even at home and has no friends or well-wishers.

He who has no worldly successor remains unknown as a stranger even in his homeland.

-2- Contentment means that a man should remain satisfied with what he gets and should not complain if he gets less. If he is not so contented he will try to satisfy his greed by committing social crimes like misappropriation, cheating and deceiving others, because greed compels one to satisfy one's wants by any means whatever. Then the satisfaction of one's want opens the way for another want and as a man's wants get satisfied his craving increases and he can never get rid of his needs or of dissatisfaction. This increasing dissatisfaction can be stopped only by contentment which makes a man carefree from all wants except the most essential ones. This is that everlasting wealth that gives satisfaction for good.

62 If you are met with a greeting, give better greetings in return. If a hand of help is extended to you, do a better favour in return, although the credit would remain with the one who was first.

63 The interceder is the wing of the seeker.

64 The people of the world are like travellers who are being carried while they are asleep.

65 A lack of friends means strangeness.

66 To miss what one needs is easier than to beg from an inappropriate person.[1]

67 Do not feel ashamed for giving little, because refusal is smaller than that.

68 Charity is the adornment of destitution, while gratefulness (to Allah) is the adornment of riches.

69 If what you aim at does not come about then do not worry as to what you were.

70 You will not find an ignorant person but at one extreme or the other (i.e. a person who neglects or a person who exaggerates).[2]

71 As intelligence increases, speech decreases.

72 Time wears our bodies, renews desires, brings death nearer and takes away aspirations. Whoever is successful with it encounters grief and whoever misses its favours also undergoes hardships.

-1- The shame that is faced in putting a request before an inappropriate person gives more mental pain than the grief in not obtaining its fulfilment. That is why non- fulfilment of a request can be tolerated but the obligation of a low and humble person is intolerable. Every self-respecting person would therefore prefer deprival to being under obligation to an inappropriate man, and will not tolerate placing his request before a low and humble person.

-2- Talkativeness is the result of diffused thinking while diffusion of thought is the result of the unripeness of wisdom. When wisdom attains perfection and understanding ripens one's mind, and thoughts are balanced, and wisdom acquires power and control over the tongue, as over other parts of the body, the tongue does not act without thinking or outside the dictates of wisdom. Obviously, uttering after thinking is short and free from extras.

As a man's intelligence increases his speaking decreases and he does not speak save at the opportune moment.

73 Whoever places himself as a leader of the people should commence with educating his own self before educating others; and his teaching should be by his own conduct before teaching by the tongue. The person who teaches and instructs his own self is more entitled to esteem then he who teaches and instructs others.

74 The breath of a man is a step towards his death.[1]

75 Every countable thing is to pass way and every expected thing must come about.

76 If matters get mixed up then the last ones should be appreciated according to the previous one.[2]

77 It is related that when Zirar bn-Hamza az-Zibaabi[3] went to Moaawiya and Moaawiya enquired from him about Ameer al-Momineen, peace be upon him, he said:

-1- That is just as each step makes way for the other and this exercise by steps is the means of nearing the goal, similarly every breath of life serves as, death-knell for the previous one and carries life towards death, as if the breath whose motion is regarded as a sign of life is in fact the sign of the passing away of one moment of life and a means of nearing the goal of death, because each breath is death for the previous one, and life is the name of those very death-carrying breaths.

Every breath is the dead body of the life that passed by. Life is the name of living by facing successive deaths.

-2- By looking at a seed a cultivator can say what plant will come out of it, what fruits, flowers or leaves it will have and what will be its expanse. In the same way, a guess can be made about the success of a student by looking at his labour and effort or about the failure of some other student by looking at his leisureliness and idleness, because he beginning is indicative of the end and the premises of the conclusion. Therefore, if the end of any matter is not visible then its beginning should be looked at. If its beginning is bad the end too would be bad and if the beginning is good the end too would be good.

An auspicious river begins from the very spring.

-3- Ziraar bn-Zamra was one of the companions of Ameer al-Momineen. After the death of Ameer al-Momineen, he went to Syria (ash-Sham) where he met Moaawiya. Moaawiya asked him "Describe Ali to me." He replied "Would you please excuse me from answering this?" But Moaawiya insisted "You must describe him." Whereupon Ziraar said:

If there is no alternative, then you should know that Ali was a man whose personality knew no limits, terrible in power, his speech was decisive, his judgements based on justice, his knowledge spread out in all directions and wisdom was manifest in all his behaviour. Among the food he liked most was the coarse kind and among the clothes,

I stand witness that I have seen him on several occasions when night had spread and he was standing in the niche (of the mosque) holding his beard. groaning like a man bitten by a snake and weeping as a grieved man. saying:

O world. O world! Get away from me. Why do you present yourself to me? Or are you eager for me? You may not get that opportunity to impress me. Deceive some other person. I have no concern with you. I have divorced you thrice whereafter there is no restitution. Your life is short, your importance is little and your liking is humble. Alas! The provision is little, the way is long, the journey is far and the goal is hard to reach.

78 ON PREDESTINATION

A man enquired from Ameer al-Momineen: Was our going to fight against the Syrians destined by Allah? Ameer al-Momineen, peace be upon him, gave a detailed reply, a selection from which is hereunder:

Woe to you. You take it as a final and unavoidable destiny[1] (according to which we are bound to act). If it were so, there would have been no

---

the short (and humble) ones. By Allah, he was among us as one of us. He used to respond to our questions and fulfil all our requests. By Allah, although he used to let us get close to him and he himself was close to us, we did not dare address him due to our feeling of awe towards him nor did we dare to speak first due to his greatness in our hearts. His smile displayed a row of pearls. He used to honour the pious; to be kind to the needy, to reed the orphan, the near of Kin or the needy man in misery on the day of hunger; to clothe the bare ones and to help the undefended person. He used to detest the world and its flowering. I stand witness that... (and so forth, as quoted above by Sayyid Razi). When Moaawiya heard this from Ziraar his eyes became full of tears and he said "May Allah have mercy on Abol-Hasan. He really was so." Then, turning to Ziraar he said "How do you feel in his absence, O Ziraar!" Ziraar replied "My grief is like that of a woman whose only child is butchered in her arms." (al-Isteeaab, vol.3, pp.1107- 1108; Hilyatol-Awliyaa, vol.2, p.84; Sifatos-Safwa, bn-Jawzi, vol.1, p.121; al-Amaal, Abo-Ali al-Qaali, vol.2, p.147; Zahr al-Aadaab, al-Hosri, vol.1, pp.40-41; Morooj az-Zahab, vol.2, p.421; ar-Riyaaz an-Nazirah, al-Mohibb at-Tabari, vol.2, p.212; bn-Abil-Hadeed, vol.18, pp.225-226).

-1- The end of this story is that after this the man enquired "What kind of destiny it was by which we had to go?" and Ameer al-Momineen said "qada" (destiny)" means command of Allah. For example, He has said "wa qala rabbuka alla tabudd illa iyyaku" (And commanded your Lord has that you shall worship not (any one) but Him" (Quraan, 17:23)). Here "qaada" stands for commanded.

question of reward or chastisement and there would have been no sense in Allah's promises or warnings. (On the other hand) Allah, the Glorified, has ordered His people to act by free will and has cautioned them and refrained them (from evil). He has placed easy obligations on them and has not put heavy obligations. He gives them much (reward) in return for little (action). He is disobeyed, not because He is overpowered. He is obeyed but not under force. He id not send prophets just for fun. He did not send down the Book for the people without purpose. He did not create the skies, the earth and all that is in between them in vain. That is the imagination of those who disbelieve; then woe to those who disbelieve- because of the fire. (Quraan, 38:27)

79 Take wise points from wherever they may be, because if a wise saying is in the bosom of a hypocrite it flutters in his bosom till it comes out and settles with others of its own category in the bosom of the believer.

80 A wise saying is a lost article of the believer. Therefore, get wise sayings even though from people of hypocrisy.

81 The worth of every man is in his attainments.[1]

Sayyid Razi says: This is the sentence whose value cannot be assessed, with which no wise saying can be weighed and with which no other sentence can be matched.

82 I impart to you five things which, if you ride your camels fast in search of them, you will find them worth it.

No one of you should repose hope save in his Lord (Allah); no one of you should fear anything save his sin; no one should feel ashamed of saying "I do not know" when he is asked a matter which he does not know; no one should feel ashamed of learning a thing that he does not know; and you

-1- The real value of a person is his knowledge (and perfection of attainments). His worth and position would be in accordance with the position of knowledge and attainment he holds. Eyes that are conscious of real values do not look at the face, features, tallness of stature, size or worldly pomp and position but look at the attainments of a person and assess his worth according to these attainments. The conclusion is that a man should strive to acquire distinction and knowledge. The worth of every person is according to the extent of his knowledge.

should practise endurance, because endurance is for belief what the head is for the body, so that just as there is no good in a body without the head there is no good in belief without endurance.

83 Ameer al-Momineen, peace be upon him, said about a man who praised him much, although he did not admire him:

I am below what you express and above what you feel in your heart.

84 The survivors of the sword (from getting killed) are large in number and have a large progeny.

85 Whoever abandons saying "I do not know" meets his destruction.

86 I love the opinion of an old man more than the determination of a young man; (or according to another version) more than the martyrdom of a young man.

87 I wonder about the man who loses hope despite the possibility of seeking forgiveness.

88 (Imam) Abu Jafar Mohammad bn-Ali al-Baqir, peace be upon both of them, has related from Ameer al-Momineen, peace be upon him, that he said:

There were two sources of deliverance from the Allah's punishment, one of which has been raised up, while the other is before you. You should therefore adhere to it. The source of deliverance, which has been raised up is the Messenger of Allah (may He bless him and his descendants), while the source of deliverance that remains is the seeking of forgiveness. Allah, the Glorified, has said: And Allah is not to chastise them while you are among them, nor is Allah to chastise them while yet they seek forgiveness. (Quraan, 8:33)

Sayyid Razi says: This is one of the most beautiful way of deducing the meaning and the most delicate manner of interpretation.

89 If a man behaves properly in matters between himself and Allah, then Allah keeps proper the matters between him and other people; and if a man keeps proper the affairs of his next life then Allah keeps proper for him the affairs of this world. Whoever is a preacher for himself is protected by Allah.

90 The perfect jurist of Islam is he who does not let people lose hope from the mercy of Allah, does not make him despondent of Allah's kindness and does not make him feel safe from Allah's punishment.

91 The hearts get disgusted as bodies get disgusted; so look for beautiful wise saying for them.

92 The most humble knowledge is that which remains on the tongue and the most honourable one is that which manifests itself through (the action of) the limbs and the organs of the body.

93 None of you should say "O Allah, I seek Your protection from trouble" because there is no one who is not involved in trouble, but whoever seeks Allah's protection he should seek it from misguiding troubles, because Allah, the Glorified, says: And know you! That your wealth and your children are a temptation. (Quraan, 8:28) and its meaning is that He tries people with wealth and progeny in order to distinguish one who is displeased with his livelihood from the one who is happy with what he has been given. Even though Allah, the Glorified, knows them more than they know themselves yet He does so to let them perform actions with which they earn reward or punishment because some of them like to have male (children) and dislike to have female (children), and some like to amass wealth, and dislike adversity.

Sayyid Razi says: This is one of the wonderful interpretations related from him.

94 Ameer al-Momineen, peace be upon him, was asked what is good and he replied:

Good is not that your wealth and progeny should be much, but good is that your knowledge should be much, your forbearance should be great, and that you should vie with other people in worship of Allah. If you do good deeds you thank Allah, but if you commit evil you seek forgiveness of Allah. In this world good is for two persons only; the man who commits sins but rectifies them by repentance; and the man who hastens towards good actions.

95 Action accompanied by fear for Allah does not fail, and how can a thing fail that has been accepted.[1]

96 The persons most attached to the prophets are those who know most what the prophets have brought. Then Ameer al-Momineen recited the verse:

Verily, of men nearest to Abraham are surely those who followed him and this (Our) Prophet (Mohammad) and those who believe (Quraan, 3:68).

Then he said:

The friend of Mohammad is he who obeys Allah, even though he may have no blood relationship, and the enemy of Mohammad is he who disobeys Allah even though he may have near kinship.

97 Ameer al-Momineen, peace be upon him, heard about a Kharijite who said the mid-night prayers and recited the Quraan, then he said:

Sleeping in a state of firm belief is better than praying in a state of doubtfulness.

98 When you hear a tradition test it according to the criterion of intelligence not that of mere hearing, because relaters of knowledge are numerous but those who guard it are few.

99 Ameer al-Momineen, peace be upon him, heard a man recite:

Verily we are Allah 's and verily to Him shall we return (Quraan, 2:l56).

Then he said:

Our saying "inna lillah" (Verily we are Allah's) is an admission of His majesty over us and our saying "wa inna ilayhi rajioon" (and verily to Him shall we return) is an admission of our being mortal.

100 Some people praised Ameer al-Momineen, peace be upon him, to his face, then he said:

O my Allah! You know me better than myself, and I know myself more than they know. O my Allah! make us better than what they think and forgive us what they do not know.

-1- As Allah says:

... Verily, Allah do accept (an offering only) from those who guard (themselves against evil). (Quraan, 5:27)

101 Fulfillment of (others) needs becomes a lasting virtue in three ways:- regarding it small so that it attains bigness, concealing it so that it may manifest itself, and doing it quickly so that it becomes pleasant.

102 Shortly a time will come for people when high positions will be given only to those who defame others, when vicious people will be regarded as witty and the just will be regarded as weak. People will regard charity as a loss, consideration for kinship as an obligation, and worship grounds for claiming greatness among others. At this time, authority will be exercised through the counsel of women, the posting of young boys in high positions and the running of the administration by eunuchs.

103 Ameer al-Momineen, peace be upon hi n, was seen in worn-out clothes with patches and when it was pointed out to him he said:

With it the heart fears, the mind feels humble and the believers emulate it. Certainly, this world and the next are two enemies against each other and two paths in different directions. Whoever likes this world and loves it hates the next and is its enemy. These two are like East and West. If the walker between them gets near to one, he gets farther from the other. After all, they are like two fellow-wives.

104 It is related by Nawf al-Bikali that: I saw that one night Ameer al-Momineen, peace be upon him, came out from his bed and looked at the stars, then he said to me: "O Nawf, are you awake or sleeping?" I said "I am awake, O Ameer al-Momineen" Then he said:

O Nawf! blessed be those who abstain from this world and are eager for the next world. They are the people who regard this earth as floor; its dust as their bed-cloth; and its water as their perfume; they recite the Quraan in low tones and supplicate in high tones and then they are cut off from the world like Esaa (Jesus).

O Nawf! The prophet Dawood (David), peace be upon him, rose up at a similar hour one night and said "This is the hour when whatever a person prays for is granted to him unless he is a tax-collector, an intelligence man, a police officer, a lute player or a drummer.

Sayyid Razi says: It is also said that "artaba" means tabl "drum" and "kubah" means lute.

105 Allah has placed on you some obligations which you should not ignore, has laid down for you limits which you should not transgress, has prohibited you from certain things which you should not violate, and has kept quiet about certain things, but He has not left them out by mistake so that you should not find them.

106 If people give up something relating to religion to set right their worldly affairs, Allah will inflict upon them something more harmful than that.

107 Often the ignorance of a learned man ruins him while the knowledge he has does not avail him.

108 In man there is a piece of flesh attached to him a vein and it is the strangest thing in him. It is the heart. It has a store of wisdom and things contrary to wisdom. If it sees a ray of hope, eagerness humiliates it and when eagerness increases, greed ruins it. If disappointment overtakes it, grief kills it. If anger rises in it, a serious rage develops. If it is blessed with pleasure, it forgets to be cautious. If it becomes fearing, it becomes heedless. If peace extends all round, it becomes neglectful. If it earns wealth, freedom from care puts it in the wrong. If trouble befalls it, impatience makes it humble. If it faces starvation, distress overtakes it. If hunger attacks it, weakness makes it sit down. If its eating increases, heaviness of stomach pains it. Thus, every shortness is harmful to it and every excess is injurious to it.

109 We (the members of the Prophet's family) are like the pillow in the middle. He who lags behind has to come forward to meet it while he who has exceeded the bounds has to return to it.

110 No one can establish the rule of Allah, the Glorified, except he who shows no relenting (in the matter of right), who does not behave like wrong doers and who does not run after objects of greed.

111 Sahl bn-Honayf al-Ansaari died at Koofa after his return from the battle of Siffeen and he was very much loved by Ameer al-Momineen, peace be upon him. On this occasion Ameer al-Momineen said:

Even if a mountain had loved me, it would have crumbled down.

Sayyid Razi says: The meaning of this is that since the trial of the man who loves Ameer al-Momineen will be so, severe troubles would leap towards him, and this is not the case except with the God-fearing, the virtuous and select good. There is another similar saying of Ameer al-Momineen's individuals, namely:

112 Whoever loves us, members of the Household (of the Prophet), should be prepared to face destitution.[1]

Sayyid Razi says: This has been interpreted in a different way as well, but on this occasion is not fit to mention here.

113 No wealth is more profitable than wisdom, no loneliness is more estranging than vanity, no wisdom is as good as tact, no honour is like fear from Allah, no companion is like the goodness of moral character, no inheritance is like civility, no guide is like promptitude, no trade is like virtuous acts, no profit is like Divine reward, no self-control is like inaction in time of doubt, no abstention is like that (which is) from prohibitions, no knowledge is like thinking, no worship is like the discharge of obligation, no belief is like modesty and endurance, no attainment is like humility, no honour is like knowledge, no power is like forbearance, and no support is more reliable than consultation.

114 At a time when virtue is in vogue in the world and among people, if a person entertains an evil suspicion about another person from whom nothing evil has ever been seen, then he has been unjust. And at a time when vice is in vogue in the world and among people, if a man entertains a good idea about another person he has flung himself in peril.

115 It was said to Ameer al-Momineen, peace be upon him: How are you, O Ameer al-Momineen? and he replied: How can he be whom life is driving towards death, whose state of healthiness can change into sickness any moment and who is to be caught (by death) from his place of safety.

-1- Perhaps the other meaning of this saying is that: "Whoever loves us should not hanker after worldly matters even though in consequence he may have to face destitution and poverty; but he should rather remain content and avoid seeking worldly benefits. "

116 There are many people who are given time (by Allah) through good treatment towards them and many who are deceived because their sinful activities are veiled (by Allah), and many who are enamoured by good talk about themselves. And Allah does not try anyone as seriously as He tries him whom He allows time (to remain sinful).

117 Two categories of persons will face ruin on account of me: he who loves me with exaggeration, and he who hates me intensely.

118 To miss an opportunity brings about grief.

119 The example of the world is like a serpent. It is soft to the touch but its inside is full of venom. An ignorant person who has fallen into deceit is attracted towards it but a wise and intelligent man keeps on his guard against it.

120 Ameer al-Momineen, peace be upon him, was asked about the Quraysh, when he replied:

As for Bani-Makhzoom they are the blossoms of the Quraysh. It is delightful to talk to their men and to marry their women. As for Bani-Abd Shams, they are farsighted and cautious about all that is hidden from them. As for ourselves (Bani-Hashim) we spend whatever we get and are very generous in offering ourselves in death. Consequently, those people are more numerous, more contriving and more ugly while we are more eloquent, well-wishing and handsome.

121 What a difference there is between two kinds of actions: an act whose pleasure passes away but its (ill) consequence remains, and the act whose hardship passes away but its reward stays.

122 Ameer al-Momineen, peace be upon him, was accompanying a funeral when he heard someone laugh. Then he said:

Is it that death has been ordained only for others? Is it that right is obligatory only on others? Is it that those whom we see departing on their journey of death will come back to us? We lay them down in their graves and then enjoy their estate (as if we will live for good after them). We have ignored every preacher, man or woman, and have exposed ourselves to every catastrophe.

123 Blessed be he who humbles himself, whose livelihood is pure, whose heart is chaste, whose habits are virtuous, who spends his savings (in the name of Allah), who prevents his tongue from speaking nonsense, who keeps people safe from evil, who is pleased with the (Prophet's) Sonna, and who is unconnected with innovation (in religion).

Sayyid Razi says: Some people attribute this and the previous saying to the Messenger of Allah (may Allah bless him and his descendants).

124 The jealousy of a woman (with co-wives) is heresy, while the jealousy of a man is a part of belief.

125 I am defining Islam as no one has defined before me: Islam is submission, submission is conviction, conviction is affirmation, affirmation is acknowledgement, acknowledgement is discharge (of obligations), and discharge of obligations is action.

126 I wonder at the miser who is speeding towards the very destitution from which he wants to run away and misses the very ease of life which he covets. Consequently he passes his life in this world like the destitute, but will have to render an account in the next world like the rich.

I wonder at the proud man who was just a drop of semen the other day and will turn into a corpse tomorrow. I wonder at the man who doubts Allah although he sees His creations. I wonder at him who has forgotten death although he sees people dying. I wonder at him who denies the second life although he has seen the first life. I wonder at him who inhabits this transient abode but ignores the everlasting abode.

127 Whoever falls short of actions falls into grief, and Allah has nothing to do with him who spares nothing from his wealth in the name of Allah.

128 Guard against cold in its (seasonal) beginning and welcome it towards its end because it effects bodies in the same way as it effects plants. In the beginning, it destroys them but in the end it gives them fresh leaves.[1]

-1- During autumn, protection from cold is necessary because with the change of weather the temperature of the body also changes and ailments such as flue, catarrh, cough etc., occur. This is because bodies are accustomed to hot weather and when suddenly cold comes on tissue become contracted and cold dryness increases in the body. Thus,

129 Greatness of the Creator appreciated by you would belittle the creatures in your view.

130 When Ameer al-Momineen, peace be upon him, returned from (the battle of) Siffeen and noticed the graves outside Koofa, he said:

O residents of houses which give a sense of loneliness, of depopulated areas and gloomy graves. O people of the dust, O victims of strangeness, O people of loneliness and O people of desolateness! You have gone ahead and preceded us while we are following you and will meet you. The houses (you left) have been inhabited by others; the wives (you left) have been married by others; the properties have been distributed (among heirs). This is the news about those around us; what is the news about things around you?

Then Ameer al-Momineen, peace be upon him, turned to his companions and said:

Beware. If they were allowed to speak they would inform you that: Verily, the best provision is fear of Allah. (Quraan, 2:197)

131 ABOUT THOSE WHO FALSELY ACCUSE THIS WORLD

Ameer al-Momineen, peace be upon him, heard a man abusing the world and said:

O you who abuse the worlds O you who have been deceived by its deceit and cheated by its wrongs. Do you covet the world and then abuse it? Do

---

bathing with cold water soon after bathing with hot water is harmful for this very reason that with hot water the tissues expand and so they at once admit the effect of cold water, and in consequence the natural heat of the body is effected. On the other hand, there is no need of protection from cold during spring season nor is it harmful for the health, because the body is already accustomed to cold. Thus, the temperate cold of the spring is not unpleasant to the body. Rather, with the decline of cold there is an increase of heat and dampness in the body as a result of which growth gets impetus, natural heat rises, the body grows, the temperaments feels pleasant and the spirit is joyful.

Similarly, there is the same effect in the plant world. Thus, during autumn due to the prevalence of coldness and dryness, the leaves wither, the vegetative power decreases, the freshness of the plants fades and there is a death-like effect on the green areas. Spring brings the message of life for them. Then with the blowing of healthy winds the blossoms begin to sprout, plants become fresh and healthy, and forests and wildernesses acquire a green hue.

you accuse it or it should accuse you? When did it bewilder you or deceive you-whether by the decay and fall of your forefathers, or by the sleeping places of your mothers under the ground? How much you looked after them in their illness and nursed them during sickness, desiring them to be cured and consulting physicians for them in the morning when your medicine did not avail them and your wailing for them did not benefit them. Your mourning over them did not prove useful to them and you could not achieve your aims. You could not ward off (death) from them with all your power. In fact, through the dying man the world presented an illustration for you and showed you by the example of his falling down how you would (also) fall.

Certainly, this world is a house of truth for him who appreciates it; a place of safety for him who understands it; a house or riches for him who collects provision from it (for the next world); and a house of instructions for him who draws instruction from it. It is the place of worship for the lovers of Allah; the place of praying for the angels of Allah; the place where the revelation of Allah descends; and the marketing place for those devoted to Allah. Herein they earned mercy and herein they acquired Paradise by way of profit.

Therefore, who can abuse it when it has announced its departure and called out that it would leave! It had given news of its own destruction and the death of its people. By its hardship it set an example of their hardships. By its pleasures it created eagerness for the pleasures (of the next world). It brings ease in the evening and grief in the morning by way of persuasion, dissuasion, alarm and warning. People abuse it on the morning of their repentance but there are others who will praise it on the Day of Judgement. The world recalled to them the next life and they bore it in mind. It related to them (things of the next life) and they acknowledged them. It preached to them and they took lesson therefrom.[1]

-1- Every speaker and preacher manifests the force of his speaking in subjects in which he is well-versed. If he has to change the subject neither will his mind move nor will his tongue be able to speak out. But he whose intellect has the capability of adaptation and

132 There is an angel of Allah who calls out every day "Beget children for death, collect wealth for destruction, and raise construction for ruin

133 This world is a place for transit, not a place for stay. The people herein are of two categories. One is the man who sold away his self (to his passions) and thus ruined it, and the other is the man who purchased his self (by control against his passions) and freed it.

134 A friend is not a friend unless he affords protection to his comrade on three occasions: in his adversity, in his absence and at his death.

135 He who is bestowed four things is not disallowed four things: he who is allowed to pray is not deprived of the response to it; he who is allowed to offer repentance is not deprived of its acceptance; he who is allowed to seed forgiveness is not deprived of forgiveness; and he who is allowed to be grateful is not deprived of furtherance of favours.

Sayyid Razi says: This is confirmed by the Book of Allah. About praying, Allah says: "call you to Me, I will answer you" (Quraan, 4:60). About forgiveness Allah says: And whoever does evil, or wrongs his own self and thereafter seeks pardon of Allah, shall find Allah Oft-forgiving, Merciful" (Quraan, 4:110). About gratefulness He says: "If you be grateful I will increase (my favours) to you" (Quraan, 14:7). About repentance He says: "Verily, repentance (Acceptable) with Allah is only for those who do evil ignorantly and then turn (to Allah) soon (after); these (are those) Allah will turn (merciful) to them; and Allah is All-knowing, All-wise" (Quraan, 4:17).

136 For the God-fearing prayers is a means of seeking nearness to Allah; and for the weak the Haj (pilgrimage to Mecca) is as good as jihad (fighting in the way of Allah). For every thing there is a levy; and the levy of the body

---

whose mind has the power of imagination can turn round his utterances in whatever manner he likes, and can show the excellence of speaking on whatever subject he desires. Consequently, when the tongue which had for so long been abusing the world and unveiling its deceitfulness starts praising the world it shows the same mastery of speaking and power of arguing that had ever been its chief distinction. And then, the use of commendatory words does not alter the principle and although the ways are different the object remains the same.

is fasting. The jihad of a woman is to afford pleasant company to her husband.

137 Seek livelihood by giving alms.

138 He who is sure of a good return is generous in giving.

139 Assistance is allowed according to need.

140 He who is moderate does not become destitute.

141 A small family is one of the ways of (securing) ease.

142 Loving one another is half of wisdom.

143 Grief is half of old age.

144 Endurance comes according to the affliction. He who beats his hand on the thigh in his affliction ruins all his good actions.

145 There is many a person who fasts whose fast is nothing but just hunger and thirst, and many an offerer of prayers whose prayer is no better than wakefulness and hardship. The sleep as well as the eating and drinking of the intelligent (god-knowing) person is far better.

146 Protect your belief by charity; guard your wealth by paying Allah's share; and ward off the waves of calamity by praying. A

147 People are of three types

147. Komayl bn-Ziyad[1] has related: Ameer al-Momineen, peace be upon him, caught hold of my hand and took me to the graveyard. When he had passed through the graveyard and left the city behind, he breathed a deep sigh and said:

O Komayl these hearts are containers. The best of them is that which preserves (its contents). So, preserve what I say to you. People are of three types: One is the scholar and divine. Then, the seeker of knowledge who is also on the way to deliverance. Then (lastly) the common rot who run after every caller and bend in the direction of every wind. They seek not

-1- Komayl bn-Ziyad an-Nakhaai was the holder of the secrets of the Imaama and one of the chief companions of Ameer al-Momineen. He held a great position in knowledge and attainment and a chief place in abstinence and Godliness. He was Ameer al-Momineen's Governor of Heet for sometime. He was killed by al-Hajjaj bn-Yoosof ath-Thaqafi in the year 83 A.H. at the age of ninety years and was buried outside Koofa.

light from the effulgence of knowledge and do not take protection of any reliable support.

O Komayl, knowledge is better than wealth. Knowledge guards you, while you have to guard the wealth. Wealth decreases by spending, while knowledge multiplies by spending, and the results of wealth die as wealth decays.

O Komayl, knowledge is belief which is acted upon. With it man acquires obedience during his life and a good name after his death. Knowledge is the ruler while wealth is ruled upon.

O Komayl, those who amass wealth are dead even though they may be living while those endowed with knowledge will remain as long as the world lives. Their bodies are not available but their figures exist in the hearts. Look, here is a heap of knowledge (and Ameer al-Momineen pointed to his bosom). I wish I could get someone to bear it. Yes, I did find (such a one); but either he was one who could not be relied upon. He would exploit the religion for worldly gains, and by virtue of Allah's favours on him he would domineer over the people and through Allah's pleas he would lord over His devotees. Or he was one who was obedient to the hearers of truth but there was no intelligence in his bosom. At the first appearance of doubt he would entertain misgivings in his heart.

So, neither this nor that was good enough. Either the man is eager for pleasures. easily led away by passions, or is covetous for collecting and hoarding wealth. Neither of them has any regard for religion in any matter. The nearest example of these is the loose cattle. This is the way that knowledge dies away with the death of its bearers.

O my Allah! Yes; but the earth is never devoid of those who maintain Allah's plea either openly and reputedly or, being afraid. as hidden in order that Allah's pleas and proofs should not be rebutted. How many are they and where are they? By Allah, they are few in number, but they are great in esteem before Allah. Through them Allah guards His pleas and proofs till they entrust them to others like themselves and sow the seeds thereof in the hearts of those who are similar to them.

Knowledge has led them to real understanding and so they have associated themselves with the spirit of conviction. They take easy what the easygoing regard as hard. They endear what the ignorant take as strange. They live in this world with their bodies here but their spirits resting in the high above. They are the vicegerents of Allah on His earth and callers to His religion. Oh, oh, how I yearn to see them!

Go away now, O Komayl wherever you wish.

148 Man is hidden under his tongue.[1]

149 He who does not know his own worth is ruined.

150 ON PREACHING

Ameer al-Momineen, peace be upon him, said to a man who had request him to preach:

Do not be like him who hopes for (bliss in) the next life without action, and delays repentance by lengthening desires, who utters words like ascetics in this world but acts like those who are eager for it; if he is allowed something from it he does not feel satisfied; if he is denied he is not content; he is not grateful for what begets and covets for increase in whatever remains with him; he refrains others but not himself; he commands others for what he himself does not do; he loves the virtuous but does not behave like them; he hates the vicious but himself is one of them; he dislikes death because of the excess of his sins but adheres to that for which he is afraid of death.

If he falls ill he feels ashamed; if he is healthy he feels secure and indulges in amusements; when he recovers from illness he feels vain about himself; when he is afflicted he loses hope; if distress befalls him he prays like a bewildered man; when he finds ease of life he falls into deceit and turns his face away; his heart overpowers him by means of imaginary things

---

-1- The meaning is that a man's worth can be known by his speech because the speech of every person is indicative of his mind and manners, and by virtue of it his feelings and temperament can be very easily assessed. Therefore, so long as he is silent his weakness as well as attainments are concealed but when he speaks his real self manifests itself.
A man is hidden under his tongue.
Unless he speaks you cannot know his worth and value.

while he cannot control his heart by his conviction; for others he is afraid of small sins, but for himself he expects more reward than his performance; if he becomes wealthy he becomes self-conscious and falls into vice; if he becomes poor he despairs and becomes weak; he is brief when he is doing a good thing but goes too far when he is begging; when passion overtakes him he is quick in committing sin but delays repentance; if hardship befalls him he goes beyond the canons of the (Islamic) community; he describes instructive events but does not take instruction himself; he preaches at length but does not accept any preaching for himself; he is tall in speaking but short in action; he aspires for things that will perish and ignores things that will last for good; he regards profit as loss and loss as profit; he fears death but does nothing in its anticipation. He regards the sins of others as big but considers the same things for himself as small; if he does something in obedience to Allah he considers it much but if others do the same he considers it small; he therefore rebukes others but flatters himself; entertainment in the company of the wealthy is dearer to him than remembrance (of Allah) with the poor; he passes verdicts against others for his own interests and does not do so against himself for other's interests; he guides others but misguides himself; he is obeyed by others but he himself disobeys (Allah); he seeks fulfillment of obligations (towards himself) but does not fulfil his obligations (towards others); he fears the people (and acts) for other than his Lord (Allah) and does not fear his Lord in his dealings with the people. *Sayyid Razi says: If this book had contained nothing save this short utterance it would have sufficed as a successful piece of preaching, a specimen of high philosophy, an object of wisdom for the onlooker and a source of instruction for the meditative watcher.*

151 Every human being has to meet the end. sweet or sour.

152 Every comer has to return and after returning it is as though he never existed.

153 The endurer does not miss success although it may take a long time.

154 He who agrees with the action of a group of persons is as though he joins them in that action. And every one who joins in wrong commits two sins; one sin for committing the wrong and the other for agreeing with it.

155 Adhere to contracts and entrust their fulfillment to steadfast persons.

156 On you lies (the obligation of) obedience to the person about whom you cannot plead the excuse of ignorance.[1]

-1- Just as Allah sent down a series of prophets by way of His Justice and mercy to guide and direct towards religion, in the same way He laid down the system of the Imaama to protect religion from alteration and change so that every Imaam may in his time save the Divine teachings from the onslaught of personal desires and give directions about the correct precepts of Islam. And just as it is obligatory to know the originator of the religion (i.e., the Prophet) in the same way it is necessary to know the protector of the religion; and he who remains ignorant of him cannot be excused because the issue of Imaama is supported by so many proofs and testimonies that no intelligent person can find any way to deny it. Thus, the Holy Prophet has said:

Whoever dies without knowing the Imaam of his times dies a pre-Islamic (jahiliyya) death. (Sharh al-Maqaasid, at-Taftazaani ash-Shaafii, vol.2, p.275; al-Jawaahir al-Moziyya, al-Khateeb al-Hanafi, vol.2, pp.457, 509).

It has also been narrated by Abdillah bn-Omar Moaawiya bn-Abi-Sofyaan and Abdillah bn-Abbaas that the Messenger of Allah, peace be upon him and his descendants, said that:

One who dies without (knowing his) Imaam and binding himself by on oath of allegiance to him will die the death of one belonging to the days of jaahiliyya, and one who withdraws his hand from obedience (to the Imaam) will find no argument (in his defence) when he stands before Allah on the Day of Judgement. (al-Mosnad, at-Tayaalisi, p.259; as-Saheeh, Muslim, vol.6, pp.22; al-Mosnad, Ahmad bn-Hambal, vol.4, p.96; as-Sonan al-Kobra, al-Bayhaqi, vol.8, p.156; at-Tafseer, bn-Katheer, vol.1, p.517; Majma" az-zaw8id, vol.5, pp.218, 224, 225)

bn Abil-Hadeed also agrees that the personality about whom no one's ignorance can be excused is that of Ameer al-Momineen. He also acknowledges the obligation to obey him and holds that he who does not believe in the issue of Imaama will not achieve deliverance. In this connection he writes:

He who is ignorant of the position of Ali, peace be upon him, as Imaam and denies its veracity or obligatory character would, according to our associates, remain in Hell for ever, his fasting or prayers being of no avail to him, because the knowledge of this matter is among the basic principles which constitute the foundations of religion. However, we do not regard one who denies his Imaama as an unbeliever but only a sinner, a transgressor or a deviator, etc. (Sharh Nahjol-Balagha, vol.18, p.373)

157 Surely, you have been made to see if (only) you care to see; surely, you have been guided if (only) you care to take guidance; and surely, you have been made to hear if (only) you care to lend your ears.

158 Admonish your brother (comrade) by good behaviour towards him, and ward off his evil by favouring him.[1]

159 He who puts himself in conditions of ill-repute should not blame those who entertain bad ideas about him.

160 Whoever obtains authority (usually) adopts partiality.

161 He who acts solely according to his own opinion gets ruined, and he who consults other people shares in their understanding.

162 He who guards his secrets retains control in his own hands.

163 Destitution is the greatest death.

164 He who fulfils the right of a man who does not fulfil his right, (is as though he) worships him.

165 There should be no obeying anyone against Allah's commands.

166 No person is to be blamed for delay in (securing) his own right but blame lies on him who takes what he is not entitled to.

-1- If evil is done in return for evil, and abuse in return for abuse, the door for animosity and quarrel is opened. But if an evil-doer is met with kindness and gentleness he too would be compelled to change his behaviour. Thus, once Imaam Hasan was passing through the market place of Madeena when a Syrian noticing his majestic personality enquired from the people who he was and on being told that he was Hasan son of Ali (peace be upon him) he was exasperated and coming close to him began to abuse him. The Imaam heard him quietly. When he finished the Imaam said "You seem to be a stranger here." He acknowledged this and the Imaam continued "Then you had better come with me and stay with me. If you have any need I shall fulfil it, and if you need financial assistance I shall render it." When he saw this kindness and fine manners in return of his harsh and hard words he was extremely ashamed, and admitting his fault sought his forgiveness. When he left the Imaam, he did not have better regard for anyone else on the surface of the globe. (al-Kaamil, al-Mobarrad, vol.1, p.235; vol.2, p.63; Nehaaya fi al-Iraab, an-Nowayri, vol.6, p.52; Mataalib as-Saaidi, bn-Talha ash-Shaafii, vol.2, pp.11-12; al-Manaaqib, bn-Shahraashoob, vol.4, p.19; al-Bihaar, al-Majlisi, vol.43, p.344)
If you are a proper human being do good to the evil-doer.

167 Vanity prevents progress.[1]

168 The Day of Judgement is near and our mutual company is short.

169 For the man who has eyes the dawn has already appeared.

170 Abstention from sin is easier than seeking help afterwards.[2]

171 Many a single eating prevents several eatings.[3]

172 People are enemies of what they do not know.[4]

173 He who has several opinions understands the pitfalls.

174 He who sharpens he teeth of anger for the sake of Allah acquires the strength to kill the stalwarts of wrong.[5]

-1- A person who seeks perfection and believes that he is still in need of it can be expected to attain the aim of perfection, but a person who is under the illusion that he has reached the zenith of progress and perfection will not feel the need to strive to attain it, but according to his own view he has already traversed all the stages of perfection and now he has no stage in sight to strive for. Thus, this vain and illusioned man will always remain deprived of perfection and this vanity will end all possibility of his rise.

-2- It is not as difficult to keep aloof from sin the first time as it is after becoming familiar with it and tasting it, because a man does not feel difficulty in doing a thing to which he has become habituated, but it is really hard to give it up. As habits become confirmed, the conscience becomes weaker and difficulties crop up in the way of repentance. To console the heart by postponing repentance is therefore usually without avail. Surely, when there is difficulty in keeping off sin even in the beginning the lengthening of the period of sins will make repentance still more difficult.

-3- This is a proverb which is used when a man runs after one advantage so vehemently that he has to give up several other advantages, like the man who eats too much or against his appetite and has to go subsequently without several meals.

-4- A man attaches great importance to the science and art which he knows and regards that science of no importance which he does not know, and belittles it. This is because whenever such a matter is discussed he is regarded not worthy of attention and is ignored, and thereby he feels slighted. This slight pains him, and a man naturally dislikes a thing that pains him and hates it. In this connection, Plato was asked "What is the reason that he who does not know hates him who does know, but he who knows does not bear malice or hatred towards him who does not know?" He replied "He who does not know realises that he suffers from a defect and thinks that he who knows must regard him low and humble on account of this defect, so he hates him. On the other hand he who knows does not have the idea that he who does not know should regard him low and so there is no reason why he should hate him.

-5- The person who rises to face wrong for the sake of Allah is afforded support and assistance from Allah and, despite lack of power and means, the forces of wrong cannot shake his determination or create a tremor in his steady feet. But if there is a tinge of personal benefit in his action he can be very easily prevented from his aim.

175 When you are afraid of something dive straight into it, because the intensity of abstaining from it is greater (worse) than what you are afraid of.

176 The means to secure high authority is breadth of chest (i. e., generosity).

177 Rebuke the evil-doer by rewarding the good-doer.[1]

178 Cut away evil from the chest of others by snatching (it) away from your own chest.[2]

179 Stubbornness destroys (good) advice.

180 Greed is a lasting slavery.

181 The result of neglect is shame, while the result of far-sightedness is safety.

182 There is no advantage in keeping quiet about an issue of wisdom, just as there is no good in speaking out an unintelligent thing.

183 If there are two different calls then one (of them) must be towards misguidance.

184 I have never entertained doubt about right since I was shown it.

185 I have neither spoken a lie nor have I been told a lie. I have neither deviated nor have I been made to deviate (others).

186 He who takes the lead in oppression has to bite his hand (in repentance) tomorrow.

187 The departure (from this world) is imminent.

-1- This means that the giving of full reward to the virtuous for their good actions and appreciating them puts the evil-doers also on the right path. This is more effective than ethical preaching, warning and rebuke. This is because by temperament man inclines towards things from which benefits accrue to him, and his ears (yearn to) resound with eulogies in praise and admiration of him.

-2- This sentence can be interpreted in two ways. One is that if you bear malice against anyone, he too will bear malice against you. Therefore, destroy the malice from his heart by removing it from your heart, since your heart is the index of other's heart. If your heart will have no malice there will remain no malice in his heart too. That is why a man assesses the purity of another person's heart by the purity of his own heart. Thus, a man asked his friend "How much do you love me?" and the reply was "4Ask your own heart." That is "I love you as much as you love me.

The second interpretation is that if you want to dissuade another person from evil, first you should refrain yourself from that evil. In this way, your advice can be effective on others, otherwise it will remain ineffective.

188 Whoever turned away from right was ruined.

189 If patience does not give relief to a man impatience kills him.

190 How strange? Could the caliphate be through the (Prophet's) companionship but not through (his) companionship and (his) kinship?

Sayyid Razi says: Verses have also been related from Ameer al-Momineen on the same matter. They are:-

If you claim to have secured authority by consultation, how did it happen when those be consulted were absent! If you have scored over your opponents by kinship then someone else has greater right for being nearer to the Holy Prophet.[1]

-1- bn-Abil-Hadeed (Izzoddeen Abdl-Hameed bn-Hibatillah al-Motazili (586/1190 655/12571) says:

The saying of Ameer al-Momineen in the form of prose and poetry was intended for Abi-Bakr and Omar. In his prose he addressed Omar, because when Abi-Bakr asked Omar (on the day of Saqeefa): "Give me your hand so that I may swear allegiance to you." Omar replied "You are the companion of the Messenger of Allah in all circumstances-comfort and hardship. So, give me your hand.

Ali, peace be upon him, says (with regard to the claim of Omar) that:

If you give arguments in favour of the Abi- Bakr's deserving the caliphate on the basis of his being the companion of the Holy Prophet in all circumstances, then why did you not hand over the caliphate to one (i.e., Ameer al-Momineen) who shares with him (Abi-Bakr) in this matter, and who had superiority over him by having a relation of kinship with the Holy Prophet?

In his poetry, Ameer al-Momineen addressed Abi-Bakr, because he argued with the Ansaar at Saqeefa saying; "We (the Quraysh) are the kin of the Messenger of Allah and the seed from which he sprung, (therefore, we are the most deserving people to succeed him).

After allegiance was sworn to Abi-Bakr (by a small group at Saqeefa) he used to argue with the Muslims that they must accept his caliphate since it had been accepted by the ahlol-halli wa al-Agd (the group who can tie and untie a matter — i.e., those who were present at Saqeefa).

Ali, peace be upon him, says (with regard to the claim of Abi-Bakr) that:

Regarding your argument with the Ansaar that you are from the seed from which the Messenger of Allah sprung, and one of his tribe, there is other one (i.e. Ameer al-Momineen himself) who has the nearest relation of kinship to the Holy Prophet. And concerning your argument that you have been accepted by the consultation of the companions of the Holy Prophet (whom you mean by ahlol-hali wal-aqd), how did it happen that most of the companions were absent (on the day of Saqeefa) and did not swear allegiance to you." (Sharh Nahjol-Balagha, vol.18, p.416)

191 In this world man is the target towards which the arrows of death fly, and is like that wealth whose destruction is quickened by hardships. (In this world) with every drink there is suffocation and with every morsel there is chocking. Here no one gets anything unless he loses something else, and not a day of his age advances till a day passes out from his life. Thus, we are helpers of death and our lives are the targets of mortality. How then can we expect everlasting life since the night and day do not raise anything high without quickly arranging for the destruction of whatever they have built and for the splitting asunder of whatever they have joined together.

192 O son of Adam, whatever you earn beyond your basic needs you will only keep vigil over it for others.

193 Hearts are imbued with passion and the power of advancing and retreating. Therefore, approach them for action at the time of their passionateness and when they are in a mood for advancing, because if hearts are forced (to do a thing) they will be blinded.

194. Ameer al-Momineen, peace be upon him, used to say: If I am angry when shall I vent my anger-when I am unable to take revenge and it be said to me "better you endure" or when I have power to take revenge and it be said to me "better forgive?

195. Ameer al-Momineen, peace be upon him, passed beside a dump of rubbish full of filth and remarked:

This is what the misers used to be niggardly about. In another tradition it is related that he said: This is what you used to dispute with each other about until yesterday!

196 The wealth that teaches you lesson does not go waste.[1]

-1- The person who gains a lesson and experience by spending money and wealth should not lament its loss but should deem the experience more valuable than the wealth because wealth is an any case wasted away while the experience will protect him against the dangers of the future. Thus, a scholar who had become destitute after having been wealthy was asked what had happened to his wealth and he replied: "I have purchased experiences with it and they proved more useful than the wealth. After losing all that I had, I have not been in the loss.

197 The hearts become tired as the bodies become tired. You should therefore search for beautiful sayings for them (to enjoy by way of refreshment).

198. When Ameer al-Momineen, peace be upon him, heard the slogan of the Kharijites: There is no verdict save of Allah, he said: This sentence is true but it is interpreted wrongly.

199 About the crowd of people:

These are the people who, when they assemble together, are overwhelming but when they disperse they cannot be recognised.

These are the people who when they assemble together cause harm but when they disperse are beneficial.

It was pointed out to him: We know their harm at the time of their assembling but what is their benefit at the time of their dispersal? Then he replied:

The workers return to their work and people get benefit out of them, like the return of the mason to the building site, that of the weaver to his loom, and that of the baker to his bakery.

200. An offender was brought before Ameer al-Momineen, peace be upon him, and there was a crowd of people with the man, so Ameer al-Momineen remarked:

Woe to the faces who are seen only on foul occasions.

201. Ameer al-Momineen,-peace be upon him, said: With every individual there are two angels who protect him; when destiny approaches they let it have its own way with him. Certainly, the appointed time is a protective shield (against the events which occur before it).

202. When Talha and az-Zobayr said to him: We are prepared to swear allegiance to you on condition that we have a share with you in this matter (of caliphate), No, but you will have a share in strengthening (the caliphate) and in affording assistance and you will both be helping me at the time of need and hardship.

203. O people, fear Allah Who is such that when you speak He hears and when you conceal (a secret) He knows it. Prepare yourself to meet death

which will overtake you even if you run away, catch you even if you stay and remember you even if you forget it.

204. If someone is not grateful to you, that should not prevent you from good actions, because (possibly) such a person will feel grateful about it who has not even drawn any benefit from it, and his gratefulness will be more than ingratitude of the denier; And Allah loves those who do good. (Quraan, 3:134,148; 5:93)

205. Every container gets narrower according to what is placed in it except knowledge which expands instead.

206 The first reward the exerciser of forbearance gets is that people become his helpers against the ignorant.

207. If you cannot forbear, feign to do so because it is seldom that a man likens himself to a group and does not become as one of them.[1]

208 Whoever takes account of his self is benefited, and whoever remains neglectful of it suffers. Whoever fears remains safe; whoever takes instruction (from things around) gets light; and whoever gets light gets understanding, and whoever gets understanding secures knowledge.

209 The world will bend towards us after having been refractory as the biting she-camel bends towards its young. [2]

Then Ameer al-Momineen recited the verse;

And intend We bestow (Our) favour upon those who were considered weak in the land! and to make them the Imams (guides in faith), and to make them the heirs. (Quraan, 28:5)

-1- It means that if a person is not temperamentally forbearant he should try to be so in the sense that he should put up a show of forbearance against his temperament. Although he may feel some difficulty in curbing his temperament, the result will be that by and by forbearance will become his temperamental trait and then no need to feign will remain, because habit slowly develops into second nature.

-2- This saying is about the awaited Imaam who is the last of the series of Imaams. On his emergence all states and governments will come to an end, and the complete picture referred to in the verse will appear before the eyes,

Whoever wants to may rule in this world but in the end the rule will be in the hands of the descendants of Ali (peace be upon them).

210 Fear Allah like the one who prepares himself after extracting himself (from worldly affairs) and after getting ready in this way makes effort; then he acts quickly during the period of this life, hastens in view of the dangers (of falling into error) and has his eye on proceeding towards the goal, on the end of his journey and on the place of his (eventual) return.

211 Generosity is the protector of honour; forbearance is the bridle of the fool; forgiveness is the levy of success; disregard is the punishment of him who betrays; and consultation is the chief way of guidance. He who is content with his own opinion faces danger. Endurance braves calamities while impatience is a helper of the hardships of the world. The best contentment is to give up desires. Many a slavish mind is subservient to overpowering longings. Capability helps preservation of experience. Love means well-utilised relationship. Do not trust one who is grieved.

212 A man's vanity for himself is one of the enemies of his intelligence.[1]

213 Ignore pain otherwise you will never be happy. (Or according to another reading): Ignore pain and grief; you will ever be happy.[2]

214 The tree whose trunk is soft has thick branches.[3]

215 Opposition destroys good counsel.

216 He who gives generously achieves position. (Or according to another interpretation): He who achieves position begins to make wrong use of it.

-1- It means that just as an envious person cannot appreciate any good in him whom he envies, similarly, vanity cannot tolerate the emergence of intelligence or the prominence of good qualities as a result of which the envious person remains devoid of those qualities which are deemed to be good by human intellect.

-2- Every individual has some shortcomings or other. If a person keeps aloof from others because of their faults and weakness, he will, by and by, lose all his friends and become lonely and forlorn in this world and thus his life will become bitter and his worries will multiply. At such a moment he should realise that in this society he cannot get angels with whom he may never have any cause of complaint, that he has to live among these very people and to pass his life with them. Therefore, as far as possible he should ignore their shortcomings and pay no regard to the troubles inflicted by them.

-3- The person who is haughty and ill-tempered can never succeed in making his surroundings pleasant. His acquaintances will feel wretched and sick of him. But if a person is good-tempered and sweet-tongued people will like to get close to him and befriend him. At the time of need they will prove to be his helpers and supporters whereby he can make his life a success.

217. Through change of circumstances the mettle of men is known.
218 Jealousy by a friend means defect in his love.
219. Most of the deficiency of intelligence occurs due to the flash of greed.[1]
220 There is no justice in passing a verdict by relying on probability.
221. The worst provision for the Day of Judgement is high-handedness over people.
222. The highest act of a noble person is to ignore what he knows.
223 Whomever modesty clothes with its dress people cannot see his defects.[2]
224 Excess of silence produces awe; justice results in more close friends; generosity hightens position; with humility blessings abound in plenty; by facing hardships leadership is achieved; by just behaviour the adversary is overpowered; and with forbearance against a fool there is increase of one's supporters against him.
225 It is strange that the jealous do not feel jealous about bodily health.[3]

-1- When a man falls into greed and avarice, he gets entangled in evils like bribery, theft, misappropriation, usury and other immoral acts of this type, while the mind is so dazzled with the brilliance of the evil desires that it fails to see the ill effects and consequences of those bad deeds and to prevent him from them or awaken him from his slumber of unmindfulness. Nevertheless, when he prepares to depart from this world and finds that whatever he had amassed was for this world only and that he cannot take it with him, then, and only then his eyes Bet opened.

-2- If a person adorns himself with the quality of modesty then it prevents him from committing evil acts. Therefore, he has no evil for the people to find in him. Even if a bad act is ever committed by him he does not commit it openly because of his feeling of modesty lest the people notice him.

-3- A jealous person feels jealous of the property and position of others but not of their health and physical power, although this blessing is the best of all others. The reason is that the effects of wealth and riches remain before the eyes through external pageantry and means of ease and comfort, whereas health is the victim of disregard for being a routine matter, and it is regarded so unimportant that a jealous person does not consider it worth his feeling of jealousy.

Thus, if he sees a labourer carrying a burden on his head all day he does not feel envious, as if health and energy is not an object of envy. Nevertheless, when he himself falls ill he realises the value and worth of healthiness. It is now that he realises that it was this health which till now carried no importance in his eyes but was the most deserving to be envied. The intention is that one should regard health as a highly valuable blessing and remain attentive towards its protection and care.

226 The greedy is in the shackles of disgrace.

227. When asked about belief

Belief means appreciation with the heart, acknowledgement with the tongues and action with the limbs.

228 He who is sorrowful for this world is in fact displeased with the dispensation of Allah. He who complains of a calamity that befalls him complains of his Lord (Allah). He who approaches a rich man and bends before him on account of his riches then two-third of his religion is gone. If a man reads the Quraan and on dying goes to Hell then it means that he was among those who treated Divine verses with mockery. If a man's heart gets attached to the world, then it catches three things, namely worry that never leaves him, greed that does not abandon him and desire which he never fulfils.

229 Contentment is as good as estate, and goodness of moral character is as good as a blessing.

230. Ameer al-Momineen, peace be upon him, was asked about Allah's saying: (Whosoever did good. whether male or female, and he be a believer, then); We will certainly make him live a life good and pure (and certainly We will give them their return with the best of what they were doing). (Quraan. 16:97) when he said: that means contentment.[1]

231 Be a sharer with him who has an abundant livelihood because he is more probable to get more riches and likely to secure an increase of the share therein.

-1- The reason for calling goodness of moral character a blessing is that just as blessing brings forth pleasure, in the same way a man can make his environment pleasant by endearing others" hearts through goodness of moral character and can thus succeed in procuring ways for his happiness and ease And contentment has been regarded as capital and estate for the reason that just as the estate and area under sway dispels need in the same way when a man adopts contentment and feels happy over his livelihood he becomes free of turning to others in the time of need.

Whoever is contented with the morsel he gets, dry or wet, is the king of all the land and sea.

232. About Allah's: Verily, Allah enjoins justice (adl) and benevolence (ihsaan) (Quraan, 16:9). Here "adl means equidistribution and ihsaan means favour.

233 He who gives with his short hand is given by a long hand.

Sayyid Razi says: The meaning of this saying is that even though what a man spends in charity from his possessions may be small, yet Allah, the Sublime, gives good reward for it. And the two hands referred to, here means two favours. Thus, Ameer al-Momineen has differentiated between the favour of man and the favour of the Lord (Allah) — exalted be the mention of His name — since he has described the first as small and the other as big. This is because the favours of Allah are ever multiplied manifold to the favours of man since Allah's favours are basic in the sense that every other favour springs from it and turns to it.

234. Ameer al-Momineen said to his son al-Hasan, peace be upon them both: Do not call out for fighting, but if you are called to it do respond, because the caller to fighting is a rebel and the rebel deserves destruction.[1]

235 The best traits of women are those which are the worst traits of men, namely: vanity, cowardice and miserliness. Thus since the woman is vain, she will not allow anyone access to herself; since she is miserly, she will preserve he own property and the property of her husband; all since she is weak-hearted, she will be frightened with everything that befalls her.

236. It was said to Ameer al-Momineen, peace be upon him: Describe the wise to us; and he said: The wise is one who places things in their proper

-1- The meaning of this is that if the enemy aims at fighting and takes the initiative in it, then one should advance to face him, but one should not initiate the attack because this would be clear high-handedness and excess, and whoever commits high-handedness and excess will be disgracefully vanquished and thrown down. That is why Ameer al-Momineen always entered the battlefield on being challenged by the enemy. He never offered the challenge from his side. In this connection, bn-Abil-Hadeed writes:

We have never heard that Ameer al-Momineen ever challenged anyone for confrontation. Rather, when either he was particularly challenged or the enemy flung a general challenge, then alone he should go out to meet the enemy and would kill him. (Sharh Nahjol-Balagha, vol.I9, p.60)

positions. Then, he was asked: Describe the ignorant to us; and he said: I have already done so.

Sayyid Razi says: The meaning is that the ignorant is one who does not place things in their proper positions. In this way, Ameer al-Momineen abstention from describing was a way of describing him because his attributes are just the opposite of the wise.

237 By Allah, this world of yours is more lowly in my view than the (left over) bone of a pig in the hand of a leper.

238 A group of people worshipped Allah out of desire for reward surely, this is the worship of traders. Another group worshipped Allah out of fear, this is the worship of slaves. Still another group worshipped Allah out of gratefulness, this is the worship of free men.

239. Woman is evil, all in all; and the worst of it is that one cannot do without her.

240. He who is a sluggard loses his rights and he who believes in the backbiter loses his friend.

241 One ill-gotten piece of stone in a house is a guarantee for its ruin.

Sayyid Razi says: In one tradition this saying is attributed to the prophet. It is no wonder that the two sayings should resemble each other because they are driven from the same source and dispersed through the same means.

242 The day of the oppressed over the oppressor will be severer than the day of the oppressor over the oppressed.[1]

-1- It is easy to bear oppression in this world but it is not easy to face its punishment in the next world, because the period of bearing oppression even though life-long is after all limited; but the punishment for oppression is Hell whose most fearful aspect is that life there will last for ever and death will not save from punishment. That is why, if an oppressor kills someone then with that killing the oppression comes to and end, and there is no further scope for any further oppression on the same person; but its punishment is that he is thrown in Hell where he suffers his punishment.

The Persian couplet says:

The effect of the oppression on us has passed away, but it will ever remain on the oppressor.

243 Fear Allah to some degree (even) though it be little; and set a curtain between you and Allah (even) though it be thin.

244 When replies are numerous the correct point remain obscure.[1]

245 Surely in every blessing there is a right of Allah. If one discharges that right Allah increases the blessing, and if one falls short of doing so one stands in danger of losing the blessing.

246 When capability increases, desire decreases.

247 Keep on guard against the slipping away of blessings because not everything that runs away comes back.

248 Generosity is more prompting to good than regard for kinship.

249 If a person has a good idea about you make his idea be true.

250 The best act is that which you have to force yourself to do.

251 I came to know Allah, the Glorified, through the breaking of determinations, change of intentions and losing of courage.[2]

252 The sourness of this world is the sweetness of the next world while the sweetness of this world is the sourness of the next one.

253 Allah has laid down Imam (belief) for purification from polytheism; salat (prayer) for purification from vanity; zakat (levy) as a means of livelihood; siyaam (fasting) as a trial of the people; Haj (pilgrimage to the House of Allah in Mecca) as a support for religion; jihad (fighting in the way of Allah) for the honour of Islam; persuasion for good (al-Amr bill-maroof) for the

-1- If replies to a question begin to be given from all sides, every reply will raise another question and thus open the door for arguing, and as the number of replies will further necessitate search for the real truth, detection of the correct reply will become more and more arduous, because everyone will try to have his reply accepted as correct as a result of which he will try to collect arguments from here and there to have his reply accepted as correct as a result of which the whole matter will become confused and this dream will turn into an aimless one because of the multiplicity of interpretations.

-2- The breaking of determinations and losing of courage can be argued to prove the existence of Allah in this way that, for example, a man determines to do a thing but before the determination is transformed into action, it changes and some other idea takes its place. This alteration of ideas and determinations and the emergence of change therein is a proof that there is some higher controlling power over us which has the capacity to bring them from non-existence to existence and again from existence into non-existence, and this is what is beyond human power. Therefore, it is necessary to acknowledge a super authority who effects change and alteration in determinations.

good of the common people; dissuasion from evil (an-nahy "anil-monkar) for the control of the mischievous; regard for kinship for increase of number; revenge for stoppage of bloodshed; the award of penalties for the realisation of importance of the prohibitions; the abstinence from drinking wine for protection of the wit; the avoidance of theft for inculcating chastity; abstinence from adultery for safeguarding descent; abstinence from sodomy for increase of progeny; tendering evidence for furnishing proof against contentions; abstinence from the lie for increasing esteem for truth; maintenance of peace (salam) for protection from danger; Imaama (Divine Leadership) for the orderliness of the community and obedience (to Imams) as a mark of respect to the Imaama.[1]

-1- Before describing some of the aims and good points of the commands of the sharia (i.e., religious law), Ameer al-Momineen has began with the aims and objects of Belief (Emaan), because Emaan serves as the basis of religious commands, and without it no need is felt for any religious code or jurisprudence. Emaan is the name of acknowledging the existence of the Creator and admission of His Singularity. When this Emaan takes root in the heart of a man then he does not agree to bow before any other being, nor is he over-awed or affected by any power or authority. Rather, getting mentally freed of all ties he regards himself a devotee of Allah and the result of this adherence to the Unity is that he is saved from the pollution of polytheism.

Prayer (salat) is the most important of all forms of worship. It consists of standing, sitting, bending and prostration, and these postures are a successful way of destroying the feeling of vanity and pride, erasing self-conceit and egotism and creating humility and submissiveness, because the actions and movements of a vain person produce pride and haughtiness while humble actions engender the quality of submissiveness and humbleness in the mind. With the exercise of these acts a man, by and by, acquires a humble temperament. This is how the Arabs who were so vain that if their whip fell off during riding they would not bend down to pick it up or if the strap of the shoe gave way they thought it insulting to bend down to mend it, began to rub their faces on dust during prostration in prayers, and place their foreheads in the position of others" feet during the congregational prayer, and in this way acquired the true spirit of Islam after abandoning the pre-Islamic vanity and partisanship.

zakat, namely that a person who is able to do so should pay annually out of his money or property a fixed share for those who are either destitute or do not have means of livelihood for a year, is an obligatory command of Islam, the purpose behind which is that no individual in the community should remain poor and they should remain safe from the evils that result from need and poverty. Besides, another objective is that wealth should keep rotating from one individual to another and should not be centred in a few persons.

Fasting (siyaam) is a form worship in which there is not an iota of show, and no motive is active in it except that of pure intention. As a result, even in seclusion when hunger perturbs a man or thirst makes him uneasy he does not extend his hand for eating, nor does the longing for water make him lose his control although if something is eaten or drunk no one is to peep into his stomach, but the purity of conscience prevents his will from deflecting. This is the greatest good of fasting that it engenders purity of will in action.

The purpose of Haj (pilgrimage to the House of Allah) is that Muslims from all corners of the globe should assemble at one place so that this world assembly should prove to be an occasion for the manifestation of Islam's greatness, the renewal of the passion for worship and the creation of bonds of mutual brotherhood.

The purpose of Jihaad (fighting in the way of Allah) is to fight with all possible might those forces which oppose Islam, so that Islam may achieve stability and progress. Although there are dangers for life in this course and difficulties crop up at every step, yet the tidings for eternal ease and everlasting life produce the courage to bear all these hardships.

The persuasion for good and dissuasion from evil are effective ways of showing others the correct path and preventing them from wrong. If a community has no persons to perform these duties nothing can save it from ruin and it falls to an extreme depth morally and socially. That is why Islam has laid great stress on it as compared to other matters, and held disregard to it as an unpardonable sin.

Doing good for kinship means that a man should do favours to his relatives and at least should not stop mutual accosting and speaking with them so that spirits may become clean and family ties may develop, and the scattered individuals may render strength to one another.

Seeking vengeance is a right given to the survivors of the person killed. They can demand a life for a life so that for fear of punishment no one would dare kill any person, and at the same time the survivor's passion for revenge should not result in the killing of more than one person. No doubt forgiveness or pardon does carry weight in its own place but where it means trampling of an individual's right or a danger to world peace it cannot be regarded as good. Rather, on such an occasion revenge is the sole way of stopping bloodshed and killing for the safety of human life. Thus, Allah says:

And for you there is (security of) Retaliation O you men of understanding, so that you may guard yourself (against evil). (Quraan, 2:179)

The purpose behind the awarding of penalties is to make the offender appreciate the seriousness of violating the prohibitions of Allah so that he may keep off the prohibitions for fear of punishments.

Wine causes diffusion of thinking, dispersion of senses and weakness of understanding. As a result, a man commits such actions which would not be expected of him in the state of being in his senses. Besides, it ruins health and renders the body liable to catch infectious diseases while, sleeplessness, nervous weakness and rheumatism are its chief effects. The sharia has prohibited it in view of these ill-effects.

Theft, that is, taking over someone else's property is an evil habit which is produced by the sway of greed and evil passions and since bringing down evil passions from the position of excess to the bounds of moderation means chastity the abstinence from theft by curbing greed and evil passions would produce chastity.

Adultery and sodomy have been prohibited in order that lineage may be regulated and the human race may continue and prosper, because the issues by adultery are not regarded legitimate for the purposes of lineage and consequently they are not entitled to inheritance, while there is no question of issues in the case of unnatural practices. Besides, as a consequence of these evil practices one contracts such diseases which cause ruination of life in addition to discontinuity of progeny.

The law of evidence is needed because if one party denies the right of another party the latter may establish it through evidence and safeguard it thereby.

Abstention from lies and falsehood has been commanded so that the standing and importance of its contrary namely truth may become prominent and in observing the benefits and advantages of truth the moral weakness of falsehood may be avoided.

salaam means peace and peace-loving and it is obvious that peaceful attitude is a successful way of protection from dangers and prevention of war and fighting. Generally, commentators have taken the word salam to mean mutual greetings and well-wishing but the context and the fact that it has been mentioned in the series of obligations does not support this interpretation. However, according to this interpretation salaam is a means of safety from dangers because it is regarded as a way of peace and peace-loving. When two Muslims meet each other they offer salam one to the other, it means that they announce the wishes of each for the welfare of the other whereafter each feels safe with the other.

Imaama (Imaama): This word has appeared in the same form in the correct copies of Nahjol-Balagha as well as in its commentaries like bn-Abil-Hadeed, vol.19, p.90. bn-Maytham, vol.5, pp.367-378; Minhaaj al-Baraa, vol.21, p.318; and other sources besides Nahjol-Balagha such as Nehaaya al-Iraab by an-Nowayri ash-Shaafii, vol.8, p.183 and al-Bihaar by al-Majlisi, vol.6, p.111.

In fact, this word of "Imaama" has been distorted to "amaana" (trust) or "amaanaat" (trusts) in some copies such as those printed in Egypt. It is very surprising to note that the word has appeared as amaana in the text of Nahjol-Balagha printed with the commentary of bn-Abil-Hadeed in Egypt in the first edition vol.4, p.350 as well as in the second edition edited by Mohammad Abol-Fazl Ibraheem, vol.19, p.86; while he himself (bn Abil-Hadeed) based his commentary on its correct reading namely Imaama as did other commentators.

However, in explanation of this sentence "Imaama for the orderliness of the community," as the theological scholars say:

Whoever has known dark experiences and has examined political principles knows, of necessity, that whenever men have among them a chief and a guide whom they obey, who restrains the oppressor from his oppression and the unjust man from his injustice

254. Ameer al-Momineen, peace be upon him, used to say: If you want an oppressor to take an oath ask him to swear like this that he is out of Allah's might and His power, because if he swears falsely in this way he will be quickly punished, while if he swears by Allah Who is such that there is no god but He, he will not be quickly punished since he is expressing the Unity of Allah, the Sublime.[1]

---

and avenges the oppressed of his oppressor, and along with that leads them to rational principles and religious duties, and restrains them from the corruptions which cause the destruction of order in their worldly affairs, and from the evils which result in wretchedness in the world to come, so that every individual might fear that punishment, then because of this they will draw near to soundness and depart from corruption. (al-Baabol-Haadi Ashar, Engl. transl. p.63)

The institution of Imaama is intended to cater for the unification of the nation and to protect the commandments of Islam from alteration and change, because if there is no head of the nation and no protector of religion neither can the order of the nation be maintained nor can the commandments of Islam remain safe from interference by others. This object can be achieved only when obedience to him is obligatory on the people, because if he is not obeyed and followed as an obligation he will neither be able to maintain justice and equity, nor secure the rights of the oppressed from the oppressor, nor issue and enforce the laws of the sharia and consequently the extinction of evil and mischief from the world cannot be expected.

-1- It is narrated that someone levied some charges against Imaam Jafar as-Saadiq before the Abbaasid Caliph Abdillah bn-Mohammad al-Mansoor. al-Mansoor sent for the Imaam and told him that such and such a person had told him such and such about him. The Imaam said it was all wrong and there was not an iota of truth therein, and desired the man to be sent for and questioned before him. Consequently, he was sent for and questioned. He said that whatever he had said was true and correct. The Imaam said to him "If you are speaking the truth then you swear as I ask you to swear." Thereafter, the Imaam made him swear by saying "I am out of Allah's might and power and I rely on my own might and power." Soon after swearing like this he got an attack of paralysis and he became motionless. The Imaam, returned with full honour and prestige. (al-Kaafi; al-Kolayni, vol.6, pp.445-446; al-Bihaar vol.47, pp.164-165, 172-175, 203-2Q4; al-Fosool al-Mohimma, bn-as-Sabbagh al-Maaliki, pp.225-226; as-Sawaaiq al-Mohriqa, bn-H. ajar ash-Shaafii, p.120; Jaami Karaamaat al-Awliyaa, an-Nabhaani ash-Shaafii, vol.2, p.4).

Such an event took place again during the reign of Haroon ar-Rasheed (149/766-193/809-the grandson of al-Mansoor) when Abdillah bn-Mosab (the grandson of Abdillah bn-az-Zobayr — the well-known enemy of Ahlil-Bayt of the Holy Prophet) slandered Yahya bn-Abdillah bn-Hasan bn-(al-Imaam) al-Hasan bn-Ali bn-Abi-Talib before Haroon ar-Rasheed by saying that he was plotting a revolution against him (Haroon). Then Yahya made Abdillah swear before Haroon in the same manner as the Imaam had done. When

255 O son of Adam, be your own representative in the matter of your property and do about it whatever you want to be done with it after your death.[1]

256. Ameer al-Momineen, peace be upon him, to said: Anger is a kind of madness because the victim to it repents afterwards. If he does not repent his madness is confirmed.

257 Health of body comes from paucity of envy.[2]

258. To Komayl bn-Ziyad an-Nakhaai:

O Komayl, direct your people to go out in the day to achieve noble traits and to go out in the night to meet the needs of those who might be sleeping, for I swear by Him Whose hearing extends to all voices if ever someone pleases another's heart, Allah will create a special thing out of this pleasing so that whenever any hardship befalls him it will come running like flowing water and drive away the hardship as wild camels are driven away.

259 When you fall in destitution, trade with Allah through charity.

260 Faithfulness with faithless people is faithlessness with Allah, while faithlessness with faithless people is faithfulness with Allah.

Abdillah swore as he was required to, the symptom of leprosy soon appeared in him in the presence of Haroon and he died after three days, while every part of his flesh cracked open and all the hair of his body fell out. After this, Haroon used to say "How soon Allah took revenge on Abdillah for Yahya!" (Maqaatil at-Talibiyyeen, Abol-Faraj al-Isfahaani, pp.472-478; Morooj az-Zahab, al-Masoodi, vol.3, pp.340-342; Taareekh Baghdad, al-Khateeb, vol.14, pp.115/12; bn-Abil-Hadeed, vol.19, pp.91-94; at-Taareekh, bn-Katheer, vol.10, pp.167-168; Taareekh al-Kholafaa, as-Seyooti, p.287).

-1- The meaning of it is that if a person desires that after his death a portion of his property should be spent on charity, he should not wait for his death but spend it wherever he desires even during his lifetime; for it is possible that after his death his successors may not act upon his will or he may not get an opportunity to will.

A Persian couplet says:

Give away money and property while you are living as after you it would be out of your control.

-2- Envy produces such a poisonous matter in the body which destroys the natural heat of the body as a result of which the body weakens and the spirit withers. That is why an envious person never prospers and melts away in the heart of envy.

261 There is many a man being gradually brought towards punishment by good treatment with him; many a man who remains in deceit because his evils are covered; and many a man who is in illusion because of good talk about him, while there is no greater ordeal by Allah, the Glorified, than the giving of time.

Sayyid Razi says: This saying has appeared earlier as well but here it contains a beautiful and useful addition.

Section wherein we have included selections from wonderful sayings of Ameer al-Momineen, peace be upon him, which require explanation

262-1. A tradition related from Ameer al-Momineen, peace be upon him, says:

When the situation is like this, then the head of the religion will rise and people will gather around him as pieces of rainless cloud collect during autumn.

Sayyid Razi says: "yaasoob[1] is the great chief who is in charge of the people's affairs, and "quza" means the pieces of cloud which have no rain.

-1- "yaasoob" is the name given to the queen bee, and the saying of Ameer al-Momineen is: "fa iza kana zalika zaraba yaasoobideen bi zanabihi. The word "zaraba" means to beat, strike, hit, etc.; "yasoobideen" means "the head of religion and the shareeaa, and "zanab" means tail, end, adherent or flower. In this sentence "yaasoobiddeen" stands for the present Imaam (al-Imaam al-Mahdi). Although this title was given by the Holy Prophet to Ameer al-Momineen specially, as he said:

O Ali, you are the yaasoob (head) of the believers while wealth is the yaasoob of the hypocrites. (al-Isteeaab, vol.4, p.1744; Osdol-Ghaaba, vol.5, p.287; al-Isaaba, vol.4, p.171; ar-Riyaaz an-Nazira, vol.2, p.155; Majma" az-Zawaaid, vol.9, p.102; bn-Abil-Hadeed, vol.1, p.12; vol.19, p.22).

Also the Holy Prophet said to Ali:

You are the yasoob of the religion. (ar-Riyaaz an-Nazira, vol.2, p.177; Taaj al-Aroos, vol.1, p.381; bn-Abil-Hadeed, vol.1, p.12; vol.19, p.224) Also the Holy Prophet said to Ali: You are the yaasoob of the Muslims (Yanaabee al-Mawadda, al-Qundoozi, p.62)

Again the Holy Prophet said:

You are the yaasoob of the Quraysh (al-Maqaasid al-Hasana, as-Sakhaawi, p.94).

Therefore, the reason for giving the Imaam this name is that just as the queen bee is pure alone and in the society of otter bees, and she collects her nectar from the blossoms and flowers keeping away from pollution, in the same way the present Imaam is free from all pollutions and is perfectly clean and pure. This saying has been interpreted in several ways:

263-2. A tradition of Ameer al-Momineen, peace be upon him, says: He is a versatile speaker.[1]

Sayyid Razi says: 'shahshah" means one expert and free in speech, and every one who is free in speech or walking is called 'shahshah" while in another sense this word means a miserly and niggardly person.

264-3. A tradition from Ameer al-Momineen, peace be upon him, says: Quarrels bring about ruin.

Sayyid Razi says: "quhm" means ruin because quarrels often drive men into ruin and grief. In the same way, it is said "quhmatul-Arab" which means the period (of drought) when the cattle owned by the nomad desert Arabs are reduced to bones, and this is their being driven to it. Another argument is also advanced in this matter; namely that hardship of the desert life drives them to hazar (a civilised region with town and villages and a settled population (as opposed to desert)).

265-4. A tradition of Ameer al-Momineen, peace be upon him, says:

When girls reach the stage of (realising) realities, relations on the father's side are preferable.

Sayyid Razi says: Instead of "nassol-hiqaq" the combination "nassal-haqaaiq" has also been related. "nass" means the last end of things or their remotest limit, such as "an-nassi feeder" means the maximum a

---

Firstly, it means that "when the present Imaam settles at his seat after his tour and rotation round the world people will gather around him.

Secondly, it means that "when the Imaam moves about on the earth along with his friends and associates..." In this case the word "zaraba" would mean moving about and the word "zanab" would mean helpers and associates.

Thirdly, it means that "when the Imaam rises with a sword in hand..." In this case the word "zanab" would mean stinging by the bee.

Fourthly, it means that "when the Imaam rises for the propagation of true faith with full fervour..." In this case the sentence is suggestive of the state of anger and the posture for attack.

-1- The reference by the versatile speaker is to Sasaa bn-Sohaan al-Abdi who was among the chief companions of Ameer al-Momineen. This saying throws light on the greatness of his speaking quality and the force of his utterances. In this connection, bn-Abil-Hadeed has written: It is enough for Sasaa's greatness that a personality like "Al-, peace be upon him, has praised him for versatility and eloquence of speech. (Sharh Nahjol-Balagha, vol.19, p.106)

beast can walk. Or you say "nasas tur-rajula anil-amrt" when you have questioned a man to the extreme to make him utter all he has. Thus "nassol-haqaaiq" means prudence because it is the last limit of childhood and is the time when a child crosses childhood into majority, and this is a very eloquent reference to the point, and strange too. Ameer al-Momineen, intends to say: When girls reach this stage their relations on father's side have a better right than their mother, provided they are those with whom marriage is prohibited like brother and uncles, to arrange for their marriages if they so desire. "al-hiqaq" also means the quarrelling of the mother with a girl's paternal relations. This quarrel is that everyone of them says he has a better right for her, That is why it is said "haqatuhu hiqaqan" on the lines of "jadaltuhu jidalan. It has also been said "nassol-hiqaq" means acquiring understanding and this is prudence, because Ameer al-Momineen refers to the stage when right and duties become applicable. The person who has related the word as "haqaaiq" intends to signify the plural of "haqiqah" (reality).

The above is what Abi-Obayd al-Qaasim bn-Salaam has stated (in Ghareeb al-hadeeth, vol.3, pp. 456-458); but I think that the intention here by the word "nassol-hiqaq" is a girl's reaching the stage when it is possible to marry her and to allow her to dispose of her rights herself on the analogy of "bil hiqaqi minal-ibili" (a camel's attaining majority) wherein of "hiqaqi" is the plural of "hiqqah" or "hiqq" and it means completion of three years (of age) and entry into the fourth, which is the time when it reaches the age when it is possible to ride on its back and to exert it in walking. "haqaaiq" too is the plural of "hiqqah. Thus, both the versions point to the sane meaning, and this interpretation is more in keeping with the way of the Arabs than the other one stated earlier.

266-5. A tradition of Ameer al-Momineen, peace be upon him, says: Faith produces a "lumazah" in the heart. As faith develops, the "lumazah" also increases

Sayyid Razi says: "lumazah" is a white spot or something like that. On that analogy if a horse has a white spot on its lower lip it is called "farusun al-mazu, that is, a white-spotted horse.

267-6. If a man has a "ad-daynoz-zanoon" (i.e. doubtful loan) it is his duty to pay zakat thereon for all the past years when he recovers it.

Sayyid Razi says: "az-zanoon" is the loan about which the lender does not know whether he will be able to recover it from the borrower, He is like the one who hopes as well as loses hope. This is the most eloquent way of expression. In this way everything about which you do not know where you stand would be zanoon. In the same strain poet al-Aasha (Maymoon bn-Qays al-Waaili (d. 7/629) says:

The az-zanoon well (i.e., the one that may or may not have water) which is also deprived of the rain of the raining clouds cannot be compared to the Euphrates whose waves are rising high and which is pushing away the boat as well as the adept swimmer.

jodd" means the well (situated in a wilderness), while zanoon is that about which it is not known whether or not it has water.

268-7. A tradition of Ameer al-Momineen, peace be upon him, relates that he arranged a force for advancing for jihad and said: iziboo (turn away) from women so far as you can.

Sayyid Razi says: It (iziboo)means that "keep off" from thoughts of women and from clinging your heart to them, and do not have union with them; because all this produces weakness in enthusiasm, affects the firmness of determination weakens against the enemy and prevents from exerting in fighting. Whatever prevents from something is called "azabd anhu" i. e., turned away from it. Thus "al-azib" and "al-azub" mean one who gives up eating and drinking.

269-8. A tradition of Ameer al-Momineen, peace be upon him, says: Like the successful shooter (al-yaasir al-faalij) who looks forward to achieving success at his first shot.

Sayyid Razi says: "al-yasirun" (pl. of al-yasir) means those who shoot with arrows on the slaughtered camel by way of gambling; while "al-falij" means successful or victorious. For example, it is said "falaja alayhim" or "falajahum" (that is, he got victory over them or overpowered them). A poet has said by way of war recital: When I noticed a successful person securing victory.

270-9. A tradition of Ameer al-Momineen, peace be upon him, runs:

When the crisis became red-hot we sought refuge with the Messenger of Allah (peace be upon him and his descendants), and none of us was closer to the enemy than he himself.

Sayyid Razi says: This means that when fear of the enemy increased and fighting became serious, the Muslims would begin to think that since the Messenger of Allah had taken up fighting himself, Allah must give them victory through him and that therefore they would be safe from all the dangers because of his existence.

And the words "izahmarral-baasu" (when the crisis became red-hot) refers to the seriousness of the matter. For this purpose several expressions have been used out of which this is the best one, since Ameer al-Momineen has likened war with fire which combines heat and redness both in action as well as colour. This is confirmed by the word of the Messenger of Allah (peace be upon him and his descendants) when on the day of Honayn he noticed people of Hawazin (tribe) fighting by said "Now watees has heated up" and watees is the place where fire is lighted. In this way, the Messenger of Allah (peace be upon him and his descendants) likened the seriousness of fighting by men to the seriousness of the fore and its flames.

This section ends and we return to the original theme of the chapter

271 When the news of the attack of Moaawiya's men on al-Anbaar reached Ameer al-Momineen, peace be upon him, he himself came out walking till he reached an-Nokhayla, where people overtook him and said "O Ameer al-Momineen, we are enough for them" then he said:

You cannot be enough for me against yourselves, so how can you be enough for me against others? Before me the people used to complain of the oppression of their rulers but now I have to complain of the wrongful actions of my people; as though I am led by them and they are the leaders or that I am the subject and they are the rulers.

The narrator says: When Ameer al-Momineen, peace be upon him, uttered this during his long speech which we have included in the collection of sermons (No.27), two men from his companions advanced towards him and one of them said: I rule no one except myself and my brother (Quraan, 5:25). So, order us with your command, O Ameer al-Momineen and we will accomplish it. Thereupon, How can you two accomplish what I aim at?

272. When al-Haarith bn-Hawd came to Ameer al-Momineen, and said: Do you believe I can ever imagine that the people of Jamal were in the wrong? O al-Haarith! You have seen below yourself but not above yourself, and so you have been confused. Certainly, you have known right, so that you can recognise the righteous. And you have not known wrong, so that you can recognise the people of wrong! Then al-Haarith said: In that case, I shall withdraw along with Saad bn-Malik and Abdillah bn-Omar; whereupon Verily, Saad and Omar have neither sides with Right nor forsaken Wrong.[1]

-1- Saad bn-Maalik (i.e. Saad bn-Abi-Waqqas, the father of Omar bn-Saad who killed Imaam Hosayn) and Abdillah bn-Omar were among those who were keeping themselves away from Ameer al-Momineen's help and support. As for Saad bn-Abi-Waqqas, after the killing of Othmaan he retired to some wilderness and passed his life there, but did not agree to swear allegiance to Ameer al-Momineen (as Caliph). But after the death of Ameer al-Momineen he used to express his repentance, saying "I held an opinion but it was a wrong opinion." (al-Mostadrak, al-Haakim, vol.3, p.116). And when Moaawiya blamed him for not supporting him in his fight with Ameer al-Momineen, Saad said:
I only repent for not having fought against the rebellious group (i.e. Moaawiya and his people). (Ahkaam al-Quraan, al-Jassas al-Hanafi, vol.2, pp.224,225; al-Foroo, bn-Moflih al-Hambali, vol.3, p.542)
As for Abdillah bn-Omar, although he had sworn allegiance, he refused to help Ameer al-Momineen in the battles putting forth the excuse: "I have sought seclusion to devote myself to worship and do not therefore want to involve myself in war and fighting
A Persian couplet says:
Intelligence regards such excuses worse than the offence itself.
Abdillah bn-Omar also frequently used to express his repentance, even up to the last moments of his life, saying:

273 The holder of authority is like the rider on a lion-he is envied for his position but he well knows his position.[1]

274 Do good with the bereaved ones of others so that good is done to your bereaved ones also.

275. When the utterance of the wise is to the point it serves as a cure, but if it is wrong it proves like an illness.[2]

276. When asked by someone to define religion for him

Come to me tomorrow so that I enlighten you in the presence of all the people, so that if your forget what I say others might retain it, because an utterance is like a fluttering prey which may be grappled with by someone but missed by others.

Sayyid Razi says: We have already stated in the earlier chapter what A Ameer al-Momineen replied to this man, namely his saying (No.31) "faith stands on four supports

277 O son of Adam, do not inflict the worry of the day that has not yet come on the day which has already come, because if that day be in your life Allah will bestow its livelihood also.

I do not find anything in myself to be distressed about in this world, except my not having fought alongside Ali bn-Abi-Talib against the rebellious group as Allah, to Whom belongs Might and Majesty, had commanded me. (al-Mostadrak, vol.3, pp.115-116; as-Sonan al-Kobra, al-Bayhaqi, vol.8, p.172; at-Tabaqaat, bn-Saad, vol.4, part.1, pp.136, 137; al-Isteeaab, vol.3, p.953; Osdol-Ghaaba, vol.3, p.229; vol.4, p.33; Majmaaz-zaw4id, vol.3, p.182; vol.7, p.242; al-Foroo, vol.3, p.543; Rooh. al-Maani, al-Aaloosi, vol.26, p.151).

1 The intention is that if a person holds high position in the royal court people look at his rank and position and honour and prestige with envy, but he himself has always the fear lest the royal pleasure turns against him and he falls in the pit of disgrace and dishonour or death and destruction, like the rider on a lion with by whom people are awed, but he himself it ever facing the danger lest the lion devours him, or throws him in some fatal pit.

-2- The group of the learned and reformers is responsible for improvement as well as deterioration because the common people are under their influence, and regard their words and action as correct and standard, rely on them and act upon them. In this way, if their teaching caters for improvement then thousands of individuals will acquire improvement and betterment thereby; but if there be evil in it then thousands of individuals will get involved in misguidance and get astrayed. That is why it is said: "When a scholar gets into evil the whole world gets into evil.

278 Have love for your friend up to a limit, for it is possible that he may turn into your enemy some day; and hate your enemy up to a limit for it is possible that he may turn into your friend some day.

279 There are two kinds of workers in the world. One is a person who works in this world for this world and his work of this world keeps him unmindful of the next world. He is afraid of destitution for those he will leave behind but feels himself safe about it. So, he spends his life after the good of others. The other is one who works in this world for what is to come hereafter, and he secures his share of this world without effort. Thus, he gets both the benefits together and becomes the owner of both the houses together. In this way, he is prestigious before Allah. If he asks Allah anything He does not deny him.

280. It is related that during the days of (Caliph) Omar bn-Khattaab, the question of the excess of the ornaments of the Kaba was mentioned to him and some people suggested: If you prepare with it an army of Muslims that will be a matter of great reward; and what would the Kaba do with the ornaments? Omar thought of doing so but asked Ameer al-Momineen, peace be upon him, when he said:

When the Quraan was descended on the Prophet, peace be upon him and his descendants, there were four kinds of property. One, the property of Muslim which he distributed among the successors according to fixed shares. Second, the tax (fay) which he distributed to those for whom it was meant. Third, the One-fifth (khums) levy for which Allah had fixed the ways of disposal. Fourth, amounts of charity (Sadaqaat) whose disposal was also fixed by Allah. The ornaments of Kaba did exist in those days but Allah left them as they were, but did not leave them by omission, nor were they unknown to Him. Therefore, you retain them where Allah and His Prophet placed them.

Thereupon, Omar bn-Khattaab said: If you had not been here we would have been humiliated; and he left the ornaments as they were.[1]

-1- Among the first three Caliphs, Omar bn-Khattaab often used to call upon Ameer al-Momineen for the solution of many unsolved problems and so as to benefit from his vast knowledge. But Abi-Bakr, due to the short period of his caliphate, and Othmaan, due to the special circumstances of his caliphate and his entourage, seldom used to call on Ameer al-Momineen and benefit from his advice. Omar used to praise Ameer al-Momineen very much for his vast knowledge, saying:

The most knowledgeable person among us in jurisprudence and judgement is Ali. (as-Saheeh al-Bokhaari, vol.6, p.23; al-Mosnad, Ahmad bn-Hambal, vol.5, p.113; al-Mostadrak, al-Haakim, vol.3, p.305; at-Tabaqaat, bn-Saad, vol.2, part 2, p.102; al-Isteeaab, vol.3, p.1102)

Certainly, there is no need for the evidence of Omar and others in this field when Omar himself and a group of the Companions confess that the Holy Prophet used to say:

Ali is the most knowledgeable in jurisprudence and judgement among my Omma (Muslim community). (Akhbaar al-Quzaat, Waki, vol.1, p.78; Masabeeh as-Sonna, al-Baghawi, vol.2, p.203; al-Isteeaab vol.1, pp.16-17; vol.3, p.1102; ar-Riyaaz an-Nazira, vol.2, p.108; as-Sonan, bn-Maaja, vol.1, p.55).

In this connection, Ahmad bn-Hambal narrates from Abi-Hazim that a certain man approached Moaawiya and put to him some questions on religion. Moaawiya said "Refer this question to Ali who possesses better knowledge." The man said "But I would rather have your reply than that of Ali." Moaawiya silenced him and said "It is the worst thing I have heard from you. You have expressed hate towards the person whom the Messenger of Allah used to coach and tutor as a mother bird feeds a nestling by putting grain after grain into the mouth of the nestling with its beak and to whom the Messenger of Allah said:

You hold the same position in relation to me as Haaroon held in relation to Moosa except that there shall, in all certainty, be no prophet after me;

and to whom Omar used to turn for the solution of unsolved problems." (Fayz al-Qadir, al-Munaawi, vol.3, p.46; ar-Riyaaz an-Nazira, vol.2, p.195; as-Sawaaiq al-Mohriqa, p.107; Fat-hol-Baari, vol.17, p.105) Also Omar used to say frequently:

Women lack the ability to give birth to such as Ali bn-Abi-Talib. Had it not been for Ali Omar would have been finished. (Taweel Mokhtalaf al-Hadeeth, bn-Qutayba, p.202; al-Isteeaab, vol.3, p.1103; Quzaat al-Andalos, al-Maaliqi, p.73; ar-Riyaaz an-Nazira, vol.2, p.194; al-Manaaqib, al-Khwaarizmi, p.39; Yanaabee al-Mawadda, p.75, 373: Fayz al-Qadir, vol.4, p.356).

He also used to say:

I seek the protection of Allah from the problems in which Abol-Hasan (Ali) is not present! (al-Isteeaab, vol.3, pp.1102-1103; at-Tabaqaat, vol.2, part 2, p.102;.Sifatos-Safwa, bn-Jawzi, vol.1, p.121; Osdol-Ghaaba, vol.4, pp.22-23; al-Isaaba, vol.2, p.509; at-Taareekh, bn-Katheer, vol.7, p.360)

Omar often addressed Ameer al-Momineen, thus:

281. It is related that two persons were brought to Ameer al-Momineen, peace be upon him. They had committed theft of public property. One of them was a slave purchased from public money and the other had been purchased by someone among the people. Then Ameer al-Momineen

---

O Abol-Hasan, I seek the protection of Allah from being in a community among which you are not found. (al-Mostadrak, vol.1, pp.457-458; at-Tafseer, Fakhroddeen ar-Raazi, vol.32, p.10; ad-Dor al-Manthoor; as-Seyooti, vol.3, p. 144; ar-Riyaaz an-Nazira, vol.2, p.197; Fayz al-Qadir, vol.3, p.46; vol.4, p. 356; as-Sawaaiq al-Mohriqa, p.107)

Above all these confession is the acknowledgement by the Holy Prophet of Ameer al-Momineen as narrated by Omar bn-Khattaab himself, Abi Saeed al-Khodri and Maaz bn-Jabal that the Holy Prophet said:

O Ali, I have exceeded you in Prophethood, for there will be no prophet after me, and you exceed others in seven noble qualities. You are: the first who believed in Allah, the best fulfiller of the promise made to Allah, the best adherer to the commandments of Allah, the most equitable distributor among the people, the best dispenser of justice (or the most clement) to the (Muslims) subjects, the one who has the best insight into controversial cases, (or the most learned in judgement), and the most conspicuous in virtue and honour before Allah. (Hilyatol-Awliyaa, vol.1, pp.65, 66; ar-Riyaaz an-Nazira, vol.2, p.198; al-Manaaqib, al-Khwaarizmi, p.61; Kanz al-Ommaal, vol. 12, p.214; bn-Abil-Hadeed, vol.13, p.230)

It is also narrated by Ameer al-Momineen, Abi-Ayyoob al-Ansaari, Maaqil bn-Yaasir and Borayda bn-Husayb that the Messenger of Allah (p.b.u.h.a.h.p.) said to Fatima (p.b.u.h.) that:

Are you not satisfied? Surely, I have married you to the foremost of my Omma who believes in Islam, and the most knowledgeable among them and superior among them in clemency. (al-Mosnad, Ahmad bn-Hambal, vol.5, p.26; al-Mosannaf, as-Sanani, vol.5, p.490; al-Isteeaab, vol.3, p.1099; Osdol-Ghaaba, vol.5, p.520; Kanz al-Ommaal, vol.12, p.205; vol.15, p.99; Majma az-Zawaaid, vol.9, pp.101, 114; as-Seera al-Halabiyya, vol.1, p.285)

After we read the following saying on the Holy Prophet, it is no surprise for us to note that the above acknowledgements of the vast knowledge of Ameer al-Momineen and his efficiency in the field of jurisprudence and judgement were made.

I am the city of knowledge and Ali is its gate; he who wants to acquire (my) knowledge must come through the gate. (al-Mostadrak, vol.3, pp.126, 127; al-Isteeaab, vol.3, p.1102; Osdol-Ghaaba, vol.4, p.22; Tahzeeb at-Tahzeeb, vol.6, pp.320-321; vol.7, p.337; Majma az-Zawaaid, vol.9, p.114; Kanz al-Ommaal, vol.12, pp.201, 212; vol.15, pp.129-130)

Also, the Holy Prophet said:

I am the store-house of wisdom and Ali is its gate. He who wants to acquire wisdom must come through the gate. (al-Jaami as-Saheeh, at-Tirmizi, vol.5, pp.37-638; Hilyatol-Awliyaa, vol.1, p.64; Masabeeh as-Sonna, al-Baghawi, vol.2, p.275; ar-Riyaaz an-Nazira, vol. 12, p.193; Kanz al-Ommaal, vol. 12, p.201)

said: As for this one who is the property of public money, there is no punishment for him for it means one property of Allah having taken another property of Allah. As for the others he should get the punishment. Consequently, his hand was cut.

282 If my steps acquire firmness out of these slippery places, I will alter several things.[1]

-1- It cannot be denied that after the Prophet of Islam changes came into existence in the religion when some people acting upon their imagination, amended or altered the commands of the shareeaa, although no one has the right to make alteration in the shareeaa, namely to ignore the clear commands of the Quraan and the Sonna and enforce commands produced by his own imagination and thinking. Thus, the Quraan contains this clear method of divorce that "(Revocable) Divorce (i.e. divorce in which resumption of conjugal relations is permissible without a marriage to another man taking place) may be twice" (Quraan, 2:229). But in view of certain supposed advantages the Caliph Omar ordered three divorces to be pronounced on a single occasion. Similarly, he introduced the system of "awl in inheritance and introduced four takbir in the funeral prayer. In the same way the Caliph Othmaan added an Azaan to the Friday prayer, ordered the offering of full prayers in place of qasr (shortened) ones, and allowed the sermon to precede the "Id prayer. In fact, hundreds of commands of this type were fabricated, as a result of which even correct commands got mixed with the wrong ones and lost their authenticity. (For changes made see: al-Ghadeer, al-Ameeni (by Abi-Bakr), vol.7, pp.74-236; (by Omar), vol.6, pp.83-325; (by Othmaan), vol.8, pp.98- 387; an-Nass wa al-Ijitihaad, Sharafoddeen (by Abi-Bakr), pp.76-154; (by Omar), pp.155-276; (by Othmaan), pp.284-289. See also Moqaddama Miraat a1-Oqool, al-Askari, vol.1 and vol.2).

Ameer al-Momineen, who was the greatest scholar of the shareeaa, used to protest against these commands and had his own views as against the Companions. In this connection, bn-Abil-Hadeed writes:

There is no possibility for us to deny that Ameer al-Momineen had views on the commands of the shareeaa and opinions at variance with those of the Companions. (Sharh Nahjol-Balagha, vol. 19, p.161)

When Amir al-Momineen assumed charge of the formal caliphate, revolts soon cropped up on all sides and he did not get rid of these troubles up to the last moment. Consequently, the altered commands could not be fully corrected and many wrong or doubtful commands gained currency in areas far removed from the centre. Nevertheless, the group of people who were associated with Ameer al-Momineen used to enquire about the commands of the shareeaa from him and recorded them, as a result of which the correct commands did not disappear and the wrong ones did not become unanimously accepted.

283 Know with full conviction that Allah has not fixed for any person more livelihood than what has been ordained in the Book of Destiny, even though his means (of seeking it) may be great, his craving for it intense and his efforts for it acute; nor does the weakness of a person or the paucity of his means stand in the way between what is ordained in the Book of Destiny and himself. He who realises it and acts upon it is the best of them all in point of comfort and benefit; while he who disregards it and doubts it exceeds all men in disadvantages. Very often a favoured person is being slowly driven (towards punishment) through those favours; and very often an afflicted person is being done good through his affliction. Therefore, O listener, increase your gratefulness, lessen your haste and stay within the bounds of your livelihood.

284 Do not turn your knowledge into ignorance or your conviction into doubt. When you gain knowledge act (upon it) and when your acquire conviction proceed (on its basis).[1]

285 Greed takes a person to the watering place but gets him back without letting him drink. It undertakes responsibility but does not fulfil it. Often the drinker gets choked before the quenching of his thirst. The greater the worth of a thing yearned for the greater is the grief for its loss. Desires blind the eyes of understanding. The destined share will reach him who does not approach it.

286 O my Allah, I seek Your protection from this that I may appear to be good in the eyes of the people whilst my inward self may be sinful before You, and that I may guard myself (from sins) only for show before the people

---

-1- Knowledge and conviction require that they should be acted upon. If they are not acted upon they cannot be called knowledge and conviction. Consequently, if a man says he knows the dangers that exist on particular path but he adopts that very path for his journey instead of the path that has no dangers, then who can say that this man had full certainty about the dangers of that path, because the consequence of such certainty should have been that he would have avoided going on that path. Similarly, the person who has belief in the resurrection and revival of life or in chastisement and reward cannot be overpowered by those things of this world that make a man neglectful to the extent of disregarding the next life, nor can he fall short in good actions for fear of chastisement and evil consequences.

although You are aware of all about me. Thus, I appear before the people in good shape although my evil deeds are placed before You. This means achieving nearness to Your creatures but remoteness from Your pleasure.

287 I swear by Him Who let us pass the dark night after which there was a bright day that such and such did not happen.[1]

288 A small action which is continued with regularity is more beneficial than a long one performed with disgust.

289 When optional issues stand in the way of obligatories, abandon them.

290 Whoever keeps in view the distance of the journey remains prepared.

291 Perception by the eyes is not real observation because the eyes sometimes deceive people; but wisdom does not deceive whomsoever it counsels.

292 Between you and the preaching there is a curtain of deception.

293 The ignorant among you get too much while the learned are just put off.

294 Knowledge dispels the excuse of those who advance excuses.

295 He whom death overtakes early seeks time while he whose death is deferred puts forth excuses for postponement (of doing good actions).

296 For every thing to which people say "how good!" there is an evil hidden in this world.

297. Ameer al-Momineen, peace be upon him, was asked about Destiny, when he said: It is a dark path-do not tread upon its it is a deep ocean-do not dive in it, and it is the secret of Allah-do not take trouble about (knowing) it.

298 When Allah intends to humiliate a person He denies him knowledge.

299 In the past I had a brother-in-faith,[2] and he was prestigious in my prestigious because the world was humble in his eyes, the needs of the

-1- Sayyid Razi has not written what it was that did not happen, leaving us only with the first part of the sentence.

-2- The man whom Ameer al-Momineen has referred to as his brother and whose qualities he has stated, has been taken by some commentators to be Abi-Zar al-Ghifaari, by some Othmaan bn-Mazoon al-Jomaahi and by some al-Miqdaad bn-Aswad al-Kindi; but it is not unlikely that no particular individual is referred to at all, because it is customary with Arabs for them to speak of a brother or a comrade although they have no particular individual in mind.

stomach did not have sway over him, he did not long for what he did not get; if he got a thing he would not ask for more; most of his time he was silent, if he spoke he silenced the other speakers, he quenched the thirst of questioners, he was weak and feeble but at the time of fighting he was like the lion of the forest or the serpent of the valley, he would not put forth an argument unless it was decisive.

He would not abuse anyone in an excusable matter unless he had heard the excuse, he would not speak of any trouble except after its disappearance, he would say what he would do, and would not say what he would not do, even if he could be exceeded in speaking, he could not be excelled in silence, he was more eager for keeping quiet than speaking and if two things confronted him he would see which was more akin to the longing of the heart and he would oppose it.

These qualities are incumbent upon you. So, you should acquire them and excel each other in them. Even if you cannot acquire them you should know that acquiring a part is better than giving up the whole.

300 Even if Allah had not warned of chastisement on those disobedient to Him, it would be obligatory by way of gratefulness for His favours that He should not be disobeyed.

301 Condoling Ashath bn-Qays about (the death of) his son:

O Ashath, if you grieve over your son, certainly it is the consequence of the blood relationship; but if you endure, then Allah provides recompense for every affliction. O Ashath, if you endure even then matters will move on as ordained by Allah but in that case you will deserve reward; while if you lose patience, matters will again move as ordained by Allah, but in this case you will be bearing the burden (of sins). O Ashath, your son (when he lived) gave you happiness while, at the same time, he was a trial and hardship and (when he died) he grieved you while, at the same time, he has proved a source of reward and mercy for you.

302. Ameer al-Momineen, peace be upon him, said on the grave of the Messenger of Allah, peace be upon him and his descendants, at the time of burial:

Certainly, endurance is good except about you; fretting is bad except over you; and the affliction about you is great while every other affliction before or after it is small.

303 Do not associate with a fool because he will beautify his actions before you and long that you too be like him.[1]

304. Ameer al-Momineen, peace be upon him, was asked about the distance between East and West when he replied: One day's travelling for the sun.

305 Your friends are three and your enemies are (also) three. Your friends are: your friend, your friend's friend and your enemy's enemy. And your enemies are: your enemy, your friend's enemy and your enemy's friend.

306. Ameer al-Momineen, peace be upon him, saw a man busy against his enemy with what was harmful to himself too, so he said: You are like one who pierces a spear through himself in order to kill the person sitting behind him.

307 How many are the objects of lessons, but how few the taking of lessons.[2]

-1- A fool considers his ways of action appropriate, and wants his friend also to adopt the same ways, so that he should become as he himself is. This does not mean that he desires that his friend should become as foolish as he is. He cannot be thinking like this, because he does not consider himself foolish. If he in fact considered himself foolish, then he would not have been foolish. Instead, he considers his ways of action as correct, and desires his friend to be equally "wise. That is why he presents his view before him in an embellished form and desires him to act upon it. It is possible his friend may be influenced by his advice and tread on the same path. Therefore, it is better to keep away from him.

-2- If the vicissitudes and changes of this world are observed, the circumstances and condition of the people attended to and their histories noted, then from every corner edifying stories can be heard which are fully capable of arousing the mind out of its forgetful slumber, or providing instruction and of imparting teaching and clear mindedness. Thus, the creation and dissolution of every thing in this world, the blossoming of flowers and their withering, the thriving of vegetation and its withering away and the subjugation of every atom to change are such instructive lessons that they are enough to curb any hope of attaining eternity in this deceitful life as long as the eyes and ears are not closed to these instructive events.

A Persian couplet says:

The world is full of stories of folk gone by, but unless one lends an ear to it, its call is weak.

308 He who goes too far in quarrelling is a sinner, but if one falls short in it, one is oppressed and it is difficult for a quarreller to fear Allah.

309 I am not worried by a fault after which I get time to offer prayer in two units (rakah) and beg safety from Allah.

310. Ameer al-Momineen, peace be upon him, was asked: How Allah would conduct the accounting of all persons despite their large number. He replied: Just as He provides them livelihood despite their large number. Then it was said to Him: How will He conduct their accounting without their seeing Him. He replied: Just as He provides them livelihood although they do not see Him.

311 Your messenger is the interpreter of your intelligence while your letter is more eloquent in expressing your true self.

312 The person who is afflicted with hardship is not in greater need of praying than the one who has been spared affliction but is not immune from it.

313 People are the progeny of the world and no one can be blamed for loving the mother.

314 The destitute is the Messenger of Allah. Whoever denies him denies Allah and whoever gives him gives Allah.

315 A self-respecting man never commits adultery.

316 The fixed limit of life is enough to remain watchful.[1]

317 A man can sleep on the death of his child, but cannot sleep at loss of property.

Sayyid Razi says: It means that a man keeps patience on the death of his children but does not do so on the loss of property.

-1- The idea here is that lighting may flash a hundred thousand times, tempests may rise, the earth may quake and mountains may collide with each other, but as long as the fixed period of life has yet to run its course no occurrence can cause any harm, nor the typhoon of death put out the flame of life; for there is a fixed hour for death, and nothing can cut it short before that time. In this way, obviously death itself is the watchman and guardian of life. The hemistich of a verse says:

What is known as death is the watchman of life.

318 Mutual affection between fathers creates a relationship between the sons. Relationship is more in need of affection than affection is of relationship.

319 Be afraid of the ideas of believers, because Allah, the Sublime, has put truth on their tongues.

320 The belief of a person cannot be regarded as true unless his trust in what is with Allah is more than his trust in what he himself has.

321. When Ameer al-Momineen, peace be upon him, came to Basra he sent Anas bn-Malik to Talha and az-Zobayr to make them recall what he (Anas) himself had heard the Messenger of Allah, peace be upon him and his descendants, say concerning them both, but he avoided doing so and when he came back to Ameer al-Momineen, he said that he had forgotten that matter. Thereupon, Ameer al-Momineen, peace be upon him said:

If you are speaking a lie Allah may afflict you with white spots (leucoderma) which even the turban may not cover.

Sayyid Razi says: White spot means leucoderma. After sometime this disease did occur to Anas's face so much so that he was never seen without a veil.[1]

-1- The occasion and circumstances surrounding this saying as related by Sayyid Razi were that when at the time of the Battle of Jamal Ameer al-Momineen sent Anas bn-Malik to Talha and az-Zobayr with the purpose that he should recall them the Prophet's saying to the effect that: "You two will fight Ali and will commit excess over him, he came back and stated that he had forgotten to mention it. Then, Ameer al-Momineen uttered these words about him. However, it is said that Ameer al-Momineen said the sentence on the occasion when he wanted Anas to confirm the Prophet's saying: "Whosoever master I am, Ali is his master. O my Allah, love him who loves Ali and hate him who hates Ali. Consequently, numerous persons have testified to this saying but Anas kept quiet. Then, Ameer al-Momineen, said to him "You too were present at Ghadeer Khom, what is keeping you silent on this occasion? and he said "I have grown old and my memory does not serve me well. Then, Ameer al-Momineen, pronounced this course. (Ansaab al-Ashraaf, al-Balazoori, (concerning the biography of Ameer al-Momineen), pp.156-157; al-Alaaq an-Nafisa, bn-Rosta, p.221; Lataaif al-Maarif, ath-Thaalibi, pp.105-106; Mohazaraat al-Odabaa, ar-Raaghib, vol.3, p.293; bn-Abil-Hadeed, vol.4, p.74; Arjah al-Mataalib, ash-Shaykh Obaydillah al-Hanafi, pp.578, 579, 580).

In this connection, bn-Qutayba (Abdillah bn-Muslim ad-Dinawari (231/828 -276/889) writes:

322 Sometimes the hearts move forward and sometimes they move backward. When they move forward get them to perform the optionals (as well), but when they move backward keep them confined to obligatories only.

323 The Quraan contains news about the past, foretellings about the future and commandments for the present.

324 Throw a stone in return from where one comes to you because evil can be met only with evil.

325 To his secretary Obaydillah bn-Abi Rafi:

Put cotton flake in the inkpot, keep the nib of your pen long, leave space between lines and close up the letters because this is good for the beauty of the writing.

326 I am the yaasoob (leader) of the believers, while wealth is the leader of the wicked.

Sayyid Razi says: It means that the believers follow me while the wicked follow wealth just as the bees follow their "yaasoob" who is their leader.[1]

People have related that Ameer al-Momineen asked Anas bn-Malik about the Prophet's saying "O my Allah, love him who loves "Al; and hates him who hates Ali," and he replied "I have grown old and I have forgotten it." Then Ali said: "If you are a liar, Allah may afflict you with white spots which even the turban may not cover.(al-Maarif, p.580) bn-Abi-Hadeed has also supported this view and, denying the incident mentioned by Sayyid Razi, writes:

The incident mentioned by Sayyid Razi that Ameer al-Momineen sent Anas bn-Malik to Talha and az-Zobayr is an unrecorded event. If Amir al-Momineen had sent him particularly to recall to them the Prophet's saying concerning them, then he could hardly have come back and said that he had forgotten it because when he left Ameer al-Momineen and went to these two persons he should have admitted and remembered the saying, and therefore how could he, on his return after an hour or a day, plead that he had forgotten it and deny it. This is something that cannot happen. (Sharh Nahjol-Balagha, vol.19, pp.217-218)

-1- We have already explained the meaning of the word "yasoob" in the foot-note of saying No.262-1, and pointed out that this title was given to Ameer al-Momineen by the Holy Prophet himself and we quoted some of his different utterances on this subject.

Here we quote one of the traditions in which this title appears. It is narrated by Abi-Layla al-Ghifaari, Abi-Zarr, Salmaan, bn-Abbaas and Hozayfa bn-Yaman that the Holy Prophet used to say:

Soon after my death there will be discord. When it occurs, adhere to Ali bn-Abi-Talib

327. Some Jews said to Ameer al-Momineen, peace be upon him: You had not buried your Prophet when you picked up differences about him, when Ameer al-Momineen replied:

We did not differ about him but we differed after him (i.e. about his succession); whereas you had not dried up your feet after coming our of the river (Nile) when you began asking your Prophet: Make you for us a god as they have gods of their own. "Verily you are a people behaving ignorantly" (Quraan, 7:138)[1]

328. Ameer al-Momineen, peace be upon him, was asked: With what did you overpower your adversaries? He answered:

Whenever I confronted a person he helped me against himself.

---

since he will be the first person to see me and the first person to shake hands with me on the Day of Judgement. He is the greatest man of truth (as-Siddeeq al-akbar), and he is the discriminator faarooq) from among this Omma who discriminates between right and wrong, and he is the yasoob (leader) of the believers while wealth is the yasoob of the hypocrites. (In addition to the references given in the above-mentioned foot-note, see also Fayz al-Qadir, vol.4, p.358; Kanz al-Ommaal, vol.12, p.214; Montakhab al-Kanz, vol.5, p.33; bn-Abil-Hadeed, vol.13, p.228: Taareekh ash-Shaam, bn Aasaakir, (on the biography of Ameer al-Momineen, vol.1, pp.74-78; as-Seera al-Halabiyya, vol.1, p.380; Zakhaair al-Oqbaa, p.56; Yanaabee al-Mawadda, p.62, 82, 201 and 251).

-1- The purpose behind this criticism by the Jews was to show that the Prophethood of the Prophet Mohammad was a controversial matter, but Ameer al-Momineen clarified the exact focus of controversy by using the word "after him" as against "about him, namely that the controversy was not about his Prophethood but about his succession and vicegerency. Then, commenting on the position of the Jews he pointed out that those who were today criticising the mutual differences among Muslims after the Prophet were of the same kind as those who had begun to waver about belief in the Unity of Allah even in the lifetime of Moses. Thus, when, on becoming free of the slavery of the Egyptians they reached the other side of the river and saw the figure of a calf in a temple in Sin, they asked Moses to get a similar figure for them, whereupon Moses rebuked them for being still as stubborn as they were in Egypt. This meant that a people who were so immersed in desire for idol-worship that even after being initiated into the belief in the Unity of Allah they became restless on seeing an idol and made the request for a similar idol to be made for themselves had no right to criticise any difference among Muslims.

Sayyid Razi says: Ameer al-Momineen is pointing out his striking of awe in the hearts.[1]

329. To his son Mohammad bn-Hanafiyya:

O my son, I fear lest destitution overtakes you. So, you should seek Allah's protection from it, because destitution is deficiency of religious belief, perplexity of intelligence, and it is conducive to hatred of obstinate people.

330. To a man who had asked him a difficult question:

Ask me for understanding but do not ask for confusion, because the ignorant person who tries to learn is like the learned man, but the learned man who tries to create confusion is like the ignorant.

331. Abdillah bn-Abbas once advised Ameer al-Momineen, peace be upon him, against his views, so he said: You have only to advise me but then I have to see (what to do); and if I act against your advice you have to follow me.[2]

332. When Ameer al-Momineen, peace be upon him, returned to Koofa from Siffeen, he passed by the residences of the Shibamites (who belonged to the tribe of Shibam) and heard the women weeping over those killed in Siffeen. At that time a Shibamite, Harb bn-Shorahbeel ash-Shibaami, who was one of the nobles of those people, came to him, and Ameer al-Momineen, peace be upon him, said to him:

-1- The man who is over-awed by his adversary is sure to be defeated because in facing a foe physical prowess is not enough but steadfastness of heart and strength of courage is also necessary. When the adversary loses courage and feels sure that he will be defeated then he will certainly be defeated. This is what happened to the adversary of Ameer al-Momineen; he was so affected by his acknowledged reputation that he was sure of death, in consequence of which his spiritual power and self confidence came to an end and eventually this mental state dragged him to his death.

-2- Abdillah bn-Abbaas had advised Ameer al-Momineen to issue a letter of appointment to Talha and az-Zobayr as the Governors of Koofa and to retain Moaawiya as the Governor of Syria till such time as his position became stabilised and the government gained strength. In reply to which Ameer al-Momineen said that he could not expose his own religion to danger for the sake of the worldly benefit of others, adding that "therefore instead of insisting on your own point you should listen to me and obey me."

Do your women have control over you as regards the weeping that I hear? Do you not refrain them from this crying?

Harb began to walk with him while Ameer al-Momineen, was on horseback, so Ameer al-Momineen, peace be upon him, said to him:

Get back because the walking of a man like you with one like me is mischief for the ruler and disgrace for the believer.

333. Ameer al-Momineen, peace be upon him, passed by the dead bodies of the Kharijites on the day of the battle of Nahrawan and said:

Woe unto you! You have been harmed by him who deceived you.

He was asked: O Ameer al-Momineen, who deceived them? Then, he replied:

Shaytan, the deceiver, and the inner spirit that leads one to evil deceived them through passions, made it easy for them to get into sins, promised them victory and eventually threw them into the Fire.

334 Beware of disobeying Allah in solitude, because the witness (of that situation) is also the judge.

335. When the news of killing of Mohammad bn-Abi Bakr[1] reached Our grief over him is as great as their (i. e. the enemy's) joy for it, except that they have lost an enemy and we have lost a friend.

-1- In the year 38 A.H. Moaawiya sent Amr bn-Aas. to Egypt with a large force. Amr bn-Aas called Moaawiya bn-Hodayj for assistance. They brought together the supporters of Othmaan and waged a war against Mohammad bn-Abi-Bakr and captured him. Moaawiya bn-Hodayj beheaded him and stitching his body into the belly of a dead ass, burnt it. Mohammad was at that time twenty-eight years old. It is reported that when the news of the tragedy reached his mother, she fell onto a great rage and indignation. And Aysha, his paternal sister, took a vow that, as long as she was alive, she would never eat roasted meat. She cursed Moaawiya bn-Abi-Sofyaan, Amr bn-Aas and Moaawiya bn-Hodayj after every prayer.

When Ameer al-Momineen heard the news of Mohammad's martyrdom he became immensely sad. He wrote in very grieved language to bn-Abbaas who was at Basra about the tragic death of Mohammad bn-Abi-Bakr.

336 The age up to which Allah accepts any excuse for a human being is sixty years.

337 He whom sin overpowers is not victorious, and he who secures victory by evil is (in fact) vanquished.

338. Allah, the Glorified, has fixed the livelihood of the destitute in the wealth of the rich. Consequently, whenever a destitute remains hungry it is because some rich person has denied (him his share). Allah, the Sublime, will question them about it.

339 Not to be in need of putting forth an excuse is better than putting forth a true excuse.[1]

340 The least right of Allah on you is that you should not make use of His favours in committing His sins.[2]

Hearing the news of Mohammad's martyrdom bn-Abbaas came from Basra to Koofa to offer his condolences to Ameer al-Momineen.

One of the spies of Ameer al-Momineen came from Syria and said:

O Ameer al-Momineen! When the news of Mohammad's murder reached Moaawiya, he went to the pulpit and praised the group who took part in his martyrdom. The people of Syria rejoiced so much at hearing the news that I had never seen them in such delight before.

Then, Ameer al-Momineen uttered the above saying. He further said that although Mohammad was his stepson, he was like his own son. (at-Tabari, vol.1, pp.3400-3414; bn al-Athir, vol.3, pp.352-359; bn-Katheer, vol.7, pp.313-317; Abol-Fidaa, vol.1, p.l79; bn-Abil Hadeed, vol.6, pp.82-100; bn-Khaldoon, vol.2, part.2, pp.l81-182; al-Isteeaab vol.3, pp.1366-1367; al-Isaaba, vol.3, pp.472-473; al-Ghaaraat, ath-Thaqafi, vol.1, pp.276-322;Taareekh al-Khamees, vol.2, pp.238-239).

We have written before (in the foot-note to Sermon 67) concerning the biography of Mohammad bn-Abi-Bakr.

-1- The meaning is that obligations should be so discharged that there is no occasion for putting forth excuses, because after all in making excuse there is a hint of shortcoming and humbleness, even though it may be true and correct.

-2- There are a few grades of denial of favours and ingratitude. The first is that a person may not be able to appreciate (the real significance of) a favour; for example, the sight of the eyes, the speech of the tongue, the hearing of the ears and the movements of the hands and feet. These are all favours bestowed by Allah but many people do not realise them to be favours, and do not entertain feelings of gratitude. The second grade is that a person may see a favour and appreciate it but may not feel grateful for it. The third grade is that a person may oppose the Bestower of the favours. The fourth grade is that instead of using the favours granted by Him a person may use them in committing sins against Allah. This is the highest grade of denial of favours.

341 When the disabled fall short in performing acts of obedience to Allah, the Glorified, it is a good opportunity given by Allah for the intelligent to perform such acts.

342 The sovereign is the watchman of Allah on earth.

343 Describing a believer

A believer has a cheerful face, a sorrowful heart, a very broad chest (full of generosity), and a very humble heart. He hates high position and dislikes renown. His grief is long, his courage is far-reaching, his silence is much and. his time is occupied. He is grateful, enduring, buried in his thoughts, sparing in his friendship (with others), of bright demeanour and of soft temperament. He is stronger than stone but humbler than a slave.

344 If a man happens to see the end of (his) life and his final fate, he will begin hating desires and their deception.

345 There are two shares in the property of every person-successors and accidents.

346 The person who is approached with a request is free until he promises.

347 He who prays but does not exert effort is like the one who shoots without a bow-string.

348 Knowledge is of two kinds-that which is absorbed and that which is just heard. The one that is heard does not give benefit unless it is absorbed.

349 Correctness of decision goes together with power. The one emerges with the other's emergence and disappears when the other disappears.[1]

350 The beauty of destitution is chastity and the beauty of riches is gratefulness.

-1- When anyone's star is auspicious and his luck is good, he steps automatically towards the goal in view, and his mind confronts no perplexity in determining the correct way of approach; but the person whose luck is about to ebb stumbles even in the light and his mental faculties become paralysed. Consequently, when the downfall of the Barmakids began, ten persons from among them assembled for consultation about a matter but were not able to take a decision even after long discussion. Seeing this Yahya said "By Allah, it is a forerunner of our decline and a sign of our downfall that even ten of us have not been able to settle a matter, although while when we were in ascendancy one of us used to solve ten problems easily.

351 The day of justice will be severer on the oppressor than the day of the oppression on the oppressed.

352 The biggest wealth is that one should not have an eye on what others possess.

353 Utterances are preserved and actions are to be tried. Every soul, for what it earned, is held in pledge! (Quraan, 74:38). People are to be made deficient (as regards their bodies) and meddled with (as regards their minds) except those whom Allah protects. The questioner among them aims at confusing and the answerer creates hardship. It is possible that the man who has the best views among them will be deviated from the soundness of his thinking by pleasure or displeasure, and it is possible that a single glance may affect even the man with the best wisdom among them or a single expression may transform him.

354 O groups of people, fear Allah, for there is many a man who aspires for what he does not get, many a builder of a house who does not live in it, and many a collector of that which he shall just leave behind. Possibly he may have collected it wrongfully or by denying a right. He acquired it unlawfully and had to bear the weight of sins on account of it. Consequently, he returned (from this world) with that weight and came before Allah with sorrow and grief. Loses he both this world and (also) the thereafter; that is a loss (which is) manifest. (Quraan, 22:11)

355 Lack of access to sins is also a kind of chastity.

356 The dignity of your face is solid but begging dissolves it away: therefore, look carefully before whom you dissolve it.

357 To praise more than what is due is sycophancy; to do it less is either because of inability to speak or of envy.

358. The most serious sin is that which the doer considers light.[1]

-1- The result of lack of restraint and care in respect of small sins is that a man becomes rather careless in the matter of sins, and, by and by, this habit produces boldness for larger sins. Then, he begins to commit them without hesitation. Therefore, one should regard small sins as a harbinger of bigger sins, and avoid them, so that the stage for committing big sins does not come.

359 He who sees his own shortcomings abstains from looking into other's shortcomings. He who feels happy with the livelihood with which Allah provides him does not grieve over what he misses. He who draws out the sword of revolt gets killed with it. He who strives without means perishes. He who enters the depths gets drowned. He who visits places of ill-repute receives blame.

He who speaks more commits more errors. He who commits more errors becomes shameless. He who is shameless will have less fear of Allah. He whose fear of Allah is less, his heart dies. He whose heart dies enters the Fire. He who observes the shortcomings of others and disapproves of them and then accepts them for himself is definitely a fool. Contentment is a capital that does not dwindle. He who remembers death much is satisfied with small favours in this world. He who knows that his speech is also a part of his action speaks less except where he has some purpose.

360 The oppressor among the people has three signs: he oppresses his superior by disobeying him, and his junior by imposing his authority and he supports other oppressors.

361 At the extremity of hardship comes relief, and at the tightening of the chains of tribulation comes ease.

362 To one of his companions

Do not devote much of your activity to your wife and your children, because if your wife and children are lovers of Allah then He will not leave His lovers uncared for, and if they be enemies of Allah then why should you worry and keep yourself busy about the enemies of Allah.

363 The greatest defect is to regard that defect (in others) which is present in yourself.[1]

-1- What worse defect can there be that a man should criticise those defects in others which exist in himself. The requirement of justice is that before casting one's eye on the defects of others one should look at his own defects and realise that a defect is a defect whether it be in others or in oneself.

A Persian couplet says:

Looking at other's defects is neither property nor manliness. Better look at your own self since you are full of defects.

364 Someone congratulated another person in the presence of Ameer al-Momineen, peace be upon him, on the birth of a son saying: Congratulations for getting a rider of horses. Then Ameer al-Momineen, said:

Do not say so; but say: You have occasion to be grateful to Allah, the Giver, and be blessed with what you have given. May he attain full life and may you be blessed with His devotion.

365. One of the officers of Ameer al-Momineen, peace be upon him, built a stately house, about which Ameer al-Momineen, said:

This is silver coins showing forth their faces. Certainly, this house speaks of your riches.

366. It was said to Ameer al-Momineen, peace be upon him: If a man is left in his house and the door is closed, from where will his livelihood reach him. And he replied: From whatever way his death reaches him.[1]

367. Condoling with people among whom one had died, This thing has not started with you nor does it end with you. This fellow of yours was used to journeying and therefore it is better to think him still to be journeying. Either he will rejoin you or else you will rejoin him.

368 O People, let Allah see you fearing at the time of happiness just as you fear Him at the time of distress. Certainly, he who is given ease (of life) and does not consider it as a means of slow approach towards tribulation (wrongly), considers himself safe against what is to be feared while he who is afflicted with straitened circumstances but does not perceive them to be a trial loses to coveted reward.

-1- If Allah considers it appropriate to keep a man living while he is confined to a closed house, then He is certainly powerful enough to provide the means of living to him, and just as a closed door cannot prevent death in the same way it cannot prevent the entry of livelihood, because the Might of Allah, the Almighty is equally capable of either.

The meaning is that a man should be content in the matter of livelihood because whatever is destined for him will in any case reach him wherever he may be.

A Persian couplet says:

Livelihood like death will reach a man even if the door be closed, but greed keeps people (unnecessarily) anxious.

369 O slaves of desires, cut them short because he who leans on the world gets nothing out of it except the pain of hardships. O people, take upon yourselves your own training and turn away from the dictates of your natural inclinations.

370 Do not regard an expression uttered by any person as evil if you can find it capable of bearing some good.

371 If you have a need from Allah, the Glorified, then begin by seeking Allah's blessing on His Messenger, may Allah bless him and his descendants, then ask your need, because Allah is too generous to accept one (seeking His blessing on His Messenger) of the two requests made to Him and deny the other.

372 He who is jealous of his esteem should keep from quarrelling.

373 To make haste before the proper time or to delay after a proper opportunity, in either case is folly.

374 Do not ask about things which may not happen because you have enough to worry about with what happens.

375 Imagination is a clear mirror, and the taking of lessons (from things around) provides warning and counsel. It is enough for improving yourself that you should avoid what you consider bad in others.

376 Knowledge is associated with action. Therefore, he who knows should act, because knowledge calls for action; if there is a response well and good, otherwise it (i.e., knowledge) departs from him.

377 O people, the wealth of this world is broken orts that brings an epidemic; therefore keep off this grazing land, leaving it is a greater favour than peacefully staying in it, and its part enough for subsistence is more blissful than its riches. Destitution has been ordained for those who are rich here, while comfort has been destined for those who keep away from it. If a person is attracted by its dazzle, it blinds both his eyes; and if a person acquires eagerness towards it, then it fills his heart with grief which keep alternating in the black part of his heart, some grief worrying him and another giving him pain. This goes on till the suffocation of death overtakes him. He is flung in the open while both the shrines of his heart

are severed. It is easy for Allah to cause him to die and for his comrades to put him in the grave.

The believer sees the world with eyes that derive instruction, and takes from it food enough for his barest needs. He hears in it with ears of hatred and enmity. If it is said (about someone) that he has become rich, it is also said that he has turned destitute ;-and if pleasure is felt on one's living, grief is felt over his death. This is the position, although the day has not yet approached when they will be disheartened.

378 Allah, the Glorified, has laid down reward for obedience to Him and punishment for committing sins against Him in order to save men from His chastisement and to drive them towards Paradise.

379 A time will come when nothing will remain of the Quraan except its writing, and nothing of Islam except its name. The mosques in those days will be busy with regards to construction but desolate with regard to guidance. Those staying in them and those visiting them will be the worst of all on earth. From them mischief will spring up and towards them all wrong will turn. If anyone isolates himself from it (mischief) they will fling him back to it and if anyone steps back from it they will push him towards it.

Says Allah, the Glorified, (in hadeeth qudsi — i.e., the tradition in which Allah Himself speaks): I swear by Myself that I shall send upon them an evil wherein the endurer would be bewildered, and He would do so. We seek Allah's pardon from stumbling through neglect.

380. It is related that it was seldom that Ameer al-Momineen, peace be upon him, ascended the pulpit and did not utter the following before his sermon: O people, fear Allah for man has not been created for naught so that he may waste himself, nor has he been left uncared for so that he may commit nonsensical acts. This world which appears beautiful to him cannot be the replacement of the next world which appears bad in his eyes, nor is the vain person who is successful in the next world even to a small extent.

381 There is no distinction higher than Islam; no honour more honourable than fear of Allah; no asylum better than self restraint; no intercessor more effective than repentance; no treasure more precious than contentment; and no wealth is a bigger remover of destitution than being satisfied with mere sustenance. He who confines himself to what is just enough for maintenance achieves comfort and prepares abode in ease. Desire is the key of grief and the conveyance of distress. Greed, vanity and jealousy are incentives to falling into sins and mischief-mongering is the collection of all bad habits.

382. To Jabir bn-Abdillah al-Ansaari: O Jabir, the mainstay of religion and the world are four persons: The scholar who acts on his knowledge; the ignorant who does not feel ashamed of learning; the generous who is not niggardly in his favours; and the destitute who does not sell his next life for his worldly benefits. Consequently, when the scholar wastes his knowledge, the ignorant feels shame in learning; and when the generous is niggardly with his favours, the destitute sells his next life for the worldly benefits.

O Jabir, if favours of Allah abound on a person the people's needs towards him also abound. Therefore, he who fulfils for Allah all that is obligatory on him in this regard will preserve them (Allah's favours) in continuance and perpetuity, while he who does not fulfil those obligations will expose them to decay and destruction.

383. Bn Jareer at-Tabari has, in his history (vol.2, p.1056; also Bn al-Atheer in his history, vol.4, p.478), related from Abdr-Rahmaan bn-Abi Layla, al-faqeeh (the theologian), who was one of those who had risen with (Abdr-Rahmaan bn-Mohammad) Bn al-Ashath to fight al-Hajjaj (bn Yoosof ath-Thaqafi), that he (Bn Abi Layla) was exhorting people to Jihad by recalling: On the occasion of the encounter with the people of Syria I heard Ameer al-Momineen, may Allah exalt his degree of rank among the righteous and may He reward him the reward of martyrs and men of truth, saying:

O believers, whoever observes excesses being committed and people being called towards evil and disapproves it with his heart is safe and free from responsibility for it, and whoever disapproves of it with his tongue would be rewarded and he is in a higher position than the former but whoever disapproves it with his sword in order that the word of Allah may remain superior and the word of the oppressors may remain inferior, catches hold of the path of guidance and stands on the right way, while his heart is lighted with conviction.

384. Another saying in the same strain runs as follows: So, among them (the Muslim community) there is he who disapproves evil with his hand, tongue and heart. This man has perfectly attained the virtuous habits. And among them there is he who disapproves evil with his tongue and heart but not with his hand. This man has attained only two virtuous habits but lacks one. And among them there is the third one who disapproves evil with his heart but not with his tongue and hand. This is the one who lacks the two better qualities out of three and holds only one. Then, among them there is also he who does not disapprove evil either with his tongue, heart or hand. He is just a dead man among the living.

All the virtuous deeds including war in the way of Allah as compared to the persuasion for good and dissuasion from evil are just like spitting in the deep ocean. The persuasion for good and dissuasion from evil do not bring death nearer nor do they lessen the livelihood. And better than all this is to utter a just expression before the tyrannical ruler.

385. It is related from Abu Johayfa who said: I heard Ameer al-Momineen, peace be upon him, saying:

The first fighting with which you will be overpowered is the fighting with hands, thereafter with your tongues and then with your hearts. Consequently, he who does not recognise virtue with his heart or does not disapprove evil will be turned upside down. Thus, his upside will be turned downwards and his low side swill be turned upwards.

386 Certainly, right is weighty and wholesome while wrong is light and epidemical.

387 Do not feel safe from the punishment of Allah even about the best man in the whole community because Allah, the Sublime, says: But no one feels

secure the plan of Allah save the people (who are the) losers. (Quraan, 7:99). Again, do not lose hope even for the worst man of the community because Allah, the Sublime says: Verily, despairs not of Allah's mercy but the disbelieving people. (Quraan, 12:87).

388 Miserliness contains all other evil vices and is the rein with which one can be led to every evil.

389 O son of Adam, livelihood is of two kinds: the livelihood which you seek and the livelihood which seeks you; if you do not reach it, it will come to you. Therefore, do not turn your one day's worry into a year's worry. Whatever you get every day should be enough for you for the day. If you have a whole year of your life even then Allah, the Sublime, will give you every next day what He has destined as your share. If you do not have a year in your life then why should you worry for what is not for you. No seeker will reach your livelihood before you nor will anyone overpower you in the matter of livelihood. Similarly, whatever has been destined as your share will not be delayed for you.

Sayyid Razi says: This saying has already appeared elsewhere in this chapter except that here it is clearer and more detailed. This is why we have repeated it according to the principle laid down in the beginning of the book.

390 Many a man faces a day after which he finds no day and many a man is in an enviable position in the earlier part of the night but is wept over by bewailing women in its later part.

391 Words are in your control until you have not uttered them; but when you have spoken them out you are under their control. Therefore, guard your tongue as you guard your gold and silver, for often one expression snatches away a blessing and invites punishment.

392 Do not say what you do not know; rather do not say all that you know, because Allah has laid down some obligations for all your limbs by means of which He will put forth arguments against you on the Day of Judgement.

393 Fear lest Allah sees you while committing His sins or misses you when it is time to obey Him and as a result thereof you become a loser. Therefore,

when you are strong be strong in obeying Allah and when you are weak be weak in committing sins of Allah.

394 Leaning towards this world despite what you see of it, is folly, and lagging behind in good deeds when you are convinced of good reward for them is obvious loss, while trusting in every one before trying in weakness.

395 It is (the proof of the) humbleness of the world before Allah that He is disobeyed only herein and His favours cannot be achieved except by abandoning it.

396 One who is in search of something will obtain it, at least a part of it.

397 That good is no good after which there is the Fire, and that hardship is no hardship after which there is Paradise. Every bliss other than Paradise is inferior and every calamity other than the Fire is comfort.

398 Beware that destitution is a calamity, but worse than destitution is ailment of the body, while worse than bodily ailment is the disease of the heart. Beware that plenty of wealth is a blessing, but better than plenty of wealth is the health of the body, while still better than the health of the body is the chastity of heart.

399 Whomever his action detains behind, his lineage cannot put him forward. In another version it is thus: Whoever misses personal attainment cannot be benefited by his forefathers" attainments.

400 The believer's time has three periods: The period when he is in communion with Allah; the period when he manages for his livelihood; and the period when he is free to en joy what is lawful and pleasant. It does not behove a wise person to be away (from his house) save for three matters, namely for purposes of earning, or going for something for the next life or for enjoying what is not prohibited.

401 Abstain from the world so that Allah may show you its real evils and do not be neglectful because (in any case) you will not be neglected.

402 Speak so that you may be known, since man is hidden under his tongue.

403 Take off the favours of the world whatever comes to you and keep away from what keeps away from you. If you cannot do so be moderate in your seeking.

404 Many an expression is more effective than an attack.

405 Every small thing that is contented upon suffices.

406 Let it be death but not humiliation. Let it be little but not through others. He who does not get while sitting will not get by standing either. The world has two days one for you and the other against you. When the day is for yours, do not feel proud but when it is against you endure it.

407 The best scent is musk; its weight is light while its smell is scentful.

408 Put off boasting, give up self-conceit and remember your grave.

409 The child has a right on the father while the father too has a right on the child. The right of the father on the child is that the latter should obey the former in every matter save in committing sins of Allah, the Glorified, while the right of the child on the father is that he should give him a beautiful name, give him good training and teach him the Quraan.

410 Evil effect of sight is right; charm is right; sorcery is right, and faal (auguring good) is right, while tayara (auguring evil)[1] is not right, and

---

-1- "faal" means something from which one augurs well while "tiyarah" means something from which one augurs evil. From the point of view of religious law auguring evil from anything has no basis and it is just the product of whim.

However, auguring well is not objectionable. For example, when after the immigration of the Prophet (from Mecca to Madeena), the Quraysh announced that whoever apprehended the Prophet would be given one hundred camels as prize. Thereupon, Borayda bn-Hosayb al-Aslami set off in his search with seventy of his men and when they met at a halting place the Prophet asked him who he was and he said he was Borayda bn-Hosayb al-Aslami. Borayda said:

The Holy Prophet was not auguring evil instead he used to augur good." On hearing this, the Prophet remarked: "barada amrand wa salaha" (our consequence will be wholesome). Then he asked him what tribe he came from and on his replying that he was from Aslam, the Prophet remarked:

'salimna" (we would be safe). Then he asked from which scion he was and when he replied that he was from Bani-Sahm, the Prophet remarked: Karaja sahmoka (your arrow has missed the aim). Borayda was much impressed by this pleasing conversation and inquired from the Prophet who he was. The Prophet replied "Mohammad bn-Abdillah. Hearing this, he spontaneously exclaimed "I do stand witness that you are the Messenger

spreading of a disease from one to the other is not right. Scent gives pleasure, honey gives pleasure, riding gives pleasure and looking at greenery gives pleasure.

411 Nearness with people in their manners brings about safety from their evil.

412 Someone uttered an expression above his position, then Ameer al-Momineen, peace be upon him, said to him: You have started flying soon after growing feathers (shaar) and commenced-grumbling before attaining youth (saqb).

Sayyid Razi says: Here 'shaair" means the first feathers that grow on a bird before it is strong enough to fly. And saqb means the young camel who does not grumble unless it becomes major.

413 Whoever hankers after contraries gets no means of success.

414. On being asked the meaning of the expression: "la hawla wala quwwata illa billah" (there is no strength nor power by means of Allah).

We are not master of anything along with Allah. and we are not master of anything save what He makes us master of. So. when He makes us master of anything of which He is a superior Master over us He also assigns some duties to us: and when He takes it away He will take away those duties as well.[1]

---

of Allah, and forsaking the prize announced by the Quraysh acquired the wealth of Belief. (al-Isteeaab, vol.1, pp.l85-186; Osdol -Ghaaba, vol.1, pp.l75-176).

-1- What Ameer al-Momineen means is that man does not enjoy regular mastery over anything, but such mastery as he is assigned by Allah, and so long as this mastery lasts the obligations of the shareeaa also continue, whereas when the mastery is taken away the obligations too are lifted off, since in such a case the laying of obligations would mean placing of responsibility beyond capacity which cannot be allowed by any or prudent person. This is why Allah has placed the responsibility of performing various acts after having conferred the necessary energy in the limbs. It follows that this responsibility would remain only so long as the energy subsists and that on the disappearance of the energy the responsibility for action would also disappear. For example, the obligation to pay zakat (tax) applies only when there is wealth; but when Allah would take away the wealth He would lift off the liability to pay zakat because in such a case the laying of obligation is against prudence.

415. Ameer al-Momineen, peace be upon him, heard Ammaar bn-Yasir (may Allah have mercy on him) conversing with al-Mogheera bn-Shoba and said: Let him alone O Ammaar, for he has entered religion only to the extent of his deriving advantage of the world, and he has wilfully involved himself in misgivings in order to adopt them as cover for his shortcomings.

416 It is good for the rich to show humility before the poor to seek reward from Allah, but better than that is the haughtiness of the poor towards the rich with trust in Allah.

417 Allah does not grant wisdom to a person except that some day He will save him from ruin with its help.

418 Whoever clashes with Truth would be knocked down by it.

419 The heart is the book of the eye.

420 Fear of Allah is the chief trait of human character.

421 Do not try the sharpness of your tongue against Him Who gave you the power to speak, nor the eloquence of your speaking against Him Who set you on the right path.

422 It is enough for your own discipline that you abstain from what you dislike from others.

423 One should endure like free peoples otherwise one should keep quite like the ignorant.

In another tradition it is related that Ameer al-Momineen, peace be upon him, said to al-Ashath bn-Qays by way of condolence on the death of his son:

Either endure like great people or else you will forget like animals.

424 It deceives, it harms and it passes away. Allah, the Sublime, did not approve it as a reward for His lovers nor as a punishment for His enemies. In fact, the people of this world are like those riders that as soon as they alighted the driver called out to them and they marched off.

425. To his son Hasan (peace be upon him): O my son, do not leave anything of this world behind you, because you will be leaving it for either of two sorts of persons: Either a person who uses it in obeying Allah, in this case he will acquire virtue through what was evil for you, or it will be a person

who uses it in disobeying Allah and in that case be will be earning evil with what you collected for him, and so you will be assisting him in his sinfulness; and neither of these two deserves to be preferred by you over yourself.

Sayyid Razi says: This saying is also related in another version namely: Whatever of this world is now with you was with others before you and it will pass to some others after you. thus, you are collecting things for either of two sorts of men: either a man who uses whatever you collected in obedience of Allah and so acquires virtues with what was evil for you, or a man who uses it in disobedience of Allah and so you will be getting evil for what you collected. And neither of these two is such that you may prefer him over yourself or you may burden yourself for him. Therefore, hope for the mercy of Allah for him who has passed away and for Divine livelihood for him who survives.

426. Someone said before Ameer al-Momineen, peace be upon him: "astaghfirollah" (I ask Allah's forgiveness), then Your mother may lose you! Do you know what "istighfaar" (asking Allah's forgiveness) is? "istighfaar" is meant for people of a high position. It is a word that stands on six supports. The first is to repent over the past; the second is to make a firm determination never to revert to it; the third is to discharge all the rights of people so that you may meet Allah quite clean with nothing to account for; the fourth is to fulfil every obligation which you ignored (in the past) so that you may now do justice with it; the fifth is to aim at the flesh grown as a result of unlawful earning, so that you may melt it by grief (of repentance) till the skin touches the bone and a new flesh grows between them; and the sixth is to make the body taste the pain of obedience as you (previously) made it taste the sweetness of disobedience. On such an occasion you may say: "astaghfirollah.

427 Clemency is (like) a kinsfolk.

428 How wretched the son of Adam (man) is! His death is hidden, his ailments are concealed, his actions are preserved, the bite of a mosquito pains him, choking cause his death and sweat gives him a bad smell.

429 It is related that Ameer al-Momineen, peace be upon him, was sitting with his companions when a beautiful woman passed by them and they began to look at her whereupon
The eyes of these men are covetous and this glancing is the cause of their becoming covetous. Whenever anyone of you sees a woman who attracts him, he should meet his wife because she is a woman like his wife. Then, one of the Kharijites said: Allah may kill this heretic. How logical he is! The people then leapt towards him to kill him but Wait a bit. There should either be abuse or else pardon from the offence.

430 It is enough if your wisdom distinguishes for you the ways of going astray from those of guidance.

431 Do good and do not regard any part of it small because its small is big and its little is much. No one of you should say that another person is more deserving than I in doing good. Otherwise, by Allah, it would really be so. There are people of good and evil. When you would leave either of the two, others will perform them.

432 Whoever set right his inward self, Allah sets right his outward self. Whoever performs acts for his religion, Allah accomplishes his acts of this world. Whoever's dealings between himself and Allah are good, Allah turns the dealings between him and other people good.

433 Forbearance is a curtain for covering, and wisdom is a sharp sword. Therefore, conceal the weaknesses in your conduct with forbearance and kill your desires with your wisdom.

434 There are some creatures of Allah whom Allah particularises with favours for the benefit of the people, therefore He stays them in their hands so long as they give them to others; but when they deny them to others He takes away the favours from them and sends them to others.

435 It does not behove a man to have trust in two positions, health and riches, because there is many a man whom you see healthy but he soon falls and many a man whom you see rich but soon turns destitute.

436 Whoever complains about a need to a believer, it is as though he has complained about it to Allah; but whoever complains about it to an unbeliever it is as though he complained about Allah.

437 On the occasion of an Eed (Muslim feast day): It is an Eed for him whose fasting Allah accepts and for whose prayers He is grateful; and (in fact) every day wherein no sin of Allah is committed is an Eed.[1]

438 On the Day of Judgement the greatest regret will be felt by the man who earned wealth through sinful ways, although it is inherited by a person who spends it in obeying Allah, the Glorified, and he will be awarded Paradise on that account while first one will go into the Fire on account of it.

439 The worst in bargaining and the most unsuccessful in striving is the man who exerts himself in seeking riches although fate does not help him in his aims and consequently he goes from this world in a sorrowful state while in the next world too he will face its ill consequences.[2]

440 Livelihood is of two kinds: the seeker and the sought. Therefore, he who hankers after this world death traces him till it turns him out of it; but he who hankers after the next world. worldly ease itself seeks him till he receives his livelihood from it.

-1- If feeling and conscience is alive even the remembrance of a sin destroys peace of mind because tranquillity and happiness are achieved only when the spirit is free from the burden of sin and one's robe is not polluted with disobedience. And this real happiness is not bound by time, but on whatever day a man desires he can avoid sin and enjoy this happiness, and this very happiness will be the real happiness and the harbinger of id.

A Persian hemistich says: Every night is the Grand Night provided you appreciate its worth.

-2- Despite efforts throughout life a man does not always achieve all the successes of life. In some occasions he succeeds as a result of effort and seeking, on many others, he has to face defeat and to give up his objectives admitting defeat before fate. A little thinking can lead to the conclusion that when things of this world cannot be achieved despite effort and seeking how can the success of the next world be achieved without striving and seeking.

A Persian couplet sags:

You hankered after the world but did not attain the object. O Allah, what would be the result when the good of the next world has not even been sought.

441 The lovers of Allah are those who look at the inward side of the world while the other people look at its outward side. they busy themselves with its remoter benefits while the other people busy themselves in the immediate benefits. They kill those things which they feared would have killed them, and they leave here in this world what they think would leave them. They took the amassing of wealth by others as a small matter and regarded it like losing. They are enemies of those things which others love while they love things which others hate. Through them, the Quraan has been learnt and they have been given knowledge through the Quraan. With them the Quraan is staying while they stand by the Quraan. They do not see any object of hope above what they hope and no object of fear above what they fear.

442 Remember that pleasures will pass away while the consequences will stay.

443 Try (a man) and you will hate him.

Sayyid Razi says; Some people say this saying is of the Prophet (p.b.u.h.a.h.p), but what confirms that it is the saying of Ameer al-Momineen (p.b.u.h.), is the statement related by Thalab from Bn al-Araabi namely that (Caliph) al-Mamoon said "If Ali had not said okhbir taqlihi" (Try a man and you will hate him)" I would have said "aqlihi takhbor (Hate a man in order to try him)

444 It is not that Allah, to Whom belongs Might and Majesty, may keep the door of gratitude open for a person and close the door of plenty upon him, or to open the door of prayer to a person and close the door of acceptance upon him, or to open the door of repentance on a person and close the door of forgiveness upon him.

445 The most appropriate person for an honourable position is he who descends from the people of honour.

446 When asked: Which of the two is better; justice or generosity?

Justice puts things in their places while generosity takes them out from their directions; justice is the general caretaker while generosity is a particular benefit. Consequently, justice is superior and more distinguished of the two.

447 People are enemies of what they do not know.

448 The whole of asceticism is confined between two expressions of the Quraan. Allah, the Glorified says: Lest distress you yourselves for what escapes you, and be overjoyous for what He has granted you (Quraan, 57:23). Whoever does not grieve over what he misses and does not revel over what comes to him acquires asceticism from both its sides.

449 What a breaker is sleep for resolutions of the day!

450 Governing power is the proving ground for people.

451 No town has greater right on you than the other. The best town for you is that which bears you.

452. When the news of the death of (Malik) al-Ashtar (may Allah have mercy on him), reached Ameer al-Momineen, peace be upon him, said:

Malik. what a man Malik was! By Allah, if he had been a mountain he would have been a big one (find), and if he been a stone he would have been hard, no horseman could have reached it and no bird could have flown over it.

Sayyid Razi says: "find" means a lonely mountain (rising in height above the range).

453 A little that lasts is better than much that brings grief.

454 If a man possesses a revealing quality wait and see his other qualities.[1]

455 To Ghaalib bn-Sasaa, the father of al-Farazdaq (the famous Arabic poet) during a conversation between them:

What about the large number of your camels?

-1- The good or bad quality that is found in a man springs from his natural temperament. If the temperament produces one quality, his other qualities will also be akin to this one because the dictates of temperament will be equally effective in either. Thus, if a man pays zakat and khoms it means that his temperament is not miserly. Therefore, it is expected that he would not be niggardly in spending in other items of charity as well. Similarly, if a man speaks a lie it can be expected that he will indulge in backbiting too, because these two habits are similar to each other.

The man replied: They have been swept away by (discharging of) obligations. O Ameer al-Momineen! Whereupon Ameer al-Momineen, peace be upon him, said:
That is the most praiseworthy way of (losing) them.

456 Whoever trades without knowing the rules of religious law will be involved in usury.

457 Whoever regards small distresses as big, Allah involves him in big ones.

458 Whoever maintains his own respect in view, his desires appear light to him.

459 Whenever a man cuts a joke he separates away a bit from his wit.

460 Your turning away from him who inclines towards you is a loss of your share of advantage, while your inclining towards him who turns away from you is humiliation for yourself.

461 Riches and destitution will follow presentation before Allah.

462 az-Zobayr remained a man from our house till his wretched son Abdillah came forth.[1]

-1- Abdillah bn-az-Zobayr bn-Awwam (1/622-73/692), whose mother was Asma, sister of Aysha (daughter of Abi-Bakr), had grown in his dislike of the Bani-Hashim especially towards Ameer al-Momineen to such a stage that he was able to change the opinion of his father, az-Zobayr, against Ameer al-Momineen although the latter was the son of his father's aunt. That is why Ameer al-Momineen said:
az-Zobayr had always been from us the Ahlil-Bayt (our household), until his ill-owned son Abdillah grew up. (al-Isteeaab, vol.3, p.906; Osdol-Ghaaba, vol.3, pp.l62-163; bn-Asakir, vol.7, p.363; bn-Abil-Hadeed, vol.2, p.l67; vol.4, p.79; vol.20, p.104)
Abdillah was one of the instigators of the battle of Jamal. His aunt Aysha, his father, az-Zobayr, and the son of his mother's uncle Talha, had fought against Ameer al-Momineen. Thus, bn-Abil-Hadeed writes:
It was Abdillah who urged az-Zobayr to fight (in the battle of Jamal), and made the march to Basra seem attractive to Aysha. (Sharh Nahjol-Balagha, vol.4 p.79)
Aysha loved her nephew Abdillah very much. To her he was like the only child of a mother, and none in those days was more beloved to her than him. (al-Aghaani, Abol-Faraj, vol.9, p.l42, bn-Abil-Hadeed, vol.20, p.l90; bn-Katheer, vol.8, p.336).
Hishaam bn-Orwa relates:
I have not heard her (Aysha) praying for anyone as. she used to pray for him (Abdillah). She gave ten thousand Dirhams (as a gift) to the one who informed her of Abdillah's safety from getting killed (by al-Ashtar in the fight of the battle of Jamal), and prostrated

to Allah in thanks-giving for his safety. (bn Aasaakir, vol.7, pp.400,402; bn-Abil-Hadeed, vol.20, p.111)

This was the reason of Abdillah's authority over her and his complete command over her affairs. He was the one who directed and guided her in the direction he wished.

However, Abdillah's hatred against the Bani-Hashim had reach such a stage that according to the narrations of a group of historians:

During his (Abdillah's) Caliphate (in Mecca) he did not send blessings on PM in his Friday prayer speech (Khotba) for forty Fridays. He used to say: "Nothing prevents. me from mentioning the Prophet's name except that there are a certain men (i.e. Bani-Hashim) who become proud (when his name is mentioned).

In another interpretation:

Nothing prevents... except that the Prophet has a bad household who will shake their heads. on the mention of his. name (Maqaatil at-Talibiyyeen, p.474; Morooj az-Zahab, vol.3, p.79;at-Taareekh, al-Yaqoobi, vol.2, p.261; al-Iqd al-fareed,vol.4, p.413; bn-Abil-Hadeed, vol.4, p.62; vol.l9, pp.91-92; vol.20, pp.l27-129)

Abdillah bn-az-Zobayr said to Abdillah bn-Abbaas:

I have been concealing my hatred toward you, the people of this house. (i.e. the Household of the Prophet) for the last forty years. (al-Masoodi, vol.3, p.80; bn-Abil-Hadeed, vol.4, p.62; vol.20, p.l48)

He also used to hate Ameer al-Momineen in particular, defame his honour, abuse and curse him. (al-Yaqoobi, vol.2, pp.261-262; al-Masoodi, vol.3, p.80: bn-Abil-Hadeed, vol.4, pp.61, 62-63, 79)

He gathered Mohammad bn al-Hanafiyya (the son of AM) and Abdillah bn-Abbaas with seventeen men from the Bani- Haashim including al-Hasan bn-Hasan bn-AM and imprisoned them in the shib (a small mountain valley) of Arim. He intended to burn them with fire, so he placed plenty of wood at the entrance of the shib. Meanwhile, al-N1ukhtar bn-Abi-Obayd ath-Thaqafi dispatched four thousand soldiers to Mecca. On their arrival, they attacked Abdillah bn-az-Zobayr unexpectedly and rescued the Bani-Haashim. Orwa bn-az-Zobayr made an excuse for his brother's (Abdillah) deed saying that this action of his brother's was a result of the Bani Haashim's refusal to swear allegiance to him (Abdillah), like the action of Omar bn-Khattaab towards the Bani-Hashim when they gathered in the house of Faatima and refused to swear allegiance to Abi-Bakr. So, Omar brought wood and intended to burn the house on them. (Maqaatil at-Talibiyyeen, p.474; al-Masoodi, vol.3, pp.767,: al-Yaqoobi, vol.2, p.261; bn Abil-Hadeed, vol.l9, p.91; vol.20, pp.l23/26 6-148; bn-Aasaakir, vol.;, p.408; al-Iqd al-fareed, vol.4, p.413; bn-Saad, vol.5), pp.73-81; at-Tabari, vol.2, pp.693-695; bn-Atheer, vol.4, pp.249 2a4; bn-Khaldoon, vol.3, pp.26-28)

In this connection, Abol-Faraj al-Isfahaani writes:

Abdillah bn-az-Zobayr always instigated others, against the Bani-Haashim and pursued them (in his aim) by every worst method; he inspired against them and spoke against them on the pulpits; and remonstrate(3 against them. Sometime bn-Abbaas or someone else from them (Bani Hashim) raised an objection against him. But afterwards he changed his way and imprisoned bn-Hanafiyya in a prison at the shib "Arim. Then, he gathered

463 What has a man to do with vanity. His origin is semen and his end is a carcass while he cannot feed himself nor ward off death.[1]

464 When asked about the greatest poet

The whole group of them did not proceed on the same lines in such a way that we can know the height of their glory; but if it has to be done then it is the "al-Malik az-Zilleel" (the mislead king).

Sayyid Razi says: Ameer al-Momineen means Imriol-Qays.[2]

---

bn-Hanafiyya along with other members of the Bani-Hashim who were present (in Mecca) in a prison and collected wood to set fire to it. This was because of the news that had reached him that Abi-Abdillah al-Jadali and other followers of bn-Hanafiyya had arrived (in Mecca) to support bn-al-Hanafiyya and fight Abdillah bn-az-Zobayr. Therefore, he hastened to do away with the prisoners. But when this news reached Abi-Abdillah al-Jadali, he came there at the time when the fire was already set on them, then he put out the fire and rescued them. (al-Afghani, p.l5)

So, all these prove the word of Ameer al-Momineen about him.

-1- If a man ponders over his original condition and the eventual breaking up and ruining of his body he will be compelled to admit his lowliness and humble position instead of being proud and vain, because he will see that there was a time when he did not exist and Allah originated his existence with a humble drop of semen which took the shape of a piece of flesh in the mother's womb and continued feeding and growing on thick blood. When on completion of the body he set foot on the earth he was so helpless and incapable that he had neither control over his hunger and thirst nor on sickness and health, nor any command over benefit or harm, or any authority over life and death, not knowing when the energy of limbs may exhaust, feeling and sense may leave, eye-sight may be taken away, power of hearing may be snatched and when death may separate the spirit from the body and leave the latter to be cut into pieces by vultures and kites or for worms to eat in the grave.

An Arabic couplet says:

How does one whose origin is semen and whose end is a carcass dare be vain?

-2- This means that a comparison can be made among the poets when their imagination runs in the same field; but when the expression of one differs from the other, and the style of one varies from that of the other it is difficult to decide who is defeat and who has won the field. Consequently, from various considerations one is preferred over the other and someone is considered greater for one consideration and the other for other consideration, as the famous saying goes:

The greatest poet of Arabia is Imriol-Qays when he rides; al-Asha when he is eager for something and an-Naabigha when he is afraid.

Nevertheless, despite this categorisation Imriol-Qays is regarded to be in a high position among poets of the first era because of the beauty of his imagination, the excellence of his description, his inimitable similes and rare metaphors, although many of his couplets

465 Is there no free man who can leave this chewed morsel (of the world) to those who like it? Certainly, the only price for yourselves is Paradise. Therefore, do not sell yourself except for Paradise.

466 Two greedy persons never get satiated, the seeker of knowledge and the seeker of this world.

467 Belief means that you should prefer truth (even) when it harms you rather than falsehood (even) when it benefits you; that your words should not be more than your action and that you should fear Allah when speaking about others.

468 Destiny holds sway over (our) predetermination till effort itself brings about ruin.

Sayyid Razi says: Something of this meaning has already appeared earlier though in words different from these.

469 Forbearance and endurance are twins and they are the product of high courage.

470 Backbiting is the tool of the helpless.

471 Many a man gets into mischief because of being spoken well about.

472 This world has been created for other than itself and has not been created for itself.

473 The Bani-Omayya (Omayyads) have a fixed period (mirwad) wherein they are having their way. But when differences arise among them, then even if the hyena attacks them it will overpower them.

Sayyid Razi says: Herein "mirwad" is a form derived from "irwad" which means to allow time, to wait for. It is an extremely eloquent and wonderful expression. It is as though Ameer al-Momineen, peace be upon him, has likened the period of Bani-Omayya to a limited area meant for the training

---

are below moral standards and speak about obscene subjects. But in spite of this obscenity the greatness of his art cannot be denied, because an artist looks at a poetic production from the point of view of art ignoring the other factors which do not affect art.

of horses for racing where they are running towards the limit, so that when they reach its extremity their organisation will be destroyed.[1]

474. Eulogising the Ansaar:

By Allah, they nurtured Islam with their generous hands and eloquent tongues as a year old calf is nurtured.

475 The eye is the strap of the rear.

Sayyid Razi says: This is a wonderful metaphor, it is as though Ameer al-Momineen, has likened the rear part of the body with a bag and the eye with a strap. When the strap is let loose the bag cannot retain anything. According to the well-known and reputed view it is the saying of the Prophet but some people have stated it to be of Ameer al-Momineen. al-Mobarrad has mentioned it in his book al-Mobarrad under the chapter Words of single letters. We too have discussed this metaphor in our book named Mojizaat al-Aathaar an-Nabawiyya.

476. A ruler came into position over them. He remained upright and made them upright till the entire religion put its bosom on the ground

-1- This is the prophecy about the decline and fall of the Omayyads that proved true, word for word. This rule was founded by Moaawiya bn-Abi-Sofyaan and ended with Marwaan bn-Mohammad al-Himaar in 132 A.H. after a life of ninety years, eleven months and thirteen days. The Omayyads period was second to none in tyranny, oppression, harshness and despotism. The despotic rulers of this period perpetrated such tyranny that it put blots on Islam, blackened the pages of history and injured the spirit of humanity. They allowed every kind of ruin and destruction only to retain their own personal authority. They led armies to Mecca, hurled fire on the Kaba, made Madeena the victim of their brute passions, and shed streams of Muslim blood. At last, this bloodshed and ruthlessness resulted in revolts and conspiracies from all sides and their internal strife and agitation and their mutual fighting paved the way for their ruin. Although political unrest had set in among them earlier yet during the days of al-Waleed bn-Yazeed open disturbances began to occur. On the other side Bani-al-Abbaas (the Abbaasids) also started preparations and during the reign of Marwaan al-Himaar they started a movement under the name of "al-Khilafa al-Ilaahiyya" (the Caliphate of Allah). For successful piloting of this movement they got a martial leader Abi-Muslim al-Khoraasaani who, in addition to his knowledge of political events and occurrences was also an expert in the art of warfare. Making Khoraasaan as the base he spread a whole net against the Omayyads and succeeded in bringing the Abbaasids to power.

In the beginning this man was quite unknown and it is for this unknowness and low position that Ameer al-Momineen likened him and his associates to the hyena as this simile is used for low and humble people.

477 A severe time will come upon the people wherein the rich will seize their possessions with their teeth (by way of miserliness) although they have not been commanded to do so. Allah the Glorified, says: Forget nor generosity among yourselves (Quraan, 2:237). During this time the wicked will rise up while the virtuous will remain low and purchases will be made from the helpless although the Prophet, peace be upon him and his descendants, has prohibited purchasing from the helpless.[1]

478 Two types of persons will fall into ruin over me: The one who loves exaggerates and the other who lays false and baseless blames.

Sayyid Razi says: This is on the lines of Ameer al-Momineen own saying which runs: "Two categories of people will be ruined over me: the one who loves exaggeratingly and the hater and malice-bearer[2]

-1- Generally purchases are made from helpless people in such a way that taking advantage of their need and necessity, things are purchased from them at cheap rates and are sold to them at high prices. No religion allows taking advantage of such helplessness and extreme need, nor is it permissible in ethics that profiteering should be resorted to at the time of others" helplessness.

2 The Holy Prophet used often to urge and order the Omma to love Ameer al-Momineen and forbid them to bear any hatred against him. Moreover, the Holy Prophet used to regard the love of Ameer al-Momineen as the sign of Faith (Emaan) and the hatred of him as the sign of hypocrisy (nifaaq) (as we have already mentioned on the foot-note of No. 45)

Now, we quote one of the traditions of the Holy Prophet with regard to this subject. If has been narrated through fourteen companions that the Holy Prophet said:

Whoever loves Ali, he surely loves me; and whoever loves me, he surely loves Allah, and whoever loves Allah, He will cause him to enter Paradise.

Whoever hates Ali, he surely hates me; and whoever hates me, he surely hates Allah, and whoever hates Allah, He will cause him to enter the Fire.

And whoever hurts Ali, he surely hurts me, and whoever hurts me, he surely hurts Allah, (surely, those who hurt Allah and His Messenger, Allah has cursed them in the present world and the world to come, and has prepared for them a humbling chastisement (Quraan, 33:57). (al-Mostadrak, vol.3, pp.127-128; 130; Hilyatol-Awliyaa, vol.1, pp.66-67; al-Isteeaab, vol.3, p.1101; Osdol-Ghaaba, vol.4, p.383; al-Isaaba, vol.3, pp.496-497; Majma" az-Zawaaid, vol. 9, pp.108-109, 129, 131, 132, 133; Kanz al-Ommaal, vol. 12, pp.202, 209, 218-219; vol.15, pp.95-96; vol.17, p.70; ar-Riyaaz an-Nazira, vol.2, pp.166, 167, 209, 214; al-Manaaqib, bn-Maghaazi, pp.103, 196, 382)

At the same time, the Holy Prophet used to caution the Omma against exaggeration in (Ameer al-Momineen's) love of him in exceeding the bounds of Islam in love for him. One

Who does so is called Ghaali, i.e. he who believes that the Holy Prophet or Ameer al-Momineen or any of the Shiite Imaams is god, or attributes to them the special attributes of Allah, or believes that the twelve Imaams are prophets, or makes any claim which they (the Holy Prophet and Imaams) did not make about themselves.

On the contrary, the Holy Prophet had also forbidden any offence or denigration concerning them (Imaams); and he used to blame those who lay false and baseless accusations against them as well as those who hate and bear malice.

It was for this reason that the Holy Prophet sometimes used to refrain from mentioning some of the excellent qualities of Ameer al-Momineen as J3bir bn-Abdillah al-Ansaari narrates:

When Ameer al-Momineen approached the Holy Prophet with the news of the conquering of Khaybar by himself (Ameer al-Momineen), the Holy Prophet said to him:

O Ali, had it not been for some groups of my Omma who may say about you, what the Christians say about "Esaa, son of Maryam. I would have said (something) about you so that you would not pass before any Muslim but that he would seize the dust from the tracks of your feet demanding blessing from it. But it suffices to say that you hold the same position in relation to me as Haroon held in relation to Moosa except that there shall, in all certainty, be no prophet after me." (Majma az-Zawaaid, vol.9, p.131; bn-Abil-Hadeed, vol.5, p.4; vol.9, p.168; vol.18, p.282; Manaaqib Ali bn-Abi-Talib, bn- Maghaazili, pp.237-239; Manaaqib Ali bn-Abi-Talib, al-Khwaarizmi, pp.75-76, 96, 220; Kifayatot-Talib fi Manaaqib Ali bn-Abi-Talib, al-Ganji, pp.264-265; Arjah al-Mataalib, pp.448, 454; Yanaabee al-Mawadda, pp.63-64, 130-131)

The Holy Prophet had also informed the Muslims Omma that there will appear two types of deviated groups among the Muslims who will exceed the bounds of Islamic principles towards understanding Ameer al-Momineen, as he himself has related:

The Messenger of Allah, peace be upon him and his descendants, called upon me and said "O All, there is a resemblance between you and Esaa son of Maryam, whom the Jews hated so much that they laid a false accusation against his mother, and whom the Christians loved so much that they assigned to him the position which is not for him."

(Then, Ameer al-Momineen continues) Beware! two types of persons will fall into ruin over me: The one who loves (me) who will eulogise me for what is not in me; and the one who hates (me) whose detestation against me will lead him to lay false and baseless accusations on me. Beware! I am not a prophet, and nothing has been revealed to me. But I act according to the Book of Allah and the Sonna of His Prophet as far as I can. (al-Mosnad, Ahmad bn-Hambal, vol.1, p.160; al-Mostadrak, al-Haakim, vol.3, p.123; Mishkaat al-Masaabeeh, vol.3, pp. 245-246; Majma az-Zawaaid, vol.9, p.133; Kanz al-Ommaal, vol.12, p.219, vol.15, p.110; bn-Katheer, vol.7, p.356)

The above mentioned sayings of Ameer al-Momineen (in this foot-note) as well as in the text have been reported from the Holy Prophet when he said to Ameer al-Momineen:

O Ali, two types of persons will fall into ruin over you: The one who loves exaggeratingly and the liar who lays false accusation. (al-Isteeaab, vol.3, p.1101)

Also, he said to him:

479 When asked on the Unity of Allah and His justice

Unity means that you do not subject Him to the limitations of your imagination and justice means that you do not lay any blame on Him.[1]

480 There is no good in silence over matters involving wisdom just as there is no good in speaking with ignorance.

481 In prayer for seeking rain:

O my Allah. send us rain by submissive clouds not by unruly ones.

Sayyid Razi says: This is an expression of wonderful eloquence, because Ameer al-Momineen, peace be upon him, has likened the cloud which is accompanied by thunder, lighting, wind and flashes with unruly camels who throw away their saddles and throw down their riders, and likened the clouds free from these terrible things to the submissive camels which are easy to milk and obedient to ride.

482 It was said to Ameer al-Momineen, peace be upon him: We wish you had changed your grey hair, O Ameer al-Momineen then he said: Dye is a way of adornment while we are in a state of grief.

Two categories will be ruined over you: The one who loves exaggeratingly and the hater who bears malice. (bn Abil-Hadeed, vol.5, p.6)

The famous scholar of tradition "Amir bn-Sharaaheel ash-Shabi (19/640-103/721) has confirmed this saying that these two categories appeared and both became disbelievers and were ruined. (al-Istl2b, vol.3, p.1130; al-Iqd al-fareed, vol.4, p.312)

-1- The belief in the Unity of Allah is not complete unless it is supported by belief in freedom of Allah from all imperfection; that is, one should regard Him above the limitations of body, shape, place or time and should not subject Him to one's own imagination and whims, because the being who is contained within imagination and whims cannot be Allah, but a creation of the human mind, while the field of mental activity remains confined to things which are seen and observed. Consequently, the greater man would try to appreciate Him through illustrations connected by the human mind or his imaginative efforts and the remoter man would get from reality. In this connection, al-Imaam Mohammad al-Baqir, says:

Whenever you contain Him in your imagination and whim he will not be Allah but a creation like yourself and revertible towards you.

Justice means that whatever the form of injustice and inequity it should be denied about Allah and He should not be given such attributes which are evil and useless and which the mind can in no way agree to attribute to Him. In this connection Allah says:

And perfect is the word of your Lord in truth and justice: There is none who can change His words, and He is the All-hearing and the All-knowing. (Quraan, 6:115)

Sayyid Razi says: Ameer al-Momineen, peace be upon him, is referring to the death of the Messenger of Allah, peace be upon him and his descendants.

483 The fighter in the way of Allah who gets martyred would not get a greater reward than he who remains chaste despite means. It is possible that a chaste person may become one of the angels.

484 Contentment is a wealth that does not exhaust.

Sayyid Razi says: Some people have related that this is the saying of the Messenger of Allah, peace be upon him and his descendants.

485 When Ameer al-Momineen, peace be upon him, put Ziyad bn-Abih in place of Abdillah bn-Abbas over Fars (in Persia) and its revenues, he had a long conversation with him in which he prohibited him from advance recovery of revenue. Therein he said:

Act on justice and keep aloof from violence and injustice because violence will lead them to forsake their abodes while injustice will prompt them to take up arms.

486 The worst sin is that which the committer takes lightly.

487 Allah has not made it obligatory on the ignorant to learn till He has made it obligatory on the learned to teach.

488 The worst comrade is he for whom formality has to be observed.[1]

Sayyid Razi says: This is because formality is inseparable from hardship and it is an evil that is caused by a comrade for whom formality is observed. Consequently, he is the worst of all comrades.

489 If a believer enrages (ihtishama) his brother, it means that he leaves him.

Sayyid Razi says: It is said "hashamahu" or "ahshamahu" to mean "He enraged him. According to another view it means "He humiliated him. While "ihtashamahu" means "He sought these for him, and that is most likely to cause him to separate.

-1- The friendship that is based on love and sincerity makes a man free from ceremonial formalities, but the friendship for which formalism is necessary is unstable and such a friend is not a true friend, because true friendship requires that a friend should not be a cause of trouble for the friend. If he is a cause of trouble, he will prove tedious and harmful and his harmfullness is a sign of his being the worst friend.

This is the end of our selection of the utterances of Ameer al-Momineen. peace be upon him. We are praiseful to Allah, the Glorified. for having enabled us to collect the scattered utterances from various sides and to bring together from different places the material that was lying far away. We intend, as we stipulated in the beginning, to leave some blank pages at the end of every chapter for the insertion of whatever we may get and the addition of whatever comes to us, for it is possible that some material which is not in our view at present or which is not available may become known to us and fall in our hands. We have no ability save through Allah. In Him we trust, and He is Sufficient for us. He is the best Supporter.

This book was completed in the month of Rajab, in the year 400 A.H.

May Allah send blessings on our master Mohammad the last of the prophets who guided us towards the best path, and his chaste descendants and his companions who are the stars of conviction.

The end